Japan
A Budget Travel
Guide

Japan
A Budget Travel
Guide

Ian L. McQueen

KODANSHA INTERNATIONAL
Tokyo • New York • London

Earlier editions of this work were published under the title *Japan: A Travel Survival Kit.*

Distributed in the United States by Kodansha America, Inc., 114 Fifth Avenue, New York, N.Y. 10011, and in the United Kingdom and continental Europe by Kodansha Europe Ltd., 95 Aldwych, London WC2B 4JF. Published by Kodansha International Ltd., 17-14, Otowa 1-chome, Bunkyo-ku, Tokyo 112, and Kodansha America, Inc.

First Kodansha International edition, 1992.
Updated edition, 1997.
97 98 99   5 4 3 2 1
ISBN 4-7700-2047-3

LCC 92-6193

CONTENTS

HOKKAIDO 363

CENTRAL HONSHU 398

KINKI DISTRICT 440

INTRODUCTION

Japan is one of the most interesting of all countries to visit. It has a long history, with many remains from past periods, like magnificent temples and castles, yet is possibly the most dynamically modern country on earth, with an incredible amount of industrialization (very much a mixed blessing). Its historic culture and society were completely different from anything known in the west, and many attitudes formed in the far past affect life today. Festivals from centuries ago are still held, linking present with past. Despite the "exotic" element of the country, however, it is one of the most accessible in terms of good transportation, plentiful accommodation, and friendly people, with no risk of eating bad food nor of personal danger.

Thousands of western travellers go to Japan every year (along with several times as many Asians from nearby countries), but only a relative few venture outside Tokyo, Kyoto, and a couple of other well-trod touristic destinations. There is nothing wrong in spending time in these places, of course, for they do house many of the country's chief attractions, but those who venture a little off the beaten path will find that they are in a country where foreigners are still quite a rare sight outside the major population centers, and the people are friendly. It is not like the outer reaches of a Himalayan kingdom, for example, scarcely known to the outside world, yet an element of discovery is still possible.

WHY A GUIDEBOOK?

It is sad but true that a considerable number of travellers arrive in Japan not really knowing where to go, what to see, where to stay, what to eat, when the weather is best, and how to see the most at the lowest cost. Japan is far from all western countries and expensive both to get to and to travel in, so few people can afford repeated trips to see what they missed the first time. The aim of this book is to prepare you before you enter Japan so that you can "hit the ground running", and to guide you around the country, to both the well known and the more obscure.

In many places I suggest obtaining more detailed information after arrival in Japan. The Japan National Tourist Organization (JNTO) has done a marvellous job of preparing large numbers of pamphlets and other types of printed information for the benefit of travellers, all of which is available at the Tourist Information Centers (detailed elsewhere), and much of which can be obtained from its overseas offices before departure. It is pointless to attempt to duplicate all the information that is thus available. (It would be impossible in any case!)

Some users of earlier editions have criticized this policy, saying that they could just get the brochures and not buy this book. However, it is doubtful that they would be aware of the full range of publications (or even their existence) without having it to refer to. More important, a certain amount of reading between the lines is advisable when using literature from any official (or semi-official) source in Japan (as in almost any country), for such literature must be non-controversial, up-beat, and appear to be even-handed to all regions of the country, even though some parts are of much less interest than others.

"Japan" to the foreign visitor depending only on "official" sources can be likened to the image on a rear-projection screen, with the visitor seeing only what it is desired that he see. It takes a while to be able to see around the screen to the full reality. Parts of the screen image—the cherry blossoms, Mt. Fuji, geisha, the castles, temples, and gardens—are certainly a part of Japan, but the reality also encompasses dreary, crowded cities, small houses, high-pressure education, social, and employment systems, lack of care for wildlife, destruction of the natural environment, etc. I want visitors following this book to be aware of the reality of Japan, to enjoy the many good things, but to go away with an objective picture of the country in its entirety.

This desire comes out of personal experience, for I came to Japan in 1970 expecting far more than the country could deliver, and was disappointed by not finding what I had been promised by so much that I had read. I feel that a visitor should be prepared for reality, and thus be able to enjoy the good without the disappointment of finding that the country is not a paradise on earth.

This attitude may not be appreciated by many Japanese, for there is a craving in the Japanese psyche to hear only good about Japan from all sources. "The Japanese" are not generally introspective nor self-critical, and do not understand that not all visitors are inclined to go along with such a mentality. There is a bit of a tendency to blend a wish for what might be into what really is. It is not uncommon to be asked "How do you like Japan?", seeking a praising answer. I have even heard an overseas visitor asked bluntly, "Don't you think Japan is a very beautiful country?" (Have you stopped beating your wife?!) How you would answer such a question is your choice. I would say, "Some parts are very beautiful, and some parts are not." I feel that it is useful to inject some reality to balance their perceptions, otherwise there would never be any incentive on the part of the Japanese for improvement.

Another problem with relying on printed material, especially that produced by local authorities, is that it is likely to be a bit inaccurate, painting a glowing picture of a minor attraction, or failing to take into account the difference in interests between those of a Japanese and a foreign traveller. (I have no vested interest in promoting one place over another.) It is also as likely as not to give no information on other places of interest located nearby but in a different political district or prefecture.

My opinions and judgments are based on first-hand experience with most places described in the book; in some cases I have used information from other travellers and other normally dependable sources. Because the book was written by one person, the standards for judging the interest of an attraction are uniform, and inherently include comparisons with the attractions of a number of other countries.

ORGANIZATION OF THE BOOK

The book is divided into two main sections. The first section gives you all the general information required for planning your travels in Japan. This includes the traditional sort of details that you would expect, such as the geography and weather, transportation services, economical accommodation and eating facilities, Customs and Immigration regulations, etc. It also takes in a glimpse of the history of the country and gives insights into the present society so you will have some understanding of the life and experiences of people you meet. It suggests ways to meet the Japanese and what to expect when talking with them.

The second section gives detailed travel information on all regions of Japan. The description begins with Tokyo and nearby area, continues northward through northern Honshu, then details Hokkaido (the northern main island). Description continues with the areas of Honshu west of Tokyo through to the far end of the island, then covers the smaller main islands of Shikoku and Kyushu. The small islands south of Kyushu are dealt with last.

As much as possible, there is detailed information on how to get from the airport or dock of every international port of entry into the nearest city, information about low-cost accommodation in that city, and information about transportation to other areas. However, for reasons detailed below, I have not otherwise given listings of places to stay because such information is just not needed.

Though written for the budget traveller, the book will prove useful to virtually any visitor to Japan, and will probably pay for itself in the first day or two whatever one's travel standards

BACKGROUND TO THE BOOK

This is the book that I wanted when I first came to Japan in 1970, inspired by the Expo '70 World Exposition at Osaka and the curiosity about Japan that it generated. The final few days of Expo were followed by several months of travel throughout Japan on a then-new and revolutionary Honda 750 motorcycle. However, no good guidebook on Japan was available, and I had to learn many things from experience. There was still no recommendable guidebook for the independent budget traveller by 1977, when the publisher of Lonely Planet Publications requested me to write

their Japan book. I had wanted to write such a book back in 1971, but had put aside the idea due to the uncertainty of finding a publisher and limited funds. This was the opportunity, and I took it.

With publication guaranteed, I returned to Japan in 1978 and repeated the travels made in 1970–71 to see which of my good experiences at that time could be repeated, gathering practical, detailed, and useful information that other travellers in Japan would need to know for economical, independent travel. The book that resulted from the travels and hundreds of hours of reading, typing, and drawing maps, titled *JAPAN: A Travel Survival Kit*, was the result.

The book apparently filled a need and established itself as the standard guidebook for independent minimum-cost travel. Total sales of the first three editions exceeded 150,000 (plus several thousand more in German translation), and sales increased year by year despite the entry of other guidebooks on to the market. This acceptance has been very heart-warming and encouraging, a reward for the countless hours spent writing and revising it.

AUTHOR'S VIEWPOINT

This may not be a feature of the usual guidebook, but I feel that it is legitimate to ask "Who wrote the book?"

The viewpoints and judgments in this book are based on appproximately 80,000 km of travel in Japan by motorcycle and car (and many more by train), from Hokkaido to Kyushu twice, and on more than 14 years of experience with the country and the people (combined with reading the views of many other knowledgeable writers). Comparisons of culture and attractions are based on travels in a good number of other countries. While writing, I have tried to maintain an objective viewpoint, balancing my memories of the sense of wonder felt at times during my first visit in 1970 (the type of experience that most visitors will likely share) against the knowledge and realistic viewpoint gained over the years.

Due to this attempt at objectivity, you will not find any guidebook cliches. I have been in the country long enough to see through the "oneness with/love of nature" and "exquisite politeness" myths that appear in too much writing about Japan. These seem to have been manufactured by some mysterious agency at some point in the past (some appear to have been developed at the time of the Tokyo Olympics), and have been dutifully perpetuated through the years by writers who come to Japan for a few days and repeat them without thought rather than write about what they would actually see if they looked objectively. (I suspect that they don't wish to go against prevailing wisdom lest they appear so unobservant as to have failed to see what those going before them claim to have seen.)

I consider my duty to be providing you, the traveller, with objective information, not to be a part of a PR machine. I would be willing to defend my viewpoint on any material written here, and believe that most objective people would largely agree with what I write. If I were criticized for any unflattering remark about a shortcoming in some aspect of Japan, my reply would be that the fault should be fixed, not that I should adjust my story. (Don't shoot the messenger!)

INTRODUCTION TO THIS KODANSHA INTERNATIONAL EDITION

This book, under the new title "*Japan: A Budget Travel Guide*", is now being published by Kodansha International. The reader is entitled to ask the reason for the change.

After the three earlier editions, the previous publisher felt that this book did not fit the format used in all its other guidebooks, particularly regarding giving detailed listings of places to stay and eat all over the country. My viewpoint was that this is quite unnecessary and a waste of space, and a parting of the ways became inevitable.

Regarding accommodation, most budget travellers stay in Youth Hostels, otherwise usually in *minshuku* and budget *ryokan*. A printed directory of every YH in the country is available, with sufficient English to be understandable (and there is a free JNTO brochure as well); information is given in this book about how to obtain both. Likewise, there are publications available in English listing economy ryokan and minshuku; there is also information given on how to obtain these. (Also, it is generally no problem finding accommodation "on the spot".) It has been my experience that there is no need to give the names of places to stay everywhere in the country. (Please note that I have given details of budget accommodation for all the sea and air ports of entry into Japan so you can get established for that crucial first day, wherever you land.)

As for food, Japan is not an underdeveloped third-world country, where you eat the local food at great risk, but one of the wealthiest in the world. There is no need for information on where you can eat safely, for it is safe (and palatable) everywhere, as in other advanced countries. Japan is also the land of the clone, so you will find the same types of eating places from one end of the country to the other. Prices are high, so the budget traveller will have a rather limited variety to choose from in any case. Any specific restaurant good enough to be identified by name would also be most likely to have prices outside the budget category (...well outside!).

The text is now organized as I had originally intended, which should make it easier for you, the reader, to find the information that you want with the least effort. The general information section has been rearranged to present the material more logically, in the order in which you will need it, first when planning your trip, then as you enter the country and begin to travel. Visa and immigration information, and that for accommodation, has been divided into two sections, one for short-term stays, one for long-term; since most visitors come for only a short stay, it can be confusing (and a waste of time) to struggle through a large amount of irrelevant information.

By all means compare the layout of, and information contained in, this book and its competitors. I hope you will find that this one fills your needs the best.

A Request

No guidebook is ever finished. Even before it can be printed, changes take place, and parts of it become out of date. However, I have tried to write in such a way that the information will remain useful for a few years. If you find any important changes, or have comments or suggestions regarding the book, please write me c/o Kodansha International.

I regret that I must decline to supply travel information that can be found in the book, and travellers already in Japan can easily obtain such information from a Tourist Information Office in person or by phone at no charge from anywhere in Japan. However, if you have a question not covered in the book and of a kind that the TIC cannot answer, I will try to give useful advice and information.

Enjoy your travels!

ABOUT THE COUNTRY

GEOGRAPHY

Japan is made up of four main islands, Honshu, Hokkaido, Kyushu, and Shikoku, plus hundreds of smaller ones. Together they stretch nearly 3000 km in the temperate and sub-tropical zones, between latitudes 20° and 45° N. (Equivalent locations are from Morocco to Lyons or Milan, or from Miami to Montreal.) Total land area is 377,435 sq km (147,435 sq mi), about 85 per cent of which is considered mountainous. Mountain ranges divide the country into four zones—the Japan Sea and Pacific Ocean sides of the north-east half, and the Japan Sea and Inland Sea sides of the south-west half—all of which have definite differences in patterns of both weather and customs of the people.

Japan is still geologically young, and volcanic eruptions are not uncommon. The Pacific Plate, one of the huge areas of the earth's crust afloat on the mantle, is slowly forcing itself under the islands of Japan, causing frequent earthquakes, mostly harmless. The volcanos, about 70 of which are considered active, are part of the "Ring of Fire" that follows a fault line (a junction of two plates) around the earth. Active volcanos include Aso-san, Unzen-dake, and Sakura-jima, all on Kyushu. Other volcanos on Honshu and other islands wake up from time to time, including some that had been thought dead. It is also theoretically possible for Mt. Fuji to erupt again, although it hasn't since 1707, and shows no signs of doing so.

Administrative and Other Divisions

Japan is divided into administrative units that, for the most part, follow natural boundaries. With the exception of Hokkaido and three other units (Tokyo, Kyoto, and Osaka), these smaller units are called "ken", and are modelled on the French prefectural system. There are 43 ken. Hokkaido was settled extensively only late in the 19th century and still has a small population relative to its size, so the entire island is a single *do*, or district; this is the last syllable of the name. Tokyo is a *to* (metropolis), while Kyoto and Osaka and their surrounding areas are both *fu*; all three compare in size with the smaller ken. When writing the names of the latter cities in Japanese, they are "Tokyo-to", "Kyoto-fu", and "Osaka-fu".

These political divisions are grouped into regions of similar geographic character; the names of these regions are used as the headings for most of the sections of this book. These regions are also the basis for dividing the country for regional maps (as in the detailed road maps referred to elsewhere in the book). (Large scale maps follow ken boundaries.)

HOKKAIDO

TOHOKU: Aomori, Iwate, Miyagi, Akita, Yamagata, Fukushima

KANTO: Ibaraki, Tochigi, Gunma, Saitama, Chiba, Tokyo, Kanagawa

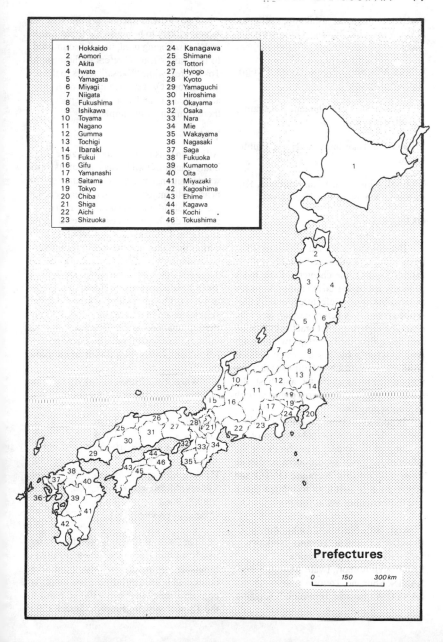

1	Hokkaido	24	Kanagawa
2	Aomori	25	Shimane
3	Akita	26	Tottori
4	Iwate	27	Hyogo
5	Yamagata	28	Kyoto
6	Miyagi	29	Yamaguchi
7	Niigata	30	Hiroshima
8	Fukushima	31	Okayama
9	Ishikawa	32	Osaka
10	Toyama	33	Nara
11	Nagano	34	Mie
12	Gumma	35	Wakayama
13	Tochigi	36	Nagasaki
14	Ibaraki	37	Saga
15	Fukui	38	Fukuoka
16	Gifu	39	Kumamoto
17	Yamanashi	40	Oita
18	Saitama	41	Miyazaki
19	Tokyo	42	Kagoshima
20	Chiba	43	Ehime
21	Shiga	44	Kagawa
22	Aichi	45	Kochi
23	Shizuoka	46	Tokushima

Prefectures

0   150   300 km

CHUBU: Toyama, Ishikawa, Niigata, Fukui, Yamanashi, Nagano, Gifu, Shizuoka, Aichi

KINKI: Mie, Shiga, Kyoto, Osaka, Hyogo, Nara, Wakayama

CHUGOKU: Tottori, Shimane, Okayama, Hiroshima, Yamaguchi

SHIKOKU: Tokushima, Kagawa, Ehime, Kochi

KYUSHU: Fukuoka, Saga, Nagasaki, Kumamoto, Oita, Miyazaki, Kagoshima

OKINAWA

Because the regional divisions (Tohoku, Chubu, Kinki, etc.) largely follow natural features, the chapters of the book generally are organized similarly. As much as possible, one prefecture (*ken*) is described completely before moving on to the next, although this is not practical when an area being described overlaps two or more *ken*, or when a *ken* has a clearly defined north and south (such as Gifu-ken) that are very different in character and best described separately, each area grouped with its similar neighbors.

In addition to these present political divisions, there are other traditional ways of dividing up the country. The names for the different groupings appear intermixed quite frequently in tourist literature (JNTO and other), so it is useful to recognize them. The most common are as follows:

TOKAI: Gifu, Shizuoka, Aichi, Mie
HOKURIKU: Fukui, Toyama, Ishikawa
SHIN-ETSU: Nagano, Niigata
SANRIKU: Aomori, Iwate, Miyagi
SANIN: Shimane, Tottori
SANYO: Yamaguchi, Hiroshima, Okayama

Anyone who spends a little time in Japan is likely to hear also the terms *Kanto* and *Kansai* being used, usually contrasted. In this case, "Kanto" refers to the general Tokyo area, while "Kansai" refers to the region around Osaka. Each has its own character, dialect, and taste preferences, and there is much rivalry implied.

TIME

All of Japan is in the same time zone, nine hours ahead of GMT. Because of its eastward position, day begins in Japan ahead of nearly all major populated areas except New Zealand and Australia. In mid-summer, the day begins excessively early, with sunrise at 4:30 and the sky becoming light earlier than this, and the evenings are very short. Japan does not use Daylight Saving Time (though there were faint rumblings in 1995 that it *might* be introduced in a couple of years), it being associated with the undesirable/unnatural reforms introduced during the Occupation, so the Japanese (and the visitor) lose much of the summer sun. ("The sun always rises earlier in the summer.")

When it is 12 noon in Tokyo, the time in other places (standard time) is:

Hong Kong	11 a.m.
London	3 a.m.
America, east coast	10 p.m.*
America, west coast	7 p.m.*
Hawaii, Alaska	5 p.m.*
Sydney, Melbourne	1 p.m.
New Zealand	3 p.m.

(* denotes previous day)

The 24-hour system is used for writing nearly all times in Japan, whether railway timetables or notices in restaurant windows, and is used throughout the book. To convert a time later than 1300 (1 p.m.) to the 12-hour system, simply subtract 1200;

thus 1730 hours is the same as 5:30 p.m. For a.m. times, no arithmetic is necessary—0900 simply means 9 a.m.

CLIMATE

Japan is generally in the temperate climate zone, but it is an unusually long country north to south. As a result, the climate varies widely at the same time of year in different latitudes, or even within the same region (coastal vs mountain, for example). There can be blizzard conditions on Hokkaido, sunny, crisply-cool weather in Tokyo and Kyoto, mild Mediterranean conditions on Kyushu, and pleasant warmth in Okinawa.

The climate of the various regions and the best times of the year for travelling in Japan are detailed in the section on Travel Planning.

HISTORY

Because written Japanese records of history don't exist prior to the Nara era (710–784 A.D.), most knowledge of Japan before that time is based on Chinese records. Archeological excavations have found traces of settlement from 100,000 years ago, but nothing further until a few thousand years ago. The earliest civilization about which much is known has been named the Jomon period, tentatively dated up to the second century B.C. There is some evidence of a Polynesian/Southeast Asian connection in the people of this period, and seeming links between Japanese and Polynesian language structures may originate with them. There were probably northern Asian elements present in Japan at this time as well. It has also been hypothesised that the Jomon were in fact the Ainu people. Jomon pottery has been found in many areas of the country, as far north as Hokkaido, and the Ainu once lived throughout much or all of Japan.

The next civilization that has been as-signed a name is the Yayoi, identified by a clearly different type of pottery. It is likely that these people were closely related to (or belonged to) the peoples of southern Korea and that there was a considerable amount of trade between the islands of Japan and the Korean peninsula, the land mass nearest to Japan. Bronze and iron were introduced into Japan at this time, although the bronze age was short lived. There is interesting evidence that settlements were invaded by warriors from Puyo (Korea) in the late fourth century; these were semi-nomadic, horse-riding people displaced from the Manchuria area who gradually conquered much of the Korean peninsula. Evidence for this is the sudden appearance of horses and armored warriors, unknown in Japan in the third century, and the commencement of the construction of large tomb mounds in many areas of Japan, a practice previously unknown in Japan but common in Korea. These mounds are found from Kyushu through to the Tokyo area. Despite the light that the contents could probably throw on Japanese history, the authorities seem reluctant to excavate, reputedly on the grounds that they may house the remains of ancestors of the present royal family. Since it is very unlikely that the royal lineage extends back so far or so extensively, cynics suggest that excavations would show, as did the Takamatsuzaka tomb in Asuka (near Nara) in 1972, a strong Korean connection. I believe many Japanese hold Koreans in low regard, therefore ties to the royal family just would not do.

The pre-invasion Japanese probably became dominant around the end of the sixth century and developed into a loosely joined nation governed from Yamato (near present-day Nara). Culture from Korea and China flowed into the country during this time, including Buddhist teachings, the Chinese writing system, and many new arts and crafts. This leads to the dawn of the Nara era (Nara-jidai).

Nara Era (710–784 A.D.)

The most famous organiser of the early Japanese state was Prince Shotoku. In his lifetime (573–620 A.D.) he introduced a constitution and concept of the state, promoted Buddhism as a state religion, greatly improved education and culture, and set up an excellent system of state administration. Many temples were built in Nara under his direction, some of which still exist, such as Horyuji (Nara). Subsequent rulers continued his program of codification of laws and administration.

This period was the first time that the capital remained in the same location after the death of the ruler. It was a prosperous time and Nara grew to a large size, much greater than the present city. The Buddhist temples gained so much power and wealth that they were a threat to the ruler, so a later ruler (Kammu) moved the capital to Heiankyo (now Kyoto) in 794 A.D., where it remained until 1868.

Heian Era (794–1192)

The first four centuries of Kyoto rule are called the Heian Period (794–1192). The early days were ones of achievement, with cultural delegations from China, conquest of the Ezo (Ainu aboriginal people) in northern Honshu, and the blending of Buddhist beliefs with those of Shinto to make the former more acceptable by representing Shinto gods as early manifestations of Buddhist incarnations.

During this time the Fujiwara family gained great power, members becoming Prime Minister, regent to the throne, and supreme advisor to the emperor. With their luxurious lifestyle and neglect of administration, corruption grew, civil war broke out between 1156 and 1160, and the Taira fam-

ily rose to power. In turn, they repeated the luxurious extravagance of their predecessors. They were overthrown by the Minamoto (better known as the Genji) in 1185 after a string of battles along the south coast of the country, ending in the battle of Dannoura (Shimonoseki) when the Taira were obliterated. This led to the Kamakura period.

Kamakura Era (1192–1333)

The Genji made their government headquarters in Kamakura (near present-day Tokyo). It was the beginning of military government or *bakufu*, under a *shogun* ("generalissimo"), which lasted with few breaks until 1868. Military outposts were set up throughout the country with the duties of maintaining order and collecting taxes.

The Minamoto lasted only 27 years, the last one being assassinated, then a Fujiwara was invited from Kyoto to fill the post of *shogun*, although control remained in the hands of the Hojo family. The imperial capital remained at Kyoto, but the emperor had become a mere figurehead, as he would remain for most of the period until 1868.

During the Kamakura period the Mongols under Kublai Khan tried in 1174 and 1181 to land at Hakata (northern Kyushu). The first wave was fought off (barely), and defensive walls (traces of which may still be seen near Fukuoka) were built in preparation for the second attempt. The walls helped somewhat, but a destructive typhoon wrecked the Mongol fleet, decimating its 100,000 warriors. This typhoon was obviously a wind (kaze) sent by the gods (kami), or a *kamikaze*. This word was revived late in World War II, in a second attempt to save Japan from invasion, to describe the suicidal attacks made by "kamikaze" pilots against American ships.

After the victory over the Mongols, the military could not reward the expectations of its soldiers, and emperor Godaigo took advantage of the unrest to restore the imperial throne to power.

Muromachi and Azuchi-Momoyama periods (1336–1600)

Godaigo failed to reward his military commanders in proportion to their services, and indulged his courtiers, so forces under the Ashikaga clan drove Godaigo out of Kyoto into the mountains of Yoshino and a new military government was set up in Kyoto (1336).

The result of this was that for the next 57 years there were two courts, after which they joined, with the military government dominant; this was the Muromachi bakufu, which lasted until 1573. The period 1336–1573 is the Muromachi era; the gold pavilion at Kinkaku-ji (Kyoto) dates from these times.

The luxury of Kyoto life led to poor administration, heavy taxes, and civil war from 1467 until 1568, when the warlord Oda Nobunaga entered Kyoto, but he was assassinated in 1582. The struggle for control of the country was taken over and completed by Toyotomi Hideyoshi. The short period 1573–1600 is the Azuchi-Momoyama era, named after the castles of Oda and Toyotomi. It is usually called only "Momoyama"; the name symbolises a colorful, flamboyant decorative style, quite in contrast with the restrained style that is normally thought of as Japanese. The original Osaka castle, of which the immense foundation stones remain (with a modern superstructure), was built in this period.

Edo Era or Tokugawa Era (1600–1867)

The time of Toyotomi Hideyoshi led up to the beginning of the best-known period in Japanese history, the Edo (or Tokugawa) era. Tokugawa Ieyasu succeeded in subduing all rivals. He set up a *bakufu* government in Edo (now Tokyo); the emperor continued to reside in Kyoto, without power. The country was divided into nearly 270 fiefs, each under a *daimyo* (feudal lord) who owed his power and allegiance to the *shogun*, Tokugawa.

During this period contact by European traders and missionaries increased to the point where the government felt the foreign influences (particularly Christianity) were a threat to the stability of the country. Christianity was suppressed with the martyring of many thousands (especially in Kyushu, the center of Catholicism). Only the Dutch were permitted to trade, and only through Nagasaki on the southern island of Kyushu; the Portuguese were banned in 1639, and the English and Spanish had been excluded earlier. (The early days of the Tokugawa era is the period fictionalized in James Clavell's novel *Shogun*; the character "Anjin" was modelled after an actual shipwrecked pilot, Will Adams.)

The following two and a half centuries saw a Japan sealed as completely as possible from contact with the outside world. Many Japanese who left and returned were executed to prevent the introduction of outside ideas (although swearing to say nothing of what they had seen while abroad was usually enough to spare their lives). Society was highly organised, with clearly defined classes (military, farmers, artisans, and merchants) with little mobility between classes. Interestingly, the merchants were the lowest class. Incredibly detailed laws decreed every aspect of life, such as the type of clothing that might be worn, the kind of food one was allowed, place of residence, movement, even the space and position in which one might sleep! Orders of the military leaders were to be obeyed instantly; hesitation or expression of displeasure or question was likely to result in death. (This historic fact might give some explanation for the tendency to this day on the part of the Japanese to show relatively little expression and to follow orders without much question.)

The isolation was brought to an end with the arrival of the Black Ships of Commodore Perry (U.S. Navy) in 1853 with a demand that Japan open its doors to trade. Yokohoma and other ports were opened within a few years. The entry of the foreign barbarians was not universally welcomed and the Choshu clan, controlling Shimonoseki Strait, then closed it, resulting in a three-day bombardment and the destruction of the shore installations by British, American, French, and Dutch ships in 1864. The Choshu then realized that Japan had to be modernized to overcome its powerless position.

Emperor Meiji had begun his reign in 1852, but was as powerless as his predecessors in the face of the Tokugawa. The Choshu joined with the Satsuma clan of Kagoshima (southern Kyushu) to press for the end of the Tokugawa government and the restoration of the emperor to full power. In the ensuing period of fighting and confusion, the *shogun* stepped down and Emperor Meiji began his amazing reign in 1868. Fighting by elements loyal to the Tokugawa continued in several parts of the country and had to be put down by force, but eventually the emperor was given full powers. This is called the Meiji Restoration, although a more apt word might be "revolution"; the period of turmoil was much more like civil war than is usually recognized.

Meiji Era (1868–1912)

During the Meiji era (1868–1912), Japan went from an isolated, feudal, agricultural nation to one of the world's most powerful and dynamic countries, with a modern navy and army (that defeated Russia in 1905), a network of railroads, industry of all kinds, and a parliament. Every effort was made to modernize all aspects of Japanese life. This resulted in some excesses as many relics of the past were intentionally destroyed, including many picturesque castles and traditional objects like bronze lanterns. (The collection in the British Museum was rescued from a scrapyard by a ship's captain.)

Taisho Era (1912–1926)

Meiji was succeeded in 1912 by Emperor Taisho, but there is little record of his rule. It seems he was mentally unstable—reportedly the result of inadvertent poisoning by a white lead compound while being suckled by a wet nurse. (The compound was commonly used by women to whiten their skin; its side effects, especially its effect on the brain, were not fully appreciated.)

Showa Era (1926–1988)

Emperor Hirohito (known after his death as Emperor Showa) succeeded to the throne in 1926 and was the longest reigning monarch in the world until his death at the beginning of 1989.

The awakened national spirit and expansion of the Meiji era had far-reaching effects beyond the Taisho era and well into the Showa era of Emperor Hirohito. The need for raw materials and markets for the growing industrial machine led to wars with China in 1894 and 1937; the former resulted in the ceding of Taiwan to Japanese control. Korea was invaded in 1910 and its queen murdered, providing the foundation for the national antipathy toward Japan that persists to this day.

The world-wide economic depression of the 1930s gave the military the opportunity to expand its control over the country, and an inculcation of a sense of racial superiority over all other peoples and races, resulting in conquests of many Asian countries in an effort to form the "Great East Asian Co-Prosperity Sphere", with Japan (naturally) at its center. (It is generally believed that the emperor had only a passive role during the pre-war period and that the military government carried out their actions in his name but without his active participation.) These actions led, however, to the ultimate disaster of World War II and the devastation of Hiroshima and Nagasaki—the first and only cities ever to be atom-bombed—and the destruction of almost all the other major cities by fire and explosive bombing. It was also the first time in its recorded history that Japan had been conquered. Occupation by Allied forces (mainly American, but including British, Australian, and New Zealand) followed.

Post-war changes have been dramatic, with rejection of military values to such an extent that the armed forces are still held in low esteem. The right-wing militaristic mentality which promoted State Shinto as a national religion has largely disappeared. A small minority still supports it, and trucks laden with loudspeakers drive through the streets of the large cities (particularly Tokyo) blaring nationalistic and military (WWII-era) music and slogans over hyperpower loudspeakers, but they are ignored by the general populace. One look at the immature young men or semi-thugs strutting on the truck roofs in their uniforms explains why. (Nevertheless, these people do, unfortunately, have considerable power. Threats to bomb theaters prevented the showing of the film "Mishima" in Japan, and the mayor of Nagasaki was shot in an assassination attempt, "punishment" for declaring that the late emperor had some responsibility for WWII.)

Prior to the war, the emperor had been revered as a living god by State Shinto. After Japan's defeat he renounced any claim to divinity, and became a constitutional monarch, like the monarch of Great Britain. The role of emperor then became that of a symbol of the Japanese state; although he is consulted and advised, the emperor has no actual power in governing the country.

Heisei Era (1989–   )

The eldest son of Emperor Hirohito, Akihito, became the emperor in a number of ceremonies in 1990 and 1991. He undertook post-graduate education in England, and is much more outgoing than his father.

Present Political System

The use of war was renounced in the new constitution, although Japan is allowed a Self-Defence Force, which today is, in fact, among the world's more powerful armed forces.

The country has an elected democratic government; the Diet has two chambers, the House of Representatives and the House of Councillors which enact laws, but the administrative arm (the civil service) is very powerful and controls many aspects of business, etc., with sufficient strength to go counter to the will of the legislative branches if it feels so inclined. The conservative Liberal-Democratic party has held power for nearly all the post-war period. It is a pro-free enterprise party (though the government gives much financial assistance and "administrative guidance" to important or new industries), and the country is firmly and reliably in the Western camp.

Interestingly, a peace treaty has never been signed with the former USSR, partly because four islands were opportunistically seized off Hokkaido that had long been Japanese, by joining the war against Japan only a couple of weeks before the end. The islands were occupied even though there had never been any agreement among the Allies for this to happen. A visit in 1991 by former President Gorbachev failed to resolve the situation, but in this period of incredible changes, anything could happen during the life of this edition of the book.

ECONOMIC CONDITIONS

The economic miracle that has taken place in Japan is well-known and needs little review. It is incredible to the visitor of today to think that all the major cities (except Kyoto, which was spared because of its historic treasures) lay in ruins 40 years ago, and that the Japanese people were on the edge of starvation for several years after the war. (The GNP per capita in 1946 was only U.S. $17.) Now the country leads the world in many industries such as cars, steel, quality cameras, and electronics. It is facing competition in many traditional fields from the NIEs (Newly Industrialized Economies) like Korea and Taiwan, which have largely taken over the labor-intensive industries like textiles and cut into the steel and shipbuilding industries. However, even the phenomenal rise in value of the yen in early 1986 (a doubling against the U.S. dollar) has failed to have noticeable effect on the health of the economy; Japanese companies just come out with more and more products of high value that remain in high demand on world markets. Whether this can continue remains to be seen; in mid-1991 labor was in short supply and the economy was booming despite a precipitous fall in share values the previous year, but there were intimations of an economic downturn near the end of the year. (It remains to be seen what effect on economic health will result from the considerable number of financial scandals that were revealed in mid-1991.)

THE PEOPLE

The origins of the Japanese people are not known with any certainty. There are elements in the language that hint at a Polynesian/Southeast Asian connection in very early times, and it seems only logical to assume that various peoples immigrated across the relatively narrow Japan Sea from the Korean Peninsula, from Siberia via Sakhalin Island, and from mainland Asia areas such as Manchuria and various parts of China. There are intriguing bits of evidence, such as tribes in the northern hills of India with several types of food, like sushi, much like that in Japan, and recent research based on similarities of components in the blood has shown an apparent close kinship between the Japanese and a group living in the Lake Baikal region of Siberia.

There are many dialects spoken in different regions of Japan. It can be proposed that the dialects developed by parallel immigration of numerous ethnic groups, each with its own language and distinctive rhythm and cadence that was carried over when the vocabulary and grammar of standard Japanese established itself throughout the country (in the same way that the English accents developed). There are many words in one dialect that are not used anywhere else, and many dialects of Japanese are totally unintelligible to people from other areas. (When people from such groups are being interviewed on TV, it is necessary to add subtitles, even though they are speaking a language written exactly the same!)

The people of one region often look quite distinct from inhabitants of another region; Kyushu people would not generally be mistaken for Tohoku people for example. (One friend from Kyushu was frequently asked what Southeast Asian country she came from.) Although foreign visitors cannot identify accents, they can notice the great variety of facial and other features around the country (for example some have narrow eyes, while others are almost as round-eyed as westerners), and there is also a large variety of skin coloring from as dark as tanned Indonesians to whiter than a pale European. (The women of Tohoku (northeast Honshu) are known for white skin and rosy cheeks). The Japanese however, do not generally remark on these differences to each other because they want to believe they are all of the same group, something very important in Japanese society.

Many Japanese like to consider themselves as a unique race, different from other Asians, but the fact is there can be no such thing as an identifiable Japanese race. They have a national culture, but the present inhabitants of the Japanese islands are a mixture of many peoples of Asian origin. In their physical appearance many Japanese *are* clearly identifiable as such, but as much as 30–50 per cent of the population could be dropped into another country of the region (Korea, China, Philippines, Thailand—even Indonesia, India, or Nepal) and be indistinguishable from the local population.

In addition to the "mainstream" (Yamato) Japanese, there are also minority peoples. The Ainu (pronounced "eye-noo") are now found only in Hokkaido, though once they lived at least as far south as the Tokyo area, and quite possibly much farther south and west than that. Formerly a hunting and fishing people with an animistic culture, their way of life was destroyed through the centuries by the ethnic Japanese, and they now live much like other Japanese. No one knows the origin of the Ainu; their language seems unrelated to any other in the world, although native Siberian tribes have a similar bear cult. They are also said to be the most hirsute people on earth. There are about 15,000 Ainu in Japan at present. Other lesser-known races or ethnic groups, each of only small numbers (Oroke, Gilyak, etc.) are also found on Hokkaido. The people of Okinawa are also of a different ethnic group. It would seem that the Yamato Japanese are not very conscious of these different groups, and believe firmly that Japan is solidly mono-ethnic. Former Prime Minister Nakasone caught much flak from Ainu when he stated to the world that Japan has no ethnic minorities.

Part of the belief still held regarding the "uniqueness" of the Japanese is a legacy of the pre-war government promotion of Shinto. Myths regarding the origins of the Japanese, e.g., that they were descendants of the Sun Goddess Amaterasuomikami, were actually taught in schools. The purpose was to instill a feeling of strong nationalism that would support a war. Japanese were encouraged to feel superior to, and separate from, other peoples; this served the ends of the militarists who were pushing Japan into conquest of other Asian countries. They have not been able to break the habit. Indeed, hundreds of books under the generic term *nihonjinron* ("study of the Japanese") perpetuate these feelings of separateness by describing ("imagining" is a better word) differences (never similarities) between the Japanese and other people. Much of this rubbish is produced by people with impressive university titles . . . which raises questions about the universities. (Not a few foreign academics have written similar material, but that fashion appears to be coming to an end.)

The characteristics of the present-day Japanese that a foreign visitor will experience are touched on are discussed in a later section, "Meeting the Japanese".

RELIGION

Shinto

Shinto—"Way of the Gods"—is the so-called native Japanese religion. It has no scriptures, and is basically an animistic belief largely concerned with obtaining the blessing of the gods for future events. Ceremonies are held to bless babies, children (Shichigosan festival), weddings, and the start of new enterprises. Even large corporations take no chances, and enlist the aid of a Shinto priest; it is not uncommon to see a Shinto ceremony for blessing a building site before construction begins.

Before the war, Shinto was glorified by the state and used to bestow a blessing from the gods on the militaristic line that the government was following. State aid was given to shrines throughout the country. After the war, however, all such aid was cut and Shinto reverted to its earlier, simpler form, supported only by donations from the faithful.

Before Shinto existed, there was a shamanistic folk faith similar to that in many other Asian countries. It still exists in isolated parts of Japan, such as Osorezan in the very north of Tohoku, and is known as minkan-shinko. (Judging by the ease with which charlatans can sell "specially blessed" items for curing ailments, there are receptive elements for this type of "religion" in the psyche of many Japanese. But then, our own countries have the equivalents.) When Shinto was first introduced, many existing shamanistic deities were given new Shinto names in a (largely successful) attempt to supplant the older religion by absorbing its gods and ceremonies. (In the same way, Christianity took over many ancient pagan festivals in Europe.)

Shinto shrines, called jinja, taisha, or jingu (depending on the rank) are generally identifiable by a torii gate—two uprights and a double cross-bar. There is often a thick braided rope made of rice straw suspended between the uprights of the torii, a shimenawa, put up after the harvest season. There are normally carved stone koma-inu (guardian lions or dogs) at the entrance, similar to those seen at Chinese shrines. If portrayed correctly, the mouth of one lion is open, the other closed. This symbolises "Ah" and "Um", the sounds of birth and death, the Beginning and the End, from Hindu mythology. The distance between them is the Path of Life, a reminder to those walking between them of the shortness of their temporal existence. (Most Japanese, however, are unaware of the significance.)

The shrine building is often very simple, although all incorporate customary design elements of symbolic importance. There is often a rope hanging down from a "rattle" suspended in the eaves. Worshippers shake it to wake up the gods and get their attention, and then clap their hands together before praying. This is almost a reflex action with most Japanese, even those who claim to have no religious faith (which is the vast majority of the population).

It is common for people to follow both Shinto and Buddhist beliefs without any conflict in their minds, as each covers certain aspects of life not touched by the other. Buddhism, with its many sects and voluminous literature, appeals more to the intellectual side of the religious nature, while the simplicity of Shinto makes it instantly accessible to all.

Buddhism

Buddhism arrived in Japan, from China, in the middle of the sixth century. Through the centuries, the original teachings of the Buddha in India had already been modified by the Chinese to suit their temperament and culture, and this derivative form which reached Japan was further molded so that foreign Buddhists scarcely recognise the Japanese faith as being part of their own. Numerous Buddhist sects have developed in Japan since its introduction; even in recent decades there have been new ones, such as Soka Gakkai.

Most Japanese families have some ties with Buddhism, if in no other way than through burial by a Buddhist priest on temple grounds. The eldest son of most families is guardian of the family altar, an ornately gilded wooden structure in the household place of honor. In it are tablets with the names of deceased family members. Regular ceremonies honor these ancestors, ceremonies which have led to the mistaken belief that the Japanese actually worship their ancestors. During the annual *obon* season (around mid-August; it varies with the lunar calendar), it is believed that the souls of the deceased return to visit. It is a happy time, with group dancing in public places everywhere in the country.

The greatest manifestation (to foreign visitors) of Buddhism in Japan is the beautiful temple buildings in Kyoto (and some in other parts of the country). The religious significance of the brilliantly gilded figures, altar fittings, and other accoutrements and decorative elements will be lost on those not familiar with Buddhist symbolism, but they can still be appreciated by a foreign onlooker as works of art. Another symbol of Buddhism and of Japan itself is the *Daibutsu*, the great bronze statue of Buddha, at Kamakura.

Others

Christians make up about 1% of the population of Japan, although adherents are found in disproportionately larger numbers in public life. The fact that it is a "foreign" faith militates against its greater acceptance (plus the fact that the Japanese are generally not a religious people).

Many new sects have sprung up in Japan in this century, a large number just since the war. Most are centered around their founder. (In the mid-eighties, one group of women committed mass suicide when their leader died.) The sects range from the weird to the wonderful, and cover the full range of faith healing, shamanism, and mysticism. Most are departures from traditional Buddhism, Shinto, and even Christianity (or combinations thereof).

WHERE TO GO

With the exception of the lucky few with large amounts of time to wander leisurely through the country, most visitors to Japan must make the best of a few days. The notes in this section are intended to help you plan an itinerary that takes in the most of what you want to see.

The answer to "where to go?" depends largely on your personal interests, but it is probably a good bet that most people who come to Japan have an impression of the country based to a large extent on the past, and wish to see what remains from the days of the samurai, plus social arts and folkloric items that have developed through the centuries, such as dances and festivals. Even though the book has been panned by the critics for historical inaccuracies, *Shogun* has probably done more to make the world aware of Japan, and had more influence on overseas perceptions of the country, than any other single source. For this reason there is a good amount of space in this book devoted to the authentic castles that still stand (there are several modern reproductions as well), historic gardens, sections of old cities that have survived into the present and so forth. The natural beauty of Japan is also well known, so there is information on the vast majority of well known beauty spots and picturesque places in the countryside. In addition, there is information on "living culture" attractions, such as festivals, which are the best single way to see both the old Japan and the modern people enjoying themselves. The following summarizes the attractions of Japan, region by region, and by type of attraction.

Cities of Interest

A few cities and clearly defined small areas are on almost every visitor's itinerary. Nearly everyone wants to visit Kyoto (and nearby attractions) and Nikko. Time permitting, many wish also to see either Hiroshima or Nagasaki for their unfortunate relationship with the A-bomb.

Kyoto, near the center of the main island (Honshu) was the imperial capital for just over 1000 years. The centuries of refined and elegant living of the people of the court, plus the practice of locating the most magnificent of everything (temples, gardens, and other structures) in the capital, have resulted in Kyoto's having the greatest concentration of temples and other "seeable" attractions in Japan, in addition to offering the opportunity of seeing a number of traditional crafts and cultural activities being performed. Nara, the site of a capital even older than Kyoto, is only an hour southward, and two of the country's finest castles are 90 minutes (or less) westward (Himeji) and one hour eastward (Hikone). The cultured pearl area of Ise is only about two hours away. Kyoto itself is less than three hours westward from Tokyo by Shinkansen superexpress train.

Nikko, less than two hours north from Tokyo by train, combines the man-made beauty of two incredibly colorful mausolea, dating back more than three centuries, with the natural attraction of a lake backdropped

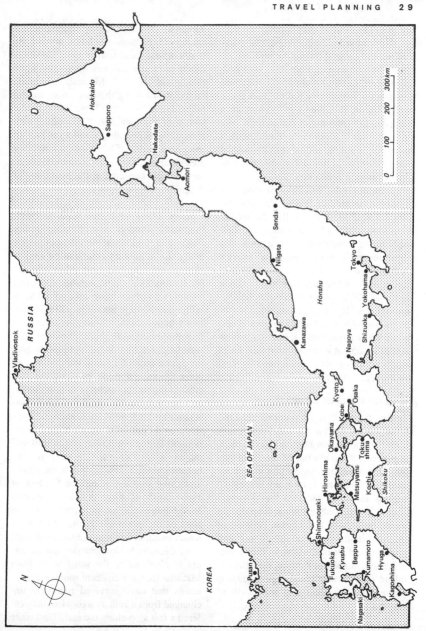

by mountains and a high waterfall.

Hiroshima and Nagasaki both have excellent museums showing the chilling effect of the A-bombs that were dropped.
Hiroshima is easily reached by Shinkansen
from both Tokyo and Kyoto, and those
with a Japan Rail Pass can even make a
long day trip there out of Kyoto (or a *very*
long one out of Tokyo). Nagasaki, with a
more scenic setting, is on the south coast of
the southern main island, Kyushu, and cannot be reached so quickly.

Tokyo, Osaka, and Nagoya have few
attractions of the "traditional" touristic nature because all were levelled during the
war. However, each (particularly the first
two) offers some modern attractions, and
there are easily reached places of interest
near all three. From Tokyo one can make
day trips to Kamakura (the great bronze
Buddha), Nikko (described above), Matsumoto (one of Japan's finest castles), Yokohama (the very fine Sankei-en garden and
some lesser attractions), Kawasaki (excellent collection of traditional farmhouses in
a park setting), and the area around Mt. Fuji
and the Izu-hanto peninsula.

Regional Attractions

To find the "real" Japan (pedants need not
write; I know that the cities and other manifestations of modern Japan are just as real),
it is necessary to get out of the cities and
into the countryside, mountains, or smaller
towns. Although there are many interesting
regions in Japan, the two that I would
choose if I had only a limited time budget
would be Tohoku and Chubu, because of
their concentration of things to see and
large areas of pleasant scenery. The former
is the northern part of Honshu, the latter the
inland (and mountainous) region roughly
between the Mt. Fuji area and north of
Nagoya.

Tohoku: This area has Mt. Bandai and a
cluster of picturesque lakes around its
northern base, other nearby mountain views
(some of clearly volcanic appearance), the
photogenic bay of Matsushima, many
scenic views along the east coast, around
lakes Tazawa-ko and Towada-ko, in the
towns of Kitakata and Kakunodate with
their many old buildings, and a valley with
more thatched-roof houses than any other
area in Japan. There are also many interesting festivals clustered at the beginning of
August.

Chubu: The Chubu area takes in much
mountain scenery, with terraced paddy
fields and traditional farmhouses along
many roads. Journeys that can be recommended are from Matsumoto (home of one
of the country's oldest and finest original
castles) through to Takayama, an old town
with many historic buildings still standing,
and a reconstructed "village" of traditional
farmhouses moved there from the surrounding countryside and arranged to give
the appearance of a functioning village of
olden times. En route between the two
cities is the natural splendor of Kamikochi,
and beyond can be found the rustic Shirakawa-go area, with its clusters of huge
three- and four-level thatch-roofed farmhouses. To the north of this area (but still
inland, accessible via Toyama) are the
beauties of the Tateyama mountain region.
Stretching into the waters of the Sea of
Japan north of there is the picturesque
Noto-hanto peninsula, and near the western
base of the peninsula is the old city of
Kanazawa that has many interesting remnants from one to two centuries ago. (It was
not bombed during the war.) South from
Matsumoto, via a different route, are three
towns that have survived relatively unchanged from a century ago when they offered a rest stop along the main land route

between Tokyo and Osaka, while a parallel valley offers some pleasant gorge and mountain scenery. (It is possible to make a loop out of the Matsumoto area that takes in all these places.)

Hokkaido: The northern main island has little historic background, having been settled by the Yamato Japanese (as distinguished from the indigenous Ainu) seriously only in the last century. Its strong suit is nature. This includes two regions of mountain terrain, around Mashu-ko lake in the east, and near lakes Toya-ko and Shikotsu-ko in the west, plus several stretches of coast worth seeing, such as the Shiretoko-hanto peninsula to the east, and the Shakotan-hanto peninsula to the west.

Kyushu: The southernmost main island has some places of historic interest (it is regarded as the cradle of Japanese civilization), but it is noteworthy more for natural scenery, like Mt. Aso and the surrounding valley that constitute the remains of the largest volcanic crater on earth, continually-erupting Sakurajima across from Kagoshima (a city of some interest), the Kirishima plateau, and the interesting coast along the SE side. The city of Nagasaki is of note for both the A-bombing and historic remains, as well as its favorable appearance, and Kagoshima offers some interesting places to see.

West from Kyoto: The south coast (Sanyo kaigan) is very heavily built up and offers little sightseeing despite bordering the Inland sea. Cities with some attractions are Okayama, Kurashiki, Onomichi, Hiroshima, and Iwakuni. The north coast (Sanin-kaigan) has only a few identifiable places to visit, but it is one of the least built-up of the "settled" areas of the country and is very pleasant to travel through. It is

comparatively flat, and would be one of the most enjoyable areas in Japan for bicycling (along with the coast between there and Kanazawa, as well as around the Noto Peninsula).

Southern Islands: The islands stretching south from Kyushu to Taiwan, which include Okinawa, are generally semi-tropical in nature, though most have individual characteristics.

Making the Most of Your Travels

Once you have made your plans and set out, my strongest suggestion is that you stay at *minshuku* (or *ryokan*) if your budget permits choosing them over youth hostels, for this will enable you to have the greatest amount of contact with "ordinary" Japanese. For very many travellers, their best memories come from the people they have met along the way. This book gives detailed information on accommodation, including how to make advance reservations (if you can maintain a schedule) along with full details regarding transportation.

As a brief summary, here are the locations of some of the best examples of things that visitors usually look for.

CASTLES	GARDENS
Himeji	Sankei-en
(Kyoto region)	(Yokohama)
Matsumoto	Ritsurin-koen
(Chubu region)	(Takamatsu)
Hikone	Genkyu-en
(Kyoto region)	(Hikone)
Matsuyama	Korakuen*
(Shikoku)	(Okayama)
Inuyama	Kenroku-en*
(Nagoya region)	(Kanazawa)
Matsue	
(Sanin coast)	

*The Japanese have assigned "ratings" to virtually everything in the country, from companies to universities to the merit of scenic places. These appear to have been handed down from on high in time immemorial, never to be questioned. Thus the top gardens, to the Japanese, are at Kanazawa, Okayama, and Mito. I found the latter to be a total disappointment, mostly open lawn (I spent considerable time looking for a non-existent "hidden" garden that would justify the fame), the one at Okayama nice in the garden section, but again largely lawn, and the one at Kanazawa large and good, but fitted with loudspeakers to extol at high volume the wonderfully peaceful atmosphere of the place, and tell how it encourages contemplation and inner peace. I have listed my preferences above based on my perceptions of what a Japanese garden should be. Comments are invited, pro or con. (No "con" has been received in the three years to 1991.)

WHEN TO GO

Climate

When to go to Japan, apart from personal convenience, is affected primarily by weather, but other factors to keep in mind are Japanese holidays and festivals.

Japan is a long country north to south, so the climate and weather vary widely. At any time there can be a great difference in conditions from one region of the country to another, and at different parts of the same region, especially in the many mountainous areas. There can be blizzard conditions on Hokkaido, sunny, crispy-cool weather in Tokyo and Kyoto, mild Mediterranean conditions on Kyushu and pleasant warmth in Okinawa.

The best single time period to visit Japan is from mid-September to mid/late-November. By then the heat and humidity of summer have passed, as have (most of!) the typhoons and rain that usually come in the late summer–early autumn. From then, starting in October in Hokkaido (the northern main island) the weather cools and the leaves change color in a display of fiery autumn foliage that is among the best to be found anywhere in the world. The change of color advances southward, earlier in high mountainous regions, more slowly along the coasts, and normally has reached Kyoto by the first half of November (although it can vary a week or two in either direction). These are the best two or three weeks of the year to visit Kyoto and it is well worth trying to get there then. However, the Japanese are also fully aware of the beauties of that season, and Kyoto is more crowded then than at any other time, so it is wise to book (even months ahead) for accommodation (or plan to use a neighboring city for accommodation). Within the next couple of weeks the leaves will have fallen everywhere, and the countryside will have faded to a dull brown, a far cry from the lush greens of summer or the almost iridescent green-gold of the rice paddies from mid-August until harvest.

Spring has long been touted as the ideal time to visit Japan. It seems that every brochure stresses the beauty of the cherry blossoms (*sakura*) as the symbol of Japan and gives the impression that this is the only time to visit. The fact is that anyone trying to see Japan at sakura time runs the risk of frustration and disappointment. True, the blossoms *are* beautiful, and when they're backdropped by or are part of a picturesque Japanese castle, the effect is incomparably lovely. But there are two factors working against a visitor with only a few days for sightseeing. First, the start of the sakura season varies from year to year over a range of several weeks, from very early April until late in the month. Second, the blossoms are fickle, remaining on a tree less than a week. In addition to the natural tendency of the petals to fall off, the perversity of nature makes this a season of strong winds and rain that remove them even more quickly. The short-lived nature of the blossoms made them a symbol of the samurai warrior, who was expected to have. a short but glorious life. For this, and as a symbol of all our lives, they have long been held dear by the Japanese.

Fortunately, with the great diversity in climate from north to south, and from coast to mountain, the blossom season extends six to eight weeks nationwide, advancing in a wave of pink and white from Kyushu north to Hokkaido.

Since *sakura* are an early blossoming species (though not the earliest, as plums come out in February), their appearance is followed by a period of several weeks while the rest of nature catches up and other greenery appears. This can be a season of windy and unsettled weather, with some beautiful days, some cloudy, some rainy. In general, spring begins chilly and clear in March and finishes warm to hot and humid in June. On Hokkaido, and in the highlands of Honshu, the temperatures are considerably lower, so that snow may remain on the ground as late as May or even June. There are some mountains where skiing is possible (for short runs) right into August.

Spring leads up to the rainy season, or *tsuyu* (also called *baiu*), which normally begins in Tokyo around June 10 and continues until about July 20, although it is earlier than this to the south and west, and from year to year. (It was not declared finished in Tohoku until well into August in 1987.) During this period rain can be expected on almost any day. However, the rainy season has been affected by the same climatic changes being felt around the globe,

and since 1978 there has been almost no rainy season. In 1978 it didn't rain at all in Tokyo, and in 1987 most of the days of the "rainy season" were gloriously blue and would have offered very good travelling conditions in many parts of the country (although they played merry hell with the water supplies of cities like Tokyo that depend on the rains to fill the reservoirs).

So, if you cannot avoid going to Japan during the rainy season, take cheer from the chance that the weather will be much better than expected. (One wit says that Japan actually has six seasons, winter, spring, rainy season, summer, typhoon season, and autumn.)

Incidentally, it is a popular belief among the Japanese that there is no rainy season on Hokkaido, but foreign residents report that a lot of water tends to fall out of the sky there at that time! Generally there is no rainy season along the Sanin-kaigan coast of western Honshu.

Summer is hot and humidly uncomfortable in the southern, coastal, and lower regions, which includes most major cities. ("Hot" is in the 90s F, 32–37° C, sometimes up to 40°.) In Hokkaido and in the highlands everywhere, summer is generally delightful, with warm to hot temperatures and low to moderate humidity. Even in northern Honshu (the Tohoku region) it gets hot, and Sapporo has its hot days, but there are often strong breezes to keep it all bearable. (Even Tokyo is usually breezy in the afternoon.) A canteen of water is a good friend when away from taps and dispensing machines, and it is not unusual to run through four to six liters of water a day. It is a good season for walking and enjoying the scenery. Birds and fantastically beautiful butterflies flitter around the lush green countryside, and the air is filled with the shrill chorus of *semi* (cicadas).

Visitors in summer should wear the

lightest garments possible; wash-and-wear clothing is *very* useful.

The warm weather usually lasts well into October, and it is still pleasant into mid-November in most areas. Despite the still scorching temperatures in the southern cities, however, swimming pools automatically close on the first day of September, and most people abruptly cease going to the beach on the same date. (At one time in the past, the entire population even changed from the clothes of one season to those of the next on the same date (Oct.1), regardless of the weather on that day, and the tradition is continued by police and "office ladies" who change into summer or winter uniforms.)

Travellers with their druthers regarding the time to start their journey and who plan to spend several months travelling around Japan would probably find the optimum route to be Hokkaido and northern Honshu through the hot season of July–August, the southern part of the country (Kyushu/Shikoku) between August and October, and the central part between September and November. For Kyoto, aim to be there in early-to-mid November; the period from from November 10 to 20 is generally the best for the autumn leaves, although this can vary by a week or more in either direction. At that time the temple areas of Kyoto must rate as some of the most beautiful places in the world, with their gorgeous combination of beautiful temples set among brilliantly colorful leaves.

Winter is generally a time of clear air, bright sun, and cool or cold weather; Tokyo has the most sunny winter days of any city in the world. Snow covers much of Hokkaido, northern Honshu, and the mountain highlands, often to a depth of several meters. Houses in the snow country may have a separate door at roof level for access during the winter! At lower altitudes, snow doesn't become a permanent feature until 100–200 km north of Tokyo. Tokyo and the other large southern cities are usually snow-free except for the occasional light falls that usually melt by midday, though in 1983–4 there were 29 days when Tokyo had snow falls. On three of those days it was more than 150mm deep and played havoc with traffic, and the snow stayed around for weeks. The following year it didn't snow once until March. Overnight temperatures are rarely much below freezing in Tokyo (although unheated apartments may seem much lower!), and daytime temperatures are commonly in the 8–10° C range. Osaka and other coastal cities in the middle and west of the main island would have similar conditions. Kyoto is higher than nearby Osaka and in low mountains, and is noticeably colder and snowier.

For ordinary touring, winter cannot be recommended very highly. Remember that when visiting temples and many other wooden-floored old buildings, it is necessary to remove your shoes and pad around in slippers, so warm socks are a must! Houses are usually not centrally heated, as fuel is expensive. Youth hostels are usually heated, especially in the colder regions, but an extra fee is levied to pay for the fuel. The large western-type hotels are invariably heated and comfortable, while public buildings, such as stores and offices, are generally overheated to the point of being sweltering.

It is said that Kyushu is semi-tropical. While the coastal areas, particularly Kagoshima, are a few degrees warmer than Honshu, it is still no tropical paradise, just pleasant; and in the mountain areas it too will be cold and snowy in winter. Okinawa and the other Ryukyu Islands are the warmest parts of Japan; their winter climate varies from cool to warm, but not quite tropical.

There are ski hills in many parts of the country, and Nagano was selected as the site for the 1998 Winter Olympics. Details of skiing for the *gaijin* visitor (and resident) can be found in a companion Kodansha International publication.

Holidays

It is useful to know the dates of Japanese holidays, because these are the times when huge numbers of people head back to their hometowns; trains are crowded and it is likely to be impossible to get reservations for any transportation or rooms. (Japanese office workers are notorious for not taking their annual holidays—possibly in order to appear keen and dedicated to the job, but more likely due to pressure from bosses—so a long holiday weekend is made more of than in western countries.)

There are 15 national holidays. The following Monday is taken as the holiday if the actual date is a Sunday, but not if it is Saturday, that being regarded as a normal working day (though growing numbers of firms are working a five-day week). On national holidays, most offices, factories, and businesses are closed, although most stores and restaurants remain open

Jan 1	New Year's Day
Jan 15	Coming-of-Age Day
Feb 11	National Foundation Day
Mar 21	Vernal Equinox Day (may change some years)
Apr 29	Green Day (Showa emperor's birthday)
May 3	Constitution Memorial Day
May 4	(unnamed "bridging" holiday)
May 5	Children's Day
July 20	Sea Day
Sept 15	Respect-for-the-Aged Day
Sept 24	Autumnal Equinox Day (date may change some years)
Oct 10	Physical Culture Day
Nov 3	Culture Day
Nov 23	Labor Thanksgiving Day
Dec 23	Emperor's Birthday

The three holiday periods to be really wary of are around New Year (roughly Dec. 28–Jan. 5), the end of April through early May, and mid-August. New Year is the biggest holiday season of the year, and many people try to return to their family home. Nearly all businesses and many restaurants are closed, busy cities like Tokyo are nearly deserted for a couple of days, and most shops are shuttered, so it is the least interesting time to visit Japan unless you have personal connections. (In recent years the degree of closing has been decreasing and the duration becoming shorter.) In the period from April 29 to May 5 there are no fewer than five holidays. It is known in Japan as "Golden Week"; many businesses give their employees the entire week off and, because the weather is usually fine, everyone travels. Or tries to! It is very difficult to obtain reservations on trains and at hotels, and train passengers without reserved seats will have a high risk of having to stand for the full journey. Worst, many youth hostels close during this period.

Although it is not a listed national holiday, be wary of the *obon* season, a week in mid-August when all Japanese try to visit the graves of their ancestors. Again, transport is very difficult to obtain. This is, however, a lively and interesting time because there is dancing on the streets and in parks every night in almost every neighborhood.

There are busy seasons also when school children go on excursions, filling up Youth Hostel accommodation in historic or nature areas (described further in the Youth Hostel section).

Festivals

Japan has a huge number of festivals, many with a known history of hundreds of years, and some that date back thousands, with evidence of religious and folk rites, such as fertility festivals.

The Tokyo Tourist Information Center (TIC) has free monthly handouts listing the festivals in Tokyo and the rest of the country, and they are posted for the Kyoto region (Kansai) on a bulletin board in the TIC in Kyoto. If you want an idea of what will be happening in a later month, the staff can copy the information sheets of the previous year; many dates remain the same from year to year.

Festivals provide an insight into Japan that cannot be gained in any other way, and it is worthwhile planning an itinerary to take in as many as possible. With few exceptions they are occasions of joy and celebration. The men (and some of the older women) get gloriously drunk and happy, and often invite any foreigners present to join in the fun and sample the contents of the cask of sake just opened. (This can make taking pictures quite difficult after a while!) A feature of nearly every festival, especially those in the country, is the drumming. The amazingly primitive rhythm is executed with great skill and precision. The drumming is apparently a carry-over from long forgotten days of the earliest inhabitants of the islands.

Festivals give some of the most lasting memories of Japan, for they are a reflection of the true Japanese spirit, a renewal of contact with their origins.

For the visitor, festivals are worth knowing about for two reasons; not only are they one of the most enjoyable types of event that one can see while in Japan, but also because the big ones are such attractions that they draw hundreds of thousands of persons from all over the country and saturate all available accommodation. For this reason, the dates of the major festivals are given in write-ups on individual areas so that travellers can try to make advance reservations in that area, or know that it will be necessary to go elsewhere to find accommodation.

SOURCES OF INFORMATION

The best single source for information on Japan is Japan National Tourist Organisation (JNTO). This is a semi-official body set up to distribute tourist information and otherwise encourage travel to Japan.

The JNTO has prepared a large number of excellent pamphlets and other publications that provide of useful information for travel in Japan, including information specially slanted toward the budget traveller. JNTO publications are available by mail from their many overseas offices (listed at the end of this section), although it is possible that a particular publication will be out of stock.

Within Japan, the JNTO operates three Tourist Information Centers (TICs), two in the Tokyo area (in central Tokyo near the Ginza district, and at Narita Airport), and one in Kyoto, not far from Kyoto station. All carry the full range of information-packed JNTO publications. These include both color brochures on the various areas of the country, and large numbers of plainer information sheets on specific cities, areas, accommodation, transportation, food, and on and on. In addition, they keep voluminous books of addresses of specialty shops, medical services, and on an unimaginable variety of other topics. If you want some special service or product, there is an excellent chance that they can locate a source and arrange a meeting, if necessary. The staff members at the TICs are also goldmines of information.

Once you have an idea of the area(s) to which you would like to travel, give your itinerary to a staff member and ask for any literature that they would recommend for sightseeing, transportation, accommodation, special attractions, etc., in that area.

Unfortunately, these three Tourist Information Centers are the only places in Japan that are equipped to give a full range of travel information in foreign languages. Information offices in other cities, at stations, for example, are there to provide details on the local area, but there is usually (some fortunate exceptions!) no one who can speak any language other than Japanese.

All three TICs can make bookings for accommodation (hotels, minshuku, and economical ryokan, though not the cheapest of places). This service is invaluable for the new arrival, for it overcomes the language problem, and the staff can give detailed directions for getting to the place.

Japan Travel-Phone

As a great courtesy to foreign visitors, the JNTO has organized *Japan Travel-Phone*, a toll-free telephone travel information service. You can call from anywhere outside of Tokyo and Kyoto at no cost to make inquiries of a tourist nature (transport schedules, sightseeing advice, etc.). It could also be useful if you were having trouble making yourself understood in some out-of-the-way place (or in a big city, for that matter!). The service operates from 0900 to 1700 Monday to Friday and 0900 to 1200 on Saturday. Outside of Tokyo or Kyoto, dial either 0088-22-4800 or 0120-44-4800. Within the Tokyo area (area code 03), dial 3201-3331; within the Kyoto area (area code 075), dial 371-5649. (The latter two are local calls at ¥10 per minute.)

Publications by JNTO/TIC

The following are useful general information booklets or other publications offered by the JNTO/TIC. The number in parentheses is the JNTO code number, and the letter is the initial letter of the languages in which it is available: English, French, German, Spanish, Portuguese, Italian, and Chinese. (The TICs usually also have non-JNTO brochures and pamphlets of particular cities and areas; ask what is currently available for areas that interest you.)

Your Guide to Japan   A 24-page booklet containing a wealth of general information about Japan - history, weather, geography, accommodation, transport, culture and the arts, and sightseeing. (101-E,F,G,S,P,I,C)

Japan Traveller's Companion   A 24-page booklet containing more specific information than the above publication, with info on transport, accommodation, sports and embassies. (105-E)

Economical Travel in Japan   A 12-page with some hints for economical travels, though rather general in coverage. (101-3-E)

The Tourist's Handbook   A booklet of useful phrases, along with the most frequently asked questions (printed in English and Japanese) that can be shown to a Japanese person, who can then choose the most appropriate answer from a list.

Tourist Map of Japan   This shows the major cities, the rail network, and large roads. It is useful for overall itinerary planning, and also has large scale maps of many cities.

Tokyo (222-E,F,G,S,P,C)

Kyoto-Nara (224-E,F,G,S,P)

Nikko (221-E,F,G,S)

Northern Japan (Hokkaido and Tohoku) (211-E)

Fuji-Hakone-Izu (223-E,F,G,S)

Central Japan (Kanto, Chubu, Kinki) (214-E)

Western Japan (Chugoku, Shikoku) (212-E)

Southern Japan (Kyushu, Okinawa) (213-E)

Hokuriku (Toyama, Ishikawa & Fukui) TO 1223-30872

Shizuoka TO 1224-07872
Tokyo map
Kyoto/Nara map

Other JNTO publications on specific topics such as accommodation and transport are listed in the appropriate sections of this book.

Other Publications

The commercial publication *Japan Visitor's Guide* has some information and maps that may be useful supplements to those mentioned in this guide, but it is best to wait until you get to Japan before obtaining a copy. It is distributed free at the Tokyo TIC and possibly at other tourist centres.

Unless the format changes, the publication *Japan Travel-Phone* has the excellent Tokyo subway and Tokyo-area transportation maps that are also printed in the JNTO map of Tokyo, in addition to an excellent transportation map of much of the Kinki district (Kyoto-Nara-Yoshino-Wakayama-Osaka-Kobe). All the maps show the station names in both *kanji* and *romaji*.

JNTO Offices Overseas

USA

Rockefeller Plaza, 630 Fifth Ave. Suite 2101, New York, NY 10111. tel (212) 757-5640

401 North Michigan Ave. Suite 770, Chicago, IL. 60611. tel (312) 222-0874.

2121 San Jacinto St. Suite 980, Dallas, TX 75201. tel (214) 754-1820.

360 Post St. Suite 601, San Francisco, CA 94108. tel (415) 989-7140.

624 South Grand Ave., Los Angeles, CA 90017. tel (213) 623-1952.

Canada

165 University Ave, Toronto, ON M5H 3B8. tel (416) 366-7140.

England

167 Regent St, London W.1. tel 734-9638.

Australia

115 Pitt St, Sydney, NSW 2000. tel (02) 232-4522.

Hong Kong

Suite 3606, Tow Exchange Square, 8 Connaught Place, Central. tel 525-5295.

Thailand

56 Suriwong Rd, Bangkok. tel 233-5108.

Switzerland

Rue de Berne 13, 1201 Geneve. tel (022) 731-81-40.

Germany

Kaiserstrasse 11, 6000 Frankfurt a/M. tel (069) 20353.

Books

There are many books about Japan on the market in Japan, whatever the subject—from gardens to food to traditional carpentry to business matters. Distribution overseas is likely to be spotty, however, and not all books listed below may be readily available. (Conversely, some books printed overseas may not be found easily in Japan, particularly those of a critical nature. The book *Yakuza*, for example, has been very difficult to find in Japan, and no Japanese publisher wished (dared) to publish it in Japanese translation because it told too much.)

A near-revolution has taken place in books about Japan in recent years. Whereas virtually all books on the country, people, and culture in the past had been praising, describing them with nothing but enthusiasm, several in recent years have taken a more neutral stance, or have been critical of various aspects of Japan once considered beyond reproach. Many of the "old school" books are translations from Japanese, and often were written by Japanese specifically to influence foreigners favorably toward Japan, although there has been no shortage of such books by foreigners beguiled by the country. A small number of the books in

English fall into the grouping *nihonjin-ron* ("theory of the Japanese"), though they are a tiny fraction of the number. The name sounds academic and commendable, but their main purpose is to convince the Japanese populace (and to reinforce existing belief) of their uniqueness in every way compared with all other peoples of the world, in language, culture, and racial make-up (or to persuade non-Japanese of the truth of these views).

If these works could be understood by foreign readers, they would be laughed at, but the difficulty of reading Japanese has made the numbers of non-Japanese readers negligible, and the risk of refutation (or of becoming widely known about in other countries) has been small. However, books in English appearing recently have taken this genre of Japanese literature to task, one giving an excellent analysis of the reality of Japanese life and society, another cutting the ground out from under the "theoretical" grounds on which *nihonjin-ron* is based, and others giving anecdotal recounting of realities.

One book by a quack named Tsunoda has been translated into English, and provides an example of the type of nonsense that is being published in Japanese. It tries to show that the Japanese brain is organized and processes information in a way different from that of all other peoples. It can be plowed through (it is hard going) by those who enjoy off-beat humor. (Keep in mind that it was not written to be amusing.)

The sad aspect of all this is that a sizeable amount of the work is being cranked out by people with impressive academic credentials and who work at some of the country's top universities; it makes one wonder about the quality of the educational system. Part of the reason is that one must support the work and theories of one's superior if one wishes to advance within the university system; original thinkers are discouraged, and attacking the theories of others, no matter how ridiculous, is anathema. There is little criticism in Japan in almost any field, it would seem.

Anyone making up a list of books to read about Japan has the option of going the "realist" or the "traditionalist" route in acquiring information about the country. The following list of books attempts to distinguish between them where this is relevant. Any competent bookstore would have listings of books available in your country and could order what it didn't stock.

People and Society

The Japanese, Jack Seward (Lotus Press, Tokyo).
More about the Japanese, Jack Seward (Lotus Press, Tokyo).
The Tourist and the Real Japan, Boye de Mente (Charles E Tuttle).

The first two were written some time ago and were getting on a bit in years, but have been updated and give many useful insights. The other may not be available any longer, but if it is, most of its comments are still valid.

The Land of the Rising Yen, George Mikes (Penguin Books). Although published in 1970, this book (if it can be found) gives a witty and perceptive look at the country and people—better than any five sociology and history books combined.

A Look Into Japan (Japan Travel Bureau). This pocket-size book answers all those "What is that?" questions asked by most travellers in Japan. Want to know the symbolism of the various positions of hands or feet on Buddhist statues; the names of the buildings in a temple/shrine; the parts making up the buildings; the parts of a room; the construction and movement of Bunraku puppets. . . ? This book has the answers.

Shadows of the Rising Sun, Jared Taylor.

This book gives an excellent overview of the country, the people, and the culture in a very objective and incisive no-nonsense manner. Taylor grew up in Japan and speaks the language like a native, so his observations cannot but be reliable.

The Japanese Mind: The Goliath Explained, R.C. Christopher (Simon & Schuster). A good book covering most aspects of Japan, though criticised from one quarter from having borrowed too liberally from the writings of others.

The Roads to Sata, Alan Booth (Weatherhill). Alan Booth walked from the top of Hokkaido to the bottom of Kyushu, then wrote about his experiences and the people he met. For anyone contemplating travel out in the boonies, this is a good introduction to the behavior and reactions of typical Japanese when a non-Japanese face shows up on their turf. It is realistic and candid, portraying both the great kindness and the subtle (and not-so-subtle) discrimination against a non-Japanese.

Images of Japanese Society, R. Mouer and Y. Sugimoto (Routledge and Kegan Paul). For a serious, objective look into the realities of Japanese society, this sociological study is the one. Unfortunately it is rather pricey, so a copy from a library would save much money.

The Myth of Japanese Uniqueness, Peter Dale, Croom Helm, (Nissan Institute for Japanese Studies, UK). For anyone really interested in Japan in depth, this book will be of great interest, for it provides an objective look at Japan while totally demolishing the writings of the *nihonjin-ron* type (which have, for years, influenced most works written on Japan by non-Japanese). It might be a bit deep for the casual visitor, but would be invaluable to anyone truly interested in Japan. It is, unfortunately, *very* expensive, over ¥10,000, so would best be borrowed (if available).

Learning How to Bow: An American Teacher in a Japanese School, Bruce S. Feiler (Ticknor & Fields, New York; U.S. $19.95). This is must reading for prospective JET teachers, but also gives a firsthand view to any interested visitor of how the education system molds its charges into enforced conformity.

Occupation, John Toland (Tom Doherty Associates, New York) 1987. Based around the War Crimes Trials, this interesting book makes real not only the physical conditions in Japan after the war, but also gives a good look into Japanese society and thinking to this day. Although a novel, it is heavily based on historic events and persons.

The Lady and the Monk, Pico Iyer (Alfred A. Knopf, New York). The story of one foreign man's search in Japan for what remains of the old culture and ways as a means of personal enlightenment, and his bumps with reality. It might be good preparation for anyone with a mystic view of Japan.

And in the other corner...

Japanese Society, Chie Nakane (Penguin Books). Rather turgid and exhausting at times, it gives a thorough examination of the social structure of Japan, but should be approached with a little scepticism, for not a few of the supposedly unique Japanese characteristics sound surprisingly like aspects of those of western and other countries.

The Chrysanthemum and the Sword, Ruth Benedict. This book is regarded as a "classic", but its conclusions are not accepted wholeheartedly these days. It was put together during WWII by interviewing Japanese immigrants, interned under the shameful U.S. program during the war, as an attempt to understand the thinking of the Japanese in Japan. It is remarkable in what it accomplished, but its observations should be taken with a little reservation.

Any books by Takeo Doi should be regarded with great scepticism. Typical of many academic writers, his writing style lacks the intellectual precision, logic, and integrity that is expected in the west (in idealized theory, at least!).

Economic

Japan: The Coming Economic Crisis, Jon Woronoff (Lotus Press). An excellent dissection of the Japanese economy, how it works, and potential problems. Fortunately for Japan and the Japanese, the worst of his predictions have failed to materialize, but the situation that he presents still exists. (Woronoff has written several other books on politics, society, and economics, several of which overlap somewhat, but all are worth reading even if with slight reservations.)

History

Japan from Prehistory to Modern Times, John Whitney Hall (Charles E Tuttle). *The Japanese*, Reischauer.

Nature

The Birds of Japan, Mark A. Brazil (Christopher Helm, London; 35 pounds). A 1991 work that will be a classic in its field. Excellent illustrations, distribution, etc. (If not at bookshops, order from Wild Bird Society of Japan, 1-1-4 Shibuya, Shibuya-ku, Tokyo 150; ¥13,700)
A Birdwatcher's Guide to Japan, Mark A. Brazil (Kodansha International).
Wild Flowers of Japan, Ran Levy (Kodansha International)

Language

Japanese Made Easy, T.A. Monane (Charles E Tuttle).
Beginning Japanese (Parts 1 and 2), Eleanor Harz Jorden (Yale University Press).

The former is a normal-size paperback giving adequate instruction for basic conversation as used for travel. The latter is a

pair of paperbacks in a choice of two formats, near-"normal" and larger. These two have much more detail in vocabulary and explanations of usage, so are better suited to a formal course of study.

Japanese in Action, Jack Seward.
This is a perenniel best-seller for understanding the language and the people.
Japanese for Busy People (Kodansha International).

Kodansha International has a full line of language books and dictionaries for the beginning to advanced student of Japanese, many of which have been given favourable reviews.

Special Interest Travel

In recent years, good numbers of books describing the touristic points of interest in a variety of parts of Japan, or on other aspects of travel in Japan, have appeared and (just as important) are being kept up to date. Among these are:

Hiking in Japan, Paul Hunt (Kodansha International; 1988).
Weekend Adventures Outside Tokyo, Tae Moriyama (Shufunotomo).
Day Walks Near Tokyo, Gary Walters (Kodansha International).
Kanazawa, Ruth Stevens (Kanazawa Tourist Assoc.).
In and Around Sendai, Vardaman, Garner & Brown.
Exploring Kamakura, Michael Cooper (Weatherhill).
A Guide to the Gardens of Kyoto, Treib and Herman (Shufunotomo).
Old Kyoto—A Guide to Traditional Shops, Restaurants and Inns (Kodansha International).
Cyclig Japan, Bryan Harrell (Kodansha International)
Trails of Two Cities : A Walker's Guide to Yokohama, Kamakura and Vicinity, John

Carroll (Kodansha International)
Japan for Kids, Kanagawa and Huey (Kodansha International)
Ski Japan!, T. R. Reid (Kodansha International)

Food

Some books have been published to help the foreign visitor select tasty dishes, or even to be able to order when there is not a word of English in the establishment.

Eating Cheap in Japan is a good inexpensive book to take along.
Reading Menus in Japanese Restaurants, Rory McGwire (ALC Press; ¥1000). The title says it all. It covers about 800 dishes available in restaurants ranging from swanky to everyman's.

Working in Japan

Two books give information that supplements the section in this book regarding employment possibilities and problems for foreigners in Japan.

The Job Hunter's Guide to Japan, Terra Brockman (Kodansha International)
Living and Working in Japan, Ron Davidson (Yohan Publications)

Bookshops

Tokyo has by far the largest number of stores selling foreign language books (mainly English) although at least one store in every major city should have at least a small selection. Two well-known chains of stores stocking foreign books are Kinokuniya and Maruzen. In Tokyo, the main Kinokuniya store is a favorite rendezvous in Shinjuku. In the Ginza area, the Jena bookstore has been a landmark for decades. Foreign language books (English) are found on the third floor. Another Tokyo bookstore is Byblos, in Takadanobaba.

Books are expensive in Japan, both imported and printed in Japan. Printing costs are high in Japan, and the exchange rate used for foreign books is more like 140-180 yen to the dollar than the actual rate.
Publishers' Addresses:

Kodansha International Ltd.
1-17-14 Otawa
Bunkyo-ku
Tokyo 112
tel. 3944-6492

Yohan Publications
3-14-9 Okubo
Shinjuku-ku
Tokyo 169
tel. 3208-0181

Shufunotomo Co. Ltd.
2-9 Kanda-Surugadai
Chiyoda-ku
Tokyo 101
tel. 3294-1118

ALC Press
2-54-12 Eifuku
Suginami-ku
Tokyo 168
tel. 3323-1101

Kanazawa Tourist Assoc.
9-13 Oyama-cho
Kanazawa

Keyaki-no-machi (In and Around Sendai)
402, 1-13-5 Yagiyama-honmachi
Taihaku-ku
Sendai

BY AIR

There are at least 12 international ports of entry by air into Japan: Tokyo, Osaka (Kansai International Airport; also serves Kyoto and Kobe), Nagoya, Niigata, Sendai, Komatsu, Fukuoka, Kumamoto, Nagasaki, Kagoshima, Naha, and Sapporo. The first six are on Honshu, the main island, the last is on Hokkaido, Naha is on Okinawa, and the rest are on Kyushu, the southernmost of the four major islands. The first three have the lion's share of international connections; the others are connected mainly with places in the region, such as Hong Kong, Guam, Saipan, Pusan, Seoul, and Shanghai. The following listing of connections is for convenience only, and is subject to change. Any travel agent would have up-to-date reference books showing the available connections.

Tokyo

Tokyo has the largest number of international flights of all cities of Japan, but nearly all go to Narita airport, nearly 60 km out in the country. Getting into central Tokyo from there takes an absolute minimum of 1-1/2 hours. (Further details are given in the Tokyo chapter.) The only international airline to fly into convenient Haneda airport is China Airlines; this airport is used by most domestic flights to Tokyo.

Osaka

Osaka's Kaisai International Airport is connected with nearly 40 cities on most continents. It is a good starting point for travel in Japan, for it is close to Kyoto, the premier tourist attraction city in the country, as well as Kobe. All three cities are on the Shinkansen, putting most of the country within a few hours' reach. The train and/or bus and/or ferry/jetfoil service to Osaka, Kyoto, Kobe, and Nara are described in the respective sections.

Nagoya

Nagoya, near the middle of the country, is connected with several cities in Asia, Oceania, and west-coast North America. The airport is about half an hour away from Nagoya station by regular airport bus. Nagoya itself is a commercial city with little of interest to tourists, but there are several attractions relatively close by, such as Takayama and Iida (in a scenic valley). All Shinkansen (bullet) and other JR trains stop there, and there are bus services east to Tokyo, west to Kyoto and Osaka.

Niigata

Niigata, on the north coast almost due north of Tokyo, has flights from Seoul, and is the port of entry from Khabarovsk for travellers using the Trans-Siberian railway or Aeroflot route from Europe. Only about a third of the passengers from Europe are able to get bookings on the ship from Nakhodka to Yokohama, and the rest must fly into Niigata. Niigata is easily reached by bus from the airport, and Tokyo is as little as 113 minutes away by Shinkansen train (the most expensive way), or in about 4-1/2 hours by a regular express. There is also bus service to Tokyo and to points north and south of Niigata.

Fukuoka

Fukuoka, in northern Kyushu, is a convenient entry point for travellers from a number of cities in Asia and Oceania. From there it is easy to circle around Kyushu, then carry on through western Japan to Kyoto, Tokyo, etc. Fukuoka is the western terminus of the Shinkansen. There is frequent bus service between the airport and Hakata station. (The station is named Hakata after the city where it is located, across a river from Fukuoka.)

Kumamoto

The rather provincial city of Kumamoto is linked to Seoul. It is a gateway to the volcano Mt. Aso, and Nagasaki is not far away in the opposite direction. A circle around the rest of Kyushu can easily be arranged.

Kagoshima

Flights link Kagoshima with Hong Kong and Seoul. This is the southernmost city in the main islands, and has several places of interest in and around it. There is regular bus service between the airport and Nishikagoshima, the main station of the city. From here you can travel up through Kyushu, seeing virtually everything of interest without backtracking.

Naha

Naha, the major city of Okinawa, is connected with Guam, Hong Kong, Honolulu, Los Angeles, San Francisco, and Taipei. Naha is a good starting point for exploring the numerous islands to the south of Kyushu. There are many flights from Naha to a number of cities on the main islands, as well as boat connections to several cities, like Tokyo, Osaka, Kobe, Kagoshima and Hakata.

Air Fares

Air fares are constantly changing, usually upwards. Check newspapers in large cities for special discounts. The best bargain fares in Asia are available in Hong Kong and Bangkok. In Europe, Amsterdam is the best bargain-hunting center. London may have good fares on a standby basis, and Frankfurt is also a place with bargain flights. Airlines with a reputation for low prices (though little else) from Europe to Asia are Biman Bangladesh Airlines, Pakistan Airlines, and Air India.

Japan was one of the last major destinations from Australia to get any sort of discount fares. Usually the only "cheap" fare is an Apex (advance-purchase excursion) return ticket, but there may be special bargains. Check with a good travel agent.

If you plan to visit Singapore, Hong Kong, or Bangkok, the best deal would be an Apex ticket to one of these destinations and a separate return ticket from there to Japan. China Airlines is popular with travel agents for this. You can buy the ticket in Australia or wait until you reach Singapore, etc. The total fare is more than the Apex fare to Tokyo but it's the cheapest way to get a stopover if you want one.

For years there was no such thing as a bargain fare out of Japan, but in recent years prices have come down considerably for advance-purchase "group" fares and other special deals. The opening of the airspace of the former USSR allowed fares to Europe to go substantially lower. The only way to find the lowest fares is to look for advertisements of travel agencies in publications like the newspapers, Tokyo Journal, and Kansai Time Out.

WARNING: The Japanese authorities do everything possible to protect their own airlines, particularly JAL. Tickets are scrutinized carefully to ensure that the maximum amount of revenue has flowed into Japanese coffers, and one must be careful not to buy a ticket that will not be honored on a flight out of Japan. Thus, it is not possible to tear out a Hong Kong–Tokyo segment ticket (for example) and fly out with the next one, for computers make it easy to check if the ticket-holder actually did use the first ticket to fly into Japan. If not, the ticket out will not be honored. This is probably contrary to IATA regulations, but too bad.

There are often advertisements in local newspapers in Japan offering unused portions of tickets for sale cheap. The seller offers to go to the airport to see the buyer through the check-in. However, I have seen the name on the ticket checked against the name on the passport *at the boarding gate* and after the seller would have left the airport. Perhaps it is possible to get away with this fiddle sometimes, but I would not put my own money on the line unless I had a sure way to contact the person selling the ticket.

BY SEA

There are no longer any regular passenger liner services between Japan and the countries of Europe and North America, although there is regular service to the neighboring countries of Taiwan, South Korea, and China (detailed below). Cruise ships stop at Tokyo, Yokohama, and Kobe from time to time, but obviously these are not scheduled (nor are they cheap), so are not a normal way to get to Japan. Visitors on ships that stop at both Tokyo/Yokohama and Kobe can leave the ship at one, travel through the country to the extent permitted by time, and rejoin it at the other.

For cruise passengers with one or two nights in the Yokohama-Tokyo area, suggested places to visit are Nikko, Kamakura, and Tokyo. If your ship calls at Kobe next, you can travel from Tokyo to Kyoto by Shinkansen train, catching a glimpse of Mt. Fuji en route (atmospherics permitting), tour Kyoto for a while, then go on to Kobe to rejoin your ship.

Apart from cruise ships there are a few cargo ships sailing the Pacific that take passengers. Most prefer to take passengers for the entire trip, to the final destination, so it may be harder to get a booking to Japan on a ship going to other ports. The best advice is to find a capable travel agent who can find a freighter that will be going to Japan. Fares vary enormously, but usually even the cheapest will be considerably more expensive than flying.

Vladivostok & the Trans-Siberian

The only regular passenger service to Japan (apart from the ferry services to/from Korea, Taipei, and China) is operated by the Russian-owned Far East Shipping Line, between Vladivostok (east coast of Russia) and Niigata or Fushiki (in Toyama).

In 1994, the scheduled number of sailings from (to) Niigata/Fushiki was June: 3 (3); July: 5 (5); August: 4 (4); September: 5: October 3 (3). The trip takes about two days, with fares ranging from ¥31,400 to ¥80,900.

The frequency of service has decreased considerably over the past few years and it may be discontinued; in previous years there were also sailings in April and May. The Trans-Siberian sector is typically nine days travelling between Moscow and Vladivostok with a break at Khabarovsk and Irkutsk.

Almost all travellers have had good comments on the ship service and most have been satisfied by the Trans-Siberian rail trip, though there were tales in past years of being unable even to obtain the meals that they had paid for.

Arrangements are made through the Japan-Soviet Tourist Bureau in Tokyo (tel (03) 5562-3382) and Osaka (tel (06) 531-7416). The Tokyo TIC (and probably Kyoto) usually has a leaflet giving more details and maps for getting to both the Tokyo and Osaka JSTB offices.

Korea

There is a daily (each direction) ferry service between Shimonoseki (at the far west of Honshu) and Pusan in Korea. The Kampu ferry (tel (0832)-24-3000) is the least expensive way of getting from Korea to Japan, the lowest fare being ¥8500. Further details of the ferry are given in the section on Shimonoseki, and the TIC in Tokyo has a handout information sheet with complete details.

Many people want to go between Tokyo and Seoul to renew visas. The cheapest way to do this is by a lengthy trip by train or train and boat to Shimonoseki, ferry to Pusan, and train or bus from there to Seoul and back. Unless you are desperate to save every last yen, you should consider flying directly between Tokyo and Seoul; the three-day excursion fare is only about ¥10,000 more than the combined surface fares, and is one heck of a lot more convenient. In addition, the horror stories of Immigration officials in Shimonoseki (well-founded) make it advisable to bypass that as a point of entry unless you have lots of money on hand when entering Japan.

Taiwan

There is a more-than-weekly boat service between Naha (Okinawa) and Taiwan, to Keelung, in northern Taiwan, and Kaohsiung, farther south. The former takes 35 hours, the latter two more. The boats also stop briefly at the islands Miyako and Ishi-

gaki en route from Naha to Taiwan (both trips), but only one stops on the return trip, at Ishigaki. The lowest fare is ¥15,600 Naha-Keelung, ¥18,000 Naha-Kaohsiung. The shipping company is Arimura Sangyo; telephone numbers are: Naha (098) 869-1320; Tokyo (03) 3562-2091; Osaka (06) 531-9267. The TIC in Tokyo has a handout detailing the current schedules, fares, visa information, and other essential information.

China

There is a weekly service in each direction between China (Shanghai) and Japan (alternating week-by-week among Yokohama, Osaka and Kobe). The trip takes just over two days for the latter two and just under three for Yokohama. Minimum fare (tatami class, which is often noisy and smoky due to students) is ¥26,910 for Yokohama, ¥20,700 for the other two. The fare includes two breakfasts. Office phone numbers are: Kobe (078) 392-1021), Tokyo (03) 3294-3351.

IMMIGRATION

Everyone entering Japan for any purpose (except U.S. military and dependents) must have a valid passport or other travel document. In principle, everyone must also have a visa, although this requirement is waived for short-term visitors from many countries, as described below. There are two general categories of visa, short-stay and long-stay. The short-stay type will be described in the first part of this section, since most readers will need information for only a short visit. Information on long-stay visas (for students, working, etc.) is given at the end.

Warning: When in Japan, always carry your passport or Alien Registration Certificate (explained in the section on long-stay visas) with you any time you are away from your accommodation. (Those under 16 are exempt from this regulation.)

Short-Stay Visits

Short-Stay (Tourist-Type) Visas

In principle, a short-stay visa is required by all persons of the type described as "Temporary Visitor" in the semi-official "A Guide to Entry, Residence and Registration Procedures in Japan for Foreign Nationals", such as visitors to the country for a relatively short period of stay of a touristic nature. Important exemptions from this rule are citizens of most English-speaking and western European countries (with the notable exceptions of Australia and South Africa), many Latin American countries, and a few other countries in Asia and Africa, who do not need to obtain a visa beforehand for the above "touristic" purposes. (But they must obtain one for any other type of activity.) Valid purposes include sightseeing, recreation, attending meetings or conventions, inspection or study tours, participation in contests (athletic and other), visiting relatives and friends, goodwill visits, and similar non-remunerative activities. If required, such visas must be obtained from a Japanese diplomatic mission prior to arrival in Japan.

Caution: Be sure that your visa is stamped in your passport, not on the application form or elsewhere. Although the latter is legal (I checked with the Ministry of Foreign Affairs), the inspector at the port of entry may be ignorant of the regulations or may just want to throw his weight around, and refuse entry. (It has happened.) Visas are issued by the Ministry of Foreign Affairs, while immigration officers are employees of the Ministry of Justice. Don't let yourself be the victim of a bureaucratic turf battle.

Shore Pass

Although the name dates from the days of ship travel, a shore pass can be very useful to many travellers in the air age. A shore pass permits a stopover of up to 72 hours in Japan, without visa, even for those who require visas to enter for longer periods of time. During this 72-hour period, the holder is free to travel anywhere within the country, so it affords the opportunity for a quick look around. It can be particularly useful for those who must obtain a visa for each entry to Japan and who are going to another country via Japan before returning to stay in Japan. Such a person can enter Japan for 72 hours on the first trip, saving the visa for the longer stay. I used one once while holding a working visa. At the time I could obtain only a single-entry re-entry permit, and wanted to stop over briefly in Japan between visits to Australia and Canada without using the re-entry permit, for these are not cheap, and my short visit was to be on a weekend when no Immigration office was open to issue another re-entry permit. A shore pass solved the problem.

To obtain a shore pass, one must have a confirmed onward-bound flight leaving within the 72-hour period. One obtains a shore pass prior to passing the Immigration inspector. At Narita airport there is a small mobile desk (quite clearly marked) at the entrance to the hall where travellers line up for Immigration procedures. (This has not always been manned, so it might be a good idea to ask your airline to advise you on what to do upon arrival, notify the authorities in advance, or whatever.)

Transit Visa

Passengers on a cruise ship that will dock at two ports in Japan can get a transit visa on landing that is valid for up to 15 days of travel through Japan to rejoin the ship at the other port. Passengers are supposedly required to designate their route, but there is no further check of their whereabouts once they are on shore. The ship's agent makes the arrangements for a transit visa.

Arrival in Japan

The passport of every entrant to Japan is stamped at the port of entry. In the stamp for an ordinary short stay, the inspector adds extra stamps in the space marked "Status" and "Duration". These are both explained below.

Status of Residence

Anyone entering for one of the "touristic" purposes described above would receive a "Temporary Visitor" status of residence. All others are of long stay type, and are detailed in the later section on that topic.

Duration

For citizens of Canada and most western European countries with a visa-waiving agreement, the period of stay (potentially; see below) is up to 3 months. It is 6 months for citizens of West Germany, U.K., Switzerland, Austria, Ireland and some others, 90 days for those from New Zealand and the USA, and up to 3 months for most other countries. The actual wording in the above-mentioned "Guide" is "6 months or less", etc. This means that the durations are nominal (unfortunately), and the inspector at the port of entry can be arbitrary in the period of stay granted.

Under the now-superseded regulations, I was entitled to a 90-day period, but one time I was forced to accept a 60-day period; when I protested (politely), I was told brusquely that I had the choice of accepting the 60-day period or going back to Korea. Immigration inspectors at Shimonoseki and Fukuoka have (in past years) had the bad reputation of this practice regardless of the period of stay requested. This is especially aggravating because there is, in effect, a "no-extension" policy (in mid-1991), as discussed below.

I do not know if the new regulations, which have eliminated the former "tourist" category, have tied the hands of these unpleasant people, nor have I had any recent reports on these ports, so cannot advise if the situation has remained as bad. (I would appreciate reports, good and bad, on experiences at these and other ports of entry.)

For citizens of a country without a visa-waiving agreement, the period of stay is nominally 90 days, and it seems that there is a better possibility of renewal (see below).

Extension of Period of Stay

The unofficial "Guide" referrred to above, in its characteristic indefinite manner, states "A foreign national who wishes to extend his period of stay should make an application for permission of extention (sic) of period of stay not later than the expiration date of the authorized period of stay." It continues later, "An application will not be necessarily approved." When I asked in mid-1991 at the Immigration office in Tokyo (Otemachi) about the current situation, I was told that no extension was being given to a Temporary Visitor who entered on a visa exemption basis, although those who obtained a tourist visa from a consular office overseas were sometimes successful. In any case, it would do no harm to give it a try if you really want to continue travelling within the country. (Up to the changes in immigration regulations in June 1990, a tourist had the possibility of obtaining extension(s) to a total of 6 months; one can hope that the policy of granting extensions to all will be reinstated.)

Applications are accepted up to a month prior to the expiration of the current period of stay, and an early application would allow for an alternative plan of action in the event that the extension was not given. If the extension is not approved, there is no option but to go to another country (Korea and Taiwan are the closest) and then re-enter. Beyond a certain number of such re-entries, one could expect to encounter reluctance or refusal. Keep in mind that the immigration officials at some ports of entry, such as Shimonoseki and Fukuoka (used often by budget travellers because they are on the lowest-cost boat and air routes between Korea and Japan), have a well-deserved reputation for being unpleasant, and could make even a first return difficult. If there is any doubt about being re-admitted, the better course is to fly in through a more cosmopolitan airport, like Tokyo or Osaka.

If an extension is permitted, there is the possibility that a letter of guarantee will be required. In such cases, the authorities prefer a Japanese as guarantor, but an obviously settled foreign resident is acceptable. A sample Letter of Guarantee is shown in the section on long-stay visas.

Potential Problems to Entry

Keep in mind that even if you have a visa, or your country has a visa-waiving agreement, you are not automatically entitled to entry into Japan when you arrive. The Inspector at the port of entry is king and can refuse entry, compelling the would-be entrant to fly back out of Japan at his own expense. Visas are issued abroad by the Ministry of Foreign Affairs (Gaimusho) at Japanese diplomatic missions, but actual permission to land is granted at the port of entry by inspectors who are under the jurisdiction of the Ministry of Justice. They have the right to demand to be shown an onward ticket, proof of adequate funds, and so on. Although most inspectors are reasonable, there have been many cases of totally ridiculous behavior. In one case, a traveller had arranged for money to be waiting for him in Japan, but because he had little in hand at the port of entry, he was refused entry. Anyone who has had dealings with banks, particularly Japanese ones, can only sympathize with the traveller's problems in having such remitted funds transferred to another country.

Having money in hand is not necessarily enough, however. One American man (perhaps not coincidentally, of African descent) married to a Japanese woman but unable to get permanent residence and thus depending on repeated tourist visas to enter and stay in Japan, arrived at Fukuoka to meet her. Despite having U.S. $2000 in cash in his pocket, he was held in a small room for six hours and not allowed to enter the country until his wife had, at easily-imagined great effort, managed to buy a $40 air ticket to Pusan at 8 o'clock on a weekend night.

Some other incidents that have occurred are related in the section on long-stay visas.

The authorities can refuse entry to Japan to any of the following:

-persons with contagious diseases or leprosy
-the mentally disturbed
-those with insufficient funds
-drug addicts and users
-ex-convicts who were sentenced to more than one year in prison
-prostitutes
-anyone deported from Japan less than a year earlier
-anyone who may cause harm to the interests and security of Japan

The latter is a wonderful catch-all, and can be interpreted as the authorities wish. In 1979 a New Zealand member of the Indian religious sect Ananda Marga was turned back at Narita even though he had a proper visa and there is no law prohibiting this group in Japan. As for prostitutes, this is a bit of a joke, because hundreds of women from Southeast Asia arrive and are met at the airport by gangsters (easily identified by appearance and behavior) who cart them off for their sordid work, and nothing is ever done to stop them. Of course no foreign "business girl" would ever declare her true occupation, for prostitution is illegal in Japan (though one would never realize it within the country!).

IMMIGRATION OFFICES

Tokyo	(03) 3213-8111 or 3664-3046
Narita	(0476) 34-2222
Yokohama	(045) 651-2851/2
Nagoya	(052) 951-2391
Osaka	(06) 941-0771
Kobe	(078) 391-6377
Sendai	(022) 256-6076
Sapporo	(011) 261-9311
Takamatsu	(0878) 22-5851
Hiroshima	(082) 221-4412
Shimonoseki	(0832) 23-1431
Fukuoka	(092) 281-7431
Kagoshima	(099) 222-5658
Naha	(098) 832-4185

Despite the negative notes included in these sections to inform the unwary of potential pitfalls, Japan is still easier to enter than many other countries.

NOTE: Information in the sections regarding visas was current as of mid-1991. It is believed to be accurate, but you should inquire of a Japanese diplomatic mission if you have any questions about current regulations.

Long-Stay Visas

For anyone wishing to enter or remain in Japan for any purpose other than one of the "touristic" reasons described above, it is necessary to obtain a visa from a Japanese diplomatic representative beforehand. There are no visa exemptions for any long-term purposes of entry.

Unlike many countries, it is not possible to be an immigrant to Japan, with the right to stay permanently, seek employment, bring in family members, etc. The only way to stay for a long time (apart from the few refugees admitted, mostly Vietnamese, and very few of them), is to be engaged in some activity that can attract a sponsor of some sort or form. Once the activity comes to an end, so does the permission to stay (unless you have been in the country long enough to obtain a permanent resident visa, or marry a Japanese) and you must then leave (unless you find another activity and sponsor). If you have a working visa and are employed by a large company, there is usually no problem continuing (but only a year at a time—no multi-year visas in most cases). Even with a visa for an activity and while legitimately following that activity, the path is not necessarily smooth; refer to the "Strange Happenings" section, below.

Long-stay visas can be obtained for many activities prior to entering Japan, while many people will have to go to Japan first to make arrangements for such a visa, then apply. The two cases are described separately.

Information in this section only supplements the section on short-stay visas; please refer to that section also.

Status of Residence

The following table lists the official name of the main categories of Status of Residence (= type of visa) given for long stays, and the nominal period of stay for each (usually renewable).

Cultural Activities	1 yr; 6 mo
College Student	1 yr; 6 mo
Pre-College Student	1 yr; 6 mo; 3 mo
Specialist in Humanities/ International Services	1 yr; 6 mo
Instructor (school teaching)	1 yr; 6 mo
Researcher	1 yr; 6 mo
Engineer	1 yr; 6 mo
Entertainer	1 yr; 3 mo
Skilled Labor	1 yr; 6 mo
Journalist	3 yr; 1 yr; 6 mo
Professor (academic research/teaching)	3 yr; 1 yr; 6 mo
Investor/Business Manager	3 yr; 1 yr; 6 mo
Religious Activities	3 yr; 1 yr; 6 mo

Periods of stay listed as more than one year usually have to be renewed annually.

The fourth of these, Specialist in Humanities/International Services, would be the category of "working" visa given to most people, including those teaching English (apart from those at government and private schools, who fall into the "Instructor" category). It covers such work as copywriting, translation, rewriting, public relations, language instruction, product development, and several others, making it a "catch-all" category.

With the revision of immigration regulations of June 1990, the authorities are tending to give visas only to university graduates (including applicants for teaching English), and potential entrants are having to show their degree (original document) when applying.

Activities falling within Cultural Activities are study of the Japanese language, traditional arts such as the tea ceremony, flower arrangement, music, dancing, traditional games (i-go), and martial arts.

While it is generally possible to obtain permission to work part-time on a student visa, if the primary intention is full-time employment it is better to get a working visa from the start.

Despite the name, the category of Pre-College Student is the one given to students enrolled in a Japanese-language course.

Visas can be arranged before or after entering Japan, as detailed in the following sections.

Arranging a Visa Before Entering Japan

Study and Working/Commercial Visas

People wishing to engage in any one of several types of activity will be able to obtain a visa without great difficulty before going to Japan, including:

-those who will be taking a recognized course of study (especially at university level) where standards are recognized internationally and entry is based on the applicant's academic record;
-those who will be teaching or performing research at a recognized institution;
-Prospective students who can arrange for a school that teaches some form of Japanese culture, as discussed above, and that can provide required documentation by correspondence;
-those engaged in "activities for the arts" (music, writing, graphic arts, etc.) organized by some Japanese institution;
-journalists;
-entertainers contracted overseas;
-skilled workers contracted overseas;
-those being transferred to Japan by their employer;

-missionaries sent by a religious organization.

In all these cases, documentation can be arranged from outside the country by the institution, future employer (which will be acting as sponsor), or company sending the employee to Japan. Someone from the organization can act as proxy and obtain a "Certificate of Eligibility for Status of Residence", which is discussed next. (General information on job-hunting is given in the later "Employment" section.)

Information on documentation required for these types of long-stay visa is given in abbreviated form in the booklet "A Guide to Entry, Residence and Registration Procedures in Japan for Foreign Nationals", described below. For detailed and up-to-date information, contact any Japanese diplomatic representative overseas (embassy or consular office). In general, an application will consist of an application form in duplicate (Form 1C), a photo 45 x 45 mm, a Letter of Guarantee, documents showing the reason for wishing to enter Japan, school records or company documents, documentation on the institution where you will study/teach or details on your company's activities in Japan, and so forth. The same office will accept the application and issue the visa.

Working Holiday Visa

An agreement between the Japanese government and those of Australia, Canada, and New Zealand set up a plan that gave young citizens (18–25; sometimes to 30) of those countries and of Japan reciprocal rights for a working holiday of up to a year, with extension at the option of the authorities. Citizens of the above countries should obtain further information from Japanese diplomatic representatives.

Arranging a Visa within Japan

It is often simplest to go to Japan and make the necessary arrangements for a long-stay visa in person. The usual procedure is to enter Japan, giving "travel" and/or "sightseeing" as the purpose of entry, thus obtaining Temporary Visitor status, then find a school, job, etc., and make the arrangements for a visa. Do not give "work" as the reason for entry, for that is a prohibited activity and you would likely be turned back at the port of entry. (See Practical Information chapter, Working section.)

After obtaining the required documents, you take them to a Japanese diplomatic representative in another country (most commonly Korea). A way of simplifying this procedure is described in the following sections "Certificate of Eligibility for Status of Residence" and "Going Abroad to Apply for a Visa".

Types of Long-Stay Visa

It should be possible to obtain up-to-date information on requirements for these types of visas and others (such as options for persons who plan to marry a Japanese) from regional Immigration offices, and perhaps in smaller district offices. The Otemachi office in Tokyo has had advisory staff who spoke English well.

Cultural Activities Visa

This is the visa category covering cultural studies (activities listed in short-term visas section, but not Japanese language). One first finds a suitable school, which will then provide letters of guarantee and other documents to satisfy the authorities. Holders of a Cultural Activities visa can not obtain working permission.

Pre-College Student Visa

As mentioned above, this is the category

given for studying Japanese. (It is also legal to study Japanese on a Temporary Visitor visa, but the short maximum period (3 months) given on one would limit the length of the course.) In the same way as for a cultural visa, one first finds a suitable school, which will then provide letters of guarantee and other documents to satisfy the authorities. Holders of a Cultural Activities visa can usually get permission to work to defray living costs. Working permission is typically good for up to twenty hours a week. However, if the study program is given only at night, it is sometimes possible to get permission to work full-time during the day, as long as there is proof that the student is actually carrying on the activity for which the visa was granted.

Specialist in Humanities/International Services Visa

This mouthful can be regarded as a working/teaching visa. Since it is usually difficult to arrange employment with a school or Japanese company from outside Japan, it would be difficult to obtain this sort of visa without first going to Japan (although there is some overseas recruitment these days; see the "Employment" section). In the same way as for a cultural visa, one first finds a suitable job from inside Japan, and the prospective employer then provides a letter of guarantee and the other documents needed to satisfy the authorities.

CERTIFICATE OF ELIGIBILITY FOR STATUS OF RESIDENCE Anyone planning to apply for a visa of the types just described will have to leave Japan to file the application. Much delay can be saved by obtaining a "Certificate of Eligibility for Status of Residence" from an Immigration Office in Japan; this process also means that only a single trip out of the country is required. To obtain this certificate, one fills in any applicable

forms and obtains all necessary documentation, then presents it all to the regional or district Immigration office closest to the proposed place of residence. The documentation usually requested (stress on "usually") is given in the "Guide", described below, but the inspector may ask for anything he wants. If the inspector is satisfied that all requirements have been met, the Certificate is issued. This signifies that the applicant will receive the visa. (This process typically takes 1–1.5 months.) The next step is to take the Certificate to a Japanese diplomatic mission in any other country, the visa is issued, and the applicant returns to Japan.

Once issued, a Certificate must be used within three months, otherwise it expires.

A Certificate can be obtained for a person not in Japan by a proxy in Japan. Categories of people allowed to act as proxies are listed in the "Guide", described below.

Going Abroad to Apply for a Visa

If it is necessary to go abroad to apply for a visa, the Japanese embassy in Seoul is the most popular for this purpose, although a Japanese diplomatic mission in any other foreign city will do just as well. So many foreigners make similar applications at Seoul that it handles them as a matter of routine. If all papers are in order, a Cultural Activities visa will usually be granted in one working day. Other types may require a few days if you have a Certificate of Eligibility, otherwise several weeks while the documents are processed back in Japan. During this period you are free to return to Japan.

When you have received your visa, check carefully what has been stamped and written in your passport. Unfortunately, there have been cases of incompetence at consular offices. One Australian businessman, for example, applied for a multiple-entry business visa, submitted all the necessary documents, waited a period of time, then received his passport back with a visa stamped in it. When he flew to Japan, he found that he had been given a single-entry tourist visa!

Be sure that your visa is stamped in your passport, not on the application form or anywhere else. The latter is legal, but inspectors at the port of entry have been known to refuse to accept it. One person received a multiple-entry visa stamped on the back of his application. He used it once to enter Japan via Narita airport, then went on to Korea. He returned to Japan via Fukuoka, and was refused entry because the visa was not in his passport. He had to go back to Korea, at his own expense, livid with rage.

Visas are issued by the Ministry of Foreign Affairs, while immigration officers are employees of the Ministry of Justice. Their aims aren't always in synchronism.

STRANGE HAPPENINGS DESPITE HAVING A PROPER VISA Once you have your work visa, remember that you still have to pass the immigration inspector at the port of entry. An inspector at Shimonoseki (the port of entry from Korea by ferry, the least expensive way to enter Japan from Korea) is known to have refused entry to one person on the grounds that he did not have enough money with him, even though he had just been given a work visa in Seoul, had a job waiting in Tokyo, and had sufficient money for the train fare to get there! Shimonoseki has a bad reputation for such goings-on, so it might be worth flying to Osaka or Tokyo, where the officials are more reasonable.

When you have entered the country, immediately check your passport to be sure that you have been given the correct status. One well-known lady journalist wrote that she had been stamped into the country once as a tourist, and once as a missionary! (She had a proper working visa.) When she brought the error to the attention of the immigration officials, they were very reluctant to admit that they had made a mistake, and even suggested that she fly out and return again!

Once you are in Japan, things will probably go smoothly. However, strange events can occur. A close friend of mine was a part-time post graduate student at Keio University, one of the best in Japan, working part-time as a teacher in a government school to support herself. After she had been in Japan for four years, routinely obtaining an extension to continue her work, she was abruptly informed during her next application that she had been in Japan solely for the purpose of making money (not "suspected", but "notified" of the "fact"), was grilled unpleasantly for several hours at the Immigration office during which she was virtually told that she was a liar, and was told that she would have to leave Japan. There were no grounds whatever for their accusations (she was living a very "student" existence), but she was nevertheless forced to leave a few months later, her Masters degree unfinished, and feeling a great deal of bitterness toward the authorities who had forced her departure and no small amount of ill will toward Japan.

Change of Status

A person entering Japan on a long-term visa may engage in only the activity allowed under his or her status. However, it is usually possible to get permission from an Immigration office to change activity (or status), but it is required to obtain this permission, as it is to engage in the same activity in a different place. For example, permission would be needed for a person with a student status who wanted to teach

English, for a teacher who wanted to change to a different school, for a person on a cultural visa studying pottery who wanted to take up lacquer-making, or a person wanting to change status from teaching to other work.

The good news is that the authorities seem to grant such requests in most cases. However, you must obtain permission first before engaging in the new activity. There is always the chance that the authorities will check whether the change has already been made, and failure to obtain prior permission might result in "unfavorable consideration" of a future request for an extension, or possibly even outright deportation. A letter of apology might be sufficient to get out of the problem, but it is best to avoid trouble in the first place.

LETTER OF RELEASE If one is working for one employer and changes to another, one is supposed to obtain a "letter of release" from the first. Sometimes, however, the departure is unfriendly, and the first employer will do nothing whatever to help. This is not a problem, for the letter is not an absolute requirement. When requesting a change of status to transfer to the new employer, it is sufficient to say "personal difficulties", or "better pay" as reasons for the change.

It is usually possible for those with a non-tourist status to change their status in Japan without leaving the country.

Re-Entry Permit

If you have a visa for a long-term status and wish to leave Japan for a short time and then return to continue the same activity, you should obtain a re-entry permit before leaving Japan. This is not a landing permit (entry is not guaranteed, as for any entry into the country, but there is normally no problem) and you must still satisfy the immigration inspector at the port of entry; it does facilitate re-entry and assures preservation of the original status. If you do not obtain the permit, however, your original status (visa) will be cancelled automatically upon your departure, and you would have to start the application process again from the beginning.

There are two types of re-entry permit, single-entry (¥3000), and multiple-entry (¥6000). Either is valid for up to one year, and less if the balance of the permitted period of stay in Japan is less. It must be used within six months of issue. Its period of validity (and that of the original visa) cannot be extended outside Japan; if it (or the visa) expires while the holder is abroad, a new visa must be obtained before the holder can return to Japan to resume the original status.

Sample Letters for Documentation Purposes

Letter of Guarantee

For any type of long-stay visa, and often for an extension of stay as a tourist, a Letter of Guarantee is required. An acceptable form of letter is provided here.

If possible the guarantor should be a Japanese citizen who has the financial resources to take on this obligation. To demonstrate this capability, the guarantor is usually required to supply a certificate of employment and recent certificate of tax payment. (It is considered a rather heavy obligation, and many Japanese are reluctant to take it on.)

For a working or language-teaching visa, the company or school can provide the letter, and for a press or commercial visa, the guarantee letter would of course be provided by the person's organisation.

The Japanese authorities always prefer to have a Japanese guarantor. In one case, a foreign employee of a very large multinational corporation presented a letter of guarantee from his company, but was asked if he couldn't find a Japanese guarantor. So he asked his secretary if she would write a letter of guarantee for him. She did and it was accepted! (A foreigner employed steadily in Japan should also be acceptable.)

To: Consul-General (Ambassador) of Japan/ Minister of Justice

    Outside Japan   Within Japan
        Letter of Guarantee

In connection with the application by Mr. (Mrs., Miss) _____ for a _____ visa, I hereby guarantee the following:

    1. Logistic support while he/she is in Japan.
    2. Transportation fee for repatriation.
    3. Any other information concerning ... will be given gladly.

Guarantor:

Name:
Nationality:
Address:
Tel:
Status of residence:
Occupation:
Relationship:

                (Signature)

    Note that it is very common practice for companies to demand that prospective employees sign a statement that they will not hold the company responsible for item 2., above, guaranteeing repatriation, thus absolving themselves of the responsibility that they have signed for.

Letter of Credit

If you have time to make preparations before leaving home base, a way that can sometimes get around the problem of finding a guarantor is to arrange a line of credit with a bank where you are known, and have it issue a "to whom it may concern" letter with a message to the effect: "This is to certify that (name) has arranged a line of credit with this institution valid until (date) for an amount sufficient to guarantee his/her repatriation from Japan." I obtained such a letter once, and it was accepted at the Tokyo Immigration office for extending a Temporary Visitor type of visa. The letter is kept on file and can be referred to again for subsequent applications for extension.

Letter of Apology

When dealing with government authorities at any level in Japan, people frequently run afoul of some regulation or other. The standard practice is to write a letter of apology, stating something to the effect that the event was an oversight, that it was unintended, that the person humbly hopes that he/she has not caused inconvenience to the department/person/ whatever, etc. If the infraction was not serious, the letter is generally accepted and the matter overlooked. (Whether anyone gives the slightest credence to the sincerity of the letter or the writer is yet to be determined. If it becomes necessary to write one, just regard it as a quirk of the system, part of the charm of the country. Just remember the operative advice: Always show sincerity, even if you have to fake it.) It seems that a letter of apology goes a long way toward getting one off the hook for a wide range of misdemeanors, but it would not be wise to explore the outer limits of this process!

Alien Registration

All aliens remaining in Japan for more than

90 continuous days (with the exception of diplomats and U.S. military personnel) must register with the authorities and obtain an Alien Registration Card (ARC). Details of the procedure follows.

****

YOU MUST CARRY YOUR ALIEN REGISTRATION CARD (OR PASSPORT) WITH YOU AT ALL TIMES!

****

You can be asked by police or other authorities to produce your ARC or passport at any time. It is not unknown for a person walking innocently down the street to be challenged. Failure to be able to show either document will most likely lead to several unpleasant hours in custody while someone else fetches it. Contrary to logic, the "offender" is usually not allowed to go and get it, even in the company of an officer, and even if the card is in a building nearby. If there is no one else who can get it, an impasse is reached. It is a needless annoyance bordering on idiocy in many cases, but one that could befall any foreigner in Japan. Although a challenge is not a regular occurrence, it happens often enough to be a concern. It is difficult to say if it is done out of perversity, or showing "authority". It is doubtful that they catch many criminals this way.

Obtaining an Alien Registration Certificate
Obtaining an ARC is simple and costs nothing, but does require three photographs—about 50 x 50 mm. It is issued by the municipal office of the city, town, or ward (ku) in which you are living. In the case of travellers, the address of a lodging place is acceptable.

Those with a long-stay visa and a reentry permit keep their ARC if they are going overseas temporarily.

A change of residence within the district must be recorded at the original issuing office. A move to another district requires re-registration in the new district within 14 days.

SUGGESTION: Before setting out on your travels, have a passport-type photo taken (plain background, facing the camera straight on), preferably on 35mm film (color or black-and-white). If having the photo taken by a studio, inform them beforehand that you need the negative; it may take some looking to find a place that will agree to give up the negative. Take it with you, and get prints of the required size as you need them. You will need photos for an ARC, and visas for travel to other countries can consume an awesome number of them.

FINGERPRINTING Persons over 14 years of age who are granted a total stay of more than one year must be fingerprinted.

This requirement is being protested increasingly often, and much unfavourable comment has been made over the years, observing (probably accurately) that Japan's control and treatment of aliens reflects an element of xenophobia that has existed in the country since it was first opened to foreigners in the 19th century, and probably much further back than that.

The ARC system was set up after the war to keep control of Koreans and Taiwanese who had been forced to go to Japan before and during the war, and it is widely believed that the card system is kept in effect to keep these minorities in a subordinate position (although changes in regulations have eased the situation for them, but not for those of other nationalities). Each year there are more and more protests about the system, with some protesters going on hunger strikes to make their point. However, rather than easing up on the system and joining the rest of the world, the Justice Ministry has actually tightened up regulations and forced at least one Korean protester to leave the country with his Japanese wife because he refused to be fingerprinted. Previously, refusal was punishable only by a fine, and there is no written regulation calling for deportation. This was a good example of the power of the bureaucracy to make their own regulations not covered by law.

The regulations requiring registration are said to be the strictest in the free world (and the most bothersome). Japan is the only country that requires fingerprinting of aliens but not its own citizens. (Some require it of both.) In Japan, only criminals are fingerprinted, and this fact, say some, indicates how highly the Japanese regard foreigners. In actuality, the fingerprints are of no practical use, for it is the photographs in documents that provide identification. Several people, including the Rev. Jesse Jackson, have compared the ARC with South Africa's pass laws. (*Those* were finally repealed). The Japanese requirements certainly emphasize the meaning of the Japanese word for foreigner, *gaijin*, which literally means "outside person", and the omnipresent sense of "us" and "them" that prevails in Japanese society.

In 1979 Japan signed an international agreement that may eventually result in the abolition of the Alien Registration procedures, but at the time of publication of each edition of this book to date this had not occurred.

Following the changes in immigration regulations of June 1990, there is only one book that gives detailed information on immigration procedures, "A Guide to Entry, Residence and Registration Procedures in Japan for Foreign Nationals". It was prepared by a "Study Group, Immigration Bureau, Ministry of Justice", which means that it can be considered a guide that is fairly reliable, but not official. (This is typical of Japan, where there are few hard-and-fast eternal verities in the field of law, and bureaucrats can make laws jump through hoops to suit their whims). It is also infuriatingly wordy while simultaneously vague (interrelated phenomena), and its many grammatical lapses need a complete rewrite to make it understandable without repeated readings. (However, introducing such improvements would require clarification of a number of items conveniently ambiguous, so might not suit the concerned ministry.)

This ¥1500 soft-cover publication is available in Tokyo at the bookstore in the building on the corner of the street on which the Otemachi Immigration office is located. The publisher is:

Nihon Kaijo Shupan k.k.
3-16-6 Minami Nagasaki
Toshima-ku
Tokyo 171
Tel. (03) 3953-5757

The cost for surface postage is an additional ¥260 in Japan. Write to the publisher for mail rates overseas.

FOREIGN DIPLOMATIC REPRESENTATIVES

Because Tokyo is the capital, all embassies and other diplomatic representatives are listed in the section covering that city. (For convenience, the Korean consular offices in other cities are listed there also.)

CUSTOMS

Japanese Customs are quite generous in their allowances, especially for liquor. You can bring in three 760-ml bottles of alcoholic beverages. Other limits are: 400 cigarettes or 100 cigars or 500 g of tobacco, with a maximum combined weight of 500 g; two ounces of perfume; two watches valued no higher than ¥30,000 each (including any in current use); and other goods with a total value of not more than ¥100,000. Inspectors are generally lenient, allowing in anything that could be considered reasonable for a person's stay in Japan; luggage often isn't opened unless they are suspicious of the contents.

Even if you don't smoke, it might be worth bringing in foreign cigarettes (American or British are the best). They are very welcome gifts to Japanese smokers, and are a nice "thank you" for assistance or when hitchhiking, either the whole packet or one at a time. They are also appreciated by foreigners in Japan, for Japanese tobacco is not the best in the world.

As for booze, it is relatively expensive in Japan (compared with the U.S., for example), so bring your limit if you like spirits or if you'll be visiting friends. Do not bother to bring in liquor with the intention of selling it. The days when anyone could sell booze at a high profit by walking into a bar are long gone. It might still be possible to unload it at a small profit, but it is not worth the bother. The Japanese themselves go overseas these days in droves and bring back their own, in adition to which the prices have remained fairly static over the years, so increasing salaries have made it relatively cheaper. The reselling racket dates back to times when the Japanese couldn't afford to go out of the country (or were virtually banned from travel), and those days are years in the past.

On arrival, a verbal declaration is usually sufficient if you have no unaccompanied baggage. If you have sent belongings separately (e.g., by mail), declare them upon arrival on the form provided (in duplicate; carbon paper only sometimes available). You show this form to Customs when the packages arrive; it is unlikely that any duty will be charged on the contents. Parcels arriving without such a customs declaration are subject to duty, although the inspectors are usually not too harsh. Packages of food and low-value items or gifts usually come through without trouble.

The Japanese authorities are very down on narcotics, marijuana, and stimulant drugs (amphetamines). Anyone caught bringing any of these products into Japan can expect no sympathy from the law, and Japanese prisons are few steps from Dark-ages conditions. (Even suspects are treated like prisoners before they are tried, and the remand stage can go on for weeks.)

Firearms are very tightly controlled in Japan; anyone caught smuggling them or ammunition can expect an unpaid vacation.

Pornography is frowned on in Japan, but what constitutes porn is laughable by Western standards. The main determinant is whether any pubic hair can be seen. Western films showing this subversive substance are defaced by little blobs that move around with the bodies, and bring more attention to what is being concealed than if it were shown. The portrayal of pubic hair in any form has traditionally been a complete no-no, although camera magazines are showing ever more. This domestic relaxation will probably have no effect on the practice of defacing imported magazines to the extent that the "offending" parts are blacked out or even abraded down to bare paper. (Some wags claim that this is another infamous hidden trade barrier to keep out products in which the Japanese are not competitive.) Because of the enforced innocence of these magazines, the unexpurgated versions are good conversation/peering pieces. If you bring one in, keep it out of sight or fold the cover over. One imaginative American sent his friend in Japan a copy of Penthouse with the cover exchanged for one from the aquatic sports magazine "Skin Diver".

One could be sympathetic to official attempts to keep the morals of the country pure if it weren't for the huge amount of blatant commercial sex and prostitution under a variety of guises (sex shows, etc.) permeating the country and the countless Japanese "comic" books (*manga*) portraying incredible scenes of rape, torture, disfigurement, and degradation of women, and these are on sale everywhere. When I took a Japanese "bondage" magazine of the type available at any local convenience store back to Canada to show friends, Canadian Customs wouldn't let it into the country!

TRANSPORTATION

Intercity Public Transportation

Japan has an excellent public transport system in all populated areas. This chapter summarizes what is available, although it cannot possibly give complete details of every train, for there are more than 28,000 a day throughout the country! If you are making travel arrangements in Japan using scheduled transportation, the simplest way is to use a travel agency. The price will usually be the same as what you would pay if you bought the ticket yourself, and agents can often offer combinations of fares and accommodation that are cheaper than the two separately (sometimes the same as the list price of the transportation alone.) The largest travel agency is the Japan Travel Bureau, a semi-official organization, which has offices in every major city throughout the country and branch offices overseas. (It is, of course, a matter of luck whether any individual office will have an English speaker on staff.)

The single most useful book for travel in Japan by public transport is *jikokuhyo*—or "book of timetables". This invaluable publication runs to over 1100 pages (it seems to gain 50 to 100 per year), with timetables for every form of scheduled transport in Japan—trains, buses, planes, ferries, even cable cars. If there were scheduled stage coaches, they'd be listed too!

There are several editions of various sizes and coverage. I recommend the large JTB version ("*ohki JTB jikokuhyo*") because its maps are more detailed, and it has

information on bus lines and ferries, which the small ones do not. (There is also a large JR version that seems identical in contents though a little different in arrangement, but I have not verified every detail.) It is issued monthly, costs about ¥900 (also increases by the year), and is available from any newsstand or bookstore. The entire book is written only in Japanese, but even if you can't read a single character you can still use it quite easily (described below).

There is a version with some English, identified on the cover as *JTB'S Mini-Timetable* but, while its publication is a kind and appreciated gesture, it lists only express train services (no local trains); long-distance ferries (no local services between adjacent islands); the expressway buses (but none of the large number of local services found through so much of the country); and airlines. The English extends basically to the romanization of the names of major places on the maps and the major cities shown in the timetables. For short or simple journeys it should be adequate, but for extensive independent travels you should learn how to use the large Japanese version.

The secret to using the all-Japanese version lies in the maps at the front of the book, which show the entire country region by region. Note that the maps are distorted to fit the pages and that north is somewhere off to the right. All but the last map show surface transportation; the last shows air connections.

On the maps, JR Shinkansen super express "bullet" trains are shown by a red line of alternating solid and hollow sections, while main JR lines are shown in solid black and JR local lines are solid light blue. Private railway lines are shown by a narrow black line with crossbars. Bus routes on ordinary roads are represented by a narrow blue line. (Expressway buses are shown on a separate map.) A cable car or funicular railway looks like a stretched coil spring, and a ferry is indicated by a thin red line in the water areas. The availability of rental cars near a station is shown by a red car symbol. Special vocabulary: a cable car system, with gondolas suspended from cables, is known as a "ropeway", while a funicular railway is a "keburu" (cable).

Areas of (Japanese) touristic interest are shaded green and have a number in green that corresponds to a brief description (in Japanese) at the top and bottom of the page. (I write "Japanese" for touristic interest because many places of interest to them would be of no appeal to the average foreign visitor, such as sites of historic battles where nothing stands today to be seen.)

The key to using these maps, including the expressway bus map, is the number (sometimes with a letter) written in red beside the transportation line. The number refers to the page that has the timetable for that service; the letter, if any, refers to the section of the page. It's that simple.

Although all place names are written only in *kanji* (Chinese characters), it is easy to match the names of large cities with the names printed in *romaji* on another map, such as one of the road maps suggested elsewhere in this book. (With a little practice, it should be possible to compensate for *jikokuhyo* map distortions and use the free JNTO map of Japan for this purpose.) Also, there is a commercial railway map available in bookstores with the name of every major station printed in *romaji*.

Following the pages of maps of the

various sections of the country, but prior to the maps for highway buses and air services, are maps detailing the transport facilities in and around Kobe/Osaka/Kyoto, Nagoya and Tokyo/Yokohama/Kawasaki. (Insets on the pages with the main maps show the subway systems of Fukuoka, Sendai, and Sapporo.)

The final two maps represent the highway bus services and all air services within Japan. Air services in Japan are organized in a hub and spoke system, as can be seen on the map, the hubs being Sapporo, Tokyo, Nagoya, Osaka, Fukuoka, and Naha (Okinawa). There are links between some points at the ends of spokes. The color of the lines representing the spokes corresponds to the airline, the names of which are all in Roman letters (e.g., JAL, ANA, etc.). Beside the name of the linked city is a number that corresponds to the part in the airlines section of the book, located at the very end of the timetable section. City names are in only.

A mid-1991 book is broken up into 20 sections, the first 18 of which are JR train services, with bits of information and advertisements scattered among them. In a typical issue (they don't change much in format), the first section gives schedules for Shinkansen, "L" Limited Express (*tokkyu*) and sleeper services. The second section shows the most convenient connections for the fastest non-Shinkansen service over long distances, such as Tokyo–Nagasaki, or Sapporo–Tokyo. Sections 3–17 give the schedule of all intercity JR services, line by line, organized by geographical area. Section 18 mainly gives the schedule of all JR lines operating in the Tokyo–Kawasaki– Yokohama and Osaka–Kyoto–Kobe metropolitan areas. Section 19 is a great catch-all of everything else, beginning with the long-distance buses; JR fare information; private transportation of all types (railways, buses, ferries, cable cars), region by region; boat services to and around Okinawa and other southern islands and bus services on the islands; long distance domestic and international ferry connections (including those to Pusan (Korea), Keelung and Kaohsiung (Taiwan), and Shanghai (China)); and excursion and sightseeing bus tours. Section 20 gives air connections, both domestic and international, with the names of starting and destination airports for international flights given in *romaji* as well as *kanji*. At the end of the book comes complete JR fare information (including all JR excursion fares with simple maps), then hotel information.

In summer issues there may be an extra section of excursion train and airline services appearing before the Shinkansen section.

As mentioned in the section on the Japanese language, *kanji* characters all have two or more pronunciations, some a multitude. In addition to the readings listed in dictionaries, place and family names can have their own individual pronunciation found nowhere else, which means that many place names just cannot be pronounced by a Japanese person unless he/she happens to know it beforehand. However, a helpful hint if you are diligent enough to be using a *jikokuhyo* and map with romanized place names to plan your travels, is that the pronunciation of all station names on JR train lines is shown in *hiragana* to the right of the timetable of a service (only on the first page of a multipage listing). With a table of the pronunciation of *hiragana* characters, it is possible to read out the name of the place.

Trains

The railway network in Japan is by far the best in Asia and can be ranked among the most comprehensive in the world. Trains in Japan are punctual, range in frequency from adequate to amazing, and in speed from pokey to phenomenal. They include the famed Shinkansen super-expresses ("bullet trains", although the Japanese do not use this term), among the fastest scheduled trains in the world. Fares are not cheap.

Nominally, all the railways in Japan are privately operated. For 115 years up to 1987, the largest system was the government-operated Japan National Railways (JNR). By that time it had accumulated a debt of approximately 5,200,000,000,000 yen (about U.S. \$50 billion at ¥105 to the dollar), and the government decided that it was time to do something about it. What they did was to "privatize" the system into eight "private" lines that made up the new Japanese Railways (JR), each of which is to theoretically become more efficient and shake off the bureaucratic mentality that got it into the original mess. One wishes them luck, but as each of the new companies has carried over its share of the debt, and a huge number of just-retired high-level bureaucrats got parachuted into the new companies just before they started, one wonders if anything will have improved.

The new lines are still coordinated, and one can buy through tickets that are valid for all regions of the country, so the overseas visitor will (we hope) see no real difference from the old JNR days.

The JR system provides long distance service throughout the country, as well as services around the cities of Tokyo and Osaka. The "true" private lines usually run only comparatively short distances—up to 100 km or so—and are usually regarded as commuter lines. Exceptions to this short haul "rule" are some private lines that run appreciable distances to resort areas near the major city on which they are centered, and the private lines in the Kinki district, which provide the fastest, cheapest, and most convenient services among the major cities of that area (Nagoya, Osaka, Kobe, Kyoto, and Nara). The private lines are discussed in more detail in the section covering intra-city transport.

The main station of a JR line is almost invariably near the center of the city. For private lines this may or may not be true. In Tokyo, for example, all the private lines end at various points at some distance from the center of Tokyo and are connected by the Yamanote loop line.

Japanese Railways (JR)
The national "private" railway system is called "JR". Fares are calculated by distance and the class of service. There is a base fare from point A to point B, to which are added surcharges for the various types of expresses (explained below), seat reservation charge, "Green-sha" (first class), and sleeper/roomette.

The JNTO booklet *The Tourist's Handbook* can be useful for buying tickets as it has English and Japanese phrases written in the format of an order form.

There are more than 25,000 JR trains every day throughout Japan. In *jikokuhyo*, JR train schedules fill more than 600 pages! There is a summary of services printed in English, and given out free by the JNTO, called *Railway Timetable* (TO 1420-60914). It gives the schedule of all Shinkansen services, *tokkyu* and *kyuko* (express) JR trains (but no locals), and many of the most important private lines, and explains the various discounts and surcharges.

The TICs in Tokyo, Kyoto, and Narita give out photocopied sheets of the schedule (and required changes of train) for travelling between Tokyo and Kyoto/Osaka by Tokaido line (non-Shinkansen trains). These trains take about 10 hours, compared with less than four by Shinkansen, but the fare is less than half. (The highway bus would generally be preferable to this method.) Other sheets from the TIC cover JR services to and from northern Honshu and to Hokkaido via the tunnel. The TIC offices are the best sources of information for most travel inquiries, but they do not sell tickets.

There are travel information centers at all major JR stations. At Tokyo station (Yaesu side), the Travel Information Service is clearly labelled in English and some staff members speak sufficient English to be helpful, but it is best to speak slowly and clearly. Travel agencies like those listed for reserved ticket sales can also supply information, though they may not have anyone who can speak English.

If you are travelling in the spring, be warned that for many years there has been a nationwide strike of JR services during this busy time. It has usually lasted only a few days, but can be a great interruption. Private railways and subways may be struck at the same time.

JR SERVICES There are several levels (i.e., speeds) of JR service, largely corresponding to the distance between the terminal points of the train. All trains have both regular and "Green Car" (first class) coaches. The only difference is softer seats, a little more room, and individual video screens in the latter. Most travellers will not bother with the substantial extra cost; the coach seats are entirely adequate.

The basic level is called *futsu* (also "kaku eki teisha" or "kakutei"); these trains stop at every station. It is the slowest service and is usually limited to relatively short runs of about 100 km. Around major cities the quality of coaches on such service is good; some country lines tend to be the dumping ground for older coaches. In the backwoods the local trains may be called *donko*, a folksy word with a descriptive sound, but a foreigner who uses it will find that the Japanese are amused.

Kyuko is translated as "ordinary express"; these trains make only a limited number of stops, skipping a number of stations en route. They run moderately long distances. With the exception of a very small number of *kaisoku* services (translated as "rapid" on timetables and notices), there is a surcharge for *kyuko* trains. The surcharges are:

Up to (km)	Yen
50	520
100	720
150	930
200	1030
200 plus	1240

The surcharge is higher for Green Cars, and there is a ¥500 seat reservation charge.

The *kaisoku* services most likely to be encountered by foreign visitors are the Tokaido-sen and Yokosuka-sen lines between Tokyo and Yokohama; the Chuo-sen line from Tokyo and Shinjuku west to Takao and Tachikawa; and the *shin-kaisoku* service on the Tokaido Honsen line from Kyoto to Osaka, Kobe, and Himeji.

Tokkyu is translated as "limited express"; such trains stop only at major cities. They are the fastest trains (other than the Shinkansen) and are used for long distance travel.

Surcharges for *tokkyu* trains (unreserved ordinary seat) are:

Up to (km)	Yen
50	720
100	1130
150	1750
200	2060
300	2270
400	2470

600	2780
over 600	3090

The surcharge is higher for Green Cars, and there is a ¥500 seat reservation charge.

OVERNIGHT SLEEPERS For long distance travel, an alternative to the super-express Shinkansen trains is one of the overnight sleeper trains. These leave in the evening, travel through the night, and reach their destination early the next morning. The main services are from Tokyo and Osaka, with stops at stations near the starting point to pick up more passengers and at several stations prior to the terminus. The most important of these services are:

Tokyo	–Nagasaki (Kyushu)
	–Kagoshima (Kyushu)
	–Kumamoto (Kyushu)
	–Miyazaki (Kyushu)
	–Hakata (Kyushu)
	–Shimonoseki (W. Honshu)
	–Hamada (Sanin coast)
	–Hiroshima
	–Okayama
	–Takamatsu (Shikoku)
Tokyo (Ueno)	–Kanazawa (Hokuriku)
	–Aomori (Tohoku; via Akita, via Morioka)
	–Sapporo (Hokkaido)
Nagoya	–Kagoshima
Osaka	–Aomori (via Akita)
	–Nagasaki
	–Kagoshima
	–Miyazaki
	–Matsue (Sanin coast)
	–Hakodate (Hokkaido)
Hakata	–Kagoshima

Surcharges for the sleeping car depends

on the type of accommodation (private compartments, upper/lower bunk, etc.); the distance travelled, and whether it is a kyuko or tokkyu train. The maximum surcharge, for a tokkyu trip of over 600 km, ranges from ¥5700 to ¥17,000, depending on whether it is a bunk, compartment, or other accommodation. These surcharges must be paid by the holders of a Japan Rail Pass.

SHINKANSEN The fastest trains in Japan are the three Shinkansen super-express train lines: the Tokaido/Sanyo line running from Tokyo to the west (to Nagoya, Kyoto, Osaka, Hiroshima, and Hakata); the Tohoku line running from Tokyo to the northeast (to Sendai and Morioka); and the Joetsu line running north from Tokyo (to Niigata). They hit a maximum of 270 km/h (168 mph), second only to the French TGV service, and long the fastest in the world. The rails are continuously welded and mounted on a concrete roadbed so there is no sway and no clickety-clack, so it is necessary to look at the speedometer in the buffet car to believe the speed at which it is travelling. With well over two billion passengers carried without a single fatality, it has an incredible safety record. A ride on one is something that should be experienced at least once. They are known to foreigners as "bullet trains" but in Japan they are just "Shinkansen", which has the prosaic meaning "new main line".

The original plan for the Tohoku line was for it to link Sapporo (Hokkaido) with Hakata (Kyushu), and construction began on the 54 km tunnel under the Tsugaru strait between Honshu and Hokkaido. After many years and ¥690 billion, the tunnel was finished in 1985. By then air travel had developed as a major means of getting to distant parts of the country, and the future of the tunnel was put in doubt, for it could never pay for itself. (There were estimates that it would cost more to lay tracks in it than it could hope to earn back, and there were semi-facetious suggestions that the tunnel would better be converted to the world's largest mushroom farm.) However, tracks were laid and there is train service linking Honshu and Hokkaido, although it is ordinary service, not Shinkansen; the Hokkaido part of the Shinkansen was never built, and the Honshu line was terminated at Morioka (between Sendai and Akita), instead of running all the way to Aomori. (It may be extended somewhat during the 90s.)

A branch off the Joetsu line is to be built from Takasaki to Nagano in time for the 1998 Winter Olympics.

There are both reserved and unreserved Shinkansen seats. It is generally advisable to get reservations if possible, especially during the holiday periods (described elsewhere in the book) when huge numbers of Japanese are on the move. At those times the unreserved coaches will be filled with standees who may have to make an entire 6+ hour trip without a seat. Reservations can be made at any JR station with a Green Window.

As with ordinary JR trains, there are both regular and Green Car coaches. Also, there are double-decker cars on some trains of the Tokaido/Sanyo and Tohoku lines, with all upper seats having a "Green Car" rating, although one frequent traveller complained that tickets were never available at stations and it appeared that travel agencies were buying them all up.

The concept of non-smoking cars is making progress. In past years, only coach 1 of a train was a non-smoker, but now car 1 and 2 of all Shinkansen trains are a non-smoker, and there are two others on nearly all trains, though the car numbers differ with the line and the types of cars making up the train. Some cars are also divided into smoking and non-smoking sections, a recent innovation. (Japan has been years behind the Western world regarding non-smokers' rights, but the situation improves by the year.) The layout of all Shinkansen trains regarding both non-smoking cars and double-decker cars is shown in a section at the back of *jikokuhyo*.

Note that trains are numbered so that car 1 is always the one pointing westward (or southward), regardless of the direction the train is travelling.

Don't look for the gourmet meals and high-class dining facilities that one might expect on such trains. A Japanese newspaper columnist once complained of "awful" coffee, "the world's worst sandwiches", and dining facilities that are "a step below most lower class slum eateries". This is an exaggeration, but the food is no more than adequate. Women also go through the train from time to time selling boxed lunches (*bento*). The best bet is to buy a bento before leaving the station, for there is more choice available.

A Japan Rail Pass is valid for use on all Shinkansen lines, and it is feasible to use it for lengthy day trips. One traveller, for example, used one to go from Kyoto to Hiroshima for a couple of hours, then took another train almost to Tokyo the same day.

All Shinkansen train schedules are listed in the JNTO publication "Railway Timetable" (available in the TIC offices in Tokyo, Narita airport, and Kyoto), and are also listed in *jikokuhyo* (though only in Japanese). Trains begin running at about 0600, and all have arrived before midnight. The following notes will be useful in understanding the different types of service.

TOKAIDO/SANYO LINE The Tokaido line (the original) runs from Tokyo to Osaka (Shin-Osaka station), and the Sanyo line from there to Hakata. It is possible to go from Tokyo to Hakata (in northern Kyushu) in as little as 5 hr 47 min. There are three services on the Tokkaido/Sanyo line, Nozomi ("Hope), Hikari ("Light"), and Kodama ("Echo"). Fares have been the same for both for the latter two.

Nozomi trains are the fastest, making the Tokyo–Shin-osaka trip in 2 hr 30 min at up tp 270 km/h, and generally running non-stop. Hikari trains are the next fastest. Those originating at Tokyo stop only at Nagoya and Kyoto between Tokyo and Osaka, and take only 2 hr 34 min for the trip to Kyoto and 3 hr exactly to Osaka. (These times may have been shortened by the time the book goes on sale. Hikari originating at Osaka generally stop only at Okayama, Hiroshima, and Hakata. From Tokyo, an average of two Hikari trains per hour continue beyond Osaka through to Hakata, and others go as far as Okayama or Hiroshima. There are several patterns of stops by various trains, some stopping at every station beyond Osaka, and others stopping only at Okayama, Hiroshima, and Kokura (also N. Kyushu). The pattern of stops evolves through the years, so it is advisable to study a timetable to get the most suitable service for your destination.

Kodama trains stop at every station along their route. Virtually all run only Tokyo–Osaka or Osaka–Hakata; a rare exception may run Tokyo–Okayama. The Tokyo–Kyoto trip by Kodama takes 3 hr 38 min.

There is a similar mixture of Hikari and Kodama trains east-bound, some Hikari going only to Osaka from Hakata, many continuing to Tokyo, many Kodama running from Hakata only to Osaka, and others originating at Osaka for Tokyo.

Trains leave Tokyo every 4 to 10 minutes typically (maximum wait 16 minutes), at comparable frequency from Osaka for

Tokyo, and somewhat less frequently to and from Hakata. There are also many extra trains on holidays and other days when heavier traffic is expected, all of which are shown in *jikokuhyo*. The first through trains leave Tokyo, Osaka, and Hakata at or just after 0600. Some Grand Hikari trains between Tokyo and Hakata have double-decker cars.

On a clear day, the Tokaido Shinkansen affords a superb view of Mt. Fuji as it passes the region of Fuji city, one of the best views available.

TOHOKU YAMAGATA LINE The Tohoku line runs northeast from Tokyo (Tokyo station) through Fukushima and Sendai to Yamagata and Morioka. (It was originally planned to go to Aomori, and thence to Sapporo on Hokkaido, but construction was suspended due to the cost. It may yet be extended in steps.)

There are three types of service, Yamabiko (the express), Aoba ("Green Leaf" [literally, "Blue Leaf", but that's another story]), the local, and Tsubasa ("Wing"). The Tsubasa trains are hitched on to Aoba and Yamabiko trains, separating at Fukushima station. The Tsubasa then goes on to Yamagata. As with Tokaido/Sanyo trains, there are various patterns of stops.

Yamabiko trains generally skip four or five stations between Tokyo and Sendai (about two hours). There are about 38 of these per day, about 26 of which continue to Morioka, most of them stopping at every station above Sendai en route (3 hr 11 min to 3 hr 22 min). In addition, there is a small number (about 13/day) that skip most or all stations between Tokyo and Sendai (as little as 1 hr 41 min), and also skip all stations from there to Morioka (2 hr 45 min total).

The Aoba trains, about 16/day, stop at all stations between Tokyo and Sendai (the terminus), taking about 2 hr 30 min.

The pattern and frequencies are about the same in the opposite direction for both types of service. There are also many extra trains on weekends in the summer, mostly between Tokyo and Sendai.

The view from the train on the Tohoku line is not nearly as good as that along the Tokaido/Sanyo lines. The tracks run through flat valley terrain quite distant from any hills of note (at least as far as Sendai), and where the track passes near built-up areas there are shields built onto the track structure to deflect train noises upward, and these impede the view.

JOETSU LINE The Joetsu line is regarded by many to be a triumph of politics over economics. Niigata is not a particularly important city by Japanese standards, but it is the home town and power base of the amazing former prime minister Kakuei Tanaka (the one found guilty of accepting a $2 million bribe from the Lockheed Aircraft Company and now out of active politics as the result of a crippling stroke). Because of this connection, it is not surprising that it was favored to be linked to Tokyo by Shinkansen line despite the likelihood that it would never make money, since about half the distance is through tunnels and very expensive to build, and the traffic is relatively light.

As with the other lines, there are two types of service. Asahi ("Sunrise", the express), and Toki ("Crane", the local). Like the others, there are several patterns of stops.

Asahi trains, about 18/day plus extras on holidays and some weekends, make the Tokyo (Tokyo station)–Niigata trip in between 1 hr 36 min and 2 hr 7 min, depending on the number of stops.

Toki trains, about 15/day, stop at all stations, and take 2 hr 20 min.

This is the line least likely to be used by foreigners because of the lack of interesting things to see in the Niigata area. However, Niigata is the port of entry for flights from Khabarovsk (Russia), so travellers arriving there can use it to reach Tokyo quickly.

Buying Tickets (All Trains)
Tickets to any station in Japan can be bought at any JR station. For short distances there are usually ticket vending machines, and for longer distances they can be bought at the ticket window.

There are no reserved seats on *futsu* trains. There are both reserved and unreserved seats on *kyuko*, *tokkyu* and Shinkansen trains. Reserved tickets can be bought any time between a month in advance and a few minutes before departure. Seats on any of these trains can be reserved at any station with a Green Window (midori-no-madoguchi), which means all major stations in the country including most stations in Tokyo. (The name refers to the green over the window or the green band around glassed-in offices.) Reserved seat tickets may also be bought at offices of Japan Travel Bureau (JTB), Kinki Nippon Tourist Corp., and Nippon Travel Agency.

Seats on the Shinkansen can be reserved in Canada and the USA, and possibly other countries, through JAL offices by passengers who will be flying by JAL to Japan.

JR FARES As noted earlier, train fares are calculated from a base fare plus added surcharges. Fares used to rise with monotonous regularity, but some (like the Tokaido Shinkansen) scarcely increased during the four years up to May 1991. Shinkansen fares are now almost as high as air fares. For up-to-date fares, refer to the JNTO publication *Railway Timetable*. Some sample fares are listed below. For journeys over 100 km, student fares are

available which give a 20 per cent discount off the regular fares. For a return JR train/ferry trip exceeding 600 km one-way there is a 20 per cent discount on the return section. One of the travel agents mentioned earlier would be able to help.

The following are some representative fares as of mid-1996.

TOKYO TO	FUTSU	SHINKANSEN
Fukushima	¥ 4,530	¥ 8,530
Sendai	¥ 5,670	¥10,390
Morioka	¥ 8,030	¥13,570
Shizuoka	¥ 3,190	¥ 6,060
Nagoya	¥ 5,970	¥10,380
Kyoto	¥ 7,830	¥12,970
Osaka	¥ 8,340	¥13,480
Hiroshima	¥11,120	¥17,700
Shimonoseki	¥12,570	¥20,180
Hakata	¥13,180	¥21,300
Niigata	¥ 5,360	¥10,080

JAPAN RAIL PASS A definite travel bargain in this country largely bereft of bargains, is the Japan Rail Pass. Exactly the same in concept as the Eurail pass, a JRP entitles the holder to use all JR train, bus, and ferry services (including *kyuko*, *tokkyu* and the Shinkansen) without surcharge, and seat reservations may also be made without charge. However, to use a berth on a sleeper, it is necessary to pay not only the berth charge, but also the associated express charge.

Passes are valid for a period of seven, 14 or 21 days and the basic passes cost ¥27,800, ¥44,200 and ¥56,600, respectively, for adults (50 per cent off for children 6 to 11). A first class "Green Car" pass is about a third higher. Since the Shinkansen round-trip fare between Tokyo and Kyoto is ¥25,940, the bargain nature of the JRP is obvious. The JR network covers most parts of the country that visitors would want to see. Note, however, that the pass is not valid on private railway lines, so there may be occasions when a pass holder has to pay separate fares.

A JRP cannot be purchased in Japan. It, or rather an Exchange Order (voucher), must be bought in a foreign country through an authorized agent—almost any travel agent should be able to arrange this. The voucher is open dated, but must be exchangeed within three months of issue.) When you reach Japan, you go to a JR Travel Service Center (at major stations) or the JR desk at Narita airport. There you fill in a Pass application and exchange the voucher. At this time you must specify the first day you want to use the pass.

Technically, foreign residents of Japan are not permitted to use a JRP. Some residents wonder if a friend could purchase a voucher overseas and bring it in with them. The validation procedure is supposed to require checking the passport of the voucher holder for the date of entry and the status of residence, to prevent residents from using a pass. The office at Narita and offices in Tokyo follow the procedure scrupulously with a checklist; offices in smaller cities might be less diligent. It would be the purchaser's gamble. If contemplating this, it would be wise to inquire of the travel agent at the time of purchase if an unused voucher would be refundable.

For more complete details, there is a brochure "Japan Rail Pass", probably also available from overseas JNTO offices.

EXCURSION TICKETS JR also has excursion tickets (*shuyuken*). There are four different types: *ippan shuyuken*, *route shuyuken*, *mini shuyuken*, and *wide shuyuken*.

Wide shuyuken This is an all-inclusive ticket for direct travel (no stopover en route) from any place to a distant point, unlimited travel on JR train and bus services within the designated area, and direct travel back to the starting point. In the north of Japan there are two 20-day schemes for travel in Hokkaido (one for all points on Hokkaido, one for the southern part only, and a variation of the first that includes an air flight in one direction), and another route in Tohoku (northern Honshu) for 10 days. In the south of Japan there is a "wide shuyuken" for travel anywhere in Kyushu for 20 days by JR train and bus, with the option of a boat trip in one direction from Beppu (Kyushu) to Kobe/Osaka, or from Beppu to Takamatsu (Shikoku). Others offer unlimited travel within Shikoku for 20 days, or unlimited travel in the Sanin area (the north coast of western Honshu).

Mini shuyuken This is similar to the wide shuyuken but covers a smaller area and has a shorter period of validity.

Route shuyuken This is for travel along certain designated routes that take in a number of places considered worth seeing, It is valid for 30 days and gives a 10 per cent discount over regular fares.

Ippan shuyuken This is an excursion ticket over a route chosen by the traveller. It must take in two or more designated areas with travel of more than 201 km (train, bus, boat) before returning to the starting point. It is good for 30 days and gives a 10 per cent discount.

There are numerous options resulting from the number of schemes. It is advisable to obtain copies of the photo-copied information sheets from the TICs in Tokyo or Kyoto. The same information is available at any JR or JTB office or travel agents but few of the staff at these places speak English, unlike in the TICs.

Excursion tickets can be purchased at any JR station in Japan with a Green Window office, or from any travel agency.

Groups of 15 or more receive a discount of about 10 per cent.

Economy Coupons are available for

JR trains plus hotels and sightseeing on approved JR routes.

Private travel agencies also offer special excursion deals that combine train fares and accommodation. It is not uncommon for travellers who opt to stay at a minshuku to find that the total cost of both train (Shinkansen) and accommodation offered in some package tours comes to no more than the posted Shinkansen fare alone.

Special Train

Special steam locomotives ("SL" in Japanese!) train excursions can be enjoyed at three places in Japan. JR phased out its last SL in December 1975, but the clamor of Japanese steam fanatics led them to revive some services on the Yamaguchi line, in western Honshu, the only line where the water towers and other required equipment still remained, and another was restarted in Kyushu in 1991.

The Yamaguchi service, using a C56 or C57 locomotive, commences operations in late July or early August and generally runs daily, though the schedule changes yearly. From September through November it runs on weekends and national holidays. Trains make one daily round trip, leaving Ogori (one stop on the Shinkansen from Shin-shimonoseki) at 10:30 and arriving at Tsuwano (65 km inland toward Masuda on the north coast) at 12:30, travelling at speeds of up to 65 km/h and stopping at eight stations on the way. The return trip leaves Tsuwano at 15:21. Trains have five coaches with a seating capacity of 400, but it is advisable to reserve ahead, for the trip is very popular. The one-way fare is about ¥1,090, and a reserved seat is an extra ¥500. Tickets can be bought at the Green Window of any JR station.

The main steam service in Kyushu makes the scenic run from Kumamoto through the valley of the great volcano,

Aso-san, to the town of Aso. The train leaves in mid-morning and returns in early afternoon, the trip up taking about 2-1/4 hours, and the down hill trip back to Kumamoto just under two hours.

Excursions run most weekends from mid-June to early August, sometimes one weekend day, sometimes both, and there may be a period of daily runs in mid-summer. Seats are available only on a reservation basis; since there are only three cars, the number of seats is very limited. The coaches are advertised as being of American type. The train is known as "Aso Boy". (Don't ask how they choose their names!) There has also been a single annual excursion in the fall between Yatsushiro and Hitoyoshi, in the south of the island.

The only line in Japan where steam locomotives were never completely phased out is the short Oigawa line (private) in Shizuoka-ken. It runs from Kanaya (about 190 km southwest of Tokyo and 12 km west of Shizuoka city) to Senzu.

The basic SL service is the "Kawaneji" train, leaving Kanaya at 1145, reaching Senzu at 1259, and returning at 1442. During the off season it runs only on weekends, but it is operated regularly during the week through July and August. The schedule is printed in *jikokuhyo*, and the Tokyo TIC or any travel agent can give more information. For the 40 km trip, either by steam or diesel, the one-way fare is ¥640.

In 1979 a C-56 type locomotive, built in Japan between 1935 and 1939 was brought back from Thailand for use on the Oigawa line. It had been used during WW II to haul war supplies on the infamous Thailand–Burma railway.

Air

There are several airlines operating on domestic routes in Japan. JAL (Japan Air Lines–*Nippon Koku*) and ANA (All Nippon Airways–*Zen Nippon Koku*) have the largest number of services, but an alphabet soup of smaller airlines are important in various regions, such as JAS, JAC, ANK, NCA, NAW, JAIR, NAL, JTA, ADK, RAC, and TAL.

Domestic air services have a hub and spoke arrangement, the hubs being Tokyo, Osaka, Sapporo, Nagoya, Okayama, and Naha (Okinawa). Thus travel between regional cities generally requires passing through one of the large airports.

At Tokyo, Haneda airport is used for all domestic flights, except for about 12 a day which link Narita airport with Sapporo, Osaka, Fukuoka and Nagoya. At Osaka, about 60 flights a day use Kansai International Airpots, permitting reasonable connections with overseas flights. The main airport at Osaka for domestic flights is Itami, served by about 120 flights a day.

Listed below are sample air fares (one way). Return fares are 10 per cent cheaper than two one-way fares.

TOKYO TO:

Sapporo	¥23,850
Nagoya	¥11,600
Osaka	¥14,600
Hiroshima	¥21,600
Fukuoka	¥25,350
Kagoshima	¥29,100
Naha	¥34,900
Nagasaki	¥29,100

SENDAI TO:

Sapporo	¥19,250

NAGOYA TO:

Sapporo	¥28,550
Sendai	¥19,250
Nagasaki	¥21,500
Kagoshima	¥21,600
Naha	¥32,750

OSAKA TO:

Sendai	¥23,400
Nagasaki	¥17,750
Kagoshima	¥18,450

HIROSHIMA TO:

Kagoshima	¥17,300

KAGOSHIMA TO:

Naha	¥21,050

Buses

Long-Distance Buses

Not so many years ago the only long-distance buses ran between Tokyo and Kyoto/Osaka along the expressway. In recent years, an extensive intercity express bus system has developed, the result of completing the expressway system from northern Honshu to southern Kyushu (ordinary highways are narrow and crowded, cities and towns are incessant, and the speed limit is only 60 km/h), and because they can offer service at lower cost than the railways. The bus generally costs a little less than the base JR train fare, about half the cost of the Shinkansen for the same distance.

In addition to these express buses, there are feeder bus lines with runs of 50 to 100 km that give access to nearby towns, resort areas, amd most places of touristic interest. A look at the maps in *jikokuhyo* shows a blue web of these services in regions of interest to tourists, making it useful to study the appropriate pages of *jikokuhyo* for bus routes when planning your travels. Some of these routes will be of special interest to readers of this book, such as the bus from Shin-shima-shima (near Matsumoto) through mountain scenery to Takamatsu. Such routes are detailed in the appropriate section of the book. (In addition, not marked on the maps, are local bus services running within virtually every city and large town and to nearby population centers.) Almost all these local services leave from near the main JR station. As with all travel planning, it will undoubtedly be necessary to get some help from fellow (Japanese) travellers. This is par for the course.

The system of fare collection on local runs is the same as is used in many cities. The passenger takes a ticket from a machine at the back entrance; the ticket shows the zone where the passenger boarded. A sign at the front of the bus shows the fare payable at that point by passengers getting off, zone by zone.

Long-distance bus services can be divided into two types, day buses and night buses.

The day buses generally make many scheduled stops at designated places beside the expressway, from which passengers walk a short distance to connect with local transportation. The night buses leave late at night and run virtually non-stop, generally reaching their destination between 0600 and 0900 the next morning for an early start on the day's sightseeing. In addition to costing less than the base train fare, a night bus saves the cost of a night's accommodation.

The following paragraphs detail some of the major bus routes in order to give an idea of the coverage available.

Day Buses

The main and best-served run is Tokyo–Nagoya–Kyoto–Osaka. From early morning, buses run from Tokyo along the Tomei expressway (kosokudoro) to Nagoya and from there to Osaka/Kyoto along the Meishin expressway, stopping at pull-offs on the highway to let off and pick up passengers. During the day it is necessary to change buses at Nagoya. (See below for details of direct night buses.) Transfers are

quite well co-ordinated, with buses leaving Nagoya for Kyoto or Osaka shortly after the arrival of most buses from Tokyo. In mid-1991, the last bus from Tokyo to connect for the trip to Osaka leaves Tokyo station at 12:00 noon, and to connect for Kyoto at 13:00 (although buses continue to depart from Tokyo until 18:38 for Nagoya, and later for closer terminal cities like Shizuoka). The same change at Nagoya is required when going from Osaka/Kyoto to Tokyo. The last connecting bus (mid-1991) from Osaka and Kyoto is at, respectively, 23:10 and 00:30. Fares are ¥5,000 for Tokyo–Nagoya, and ¥2200/2600 for Nagoya–Kyoto/Osaka. There is a discount of about 25 percent on the return portion of a round-trip ticket.

Other day bus runs cover all parts of the country, and listings take up eight pages of *jikokuhyo*. Some likely to be of special interest to travellers include Tokyo–Mt. Fuji area, Tokyo–Hakone area, Tokyo–Matsumoto, Tokyo–Ina and Ina–Nagoya.

Night Buses

There are night buses (*yakobin busu*) for long-distance travel between points throughout the country. Judging from the Tokyo Kyoto JR bus that I have experienced, they are quite comfortable, with reclining seats, so sleeping is not too difficult and they are definitely more comfortable than sitting up on a night train over the same distance. If available, the preferred seat for longest legroom is probably the one immediately in front of the toilet.

The only direct buses between Tokyo and Kyoto/Osaka (no change at Nagoya) run at night, leaving late in the evening and arriving early next morning. There are buses operated by JR and other companies. They leave at only one or two departure times on each route. The night bus is popular, so it is suggested to make a reservation as far in advance as possible. Reservations can be made up to eight days in advance at any JTB office or at the Green Window of large JR stations.

Departure/arrival times and fares (mid-1991) for the JR buses are:

Tokyo stn (Yaesu side)–Kyoto (2200/0600 and 2300/0650): ¥8,030
Tokyo stn (Yaesu side)–Nara (2200/0730): ¥8240
Shinjuku stn–Kyoto (2310/0620): ¥8,030

These buses are operated by JR, and a Japan Rail Pass is valid on them; though travellers would normally take the Shinkansen for comfort and speed, the bus might be convenient if you wanted to stay in Kyoto (say) until late evening past the last Shinkansen departure but wanted to be in Tokyo early the next morning. Information in English for Tokyo–Nagoya–Kyoto/Osaka services is available in handout literature from the Tokyo and Kyoto TICs, and they can give information on any other bus routes. Large travel agencies can also give assistance, though there is the likelihood of a language problem.

Between Tokyo and the Kansai area (Kyoto/Osaka/Nara) there are the following alternative non-JR services:

Shinjuku stn (South exit)–Osaka stn (2300/0640): ¥8,450
Shinjuku Keio Plaza Hotel–Nara stn (2300/0647): ¥8,240
Shinjuku Expressway bus terminal–Kyoto stn (2245/0555): ¥8,030
Disneyland (Chiba Chuo stn)–Nara stn (2110 (2210)/0702): ¥8,500
Disneyland (Chiba Chuo stn)–Kyoto stn (2100 (2200)/0615: ¥8,300

The listing of all night buses for all regions from Hokkaido to Kyushu fills six

pages of *jikokuhyo*. The following is just a selection, with sample departure/arrival times and cost, to illustrate the variety available. "Tokyo" in the following listing includes departures from Tokyo, Shinjuku, Shibuya and Ikebukuro stations; in some cases there are services to the same destination from more than one starting point. There are also night buses departing from Yokohama.

Tokyo–Aomori	2130/0700:	¥10,000
Tokyo–Sakata		
Tokyo–Hirosaki		
Tokyo–Hachinohe		
Tokyo–Morioka		
Tokyo–Miyoshi		
Tokyo–Yamagata		
Tokyo–Sendai	2130/0540:	¥6,100
Narita airport–Sendai		
Tokyo–Niigata		
Tokyo–Kanazawa		
Tokyo–Fukui		
Tokyo–Gifu		
Tokyo–Kobe		
Tokyo–Himeji		
Tokyo–Okayama		
Tokyo–Hiroshima	2000/0800:	¥11,840
Tokyo–Shimonoseki	1830/0825:	¥13,700
Tokyo–Shikoku (several cities)		
Kyoto–Hiroshima	2315/0600:	¥5,500
Kyoto–Nagasaki	2030/0740:	¥11,100
Kyoto–Kumamoto	2050/0735:	¥10,800
Kyoto–Hakata	2200/0725:	¥10,500
Nara–Hakata	2130/0730:	¥10,500
Osaka–Shimonoseki	2300/0805:	¥9,000
Osaka–Kagoshima	2000/0740:	¥12,000
Hiroshima–Nagasaki	2230/0600:	¥6,500
Hakata–Kagoshima	2345/0600:	¥5,300

Ferries

There are many ferries linking up widespread parts of Japan. The word may conjure up the image of a short trip on a small boat across placid and sheltered waters, but in actual fact many Japanese ferries are large ocean-going ships of 10,000 tonnes or so, and voyages may last up to 30 hours. Such ships are equipped with restaurant and bar facilities and usually have baths as well.

The cost for the lowest priced class is usually lower than competing land transport and is often more enjoyable, with the bonus of an economical "sea cruise". The cheapest fare is for an open room with tatami floors that are shared by all passengers. During the busy summer season these may be crowded and smoky, while at other times they may be nearly empty. There are other classes including private cabins.

The only "hazard" of the tatami class is that there may very well be several parties of noisy *sake-* and *shochu*-tippling merry-makers nearby, particularly after harvest season when farmers who have brought in their crops set off for their annual vacation. These groups of people are the "real" Japanese, rustic and unsophisticated, quite bawdy, and an eye-opener for the person who knows only the prim and proper Japanese businessmen. The drunker they get, the happier they get and the louder they sing. They usually know many folk songs (which all tend to sound alike!), and when truly in their cups, their dances become extremely earthy with blatant sexual themes. Even though it may be at the cost of a few hours sleep, this is a good way to get to know another side of the complex personality of Japan and to meet the most genuine people in the country. Any gregarious traveller is sure to be invited to join them.

Many ferries leave at night so you can save the cost of accommodation, but it can mean that the ship passes through scenic waters in the dark. In the summer, however, the sky becomes light as early as 0400, and much of the best part of the Inland Sea can be seen from one ferry (detailed later).

Many ferries carry motor vehicles—cars and motorcycles. The charge for a motorcycle is about 1-1/2 times the "tatami" class passenger fare. Anyone travelling by bicycle would have no trouble taking the bike along on any boat, especially if it's a collapsible model in a carrying bag.

In addition to long-distance ferries, there are many boats operating in the Inland Sea between Shikoku and Honshu, and between Kyushu and Shikoku. There are also many ships that operate between the main islands and small islands offshore, and sightseeing excursion boats that cruise for relatively short distances along the coast or loop back to the point of origin. There are also several ships that operate among the chain of islands that extends south from Kagoshima to Okinawa. These services are described in the sections covering the port cities.

Following is a list of the main long-distance ferries, with the cheapest "tatami" class fares.

OTARU (Hokkaido) TO:

Niigata	¥5,150
Tsuruga	¥6,590
Maizuru	¥6,590

NAOETSU (Honshu) TO:

Muroran (Hokkaido)	¥5,150
Iwanai (Hokkaido)	¥5,150

SENDAI (N. Honshu) TO:

Tomakomai (Hokkaido)	¥7,500

OARAI (N. Honshu) TO:

Muroran	¥9,570
Tomakomai	¥9,570

TOKYO TO:

Tomakomai	¥11,840

Kushiro (Hokkaido)	¥14,420
Nachi-katsuura	¥10,500
Kochi (Shikoku)	¥16,000
Tokushima (Shikoku)	¥8,200
Kitakyushu (N. Kyushu)	¥12,000
Naha (Okinawa)	¥19,670

KAWASAKI TO:

Hyuga (E. Kyushu)	¥17,710

NAGOYA TO:

Sendai	¥9,580
Tomakomai	¥15,450

OSAKA TO:

Takamatsu (Shikoku)	¥2,800
Matsuyama (NW. Shikoku)	¥4,900
Beppu (E. Kyushu)	¥6,900
Kochi (S. Shikoku)	¥4,530
Shin-moji (N. Kyushu)	¥5,600
Naha	¥15,450
Miyazaki (E. Kyushu)	¥8,230
Shibushi (S. Kyushu)	¥11,100

KOBE TO:

Oita (E. Kyushu)	¥5,870
Hyuga	¥7,620
Matsuyama	¥4,170
Naha	¥15,450
Shin-moji	¥5,600

IZUMI-OTSU (*near Osaka*) *TO*:

Shin-moji	¥5,600

HIROSHIMA TO:

Beppu	¥4,000

HAKATA TO:

Naha	¥12,970

KAGOSHIMA TO:

Naha	¥11,840

KITAKYUSHU:

Tokushima	¥5,800

For up-to-date information on scheduled passenger shipping, there are several useful sources.

The English-language brochure "Long Distance Passenger & Car Ferries" has a map and listings of all routes, fares, and sailing frequency (though not days), together with office phone numbers. This is published by the Japan Long Distance Ferry Association (Iino Bldg. Rm. 920, 2-1-1 Uchisaiwaicho, Chiyoda-ku, Tokyo; tel (03) 3501-0889).

We can only hope that they will continue to do so long into the future.

Jikokuhyo, the bible of all scheduled transport in Japan, shows ferry routes on maps at the front of the book. Ferries are shown as thin red lines, each with a number and a letter, which refer to the page and section in which the schedule and fare are printed. Although secondary in importance for non-Japanese, *jikokuhyo* is updated monthly, a benefit since ferry schedules change with some regularity.

Also check for free info sheets from the TICs listing boat services.

Intracity Public Transportation

Trains—Urban & Suburban

In the Tokyo and Osaka area, JR trains operate as part of the city mass transit system, where they are called *kokuden* trains. Loop lines circle the central district of both cities, while other JR lines and private railway lines act as feeder systems from the outlying areas into the central districts. In Tokyo the loop line is called the Yamanote line; in Osaka it is the Kanjo line. Several other cities are also served by JR and private railways in a similar manner.

The private railway lines usually run for comparatively short distances, less than 100 km, and link the major cities with surrounding suburban areas or nearby resorts.

In the Tokyo area, for example, 11 private railways connect directly to the Yamanote loop line—some serving as continuations of subway lines.

In the early days of railway building, the founders discovered that it was good business to build department stores over the large stations, hence many well-known stores, such as Keio, Odakyu, or Hankyu bear the name of the lines with which they are associated.

In many cases, private railways run virtually parallel to JR lines and serve the same destinations. The private lines are usually less expensive, sometimes as low as half the JR fare, and also have a reputation for better service, cleaner equipment and more polite personnel, though this may not always be true.

Details of the rail services in each city or region are given in the appropriate chapter.

Subways

There are subway systems in Sapporo, Sendai, Toyko, Yokohama, Nagoya, Kyoto, Osaka, Kobe, and Fukuoka. They offer a convenient and quick means of getting around these cities because they run free of traffic congestion.

In each city the stations are well marked above ground and can usually be used by foreigners without difficulty because there is adequate information in English. City maps show the locations of stations. In most of these cities the subways are augmented to a greater or lesser extent by private and JR railway lines. Subway maps, sometimes with romanised names, are usually available free at stations, and tourist literature (particularly for Tokyo) often has maps.

Commuter Passes

Passes valid for one, three, or six months are available for all forms of public transport in Tokyo and other major cities. A single pass valid for travel on two separate systems (JR plus subway, for example), can be purchased at the office of either of the destination stations (except for small stations).

Day Passes

The subways of Tokyo (and probably some other systems) offer a day pass valid for unlimited use of all subway lines for one day.

Bus

Every Japanese city of any size has extensive bus services. Unfortunately it is difficult to use them because their destinations are written only in Japanese and the drivers don't usually speak English. An exception is that buses in Nikko have signs in English because so many foreign tourists use them. It is necessary to know bus routes in advance, which means that only long-term residents will get much use from them. Buses are also subject to traffic delays, so they are usually much slower than trains and subways.

Two systems of fare collection are used. In Tokyo and some other cities, the fare is a flat sum paid on entering. The fare is normally clearly marked on the cash box beside the driver. Exact fare is dropped into the large opening. If change is required, there is a slot (marked for 10, 100, and 500 yen coins) into which coins are fed; change is returned from a small chute. (Older ones might give ¥10 coins in change from a ¥100 coin.) There may be two slots on top of the cash box—the left one is for tickets, the right for coins.

In many other city and country runs the fare depends on the distance travelled. Passengers enter by the rear door and take a ticket from a dispenser beside the steps. On the ticket is a number indicating the fare zone at the place of boarding. At the front of the bus is an illuminated sign that shows the fare to be paid for each starting zone if you leave the bus at that point. The fares advance as the bus moves along. Pay at the front when you leave.

Most buses in Japan have recorded messages identifying the next stop, which is very helpful if you know the name of your stop. A separate fare must be paid for each bus boarded, except in Nagasaki, which is the only city that has adopted a system of transfers.

Taxis

Taxis are expensive in Japan, like everything else. Fares are similar throughout the country, and somewhat higher in the larger cities.

The flagfall is ¥650 for the first two km, then ¥80 for each additional 280 metres (or two minutes) in Tokyo; slightly farther in other cities, plus a time charge when the taxi is moving at less than 10 km/h. The flagfall cost is displayed prominently in both windows on the left side of the vehicle and sometimes in the rear window.

A red-light sign in the left front window indicates an available taxi, green means that a night surcharge is in effect, and yellow indicates that it is answering a radio call.

Taxis can be flagged down on the street. It is (in theory) sufficient to stand at the edge of the road with an outstretched arm, fingers bent slightly downward. Never whistle. Most taxi drivers are polite and patient (some are very friendly), but some give others a bad name by passing by a foreigner and picking up nearby Japanese. (The occasional one may be quite surly with foreigners he deigns to pick up, but these may be just as unpleasant to Japanese customers.) Taxis can be summoned by

phone in cities; there is a 20 per cent surcharge for this service.

There are taxi stands near most stations and drivers are reluctant (or prohibited) to stop on the street near them. At night, in busy areas of Tokyo like Ginza or Roppongi, a taxi stop is often the only place you can get a taxi.

From 2300 to 0500 there is a surcharge of 30 per cent. That, at least, is the official rate. Because the subways and trains stop running soon after midnight, drivers have a seller's market, and it is often difficult to get a taxi after 2200, especially on rainy nights. One major cause of the problem is that companies give taxi coupons to employees, and the employees don't mind giving two or more coupons to guarantee a ride. This they indicate by the number of fingers that they hold up.

Japanese taxi drivers are not linguists and most do not speak English, although I have been pleasantly surprised on occasion. Say your destination in Japanese, if possible, otherwise have it written in Japanese by someone so you can show it to the driver. Hotels have cards with their address in Japanese to help guests get back. Pick one up on the way out. Sometimes the hotel name is different in English and Japanese—for example, the Imperial (in Tokyo) is "Teikoku hoteru" to the Japanese. Addresses are notoriously difficult to find in Japan, so don't get upset and berate the driver if he takes a long time and has to stop at one or more police boxes to get you to your destination. This is simply standard operating procedure.

Tipping is not the practice in Japan unless the driver has performed some unusual service, like helping with heavy baggage, or has spent a long time finding a difficult address. A driver might even refuse to accept the money, although reports of this happening are not so frequent these days.

Do not try to open or close the left rear door. It is operated by the driver in almost all taxis. They get quite angry if customers close the door, because it damages the mechanism. (This knowledge has been used on occasion to show displeasure with egregiously bad or surly service.)

Rickshaws

There are only a few rickshaws in use in Japan. They can be seen every day in the back streets around the Ginza, usually around dusk. When traffic is clear, the vehicle moves along surprisingly fast and smoothly. These rickshaws are not for rent by the general public—they carry geisha to teahouses and restaurants where they will entertain in traditional style with songs, dances, and stories.

At various places around Japan a few rickshaws have been dusted off and revived as tourist attractions, but they are as much a novelty to the modern Japanese as they are to westerners. I have seen them at the charming old town of Kurashiki (near Okayama), at Furukawa (near Takayama), and at Nagasaki, but reports are that tourists don't use them enough for the operators to make a living.

The rickshaw has its origin in Japan (not China), and the name is a corruption of the Japanese "jin riki sha" meaning "man powered carriage". However, Neil Pedlar wrote in an article in *The Japan Times* that the rickshaw was probably invented by an American, Jonathon Goble, who came to Yokohama as a missionary, wanted a carriage for his wife, and commissioned one from a local craftsman (who then made many more). Further, the rickshaw is a copy of a vehicle called a "brouette" first used in Paris in 1669! Goble copied the design from an encyclopedia.

Independent Road Travel

Most travellers in Japan have only a few days or weeks, and are quite satisfied to use public transportation. Some, however, have more time to spend because they have a long holiday or are studying/working in the country for an extended period and would like to have the freedom offered by their own transportation. There is no better way to see Japan completely and thoroughly than by car or motorcycle. A bicycle is also well worth considering if time, interest, and physical health are sufficient. The first notes are for motorists, followed by information specifically for cyclists.

Driving Conditions

Ordinary Roads

Roads in Japan are generally as good as they need be. This means that all roads are hard surfaced except for the rarely travelled ones high in the mountains. With the exception of expressways, roads are narrow relative to the heavy traffic that they carry, and minor country roads are so narrow that one car may have to pull off the road to let another pass. The main roads are built up to such an extent that they seem at times to be one continuous town. Traffic lights are very frequent along these highways and seem to be always red. It would appear that traffic-controlled lights for sideroads have never been heard of, and the lights continue to operate through the night even when there is negligible traffic onto the main highways from such roads. The result is that it is impossible to make good time over long distances. A typical good day's driving on ordinary roads, even by motorcycle, will cover only 200–250 km, and this will require eight to 10 hours. The best that I managed by motorcycle was 400 km in 16 fatiguing (and dirty) hours.

Passing slow vehicles is a near impossibility. Apart from the almost inevitable endless line of vehicles ahead and heavy oncoming traffic, there are few passing zones. Where there are straight and flat stretches (quite common in parts of Hokkaido and Tohoku) there will normally be a solid line on the road indicating no passing. Conversely and senselessly, when these roads get into the mountains and visibility is poor, dotted lines commonly extend around blind corners!

Important to those on two wheels is that the main trunk roads (non-expressway), those with single-digit and low two-digit route numbers, have incredibly filthy air from the huge number of diesel vehicles. This makes the ride unpleasant, clothes and any exposed skin become dirty, and it can do the lungs no good whatever.

The single greatest frustration when driving in Japan—even a danger to one's mental health - is the speed limit. Incredible as it may sound, the maximum on highways in open areas is only 60 km/h (38 mph). This limit, laughably low by international standards, is the maximum allowable, but it seems that the authorities feel that even this heady speed is rather risky, so it is common to find limits as low as 50 or even 40 km/h in open areas in the countryside. Even more ridiculous: going up mountain roads, one sometimes finds signs calling for a reduction in speed!

Unfortunately, these limits are strictly, if unpredictably, enforced. A speed trap will always be located in the only straight and level section of an otherwise twisty and hilly road, where the temptation is greatest to ease the frustration of being held back by slow and hilly stretches of road.

Offenders are flagged down by a red and white banded pole held touching the road. There is usually an "office" complete with table and chairs set up in the wilderness to mass-process the victims, with 10 or more police sitting there writing out tickets. This waste of manpower explains why patrol cars are rarely seen on any but main highways, and why driving habits on mountain and winding roads are so bad. It is very questionable that this enforcement has any relationship to road safety and probably has everything to do with making money.

AUTOMOBILE ASSOCIATION The Japan Automobile Federation (JAF) (tel. (03) 5976-9730) has a booklet which details the traffic laws. It is available by mail within Japan for ¥1120 (including postage) from: JAF, 3-5-8 Shiba Koen, Minato-ku, Tokyo 105 (tel. (03) 3976-9730), or in person from JAF headquarters (opposite the entrance to Tokyo Tower) for ¥1000.

Motorists may wish to consider membership in the JAF. It offers the same sort of road service as similar associations in other countries. Reciprocal benefits are given to members of the automobile associations of Australia, Canada, Germany, Great Britain, Holland, Hong Kong, New Zealand, Singapore, and the USA. Membership also gives a discount when buying JAF publications, and members can have strip maps made up for their journeys around Japan. Membership costs ¥4000 per year plus a joining fee of ¥2000.

Expressways
For drivers in a hurry to get from point A to point B, there is no substitute for the expressways. These now link Akita, at the far north of Honshu, to Yatsushiro, at the south of Kyushu, a distance of 2002 km. In addition, there are feeder expressways from country areas, and in metropolitan areas there are several, often parallel to each other though separated by a few km. They are the only way to get through major cities quickly (though expensively).

Tolls are exceptionally high by world standards. For a car, from Tokyo to Nagoya (360 km) costs over ¥6,000, which is substantially higher than the bus fare and a good fraction of the cost by Shinkansen. It is less for a motorcycle, but not much. Speed limits on expressways are 100 km/h; they are the only roads in Japan with such "high" limits.

Interchanges ("inta" in Japanese) are indicated in advance in both *romaji* and *kanji*, but at the exit it may be only in *kanji*, so memorize the characters of your exit when they first appear. It is also advisable to know the name of the desired exit in advance. For example, on the Meishin expressway (Nagoya–Kobe), the exit for Osaka is not named Osaka, but Toyonaka (which I found out by overshooting and exiting at Amagasaki, a good distance further on). Road maps show the name of each interchange, but usually only in *kanji*. Expressway signs in cities are largely only in *kanji*, so it is essential to know the characters for your destination before starting out. For a year or so nationalism (or whatever) was leading the authorities to remove all *romaji* from signs, but Japan has been overtaken by an "internationization" (whatever that may be) wave, and the *kanji*-only policy conflicted with this new aim. As a result, major road signs generally have city names in *romaji*, to the great relief of foreign drivers here.

Driving Habits

The average Japanese driver is reasonably competent. There isn't the long history of mass motoring in Japan that there is in Europe and elsewhere—very few people owned cars prior to the mid-1960s, and the Japanese car industry was virtually non-existent—with the result that Japanese driving for a while was abysmal. Fortunately, the gross stupidity that seemed prevalent in the early 1970s and earlier has been toned down in recent years, probably as a result of improved driver education and police law enforcement. Or perhaps most of the really dumb ones just wiped themselves out. That is not to say that present driving habits are as good as they should be, but that that they could be worse.

In order to obtain a licence, prospects must take 35 hours of lessons, but one wonders what the time is spent on, for so many drivers make the same, dangerous, errors. The following notes are intended to prepare anyone planning to drive in Japan for possible dangers, but should be noted especially by motorcyclists and bicyclists, for they (we) are most vulnerable to the actions of vehicle drivers.

The main problem with drivers in Japan is a lack of foresight. Too many do not think ahead to predict what might happen, and consequently have to slam on the brakes to avoid a collision (in which they are not always successful). Many drive so they are almost touching the vehicle ahead, depending on their reflexes alone to save them if a sudden stop is called for. This is probably a problem in most countries, but it seems to be a national characteristic in Japan, where every other aspect of life is overseen and controlled by parents, teachers, or boss, and driving is one of the few activities where one has the freedom to do as one wishes. Not all can handle the freedom. (The need for sudden braking could, of course, just be a consequence of the low speed limits that prevent drivers from gaining an appreciation of the increased distance required to stop from high speed.)

When moving away from the curb, many drivers pull a meter into the road before looking behind them to see if anything is coming. Going around corners in the city at quite high speed, without thinking that there might be a pedestrian or car in the way, is too common. Too many drivers change lanes without looking, and, once a vehicle they are passing is out of peripheral vision, many drivers immediately begin to cut over, forcing the other driver to brake abruptly.

Beware of drivers continuing through red lights. A large percentage of Japanese drivers seems to hold the belief that if an up-coming light has been green at any time while in their view, they have the right to continue through it even if it has been red for several seconds. This makes things interesting when one road has the green light, yet cars from the cross-street continue to stream across in front.

Vestiges of the old days can be found on almost any mountain road, where every Japanese male driver seems to go silly, thinking himself highly skilled with the trained reflexes of a racing driver. The fact is that the low speed limits throughout Japan prevent them from gaining any experience at high speeds on any kind of road, let alone twisty mountain ones. Almost every driver cuts straight through curves, so it is advisable to sound your horn at every blind corner. Evidence of the bad driving is that there is scarcely a meter of guard rail in all Japan that isn't scraped or bent. Containers of flowers by the roadside, often with some personal possessions and a flat stick with a name written on it, are mute testimony to a fatal accident, and are a common sight.

Right of way at an intersection of equal-size roads that have no markings goes to the vehicle on the left. Where a small road enters a larger road, all vehicles on the larger road have priority. That, at least, is the law, and it is useful to know in theory, but many Japanese appear to be unsure whether right of way is to the left or right and in practice there seems to be no clear rule. An objective evaluation is that the right of way lies with the bigger vehicle. Not for nothing has the *nihonglish* word *dumpu* evolved—it means a belligerent and reckless driver, and is a corruption of the English "dump truck".

Although most truck drivers are careful and sane, their numbers include some of the most dangerous drivers in the country. Too many drive in an irresponsibly "playful" manner, indulging in games of chase, driving almost touching the vehicle ahead, and unmindful of the mass of their vehicle. I have seen a multi-tonne concrete mixer being driven through maneuvers in heavy traffic that I would hesitate to perform in a sports car on an open track. One of the worst smashups in Japanese road history is believed to have been caused by the driver of a large truck loaded with chemicals playing "tag" with other drivers. The rear-end collision that he caused in a tunnel of the Tomei Expressway (Toyko–Nagoya) killed seven people and destroyed 173 cars in the pile-up and ensuing fire. (A common cause of accidents on expressways, especially at night, is drivers high on amphetamines, taken to keep them awake during long drives.)

Again, most drivers in Japan are okay, but watch out for the crazies. Actually, in fairness to Japanese drivers, one must remark that they are generally exceptionally well behaved in view of the small number of police patrolling the roads. For all the tight controls exerted by the police in many aspects of life in Japan, their road law enforcement is quite ineffective (to the critical eyes of a foreigner). Apart from the radar traps mentioned earlier, and some motorcycle cops monitoring speed, there seems to be negligible effort to stop drivers who are doing the dangerous things just described. Every weekend in Tokyo (and probably in other large cities), groups of motorcycle freaks called *bo-so-zoku* tear around the streets at night at high speed, making as much noise as possible. It is well known that they use the same streets week after week, yet the law enforcement seems to end at sundown. (Sometimes "law enfarcement" seems the more appropriate term.)

The amazing thing is that there are relatively few actual accidents. As long as everyone has the same habits and expectations, a certain "rhythm" of driving seems to develop and be expected. It would appear that drivers just assume that it is up to them to allow for the problems caused by others.

Despite the problems and frustrations, the rewards in the "good parts" can make driving worthwhile, and independent driving through Japan can be recommended as the best way to see the country if time and costs permit.

For less exasperating driving conditions and the chance to see a more "typical" Japan, it is preferable to use the less travelled highways (generally inland). Often they are little slower than the main roads and vastly more enjoyable, for the scenery is more what one thinks of as traditional Japan, with less of the ugliness that characterizes the average Japanese cities and towns that the main roads pass through continally.

Fuel

Fuel is readily available almost everywhere in Japan, the only exception being in remote areas with little traffic. Fuel has always been expensive in Japan. The cost of regular has been in the range of ¥120 per litre in recent years, while motor oil is incredibly expensive, up to ¥1000–1500 per litre. (There is no law on the books prohibiting the import of gasoline and refined petroleum products, but when one entrepreneur brought in a tanker full of gaso-

line for sale at his gas stations at lower cost, he was prohibited from landing it by administrative decree, and was forced to sell it to one of the major refining companies. For "orderly marketing".)

WARNING: The penalties for driving after drinking are very severe and can result in on-the-spot cancellation of licence for a year, with a good likelihood of jail or a stiff fine. Don't risk it.

Navigation

Finding your way around Japan, especially outside the cities, is not too difficult. International road signs, as found in Europe, are used for information, warning, and prohibitions, so there is no need to be able to read Japanese. Where words are used on the sign there are often also numbers indicating times, dates, or speeds, so they can usually be understood.

As mentioned above, many signs have both *kanji* and *romaji*, and it is generally possible to find one's way using only the *romaji* signs, but the critical one that you need to know to make an exit or other sudden decision will invariably be only in *kanji*. When you see a sign in both scripts with your destination written on it, memorise the *kanji*! You will then be ready.

When driving in large cities in residential areas, never try to take short cuts. Except in Kyoto and Sapporo, there are scarcely any two streets that run parallel for more than a few hundred meters, and you can get completely lost in a very short time. If you find you are lost, swallow your pride and go back the way you came, hoping not to encounter any one-way streets. (On several occasions I have had to navigate in Tokyo with a compass!)

Maps

Road maps are given out free by some service stations, but generally they have to be purchased at appreciable cost. There are no maps that are labelled extensively in *romaji*; the best you can look for is maps with key cities, and perhaps some lesser ones, marked in both scripts. A further complication is that the city names are printed in *kanji* (characters) while railway stations are shown in *hiragana* (phonetic symbols representing syllables), so that one cannot be used to locate the name of a place written in the other script. (See the note in *jikokuhyo* about *hiragana* spellings for names in *kanji*.)

Maps are available from several sources. You can check if gas stations have local maps. Maps of the whole country (by region) are available at the head offices (or travel advisory offices) of some of the oil companies. It would be best to check with the TIC as to which companies still have this service.

The JAF sells a book of maps that cover the entire country. The maps are to a suitably large scale, and have many places identified in *romaji* as well as *kanji*. Being in a single book and relatively small, the maps are convenient to use, although it can be difficult to follow a route that extends over several pages. The books cost ¥2000 (less 10 per cent for members of JAF or any of the nine affiliated foreign associations). JAF also sells a series of individual regional maps at ¥450 each.

I used the *Routiere* series for my travels. These have enough names in *romaji* to be useful, and are printed on paper-like plastic that was not affected by periodic soakings. They are many times the size of the maps in the JAF book, so each map covers a larger area. This makes them more convenient for planning longer trips, but a set of nine to cover the entire country becomes quite costly at ¥800 each. There is another series of maps also printed on

plastic under the brand name of *Area*, but these have no *romaji* whatever. (The same company has another set of maps, one for each prefecture. Don't get them. You'd have to buy 46!) If a set of maps is too pricy, you can get by adequately with one map of the entire country (¥800), but it lacks small details. This is number 10 of the *Routiere* series. (Ask for "Zenkoku no chizu".) Maps are available at any large bookstore.

A hint on map reading: the legend that explains the meanings of the symbols is in Japanese only. Roads marked in pale pink or pale green are unpaved, usually high in the mountains, and their surface is usually rough (or muddy) and treacherous for motorcyclists (voice of experience!). It is difficult to go even 10 km/h on these roads.

If you ever have to use a hand-out map of, for example, a regional touristic attraction, and it has lots of cute little illustrations of buildings, animals, etc., do not trust it to be true to scale, or even correct as to the number of streets and their relationship to each other.

See also the section on bicycling, for there are maps published for cyclists that are equally suited to motorists. The only drawback is that they cover only the central part of the country.

Driving Licences

A domestic licence of most countries or an International Driving Permit can be used for up to six months in Japan. If you are staying in the country longer, however, it will be necessary to obtain a Japanese driving licence. This is a fairly simple procedure. Arm yourself with a couple of 25 x 30 mm photos, your Alien Registration Card (or Certificate of Residence), a few thousand yen and your valid foreign licence, and go to the *shikenjo* (licence office).

In Tokyo this is near Samezu station of

the Keihin Kyuko line (out of Shinagawa station). A sign at the entrance of this office will direct you to the counter where an English speaking person will explain the rest of the procedure, which is all routine and involves nothing more difficult than a simple eye test (glasses are allowed). An International Driving Permit can be obtained easily at the same office after you have been issued your Japanese licence. (Details for reaching the office are given in the Tokyo section.)

Residents should note that the licence runs approximately two years, to your birthdate. No renewal notice is sent out, so you must keep track yourself.

Make sure you obtain your driving licence before coming to Japan as getting one in the country is a long drawn-out and very expensive affair.

Travellers who are passing through Singapore and who will be away from their own countries for several years may find it useful to obtain a Singapore driving licence (very simple on presentation of your valid licence). The Singapore licence can be renewed easily by mail, something that might be difficult in your own country if you have no permanent address. With the Singapore licence it is possible to obtain a Japanese or other licence as required. If the licence from home is valid for motorcycles it should be endorsed for the same in Singapore (as should an International Driving Permit from there or anywhere else). This procedure might be possible in other countries as well, but I know about Singapore personally.

Motorcycle Licences

A visitor planning to tour Japan by motorcycle may ride any size of bike during the first six months while using his overseas licence. However, Japanese motorcycle licences are graded by the size of the bike for

which they are valid, and the maximum size for which a Japanese licence can be obtained by showing a foreign licence is 400cc. For larger bikes a test is required. In Tokyo, at the Samezu office test site (and probably typical of elsewhere), this test is designed to be as difficult as possible, seemingly to minimize the number of riders who can have one. The test, among other things, requires one to pick up a fallen-over 750 Honda, with the cute trick that it is an old police bike with a guard bar right where one would normally support the partially raised bike with a leg. (I have picked up a standard Honda 750—with a full load of luggage—any number of times without difficulty, but had much trouble with their bike.) Other tests are to ride their bike through a tight obstacle course, down a 300 mm wide checkered steel plate, slowly, after passing first over a sharp bump while getting onto the plate, and several other difficult tricks, most of which are irrelevant to actual road riding. The Samezu test ground is right beside the harbor, so there is often a very stiff wind making precision riding that much more difficult, and some of the bikes are slightly out of alignment, so they pull to one side, requiring the rider to sit off center to keep it going straight. (I gave up after two tries, and I have about 50,000 kilometers of experience riding a 750.)

Private Motor Vehicles

Cars

Generally the only foreigners in Japan who buy new cars are those who will be staying for a year or more and who have been sent by their company. A used car can save them money, and can also be considered by shorter-term visitors who want closed-in private transportation.

NEW CARS If you are staying in Japan for some time, ask friends if a car is really useful; they may advise, from experience, that a car is often more bother than it is worth in the city, and getting out of the city into the countryside takes considerable time. Within cities it is often more convenient to use public transport and taxis. Parking places are difficult to find, on-street parking is being actively discouraged by the authorities, and commercial parking garages are expensive. It can be preferable and cheaper to use public transport to reach a vacation area and then use a rental car.

For those wishing to buy, there is (needless to say) an excellent choice of Japanese-made cars available, plus a number of imported models, though the latter are mostly sold for prestige, and their price in Japan may bear no relationship to that in their home countries.

IMPORTING CARS It is possible to import motor vehicles (cars and motorcycles) into Japan for periods of one year on a carnet (explained later), or permanently if for more than a year. However, neither is recommended. Shipping rates are high, customs clearance, port clearance, and other charges will add substantially to the cost, and if it is being imported for more than a year, tax (though not duty) will have to be paid, this being computed on the cost of the vehicle plus shipping costs. In addition to these and other likely charges, many mechanical modifications will have to be made to bring the vehicle into conformity with Japanese safety and anti-pollution requirements. This is guaranteed to be expensive. Unless there is a special reason for wanting a foreign car in Japan, it is simpler and cheaper to buy a Japanese model in Japan. Leave the overpriced and oversized foreign imports to the ostentatious local residents who have more money than sense. (Interestingly, large American cars are reputedly most popular with gangsters,

politicians, and doctors.)

Anyone still wishing to import a vehicle into Japan should contact a Japanese government representative overseas for up-to-date information on regulations. U.S. military personnel should inquire from their service regarding import regulations, for they have some advantages not given to civilians. However, there is a good selection of used cars being sold by other service personnel who are leaving Japan. and their prices are low. (Unfortunately, non-military people are not allowed to buy them for they have a special licensing arrangement.)

EXPORTING CARS With the advent of design rules in various countries, cars built to Japanese specifications cannot generally be exported to them. As for exporting a car to a country without such design rules, the Japanese model might be more expensive than the model of car exported commercially to that country because of the anti-pollution equipment required on the Japanese model. Because of agreements between overseas importers and Japanese producers, it is usually not possible to buy the export model of the type required for the USA market, for example, in Japan. In addition, Japanese cars are (mysteriously) often less expensive overseas than in Japan.

Notes in the section on motorcycles describe a *carnet*, a document that can be useful for anyone taking a car overseas for travel in a country other than the country of residence.

SECOND-HAND CARS Buying a second-hand car can be a money saver for the long term resident, and there are some good buys for someone who wants a car for only a few months of travel in Japan. Buying second-hand involves the same worries as in any country—Japanese used car salesmen enjoy the same reputation for high business principles as do their brethren around the world. However a used car in Japan is likely to be safer than one bought in a country where there is no system of compulsory vehicle inspection.

As a car gets older, the repairs required to meet the requirements of the bienniel *shaken* inspection (explained below) become progressively more expensive, and a point is reached where the owner finds it cheaper to get rid of the car and buy another. (This enforced scrapping is probably a contributor to the good health of the Japanese auto industry: make 'em buy a new one!) Old cars with only a short time before the next inspection have little value, and can be purchased cheaply. Finding them would require the assistance of a Japanese person, however.

BUYING Buying a new vehicle is much less difficult than a second-hand purchase because the price and conditions are more or less fixed, and finding a dealer is easy.

When buying a second-hand car or motorcycle, language may be the main problem because it is necessary to look around, use Japanese newspaper listings, and negotiate with someone who probably doesn't speak English. A person belonging to one of the English conversation groups found in any large city might be willing to help with this in return for the language practice.

Used cars for sale by foreigners are advertised in *Tokyo Weekender* and other local papers aimed at the resident foreigner. Such advertisers would be easiest to deal with because they will more than likely speak English, but it is still necessary to negotiate the hurdle of change of registration.

SHAKEN One of the things to know about the regulations regarding cars and motorcycles is the *shaken* system. This is a combined road tax, registration fee, insurance premium, and vehicle inspection. It is an expense every two years whether ownership changes or not. The reason why the word brings cringes to car owners is that the inspection usually requires money to bring the vehicle up to the standard.

The shaken system is disliked because it amounts to government-sanctioned extortion that benefits the great number of service centers that make the inspections. Even if no work is needed on the car and the check takes only a short time, the motorist is liable for the full charge just to have the papers filled out. Its purpose is supposedly a safety measure, but a study showed that only about 0.0015% of motor vehicle accidents (apart from those due to tire problems) were caused as a result of mechanical failure. This being Japan, however, it is unlikely that the system will change.

Motorcycles under 250cc are exempt from the inspection, but insurance is still compulsory.

Motorcycles

A person who likes motorcycles can have a very enjoyable time touring Japan by bike. The weather is favourable (or at least bearable for a minimum of eight months), there is the individual freedom afforded by any motor vehicle, plus the added advantage of being able to get through spaces that can stall a car for long periods when traffic gets snarled (which is quite often). I once got my bike across construction scaffolding where a road in the mountains had completely slipped away and down the side of a hill. Another advantage of bikes in Japan is that they can be parked almost anywhere—even on the sidewalk (police never bother them).

Most bikes in Japan are used for utilitarian purposes, like deliveries. Except in metropolitan areas (where wealth is concentrated), large bikes (over 250cc) are quite rare. Although many fire-breathing super bikes are built in Japan, most are exported. There are no Japanese-made bikes for sale in Japan (new) that are bigger than 750cc. Any seen here have been exported, then re-imported, for there is no restriction on engine size for imported bikes.

The optimum size of a bike for touring Japan is 250cc. This is the smallest size allowed on expressways and the largest allowed on the major streets of Tokyo between 2300 and 0600. An absurd law prohibits large bikes from using the major arteries between these hours on the flimsy logic that banning bikes over 250cc on these streets will stop the bosozoku (described earlier) who ride around early in the morning making as much noise as they can to bother the populace. The law penalizes law-abiding riders, for there are few parallel routes, while the bosozoku just scoff at it and ride with impunity.

Best of all, a 250cc bike is the largest size that is not subject to *shaken*. Because of the low speed limits there is little sense buying anything bigger anyway. A lady friend once rode the full length of the country on a 50cc bike without problems. (Note, however, that any bike of 125cc or below is supposed to hug the side of the road and not ride in the lanes, a dangerous requirement in view of the way car drivers disregard space requirements of two wheelers. And the edge of the road is often very rough.)

My most earnest advice is to avoid even considering the purchase of one of the countless models of cute little mini-motorscooters that have multiplied like rabbits in the past few years. Though their prices are attractive, they are hazardous to drive, for 60 per cent of them (or more) are assembled with the rear wheel cocked out of line with the frame. The result is that the back end continually tries to go off to one side, and riding one requires constant leaning to balance it. Looking at scooter riders in Japan might lead you to believe that every one of them suffers from curvature of the spine or a dislocated shoulder!

If you wish to buy a large (over 250cc bike new, the best dealers will be in the large cities—Tokyo, Osaka, etc. Large dealers are better able to give discounts, or may include accessories instead of a price reduction. The dealer can take care of the paperwork for registration, insurance, etc.

Honda has the largest dealer network in the country, followed by Yamaha, then Suzuki. Kawasaki dealers seem comparatively rare. Remember that dealers in smaller centers don't normally work on large bikes, so spare parts will not likely be sitting on the shelf in such places.

After considering the cost of a new bike you may decide to buy a second-hand one and sell it later. However, even used bikes are rather expensive in Japan. (Conversely, it is difficult to get a good price when selling.) This may seem surprising because Japan must be the ultimate throwaway society; things are usually discarded at the first sign of trouble.

Prices for used bikes have strange patterns. For example a used 400cc bike won't be much cheaper than a used 750cc (because the demand for the latter is less), and the price of bikes up to 250cc is also not low because they escape the very high recurring cost of *shaken*.

If buying a used bike in Tokyo first check the *Tokyo Weekender*. Since advertisers are usually other foreigners there should be no language problem in negotiating. You could even run an advertisement yourself, stating what size bike you want (and the date of your arrival in Japan if you're doing it from another country). Also consider an ad in Tokyo Journal. The address of each is given the Tokyo section.

The Tokyo TIC used to allow personal ads on its bulletin board, but has stopped this at the time of writing. It may change policy again in future, so it does no harm to have a look. Supermarkets used by foreigners also may have bulletin boards with bike ads. Servicemen at U.S. bases around Japan—there are several within an hour or so of Tokyo—sometimes have bikes for sale, but you would have to be sure that the registration could be transferred to a civilian.

The largest concentration of used bike shops is in the Ueno area of Tokyo, along the streets parallel to Showa-dori; this runs north-south past Ueno station (JR) and near Ueno subway station (Hibiya and Ginza lines). The dealers are to the north of the station.

Japanese newspapers also have bikes advertised and there are many motorcycle magazines with pages of bikes for sale. As with buying a car, you can get help over the language barrier with the aid of someone from an English-language study group.

Be sure to test ride any bike. There is a 50–50 chance it will pull to one side. Don't reject it immediately, as roughly half the bikes in Japan suffer from this malady. The most likely cause is simply that the rear wheel has been cocked sideways when adjusting the chain tension—one side has been tightened more than the other. This is easy to check by looking at the index marks on the arm, and easy to correct.

If you're touring Japan by bike it is advisable to carry a tire repair kit and pump. There is nothing worse than getting a flat high up on a mountain road. (This recommendation comes from personal experience!)

When having a bike serviced in a small town, keep an eye on what's going on. I once had an oil change performed in a town on Hokkaido. When I wasn't watching, the "mechanic" tightened the drain plug with an immense wrench. At the next oil change, the plug didn't come out—the entire bottom of the oil tank broke off!

Elastic luggage straps are very useful and are available from motorcycle accessory shops. Worth looking for in small local bike shops are "cottage industry" straps cut from old inner tubes, as they are long and very strong.

Another tip is to put your clothing in individual plastic bags fastened with elastic bands before putting them in your pack. This keeps them dry if you get rained on (not uncommon!). Rain gear is useful to carry with you, but it might be cheaper in other countries; a vinyl jacket and pants costs about ¥1500.

Helmets are required by law for all riders. A name-brand helmet with chin guard costs about ¥10,000 after discount.

RENTAL MOTORCYCLES Rental Motorcycles are not available for rental for long-distance touring, though in some popular tourist destinations they may be obtained for local sightseeing.

TRANECYCLIST INTERNATIONAL An organization worth knowing about, TC-International is the Japan chapter of an international association of touring motorcyclists (18 countries so far). The newsletter of TC-I (for short) has news of enthusiasts who are touring the world, or their own countries. (Editor Volker Lenzner is obviously a workaholic, judging by the publications and correspondence that he puts out!) The club enables socializing with fellow motorcycle enthusiasts in Japan. The feature of the club in Japan that would be greatest potential interest to overseas cyclists is the exchange program. Some Japanese riders will lend their personal machines to foreign members in return for the reciprocal right when they visit overseas. For details, send a self-addressed envelope and one international postal reply coupon (or a U.S. $1 bill) to Transcyclist International, CPO Box 2064, Tokyo 100-91.

Road Dangers

Japan is probably no more dangerous than other countries for motorcyclists, but you must be aware of a few local idiocies. Car and truck drivers in Japan have no appreciation of the space needs of bikes (or any other vehicles, for that matter) and drive close behind, unable to tolerate the sight of a clear space ahead of the vehicle in front. They will also go to ridiculous extremes to squeeze past a motorcycle, even if there is no space in front of it. An unsettling number of drivers will pass in traffic only a few tens of centimeters away, totally oblivious of the fact that a bike sometimes has to veer suddenly to avoid something. (I have kicked the door of the occasional offender.) It is not at all uncommon in city driving for a car to pass shortly before a corner, then abruptly cut across in front and make a left turn at the corner, instead of waiting a couple of seconds, pulling in behind, and making the turn leisurely. Expect something silly at any and all times and you should be able to remain accident-free.

Many car drivers simply don't know the law regarding motorcycles. Small bikes are required to hug the edge of the road and not exceed 50 km/h. Ignorant motorists—found in large numbers in small towns and remote areas—rarely see a bike bigger than 125cc and just don't know that larger bikes have the same right to travel down the middle of the lane as a car does.

The necessity to stay by the edge of the road is a danger from another source; the edge is often uneven due to deformation of the asphalt by being softened while hot and then pounded and squeezed into mounds at the edges (and sometimes in the actual road lanes) by heavy trucks. These ragged edges, along with uncertain shapes and slope of the gutter, can make riding hazardous.

Another road surface danger is the fact that many curves on mountain roads are cambered *toward* the edge, not (safely) toward the hillside.

Riders must always beware of taxis. Without warning they will cut across to the curb to pick up a fare, no matter how many lanes of traffic they have to cross. You must be on the watch for prospective passengers as much as the taxi drivers. Another type of problem driver too-often encountered is the one who pulls out from the curb or from a sideroad right in front of a motorcycle, even if the bike has the right of way and the road is completely clear once it has passed. It is also necessary to watch out for car doors opening in front of you, for few drivers look back to see if anything is coming.

The worst danger, however, is probably the riders of mini-motorscooters, for they ride the way they walk in crowds, cutting in with no concept of the space needed for their own safety or that of other cyclists (both motor and pedal variety), nor of good road manners, stopping directly in front of other motorcycles at traffic lights.

The best safety measure is to be sensible and drive carefully. Just remember the old saying: "There are old motorcyclists, and there are bold motorcyclists, but there are no old, bold motorcyclists."

THE H-D PHENOMENON An interesting sight in and around Tokyo and other large cities is the numerous Harley-Davidsons, the largest touring machines, loaded down with every available accessory and their riders dressed to resemble American highway patrol police, right down to shoulder patches and badges on their tailor-made uniforms. (The badges are on sale in Ueno with a choice of cities and states.) The H-D phenomenon is almost worth a trip to Japan just to observe, especially when you know how many thousands of dollars these get-ups represent. (There are also numbers of other foreign exotica, but their prices keep them out of the reach of the hoi polloi.)

EXPORTING A MOTORCYCLE Taking a bike overseas Many years ago there was no problem with buying a bike in Japan, riding it while there, then taking it home. However, there are now so many different design regulations in various countries regarding lighting, switch operation patterns, reflectors and other things that a domestic model bike cannot be registered in the U.S. (for example), while the U.S. export model cannot be ridden on Japanese highways. Export models that are manufactured in Japan can be bought in Japan and delivered to a shipping company for shipping home. Some large-model bikes are being made in the USA and may not be available in Japan at all. The domestic models could, of course, be modified to meet foreign regulations, but the cost of this, together with all the shipping expenses, would very likely push the total price higher than what you would pay at home.

If you want a new bike duty free and are travelling through Singapore at a later date, it would almost certainly be cheaper to buy one there. There is no duty payable if the bike is exported within a certain period of time, and it shouldn't be as expensive to ship from there as it is from Japan. (Even this way the shipping costs could still make the total price higher than buying new in most countries. Unless you plan to use a bike for touring in the Singapore–Malaysia–Thailand area, check beforehand

regarding the prices in the country to which you would take it.) Note also, if you do have thoughts of buying in Singapore, that shops there normally do not stock large bikes (much over 250–400cc, so it would likely be necessary to order well in advance to allow them enough time to get delivery from overseas.

Carnet

If you buy a car or motorcycle in Japan and wish to take it to another country for a period of less than a year, you can obtain a carnet (short for carnet de passages en douane) from the JAF that lets you do so without the problem of paying the duty in cash (almost always in U.S. dollars) and trying to get it back (in dollars) when leaving. The carnet is a book of several pages, each of which guarantees that the JAF will pay the duties owed if the vehicle is sold in the other country. The JAF does not do this out of the kindness of its heart of course— you must leave a cash deposit equal to the highest amount of duty that would be charged in any of the countries to which you tell them you plan to take the vehicle. For countries like Indonesia, the duty rate may be as high as 160 per cent of the purchase price of the vehicle. There is nothing in the carnet that identifies the countries for which it is valid nor the amount of deposit made to the JAF, and there is no compulsion to state every country to which it will be taken. When you finish your foreign travels, you send the carnet back to the JAF and obtain a refund of your deposit. It is not necessary to belong to the JAF to arrange a carnet.

Worth noting is that a carnet bought in Japan is extremely expensive—the administrative charges are possibly the highest in the world. For five pages (one page per entry into a country) the charge is ¥9000; for 10 pages, ¥15,000; for 25 pages,

¥20,000. Also some countries near Japan, like Taiwan, Hong Kong, Singapore, and Malaysia have, in the past, allowed a Japan-registered motorcycle to enter without a carnet or other formalities. Check with the diplomatic missions of those countries if you plan to go there.

A carnet can be arranged through Singapore, both for bikes bought in Singapore and those bought in Japan. Not only are the administration charges lower, but they will probably accept a guarantee letter from your bank in lieu of a cash deposit. A carnet can be arranged through the Automobile Association of Singapore (336 River Valley Rd, Singapore 9). They might even be able to issue a carnet by mail for a bike bought in Japan.

This section may not paint the most glowing picture of motorcycling in Japan, what with the problems of purchasing a machine, and the driving hazards. Despite all this, however, touring by motorcycle is one of the most enjoyable ways to see Japan. I've gone around the country twice this way and had very good experiences.

Rental Cars

For those not on the tightest of budgets, a rental car can be a viable way of travelling in Japan, avoiding the inevitable inconveniences of using public transportation, and providing the opportunity to sightsee the less accessible back areas that often offer the most interesting sightseeing. Costs are reasonable, especially if shared with two or three others. Rental cars are available near most major stations and elsewhere throughout the country.

It is not recommended to rent a car in a city like Tokyo because it can take hours to get out due to the absurdly low speed limits (usually 40 or 50 km/hr), the extremely crowded conditions on ordinary roads (tolls are extortionate on the expressways), and

because there are usually long dull stretches before reaching "the good bits". Rather, it is preferable to take public transportation to the starting point and pick up a rental car there. Cars can be reserved in one city and picked up in another.

Two of the main companies are Nippon Rent-a-Car (associated with Hertz, which allows world-wide reservations) and Toyota. Both have brochures in English, available at their desks at Narita airport, and at the TICs. Cars of several sizes and most cost ranges are available.

The following rates for Nippon (Hertz) are representative (and subject to change). These rates are for unlimited distance (no per-km charge), although the car must be returned with a full tank. Different companies have different policies regarding distance charges; unlimited travel is generally cheaper in practice. Vehicles can be rented for six hour, 12 hour or multiples of 24 hour periods. The first price in the following list is for the first 24 hours, the second price is for each additional day. There is an additional ¥1000 for insurance.

1300	¥8,800	¥7,200
1500	¥13,500	¥10,300
1800	¥16,500	¥11,700
2000	¥18,500	¥13,400

A discount is often available. When I rented a Nippon (Hertz) vehicle for one day, I was signed up on the spot for their "No. 1 Club", which entitled me immediately to a 20% discount. The other companies had similar schemes to reduce actual rental costs without actually cutting their listed rates. Such plans come and go and may not always be in effect.

It is generally possible to rent a car in one city and leave it in another, but a stiff charge may be added.

Cars can be reserved for pick-up almost anywhere in Japan through both companies by contacting the following offices:

	NIPPON	TOYOTA
Tokyo	(03) 3496-0919	3264-2834
Osaka	(06) 344-0919	372-6600
Nagoya	(052) 203-0919	882-0100
Fukuoka	(092) 721-0919	282-0100
Sapporo	(011) 251-0919	
Sendai	(0222) 63-0919	
Yokohama	(045) 251-0919	
Kyoto	(075) 671-0919	
Hiroshima	(082) 245-0919	
Takamatsu	(0878) 51-0919	
Miyazaki	(0985) 51-0919	
Okinawa	(098) 863-0919	

Other car rental companies are:

	TOKYO	OSAKA
Japaren	5397-8807	632-4881
Mitsubishi Rent-a-Car	3213-8071	321-5556
Nissan Rent-a-Car	5424-4123	371-4123
ACU Rent-a-Car	3364-2211	

There are also car rental offices at some railway stations; these are indicated in *jikokuhyo*.

I rented a car for ten days one year to travel around the Tohoku area, taking the Shinkansen from Tokyo to Sendai, renting and returning the car there, and returning again to Tokyo by train. This made the most of a short summer vacation period.

Hire Cars

Hire cars with drivers can be arranged through travel agencies or the larger hotels that cater to foreign tourists. They can also be contacted directly in the following cities:

In Tokyo: Kokusai Hire-Car Service, 3242-5931.
In Osaka: Nihon Kotsu Hire-Car Service, (06) 531-5430.

English-speaking drivers are available. The cost of a hire car is about double that of a taxi, and not for budget travellers!

Bicycles

Anyone in good health with the time and desire to see Japan in depth and at low cost should consider the bicycle. It offers the maximum interaction with nature and people in the countryside, and the greatest convenience in seeing many cities like Kyoto.

A bicycle is a practical proposition because it can be dismantled and packed into a special carrying bag that may be taken into the passenger compartment of a train or put in a car, to bypass boring stretches of countryside or to get out of the major cities more easily.

If you already own a good touring bike, you can transport it to Japan by air freight, by mail (if the frame isn't too big), or as part of your checked luggage (either dismantled and packed, or assembled; policies vary with the airline, so speak to the agent of the one that you will be using).

BUYING BIKES Japan is one of the world's major bicycle producers, and there are many high-quality machines available, but they generally are expensive. Standard good-quality bikes are mostly ¥40,000-and-up, and a custom-made one is difficult to find for ¥80,000.

A major problem is that stock bikes sold in Japan are sized for the Japanese. Not only are the Japanese shorter than westerners, but the *skelic ratio* of the Japanese is different from that of foreigners, a technical way of saying that the Japanese have legs that are short relative to body length. Thus, even though catalogs may show some models as suitable for people up to 182 cm, keep in mind that this means 182cm-tall Japanese. Westerners of the same height would find that they could never straighten their legs. The good news is that anyone under about 175 cm (5'9") tall will have a huge number to choose from. Compared with bikes made to westerners' proportions there will still be differences in the length of the top tube relative to that of the main down tube, but this should not be a major problem.

For those who can comfortably use a domestic model, the bikes made by Bridgestone, Fuji, Maruishi, Miyata, Nishiki, Sekine, Silk, Tsunoda, and National (among others) are all well regarded. Brochures of these manufacturers (and others) can be obtained by writing to: Japan Bicycle Promotion Institute (Att: Mr. H Kono or Mr. H Ise), Nihon Jitensha Kaikan 3 Bldg, 1-9-3 Akasaka, Minato-ku, Tokyo 107. Tel. (03) 5572-6410; both men speak good English.

Although many bikes are made for export, it is difficult to find these in Japan because they are too large for nearly all Japanese cyclists. Another problem when searching for a bike is that most dealers do not speak English. I have found one shop in Tokyo where there are usually a few large-frame bikes in stock. (If business increases, this situation will probably become better.) The proprietor, Tsuneyuki Sumiyoshi, is a young man who speaks English quite well, and should be able to handle correspondence. In September 1987 he was offering large bikes (frames in the 580 mm range), with CrMo tubing frame, quick-release fittings, and 700C rims/tires, in the ¥56,000 range. The address is: Pro-T Dryad Cycle, 1-6-28 Nakamichi, Meguro-ku, Tokyo (tel. (03) 3714-1651). If you write, please enclose a U.S. $1 note (or equivalent in a convertible currency), since postage costs out of Japan are high. He should be willing to credit this against a purchase. To reach the shop, go to Meguro station (Yamanote line), then take any bus between 1 and 6,

and get off at the third stop. This is past a major cross road and just past the crest of a longish hill. The next landmark is a small street on the right side (when going up the hill) between a Mitsubishi bank and a small police station. About 120 metres up this street is a small street to the left, with a dry-cleaning shop on the far left corner. The bike shop is just around the corner, on the left.

Another place where large-frame bikes are usually kept in stock is at bicycle shops near U.S. military bases. I found two such shops along the main street in front of Fussa Gate of Yokota Air Force Base. The bikes were of good (but not top) quality, sizes were like those that one would find in an overseas store, and prices were reasonable, in the ¥30–40,000 range. Because the U.S. servicemen are paid in dollars, and the yen has gone up so much relative to the dollar, the shops must sell at very low prices if they are to maintain any sales at all to servicemen. An advantage of these shops is that they are accustomed to dealing with Americans, and can communicate well in English.

To get to these shops, take a Chuo orange express train from Tokyo or Shinjuku station as far as Tachikawa. If your train has the terminus Okutama or Ome, continue on the train. If it has any other destination (Takao, etc.), exit at Tachikawa, go to platform 1, and take the local train. Go seven stations to Fussa. On the side of Fussa station with the large taxi stand, either take a taxi to Fussa Gate (minimum fare), or walk about 10 minutes along the small street to the right of the taxi area. When you reach the large road running along the fence around the base, turn right and look for the shops.

CUSTOM-MADE BIKES Bikes can be custom-made to order. The problems are that it takes one to three months for delivery (slowest in the spring, before the summer riding season), and that there is still a limited number of sizes. Frames are made up from tubing "kits" comprising tubes cut to length, and the fittings for the joints. The latter determine the range of sizes and angles, and thus the proportions, and the longest down-tube for which a kit is available is only 610 mm (24 inches). This is moderately large, but still not enough for the tallest westerners. It is realistic to order a custom frame only when in Japan, for it is necessary to determine if the proportions are suitable. With the value of the yen high, the price will not be attractive compared with an equivalent frame made in Europe. (Bring your own frame and fit it out in Japan!)

USED BIKES Second-hand bikes are available in Japan but, as with buying anything else, the language problem has to be overcome. Several bicycle magazines have ads. A Japanese friend or someone from an English school might be willing to assist. Other sources are police-recovered bicycle sales and suburban "junk yards" that sell a great variety of second-hand merchandise.

RENTAL BIKES At the time of writing this revision, there are no rental bikes available for prolonged touring in Honshu. An Australian living in Hokkaido has been organizing tours, and has some bikes for rent for use in Hokkaido. Write to Oikaze (see below) for details on the latest situation. If it appears that sufficient numbers of visitors would want to tour by rented bike, there is the possibility that someone could be encouraged to organize such a service. If you would potentially be interested in touring Japan in this way, send a "vote" by writing to Oikaze so that the editor can judge the amount of interest.

Bikes are available for rent by the day at a number of places in Japan. All the Cycling Inns (described in the section on Places to Stay) have bikes for rent at reasonable rates; so do several youth hostels. The *Youth Hostel Handbook* indicates these with a symbol in the write-up on the individual hostels, but does not have a central listing of such hostels, although another of their publications *Hostelling Way in Japan* does; the booklet is free on request from the national HQ in Tokyo. Several shops in Kyoto have rental bikes, but these (like most in Japan) are single-speed clunkers.

Types of Bike

There are four main types of bike sold in Japan: Camping, Touring (or Randonneur), Sportif and Racing.

Camping bikes are very strong, but heavy and slow, and are built to carry large loads of camping gear over bad roads. They make a sight in warm weather with loads of everything imaginable slung on everywhere, including bags hung from the axles. It is not a recommended type for overseas visitors.

Racing bikes are also unsuitable for touring, being uncomfortable, twitchy in handling, lacking in comforts like mudguards, fragile (especially the tires) and expensive. Road Racer bikes are between Sportif and Racing machines and can only be recommended for one-day runs.

The Touring and Sportif models are both quite light, typically 11–12 and 12–14 kg respectively. The major difference between them is the gearing. Touring bikes have a wider spread between the two front sprockets and may also have lower low ratios in the rear cluster. The end effect is that Touring bikes are a little stronger and are able to carry more on rougher roads, while the Sportif types are intended for higher speeds with less luggage.

Mountain bikes have come on to the market in recent years, but would probably be better regarded as sports machines than touring bikes.

Many bikes of all the main types are designed for quick disassembly, a definite plus feature. Such bikes are called *rinko* (short for *rinkosha*); in catalogs they are usually indicated by a wrench symbol. The main differences are that the balls of the steering column are captive, so they cannot fall out when the handle-bar stem is pulled out, the fenders remove more easily (some are in two parts, the outer section of which comes off), the axles have quick-release handles instead of nuts, etc.

If you get a bike custom made, these extras cost little but add much to convenience.

A feature that improves the quality (at increased cost) is a frame made of chrome-molybdenum (Cr-Mo) alloy tubing (instead of carbon steel), and "double-butted" tubes (thinner metal in the middle of the length of a tube), both of which make the frame lighter. Aluminum rims are essential for light weight. The best tires for touring are "clincher" types, rather than "tubular" (aka "sew-ups") that are delicate and a bother to repair. (Their advantage is minimum rolling resistance, but their owners seem to spend all their spare time repairing them.)

Taking Bikes on Trains

A bike that has been dismantled and put into a special carrying bag can be taken on any train. These are available from virtually any bike shop. When you enter a station you will be asked your destination and for a payment of ¥300. A tag will be made out indicating the destination. (This, at least, is the principle, but people regularly carry larger packages onto trains without surcharge.)

Japan Cycling Association

Cycle enthusiasts staying in Japan might be interested in membership in the Japan Cycling Association. The JCA has various functions and activities like weekend rides. For information on joining, call Mr. Kono or Mr. Ise at the Japan Bicycle Promotion Institute (tel (03) 5572-6410).

Information Resources

An American bike addict of many years' residence in Japan, Bryan Harrell, has published a newsletter on cycling in Japan for a number of years. The important information disseminated over the years has been assembled into a book, *Cycling Japan* (Kodansha International). It includes places to go, information on bike shops, budget lodgings, and bilingual maps.

To obtain a copy of Mr. Harrell's newsletter, Oikaze (rough translation: "Tailwind"), write to Oikaze, Futatsubashi #26, 2-14-4-306 Tomigaya-cho, Shibuya-ku, Tokyo 151 (tel. (03) 3468-1729). Subscriptions have been US$20 for air mail overseas delivery of six copies a year, but it would be best to send US$1 in cash or cheque (payable in the USA) to cover the mailing cost of a sample and information on availability of the newsletter. Do not send any remittance through a bank, for all proceeds would be eaten up as a "cashing charge".

TEST RIDING If you wish to try out a variety of bikes before buying one, there are two complexes, near Tokyo (Izu-hanto peninsula) and Osaka, with a vast number of rental bikes of different types plus a variety of tracks on which to try them out. The name in Japanese: *Cycling Sports Center*! There is also overnight accommodation (advance reservation recommended), and there are other sports and recreation facilities. For information, contact the Japan Bicycle Promotion Institute.

MAPS The general road maps suggested earlier for motor vehicles are equally useful for cyclists. In addition there are three maps that have been made up specifically with the cyclist in mind. They show the location of every youth hostel, places that rent bicycles (shown by a red bicycle symbol, with telephone number), special bicycle roads and touring routes, "Kokumin-shukusha" (accommodation), road gradients—even a star rating system for the difficulty of the touring courses. Of all the maps available for touring by road in Japan, these have by far the largest number of places identified in *romaji* as well as in *kanji*. The disappointing thing is that they only cover the central third of Honshu. Further maps in the series are intended to cover all Japan, eventually.

The maps are printed by the Bridgestone company and are called *sai-ku-rin-gu mappu* (cycling map); English is written on the back of the folder, but the front is only in Japanese. They cost ¥650 each and should be available at bookstores. If you have trouble obtaining copies, contact the Japan Dicycle Promotion Institute.

Hitching

For saving money and getting to know some Japanese people, there is no better way of getting around Japan than by hitching. The Japanese must be the kindest people in the world to thumbing foreigners, and the main difficulty is to avoid taking unfair advantage of them. Tales abound of drivers going hours—even days—out of their way to take travellers to their destinations, all the while buying their meals and sometimes even taking them home overnight. The official tourist authorities wish to discourage hitching, but travellers have been doing it for years and gaining insights and experience in addition to simply a ride.

The Japanese themselves rarely hitchhike and many drivers are not familiar with the meaning of an outstretched thumb. Many a foreigner has found himself taken to the next town and dropped off at the railway station!

It is useful to make up a large sign in *kanji* showing your destination, with the addition of the characters for *homen* (方面) which means "area", otherwise a literal-minded driver may go past believing that only that destination will do, when he is going a slightly shorter distance. So carry stiff paper or cardboard and a felt tip pen. Another tip is to stand at traffic lights in towns (there are many) and ask drivers if they are going your way. Neighbourhood children may be willing to help. In country areas hitching is no problem because it is easy to reach the highway and vehicles have space to stop. It is illegal to hitch at the edge of the road on an expressway, and the police to prevent it, so the best way to get started is to stand before or at the entrance toll gate. Attendants have been known to help by asking drivers if they can give you a lift to your destination.

Once you have a ride, ask where the driver is going. If he plans to exit before your destination, ask him to let you off at the next rest stop by saying *tsugi no kyukeijo* (or "rest area") *de orosh'te kudasai*. You can then ask around truck drivers (they usually stand around in groups talking), or other motorists. (Your driver may help.) Failing that ploy, you can stand with your sign near the exit from the parking lot where it leads back to the road.

For straight-through long drives it is hard to beat trucks on the expressways, particularly at night when the long-distance truckers are in action. Drivers who have given a lift will frequently try to arrange a continuation with a truck going beyond their stopping point. Though they rarely speak more than a few words of English, they are invariably good natured and interested in their passenger. Often this is their first meeting with a foreigner. It gives them added prestige to be able to show off a *gaijin* in the cab of their truck.

They are usually quite earthy and the closest inheritors of the ancient Japanese spirit. They will most likely know and sing traditional folk songs and be familiar with other elements of the true folk culture, in contrast to the court culture that produced such arts as the refined tea ceremony and koto playing.

Whoever your driver, you will probably be treated with such kindness that you are sure to want to return the favor in some way. This will be difficult, as they normally refuse to take money and will not let you pay for their meals; usually they will want to treat you! Before setting out, stock up on fruit, candy or *sembei* (rice crackers) and feed them to your driver as you go along; you can leave the rest of the box or package when you get out. Foreign cigarettes are also very popular (the Japanese smoke like chimneys)—bring them as your duty free allowance.

Be sure to try to talk to your driver; he will appreciate some attempt at communication even if he speaks no English. If two people are hitching together it is all too tempting to talk to each other all the time, and if the driver is alone he may get annoyed at being ignored after his kindness in stopping.

Any women hitching alone or in pairs who may have some doubts about the whole business would be well advised to stick to trucks with green number plates—they are company owned and the drivers are much more likely to behave themselves. Usually the drivers do not cause any problems, but some women have found themselves with a Romeo who has got the distorted idea from a film or magazine that all western women give their favours upon request. (Some of the Japanese media are libellous in their "information" about foreigners.) If you find yourself in this situation, and unable to persuade lover-boy that "no" means "no", you can try showing the message at the back of the book to him. It is written in Japanese, and says (roughly) that he has been misled by movies or books, and that Western women do not do it with casual strangers. This message is included at the suggestion of women who have had such an unpleasant experience.

Another potential risk for Western women is the young Japanese male in his jazzed up car who wishes to impress her with his highly developed driving skills and finely honed reflexes. The fact is that, because of the low speed limits, he will have had very little experience with fast driving of any kind, especially on twisty roads. The presence of a western woman is likely to make him do something foolish, especially on mountain roads where young Japanese male drivers go silly anyway. One woman was given a ride, and the driver did the predictable. When she protested, he reassured that he had trained as a racing driver. Within five minutes they were in the ditch. Fortunately they were not injured.

The problem with such a driver is that asking him to go slower may cause him to speed up. As a last-ditch effort, if this happens, show the driver the second message at the back of the book. It translates approximately, "I have all the confidence in the world in your driving, but you have a nice car and I get sick very easily." It might do some good.

Please don't ask the TIC for advice on hitching; it is not legal, they say, and they don't wish to get involved.

The following directions explain how to get to the entrances of the main expressways from the major cities of Japan.

Tokyo (northbound): For many years, the Tohoku Expressway (Tohoku Kosoku doro) began at the city of Iwatsuki, more than 30 km north of Tokyo. Only in 1987 was the road complex completed through the city, so that there was an expressway system from the north of Honshu to the south of Kyushu. The following instructions for hitching northward from Tokyo date from the earlier era, but perusal of a map does not indicate any other places where an entrance is located near a train station, so I am sticking with the old explanation. If any traveller finds a nearer starting point, please write.

Take the JR Keihin-Tohoku line to Omiya. Exit from the platform at the end closest to the front of the train; immediately to the left will be stairs down to the Tobusen line. Take it to Iwatsuki, the fifth stop; the train fares will total around ¥600.

Exiting from the front of the station, walk down the main street until you reach the second large street on the right; ignore the side alleys. Walking for 10–15 minutes will take you under the overhead roadway, to the expressway entrance.

Tokyo (southbound): Take the Shin-tamagawa line to Yoga, the fifth station after Shibuya. Shin-tamagawa line is a continuation of the Hanzomon subway line, so a train can be caught at any station along the line. At Shibuya station, the entrance is close to the statue of Hachiko, the famous dog. At Yoga, the overhead roadway of the Tomei Expressway (Tomei Kosokudoro) is about half a km to the south of the station; there is a police box near the station if directions are needed. Ask: *kosoku doro wa, dochira?*

When you reach the roadway, pass under it and turn to the right. A few hundred metres alongside the roadway, a ramp rises to the right up to the entrance; a service road continues straight. You can stand in the vee between the roads (but be ready to run quickly if a car stops because the ramp is narrow and there is a risk of causing an accident); or you can take the safer course and stand further back on the service road before the ramp splits off. It might also be possible to enlist the help of toll gate operators.

Nagoya: Take the subway bound for Hoshigaoka or Fujigaoka; the destination is Hongo station but many trains terminate before there at Hoshigaoka. In such a case, change to a following train that goes all the way. The entrance ramps for both northbound and southbound traffic are near Hongo station.

Kyoto: From the front of Kyoto station take bus No 19 or 20 and watch for signs by the roadside for the Meishin Expressway. Get off and select the correct ramp for the desired destinations, Osaka, Kobe and points south, or Nagoya/Tokyo and points north.

Note that it is not worthwhile trying to hitch within the area bounded by Kyoto-Osaka-Kobe; they form one vast conurbation and trying to find your way by road is more bother than it's worth. Trains are much quicker and more convenient, even if you have your own vehicle.

Because of the great build-up of towns around Kyoto, when heading toward the north coast, it is simplest to take the JNR train to Kamioka and start hitching from there.

Walking

Few visitors to Japan are likely to have time to walk through the country, but it can be done. As related in his interesting book *The Roads to Sata*, Japan resident Alan Booth covered the distance from the far north of Hokkaido to the far south of Kyushu in four months (in 1977). His experiences are actually typical of what any other traveller can expect to encounter while travelling in Japan, so his book can be recommended to any prospective traveller (to dispel illusions, if nothing else).

ACCOMMODATION

The travel industry is well established in Japan and there is acceptable to excellent accommodation throughout the country. In the big cities, like Tokyo, there are hotels that match the world's best, plus a variety of alternatives down the price scale. In provincial cities there are usually some facilities with a claim to being of a type that is familiar to westerners, and virtually everywhere there is Japanese-style accommodation of reasonable to good quality. (When good, such places provide some of the best memories of travel in Japan.)

For budget travellers the sad word is that there is absolutely no dirt-cheap accommodation of the kind found in most of the rest of Asia, such as the Chinese hotels, losmen, etc. The cheapest room anywhere will be from about ¥1500 per person, per night.

Visitors planning to stay at luxury-style hotels will no doubt have made reservations before leaving for Japan, so information on them is not really relevant here. Most of the information on the following pages deals with accommodation more in the range of budget travellers. (There is a counter at Tokyo's Narita airport for arranging accommodation at high-quality hotels, and the other major airports offer a similar service.)

For the most part, this book has no listings of places to stay in write-ups on individual cities. There are several reasons. Japan is a country of many cities, few of which would be of interest to a foreign visitor, so there is no sense listing accommodation in such places. All the youth hostels are listed in an easily-obtained publication, and there are hand-out publications listing reasonably low-priced hotels, *ryokan* (inns), and *minshuku* (private homes) in nearly every area of the country. It is not practical to repeat all this information. Another factor is the fact that Japan is the land of the clone, and the location and types of accommodation are quite similar from one end of the country to the other. Once you have learned minshuku-spotting, for example, the rules of the game are much the same everywhere. (Also, it would require an impractical amount of time and work to update the book for each new edition.)

I have, however, included information for locating several youth hostels, *ryokan*, and *minshuku* in areas of greatest interest to overseas visitors. The phone number is given for at least one youth hostel in or near every port of entry into Japan, along with instructions for reaching it. After a traveller has been in Japan for a few days, the system of finding a place to stay becomes more familiar.

The Japan National Tourist Organization (JNTO) has prepared several booklets and brochures on accommodation. These are available from the Tourist Information Centers (TICs), and should be available by mail as well. One of these publications that has been avalable in the past is *Reasonable Accommodations in Japan*, with listings of economical places to stay in a number of cities around Japan. Check if it is still offered. "Reasonable" in this case means ¥5,000 and up per person. Accommodation charges quoted in Japan nearly always mean "per person".

If you arrive in a fair-sized city without

having booked accommodation, you can usually get assistance at the main railway station. Most have an office (*annai-jo*) that can help you find a place to stay, although the office may close soon after 2100, and their listings may not include the least-expensive places available. (Many list only *ryokan*, not minshuku, although many so-called *ryokan* offer little more than an average *minshuku*. These terms are defined later.) Some hints on finding low-cost places are given in the section on *ryokan*.

A note about laundry: Anyone staying at hotels or *ryokan* can have their laundry done by the hotel. Dry cleaning shops and depots are common in every suburban area. Travellers using youth hostels, etc., will have to do their own washing, in many cases in a wash basin or sink using cold water (not very pleasant in unheated washrooms in mid-winter!). A manicure brush is useful for scrubbing.

The coin-operated washing machine reached Japan several years ago and can be found in conjunction with "sento" (neighborhood public baths), in the larger cities, at least. Many youth hostels have washing machines for the use of their guests.

Youth Hostels

For budget-watching travellers in Japan, economical accommodation means Youth Hostels. There are about 450 of them (down from a former 520) scattered nearly everywhere in Japan that people normally want to go. They are clean and respectable and reasonably priced—by Japanese standards anyway—typically ¥1600–3,000. There is usually no other accommodation at prices as low. The cheapest *ryokan* and *minshuku* are approximately double the YH cost.

To stay at most youth hostels in Japan you need a valid membership card issued by a Youth Hostel association belonging to the International Youth Hostel Federation (IYHF). It is best to buy a membership card in your home country, but if this isn't possible, then an International Guest Card (IGC) can be purchased from national headquarters in Tokyo or from the prefectural head office. The price is ¥2,800. Some hostels, detailed below, do not require a YH membership card; a foreign passport is adequate.

The International Guest Card is also available as a replacement in case you lose your card. The purchase price (less ¥100) will be refunded, within Japan, after a replacement card has been received from the original issuing office and shown at the Tokyo head office.

Despite the name, there is no age limit on who may use the hostels. There are, however, more regulations than at other types of accommodation. Until recently there was curfew at 2100, hostels were closed between 1000 and 1500. and hostellers were segregated by sex. Some of these restrictions have now been eased at some hostels, but it is still case-by-case which rules are relaxed, and at which hostels. (Hokkaido seems more relaxed.)

A regulation sleeping sheet is required at nearly every hostel. (These can be rented but the cost soon mounts up, so its better to have your own.) Only a few hostels permit a sleeping bag to be used.

A perfectly usable listing of all the hostels is given in the free JNTO publication "Youth Hostel Map of Japan" (#304-E). It is available from the TIC offices in Japan, and should be available by mail from overseas JNTO offices. It is less detailed than the YH publication (below) regarding access (no map), and it does not show prices, but it is all in English and quite sufficient for the purpose.

A more detailed listing of hostels is the

(Japan) Youth Hostel Handbook. It costs around ¥300. The book is written mostly in Japanese, but there is adequate explanation in English and profuse use of symbols so that foreigners can use it easily. It lists every hostel in Japan by district, with maps at the front guiding you to the page on which to look. On the appropriate page there is a short write-up for the hostel, with a small map, telephone number, and various details (the number of beds, costs of meals and heating, dates when open and the type of hostel). The name is given in *romaji*, but the address is only in Japanese. (This is a retrograde step, for former editions had the address in *romaji* as well; it is now very difficult to locate a hostel without help in reading *kanji*.)

The YH Handbook is available at the national headquarters in Tokyo, at the YH branch office in the 2nd basement of the Sogo department store in Yurakucho (near the TIC in central Tokyo), in the Sogo department store near Osaka station, and at many hostels around the country. Hours at the headquarters are 09:30 to 17:30 on weekdays, and the Yurakucho office is open daily from 10:30 to 19:30 except on Sundays, holidays, and when the store is closed (Tuesday). It can also be ordered and sent by mail. Within Japan the cost is ¥610, including postage. If entering Japan through a city other than Tokyo, you could have one sent to poste restante at a major post office. A copy could also be ordered from overseas. For payment, my suggestion is to send a ¥1,000 note (if available from a bank) or a US$10 bill (or equivalent in a convertible currency) to cover the cost and postage. The address of the head office is:

Japan Youth Hostel Association
Travel Center
Suidobashi Nishiguchi Kaikan Bldg.
2-20-7 Misakicho
Chiyoda-ku
Tokyo 191
Tel. (03) 3288-1417

The YH offices also have a booklet *Hostelling Way in Japan*, free to members. It has much more info on hostel rules, rail fares, a list of hostels with bicycle rentals, distances between cities and much more, but prices may not be current.

The third, and least satisfactory, listing of hostels is the *IYHF Handbook Vol II* which lists hostels in Africa, America, Asia and Australasia. This booklet, ¥600 in Japan, lists less than half the hostels in Japan, gives no instructions in Japanese, and is not detailed in its description of locations. For travel in Japan it is a waste of money.

There are eight types of hostel in Japan. The present Handbook does not give a breakdown of numbers, but in the days when there were 520 hostels, it was: built and managed by the JYHA (51); built privately (107); built with government subsidy—municipal (75); managed by other youth organisation (55); private house (61); temple (76); shrine (7); and *ryokan* (144).

As a general rule it is best to avoid JYHA hostels. While they may have the best facilities, too often the staff tend to be unfriendly, officious, or even rude, apparently having the attitude that they are doing a favor to the hostellers allowed to stay there. (The suggested name "youth hostile" came to mind a few times.) No doubt there are good JYHA hostels, and perhaps it is unfair to judge them by the few that I have experienced, but given the opportunity it is preferable to stay at other types, especially the temples, shrines, private homes, and *ryokan*. Staff at them are usually friendly and the atmosphere relaxed.

Hostellers staying at Buddhist temple hostels may be wakened abruptly at 0630 by drumming. This happens at Jofuku-ji, a Zen temple in a particularly beautiful valley on Shikoku island. The priest there speaks English and invites visitors to join in *zazen* meditation.

Visitors may use the 75 municipal hostels without having a YH card—a passport is adequate. Useful ones to know about are Hinoyama YH at Shimonoseki (the port for the ferry from Pusan, Korea), Tokyo International (Kokusai) YH, the hostel at Narita, and both Nagai YH and Hattori-ryokuchi YH at Osaka.

Generally very little English is spoken at any of the hostels or at the head office. If corresponding with the head office, always send International Postage Reply Coupons for the return postage. YH associations everywhere operate on tight budgets and cannot afford to pay return postage.

It is generally possible to get a bed at most hostels throughout the year without reservations. However, reservations are advised whenever possible, and it is definitely advisable to make advance bookings during the busy seasons (New Year holidays, March, late April to mid-May, and the July/August school holidays), especially around Kyoto/Nara and in mountain resort areas.

The simplest way to ensure a place to stay is to telephone a day or two in advance and make a reservation. Another reason for planning ahead is that some hostels inconveniently take holidays that are not listed in the Handbook (voice of experience, after more than once showing up at the door after dark and finding the building likewise dark). Japanese hostellers are helpful and someone will call for you to get you over the language hurdle. Just feed them the coins.

Booking by computer was once possible, but it is now necessary for the hosteller to make the reservation by return postage

paid postcards. Pre-printed JYH cards have spaces for all the required information and are available from the JYH head and branch offices (and at many hostels). They cost ¥80 for ten (plus postage if they are ordered by mail), and each will require two ¥50 stamps. An alternative is to use blank reply cards sold by the post office (¥100 each, ¥50 for sending the double card, and ¥50 for the return portion).

If you are planning to eat the hostel supper on the first night it is essential to phone ahead, or arrive early enough to permit the cook to prepare the extra food. Hostel meals are nutritionally adequate but very few are gastronomic delights. A typical meal consists of: 1 breaded pork cutlet (fatty); a portion of shredded cabbage; a piece of fish sausage; miso soup; 3 slices of cucumber; 1/8 of a tomato; 8 french fries; 1/3 of a banana; 1 mandarin orange; 14 pieces of cold macaroni with mayonaise; and as much rice as you can eat.

Many hostels have "jisui" (members' cooking), which means that hostellers can have the use of a gas cooker and pots and pans. The gas is usually metered, so it can be a contest to try to finish cooking the meal with one 10 yen coin. There is a small charge, ¥20–30, for the use of the kitchen.

Staying at youth hostels offers other advantages in addition to the relatively low cost, in particular the opportunity to observe what Japanese homes and people are like. Although the hostels are institutional in nature, and many buildings are modern structures with not a hint of Japanese tradition in them, many others are like enlargements of the traditional Japanese house. In a traditional-building type of hostel, there are soft tatami mat floors, sliding *shoji* doors, and many other typical architectural details. The bath will be like that of an average home (though probably larger), and hostellers sleep on mats laid out on the tatami. The modern buildings usually have furniture to match and western-style bunk beds. The photo with the description of the hostel in the Handbook shows the building, and this can often give a good clue as to the type of facilities.

Staying at hostels also provides the chance to meet a number of young Japanese and find out what makes them tick. While few can converse in depth in foreign languages, it is usually possible to carry on simple conversations with them. One feature immediately noticeable to westerners is the general lack of social mingling of the sexes. To overcome this shyness there may be a "Meeting", the Japanese word used to describe an hour-long get-together in the evening. This typically takes the form of a talk about the attractions of the nearby area, transport facilities, etc., followed by party games which serve the purpose of breaking down the barriers of shyness. Most westerners opt out after their first experience, unless dragged into attending, as it is all in Japanese and often childish. During the summer there are often unscheduled and informal activities like bonfires, fireworks, playing traditional games, or dancing to the music of a portable cassette player.

Most hostels are goldmines of information on attractions in the surrounding area. There are usually bulletin boards covered with train, bus, and boat schedules and other useful info. Usually it's all in Japanese but you should be able to get some help in deciphering it.

Virtually all hostels have posted rules and hours for eating, bathing, lights out, and getting up. At busy hostels these are usually rigidly adhered to, but during the off-season or when there are few people staying there, the rules may be greatly relaxed, especially for foreigners, who often receive deferential treatment everywhere in Japan.

In recent years several rules have been relaxed at the 75 or so municipal hostels: curfew has been extended from 2100 to 2230, with lights out at 2300. A radical departure from the past is that alcohol is allowed in some hostels as long as the drinkers don't disturb other guests. Whenever possible, married couples will be given rooms together in these hostels. The curfew is usually no hardship, by the way, for many hostels are located in out-of-the-way places, and they roll up the sidewalks soon after sundown in most Japanese towns.)

Bathing usually has its rules too. At some hostels you can take a bath at any time during the evening, while at others you may not use the bath outside the prescribed hours even though the tub is sitting unused and full of water that will go to waste. It is almost impossible to take a bath or shower in the morning. To do so would run counter to centuries of tradition.

Being public institutions, municipally-owned hostels often have magnificent locations on prime real estate. Hinoyama YH at Shimonoseki commands a superb view of the Kanmon Strait, which separates Honshu from Kyushu, and the graceful suspension bridge which spans the gap. Ura-Bandai YH (1606-Tohoku) is only a short distance from an emerald-green lake and numerous other smaller ponds of similar intense color. It also features a good view of the jagged top of Mt. Bandai. There are many other hostels around the country with equally fine settings.

If you stay in a hostel where you must share a room with Japanese hostellers you may find you have to fight a guerilla action to get a window open for fresh air during the night, even in mid-summer. There seems to be a perpetuation of the idea held in medieval Europe that night air is somehow dangerous and must be shut out at all costs, even on a hot night in a small eight-bunk room. The modern hostels with solid concrete walls and close-fitting doors and windows are the worst in this respect. The older, more traditional buildings are sufficiently drafty that this is not so much of a problem (though they're also cooler in winter!).

Another possible inconvenience is the noise of other hostellers, which may keep you awake at night or wake you very early in the morning. The polite way to ask them to be quiet is to say "Shizuka-ni sh'te kudasai". For a much stronger effect, say "Shizuka-ni shiro!" in a firm tone. Girls are by far the worst in this regard, for they get up at daybreak and spend the next two hours putting on make-up, chattering like magpies all the while despite repeated requests to be quiet.

Minshuku

Second to the Youth Hostels in budget-kindness are *minshuku*.

A *minshuku* (pronounced "minsh'ku") is a family home that takes guests. (Some are quite large multi-room buildings constructed specifically for public accommodation.) There are *minshuku* in every area with tourist attractions, such as historic towns, coastal villages, hot spring resorts, ski areas, etc., operated by local people such as fishermen, farmers, and townspeople. Short-time visitors to Japan usually have little opportunity to see the inside of a Japanese house, and even fewer have a chance to stay overnight. *Minshuku* make this a simple possibility.

Some *minshuku* are interesting in themselves and are an actual attraction for visitors. At Shirakawa (Gifu-ken) there are many huge old thatched-roof houses in an isolated valley. Many of them are *minshuku* and afford the opportunity to spend the

night in a very unusual farmhouse, even by Japanese standards, one that may even be a couple of hundred years old.

For travellers not on an absolutely bare-bones (i.e., youth hostels only) budget, *minshuku* are the best places to stay to gain an impression of what part of everyday Japan is like.

In a *minshuku* a guest is often made to feel almost like part of the family, and it is a unique way to experience the warmth of ordinary Japanese. Foreigners staying at *minshuku*, especially those in out of the way places, are quite rare. You might actually be the first ever to stay at a particular home. The hosts may have a few misgivings at first because many Japanese have never met (or even seen) a foreigner, but if you can reassure them that you won't use soap in the bathtub, or wear the *benjo* (toilet) slippers in the house, then they will relax and there should be no problems beyond the usual ones of trying to make yourself understood in a foreign language in a foreign country. But that's what makes it all fun! The *minshuku* owners whom I have encountered have ranged between accepting of a foreigner and very good-natured. The big problem may be that they are too kind - there are many stories of hosts pouring drinks all evening (at no charge) because of the honor of the visit!

Minshuku are not hotels, so there is minimal "maid service". Guests may have to make their own beds at night and put the bedding away in the morning, provide their own towels, etc., although it has been my experience that the hosts have done all these things as a matter of course. Charges are relatively uniform throughout Japan, in the range ¥6,000–10,000 per person, per night, including supper and breakfast. It is possible to negotiate a reduction if meals are not needed, but they often are based on local delicacies and it may be one of the few opportunities to sample typical Japanese cooking.

As with *ryokan*, you can usually find a *minshuku* from a railway station of any size. There is normally an information office (*annai-jo*) with listings of *minshuku* in the surrounding area (in areas of some touristic interest, at least). They will phone ahead and make bookings, also giving warning that a foreigner is on the way.

Travellers who begin their travels from Tokyo can make reservations by computer. There are several offices in Tokyo that can do this, but the most convenient is Travel Nippon, on the 5th floor of the Yurakucho Bldg (near the TIC), because they speak English. The address is: Travel Nippon, 2-2-1 Yurakucho, Chiyoda-ku, Tokyo. Tel (03) 3572-1461; open Monday to Saturday from 09:15 to 17:30 and they speak English.

Bookings for *minshuku* can also be made in every part of the country at any travel agent, especially JTB.

A very good leaflet is available in English listing a large number of *minshuku* in nearly all regions of the country that are better prepared than average to take foreign guests; a map shows their general location. It can be obtained from:

Japan Minshuku Association
Sukegawa Bldg. 1F
4-10-15 Takadanobaba
Shinjuku-ku
Tokyo 169
tel. 3364-1855

It also describes a minshuku and how to behave at one (folding bedding, eating, etc.).

Ryokan

There are 80,000 or so *ryokan* scattered around Japan. Establishments called "ryokan" have a wide range of facilities. At its best, a *ryokan* embodies the finest Japanese hospitality and elegance, providing a simple but flawless traditional Japanese style room with high-quality furnishings and the best in food and service. The senses should be pleased or soothed in all ways including visually, so a good *ryokan* should have a beautiful garden; not necessarily large, but definitely elegant. Unfortunately, such an ideal place is far removed from the realities of the budget traveller's wallet, and there is a high probability that a foreigner who showed up at the door of such a place would be turned away. It is not (necessarily) because of xenophobia, but simply because they are very exclusive—even Japanese cannot book into them unless introduced by someone of high enough position and who is able to give assurance that the visitor is worthy of being allowed to stay there. Other *ryokan* do not want foreigners to stay because of bad experiences in the past with overseas visitors who didn't know how to behave, didn't understand the system, or made demands that the staff were not able to meet. (In general Japanese are convinced that their way of life is completely beyond the understanding of foreigners, and that foreigners of any kind will just not fit in. If you can make yourself understood in Japanese, many more *ryokan* will be open to you.)

There are, fortunately, many other establishments also called "ryokan" that are more affordable than the "ultimate" accommodation described above. They are likely to be much more simple than the ideal but can provide some excellent memories of Japan.

The "third level", usually the least expensive type of *ryokan*, has no advantage over any other category of accommodation; the facilities may be poorer than those of a typical *minshuku* without the friendliness. There is no harm in asking to have a look at a room when considering a low-cost *ryokan*.

The JNTO has prepared a booklet containing listings of *ryokan* that are accustomed to or prepared to accept foreign visitors and which have acceptable facilities. Titled *Japan Ryokan Guide* it is available from JNTO offices and the TICs in Tokyo and Kyoto. Prices for various types of accommodation are listed along with the contact address and the means of getting there. The prices are considerably higher than those listed for hotels in the companion JNTO hotel booklet, rarely under ¥10,000 per person with two meals.

Some *ryokan* participate in the Japanese Inn Group, as well as the Welcome Inn program, discussed in the section "Inn Booking Services".

Bookings for *ryokan* can be made in every part of the country at almost any travel agent, especially JTB, but these may not be the least expensive ones, since there must be sufficient for the agent to receive a commission. Also, as mentioned above, every railway station of any size has an information office (*ryoko annai-jo*) that has listings of all accommodation in the surrounding vicinity. They can make reservations on the spot, but it is rare to find anyone who can speak English at these offices; also, remember that they don't always list the lowest-priced places.

There are usually many *ryokan* in the vicinity of any major station so if you want to find your own, try walking around the area. Look for large numbers of shoes at the entranceway, or entrances that are wide and open, as distinct from the rather secluded entrances to the average private house. People at small tobacco shops or other local businesses can often help in finding a *ryokan*.

Pensions

The word "pension" has been borrowed from the French, but has acquired the connotation in Japan of accommodation in a country location, with a strong association with sports, such as tennis, (prohibitively expensive in urban areas). They are commonly located in fairly remote areas, many situated near ski slopes. Other sporting facilities typically include boating, swimming, walking trails, table tennis, cycling, and so on. Good food, sometimes gourmet style, is often a specialty as well.

Pensions are generally operated by younger people, often quite individualistic types, so the spirit is more open and unrestricted than youth hostels, while the facilities are more elaborate and luxurious than those of a *minshuku* and more homey than a hotel. Prices are higher than those of a *minshuku*: the cheapest are about ¥3,400/5,400/7,900 for single/double/triple plus ¥1,500 for dinner, while more expensive ones run up to ¥5,200/7,200/9,700.

The pension idea has been operating in Japan only since about 1973, but there are already more than 200 around the country, from southern Kyushu to Tohoku. The pensions are not especially set up for foreign guests, but anyone with a sense of fun and adaptability will be able to get by and enjoy the features offered.

Pensions are listed, often with photos or sketches, in a book called *Japan Pension Guide* (revised annually), which is available at bookshops for about ¥700. It is written only in Japanese but you should be able to understand the important features—like price. The TICs in Tokyo and Kyoto can give further information and assistance. In Tokyo, a Japanese-speaking friend can also make inquiries from (03) 3295-6333.

Some pensions participate in the Japanese Inn Group, discussed in the following section "Inn Booking Services".

Inn Booking Services

There are at least three ways of simplifying making reservations for *minshuku/ ryokan*-type accommodation.

WELCOME INN PROGRAM This is an admirable program that enables making reservations at a large number of economical *ryokan*, *minshuku*, hotels, pensions, and *kokumin-shukusha* (explained below) throughout the country at no charge.

Within Japan, it is necessary to make reservations in person at one of the Tourist Information Centers, in Tokyo, Kyoto, or Narita airport. A maximum of three reservations can be made at a time (more if you line up again). Unfortunately, no phone or mail applications are accepted, so it is not possible to use it to arrange accommodation beyond the initial three places while on the road.

Outside Japan, travellers with confirmed flight bookings can write and request reservations for up to three places.

Write to:

Welcome Inn Reservation Center
c/o International Tourism Center of Japan
Tokyo Kotsu Kaikan 9Fl
2-10-1 Yurakucho
Chiyoda-ku
Tokyo 100
Tel: (03) 3211-4201
FAX: (03) 3211-9009

Their booklet, "Directory of Welcome Inns", is available at the TICs. It is not a JNTO publication, but it should be available from JNTO overseas offices since the program closely involves JNTO.

JAPANESE INN GROUP The *Japanese Inn Group* comprises about 80 economy *ryokan*,

minshuku, hotels, pensions, and guest houses that are prepared (i.e., welcoming, as well as having some knowledge of what foreigners are like) to accept foreigners. Their rates are in the range ¥3000– 4500 single/¥5000–9000 double for the room, meals extra (not compulsory).

Within Japan, reservations can be made by mail or FAX using its publication, "Japanese Inn Group", for mail addresses, and phone and FAX numbers. (It also has information on facilities, charges, access maps, etc.) From outside the country, reservations can be made through the coordinator:

Japanese Inn Group
c/o Hiraiwa *Ryokan*
314 Hayao-cho
Kaminokuchi-agaru
Ninomiyacho-dori
Shimogyo-ku
Kyoto 600
Tel: (075) 351-6748
FAX: (075) 351-6969

The American Express Assured Reservation Service can be used to guarantee that your room will be kept whatever time you arrive. (A no-show will be billed unless you cancel your reservation before 1800 of the day of the reservation.)

If you request the booklet to be mailed overseas, it would be a nice gesture to send the approximate equivalent of ¥200 in a convertible currency with your request. The booklet is usually available at the TICs, but it is not a JNTO publication, so will not be available from their overseas offices.

Their application form is reproduced in this book and may be used for your application.

EXCURSION FARES Most travel agencies offer combined train and accommodation "specials" for travel to Kyoto (and other places) in which the costs of the train and *ryokan* or hotel (and probably pension) are combined into a reduced-price package. On one trip that I made, the combined cost of Tokyo-Kyoto Shinkansen fare (return) plus one night in an economy *ryokan* of reasonable quality was less than the cost of the normal return Shinkansen fare. Individual travel agents make their own arrangements; the best known for such packages is JTB (Japan Travel Bureau), the largest in the country.

Temples and Shrines

Many Buddhist temples can accommodate visitors overnight, and at some of these you may participate in prayer and religious observations such as *zazen* meditation. At others the accommodation can be regarded just as a room—usually traditional tatami style—that happens to be on temple grounds. Most temples are very graceful structures, representative of what foreigners think of as the traditional Japan, so it is a good idea to stay at one at least once during a visit to Japan. A few Shinto shrines also offer accommodation.

It is easy to find a temple or shrine that accepts guests; about 75 function as youth hostels (along with their religious purposes of course), and they're all listed in the YH Handbook with a symbol. A swastika, an ancient Indian religious symbol, identifies a temple, while a shrine has a *torii* gate. A few temples are modern concrete structures, but most are traditional wooden buildings that embody the finest skills in Japanese woodworking. In the following, the temples with numbers in brackets are those in the YH Handbook.

Many temples are quite historic. Zuiryu-ji (3207, Takaoka) is about 350 years old and has several large buildings. Other temples are set in beautiful sur-

roundings, such as Jofuku-ji on Shikoku (7404) which is on a hillside overlooking a valley. Jofuku-ji is a Zen temple and one of the young priests speaks good English and invites his guests to join in *zazen* meditation. Because it is a "family" temple it is small, and no advance arrangements need to be made to stay overnight, though a phone call in advance would be prudent, as with any hostel.

There are five temples in the Kyoto area that accept lodgers. They are: Enryaku-ji (on Mt. Hiei—the number one temple of the Tendai sect, with a history of 1200 years); Myoren-ji (noted for its beautiful garden); Komyo-ji Shukubo, Daishin-in (a former detached palace of the emperor Hanazono that was later rebuilt as a Zen temple); and Inari-taisha Sanshuden. The last named is actually a shrine, not a temple, and is the most important of the many Inari shrines in Japan. It is noted for its more than 1000 torii gates that have been placed along paths that wind up the mountain.

The prices (accommodation only) range from ¥1500 to ¥3500. Some offer meals as well. To stay at any of these temples, it is best to make arrangements through the TIC in Kyoto (tel. 075-371-5649). They will also give any information that may be necessary so that you will know what is expected of you. (Many more temples used to accept foreign guests, but they had so many problems with some of them that they closed their doors to all foreigners.)

In the area around Koya-san (reasonably close to Nara) there are more than 50 temple lodgings available, virtually covering the mountain. Koya-san is very important in the Buddhist history of Japan and is very popular with pilgrims so accommodation may be hard to obtain. Costs are ¥4500 and up, with two meals. Reservations can be made through the JTB, or through the Koyasan Tourist Association, 600 Koyasan, Koya-cho, Into-gun, Wakayama-ken. Tel (07365) 6-2616.

Hotels

Hotels as they are known in the west, with beds, familiar furniture, and amenities, can be found in the major cities (especially ones frequented by foreign business people), as well as in popular resort and tourist areas. In smaller centers a "hotel" is likely to have a mixture of western and Japanese style rooms, with an equal confusion about what is expected in service. The quality of facilities and service in Japan can vary from internationally accepted levels in the major centers to something much less pretentious (but nearly as expensive) in more remote areas. Prices at hotels in Tokyo range from ¥5500 to ¥23,000 single/¥8500 to ¥30,000 (the higher prices "and up").

A listing of the 360 or so government-registered hotels of the Japan Hotel Association (generally good quality and international standard) is contained in the JNTO publication *Hotels in Japan*. The places listed usually have air conditioning/central heating, and other modern facilities, and their prices are not in the "budget" category.

Note that the word "hotel" in Japan refers more often to a special type of accommodation that lets rooms for one to two hours to couples visiting with negligible luggage. If you are seeking the "respectable" type of establishment, you may have to make this clear, for the seamier type of place is what you are more likely to encounter in smaller cities and local neighborhoods. (Actually, this short-term type of establishment can be useful for the ordinary traveller for overnight accommodation, and is described in detail under "Love Hotels".)

Business Hotels

This type of accommodation is intended primarily for travelling businessmen who want respectable and clean accommodation without the high cost of luxury hotels. It achieves economy by eliminating frills like room service—each floor has vending machines for drinks, etc. The rooms vary widely in size, but generally tend to be on the small side, with the worst ones being ridiculously cramped. It is worth asking to have a look at the room in advance if you suffer from claustrophobia. Costs vary from ¥2000 to ¥5000 for a single; doubles cost somewhat more.

At least two books that list business hotels around Japan are available at bookshops. The larger is called *Zenkoku Business Hotel* and the smaller *Mini-mini Zenkoku Business Hotel*. The former lists 1600 BH's around Japan, the latter nearly 620, with 68 in the Tokyo area alone. Both are written only in Japanese so a little work is involved in using it, but it is not difficult to match the *kanji* of place names on a map with those in the books. Organization is by *ken* (prefecture).

Capsule Hotels

While not practical for most travellers, it is useful to at least know of the existence of capsule hotels. These are tiny crawl-only "rooms" as wide as a bed. They are air conditioned so that the air remains fresh when the door is closed. They are found near major stations in large cities where office workers who missed the last train can stay at moderate cost (though still in the several thousand yen range). The compartments are sized for Japanese, and tall foreigners might find that their feet hang outside the door. (No consideration has been given to the fact that there are now large numbers of tall Japanese as well.)

Love Hotels

This type of public accommodation is available throughout Japan, but due to its very nature it gets much less promotion as a "place to stay" than the more socially acceptable *ryokan* and *minshuku*, etc. Another Japanese term for it sounds like "Abek Hoteru". Japanese has no "v", so "abek" is the French "avec" ("with"). These places rent rooms for short periods (as little as 30 minutes for a "quickie", and post rates for two hours and overnight. However, they may be used purely as overnight accommodation, as long as you are aware of their peculiarities.

The busy period is during the day and the early evening; business generally begins to slacken off in the later evening, and they will usually rent rooms for the night for little more than the short-term charge of earlier in the day. So if you can wait until quite late in the evening (after 2200 or 2300), you can obtain quarters that are usually comfortable, clean (though perhaps decorated in a rather garish style with with lots of red, pink, and purple), and more spacious than in most other accommodation in Japan, at a cost of about ¥5000–8000 a night. You will probably have to vacate the room quite early in the morning though, otherwise it may be necessary to pay the hourly rate for every hour of extra sleep-in.

Many love hotels have facilities rather out of the ordinary, such as floor-to-ceiling mirrors, often with a mirrored ceiling for good measure. The decor may resemble the harem of a sultan or other equally lush and plush places. A common feature is a color videotape recorder and camera for instant replay of the action, plus a library of porno videos for rent, a condom vendor, etc.

Once you learn to recognise the word "hoteru" in *katakana* you will find them everywhere. Outside a sign usually shows two prices—one for a "rest" (*gokyukei*), usually two hours, the other for a "stay" (*goshukuhaku*), which normally means a longer period (and is usually the rate applied to an overnight stay). The price is quoted for one room, not per person as is the case at most other types of accommodation, so it can be an economical type of place to stay if you can wait long enough at night. (Most places have a sign indicating a maximum of two persons per room.)

The love hotel can actually be a "life saver", as I found one summer when I ventured back into Tohoku to see a number of grand festivals that take place there in early August. Thousands of tourists flock there from everywhere in the country, and they had made reservations for accommodation months in advance. There was nothing to be had, even at the information office at the station in each city having the festival (there are several successive days with such festivals). I had a car (rented) and just drove 10 to 20 km out of the city until I spotted the love hotel area, then drove around until I found a free parking space (generally under the individual room in those particular hotels), unloaded the car, and moved in. In the morning someone came around and collected the money.

Entry to a "hoteru" has traditionally been the ultimate in discretion. After passing through a narrow entrance (or driving into an underground garage), the customers can no longer be seen from the street. Usually the person admitting them is out of sight behind a curtain. After the use of the room, the fee is paid to an anonymous hand. In theory one is not expected to see the staff and supposedly vice-versa, and supposedly customers never see each other either. (In most motels, each room has a separate entrance for maximum privacy). These days, however, many hotels have a lobby in which couples pass each other.

(Use of love hotels is no longer as furtive as it once was, and newspapers report that young people sometimes go together in groups.)

Outside the cities there are also "moteru" for the motorised trade. While Japan does have motels of the kind found in western countries purely for accommodation, the majority are of the love hotel variety. There is usually no mistaking one type from the other, as the exteriors of love hotels and motels are often the ultimate in bad taste, with garish pink neon signs bordering the roof, flashing signs, and outlandish architecture. There is one in Tokyo in the shape of a ship, while another in the same city is known throughout the country for its pseudo-feudal castle architecture, complete with turrets and other gewgaws.

Saunas

In cases of desperation when all normal accommodation is full, an emergency fallback (in cities, at least) is a sauna (for men certainly, and possibly for women, depending on the establishment). This is a place with showers, steam room, etc., but included is a couch where one can stretch out and have a reasonably comfortable night's sleep. (Friends have done this, but I have not yet been desperate enough to have to; with a motorcycle I was able to drive and find a love hotel, but not all travellers have this option.)

Foreigner Houses

This is the generic name for a number of houses in large cities like Tokyo that have several rooms available for rent for various periods. They have the advantage that there is no key money nor any of the other gouges encountered if apartment-hunting. Although more of interest for long-term residents, these houses are also suitable for visitors if space is available.

Many residents of these establishments find that the house becomes a community, and people often linger on for months rather than look for an apartment of their own.

A warning is that the trend is for increasing rents and for decreasing space per person so that many people may be sharing the same small room. Check out the accommodations before committing yourself.

Camping

Camping has not caught on in Japan to the same extent that it has in western countries, because there isn't the same reliance on car transport, but the number of camping grounds is increasing yearly. The JNTO publication *Camping in Japan* is an excellent list of camping grounds and is available from the TICs in Tokyo and Kyoto.

Camping facilities vary from spartan to ultra-elaborate, with prices to match. Some have only tent sites and a source of fresh water, while others have bungalows and cottages as well. Most grounds are open only in July and August. In Japan summer is, by definition, only those two months, even though the weather is warm through June, much of September, and is pleasant well into October.

Many young Japanese set up their tents in almost any open space in the country. This is forbidden in national parks, and the intensive cultivation of land makes it difficult to find open and flat space in many areas, but tents in vacant fields are a common sight. Probably the campers ask permission before setting up camp; this could be a problem for someone not able to speak Japanese. (I have met foreigners doing this, and they had encountered no hostility.)

Cycling Inns

There is a small network of cycling inns which have been set up specifically for bicycle travellers, both those on their own bikes and those who rent bikes at the inns. The facilities and costs are similar to those at the youth hostels, except that there is usually a workshop for bike repairs as well. The buildings are all new within the last few years, and the aim is to eventually have one every 100 km or so; at the moment there are about 20 of them.

The inns have been built in regions of natural beauty that invite exploration by bike; often there are specially constructed cycle paths that are separate from regular highways. In many cases it would be worth a trip to the area for sightseeing. Rental charges are reasonable, from as low as ¥200 for four hours plus ¥50 per additional hour, to a maximum of ¥250 per hour.

Information about locations and bike rentals can be obtained from a booklet issued by the Japan Cycling Association called *sai-ku-ring-gu ta-mi-na-ru* ("cycling terminal"). Although it is in Japanese only, approximate locations are shown on a sketch map at the front. Detailed addresses and specific information on how to get there from the nearest railway station is given with the description of each inn and its facilities. Copies can be obtained from the JCA. It may be easier to contact the Japan Bicycle Promotion Institute first as they have English-speaking staff who can give information and assistance. Write to: Mr. H. Kono or Mr. H. Ise, Japan Bicycle Promotion Institute, Nihon Jitensha Kaikan Bldg, 1-9-3 Akasaka, Minato-ku, Tokyo. Tel. 03-5572-6410.

Kokumin-shukusha (People's Lodgings)

People's Lodgings are accommodation and recreation facilities in a number of popular resort and natural park areas throughout Japan. They have been built by local authorities under the guidance of the Ministry of Health and Welfare as a means of bringing a vacation in attractive surroundings within the reach of most Japanese. The room charge of about ¥6,500 a night with two meals is lower than that of most *ryokan*.

The Lodgings are open to anyone, Japanese or foreigners, and no membership in any organisation is required. During the summer and busy travel seasons they tend to be fully booked, or it may be necessary to share a room. Otherwise, anyone showing up at the door will be given a room and couples will be put together if possible.

Bookings are most easily made through JTB, which issues vouchers for reserved rooms, but this system is in effect for only about 70 per cent of the Lodgings and it may take up to a week. Bookings can also be made privately by mail or phone, provided you can speak or write Japanese. The TICs have a complete listing of all Lodgings in Japan; it runs to several pages and is not a published booklet, so it is necessary to inquire in person.

Kokumin-kyukamura

These "Vacation Villages" are intended mainly for stays of several days for workers who want a quiet, relaxing rest. They are primarily in quiet locations, sometimes near famous resort or sightseeing areas, sometimes in rather remote regions. There are 27 throughout Japan; 19 have camping grounds with good facilities and about half have sporting facilities. Rates run to ¥10,000 per person with two meals. Usually two or more different menus are available at different prices.

The Villages haven't been used much by foreigners and there is no quick booking system available. There is an office in Tokyo, but the simplest way is to go to the Tokyo TIC, explain your travel plans, and ask their advice.

Seishonen Ryokamura

This "Youth Village" program, which began in the late 1960s, would provide a good way to see Japanese life in the more remote areas, as all 50 or so villages are located in fairly isolated parts of the country. They are situated in actual villages or towns (or nearby) that have been losing population and are in danger of becoming ghost towns.

Often there is a central lodge plus a very simple camping ground. Rates are similar to those of *minshuku*, from ¥7,000 with two meals.

As with Vacation Villages it would be best for any foreigner who is interested in staying at a Youth Village to contact the TIC in Tokyo and discuss travel plans. They can make suitable recommendations and suggestions. Staff at the TIC warn that hosts at the Youth Villages are not familiar with foreigners, so a little knowledge of Japanese would be useful.

Servas

Travellers who are sincerely interested in meeting Japanese families and interacting with them have the opportunity to stay in Japanese homes free of charge, through the international organisation Servas. This organization is described along with other ways of meeting Japanese. As described in the section covering that topic, the program should not be looked on as a cheap way to travel, for people who stay with families are expected to participate in some aspects of daily life.

Communes

There are several communes scattered around Japan, some of which welcome guests. These are described under the section Meeting the Japanese.

FOOD

Travellers in Japan will encounter few difficulties in finding palatable food. I can no longer write "at reasonable cost" because of the great rise in the value of the yen vis a vis almost all other currencies, but the following notes will give you the picture on food so you can eat at the lowest feasible cost.

There has been some criticism of earlier editions of this book because there have been no specific recommendations as to restaurants. There is more than one reason for this. First, Japan is the land of the clone. Once you have identified one type of food, you will be able to find it from one end of the country to the other, and prices will be much the same everywhere (slightly higher in metropolitan areas). Next, the sanitation standards are more than adequate in virtually any place you will go, so there is no need to recommend specific places just because they will not give you food poisoning. Such dangers do not normally exist. And there are restaurants in just about every part of every town or city, so finding one will be no problem. There are tens of thousands.

Western restaurant-type food is available at the large tourist hotels and restaurants in the larger cities, but it will be very expensive and cannot be considered when travelling on a budget. If you want to eat at moderate cost you must eat as the locals do.

Typical Japanese cooking centers on a bowl of rice (*gohan*), usually has a bowl of *miso shiru* soup (based on soybeans, and a good source of protein), and features one or more kinds of vegetable, plus a portion (generally small) of fish or meat. More economical dishes are based on noodles, either *soba* (greyish; buckwheat), *ramen* (yellow), or *udon* (white; wheat). Semi-western food can be found in most centers of population of any size. Typical offerings are hamburger steak, macaroni and spaghetti dishes, pilaffs, dorias, and gratins, usually with a choice of bread or rice. Interestingly, rice served with such dishes comes on a flat plate and is called "raisu" not "gohan". Also interesting is the thinking by the Japanese that bread, not potatoes, is the equivalent of rice, so that is the option with many dishes: rice or bread.

Japanese food is not spicy, so there is no problem for delicate tongues or stomachs. The weird foods that you may have read about, such as grasshoppers or chocolate-covered ants, are just as strange to the average Japanese as they are to foreigners. Yes, the Japanese do eat raw fish (*sashimi*), but it must be fresh to be eaten this way. If it seems a strange practice just remember how westerners eat oysters. Good *sashimi* has a weak flavor with no "fishy" taste or smell. Sushi (raw fish or other ingredient with rice), on the other hand, has more flavor. The only other common food that foreigners may find revulsive is *natto*: fermented soybeans that look, smell, taste, and feel like something moist that was forgotten on a back shelf for too long. (But don't let any Japanese make you feel "inadequate" if you can't eat it; approximately half the Japanese population find it just as unappealing as you do.)

Fish is the major source of protein. Beef is very expensive ("outrageously" is the word used in previous editions, but imports are being admitted more and prices are becoming less expensive), the result of deliberate and scandalous government policy to protect small and inefficient domestic producers who raise only one or two animals on miniscule plots of land. (This also protects the farmers' votes on which the government has remained in power for 30+ years.) Imported beef is sold and resold among dealers (often without leaving the freezer) until it sells in the shops for the going rate, which is approximately

ten times the original purchase price. Similarly, the price of rice is about six times the world level because the government buys everything produced at a fixed and high price, and refuses to permit a single grain of table rice to be imported.

Along these lines, if you wonder why bread is so expensive, it is because the government buys large amounts overseas at less than ¥30,000/ton, sells it to local mills for ¥84,000/ton, and uses the surplus to buy wheat from Japanese farmers at ¥147,000/ton.

Beef is not a traditional item of the Japanese diet. Until the country was opened to the western barbarians in the 1860s, the Buddhist Japanese would have been horrified at the thought of killing an animal so that it could be eaten. The famous Kobe and Matsuzaka beef are a relatively recent innovation in the diet. The meat is tasty and tender (and very, very expensive) but to the eyes of a lean-meat eater it is very fatty ("marbled" is the term used).

All dishes of a Japanese meal should be served at the same time so that you have a full choice at any one time, and should not arrive in dribs and drabs. In a good restaurant this will be true, but more than one diner at less illustrious restaurants has found his dishes arriving at widespread intervals. (This is especially likely to happen, if at all, in "western" style Japanese restaurants.)

Those who have sampled Japanese cooking in restaurants in a western country, particularly the USA, may be surprised to find that there is no similarity to what they find in Japan. The fancy, flashy "Japanese steak house" is an American invention. Food served at a good traditional (read "very expensive") *kaiseki* restaurant will be as much a treat for the eye as the tongue, with service that is very restrained and elegant. Vegetables are sliced in intricate shapes, and everything is decoratively arranged. Of course less pretentious restaurants for budget eaters are much more basic and utilitarian (and likely to be quite noisy, as much from the staff as the customers). You get what you pay for (if you're lucky). This is the type of restaurant where one course may be three slices of green bean decoratively arranged on a small dish.

Menus

One of the biggest problems can be understanding what food is available. Little "hole in the wall" eateries will have vertical strips of cardboard listing items and prices posted on the wall (but only in Japanese), while better establishments will have a conventional menu, but usually also only in *kanji*. However, a good number of restaurants in metropolitan areas will have menus with sufficient English to be understandable (though invariably with large numbers of strange spelling—but at least they're trying). Choosing a meal is no great problem, however, even though staff rarely understand English. Most restaurants have very realistic wax replicas of various dishes on display, usually in the front window, for inspection by the passing public, so you can summon a waitress and point at what looks good. Also, in 1991, a book on reading menus was released for sale. It is listed in the "books" section.

Chopsticks

Western cutlery is available at many restaurants, but it is advisable to know how to use chopsticks, for these are what Japanese food is intended to be eaten with. Japanese chopsticks (*hashi*) are shorter than the Chinese variety, and easier to manipulate. (It is best to learn how to use them before leaving home so you can just enjoy the taste without having to worry if you are going to get enough into your mouth to survive.)

Most inexpensive restaurants provide disposable chopsticks that are used once and then thrown away. The two sticks are still one piece of wood, and are split apart before use. (The consumption of these, 80 million chopsticks/day according to one source, is under fire from conservationists because of the waste of wood it represents.)

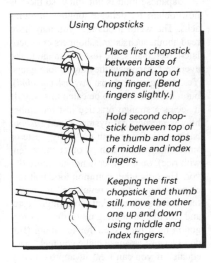

Using Chopsticks

Place first chopstick between base of thumb and top of ring finger. (Bend fingers slightly.)

Hold second chopstick between top of the thumb and tops of middle and index fingers.

Keeping the first chopstick and thumb still, move the other one up and down using middle and index fingers.

While you are eating with chopsticks, there are certain happenings that you (and every other foreigner) can reliably expect to occur. Any Japanese nearby who can speak some English is almost sure to compliment you with a phrase like: "You can use chopsticks very well." This is often said with wonderment, because it is one of the fondly held beliefs that only Japanese (well . . . maybe some other Asians also) can use chopsticks, as if the ability were an in-born, genetically-inherited trait. (This is one of the several situations that arise in Japan when you don't know whether to laugh for the humor or cry for the misinformation.) If this happens to you, and you wish to reply, you are free to confront him with the fact that a survey in the mid-60s of 10,000 people showed that younger Japanese are becoming progressively less proficient in their use, the early-20 group scoring only about 50%, and the early-30s about 63%. The less proficient got them crossed, dropped things (well-known phenomenon to foreign users!), held them in their fist, and even used them to "spear" their food. This seems to be partly the result of using spoons with school lunches. As mentioned elsewhere in the book, the Japanese hold many mystical beliefs about themselves (which do not stand up to the light of investigation . . . but they do not investigate).

Some typical Japanese dishes are:

Sashimi: slices of raw fish of various kinds. (Prices vary with type of fish; usually not cheap.)

Sushi: raw or cooked fish, vegetables, egg, etc., on or in rice. (Varying prices; many types reasonable in cost.)

Tempura: batter-dipped and deep-fried fish and vegetables; of Portuguese origin. (The accent is on the first syllable. Many types reasonable in cost.)

Sukiyaki: vegetables, thinly sliced beef, *shirataki* (like vermacelli), *tofu* (soya bean curd), all cooked together at the table in a broth of water, sake, sugar, and soya sauce. (Pronounced "ski'yaki". A winter dish; up-market prices.)

Jingis Khan: similar to *sukiyaki*, but the pot has a dome in the center surrounded by a trough; the vegetables are cooked in the broth while the meat (mutton) is cooking on the dome. (A Hokkaido dish; up-market.)

Shabu-shabu: similar to *sukiyaki* except that ingredients are cooked in water, and get most of their flavor from spice dips. (A winter dish; up-market.)

Domburi: a bowl of rice with added chicken, egg, meat, etc. (Not expensive.)

Okonomiyaki: a type of pancake usually cooked on a griddle at the table by the diners themselves; various ingredients are mixed into the batter, e.g., shrimp, squid, beef. (Not expensive. Best in cold weather because of heat from griddle at table. A good "social" dish.)

Economy Eating

For simple meals and lunches while on the move, some suggestions include *tempura* and *onigiri*. In most towns there will be a *tempuraya* (tempura shop) with freshly cooked pieces of fish, vegetables, meat (called "katsu", a corruption of the word "cutlet"), and *korokke* (croquets; potato cakes) on display on trays in the window. They are tasty and filling (if a bit calorie-laden because of the deep-fat frying), and not expensive.

A very traditional food for lunches is *onigiri*, basically a ball of rice with a piece of fish or vegetable in the center; the outside is wrapped in a sheet of crisp seaweed. The tastiest has *sake* (pronounced "shakay") inside; it is salmon.

Nearly all department stores and office buildings have restaurants in the basement and offer reasonable cost meals, especially at lunchtime. You can order individual items, but the cheapest way is to order *teishoku*, the day's set lunch; it will usually be on display. A typical *teishoku* will have a bowl of rice, *miso shiru* soup, a plate of vegetables, meat or fish, salad, and dessert.

Near most railway and subway stations, there are usually restaurants of many types such as simple noodle shops where everyone stands, Korean barbecues, semi-western style restaurants, sushi shops, coffee shops (*kissaten*), and others. Simple meals begin around ¥500–600. Places catering mainly to drinkers often prove more costly because each item ordered, such as a skewer of meat, is served and charged for separately, and is regarded more as a snack to accompany drinks than as a meal in itself.

The pizza chains Shakey's and Pizza Hut offer a real bargain between 1100 and 1400 every day except Sundays and holidays—all the pizza you can eat for a fixed price (about ¥600). The nutritional value is suspect, but it is certainly very filling and there's lots of cheese. (There was a restaurant in Kyoto, Trecca, that had the same offer, but it closed for an indefinite period. It may have resurfaced.)

For familiar, filling, and not-expensive food, there are hundreds of McDonald's hamburger shops around the country, at least one in almost every city of any size. The food is identical with that served in every McDonald's anywhere in the world (identical specifications). Other familiar chains of American origin (though operated under Japanese franchise) are Wendy's Hamburgers and Kentucky Fried Chicken. These places, particularly the hamburger shops, are probably the most economical places to eat in Japan, particularly for beef.

A type of restaurant found on the outskirts of large cities is the "family restaurant", such as Denny's, Royal Host, and Sunday Sun. These have a modern, clean decor, and multicolor illustrated menus combining both traditional Japanese dishes and Western types of food. The servings are usually quite generous relative to price, and the taste is normally good. These restaurants always have largish parking lots and are aimed at mobile customers. For this reason they will not generally be found in central parts of cities.

If you have cooking facilities where you're staying, at youth hostels, for example, you can economise. Residential neighborhoods have vegetable, fruit, and meat shops, and supermarkets have spread widely since their introduction in the late

1960s. As well as eggs, meat, fish, chicken, vegetables, cheese and milk, etc., you can get a large variety of instant *ramen* (dried bundles of noodles) that cook in a few minutes. After cooking the noodles until they separate and soften, add the provided seasonings to make a broth. Served with a couple of boiled eggs, one has the nutrition of the eggs and the filling-up of the noodles. (The broth has much salt, so be careful if you're hypertensive.) Supermarkets also usually offer a good selection of prepared food such as sushi, tempura (meat, fish, squid, vegetables, etc.), and croquets (potato with or without corn, curry, etc.).

For those on a super tight budget, bakeries slice the heels (*pan no mimi*) off loaves of bread, and you can get a bag of them at little or no cost. Peanut butter and jam are available. Jam from Romania and Bulgaria is probably the best in Japan and widely available; try the bargain sections of department stores (supermarkets are more nationalistic and usually sell only the domestic product, which generally is lacking in fruit).

For more detailed information, a good inexpensive book is *Eating Cheap in Japan*.

Coffee Shops

Visitors are always shocked at the price of a cup of coffee at coffee shops, ¥250–1,000. The usual excuse for the high cost is that you are paying for the space and the congenial surroundings. You can stay all day for the price of a single cup, and young people often have coffee-shop dates. For just coffee without the luxurious surroundings, chains like Lotteria can be suggested. Their offering, however will probably not be as tasty as the selection at the "dedicated" coffee shops. (Many Japanese coffee shops are true "coffee gourmet" heavens, and nearly all serve very high quality coffee.)

Many coffee shops offer a real bargain for breakfast, "morning service", which includes toast (and sometimes an egg) for the usual price of a cup of coffee alone.

Sociology in action: coffee shops also tend to be where teenage girls go to smoke.

Specialty Restaurants

There are many kinds of specialty restaurants in Japan. Typical is a *robata-yaki*. Generally rustic in decor, they display the raw materials that are available, like whole fish, potatoes, etc.; customers pick out the one they want, and it is cooked for them. If you want to visit such a restaurant, it is invaluable to have a Japanese companion.

Pastries

Japanese pastries are rated well by many a pastry lover.

Etiquette

It is acceptable to slurp noodles; the attitude is that it makes them taste better. Otherwise Japanese table manners are not so different from those in the west. Observe other diners and follow their lead, especially when drinking. (Details on drinking appear in the entertainment section, since few budget travellers will be indulging in a variety of alcoholic beverages.)

Dietary Problems

If you are not supposed to eat certain foods because of your religion (pork, for example), or meat of any kind (vegetarian), you have the potential for a large problem. The Japanese are generally incapable of understanding that some people have dietary preferences or taboos. It all begins at school, when the pupils are compelled to eat everything put in their school lunches, whether they detest a food or not.

Even if you request that the cook leave out all meat, for example, there is still the chance of finding some in the finished dish. Any complaint will likely be met by the equivalent of a cheerful, "Well, it's only a bit of pork!", with the intimation that it won't hurt you. (Indian restaurants, found in the larger cities, are one sure source of meat-free food, but they will be out of the "economy" class of eatery.)

Monosodium glutamate is widely used, so if you have a reaction to it, you must be careful of what you eat. A friend who has this problem advises that the only really safe food is fresh vegetables, fish, or fruit. Even raw meat seems to give the same reaction; apparently chemicals are put in to tenderize it. The worst foods for MSG are soups and sauces, and any food in Chinese-type restaurants is especially suspect. Even the salt in shakers is not to be trusted. Asking the waitress if food contains MSG will do no good, for she will automatically say there is not, and requesting that the cook not use any will have no effect. The label on packaged food (if you can read it) does not need to indicate MSG content, though the word "amino" in katakana in the list of ingredients usually indicates its presence.

Japanese cooking has tradionally used a large amount of salt, both as salt and in soya sauce (annual per capita consumption: 10 liters!). Stroke has also been the second most common cause of death in Japan. The word is now getting out among the population of the effect of excessive consumption of salt, and people are cutting down, but prepared food of all kinds (canned and in restaurants) still contains more than is healthy. Those on a low-salt diet must be careful.

Drinking

Just about every type of restaurant offers beer to drink with meals. Depending on the type of place, sake (rice beer) will usually also be readily available, as will whisky (usually drunk with water (*mizuwari*) or a mixer). Restaurants serving western-type food will usually have wine as well. As described elsewhere, Japanese wine is generally unremarkable, especially that served in ordinary restaurants. Gastronomes will be delighted (?) to learn that the average Japanese restaurateur believes that red, as well as white, wine should be served cold. (It probably makes the Japanese brands more palatable.) If you are fussy about your wine, you should ask to feel the bottle before it is opened. The various alcoholic beverages available in Japan are discussed in the Entertainment section.

Tipping

Japan has the distinction of being one of the few developed countries where tipping is not generally expected. If a service charge is expected, it will automatically be added to your bill (another way of saying it is compulsory). Quite separate from the service charge is the 10 per cent tax incurred if restaurant or bar bills exceed ¥1200.

Only at expensive nightclubs, which are a western type of import and which have largely disappeared in recent years, is tipping of waiters normal. Even nightclub hostesses do not expect tips if you pay the hostess charge and buy their drinks; this will amount to plenty in any case!

MONEY AND BANKING

Currency

The name of the Japanese currency is the *yen*—which is about as much as anyone can say about it with any certainty. In the past fifteen years the value of the yen has ranged from more than ¥280 to the US dollar to less than ¥85.

In terms of actual purchasing power in Japan, compared with what a US dollar will

buy in the US, the "true" value of the yen is between 150 and 600 yen to the dollar, though the rate through 1994 was varying above and below only 100. This makes Japan very expensive for foreign visitors. An explanation of this disparity is beyond the scope of this book!

There are coins of 1, 5, 10, 50, 100, and 500 yen; the banknotes in common circulation are for 1000, 5000, and 10,000 yen. (The banknotes all have arabic numerals and can easily be identified, in addition to which the size is proportional to the value.) Notes for 500 yen are virtually collector's items; they might be seen occasionally in Hokkaido. There is speculation that it will be phased out officially, and that a ¥50,000 or ¥100,000 note will be introduced.

The ¥1 coin is aluminum, the five is brass, with a hole. The brown solid coin is ¥10, and the ¥50 coin is nickel, with a hole. The ¥100 and ¥500 are nickel, and solid, the latter physically larger; both are clearly identified in arabic numerals. Formerly a seldom-used bother, the one-yen coin is now essential because of the odd amounts resulting from the unpopular 3% "consumption tax" on most goods and services that was introduced a few years ago.

The value of any other currency vis a vis the yen will be in proportion to its value against the US dollar and the relationship of the latter to the yen.

Most other products, including food, are very expensive, the result of small-scale and inefficient production. Rice, for example, could be bought in the U.S., Australia, Thailand, etc., for about a sixth the price charged in Japan. (Japanese families pay about 25 per cent of their income for food, compared with about 15 per cent in the USA.) However, since it is the products in demand overseas that determine the demand for the yen, this knowledge will be only academic. As one resident expressed it, "Happiness comes from regarding a ¥1000 note as one would a dollar."

Changing Money

Only yen may be spent in Japan. It is against the law for foreign currencies to be used so, unlike in many other countries in Asia, the U.S. greenback is not a second currency, and the average shopkeeper would not recognise one.

Foreign currencies can be changed only at banks with a sign "Authorised Foreign Exchange Bank", or at a few authorised stores that have a large tourist trade; they will have a similar sign posted. Both cash and travellers' cheques may be exchanged. In metropolitan areas, authorised banks are thick on the ground, but don't get caught short of yen out in the boonies, for it can be a real hassle exchanging money.

The currencies of the following countries may be exchanged in Japan: Australia, Austria, Belgium, Canada, Denmark, Netherlands, France, Germany, Hong Kong, Italy, Norway, UK, Portugal, Sweden, Switzerland, and the USA. Travellers' cheques in the currency of the following countries can be exchanged: Australia, Canada, France, Germany, India, Italy, UK, Switzerland, and the USA. Note that, while these currencies may be exchanged for yen, don't walk into a bank in a small city and try to exchange Canadian banknotes, for example. The bank will only accept them for clearance and send them to its head office, a process that would take several days (at best).

The currency of Taiwan is worthless in Japan, so be sure to change everything to a convertible currency (Japanese, American, etc.) before leaving Taiwan. The currency of Korea is almost in the same boat, as it cannot be exchanged at the usual banks in Japan. However, if you have Korean *won*

and have exchange certificates proving the money was changed through an authorised Korean Bank, you can convert them to yen, etc., at one of the three offices of the Korea Exchange Bank. They are located in Tokyo (in the Marunouchi financial district, quite close to the TIC), Osaka, and Fukuoka.

If going to Korea, convert your yen to U.S. dollars; in past years they have received a premium on the black market (quite open in Seoul—just ask among other travellers), whereas Japanese money has been worth little more than the official rate.

Travellers' cheques denominated in yen may be of little more use in Japan than foreign currency. There are many stories of clerks in bank branches outside the major cities who didn't know what to do with yen travellers' cheques issued by their own bank. Banks are even more unwilling to cash the "paper" of another bank, accepting them only for collection, so unless there is a branch of the bank that issued the yen cheques, you may have trouble getting any yen. Also, the major banks that issue travellers' cheques often don't have branches in the smaller cities, so check carefully where they can be cashed.

Banks

There are two ways to avoid carrying large amounts of cash. The first method, and probably the simplest, is to open a Post Office savings account. With such an account you can withdraw money from almost every post office in Japan, during normal business hours. (They also use a cash dispenser system.) Since there are far more post offices than banks, this method is most useful. An account can be opened at any but the smallest post office; certainly there is no problem at the central post office, Tokyo (near Tokyo station). The magic words are *yubin chokin-o hajimetai*. That should be enough to open an account.

The other way to keep money in Japan is to open a passbook savings account with a large bank, one that has branches nationwide, such as Tokyo-Mitsubishi, Sakura, Dai-ichi Kangyo, etc., and obtain a "cash card" for the account. You will be able to withdraw funds at any branch of the bank with the passbook by the "invisible signature" system, or from cash dispensing machines at almost any bank throughout the country using the cash card. (There is a ¥100 charge if the machine at a different bank is used). A cash card gets around the problem that many large banks, like Tokyo-Mitsubishi, have few branches outside the largest cities (which caused me some problems when I was travelling around). Of the banks, the Dai-ichi Kangyo has the largest number of branches through the country. (I opened my account with the Tokyo-Mitsubishi Bank at the Tokyo head office (near Tokyo station) and found that staff spoke enough English to do this without difficulty.)

It is possible to open a U.S. dollar savings account in Japan. This is probably of greater use to residents rather than visitors. It allows easy transfer of money in and out of Japan without having to exchange it each time. Banks might be unwilling to open an account for a stranger, but by looking around there should be no trouble finding a branch willing to help. Interest rates paid on dollar accounts are usually higher than for yen accounts (which are laughably low in any case), but a tax may be imposed, and some banks deduct a handling fee of 1/10 of 1 per cent per transaction (or a minimum charge of ¥750 to ¥1000, whichever is greater.)

HANKO Japanese bank customers must use a small seal, or stamp (*hanko*) on documents for all their financial transactions. They are not permitted to use a signature. However, non-Japanese are not subject to this restriction, and a signature is acceptable. (This requirement for using a *hanko* is one of the many aspects of Japan that foreigners find truly strange. If someone else gets hold of your *hanko* , they can withdraw all your money, sell your house, and do great amounts of other mischief as long as it can be kept secret from you until the transaction is complete. Numbers of persons have been murdered and their money and property taken by the killer(s), who had stolen the *hanko*.)

Cheques

It is possible to open a chequing account and write cheques, but the use of cheques is so uncommon in Japan that it would be difficult having them accepted. The universal private use of cheques as we know it in western countries is totally foreign to Japan. (Businesses do issue them.) Instead, to pay a debt or account, the Japanese arrange a transfer to the account of the creditor at the cost of ¥600 (!) per transaction, or else send cash by registered mail at the cost of postage plus ¥350. The cheapest way to remit money within the country is by a postal money order (*yubin gawase*).

Transferring Money Internationally

Despite the use of computers and other modern technology, the Japanese banking system is slow and inefficient in many ways. Transferring money to and from Japan is expensive compared with many other countries. Inbound, unexpected service charges pop up, such as a couple of thousand yen "cashing charge" for an overseas draft, even for a draft drawn on the very branch at which it is being cashed. Not for no reason are the Japanese banks the largest in the world. This section will help you minimize charges and aggravations.

TO JAPAN If there is no rush for money, the simplest way is to have a yen money order or draft (issued by a post office or bank) sent by mail to the address that you specify. (You can also carry a draft payable to yourself when coming to Japan. This may be a cheaper way of bringing in your money than travellers' cheques. Compare the total charge for TCs and a draft.)

A money order can be cashed only at the bank (post office) designated on the money order, though it can be sent from another branch for collection at the cost of a few days' delay (and possibly a handling charge). Although *most* mail gets through in Japan, it would be safer to send any draft or other remittance by registered mail, especially if it is to a Poste Restante (General Delivery) address.

Money can be sent directly from an overseas bank to its correspondent bank (or branch, if it has one), either by mail transfer (slower but cheaper) or by cable transfer (faster but at a price). It would be a good idea to talk with someone in your home bank before setting out, asking their advice on the best method of transferring money. Be sure that the sending bank understands *very clearly exactly* where the money is to be sent to: city, bank name, and branch. This is the voice of experience!

Forget trying to cash a cheque drawn on a bank in another country. A Canadian who was sent a $50 cheque as a present took it to his bank in a smaller city for processing. A few weeks later the bank called and asked him to pay them ¥1000. When he queried this, he found that their handling charges had eaten up all of his $50 *plus* a further ¥1000!

FROM JAPAN The least expensive way to send money out of Japan is via larger post offices, about 6300 of them throughout the country. The post office itself sends the remittance, either to an address or into a giro account (where these are in use). For an "address" remittance the charge is ¥1000 for the first ¥100,000, ¥1500 up to ¥200,000, ¥2000 up to ¥500,000, and ¥500 more for each additional ¥500,000 beyond that. Into giro accounts the charge is less. The process typically takes a couple of weeks. (The post office also offers faster telegraph and Telex transfers at higher cost.) For transfer to the USA (only) you can receive the money order directly and send it yourself, at a saving of ¥500.

Post offices will also exchange US, Canadian, Australian, British, French, German, and Swiss currencies, though only US banknotes will be on hand for sale at most branches. They also offer travellers' cheques issued by Visa, MasterCard, American Express, Citicorp, and Westpac in the same currencies plus yen.

Banks charge ¥2500 to ¥3500 per draft, lower rates being offered by some foreign banks, like Standard Chartered. For large amounts of money, a bank draft would be less costly than a postal money order. The foreign banks write a draft on the spot, whereas any branch of a Japanese bank apart from the head office will take several days to supply one. For a draft in a less-frequently traded currency, such as Italian lira, it might be necessary to search out a bank of that country.

For small amounts it may be cheapest to remit US dollar banknotes by registered mail (to a trustworthy recipient). American banknotes may be purchased over the counter at nearly all foreign exchange banks (though with the inevitable wait) as long as the bank has them in stock, as well as at large post offices. In Tokyo, the Bank of Tokyo in Marunouchi specializes in foreign currencies, and normally has available the banknotes of all major countries. Only notes of larger denomination may be available, such as a 10 pound British note.

If you have an account in a home-country branch of several foreign banks, such as the Bank of America, you can deposit dollars into the USA account by paying yen at the Tokyo branch. If you supply an encoded deposit slip for your account, there is no transfer charge.

In recent years the foreign exchange regulations have been relaxed greatly. For the amount of money that most travellers are likely to be dealing with, there are effectively no restrictions in changing money in either direction. An exchange receipt is given with each transaction. Up to ¥3,000,000 may be exchanged without documentation, but if your exchange dealings are in this range, it is wise to hold on to the receipts.

Bank Hours

Banks are open Monday to Friday between 0900 and 1500, but closed Saturdays. Banks issue cash cards that can be used with cash dispensers (which are located in a "Cashing Corner"), but the machines generally do not work with ordinary credit cards. (Some department stores have machines that will issue cash against a credit card, but you will have to check if a foreign card, like Visa or MasterCard, is acceptable.) The machines generally operate only 0845-1900 weekdays, 0900-1700 Saturdays and Sundays, and are closed on holidays, thus defeating the purpose of such machines as understood in most Western countries. Hours may be even more restricted in smaller cities. Outside banking hours there is a ¥100 charge to use a machine.

Bank Service

The first time that you use a Japanese bank, you will wonder how this country has advanced so far. Service is incredibly slow.

Nothing is ever finalized by one trip to the counter, as with overseas banks. One gives the withdrawal slip or whatever to the teller, receives a numbered token, then waits five to fifteen minutes for the number or name to be called. Take something to read.

Credit Cards

Several international credit cards can be used in Japan. These include Diner's Club, American Express, Master, and Visa; inquire before leaving home about the usability of any other card if you have one from another large credit card organization. Establishments accepting credit cards have signs prominently displayed. Usually the places that accept them are high-priced, aimed at the expense account or wealthy traveller. When using a credit card you are unlikely to obtain a discount of any size because the shops must pay a commission to the card company.

COMMUNICATIONS

Postal

The Japanese Post Office is generally reliable and efficient, though its rates are high, and it has been known to lose letters (as I can certify). Post Offices keep quite generous hours. District post offices are open 0800 to 1900 on weekdays and from 0800 to 1500 on Saturdays (longer hours at times of heavy traffic, as for New Year cards). Express mail is also accepted from 0900 to 1230 on Sundays and national holidays. "District post office" means the main post office of the ward (*ku*). Local post offices are open 0900 to 1700 on weekdays, and are closed Saturdays, Sundays, and holidays. Local post offices can handle letters, registered mail, and small packets for overseas destinations (air and surface), but parcels can be sent overseas only from a district post office.

The central post offices of Tokyo and Kyoto (and possibly other large cities, like Osaka, Nagoya, etc.) have some counters open 24 hours a day, so you can send letters and parcels, and collect poste restante and registered mail.

Mail can be addressed into, out of, and within Japan in *romaji* (Roman letters). To avoid letters going astray, write or print clearly, as mail sorters and carriers are not linguists.

In Tokyo there is a special post office for overseas mail, Tokyo International Post Office (*Kok'sai Yubin-kyoku*). They know all regulations regarding foreign mail and can give information in English. It is located in Otemachi (near Tokyo station) and is shown on the TIC Tokyo guide map. In theory you can obtain information in English by phone; tel 3241-4877.

For wrapping parcels, most post offices supply free twine. If you need cardboard boxes, pharmacies, grocery stores and many other shops discard them every day. Post offices sell cartons, but the largest is not very large.

Airmail envelopes should not be used for domestic mail. There may be a surcharge for colored envelopes, as they require special handling. Stickers may be attached to postcards as long as they don't add appreciably to the weight or thickness.

Philatelists may be interested to know that Japan, like every other country, regularly issues commemorative stamps (*kinen kitte*). These are sold at every post office in the country on the day of issue, but usually they disappear quickly the same day. After that they can be purchased (until sold out) at Tokyo CPO, near Tokyo station, Marunouchi side. The philatelic counter is near the center of the long counter on the ground floor. Stamps available are displayed on a board, and the way of filling in an order slip is easy to figure out.

Intelpost FAX service via the post office is detailed in the section on telecommunications.

Receiving Mail

Mail can be sent *c/o Poste Restante* (General Delivery) to any post office in Japan, but preferably to the Central Post Office of the city, which is usually very close to the main railway station. Things to note are: 1. letters are usually held for only 30 days before being returned to the sender; and 2. the Japanese seldom use the service and most people don't know that it exists. Postal clerks in smaller post offices may even be unsure where to put such letters, so there is a risk that they will go astray. At the post office, ask for either *tome oki* or *kyoku dome* and have your passport or other identification ready.

American Express offices hold mail for customers. They may ask for proof that you are a customer, but this can simply mean someone who has bought their travellers' cheques. Mail is normally held for 30 days, but they will hold it longer if it is marked "Please hold for arrival".

The addresses of branches that hold mail are:

Tokyo
c/o American Express, Denki Bldg (south wing; 1 Fl), 1-7-1 Yurakucho, Chiyoda-ku, Tokyo 100. (tel (03) 3214-0280; toll-free: 0120-020-120)
Osaka
c/o American Express, Osaka Dai-ichi Seimei Bldg 3 Fl), 1-8-17 Umeda, Kita-ku, Osaka 530 (tel (06) 341-4102)
Okinawa
c/o American Express, Awase Shopping Center, 241 Aza Yamazoto, Okinawa-shi 904

To reach the Tokyo office, take the Ginza subway line to Toranomon and leave the station via exit 3. The Mitsui Building is straight ahead. In Osaka, the office is near Osaka station.

Some embassies will hold mail for their passport holders, but they may normally return it after 30 days, unless it is marked "Please hold for arrival". The embassies of Australia, Canada, South Africa, New Zealand, and USA will hold mail, but the UK embassy will not.

Some banks will hold mail for their customers. For example, the Royal Bank of Canada will, but First National City Bank would not.

Hotels and youth hostels will hold mail for their guests. Hotels are usually quite safe addresses for mail, but the hostels vary. In my own experience I had mail arrive safely, but a friend who had her mail sent to one YH found that every one had been opened (though nothing was missing). This is not typical however.

Postal Rates

Because very few employees at post offices speak any English, making it difficult to obtain information on postal rates, the following list may prove useful.

OVERSEAS MAIL

AIR MAIL

	Letters		Small Packets	
Region*	First10g	Add' 10g	First 80g	Add' 20g
Zone 1	¥ 90	¥ 60	¥160	¥30
Zone 2	¥110	¥ 80	¥200	¥40
Zone 3	¥130	¥100	¥240	¥50

*Zone 1: Asia, Guam, Midway
*Zone 2: North America, Oceania, Middle
       East, Central America, Europe

*Zone 3: Africa, South America

Maximum weight:
  Letter: 2000g
  Small packet: 500g, (PNG, Myanmar, Cuba)
             1000g, (Italy, Paraguay)
             2000g, (others) depending on destination.

Aerograms: ¥90 for all regions.

Postcards: ¥70 for all regions (airmail).

Registration: ¥410 for both letters and small packets.

****

SURFACE MAIL

Letters
Up to (g)

20	¥ 90
50	¥ 160
100	¥ 270
250	¥ 540
500	¥1040
1000	¥1800
2000	¥2930

Including Oceania (Australia, NZ) and Asia (China, SE Asia, SW Asia)

Small Packets

All Countries
Up to (g)

100	¥ 130
250	¥ 220
500	¥ 430
1000	¥ 770

2000	¥1080

Registration: As for air mail.

INTERNATIONAL POSTAL REPLY COUPONS (KOKUSAI HENSHIN KITTEKEN)

These coupons are available for prepaying postage from foreign countries. Unfortunately, they are very expensive for the value received, one ¥150 coupon being exchangeable for the equivalent of the cost of seamail postage for an ordinary letter. An airmail letter would require two or more. (It can be simpler and much cheaper to send U.S. $1 bills for somewhat more than the estimated cost.)

****

PARCEL POST

Region

	Surface		Air		SAL*	
	500g	Each add'l 500g	1000g	Each add'l 1000g	1000g	Each add'l 1000g
1	¥1700	¥ 350	¥1800	¥ 600	¥1500	¥250
2	¥2100	¥ 600	¥2200	¥ 700	¥1700	¥400
3	¥2500	¥ 850	¥2700	¥1150	¥1800	¥550
4	¥3200	¥1400	¥3400	¥1600	¥2200	¥450

**Via Siberia: ¥2300/800

Zone 1: East Asia
Zone 2: Southeast Asia, Southwest Asia
Zone 3: North America, Oceania, Middle East, Europe, Central America, former USSR
Zone 4: Africa, South America

*SAL (Surface Air Lifted): By air to destination country; by land from there.

DOMESTIC MAIL

Letters (First Class)*

Up to (g)

25*	¥ 80
50*	¥ 90
50	¥ 130
100	¥ 190
250	¥ 270
500	¥ 390
1000	¥ 700
2000	¥ 950
3000	¥1,150
4000	¥1,350

*Dimensions must be within 90 x 140 mm minimum, 120 x 235 x 10 mm maximum

Registration: ¥420 min. (up to ¥10,000; ¥10/¥5000 extra up to ¥500,000)
Express (Special Delivery): ¥350

up to 250g	¥270
to 1000g	¥370
to 4000g	¥630

Parcels

Cost depends on distance; the following are min/max prices.

Weight (kg)	Cost
2	¥510–1,020
4	¥630–1,180
6	¥750–1,340
8	¥870–1,500
10	¥930–1,580
12	¥830–1,380

Telecommunications

Telephones

The telephone system in Japan is very well developed, and it is easy to phone anywhere in the country or the world.

Local calls cost ¥10 per minute. If no more coins are put in, the call will be terminated at the end of that time. Extra coins can be fed in advance; some phones accept only ¥10 coins, while others take both 10s and 100s. Because of the large number of types of phone and the lack of English instructions on most, a few notes will be useful.

There are several types of public (pay) phones. The most common type of phone is olive green. There are two types: some accept ¥10 and ¥100 coins plus "phone cards", while others accept only the cards. These phones can be used for calls anywhere in Japan, and a green phone with a gold front plate and a symbol of a globe and telephone can be used for international calls (see below). Excess coins can be deposited to ensure that the call will not be terminated; the surplus will be refunded at the end of the call. ¥100 coins will be used in preference to ¥10 coins if both are deposited.

The phone card is a type of credit card ("debit card", technically) for a fixed amount (¥500, ¥1000, etc.) purchased at tobacco and other shops. The card is put into a slot and the cost of the call is automatically deducted during the call from the credit value contained in magnetic memory on the card. The amount of credit remaining is shown by an indicator on the phone (in units of ¥10), and the card is returned at the end of the call for further use until its value is used up. Phone cards are particular useful for expensive calls, such as international calls.

Other types of phone have been used commonly in the past, and may still be encountered in various parts of the country for some time to come. Red phones, sometimes with a gold band, can be used for local or intercity calls. They can hold six ¥10 coins, take them one at a time as the time period expires, and return any unused coins. They are found in many shops, stations, etc.

Blue phones are identical in function to large red phones, although rare examples also take ¥100 coins.

Pink pay phones are found in private homes and operate exactly the same as red ones.

Yellow phones are the same in function as red ones, except that they can hold up to ten ¥10 coins and nine ¥100 coins. Like green phones, they are useful for intercity direct-dialled calls.

Green, yellow, and blue phones can be used for making emergency calls without coins. Emergency numbers for use anywhere in Japan are: Police 110; Ambulance 119. However the person answering will probably only speak Japanese.

A full Japanese phone number has nine or ten digits, usually in three groups. The first group is the area code and is used only when dialling from another zone; usually only the second two groups are written. If, however, all three are shown, for some peculiar reason brackets are often written around the second group, not around the area code as is usually done in other countries. The latter method is sometimes used in Japan and is used in this book.

Long-distance calls within Japan (more than 60 km) are cheaper on Saturdays, Sundays, and national holidays, and between 1900 and 0800. The discount is about 40 per cent. For information on long-distance calls within Japan, call 0120-

019019 (toll free).

International

In theory, calls can be made to any country, although it is doubtful that a call would actually be completed to North Korea or the like. Calls can be made through an operator or by dialling directly. To call the overseas operator, dial 0051 from anywhere in Japan. For information about overseas calls, ring 0057. Rates have been quite high in the past, though they are now not much different from those in the USA.

Collect calls can be made to Canada, USA, South Korea, Hong Kong, Taiwan, Australia, and western Europe.

ISD (International Subscriber Dialling) calls can be made from any private telephone not specifically disabled, from hotels, and from many pay phones (any green phone with a gold front plate and a symbol of a globe and telephone, plus yellow phones). Just have a phone card or a good supply of ¥100 coins! To begin a directly-dialled overseas call from one of these phones, first dial "001", then the country code, and then the number.

Calls are billed in units of six seconds. This means that a brief call, such as a "yes" or "no" answer, can be made very cheaply; there is no one-minute or three-minute minimum.

Telegrams

Within Japan, telegrams can be sent in roman letters from major post offices and offices of the telegraph company, NTT.

Overseas telegrams can be sent to most countries of the world and are accepted in roman letters at telegraph, telephone, or post offices. Hotels catering to foreign customers can also help.

Any group of 10 letters is accepted as one word, so words may be run together to economise (as long as the recipient can successfully separate them; remember that letters can get mistransmitted).

Intelpost

In effect, "International Electronic Mail" is a fancy name for facsimile (FAX) transmission of messages by the post office to a corresponding post office in the receiving country, from where it is delivered to the addressee. Messages can be left at large post offices in major cities, such as the international post office branch in Tokyo. The service is available to a large number of countries around the world.

HEALTH AND SAFETY

Food and Water

It is very unlikely that anyone will become ill in Japan as the result of eating or drinking. Food sold is of high standard, milk sold everywhere is pasteurized (UHT method), and tap water can be drunk anywhere in the country. The digestive troubles that you expect in most of Asia are virtually unknown. Food from mobile stalls, often seen at night near railway stations, is safe to eat.

Consumption of water in another manner, however, *can* be harmful. Swimming cannot be recommended in most populated areas of Japan, even at beaches rated as "suitable" or "very suitable" by the Environment Agency. A few years ago, doctors at the U.S. Navy base at Yokosuka made their own assessments, using American standards, of 32 beaches in the Shonan and Miura-hanto areas near Tokyo that were given the two above ratings—and warned base personnel against swimming at 25 of them. Several of the "very suitable" beaches were rated as "particularly bad".

In addition to polluted water, beaches are usually covered with rubbish abandoned to the elements by the thousands of daily holiday-makers. Oneness with nature in action.

Medical

The standards of health care in Japan are good, as reflected in longevity. According to government statistics (1987), the average expectancy for men is 75.6 years, 81.4 for women, which is the highest in the world. Medical personnel are generally trained to high standards and many Japanese doctors would rate high in any country. Likewise, there are many good hospitals with up-to-date equipment and facilities.

The other side of the coin is that Japan has its full share of quacks and unqualified practitioners who, if they got through medical school at all, did so more through money and influence than by merit. So if any serious procedure, like an operation, is suggested, be sure to get a second opinion even if the first doctor complains about losing face. Better his face than your health and wealth. More than a few foreign residents plan to go home if serious medical attention is required.

Most residents after a while hear of hospital "horror stories". One that I can trace to the source involved a foreign resident who was operated on for a ruptured appendix with only a local anaesthetic. Part-way through the operation, while his innards were literally laid on the table beside him, his wife was taken into the operating room and greeted by the horrific sight. (He did live, fortunately.) On another occasion, the victim of a stabbing was taken by ambulance from one hospital to another over a period of two hours, and was rejected at each because it was "busy". Hè died.

On balance, several people have written to the English-language papers praising the staff of various hospitals for the excellent service during treatment.

Hospital charges tend to be very high, and there is a tendency to keep patients longer than necessary (by western standards) in order to increase the hospital's income, especially at hospitals that are privately owned by doctors.

Several hospitals in the large cities were founded by various Christian groups; their approach to medical care would be more familiar to westerners, so anyone needing hospital care should try to contact them. Also in the larger cities there are several western doctors with whom foreigners will be able to talk more easily. The Tokyo TIC can give more information on these doctors and hospitals.

Hope that you do not suffer a heart attack or similar health emergency while in Japan, for ambulance personnel are prohibited from giving any paramedical treatment during the trip to the hospital. Doctors have locked up all rights to giving medical treatment, regardless of the effect on the health and well-being of the populace.

The common types of shots normally required for overseas travel can be obtained conveniently in Tokyo at the Kotsu Kaikan ("Travel Building") not far from the Tokyo TIC in Yurakucho. Slotted into this building along with travel agents, *minshuku*, and *ryokan* booking offices and other travel-related businesses, is an office where qualified personnel spend every working day jabbing or zapping (pressure spray injections). Costs are reasonable and they issue you with a card recording the shots.

A lower-priced but less convenient alternative for shots is the Tokyo Port Authority or the health facility at Narita airport. For the more obscure shots, these may be the only places.

Dental

Japanese dentists are equipped with the most modern instruments and facilities in the world, and much dental research is carried out in universities. Dental care is covered by national health insurance, so the standard of dental care is good. What makes Japanese teeth look bad (apart from older people in the country who have had their teeth replaced seemingly totally with gold) is hereditary malocclusion, so very large numbers of people have crooked teeth. Orthodonty is not covered by the health insurance, and the snaggle-tooth look is regarded as "cute".

Dental work for foreigners visiting in Japan will not be cheap. Getting an appointment can be a problem. There are dentists in large international hotels who take casual patients. In Tokyo and Kyoto, the TICs can give further advice.

Health Insurance

It is advisable to take out a medical insurance policy before coming to Japan because costs in Japan are extremely high. To be a doctor or dentist is to be in one of the most lucrative professions in Japan. This is reflected in the fact that prospective students at some medical schools must make a "gift" to the college of up to ¥40 million before they are admitted, and the average total cost for six years of study is ¥19 million. This of course means that only the children of wealthy parents will get into these schools, and it is the patients who have to ultimately pay off that scandalous "bribe" for entry. Being Japan this practice will probably continue ad infinitum; service for the general good is not a generally admired concept.

Private health insurance can be purchased within Japan; AIU was one of the pioneers in this line of coverage.

Foreign residents of Japan (non-tourist visa) may be eligible for Japanese health insurance, but this varies from one locality to another.

Personal Hygiene and Care

Birth Control

The main methods of contraception in Japan are the condom, pessaries (tablets) that are inserted prior to intercourse (two such brands are CCC and Sampoon), gels and foams, and the diaphragm; the latter is the least popular. The message is that contraception is the responsibility of the male, and few Japanese women will be "prepared" for spontaneous sexual activity.

Abortions are readily available at moderate cost and with no difficulty for both Japanese and foreign women.

The Pill is not generally available to Japanese women, so foreign women in Japan using it should make sure that they have their own supply. Foreign brands are not sold in Japan, and the only type sold in Japan is a very high dosage type intended for cycle regularizing, not contraception. Any woman using the pill should bring adequate supplies with her to Japan and arrange for supplies to be sent by mail from overseas if more are needed. The pill is not available in Japan because of lobbying by gynecologists who would lose a lucrative business if the number of abortions that they performed were reduced. Because the number of these specialists is decreasing anyway, there will be less opposition to selling the pill in Japan (the country has a huge export trade in them), and there is talk of allowing their use eventually.

Familiar (foreign) brands of sanitary protection will be found only at pharmacies like the American Pharmacy that cater to foreign clientele; Tampax is the only internationally-known brand distributed nationwide.

Mental Health

If you get the "coming unstuck" feeling, need advice or help in personal matters, or just need someone to talk to for any reason, there is a small choice of agencies who can help.

Tokyo English Lifeline (TELL) offers confidential and anonymous counselling by telephone; they can also refer callers to other agencies that might be able to help. In Tokyo the number is (03) 3264-4347. Another useful organisation is Tokyo Community Counselling Service; it refers callers to professional counsellors in a variety of fields; tel (03) 3403-7106.

Tokyo Tapes offers an extremely useful and comprehensive range of tape recorded information. Callers phone and request one or more tapes by number. For a listing of tapes by number, tel (03) 3262-0224 and ask for tape 302. The listing is also available from Tokyo Tapes, 610 Homat Commodore, 5-13-28 Roppongi, Minato-ku, Tokyo 106; and from the sponsoring organisations, the Franciscan Chapel Center, St Alban's, St Paul's Lutheran, Tokyo Baptist, and Tokyo Union churches.

Toilets

Most toilets in Japan are the Asian squatting type. These are supposedly physiologically the best kind and are personally hygienic because no part of the body comes in contact with it. Whether the squatting position is as advantageous as purported is difficult to say; negative evidence is that about a third of the population develops hemorrhoids. Many Westerners find them uncomfortable and undignified, and anyone with difficulty squatting and rising will have problems. However, unless you continually travel first class, you will face the need to use one at some time. Face the raised part, and be careful not to let anything fall out of your pockets; some people completely remove their trousers to avoid such an occurrence.

Most public toilets have no paper, so it is wise to have your own when travelling away from familiar territory. There are often vending machines for tissues at the entrance. Where paper is provided, it is almost uniformly of extremely poor quality.

All Western-style hotels, some *ryokan*, and most large and modern office buildings and department stores have clean, western-style facilities. Some Westerners who are remaining in one city for some time make mental notes of their location and plan their daily itinerary to include a visit to one.

In private homes, youth hostels, *ryokan*, *minshuku*, and other residential places, there will be a separate pair of slippers at the entrance to the toilet area. Take off the house slippers and change into the toilet ones. Don't forget to change back again when leaving, and never wear the house slippers into the toilet—both are social gaffes without peer. It all becomes instinctive after a while.

Don't be surprised or shocked at the sight of men urinating in public, especially at night after coming out of a bar after an evening of hard drinking. Even in daylight it is not unknown to see one facing a wall. (One cabinet minister was photographed taking a leak against a tree in public a few years back.)

VD and AIDS

Venereal diseases exist in Japan, although the rate of occurrence is not notably high. Despite the denials by some government ministers of the very existence of prostitution in Japan, sexual services are very readily available. One of the more popular places for this activity is the "soaplands" described elsewhere, and health surveys have found that about 70 per cent of men contracting one or other of these diseases was infected at such a place.

Although not many more than 40 AIDS sufferers had been reported identified by the government by mid-1987, of whom 27 had died, and 298 carriers had been identified, there are suspicions that there is a greater risk of the disease than is acknowledged by the authorities and that the number of infected persons is higher.

One such risk is that some of the numerous men who have made "sex tour" journeys to the fleshpots of nearby Asian countries have been infected with AIDS and will eventually develop the disease. (The "working girls" of Thailand have a very high rate of AIDS infection.) There is no reason why some of those travellers will not infect some of the girls working in commercial-sex establishments in Japan. Any heterosexual male indulging in this aspect of Japanese life should take necessary precautions against acquiring an unwanted souvenir of Japan. (Many prostitutes require use of a condom.) A potential side-benefit of the exclusionary nature of Japanese society is that many sex establishments make foreigners unwelcome, especially since the AIDS scare began.

According to a knowledgeable source, about 10,000 of the estimated 300,000 male homosexuals are AIDS virus carriers, and current medical thinking is that 5 to 20% of these could develop full-blown AIDS within five years. Thus, anyone inclined to this lifestyle should take note, and also be aware that many establishments catering to homosexuals seem to consider that they are doing all that is necessary to prevent the spread of AIDS by barring the entry of foreigners. (Many Japanese homosexuals apparently still believe that AIDS is only a "white man's disease", an attitude not difficult to acquire given the type of coverage of the disease in Japanese media.)

All blood used for transfusions is checked for AIDS contamination.

Smoking

About 66% of Japanese males smoke, the highest percentage in the world (although this is down from 80% in 1966). Not unexpectedly, the number of deaths due to lung cancer has quadrupled since 1950. As with smoke everywhere, the problem does not end with the smoker, but the pollution affects everyone in the vicinity. Japan is about 20 years behind the advanced western countries in making public areas smoke-free, although some progress has been made. Anyone in Japan is likely to be subjected to second-hand smoke in intercity trains, restaurants, and almost any public area. (Most trains do have non-smoking cars, and their numbers have been increasing.)

Public Baths

The Japanese bath is promoted as an aid to relaxation, etc., and certainly can be a very enjoyable experience. As for public baths (sento), though, some caveats may be in order, particularly for women.

Many baths provide small stools for patrons to sit on while washing. There are rumors that some sexual diseases may be transmitted by sitting on them. This is not confirmed fact, but it would be wise for a woman to use caution and squat while washing, as many Japanese women do, rather than sit on the stool.

Also likely to be of more concern to women than to men is the practice of Japanese mothers of taking their babies into the bath with them. Anyone familiar with the physiological reaction of an infant when placed in warm water will understand why some women do not like to use the large communal pool.

There are reports that athletes' foot is prevalent. Again, the public bath is suspect. Use caution.

Natural Hazards

Japan is a relatively benign country, but there are several hazards that can threaten one's safety, or even life. These notes will give some warning as to hazards to watch out for.

Radon Gas

In other countries the radioactive gas radon is regarded as a serious health hazard due to its ability to be drawn into the lungs and possibly trigger cancer. (It is emitted slowly from granite and other rocks, and can collect in basements. Campaigns are being carried out in Canada and elsewhere to minimize this build-up.) In Japan it occurs in some hot spring waters, and is actually touted as a health *cure* for a huge range of illnesses! Why it is safe only in Japan is truly wondrous. The amount breathed in during one visit to such a hot spring would probably be negligible, but a word to the wise is not out of place.

Wildlife

Snakes

There are two kinds of poisonous land snake in Japan, the *mamushi* and the *habu*, both potentially deadly. All the main islands are the habitat of the *mamushi*, while the *habu* is found only on the islands south of Kyushu, between Kagoshima and Okinawa. Like most snakes, they will usually try to escape from people if they are not cornered or startled. Snakes are deaf and cannot hear people's approach in advance, so it's quite easy to be upon one before it has a chance to hide. It is best to walk heavily, perhaps tapping the ground with a

walking stick, because they can feel vibrations in the ground and get out of the way.

The *mamushi* usually grows to a length of 700 mm or so, and has a diamond-shaped head and a moderately thick body covered with a pattern of dark circles with lighter centers. It can be found in any grassy area, and a friend informed me that his friends were wary of walking in tall grass in riverside recreation areas not far from Tokyo. The habu is larger, up to two meters long, and has the stronger venom of the two. It has a diamond-shaped head and a pattern of diamonds on its body. It is found in both trees and grass, and is always present in pineapple fields.

Bite victims can be saved if they can receive anti-venin in time. The limb should have a tournequet of sufficient tightness to minimize circulation of the venom without cutting off all circulation. The larger islands have treatment centers for *habu* bites.

Bears

Bears kill a few people every year, almost always intruders in the animals' habitat. Most bears, and most attacks, occur in Hokkaido. Attacks are most frequent when the mother has a cub.

Foxes

In recent years, many tourist promoters have been publicizing the Hokkaido fox (*kita-kitsune*) as a symbol (read "gimmick", *cute* sub-variety) of Hokkaido because of its friendly nature. For example, a farm for the foxes opened at Rubeshibe in April 1983 and became popular quickly. (Anything "cute" is sure-fire in Japan.)

If you go there, do not touch any of the foxes. The majority carry the parasitic worm echinococcus that causes a serious disease of the liver in humans, and it can be transferred just by contact. The promoters are doubtless aware of this, but commerce comes before health.

Wasps

As if any other worries were needed, there can be a danger from wasps in wild areas, particularly in the period from mid-August to early September when they are breeding and protecting the queen. In 1986, four persons died in Hokkaido of shock or other effects related to wasp stings. This was described as "very rare" by the police, but the newspaper report continued with the news that 31 people had died in 1985 after being stung by wasps and "horntails". Persons with allergies are most susceptible to ill effects from the venom. Beware of nests.

Mosquitos

Like most countries of the world, Japan has mosquitoes; not in huge swarms, but enough to make it advisable to use insect repellent. Their bites are relatively innocuous, but you can find mosquitos (or vice versa) from summer at least to late November.

Water Safety

Beaches

Lifesaving is very much lacking at public beaches in Japan, and there are often up to 50 or more drownings on a summer weekend. Many of these are due to swimming after drinking, but many of Japan's popular swimming beaches have dangerous undertows. (If you get caught in one, swim with it into deeper water, and work your way back to shore at a calmer place. Never try to swim against it.) If you go into the water, be sure that you are with a buddy who can swim well.

Sea snakes

All sea snakes are deadly venomous. Fortunately, they are found only in tropical wa-

ters, and they usually do not bother people who do not bother them. Nearly all are brilliantly colored and easy to see.

Jellyfish

A seasonal ocean hazard is jellyfish. In June 1987 about 300 persons were treated for stings on one weekend. (That is the only year in which I have seen any such reports.)

Sharks

Sharks are not regarded as a hazard in Japanese waters, although one unfortunate girl was killed by one in the early 80s while being pulled behind a boat off the south coast of Kyushu. The southern islands are close enough to the tropics that they are within the ambit of several species.

Earthquakes

Earthquakes are common throughout Japan due to its geology. Most quakes are very mild, a mere tremble (the vast majority only show up on instruments), and not enough to cause any damage.

The most famous disaster was the Kanto earthquake of 1923 when about 40,000 people were killed in the Tokyo and Kanto area. Buildings of that day were mostly flimsy wooden structures and many of the deaths were the result of fires that followed the quake. All buildings in the Tokyo area must now be built to resist earthquake damage, so an equally strong quake today would probably cause a lower death toll despite the vast increase in population. Nevertheless, in January 1995, an earthquake of a magnitude of 7.2 in the Kobe area killed about 5,900 people and caused thousands to be homeless. The Japanese government now realize the necessity for reconsidering its construction standards.

If you are caught in a strong quake, the best actions to take are: 1) Do not use elevators. 2) Stand near a supporting pillar or in a doorway, and far from the center of the room; the former will be the strongest part of the structure, and the center of a room is the part most likely to collapse. Ducking under a desk or table is a good second-best, and better than no protection at all from falling debris. 3) Get outdoors if possible and move as far as possible away from buildings.

Fire

Modern hotels in Japan meet good standards of fire safety. There are stringent statutes on the books, and most hotels meet the requirements. Any of the large international hotels can be expected to meet high standards, as can the majority of hotels aimed more at domestic travellers. However, tragic fires, with large loss of life, have shown that not all is perfect.

A fire in the Hotel New Japan (Tokyo) in 1982 took 33 lives because there were no sprinklers nor fire-blocking doors. The manager had, for several years, ignored repeated instructions by the fire department to install sprinklers and take other measures to improve fire safety, and the authorities had been lax in enforcing the regulations.

A fire at one elderly *onsen* (hotspring resort) inn in Atagawa (Shizuoka-ken) in February 1986 took 24 lives. In this case the building was old and constructed of wood, a left-over from the ticky-tacky era of construction in Japan, and a classic firetrap. (Another onsen hotel fire at Kawazu (same prefecture) later killed 57.) As it turns out, hostelries older than a certain age (and thus the most hazardous) are exempted from the law requiring them to install sprinklers "because of the high costs that would result". In addition, in this case, the fire alarm system had been disabled by the staff ("because it had gone off several times, giving a false alarm"), the emergency doors were locked, and the only staff members with keys for the doors (if they knew where the keys were) had fled as soon as the fire was identified.

Some precautions to take are:

-Try to find out if the sprinkler system (if installed) actually works. Likewise, the fire alarm system. (The problem here is that it is simple for staff to say "yes" to a question whatever the truth.)

-Learn the location of fire exits in any new accommodation.

-Check personally that fire exit doors can be opened from the inside without use of a key. If the doors are locked and a custodian keeps the keys and "will open the door if necessary", consider either demanding the key or looking for another place to stay. Don't let Japanese lack of foresight take your life.

-Look at the staff and decide if they seem to have the welfare of their guests at heart (or the wit to be of any use in an emergency). Greed and carelessness of life are not totally absent from Japan.

Hotels in *onsen* and other resort areas should be regarded as particularly hazardous in general because the main aim of most of the male visitors is revelry, which invariably involves large volumes of alcohol. In view of the very heavy smoking by the male population, the use of tatami (grass) mats in the rooms, and general carelessness when having a good time (true in any country), the potential for a blaze is higher than in most other places in the country.

Movie theaters are a potential hazard in Japan, and it is surprising that there has not been at least one disastrous fire in one in recent years. It is common practice of theater managers to allow up to double the seating capacity into the building, to the point that every aisle is packed with people. And, despite signs prohibiting smoking, people (often petty gangsters) light up with seeming impunity. If faced with the prospect of a jammed cinema, it might be wiser to pass up that performance.

Doors

Causing all the aforementioned to pale into insignificance as a hazard is the warning that anyone taller than 175 cm must be on constant guard for low doorways. Until recently the Japanese were a very short people and doorways were made to suit. The frames for doors and sliding room dividers (*shoji*) seem to have a uniform height of 180 cm. Train entrances are also low.

Tables

It sounds facetious, but tables in restaurants and other public places are also a hazard, to all long-legged foreigners. There is a crossbar (or shelf) under just about every table, positioned exactly where any such tall person will crack his or her kneecap on it. Slide under slowly! (This never seems to bother the Japanese, obviously because of their shorter legs.)

Hazards from Your Fellow Man

Japan is one of the safest countries in the world. Most visitors will not likely encounter any trouble or problem during a visit. However, like so many other aspects of Japan, safety in the country has been exaggerated and distorted by a succession of articles in the foreign press (and just possibly abetted by domestic sources). Based on the reasoning that the more one knows the better-off one is, the following is the actual situation regarding safety in Japan. The information may run counter to popular belief, but is accurate.

Theft

For theft of personal belongings, such as cameras, Japan is one of the lowest-risk countries in the world. Probably the riskiest places are those with large numbers of tourists, such as the airports. (A sign at the Tokyo City Air Terminal warns of pickpockets; though not stated, these are most likely to be from third-world countries rather than Japan.) Generally though, particularly away from the large cities, you could leave a suitcase unattended for hours almost anywhere and find it still there and untampered with when you returned. There are even tales of absent-minded people leaving cameras on park benches and returning hours later to find them still there, but it isn't recommended to try it. The average Japanese is just very honest. Lost goods will more than likely be turned in to the police or transport authority, so if you leave something valuable behind on a train don't give up, as there is a good chance it has been handed in.

The remarks on theft and honesty do not apply to umbrellas; these will disappear without a trace if left in an unlocked drip tray on a rainy day.

Bicycles and motorcycles should be locked whenever left untended. My Honda 550 was wheeled away from in front of my house one night and was found some days later minus some rather costly parts. A friend who knows the motorcycle scene reports that there are professional motorcycle thieves in operation who just load parked bikes into their truck and take off in a minute or two. They are most interested in the newest, flashiest models.

Bicycles are also susceptible to "disappearance".

Your belongings are usually safe in your room in a youth hostel if you are sharing with Japanese. They leave their belongings unattended in a way that would horrify most westerners. It is usually more necessary to be wary of other foreigners than of Japanese.

Burglaries are quite common in the big cities, although they are rarely reported in the English-language papers. Readers planning to reside a while should take all the usual precautions applicable in any western city. In small towns you may find that the locals don't bother locking their doors very much, but don't be insulted if they do start locking up when a foreigner moves into the neighborhood!

Physical Safety

Japan is one of the safest countries in the world for foreigners and locals alike for assault and rape. In general it is safe to walk on *most* streets of any city or town without risk of assault, mugging, or worse. However, the situation is not perfect, and a few realistic observations would not go amiss.

Violent crime is quite uncommon in daily life. (Disregard the dozens of hoodlums who have been murdered in gangland wars. These incidents usually do not affect the general populace. If they did, the police would start hassling the hoods instead of giving them relatively free rein.)

There have been sufficient letters in the English-language newspapers, and word-of-mouth reports from persons close to the events, about unprovoked attacks on foreigners to make it apparent that the potential for danger does exist, and that one should be prepared to avoid it. Some men have written that they have been set upon by drunks or mentally deficient laborer types (usually combinations thereof) and, unfortunately, more than a few women (particularly those living in "foreigner house" type of private accommodation) have also been subject to unwanted atten-

tion in the form of being kicked or punched for doing nothing more than walking down the street.

The motives are probably a combination of disliking foreigners (a sentiment just beneath the surface in parts of Japanese society) and, in the case of the women, resentment of their freedom and failure to conform to the restrictions that the feeble minds of the assailants think to be appropriate to all women. (They have to feel superior to *somebody*.)

Fortunately, when such attacks occur, the booze has often diminished the ability of the attacker sufficiently that he is more of an annoyance than a danger, but this is not always the case.

A teen-age American girl resident in Japan once wrote to a Tokyo newspaper reporting that she had been attacked by a man with the intention of rape when she was walking home (a considerable distance) in the wee-smalls of the morning. (She knew what he planned because he knew all the English words and was telling her what he was going to do to her.) In response, several other readers wrote to say that she had been very foolish to be out alone at such an hour, and that the safety of Japanese cities was more of a myth than reality. It has also been written that many women who do report being raped or otherwise assaulted receive little sympathy from the police, and many have been made to feel as if *they* had been responsible for the attack. (Others have reported very sympathetic treatment; like everything in Japan, it's very much case-by-case.) The effect, whatever the percentage of considerate treatment, is that a large percentage of rapes are believed to go unreported. One reason is that the women do not want the "shame" to become general knowledge, and so keep quiet.

Because of the random nature of such attacks, the best defence is simply to be aware that such things can happen and to avoid being in isolated places where they would be likely to happen, particularly after most people have gone to sleep, or to travel with someone who can be of some protection.

If, by the way, things ever get to the physical stage, there are two things to remember. First, all too often no one will come to your aid. In Japan one just doesn't get involved in the affairs of anyone other than family or acquaintances. Secondly, if the police are involved, any foreigner present is automatically suspected of being the culprit (regardless of circumstances and protestations), and is likely to be taken to the police station even if he is an innocent bystander. (This may sound like paranoia, but there have been enough reports of it actually happening over the years that one must see a pattern in police actions.)

There have been other disturbing reports of actual refusal of Japanese to provide any help even when implored directly. One foreign woman reported having been followed for a considerable time in the downtown area of Tokyo by a man who would not leave her alone. She went into a hotel and asked for help, requesting that they call the police. The staff refused. A foreign man was similarly beset in a train station, this time by two drunken laborers, and the railway personnel simply refused to call the police and would not give him help. In another case that became well known in 1987, a Japanese woman was being molested by a drunk Japanese man, a high-school physical education teacher. In desperation she pushed him away, with the result that he fell onto the tracks and was killed by a train. Editorials commented that it would not have happened if the many bystanders had taken a hand and helped her, instead of ignoring her cries for help.

A possible explanation for part of the problems that western women have in Japan is the many books and movies that present a very distorted view of westerners in general, especially their sexual habits. "Comic" books (*manga*) are notorious for their vivid depiction of rapes, torturing of women, etc., so it is easy to understand how so many men can get twisted ideas both about western women, and about the relationship between men and women in general. There is an anti-foreigner bias in much of the media and films, so things that would never see the light of day in the western world are common in Japan. (The term "yellow journalism" comes to mind.)

The sight of a foreign woman can have a strange effect on many Japanese men. It is not uncommon for foreign women to be openly propositioned, and it is (unfortunately) not at all uncommon for men to expose themselves to them on trains, in parks, and even on the streets. (They do it also to Japanese women, but it seems that they get bonus points from the perverts association if they can do it to a western woman.) One American friend who was walking home in the evening was spotted by a man driving by. He stopped his car and got out, opened his fly and chased her a considerable distance to her house, masturbating all the way. (When her neighbors heard her call for assistance, they turned off their lights!)

Another friend, a blonde German woman, was on holiday in northern Japan. While walking around the perimeter of Lake Tazawa, within one hour three cars driven by young men stopped a short distance after passing her, the drivers got out, and each one pulled down his pants to expose himself. She returned to town in disgust.

By comparison with such excitement, the numerous subway gropers and flashers are almost tame. Most of these characters are not racist in outlook, and are just as happy with Japanese women as foreign. Any Japanese woman can tell that such men are active on almost all train lines, particularly during the rush periods. One flasher in Osaka became famous because he wore a ribbon of a different color each day of the week on his exposed member.

What to do in such cases? If possible, try to ignore the incident. This may be sufficient to discourage him. Pointing and laughing hysterically might have a deflating effect. In other circumstances, it might be necessary just to run. Yell and make as much fuss as possible. Depending on the circumstances, some appropriate words for the occasion are:

> *chikan* (pervert)
> *omawari-san* (police!)

However, advice often seen is that it is better for a woman to scream "kaji!". This means "fire", and the word is more likely to get attention than any other.

For subway gropers, various suggestions have been to shout "chikan" and to step on his instep.

To put matters in perspective, how many foreign men have been brainwashed by the false image of the seductive and pliable "Asian woman".

SHOPPING

Even back in the good old days, when a U.S. dollar was worth vastly more yen and yen price tags were lower, there were relatively few bargains in Japan. The only good buys (pricewise) were in cameras and other optical goods, electronic products (radios, hi fi gear, etc.), watches, motorcycles, cars, and oil tankers.

Well you can forget about the oil tankers now—the Koreans are building them cheaper.

As for the other goods, prices have gone up with inflation, as they have everywhere, and the value of the yen has skyrocketed, so that there are even fewer "bargains" today, if the word means only low prices.

However, the quality of Japanese manufactured goods has been excellent for years and has continued to improve, and there are features undreamed-of only a few years ago, so you are paying more but getting value for money.

It comes as a surprise to most westerners to find that many Japanese-made goods cost more in Japan than they do at home. There is more than one reason. One (and the one heard always from Japanese sources) is that the distribution system in Japan is notoriously long and complex, with many links in the chain, each of which tacks on its mark-up. Foreign importers can usually buy in huge volume and distribute the goods more efficiently and therefore more cheaply. Another reason is that large Japanese companies selling overseas always go for market share, even at the expense of profits, so they are willing to sell abroad at negligible profit (if necessary) in order to keep a foothold. There are suspicions that they are selling many products in the U.S. market (and probably others) at a loss, but this is denied, for that practice is known as "dumping" and is illegal in the U.S. Where the truth lies is not for us to learn easily, but the fact is that even where import duties are applied, prices are often lower overseas than in Japan.

Japan's distribution system is actually a form of social welfare. Many of the people employed in sales and distribution have relatively few skills, do not work for companies that can pay large retirement pensions, and are actually surplus to the task of distributing the goods, but are supported by the system as a type of tax.

Something to keep in mind when looking for Japanese products is that a large number of Japanese goods sold overseas are made for export only and are never seen on the domestic market. An example is the miniature cast-iron grill called a "hibachi"; this item has never been used in Japan, and can be found in Japan only in stores selling to U.S. service people. (A true hibachi is a large ceramic pot that holds burning charcoal for heating purposes.) So if a friend at home asks you to buy something that is made in Japan, in most cases you would be advised to decline politely. Unless it is something used in Japan, it will probably be impossible to find, and if it is a common and competitive product (like a camera), it may well be cheaper at home (if home is a country that does not impose large duties and taxes).

One of the big surprises about Japan is that much of its industry is small and inefficient. (In 1986, over 81 per cent of Japan's exports were accounted for by only three categories of industry: steel, automobiles, and high-technology goods.) The large assemblers of components, like the car manufacturers, buy many of their parts from very small companies (usually family workshops) that may have only a few pieces of machinery and depend on long working hours by family members to survive financially.

There are many hand-made artistic and decorative items still being made with the exquisite attention to detail for which Japan has long been famous. They exhibit the best workmanship imaginable—flawless lacquerware, hand-forged swords and knives, incredibly beautiful hand-woven fabrics and textiles—the list goes on and on. Naturally, the prices for time-consuming hand labor will make these items costly, but the quality of the work justifies the price. The coexistence of the finest centuries-old artistry with some of the world's

most modern mass-produced goods is one of the fascinations of Japan.

While Japanese stores are usually very competitive with each other, especially for items like cameras and electronic goods, there is very little bargaining, and certainly none of the camel-market haggling of some countries. The Japanese regard this with contempt, as bad manners. The way to try for a discount is simply to ask politely if they can make it a little cheaper. Often the quoted price is the lowest that they can offer, although I have had one go down when I mentioned that another competing store already was selling for less than that. If the clerk can do not better on price, there is the chance that he can throw in an accessory to sweeten the deal.

When shopping for a camera, or other expensive item, it is generally not a good idea to go with a Japanese friend. Because the Japanese have little tradition of bargaining, they tend to pay the first price asked. If you are with a Japanese friend and the price you are offered with him is not as good as you've seen elsewhere, just politely postpone the purchase. Don't bluntly say you can get it cheaper somewhere else, as things aren't done that way in Japan; say you'd like to think it over.

Customs Inspection at Home

You should determine in advance what you are allowed to take back to your home country without incurring duties. Check with your embassy if you are in doubt.

Americans should take note of U.S. trade mark regulations. In addition to the dollar limit on what can be taken back duty-free, many goods of foreign origin are registered with the U.S. Customs service by trademark. These companies have the right to limit the volume of private imports of goods bearing that trademark; some companies totally ban private imports, while others place no restrictions on such activities. Items made in Japan that fall into this category include cameras, binoculars, lenses, and hi fi gear. The booklet *Trademark Information* can be picked up at the U.S. embassy in Tokyo, or ordered by mail from: Department of the Treasury, U.S. Customs Service, Washington DC 20229, or the U.S. Government Printing Office, Washington DC 20402.

Tax-Free Buying

Most goods sold in Japan have a national sales tax of 10–35 per cent imposed on them; list prices and price tags in most shops include this tax. Foreign tourists can purchase many types of goods free of this tax. A card is stapled into your passport at the time of the purchase and is removed by Customs at the port of departure. You may be asked to show that you have the item in your possession so as to ensure that the goods are taken out of the country.

Only some stores, generally located in popular tourist areas, offer goods on a tax-free (*menzei*) basis; many of these, such as camera shops, will have a prominent "Tax Free" sign. The serial number of an item must have been registered with the tax office to allow its sale tax-free. Thus, a shop selling to the domestic market would not stock tax-free items.

The tax-free price is not the lowest possible price; it is only the starting point for negotiations. For items such as cameras, you can obtain a further discount of 5–25 per cent, depending on the brand and the store.

Some "sharper" operators trade on the gullibility of tourists and sell "tax-free" but with no discount from list prices. (Shops at Narita Airport tend to operate on this system, but it must be remembered that they pay high rents.) Most shops in a competitive environment, though, will give good discounts, especially in Shinjuku (Tokyo) where competition is cutthroat.

Something to keep in mind is that the final price available from some shops selling at domestic, with-tax (*kazei*), prices can actually be lower than the final price at tax-free stores (especially for cameras). The sales tax is levied on the manufacturer's price, not the selling price, and the manufacturer may offer a large lot of merchandise at a special low price to increase sales volume, with the result that the final price is cheaper than what the tax-free stores can offer. You must check around for the best price.

Although tax-free purchasing is intended for tourists and other short-term visitors, those on working visas may be able to buy tax-free during the first six months or when planning to leave Japan.

Popular Purchases

Cameras

Cameras and lenses are among Japan's best-known products, with a reputation for quality and many features at reasonable prices relative to the performance. Before the rise in the value of the yen, the industry had virtually eliminated all international competition in 35 mm cameras, and it dominates most of the other camera markets as well. Although prices have risen in recent years, they are lower than what could be expected purely in terms of the exchange rates.

Japanese-made cameras are often cheaper (10–20 per cent) in Hong Kong and Singapore, so it is worth buying at one of those places if you are going through there first. If Japan is your first stop, the ability to use the camera while in Japan will probably outweigh any savings. And, if the camera is a new model, it may not be available in another country.

The lowest prices in Japan can be found in Tokyo, especially in Shinjuku, a sub-city with many large stores of all kinds. Some shops in the Ginza area sell at reasonable prices, but others are fully aware that many well-heeled foreign tourists pass by their doors and feel no need to reduce their prices excessively. Some shops in Akihabara, the electronics area, also sell the most popular models of camera.

The Yodobashi and Sakuraya stores in Shinjuku are close to the Takano Building, and are easy to find from the station (JR Yamanote line or Marunouchi subway line) once you are above ground on the east side. Both are brightly lit and the store jingles are repetitious, incessant, and loud.

There are other branches of these two stores, plus those of Doi Camera, on both the east and west side of Shinjuku station.

As with most purchases, you should compare prices carefully if you want a bargain. Make sure you are comparing identical equipment, i.e., the same model with the same lens. Sometimes you can get a better price on a camera by buying only the body at one store, and the lens at another. If you have time to check around, you should compare the prices of buying both as a unit and separately.

Keep in mind that some stores offer lower prices by selling a camera body by a famous manufacturer along with a lens that is not made by the same manufacturer. Unless you know the brand name of the lens, it is better not to accept it. There are several independent companies that manufacture excellent lenses, but there are some smaller companies that make lenses of unknown quality. If you spend the money for a good camera, be sure that the lens matches it in quality.

Many brands of Japanese-made photographic equipment are not available in Japan. For example, one company may make the lenses sold under several different names overseas; the only private brand lenses normally available in Japan are Komura, Sigma, Tamron, and Tokina. Some companies put different nameplates on the same model of camera in different markets, and some models are never sold in Japan.

If you buy a camera, it is wise to check immediately that it is giving correct exposure and is functioning properly. Servicing is faster and much easier in Japan than elsewhere. The best way to check it (other than the simple test of operating the shutter on all speeds at the store) is to run a roll of color slide film through the camera (Kodachrome 25 or 64 films can be recommended; don't use print film) and check if the pictures are satisfactorily exposed. Test pictures should be taken of normal subjects that are evenly lighted and that do not contain large areas that are very bright or very dark. If the camera has shutter speeds that can be varied manually, use the full range of them and make a record of the setting for each shot to match them to the pictures later. If only the aperture can be varied, use the full range available. If you buy extra lenses, test them all, using the full method just described. For information regarding overnight processing of the film, see the Photography section.

For years there have been stories circulating about where manufacturers "dump" their "substandard" cameras. This is one of those old myths that never die. No reputable manufacturer allows a defective piece of equipment out the factory door. They have too much to lose by playing tricks.

Electronics & Stereo Equipment

Electronics stores in Japan, especially in Tokyo, are a gadget-lover's paradise. But before rushing in with a bulging wallet, be warned of all these pitfalls.

First, electronic products, like many other Japanese goods, are often cheaper in other countries, whether it's U.S. discount stores, duty-free stores, Hong Kong, or Singapore. In other words know your prices. (But the very latest models may not be available elsewhere.)

Next, remember that many electronic goodies are heavy, bulky, or both. With the more generous baggage allowances, this may not be a problem; check with your airline to determine the weight and size limitations. As for sending by surface mail, determine the weight limit for parcel post to your destination; for some countries it is only 10 kg (22 pounds), while for other countries it is an adequate 20 kg. Sea freight charges are not cheap; the cost just for having something crated, hauling it to the docks, and customs inspection amount to about ¥20,000; then there are the actual shipping costs, documentation charges, and possible customs clearance charges at the other end. If your baggage allowance of mail can't handle the job, the cheapest way to send an item may be air freight or air express shipment.

If you still want to buy, you'll find that many items on display are made for Japan only. Japan's electrical supply is 100 volts, with a frequency of 50 or 60 Hz (depending on the region; most appliances are convertible to either). Low-power equipment may work satisfactorily on 117 V (as in North America) but with no guarantee against damage. The frequency affects motor speeds. (In Australia, UK, Europe and most other countries, supplies are 220–240 V at 50 Hz.)

Japanese TV channels and some other specifications are different from those of most other countries, as is their FM radio band (76–90 MHz), so the Japanese domestic models are unusable elsewhere. Many portable radios now have an FM band covering both domestic and foreign bands, 76–108 MHz.

Because the local models are not usually exported, getting service and parts for them overseas could be a problem; however, many Japan-only models have export equivalents with adjustable settings.

If you are buying FM stereo equipment, note there is a specification called the "stereo de-emphasis time constant". In Australia, UK, and Europe it is 50 microseconds; in North America it is 75. The modification is simple, but would cost a serviceman's time to change. It would be simpler to buy the right model in the first place; some have a switch at the back that allows selection between the two.

Good selections of export models can be found at stores like LAOX and Yamagiwa in Akihabara (see below); they have set up a Tax Free department. Some Tax Free shops also specialise in selling the export models. Several shops in the Ginza area (along the main streets, and in the International Arcade) stock a few types of electronic equipment, especially portable items like tape recorders and radios, along with camera gear, but the range is usually limited and the higher quality models may be a little rare. Prices tend to be higher than in the "discount" areas because Ginza real estate is the most expensive in the world.

The best place in Tokyo to buy domestic models of electronic equipment is Akihabara. (The name means "Autumn Leaf Field".) The station of the JR Yamanote and Keihin-Tohoku lines exits directly into the midst of the activity. Akihabara station of the Hibiya subway line exits onto a street parallel to and one long block away from the electrical area; this street passes under the JR tracks en route. In this district there are hundreds of shops of all sizes selling everything electrical that is made in Japan. Among the stores selling tax-free goods are Laox and Yamagiwa.

Recordings

The music of a country you visit is always a good souvenir. Some Japanese music is very much an acquired taste, particularly the screechy *gagaku*, but other types can be appreciated by almost any western ear for its often haunting beauty.

Very pleasing is the music of the *koto*, a long, board-like stringed instrument played while seated on the floor, and the *shakuhachi*, or bamboo Japanese flute. The koto and shakuhachi are often combined and complement each other.

One of the most beautiful of all Japanese compositions is *Kojo no tsuki* - or "Moon over Castle ruins"; another is *Sakura Sakura*. Both should be enjoyable for any listener and are included on almost every disc of traditional Japanese music.

The CD has just about pushed vinyl discs off the shelves in Japan, just as in Western countries. Prices are typically in the ¥2000 range, although discs in the ¥800–1000 range are appearing.

Japanese phonograph records were very expensive by world standards, but the quality of the records (if you can find any) was also among the best in the world.

Clothes

Japan is not a place where you would normally look for clothes, although residents can find some good buys when they become familiar with the market. The main problem is that most off-the-rack clothes do not fit well because the physique of the average Japanese is quite different from that of most westerners (long torso/short legs relative to height). Also, regarding women's clothes, the taste in fashion in Japan is quite different from what most foreign women would want to wear. The good news is, though, that if you do manage to find some-

thing that you like and that fits, it will be of good quality and well made. The Japanese comment that clothing abroad, particularly the USA, is of rather low quality, though less expensive. They are probably comparing expensive Japanese-made garments with low-priced Korea/Taiwan/Hong Kong/China products. These can also be found in Japan.

Finding shoes to fit the average large western foot is also a problem in Japan. If you do need to buy shoes while in Japan, you could try Big Shoes Akasaka, 3-21-18 Akasaka, near Akasaka-Mitsuke subway station; Ginza Washington Shoe Store, Ginza 5-chome, diagonally opposite Matsuzakaya department store in Ginza; branches of the Isetan department store; and Ten Shoe Store, Shinjuku west side, north of the big intersection.

If you're coming through Korea, or planning a trip there from Japan, you will find that you can have clothes and shoes custom-made there cheaper than most off-the-rack clothing in Japan. But carry shoes in, for they are subject to high duty if stopped by the postal Customs office.

Antiques

The post-war days when Japanese antiques were sold for a song are long gone. The song has become an operatic chorus with full orchestral backing, and prices for almost anything really good will be from high to astronomical. They are high enough that Japanese buyers have been going overseas for a number of years and buying back Japanese items at foreign auctions. If you don't know your Japanese antiques, it is best to avoid spending large sums. If you see something that you really like, then buy it, but remember that Japanese dealers know the value of their merchandise. Prices can vary, depending on how the dealer sizes up the customer.

There are regular flea markets in Tokyo and Kyoto where stallholders set up business. The chances of finding a treasure are quite remote, as these people are not as naive as they might let on.

One warning: if you wish to examine a piece of pottery or glassware, ask the stallholder to hand it to you. The occasional unscrupulous one carefully assembles the pieces of a broken item so that it collapses as soon as anyone touches it, so the customer then has to pay for it.

Eyeglasses

Glasses are expensive in Japan. It is better to get them in Hong Kong, Singapore, or Korea, but if this is not possible, lower than usual prices are available at a type of "self-service glasses supermarket". The company, Megane no Drug, has several branches in Tokyo (and perhaps elsewhere); tel (03) 3735-0022 for information.

Calculators

For years there were no inexpensive calculators on sale in Japan such as could be found in Hong Kong and Singapore. Since about 1980, however, a large variety of down-market models has become available, priced from about ¥1000. There is a limited variety of multi-function scientific models, but most calculators are fairly basic four-function types, many in garish pink cases with cutsie-poo animals for children and young women.

Computers

There are many microcomputers made in Japan, but this a product in which the Japanese uncharacteristically have largely missed the boat. There are no bargains compared with what is available in the market in most western countries (especially the U.S.). We who live in Japan sigh in envy at the low prices shown in *Byte*

magazine and others. For a long time, floppy discs made in Japan were selling in the U.S. at about one-fifth the price in Japan. (But there is no dumping, they assure us.) The only type of computer that an overseas visitor might want would be a laptop model, but even these would most likely be much more expensive in Japan than elsewhere. The best places for computer goodies in eastern Asia are Hong Kong and Singapore. (But keep in mind the possible need for servicing for whatever you buy. And if your purchase can't be carried by hand, the shipping costs will probably make it more costly than the same or equivalent at home.)

A large number of Japanese-made computers use their own operating system, one that is not compatible with established standards in the rest of the world, so they will not work with any software other than that written specifically for them.

Watches

The electronics revolution has struck the timekeeping industry as well. There is an amazing variety of electronic watches, and they are on sale "everywhere". The lowest priced models are sold in simple and inexpensive blister-pack packaging hung on display racks. Names that have established themselves in this field are Casio and Alba. Cheapie types sell at back street discount shops for as little as ¥500, while the advertised brand models begin in the ¥1800 range and stopwatch-option models start from around ¥2500. A huge variety of more expensive digital and analog style electronic watches is also available, but they have "jewellery" designs and prices.

Have a good look when selecting a watch. A Casio watch that I bought had a shiny case that looked like metal, but it was only metal-plated plastic. After a while the plating wore off on the corners, leaving sharp metal edges that scratched my wrist. That watch, and another by the same maker, although excellent time-keepers, proved to be unable to exclude moisture from an ordinary sweaty wrist, and gave up the ghost. Either select a water-resistant model or (as I did with the replacement watch), put water-proof tape across the back to seal the joint of the case.)

Conventional mechanical watches are also manufactured in large numbers and varieties of design and price. These tend to be "prestige" models, and those made by Seiko and Citizen sell generally for rather high prices. The best single area for watch shopping is Shinjuku, both in the camera stores and in some specialist timepiece shops (on both sides of the tracks). Reasonable prices may also be found in the Akihabara area and even the up-market Ginza area.

Books

The Japanese printing industry produces some of the finest quality color printing in the world. Many books are published in English every year, including collections of photographs of Japan and works on other subjects related to the country. They make excellent souvenirs of a visit to Japan.

Actually, and not being facetious, probably the best way to see the beauty of Japan is via the pages of these often gorgeous picture books. First, the photographer takes the viewer into parts of the country inaccessible to most travellers. Second, the everyday reality of Japan is that the once-large expanses of physical beauty of the last century have been whittled away by decades of development, so it is usually necessary when sightseeing to concentrate one's view on a particular small part of the overall scene in order to see only the beautiful part and exclude the ugly. The Japanese in general are adept at

this, and the photographers do the selecting and screening job for the viewers of their books. (This selective vision process partially explains also the esthetic sense of the Japanese and their ability to enjoy small, concentrated areas of beauty, such as the stereotypical Japanese garden.) The picture books are an easy vehicle for admiring selectively.

Maruzen and Kinokuniya sell English language books in a number of cities. In Tokyo there are also Jena, Kitazawa, and Yaesu bookstores, the Tuttle shop (which displays titles of that publishing company), plus stores in the arcades of most of the large international hotels; the arcade in the Imperial Hotel probably offers the greatest selection.

Books imported from overseas are very expensive. The bookstores are still converting overseas prices to yen at a rate of about ¥145 to the U.S. dollar, a rate favorable to the stores.

Lacquerware (*makie*)

Japanese lacquerware is one of the most beautiful things you can buy in Japan. Every region produces many different objects—bowls, vases, plates, wall plaques, trays—so the variety is enormous. Some cities known for lacquerware are Kyoto, Kanazawa, Wajima, and Kamakura. Quality objects can be found in most large department stores, as well as in specialty shops. Prices of the finest pieces, with flawlessly smooth finish, gold designs, etc., can run into hundreds of thousands of yen, but smaller and less pretentious pieces can be bought for a couple of thousand. It is better not to buy extremely expensive pieces unless they will be taken to an area of relatively high humidity; in dry climates, the lacquer, or underlying wood, may crack.

Cloisonne

This is produced by soldering fine wire to a metal base to trace the outline of a pattern, then filling in the spaces with material that is fired to a glassy finish. Cloisonne is a popular purchase in Japan.

Damascene

A steel base is criss-crossed with fine lines, then pre-cut patterns of gold and silver foil are beaten onto the base. The base is etched with nitric acid, lacquer is baked onto the entire surface, then the pattern is polished out. The revealed gold and silver may then be engraved further.

Dolls

Delicate Japanese dolls make a beautiful decoration in any home. There are several styles of doll made in Japan, such as Hakata clay figurines, and the more familiar kimono-clad women with fine porcelain faces and hands. The latter vary in fineness of sculpturing, so it is wise to compare. Department, specialty, and tourist stores sell them. The few that I have bought have all come from Takashimaya department store, Nihombashi (Tokyo); they had the best selection at the time that I was looking.

Pearls

The process for culturing pearls was developed by a Japanese (Mikimoto), and they remain one of the favorite purchases in Japan. Mikimoto is still the world leader in fine pearls, but many other companies also produce good quality pearls.

In the Ise area (accessible as a day-trip from Kyoto/Nara) you can see how the oysters are induced to produce pearls, as well as seeing the largest number of these gems that you are ever likely to encounter in your life. It is a good opportunity to get an idea of the range of colors available before buying: gold, silver, grey, black, and white. It wouldn't hurt to check prices in Tokyo in advance to see if they are better at the source, but be sure you have exactly the same specifications of size, number, color, etc., so the comparison is valid. The value of the pearls varies with rarity, of course, so large pearls and some colors are worth more. Because of increasing pollution off the coast of Japan, producers are now harvesting the pearls earlier, so many pearls are being produced with a thinner coating of nacre on the irritant that is placed inside the oyster than in former years. Whether new growing areas in other parts of the world will maintain the supply of large pearls, or whether the larger ones would be a good investment, is hard to say.

Americans buying pearls should note a quirk in the law that sets a 2-1/2 per cent duty rate on unknotted strings of pearls, but 27-1/2 per cent for knotted strings.

Cars, Motorcycles & Bicycles

Information regarding the purchase of vehicles is given in the Independent Road Travel section.

Swords (*katana*)

Japanese swords are the finest weapons of their kind ever made anywhere in the world. Because of the great skill and workmanship involved in making these "jewels of steel", good swords have very high prices, often millions of yen. Few foreigners can appreciate the fine details of a good sword, such as the pattern in the grain of the steel of the blade. Consequently they do not attach the mystique to a sword that the Japanese do, and would not wish to pay the high prices demanded. "Swords" selling for ¥10,000 or so are nothing but toys, pieces of ordinary steel shaped like a sword and chrome-plated to give the outward appearance of the mirror-like side of a real sword. They are only for yokels.

Though not quite the same in purpose or construction, a good Japanese kitchen knife employs some of the features of sword-making in its manufacture, and can be an interesting, functional and cheaper souvenir than a sword. The most useful type is intended for cutting sushi, and has a blade 250–300 mm long. Better ones are made of two pieces of steel forged together, one hard but somewhat brittle for the cutting edge, the other softer and more flexible for the rest of the blade. This is the same type of construction used for a sword blade (except that swords are usually made of at least four separate pieces of steel), and the boundary between the two types of steel can be seen on close inspection.

Prices of good knives run from about ¥4500 upward, the more costly ones being of higher quality. Knives of all qualities made of ordinary carbon steel (the traditional material) have some tendency to rust, and may impart a slight metallic taste if used to cut acidic foods. Blades with sufficient alloying to make them rust-resistant do not cost much more, and can be more strongly recommended. Knives are almost universally right-handed. (It is considered something not quite normal to be left-handed in Japan.) One of these knives should last a lifetime if not abused, and can be sharpened to razor sharpness. Such knives are sold by both specialty shops and department stores, and may also be available from hardware stores.

Kimono

Although the kimono (pronounced ki-mo-no, with equal stress on all syllables) looks beautiful on Japanese women, it does not adapt well to being worn by taller western women. (A Japanese woman confided that a kimono will tend to pull open at the top if worn by a woman with breasts of any appreciable size.)

Putting on and wearing a kimono correctly is time-consuming; even Japanese women must take many hours of lessons to learn how. So-called kimono sold in tourist shops have only a passing resemblance to the real thing. If it is emblazoned with images of Mt. Fuji, shrines, temples, cherry blossoms, and Tokyo Tower, you can be sure it is not authentic.

Unfortunately, the beautiful cloth for kimono is too narrow to make into western style clothing; it could, however, be employed usefully for wall hangings or the like, and would get more exposure in this way than if worn. Good kimono cloth is extremely expensive. It may be seen in any large department store, and some smaller shops sell nothing but cloth and accessories.

Another material to consider for wall hangings is the sash (obi); some of them are also very attractive and costly.

Incidentally, although all kimono tend to look much alike to untrained eyes, there are several styles for various occasions. The length of the sleeves is one style difference; formal kimono have very long sleeves. Other differences are the coloring and the type of pattern.

Wedding kimono, the most spectacularly brilliant of all kimono, may be bought in stores in Tokyo and Kyoto at very reasonable prices. These are rental kimono that are no longer usable in business (although they appear perfect to the unknowing eye). They have no other application in Japanese life, so a kimono that might have cost a million yen new can be purchased typically for ¥10,000. Ask at the TIC offices for information on stores that stock them. (One place is shops in the nearby International Arcade.) Residents should keep their eyes open for occasional advertisements in the newspapers by department stores (in Tokyo, usually Takashimaya, Ni-hombashi store) for sales of these garments.

Model Equipment

For the model enthusiast there is a great variety of Japanese-made equipment, including engines, radio control sets, kits, etc. Most popular in recent years have been the 1/12th and 1/10th scale electric-powered radio-controlled car and buggy kits, as they are quiet and clean, and can be run almost anywhere. Engine-powered vehicles are also popular but are more of a specialty item because of the greater skill required to start and adjust the engine, although new models with recoil pull starters have simplified starting greatly. The more advanced models of these vehicles are far past the "toy" stage, being well engineered miniatures with tiny ball bearings, die-cast aluminium all-independent suspension systems with functioning shock absorbers, etc.

There is also a huge variety of aircraft and model boat kits, engines, and fittings available, far more than any one shop would have in stock. A good dealer will have catalogs of the equipment available. Japanese balsa model airplane kits have a very good reputation for quality, with perfect die-cutting, sawing, etc.

Most of the radio control sets sold are for Japanese frequencies (40 MHz), plus simple sets on the six "international" 27 MHz frequencies (usable for model cars and boats only, in most countries), but most shops can normally obtain export models of the most famous brands (Futaba, JR, Sanwa, etc.) in a few days. Be sure that the model you choose can be used legally in your country (some inexpensive models sold in Japan don't meet requirements of countries like the U.S., and the allowable frequencies are different from one country to another), and check the prices against those at home to make sure that you are not paying the same or more; many Japanese-made sets sell for substantially less in the USA, for example, than in Japan.

Japanese engines have built up a reputation for quality around the world. The best known brands, with models of almost every size, are Enya and O.S. The most exotic (and expensive) of these are a five-cylinder radial, and a four-cylinder opposed engine, both masterpieces of the machinist's art. Saito specializes only in 4-stroke engines, and also has a good reputation. (Their first model product was, and is, live steam equipment for boats: boilers and engines of various sizes and configurations are available.)

Of the many hobby shops in the Tokyo area, some with staff who speak some English are: Aile Ken 4, across from the Sweden Center (near Roppongi station; tel. 3402-0004 to ask if Ken will be in the shop); Tenshodo, in the Ginza area (on the north side of Harumi-dori, above the jewellery shop of the same name, approximately across the street from Jena bookstore); Asami, in Akihabara, on the 4th floor of a narrow, curved-front building a few shops past the T-Zone shop on Chuo dori in the direction toward Ueno; and Futaba Sangyo, also in Akihabara, in the building just before Mansei-bashi bridge (in the direction toward Ginza), across Chuo-dori from the police station.

Exquisitely detailed miniature railroad equipment is also sold in Japan, particularly HO and N scale. Some locomotives sell for as much as ¥150,000 each and are miniature masterpieces of the model maker's art. More reasonably priced model equipment is also available. Three places to look are: Tenshodo (see above); Itoya, also in the Ginza area, but on Chuo-dori north of, and on the same side of the street as, Mitsukoshi department store; and Tokyu Hands, in Shibuya, a famous department-store sized emporium of handicraft materials of every imaginable sort, and an experience in its own right. (Itoya is basically a stationery store, but always has an amazing number of specialty items rarely seen elsewhere.)

Novelties

Although Japan no longer produces the cheap toys that it was once known for during the Occupation era, several gew-gaws of various types can still be found, but you'll come across them at random. Keep your eyes open. Many visitors want to know where they can buy the plastic models of food that are seen in the window of nearly every restaurant. One place where they are sold is the Kappabashi area of Tokyo. Details are given in the Tokyo section.

Toys

A large variety of toys is made in Japan. In addition to local stores serving nearby residents, and the toy department of large department stores, there are specialist toy stores in Tokyo (and probably in the other large cities). In Tokyo, one is found in the Ginza area, southward a block or so on Chuo-dori (toward Shimbashi) and on the right from Ginza crossing. (This is in the general vicinity of the TIC, so you can get directions during a visit.) Another store is located on Omote-sando, near Harajuku, so it can be visited along with Meiji-jingu shrine.

MISCELLANEOUS INFORMATION

Addresses

Visitors to Japan should know from the outset that it is almost impossible to find a place just from the address. Even Japanese find it very difficult.

Addresses are not by street. In fact, most streets have no name at all; only the most major avenues have names, and even then, some Japanese may not be familiar with them. Addresses are by district, not by street. The smallest district is the *chome*, usually only a few blocks in area. Within the chome, each building has a one-digit or hyphenated two-digit number, e.g., 4-4. What makes the system interesting is that until 1955, the numbers were assigned by chronological order of construction, not by location!

The next larger unit may have one of several names: *cho*, *machi*, or no name at all. Next comes *ku* which is the equivalent of a ward. In Tokyo, well known ward names are Chiyoda-ku, Chuo-ku (Central Ward), Minato-ku (Harbour Ward) and Shinjuku-ku. For example an address of the form "1-2-3 Nishi-meguro" means the same as "2-3 Nishi-meguro 1-chome"; the "2-3" is the building number. (The form with the *chome* written separately is for use only by foreigners, and the simpler form will get a letter to its destination just as well.)

Japanese addresses are often written in with commas in the middle of a line, such as "1-2-3, Nishi-meguro". When the whole address is printed on a single line, this can be confusing to a reader who is unfamiliar with the system. To avoid this problem, addresses in this book are generally written with no such comma, and the "chome" number will appear first.

Published maps are available that show the breakdown of every chome, building by building, but few foreigners bother with them. It is almost universal, however, for any business, store, etc., to print a small map on its business card (*meishi*) or advertisements, showing the location relative to the nearest railway or subway station.

There was an effort during the Occupation to assign numbers and letters to the major thoroughfares of Tokyo. But this attempt to rationalise a non-system was definitely not appreciated and was dropped when the Japanese were given full control of their own affairs in 1953.

The names of cities are properly followed by the suffix *shi*, as in "Yokohama-shi". The word means "city", and is tagged on to distinguish between cities and prefectures (*ken*) of the same name; there is an Okayama-shi and Okayama-ken, for example. The cities of Kyoto and Osaka are special administrative districts known as *fu*, and Tokyo is a *to* (capital); they are not *shi*.

In the countryside there are many *mura* (villages). Another word found often in addresses in the countryside is "gun", which corresponds to "county", one step smaller than *ken*.

For mail, there is a three-digit postal code.

Electricity

Electricity service everywhere in Japan is 100 volts AC, an odd voltage used nowhere else in the world except Korea (and they're changing to 220 V). Northeast of an imaginary east-west line just southwest Tokyo, the frequency is 50 Hz (cycles/sec); southwest of the line it is 60 Hz. Most 117-volt equipment such as shavers and hair dryers, designed for use in North America, will work satisfactorily, if a little slowly or with reduced heat output. The plug is identical to that used in Canada and the USA, with two flat pins.

Photography

Japan is the land of photographers. Whatever the occasion, the Japanese take a photograph of it, with themselves or family or friends in it—front and center. Taking photos is part of the social process, as the participants in the occasion almost invariably get together a few weeks later and show/exchange photos. If they then photograph the reunion as avidly, they have the makings of an infinitely long chain of social gatherings.

The implication of this is that film is consumed in huge amounts and is available everywhere in the country. Prices are reasonable, probably comparable with those in the U.S., a bit higher than in Hong Kong and Singapore, and lower than in many other countries.

The three major film companies are the great yellow father, Kodak, and the two Japanese companies, Fuji and Sakura (Konica). Polaroid film for recent model cameras is also available. (Film is also still sold for Kodak instant cameras, a commodity no longer available in the U.S. due to the judgment of a patent suit by Polaroid against Kodak. However, U.S. Customs officers would have the right to seize the film if they found it in someone's luggage.)

The vast majority of film sold for the amateur market is for color prints. Color slides are not popular (no prints to share with others!), and represent only about 10 per cent of film sales. This means that slide film can be difficult to find outside the big cities.

Kodak films are a known quantity around the world, with a well-deserved reputation for quality products. Color print films of both Fuji and Sakura are both well regarded, giving good color and grain in all speed types.

Color slide films from Fuji have been building up a good reputation overseas, but Sakura color slide films have not yet established themselves as being in the same league as the other two.

Processing

Prints

Because of the vast number of color prints made every year, processing is available "everywhere" and at reasonable cost; color prints cost as little as ¥20. Films left at local camera shops will usually be processed and returned in one to two days, although there are companies that will do it in as little as an hour. (If the chemicals are changed on schedule, the results can be quite OK, but if not, the colors can be rather strange. If time permits, there is the likelihood of better quality if the lab has more time.) There are depots around the larger cities where film may be left in the morning and picked up the same day.

Slides

All slide films can be sent for processing by any camera shop in the country. The seven-hour developing depots can get Ektachrome and the Japanese slide films developed in three to four days. For faster service of Kodak slide films (Kodachrome ordinarily takes six to eight days), take your film to the Kodak depot in the Ginza and ask for fast processing. They can have the films back in two days.

Kodachrome with prepaid processing, is not sold in Japan. In the U.S., camera stores sell mailers for processing processing 20 and 36 exposure rolls of 35mm Kodak color slide films. From mail order stores (they could ship to Japan residents), those for 36 exposures are available for under $3.50. The processing cost in Japan is about ¥1300 per roll. (Such mailers are also available in Hong Kong, but not Singapore.) These mailers, and developing of Kodachrome film sold with development included in the price, are honored in Japan and should be sent to: Far East Laboratories, Ltd., 2-14-1 Higashi-gotanda, Shinagawa-ku,Tokyo. They could also be left at the Kodak depots in Ginza or Aoyama.

X-Rays

X-ray baggage inspection machines in most airports are claimed to be safe for films up to ISO 400, and are probasbly OK for a few inspections. The dosages are cumulative, so if you will be going through a number of inspections, it would be wise to have the camera(s) and film inspected by hand.

Selling Goods in Japan

Years ago there was a lucrative black market in bottles of foreign whiskey, especially Johnnie Walker Black Label, which sold then in shops for ¥10,000 a bottle. Now the price has dropped to below ¥5000, and the Japanese go overseas and bring their own back. It is not worth trying to bring bottles into Japan and trying to sell them. It might be possible to find buyers in bars (or the bar owner might buy them), but you would probably be lucky to get your money back. Don't waste your time.

There also used to be a good market for gold Swiss watches (Rolex and Omega especially), but nowadays the Japanese travel abroad a lot and buy their own. (Overseas they have become a nation of "power shoppers".)

There are some items that would be salable in Japan, but the profit to be made is rather small. Unusual artefacts may find ready buyers; one person landed carrying a bundle of spears from Papua New Guinea and sold them easily. Top class world-famous goods may find buyers. One entrepreneur was bringing in Fender electric guitars (the latest models not yet available in Japan) and selling them at a good price. Several kinds of old model Japanese-made cameras sell for high prices in Japan, particularly Canon and Nikon rangefinder models. Stores ask very high prices for them; what they would be willing to pay is another matter.

Some Japanese will pay large sums for expensive foreign-made cameras such as Leica, Hasselblad, and Rollei, despite the fact that Japan makes the majority of high quality cameras. This seems to be part of a national inferiority complex that manifests itself in excessive adulation of foreign products simply because they are foreign (or simply vanity, wanting to have something different). It seems the added prestige of having a foreign model slung around one's neck is worth the extra cost. If you bring one of these cameras into Japan in good condition you could probably sell it, but again, it could take too long to be worth the effort. Professional photographers might provide one market.

ENTERTAINMENT

For the foreigner visiting Japan, "entertainment" covers a wide range (provided one's wallet is equally ample). The following section is a compendium of the various amusements available.

Performances

The Traditional Arts

Kabuki

This is a very Japanese form of theater, with spectacular costumes, highly stylised actions, and fantastic stage effects. Plots are often thin, or even incomprehensible, possibly based on a folk tale, but Kabuki is worth seeing at least once for the visuals alone. There are performances through much of the year at Kabuki-za in Tokyo, which is described in more detail in the Tokyo section. For the Kyoto and Osaka areas, consult the TIC in Kyoto or a tourist information publication like *Tour Companion* for information on current performances.

Noh

This is another form of drama, more restrained and refined than Kabuki. There are theaters in the large cities, with performances at various times through the year.

The above two sources can give current information.

Bunraku

The featured performers are not humans, but life-like puppets manipulated by (typically) three persons. The limbs, eyes, and mouth all move and, even though the puppeteers can be seen plainly, the dolls take on a life of their own. This art form originated in Osaka, and a new theater was built just for these performances, but Bunraku appears from time to time in Tokyo as well. The above two sources can give current information. (There is another puppet tradition in Japan, that of Awaji-shima island, one entrance to the Inland Sea area; it is described in the section covering that region.)

Traditional Dances

At various times through the year in Kyoto, there are performances of traditional dances, typically in the cherry blossom time and in the autumn. The above two sources can give current information.

Stage Shows

There are several stage shows in the large cities. One favourite for decades has been the Takarazuka Revue, a flashy stage show featuring women in all parts. There are theaters in Tokyo and the original site, Takarazuka (out of Osaka). It's totally innocent, but well polished.

Pop Road Shows

A large number of Western pop performers visit Japan, but tickets are often difficult to get, and are expensive.

Classical Concerts

There are several excellent symphony orchestras, chamber groups, and other classical groups, both based in Tokyo and visiting from overseas, and a large number of very impressive concert halls. Unfortunately, prices are out of the range of the usual traveller.

Media

Newspapers

There are five English-language daily papers. Papers are sold in the large hotels in the major cities and at many newsstands at the larger stations, as well as at many bookstores. Outside the main cities it can be difficult to find any of them, and they may be a day or two old. Prices of all papers except the *International Herald Tribune* (¥450) are in the ¥120 to ¥140 range per copy.

the *Japan Times* is the oldest English paper in Japan, and the only independent; the others are all off-shoots of parent Japanese-language papers. The Japan Times has arguably the best general coverage, and has become quite a good paper in recent years, though it does tend to follow the government line a bit. It is much thinner than big-city papers in foreign countries, but it has relatively few advertisements and its pages are almost solid news. Its world news coverage is good (true for all the papers), though biassed toward U.S. sources. (The world in North America generally ends at the northern and southern borders.)

The Mainichi Daily News is a morning paper competing with *The Japan Times*. It has many of the same articles, and differs mainly in its way of covering local events, columnists, etc. (The name means "every day daily news".)

The Asahi Evening News can use virtually the same comments as the Mainichi, except that it is an evening paper (available from noon). (The name means "sunrise evening news".)

The Daily Yomiuri is not quite in the same league as the others, being smaller and less pretentious, although it also has a lower price. It used to have stories as much as a day or two later than the other papers, but there has been a good effort to improve it in recent years.

Magazines

All the major foreign magazines, like *Time*, *Newsweek*, *The Economist*, etc., plus several European-language magazines, are available at large bookstores and hotel bookstands in the big cities. There are several magazines produced in Japan that are worth reading for a feeling of life in Japan. These include *Tokyo Journal* (Tokyo), *Kansai Time Out* (Kobe–Osaka–Kyoto area), and *Intersect* (national).

There are other magazines available that cover various aspects of Japanese society, history, and the like. These can be interesting and informative. However, it is necessary to have a certain amount of scepticism when reading such magazines, for some are not to be taken entirely seriously, seemingly being products of the *nihonjin-ron* establishment and published to promote the concept of "unique Japan". Occasionally their writers get so carried away with the "everything Japanese is better" theme that they can be unwittingly funny. One example: *The East* (one of the seeming "propaganda" outlets) had an article describing some additions to the list of 1945 standard *kanji* that must be learned in order to be literate in Japanese (and which are combined in compounds of two, three, and more to make up the words of the language, all of which must all be learned individually, including pronunciation, at easily imagined effort). It had the memorable quote, "Thus those who have mastered the 1,945 characters have finished learning the Japanese writing system. Once again, it is easier to learn Japanese than it is to learn English, which consists of hundreds of thousands of words." (Many Japanese cannot or do not distinguish between the writing system and the language.)

There are so many magazines now competing in a limited field that it is difficult to predict how many will survive, although it seems that many of these efforts are put out even at a loss for the prestige (or for publicity purposes) of the publisher. There is no shortage of would-be publishers who want to "explain" Japan and the Japanese.

Radio

The only regular broadcasts completely in English are those of the Far East Network (FEN) for the American armed forces and a new FM station, called InterFM, at 76.1MHz. (Some Japanese FM pop stations have much of their patter in English.) While FEN's broadcasts are slanted towards the interests and tastes of people in the services (very heavy on rock music and sport), it also has hourly news broadcasts and some news and commentary shows. The schedule of these has been changed so many times over the years that there is no way that a mention here would remain correct.

Mystery, adventure, and comedy programs from the golden days of radio, the '40s and '50s, have been broadcast for many years and are likely to continue. Listening areas and frequencies (kHz) are: Tokyo (810); Sasebo, Kyushu; Iwakuni, near Hiroshima; and Misawa, Northern Honshu (1575); and Okinawa (648). Tokyo area programs for both FEN and InterFM are listed daily in the *Japan Times*.

There are a few minutes of news in English each day on NHK, the government broadcasting organization.

The Japanese AM stations are heavily biased toward pop music, Japanese style (very much an acquired taste), although there is a substantial amount of the western variety as well. Program notes are published in the English-language dailies.

FM fans will be astounded to find that for all the entertainment electronic equipment produced in Japan, there is a miniscule number of FM stations in the large cities like Tokyo and Osaka. (One in Yokohama can also be heard in Tokyo.) The nationally-owned NHK station broadcasts several hours of classical, pop, jazz, and "easy listening" music each day. There is very little of traditional Japanese music, such as koto, except for a couple of hours on the weekend. The others are very heavily into "pop". The FM frequencies used in Japan are 76–90 MHz, below the international standard FM band 88–108 MHz found on most radios, so a special radio tuned to the local bands, or a converter, is necessary to pick up the broadcasts. If you want to buy good Japanese hi-fi gear to take home, buy the foreign frequency model and use a converter while in Japan, or look for a model that covers both bands.

TV

Most programming in Japan is in Japanese only. Imported programs and films are dubbed, but a new development in the electronics field, multiplex broadcasting of TV soundtracks, often allows hearing the original soundtrack of the film or program instead of the dubbed version, by use of an adaptor (although there may be some lack of continuity if segments have been cut). Films on cable TV (to some apartment buildings and most hotels catering to foreigners, and only in recent years to private homes) usually have their original sound-tracks. Programs can also be picked up from a satellite using a dish, though an un-scrambler is required.

Watching the Japanese programs, even if you can't understand a word of the dialogue, can give many insights into modern Japanese life. The role of women is clearly seen on one program after another—they are usually there only to provide a little scenery and to say *hai* (yes!) in obsequious agreement with every statement of the male who is, by definition, the most important and intelligent person on the screen.

Sports

Sumo

Not well known to foreigners except for its "fat wrestlers", Sumo is a very Japanese sport (with relatives in Mongolia) and in-teresting to watch. Two men face each other in an earth circle and grapple when they both feel ready. The loser is the first one pushed or thrown out of the circle or who touches the ground with any part of his body other than his feet. The action lasts from a second to a couple of minutes per bout.

There are six *basho* (tournaments) per year according to the following schedule: early January (Tokyo); mid-March (Osaka); early May (Tokyo); early July (Nagoya); mid-September (Tokyo); mid-November (Fukuoka).

Seats cost from mid-hundreds to mid-thousands, but the best view is that on TV, broadcast live from 1600–1800, with a summary of all 15 bouts late in the evening.

Baseball

The Japanese are as baseball-mad as the Americans, and fans of the sport might enjoy seeing a game while in Japan, ei-ther live or on TV. The players are good,

although it is admitted that the U.S. leagues are at a higher level. The mentality behind the game is very different from that in North America, and several books are available on the subject. *Slugging It Out in Japan*, by Warren Cromartie (published by Kodansha International), is the biggest eye-opener.

Skiing

Japan offers good skiing. The hills are often very crowded, and there may be a problem finding accommodation, but it is possible to avoid much of this with plan-ning. T.R. Reid's book *Ski Japan!* (Kodan-sha International) is a complete guide to skiing for foreigners in Japan, detailing more than 90 ski areas, including 20 world-class resorts. Also, the Beltop travel agency in Tokyo (tel (03) 3211-6555) is owned by a European and organizes ski tours with foreign tastes in mind. Information on ski areas and resorts is also available from the Tourist Information Center, and many of the areas are mentioned in the descriptions later in the book.

Gambling

There are three types of gambling permit-ted in Japan, two legally: horseracing, mo-torboat racing, and *pachinko*.

Horse Racing

Betting is permitted on horse races, which is the main reason for its popularity, in par-ticular with the laboring types who are not likely attracted to the sport from any appre-ciation of the beauty of the animals in ac-tion. They can be seen on days on or near the weekend, clutching a racing form or re-turning from the track bleary eyed from a day of serious drinking. The horses are of reasonably good breeding, though whether their performances would be in the world league is a bit doubtful.

Motorboat Racing

The boats are small outboard craft, and races are held on rivers and other bodies of water near the larger cities. Generally the same type of people attend race meets as for horse racing, and for much the same reasons.

Pachinko

Pachinko is a vertical pinball fame. *Pachinko* halls can be found in amazing numbers throughout Japan, always near railway stations in cities, and beside the roads in more remote places. The overseas visitor well asks what attraction there can possibly be to cause vast numbers of people to sit in rows for hours on end in garishly brightly lighted and extremely noisy galleries watching with great concentration as one steel ball after another arcs up from the automatic propulsion mechanism and then bounces from one steel pin to another on its way down, sometimes dropping into a hole that will cause additional balls to be won. The answer is that the prize that they may have won at the end of the session, such as a bar of chocolate or a jar of instant coffee, isn't the aim of the exercise. The winner can receive a slip of paper in lieu of the prize and take it to a little window in a nearby backstreet or alley where the slip is redeemed for cash. These places are easily identifiable by any person with a hint of intelligence by the line-up of people waiting. No, it's not legal, and no, nothing is ever done about it. However, there is no corruption in Japan.

Personal Entertainment

There is very little entertaining and socializing in people's homes in Japan (except for close friends). Most entertainment takes place in places serving alcohol, so we will start this section with a description of what booze is available, then move on to the types of places that serve it, then the types of entertainment that may be associated with it (or be led to by it . . .).

Drinks and Drinking

Alcoholic drinks of all kinds are readily available everywhere in Japan, but may be rather expensive compared with many western countries. They are sold in local shops virtually without restrictions, and are generally available at any hour from vending machines. Beer, sake, and whisky are usually available at almost any eating establishment. Imported whiskies and wines are available, especially in larger cities, but there are few bargains.

The following describes what is available.

Beer

Beer is the favorite alcoholic drink in Japan. Japanese beers are well regarded by beer connoisseurs, and are generally brewed in a German or Czech style. Well-known brands are Kirin, Sapporo, Suntory, and Asahi. A typical price for a large bottle (633mL) in a restaurant is ¥700, while it is about ¥330 at neighborhood shops, and a 500mL can is about ¥295 from a vending machine.

Sake

Sake (pronounced "sa-kay", not "sah-key") is the traditional Japanese drink. It is very pleasant with Japanese food and on its own. Sake is brewed by fermenting a mash of rice that has been cooked with water, and thus is more like beer than wine, except that the alcohol content goes as high as 17 per cent (considerably more than the typical 12 per cent in wines). It is certainly possible to get very drunk on it, but it is not quite as potent as much folklore would lead one to believe. (Such tales probably date back to Occupation days and are based on mistaking sake for much more powerful *shochu*.)

Sake is served hot in small 180 mL flasks, from which it is poured into tiny cups. The flask is called a *tokkuri* and is usually a decorative item made of pottery; it makes a good memento of Japan, along with a set of cups (*sakazuki*).

There are several types of sake depending on the kind and part of the rice grain used. Sake from different regions of Japan has different characteristics and tastes, so these designations do not indicate the flavor, only the quality. In addition to the standard types of sake, there are many specialty or regional types. Only two out of this many are *amazake* (sweet sake) and *nigorizake* (sake with suspended rice solids).

In shops, sake is sold in large 1800 mL bottles, as well as in smaller sizes. The size is a traditional measure called *issho*. At festivals a common sight is a large wooden keg of sake, opened by simply smashing in the lid; the contents are handed out freely in a square wooden box with neatly dovetailed leakproof joints. These boxes are of 180 mL capacity and were the traditional way of measuring granulated solids, like rice, as well as liquids. These boxes (*masu*) make good souvenirs of Japan; the 180 mL size is called *ichi-go*.

Shochu

Another Japanese alcoholic drink popular these days is *shochu*. It is a distilled liquor made from rice, wheat, sweet potatoes, sugar cane—anything containing sugar that can be fermented. The Kagoshima area of Kyushu is the *shochu* capital of Japan, though it is also made in many other areas. The distillation process is a copy of brandy-making that was introduced by foreign mis-

sionaries in the late 1500s, and shochu was once the beverage of feudal lords and the upper classes.

Earlier this century, *shochu* was popular throughout Japan. However, at the end of the war, materials for high quality shochu were not available and bootleggers blended it with anything on hand, including highly poisonous methyl alcohol. From then on it gained a bad reputation as a low-class drink associated with *jikatabi* (manual laborers nick-named for their split-toed boots) who get blotto on it regularly.

In recent years new processing methods have been introduced that eliminate most of the impurities that cause bad hangovers. Good *shochu* is little more than alcohol and water, 25–35 per cent (50–70 proof); the strength will be marked somewhere on the label. The leading brand is Jun ("purity"). It is very low in price, ¥600 for a 720 mL bottle, a fraction of the cost of whisky. It substitutes well for vodka in any mixed drink.

A popular home-made drink that visitors lucky enough to be invited into a private home may be offered is *umeshu*, which translates as "plum wine". It is made by soaking green, sour, plums in *shochu* to which has been added lots of sugar. The process is started in late June or early July and lasts at least three months. The result is delicious but very sweet and potent.

Wine

Because there is no long history of making it, Japanese wines have not reached the high levels of quality achieved in beer and whisky. Most of the best-known and widely-advertised brands are very ordinary.

Because of high costs in Japan, there is no incentive to make the necessary investments for improved processing facilities. Wines can be imported cheaper.

As for Japanese wine, the Austrian

tainted-wine scandal had interesting ramifications locally. Soon after the news about this scandal came in from abroad, a government agency, with simply amazing promptness, went around putting stickers on made-in-Japan wine with the Japanese word equivalent to "Safe". A little later it became known that wine sold in Japan needs to contain only *five* per cent Japanese-made wine to be called Japanese wine, and many companies import low-cost bulk wines from a variety of countries, like Chile, Bulgaria . . . and Austria. One company, Manns, actually had bottled and sold wine containing the glycol-tainted wine. When news came out of Europe about such wine, company representatives secretly went around to stores and took all these bottles off the shelves, then the company advertised that people who drank their wines were safe from glycol! (Company executives were fined a total of ¥30,000. By comparison, one old gent who made home-brew sake was fined ¥300,000 for his crime.) As a footnote, it was amusing to learn that the glycol about which the fuss was made is less poisonous than ethyl alcohol!

There is a fairly good selection of imported wines from many countries on sale in the metropolitan areas, particularly in some of the large department stores. Even local stores in many neighborhoods often have a number of wines from countries like France, Australia, and the U.S. (California). Prices are sometimes as low as ¥500 or less. but this is unusual; the typical range for inexpensive but good wines would be ¥1200 to ¥1500. (With the high yen, some reasonably good wine may be available at special sales for under ¥600 a bottle.) The Australian wines selling in this range have been the standard lines of good and reliable quality, but not outstanding, and sell for about double their home price—for Japan,

a remarkably small ratio.

Whisky and Other Spirits

Imported whiskies are available, especially in larger cities, so you should be able to find your favorite if you want it. Unfortunately, there are few bargains. Johnnie Walker Black Label (760 mL bottle) generally sells for ¥5800 and up, nearly always more, but can be found by the knowledgeable for under ¥5000; Red Label costs ¥2900 or more. Due to the prestige accorded to imported liquors, the price of foreign whiskies has scarcely changed despite the near-doubling in value of the yen. Rather than being something for drinking oneself, they are regarded as being for gifts. If the price were to be cut, the value as a gift would also be devalued. When the price of one imported scotch *was* cut, the sales actually fell! (The Japanese mentality gives foreign marketing people nightmares.) For years the government also did its bit by having different grades of liquor for taxation purposes and, by pure coincidence, imported scotch was virtually the only "high-grade", liquor and attracted a much higher rate than any Japanese-made product. Purely coincidental, of course. Fortunately for those who like whisky, some of the local products are regarded as good. Suntory Black Label is said to compare well with imported Scotch and costs less. (Other Suntory products are also well regarded. Try different makers' products as well. I'm a wino, not a spirits drinker, so can offer no guidance.)

Brandy and cognac are incredibly expensive in Japan. (The prices have no relationship to their price in country of origin nor taxes, but purely what the market will bear.) If you like them, or have a Japanese friend who does, be sure to bring your limit in duty free.

Drinking Customs

When drinking beer, sake, etc., with a Japanese person, the proper etiquette is to fill his glass or cup after he has filled yours. While he is pouring, hold your cup or glass up so that he can fill it more easily. If you don't want any more, put your hand over the glass. If you are new at the game, a Japanese may think you're unfamiliar with the "rules" and may fill his own glass. This is normally considered bad manners and the Japanese say "te jyaku" which means "who fills his glass with one hand, drains it with the other"; in other words an alcoholic. Before he can pour anything into his glass, take the bottle from him, and fill it for him. This may result in a mock fight, but the gesture will be appreciated.

When drinking in company, it is an honor for the senior person to offer his cup to a guest, then fill it. The guest then rinses the cup and returns it to its owner, and fills it for him. Actually, among the Japanese it is the inferior who offers the cup to his superior, but in the case of visiting foreigners the normal practice may be reversed—for the host may be implying that the guest is the honored superior.

When drinking with Japanese people, particularly those who are making a good salary, it will be difficult to pay any share of the bill (the "guest" treatment described elsewhere). Customarily one person, often the most senior, will pick up the tab and pay everything. It is necessary to think up some way to repay the favor at a later date. (Among friends this is just a convenience and they will divide the bill later; they may do so at the table if they know each other well or if there is time.)

With students and other people who are not very wealthy, the bill is usually split up according to who had what. As a foreigner you may sometimes have trouble paying for your share, but if you are drinking among friends they will not put up a fuss—it is only strangers who want to give the foreigner a good impression who will insist on paying the whole shot.

Getting drunk is one of the few safety valves open to Japanese to escape the manifold duties and obligations they must continually observe. Because of this, almost any behavior while drunk is excused. Consequently, hordes of faceless salary men, who show little individuality or personality during working hours, get quite thoroughly smashed quite frequently, sometimes nightly. They sing loudly, sometimes perform dances that can only be described as bawdy, and carry on in a manner quite "un-Japanese". Getting drunk is a very popular activity in Japan, and doing it with a group is almost a ritual, helping to cement interpersonal relations with co-workers, etc. Records in China mention that the Japanese were much given to drink at festivals 2000 years ago, so the process has a long history.

Virtually the only (though common) ill-effect of this excess drinking is that many drinkers don't know their limit and cannot hold their liquor (literally). The results of their overindulgence, known locally as "platform pizzas", may be seen on streets, railway platforms, and even inside railway cars, especially on Friday and Saturday nights. If you see people avoiding one end of a train car, you can suspect that that is the reason.

Drinking Places

There are two main types of drinking establishments in Japan, those strictly for drinking (usually with music and comfortable surroundings), and those for drinking with pleasant female companionship, i.e., hostesses.

Bars, pubs, and other drinking places range in price from reasonable to astronomical. The appearance of the place does not necessarily give an accurate indication of the prices to be paid. A place that looks expensive probably will be; nightclubs and similar places are guaranteed to take a huge bite out of a wallet. However, looking modest or even rundown is no guarantee that it will be cheap; some simple looking places are extremely expensive, either because of special service, atmosphere, or whatever that appeals to Japanese on huge expense accounts. There are stories of innocent *gaijin* (Westerners) walking into such joints, ordering a single beer, and being presented with a bill for ¥38,000!

To avoid such over-charging, stand bars are the answer. Many are operated by large companies in the liquor business, like Suntory and Nikka. Otherwise the safest course as soon as you enter an unknown bar is to ask the price of a drink and check if there is a cover charge; some places charge a couple of thousand yen as soon as a customer sits down. A favorite lurk of even better quality places is a dish of peanuts or other nibbles (called a "charm" in Japanese) that the customer is obliged to pay for at a price equal to a couple of drinks. Foreigners can sometimes get away from this racket by politely indicating that they don't want it and feigning lack of understanding about the system.

Places with hostesses are always going to be much more expensive than those for drinking only. Customers are charged for the time that girls sit with them. Anyone going in only to drink, without benefit of hostess, would probably be unwelcome.

Hostesses are part of the Japanese system of male ego-boosting; they flatter and flirt, and act as a listening post for the man's frustrations in life. (The sweet words that they utter are accepted by the man as completely true and his proper due.) Often these women are available for other outside

activities, usually on a paid basis, but sometimes on a purely friendly basis if she likes the customer. Boye de Mente's book *Bachelor's Japan* gives some specific advice on this topic. Though the book is long in the tooth, its message is still valid.

The services offered by hostesses range from sitting opposite the customer and simply pouring his drinks, to sitting on the customer's lap without benefit of undergarments and doing everything. The latter type of place is usually garishly decorated with bright lights (often pink) and are further identified by touts outside who try to entice customers in. Such places are never cheap. (With the AIDS scare, many such places will probably not admit foreigners because they are regarded as the only likely source of the disease.)

Beer halls are popular and relatively inexpensive places for a drink (and for eating). They can be recognised partly by the prominent jugs and bottles of beer in the window, although many restaurants also offer beer and have similar window displays; there is often a rather thin line between a restaurant and a beer hall, as both serve food as well as drinks. (The words for large, medium and small mugs of beer are *dai*, *chu* and *sho*.)

During the warm months many department stores open beer gardens on the roof, often with live entertainment. Prices are reasonable, the height of the buildings gives relief from the hot air at ground level, and it's a good place to see Japanese having a good time.

Almost any restaurant of any size will offer alcoholic drinks with the meal, particularly beer and sake. For economical drinking, with a simple list of drinks such as sake and beer, and simple decor (sometimes scruffy), investigate the "working-man's nightclub" or *akachochin*. These are found in many places and almost invariably near stations. The name literally means "red lantern", which is what will be found outside the establishment to identify it.

There are hundreds of gay bars in areas like Shinjuku (Tokyo) and in other large cities. There is considerable prestige in having a western boyfriend, so a welcome is assured for those so inclined. (The Tokyo Gay Support Group can give references.)

Note: Many clubs and almost any activity involving commercial sex are under control of gangsters. Foreigners with little knowledge of the language are very susceptible to being suckered into exorbitant bar bills for which payment is extorted, by violence if necessary. Any club where large numbers of girls are available is not going to be cheap; even quite legitimate places can be ridiculously expensive.

The following exhaustive description of Japanese drinking establishments, which is far more informative than any summary that I could assemble, comes courtesy of Bill Lisse, who wrote it for the newsletter of the Japan Association of Translators in Tokyo (JATT), and is obviously based on intensive (and enjoyable) research. This is its original form, and contains the complete, unexpurgated text in all its ribald glory.

The Stuff Dreams Are Made Of

Part of the August meeting was devoted to a discussion of the meanings and appropriate translations of various types of drinkeries in Japan. While most of us never have to translate material in which this is a problem, it might be interesting to be in on what is really going on in the Japanese evening. This month, let's take a tongue-in-cheek look at some of the strange and often confusing terminology used in this field, in the form of a mini-survey covering places ranging from yatai *to high-class (sic) clubs. Keep in mind that, while these places are not selling spring as do many of the newer type of non-drinkeries that have made a splash (squish?) lately, most of them do sell dreams, and this can affect both terminology and the behavior of patrons and employees. [Note: "Selling spring" is a euphemism for prostitution, and to "sell dreams" isn't far from it. I.M.]*

Yatai. At the bottom of the class ranking, we have those street stalls which serve up sake combined with oden, yakitori, *etc., flavored with lively conversation by the inevitable regular customers. If the argument is made that this is an outdoor restaurant (?) that just happens to sell sake, try counting the number of non-drinking customers some evening.*

Akachochin [literally, "red lantern", for the lantern of that color suspended outside the shop to identify it; I.M.] Although there are many varieties, this type of place can probably be described as a yatai *brought in out of the elements. Here, the ratio of customers wearing* jikatabi *[manual laborers' split-toed shoes; I.M.] and* haramaki *[thick "belly-warmer" band worn particularly by manual laborers, even in the hottest weather; I.M.] is lower than the usual* yatai, *however. For obvious reasons, the menu here is more broad-ranging than the* yatai. *Akachochin are referred to as such even if they happen to be* shirochochin *["white lantern"; I.M.] and, although some claim that the latter have more class, the author has yet to experience this difference.*

Snakku [pron. "snack"; I.M.] Here we open a real can of worms. It shouldn't come as a shock to most us that a snakku is not in the business of selling food. The product they and most drinking places in Japan are providing is a "stage" for customers (even if they don't have a karaoke [described elsewhere; I.M.] and a dream—the dream that, just maybe, it's going to happen tonight. This category exists because of laws which allow snakku to stay open until any hour. These places range from the neighborhood snakku to what should actually be called a kurabu ["club"; I.M.], if it were not for the fact that this type of snakku can stay open beyond the legal closing time for the usual kurabu. The very common presence of hostesses makes distinction even more difficult... Color a snakku "bar" if you need to describe it to someone who has never been to one. An interesting note here is that the "hostesses" at a snakku are not legally allowed to sit with customers, although this doesn't reflect the actual situation, as a visit to a snakku in Yokohama's Kannai or Fukutomi-cho district (or anywhere else, for that matter) will reveal.

Ba. The ba [bar; I.M.] is a dead or dying word and type of drinkery, it giving way to more fashionable names described elsewhere. Sad, since this is the only name that rings true to foreigners (or at least Americans). The ba usually has hostesses and, unless it is actually a snakku in disguise, it closes early (11:30 pm or so).

Come to the kyabare. Never having been in any place called a cabaret in English, I must resort to a description of what the [word here written in Japanese katakana; I.M.] is, breaking this genre into several sub-groups for clarity.

Kyabare (no qualifier). Here we have the only type of drinking establishment to which many local businessmen feel they can take their foreign clients, hence its familiarity to the foreigner. This classification covers all the big name kyabare in Akasaka [already largely vanished; I.M.] and usually has a floor show with well known performers and sometimes hundreds of hostesses.

Tashishu kyabare. Here is a dying name as well. The qualifier tashishu, one can only imagine, is designed to lend a feeling of economy and friendliness. This type of place has a bevy (flock? gaggle?) of hostesses, sometimes wearing radio pagers. Performers range from strippers to once-popular singers who can't work TV any longer. Noise pollution is the order of the day and the general atmosphere is that of the early 1960s. In short, if three or four Nikkatsu [film studio; I.M.] actors of that period popped out of the woodwork, nobody would blink an eye. In fact, such places were often used in Nikkatsu movies of that era. I hate to do this, but "sleezy nightclub" has a good ring for this one.

Pinku kyabare & pinku saron [pink cabaret/salon; I.M.] I may get some arguments that these establishments should not be listed as "watering holes", but there are customers who actually go into them to drink. These places are much older and better established [both the furnishings and the employees] than the places in Kabuki-cho (notorious "entertainment" area of Shinjuku; I.M.) that get so much space in weekly magazines, and it would be hard to classify the Kabuki-cho places as anything but packaging variations for the world's oldest profession. The "back room" is unheard of in a pink kyabare; darken the house lights and it's showtime. Without going into details as to what goes on at a pink saron, suffice it to say that the activities at the tables would bring tears to the eyes of a connoisseur of classical Japanese wind instruments. If the reader is unfamiliar with this type of establishment, it may come as a surprise that the largest chain of such places advertises on nationwide TV practically nightly. Any large train station worth its name has a few of these places, recognizable usually by a barker and a sign outside describing prices, which increase as the evening gets later (i.e., as the prospective customers get more desperate). Trying to translate this one would probably require a ten-line footnote. Good luck.

Foreigners are often excluded from such places and even I've been told "Japanese only", in spite of what I thought was pretty good Japanese. The explanation (in Japanese) was that the girls don't speak English. I countered by asking whether they wouldn't be too busy to speak anyway, but this attempt at humor fell on deaf ears—ears which only later I found out were themselves non-Japanese ears, strangely enough. [Many such establishments are operated by Koreans, along with pachinko parlors and soaplands, because discrimination against Koreans keeps them out of good jobs in most respectable lines of work. I.M.]

Kurabu. Nothing very special here. Hostesses and high prices. (Incidentally, places called ba, kurabu and even snakku can be more expensive than painting the town pink.) Probably bar would suffice for description, if we allow that this doesn't do justice to the dream dynamics at work here also. I cringe at the often heard "hostess club", probably because there is an animal known as a "hosto kurabu", intended for the pleasure of yukan madamu and off-duty soap ladies having such inclinations. ["Soap ladies": see "soaplands" elsewhere; I.M.]

Gei ba. Very expensive and not resembling very much the U.S. equivalent, one difference being that the Japanese version seems to be enjoyed by many non-gays and even women. Since I've only been to one of these, I am afraid I wouldn't be of much aid in a translation. What's wrong with gay bar?

Izakaya. This type of place has experienced radical changes in the past few years, accompanied by a doubling of the average age of patrons. The typical izakaya today is a franchise business much the same as a bentoya (bento = "box lunch"; ya = "shop"), and aims at the young and sometimes amateur-rank drinker. Menus with hundreds of items are common and the bill at the end of the evening is usually very small. I've got no good term for this one. Any takers?

Cafe Bar. The author admits to never having actually seen a cafe bar but superficial research indicates that the cafe bar (a very recent name, by the way) has lots of chrome and brass, no hostesses and aims at a fairly young clientele. This may very well come closer to the U.S. concept of bar than any other type of place covered here. I am open for suggestions or correction on this.

Pabu. Even someone who has never been to England can imagine that a pub is not a pub. All varieties are available, with or without karaoke, overt or covert hostessess, refined clientele or yakuza, etc. The name you choose will depend upon just which pub you are describing.

Hybrids. Just when you think you know all the names, someone comes along and uses a combination of two or three. Some examples:

Night Pub. The implication here is that it is something other than a pub during the daylight hours (usually a coffee shop).

Pub Snack. This can have the elements of both. The aim might be to avoid leaving out potential customers. You pays your money and takes your dream.

Coffee Snack. Same as above in some cases,

but this may be a legitimate coffee shop.

Supper Club. *Beware! Most supper clubs I've been in have had hostesses, karaoke and definitely no supper.*

The above just scratches the surface. Any ideas or corrections are appreciated.
The end

Sex

Sex is an entertainment commodity in Japan. In addition to strip shows that leave little to the imagination, sexual services of many types are readily available.

Prostitution was declared illegal in 1958. The former red-light districts are no longer official, but after a history of hundreds of years, brothels have just taken a different form. Today, a man with the yen for such things can have his full desires accommodated in a "soapland" or by negotiating with an obliging hostess at a bar or club, or a lesser variety in a "Pink Saron". In some areas streetwalkers are to be found. (Investigate Roppongi (Tokyo) on a late weekend night for the expensive type, both domestic and foreign variety.) Though few westerners will bother going, hotspring resorts are known for more than sitting in hot water.

Soapland

In early 1985 the establishments formerly known as *toruko* (corruption of "Turk", as in "Turkish bath") were required by law to change the name of their establishments to *Soapland* following protests from the country's Turkish community. Apparently even the Turkish embassy was receiving phone calls from potential customers wanting a run-down on their "services", a problem not aided by one establishment that actually called itself "The Turkish Embassy"!

Although seemingly places for bathing and cleansing, "soapland" establishments are designed to satisfy needs deeper than outward cleanliness. The "attendant" soaps all of her customer's body, often applying the soap by first lathering her own nude body and acting like a human sponge. She is then well positioned to take care of any matters that arise.

The best-known Toruko/Soapland areas in Japan are the Horinouchi district of Kawasaki and the Sakae-cho district of Chiba (both in the Tokyo region), Gifu (near Nagoya), and Ogoto (on the western shore of Biwa-ko lake, in the Kyoto/Osaka area). They are found throughout the country.

Soaplands are for the well-heeled only, and can cost up to ¥30,000 for high-class services. The help of a Japanese would be most essential in finding one and obtaining admittance, as foreigners are often unwelcome at such facilities, largely because of the language problem that can give rise to many difficulties about charges, in addition to the association of AIDS with foreigners.

Note: Soapland should not be confused with *sento* (local public baths), *onsen* (hotspring resorts), or *sauna* (which do have genuine massage)—all legitimate establishments. (Although the onsen are also noted for catering to male desires.)

Pink Saron or "Pinsaro"

Obviously this is a mispronunciation of "Pink Salon". These are bars with hostesses. There is a flat fee for drinks and nibbles (say ¥3000), but the tender ministrations of the hostess can become a lot more personal if extra money changes hands. This can run the gamut from a lapful of underwearless hostess, to "relief massage", or more. (See also Bill Lisse's discourse, previous pages.)

Pink Sarons were once plentiful in large cities and elsewhere, usually near large railway stations and identifiable by garish pink signs and touts standing outside. The interior is very dark to give the hostesses some privacy for their work. Although the touted price is in the ¥3000, the full treatment will run considerably higher, generally ¥8000–10,000.

Hostesses

Hostesses in bars and clubs are there to please their male customers by boosting their frail egos with flattery and attention. Although there are bars where the girls merely sit opposite their customers and do nothing more than pour drinks and make conversation, more usually the girls will allow the customer to become more physical and can often be induced to accompany him afterward. It is frequently necessary to pay the establishment a "ransom" if leaving with a hostess before closing time.

Call Girls

In the large cities, many play-for-pay girls are available with just a phone call. Small stickers with a provocative picture of a woman (semi or completely nude), a phone number, a price and time along with extra comments like "Two times OK", and "Hot!" (in Japanese), can be found in phone booths in many parts of large cities. Prostitution is illegal, including call-girl operations, but these stickers nevertheless can often be found close to police boxes. However, by definition, there is no corruption in Japan.

Live Sex Shows

An amusement that can still be found at hotspring resort towns, as well as in the larger cities, is live sex shows. A couple performs on stage before the delighted audience and in some cases members of the audience are invited to strip off and join in. As one newspaper expressed it, for the man who is able to function before a crowd, there's no cheaper way in Japan to get some action.

Because women of European origin are greatly preferred as partners for such shows, there is sure employment for anyone wishing to partake. Arrest and deportation is a risk of the business but it seems the police don't go far out of their way to stamp out such activities.

Equal Opportunity

The places just described are all for men. There are clubs for women where handsome young men give them total attention and offer similar services. However, they are reportedly very expensive. (For men contemplating this sort of work, the ability to speak good Japanese is a prerequisite.)

The following section is aimed at giving you a "background briefing" on the types of experience that most foreign visitors to Japan will have, and why, with particular reference to interaction with the people (how their characteristics, attitudes, behavior, etc., are likely to affect you), along with some information on the "physical realities" of Japan. One purpose is to give you some understanding of how to interact and behave with the people, the other to give you some perspective on what you will likely find. This is such an all-encompassing subject that the write-up may tend to wander about a bit, but the information (based on the experiences of a number of foreigners who have spent varying amounts of time in Japan) should help you to understand the culture and the people.

LIVING IN JAPAN

Japan can be an interesting and enjoyable country in which to spend an extended time. It is definitely foreign, very Asian, offering a new culture, society, and personal relationships to explore, yet it is generally a comfortable place to live because the basic services that foreigners want/need are generally available, and it has absorbed sufficient of the West that it is approachable. It can be a good place to live and grow personally.

Always keep in mind that although many aspects of western life have been borrowed, the background on which they are based is often unknown or imperfectly understood, and has often been absorbed only superficially. This characteristic has mani-fested itself in many ways for centuries, as evidenced in religion, for example. Buddhism in Japan bears almost no resemblance to that in any other country. The Japanese have taken certain tennets of the faith, often remote from the core, discarded the main, central, parts, and then built an entire new structure around this new center to suit the Japanese nature and history. The tradition continues today. (It is also not unique to Japan.)

Reactions to Japan

Most foreigners who remain in Japan for an extended period of time resident in one place typically go through a number of identifiable stages in their outlook on the country. Writers commenting on the phenomenon (usually in a humorous manner) have identified up to five stages, but they can be summarized adequately by three:

1. The "wonderland" (or "rosy-colored glasses") phase.
2. The "disillusionment" phase.
3. The "acceptance of reality" phase.

The first phase is characterized by adoration of everything Japanese, when everything is new and superficially so much better than in any other country in culture, politeness, arts, design, social organization, social relationships, et cetera, et cetera, ad nauseum. More than a few are so enamored that they try to live in a totally Japanese lifestyle, eating only Japanese food, socializing only with Japanese, striving to learn the language, and endeavoring to become part of Japanese society.

The second phase comes from the disappointment, often acute, of finding that the gushing reports about Japan that they had read overseas were inaccurate, incomplete, biased, misleading, simplified, misguided, ill-informed, etc., and the crowded reality and ugliness of the cities, the difference in behavior of the people from what they had expected, etc., becomes overwhelming. The most serious cases are those who have tried to become Japanese in every aspect of life, only to find that the Japanese don't *want* them to be part of Japanese society. Like a pendulum released from one side, their emotions swing to the far extreme in overreaction, to dislike (often extreme) of the country and every aspect of it.

The third phase is where the pendulum comes to rest, balanced by the realization that (on one hand) there *are* many aspects of Japan that are very interesting and worthwhile (some of which *are* worth copying in other countries), and that (on the other) there are many serious shortcomings in the country that should be put right. It is at this stage that one can enjoy and accept the many good experiences that Japan offers, while keeping a balanced overall view.

After the sand castle has collapsed, one can sit back and analyze, and finally realize that what Japan offers is as much a voyage of self-discovery and self-realization as of exploration of the country itself. (Although the ultimate phase for most foreigners is the one in which they are looking for a shipping company to get their possessions home.)

"Guest Treatment"

The usual reaction by visitors given information like the above after only a few days in Japan is to express disbelief, telling of the great treatment that they have received,

how wonderful the Japanese people are, etc.

Yes, they are wonderful . . . while the foreigner is perceived as a "guest" who is just passing through for a short time, then leaving. Those in Japan for only a short time will receive this "guest treatment" throughout their entire visit. The attitude becomes much less warm when the foreigner lets it be known that he/she has been in the country for a long time, or plans to be. Generally this change is not to hostility, only to neutrality, with special benefits no longer conferred. (One sometimes begins to wonder if there is a government department instructing the populace to give such excellent treatment to visitors, since it is so uniform throughout the country; many foreign travel writers visiting Japan seem never to get beyond it).

Unrealistic Expectations

The major cause for disappointment with the realities of Japan and the Japanese is that much of the information about Japan available overseas is inaccurate, distorted, superficial, or incomplete, and foreigners may come to Japan with unrealistic expectations. There are several reasons for this.

Information from Japanese sources presents only a Japanese point of view. While the writers have the advantage of knowing the language perfectly, and have the ability to ferret out facts that we outsiders cannot, working against objectivity is the fact that the Japanese try at all times to present only the positive where Japan is concerned. Negative aspects of any issue are normally kept from view. (This is an aspect encountered throughout Japanese society, so it is not necessarily an attempt to mislead non-Japanese; it may only seem so.)

This sort of thing is encountered in many ways in society; the Japanese are very adept at seeing only what they want to see, and ignoring the rest (or pretending that it doesn't exist). Thus, they are wondrously able to isolate and admire the one beautiful element in a view, and ignore the gas stations, fast food shops, old and shabby buildings, litter, etc., surrounding it; the principle of the Japanese garden is based on this ability to concentrate one's attention on the beauty of only a small area.

One way to look on information about Japan from Japanese sources is to think of "Japan" as an image on a rear-projection screen, with only pictures favorable to Japan being shown. These images are generated by publications prepared in Japan that are aimed at overseas readers, and by foreign writers under the Japanese influence (. . . or paycheque). Only those who stay in the country long enough will "get around the screen" and have the chance to see the good, the bad, and (thanks, Clint) the ugly. One will then find that these good but cliched aspects of Japan *do* exist, and are definitely a part of the country and its society (and very much worth experiencing), but that they are only a part of the overall picture. This is the point of view that many foreigners living in Japan come to: appreciative of the good, but aware of the shortcomings.

It seems that many articles are written by overseas writers who have had only a week or two (sometimes a day or two . . .) to see the country, and who have been "guided" by official or semi-official personnel and given the "screen" treatment. Another possible reason for inaccurate articles is that the writers read what earlier scribes have written, and are afraid to say anything contrary to the "accepted" view lest they appear to show their ignorance and inability to see for themselves all the wonderful qualities reported earlier by others. Whichever, the effect is seen in the same cliche words and phrases (so much loved by the cynical foreign resident!) that pop up with monotonous regularity, such as the Japanese oneness with nature, the four distinct seasons, beautiful Japanese scenery, exquisite Japanese politeness, and on and on.

Another factor distorting information from Japan, when it involves comparisons of some aspect of Japanese culture, practices, etc., with the equivalent in another culture, is that most Japanese (even up to the level of university professor) have a rather vague, and often inaccurate, knowledge and understanding of the outside world. The news media do present much news from overseas, and there are many TV programs giving coverage to other countries, but a substantial number of these carry a slant (intentional or otherwise) that distorts reality. Commentators on radio and TV programs attempting to explain the west not infrequently display incredible ignorance of the subject on which they are pontificating, even supposed "experts".

The message from this is that if your senses say that something about Japan is so, but a Japanese source says otherwise, don't discard your original impression immediately without further input. You could be correct.

The Japanese People

The "National Personality"

As seen in formal business situations, the Japanese may seem a stolid people with little spontaneity, personality, "spark", or dynamism. Various explanations can be offered for this reticent behavior. One is that it has long been a virtue in Japanese society to be self-effacing and stoic. Another is that in the Tokugawa days a change in expression or hesitation of any kind when receiving an order could be grounds for death on the spot. Present day Japan is still very hierarchical, so workers in offices, students in school, and anyone else lower on the organizational ladder still are expected to jump when instructed by a superior. (The entire language is based on preserving careful distinctions of rank.) The school system, the working environment, and society in general, act to inhibit spontaneity and individuality. The attitude is summed up by the old saying "The nail that sticks up gets hammered down".

In relaxed surroundings, however, they can be quite different. Japanese men become boisterous when drinking, and the facade slips. (This is the only time they may voice their honest opinions without fear of retribution.) Anyone who has experienced a *karaoke* bar knows that the Japanese can put the reticence aside completely; in these places, where recorded music provides the accompaniment, customers (well lubricated) almost fight each other to pick the microphone and sing along with the music (for hours on end if given the chance), not shy in the least, and oblivious to any shortcomings in their crooning talents.

Women are expected to be shy and demure, and in the same "formal" circumstances of an office, etc., are rather quiet. Ouside such circumstances, they are a little more outgoing, but still in much more of a shell than their western counterparts. It is only with a small group of close friends that they can be more natural.

The "ideal" for women is that they remain as childlike and dependent as possible. A look at the pop singers on TV will show the type, dressed in adolescent (or more juvenile) styles, and acting childish. There is, incidentally, nothing genetically wrong with women's voices. The high-pitched PA and radio announcements that would give a dog an ear-ache are only representative of what they are taught as being

desirable. It can be very interesting for a foreigner who is talking with a Japanese woman in normal tones to hear her voice go up an octave when she addresses a Japanese.

Behavior with Others

Behavior in Japan is mainly situational, not determined by a universally applicable set of standards. Whereas the average westerner is generally guided by Judeo-Christian ethical values of correct behavior (reflected in the concept of "common courtesy"), such over-riding principles do not exist in Japanese society. One knows how to behave in this or that situation, with people of higher, equal, or lower rank, but there is no overall idea of doing "right" on principle (ethics) or general notion of how to behave in unusual circumstances (such as encountering a foreigner for the first time in one's life in some remote part of the country!).

Within the business world, the Japanese exchange *meishi* (business cards) so that each person knows where he stands in relation to the other and can choose his behavior and language accordingly. There are completely different verbs for use with people of different status.

This seeking of information about another person is a possible explanation for the usual litany of questions that a foreigner tends to be asked on first meeting a Japanese, such as one's age. (Another explanation is that they have all learned the same list of questions in their English class; I encountered one student who read all the standard questions from a sheet of paper handed out at school. Slow wit kept me from asking for it to keep as evidence.)

One of the great achievements of Japanese society is to have developed a social structure, with codified ways of interacting, that minimizes interpersonal strife and gives the ability to live in crowded conditions without serious conflict. (As one learns more about the country, one finds out that there *are* disputes among neighbors about all the same petty matters that cause problems in any society, but they usually "keep their cool" and remain relatively civil.) This can lead to rather formalized, even stultified, conversations, with little or no spontaneity, but it does keep things moving along without friction.

The "system" can cause problems when a foreign visitor is dealing with a Japanese who has had little contact with non-Japanese, for neither knows the "ground-rules" of the other. Tales of misunderstandings are rife. For example, Japanese have a trait of talking and acting in such a way as to maintain the greatest degree of harmony, even if it means not telling the truth. In the case of two Japanese, they both know it is not the truth, but they see it as a way to avoid saying something unpleasant to each other, and both try to maintain the required harmony. (This has been called "mutually comprehensible deception".) A foreigner encountering such actions would tend to interpret this as insincerity (or duplicity, or worse), but it could be a classic case of cross-cultural misunderstanding.

Related to this system is the "Japanese smile" that can hide all real feelings.

Partly as a result of the system of personal relations, Japan is one of the safest countries in the world in which to live, and violence is quite uncommon. The average Japanese is easy-going, not fanatical about anything, just working hard to move up the promotional ladder and make a good life. However, there does exist a potential for violence. In the past couple of decades student politics has flared up with occasional mayhem, mostly limited to radical leftist factions murdering each other. (Even most student radicals appear to shed their views like a dirty shirt when they graduate and join a company to become a typical salaryman.) There are a couple of "yes, buts" to complete this picture. Under the surface, many/most Japanese are actually very emotional and high-strung. (They rank by far the highest in the developed world in psychoses.) If pushed beyond the breaking point, they can "snap" and become quite irrational. It doesn't happen often, but it is possible. The other "yes, but" is that there have been physical assaults on foreigners. This matter is discussed in the section on Dangers.

Personal Characteristics

In addition to a live-and-let-live attitude, the Japanese have a self-indulgent, selfish side to their nature. This is recognised by the Japanese themselves; in one survey, they chose it as one category defining their nation, so it is no insult to mention it here. It is apparently an extension of the "us" and "them" mentality; everyone looks after one's own group and has little or no concern for others. Charities as known in the west are almost non-existent.

An offshoot of this touches on the oft-heard cliche about their "oneness with nature". For the most part they (as a group) have no more appreciation of nature than any westerner of reasonable sensitivity. The average Japanese thoughtlessly drops cigarette packets, wrappers, bottles, and cans wherever he happens to be. A depressing number of beautiful gardens, temples, venerable tea houses, etc., have loudspeaker systems extolling at top volume the tranquility of the place, and destroying the contemplative mood that each was intended to engender.

The Japanese are also the worst offenders against the endangered species of the world. While most other countries have virtually banned their import, pelts of rare animals and many other such natural products are imported without qualm. (In recent years the import of ivory was finally banned, and it seems as if the same will happen for the shells of hawksbill turtles. It remains to be seen what eventuates in the driftnet fishing scene.) One tropical fish dealer caught with a specimen of a rare and endangered species stated that without selling them he couldn't make a living!

The Japanese are the last nation in the world to hunt whales on a large scale, defending the practice on the specious grounds that it is a needed source of protein, that it has become a Japanese tradition to eat whalemeat, and that many people would lose their jobs if it were abolished. At the time of making this revision, whaling has been banned internationally, but the Japanese are killing several hundred whales nonetheless each year for "scientific purposes", after which they are made available for sale "in order not to waste the carcass". This is being portrayed as "scientific whaling".

Almost any writings about Japan for foreign readers stress the cultural life of the Japanese. As a result, one gets the impression that everyone in Japan is adept in the arts, and spends every spare moment while not working indulging in one traditional art after another. This is not an accurate portrayal. Many Japanese, particularly housewives, do spend much time and money studying the arts like *ikebana* (flower arrangement), and refine their mind through the tea ceremony, but the average Japanese probably has little more interest in such arts (and Kabuki, Noh, etc.) than a Western counterpart would in opera. (Most males seem to spend most of their spare time watching sports on TV, or sleeping.) For this reason, Westerners should not come to Japan with a "cultural cringe"; there is

much to be admired and there are many things that Westerners can learn from Japan, but the average educated Westerner probably also has a reasonable level of "culcha". (It is important to remain objective.)

One of the myths about Japanese behavior that should be permanently laid to rest is their "politeness". As anyone who has travelled by commuter train in Japan can aver, the Japanese are not an excessively polite people in public. Any hint of manners vanishes in the attempt to get into or out of the train. When I return to Canada and travel on the subways of Montreal or Toronto I am always struck by the overall courtesy of the populace in comparision to the supposedly polite Japanese. I am astounded to see that Western men still give up seats to women, a practice unheard of in Japan unless the woman is faced with imminent collapse.

The best summation of Japanese politeness is that "Japanese are polite only with their shoes off", meaning they are exceedingly polite to people they know well enough to be indoors with (where shoes are removed).

Bowing to show respect is largely a conditioned reflex. Mothers push their children's heads down in a bow before they can even talk. The depth of a bow is more an indication of the rank or business importance of the recipient than a genuine measure of the bower's esteem, and the observant person can learn much about the true feelings of the person doing the bowing by watching the expression on his face.

Attitude to Foreigners

The Japanese word for "foreigner" is *gaijin*, a word heard often while travelling around the country, as one person points out the obvious to another, namely that there is a foreigner nearby. Japan is very much a "them and us" country, and a fuss is constantly made about anyone out of the ordinary. The "us" can be a family, a school, a company, or a department. The "out" group is *gai*, so a foreign person is a *gai-jin*, an "outside person". The observant foreigner resident in Japan for a while could be forgiven for thinking that the Japanese go out of their way to find ways in which they can categorize themselves (and others). In recent years a complete pseudo-science of personal classification based on blood type has grown up, despite the fact that there is not a shred of evidence to support the idea. An applicant may be refused a job if he or she does not fit in with the preconceived notion of the desirable blood type for the work.

Although they generally regard themselves as superior to all other peoples, the Japanese are generally friendly and kind to foreign visitors. As for foreigners of European extraction, they are generally given far better treatment than are fellow Japanese; non-Japanese Asians or those of non-white races, such as Africans, may not receive a fraction of such overwhelming good treatment. Foreigners of Japanese ancestry fall into yet another category, expected (due to other non-rational, nationalistic beliefs) to have inherited Japanese characteristics simply by birth (ability to speak the language automatically, be able to use chopsticks, etc.), yet being treated like other foreigners (semi-pariahs) when they are looking for an apartment, etc.

The Japanese (in general, with many fortunate exceptions) are very much of two minds about foreigners, both not really liking them while simultaneously holding those of European origin in exaggeratedly high esteem (most of the time, anyway), because it was hundreds of experts from Europe and America who brought knowledge of the modern world to Japan during

the Meiji era. Also it was people of European origin who defeated the Japanese during WWII, and the Japanese respect a winner. Not liking foreigners is a carry-over from the Tokugawa era, when contact with the outside world was banned. One suspects that the propaganda from before and during the last war is still exerting an influence on the populace. (Many of those high in the ruling LDP party are rightists largely still of the same mindset as those who ran the country during these periods.)

It is not uncommon to find that newspapers, magazines, films, and TV frequently present a distorted view of foreigners and foreign cultures. A repeated unfunny joke is the supposedly knowledgeable "experts" on radio and TV talking about this or that aspect of western culture, and who spout nonsense that would draw guffaws if they could be understood by non-Japanese. The written word is not necessarily any better at informing the populace of the outside world, for there is virtually an industry producing books purporting to explain the Japanese (to the Japanese) in which some quite absurd assertions are made about the supposed uniqueness of the Japanese vis a vis all other peoples; they are absurd because they are often based on mythic perception of what Japan is and on very poor knowledge of what the rest of the world is really like. This type of pseudo-study has the generic title *nihonjin-ron* ("theory of the Japanese").

A disturbing occurrence in recent years has been the release of large numbers of anti-semetic books, this despite the presence of only a tiny number of Jews in the country, all foreigners.

Fortunately there *are* some magazines and other publications, as well as a fair number of TV programs, that do give an accurate portrayal of the rest of the world, so the general population has a mental mixture of fact and fiction about the outside world.

Meeting the Japanese

Enough of the background. Let's get on to some tips that will be helpful when meeting Japanese.

It is unfortunate that most visitors to a foreign country such as Japan have little opportunity to meet the people who live there. They are always on the move and there is often a language barrier. Yet it is only through such contact, of course, that a visitor has a chance to learn of their daily life, work, pleasures, and problems. Leaving Japan without meeting any of its people, other than hotel employees, etc., is like wearing earplugs to Carnegie Hall or a blindfold to the Louvre. Because of the education system inflicted on the Japanese (they study to pass exams, not to learn), most of them have little ability to speak English despite untold hours of instruction at school. The emphasis is all on written, not spoken, work, with endless grammatical drills that have little relationship to normal communication. The effect is that communication with the typical person in Japan can be difficult. (Not helping learning of English in the least is the ubiquitous and huge volume of incorrect/weird "English" printed on shopping bags, T-shirts, and other clothing, and used as slogans in advertisements seen on signs, billboards, packages, in magazines, and on and on. It seems that a prerequisite to writing English is to have failed the subject at school.)

There is, however, a variety of programs aimed at introducing visitors to Japanese who do speak foreign languages. Because English is the most widely spoken language in the world, it is the one that most Japanese learn. (This is a source of annoyance for many Europeans who encounter Japanese who think that everyone with "white" skin speaks English.) Through several independent programs in operation around the country, you can visit a Japanese home for a couple of hours in the evening, meet Japanese people who are willing to act as guides and escorts at no charge, simply chat over a cup of coffee, or even stay with Japanese families in their homes around Japan, at no charge.

Etiquette

My suggestion if you are meeting a Japanese person for the first time in "formal circumstances" is to incline your head slightly, in a semi-bow, and to use normal western courtesy. Don't try to mimic Japanese bowing, because it is an art in itself, and don't attempt to shake hands unless the Japanese person offers a hand first, as they are generally not accustomed to the habit. (Interestingly, however, it is not unknown for Japanese businessmen and politicians to shake hands among each other these days, even when no foreigner is involved.)

Meeting a foreigner is stressful for many Japanese who have not had much contact with "outside people", and they are likely to be very nervous. Conversation is likely to be a bit strained. Don't worry about it, and try to find some topic of common interest. Don't ask really personal questions unless the Japanese person has relaxed and seems willing to talk about his/her family, personal life, etc. Sometimes such chats never rise above being a game of verbal patty-cake, exchanging words but little more. (Those teaching English to advanced classes, or to private students, often find that their students become very open and talk about very personal details without embarassment.) Most Japanese who participate in a program of introducing Japanese and foreigners have a genuine interest in meeting people from overseas, and are quite open in their conversation. The most extreme of the latter are some Japanese who have had much contact with foreigners and who speak English very well. They may tend to adopt what they have observed as being western ways of talking and behaving, requesting that you call them by their first names (unimaginable within Japanese society!), etc. Play it by ear in this case, but it is still better not to be too personal.

In homes, one usually sits on the floor, an uncomfortable position for foreigners for extended periods. If you are invited to a home, try to keep your legs under you as long as possible; if it is necessary to stretch out, avoid pointing your feet at anyone (very rude). Most Japanese will realise that foreigners become uncomfortable and will make allowances for deviation from ideal Japanese manners.

Blowing your nose at the table is a Class A social gaffe.

Home Visit System

The Home Visit System is a voluntary program through which Japanese families in several cities receive foreign visitors into their homes. The system is "semi-official" in that it is publicised in a brochure issued by the semi-government Japan National Tourist Organization (JNTO). Visits are normally arranged for a couple of hours in the evening. Food is not served, but green tea and sweets will usually be part of the evening. Hosts will show guests around the house, if desired, perhaps showing the finer points of Japanese house design (if it is not a modern western type!) and the garden, if there is space for one; Japanese houses are usually rather small. The homes open under this program are often those of well-to-do Japanese, so they will tend to be more spacious and elegant than average. The Japanese usually do not invite guests into

their homes because they consider their houses to small and humble. (In addition, they are quite likely to be very jumbled with furnishings, and rather untidy.)

There is no charge for a visit. It is customary among Japanese to take a small gift to the host or hostess whenever visiting, even among close friends. Flowers, fruit, or candy are suggestions. The Japanese participate in the program just for the pleasure it gives the guests, and the international contact it gives them. (Be punctual!)

The program is operating in Tokyo, Yokohama, Nagoya, Kyoto, Otsu (near Kyoto), Osaka, Kobe, and Kagoshima. Details about arranging visits are given in the sections covering each city. If possible, obtain a copy of the JNTO publication "Home Visit System", which contains more information and useful tips. Most hosts speak English, but in each city there are some who speak other languages.

Almost every visitor who has made such a visit has spoken very warmly of the experience.

Clubs and Organizations

Several international organizations, like Toastmasters and Lions International, have affiliates in Japan. With prior preparation it should be possible to arrange to meet Japanese members who speak English. If you have a hobby or special interest, it is possible to arrange a meeting with Japanese with the same interest. In the case of more obscure activities, one might get a Japanese person to see what specialty magazines are published in the field, and then contact the editorial office to see if they could help make contact.

Conversation "Lounges"

In Tokyo (and possibly the other large cities) there are several "conversation lounges". The purpose is to give an opportunity for Japanese (and other residents) to meet and talk in English. Most have coffee and light snacks at low (or no) charge. Those in Tokyo are advertised in *Tokyo Journal*.

Servas

Anyone travelling around Japan who really wants to get to know the Japanese more than superficially should look into the international organization *Servas*. If accepted as members of Servas, travellers may stay at the homes of Japanese families in many parts of the country, both rural and urban, for up to three days at no charge, sharing the family's home and life. Anyone looking for a free ride should read no further. Servas travellers staying with Japanese families are expected to spend much of their time talking with their hosts and otherwise participating in their lives. Only people who have a sincere interest in learning about Japanese family life and exchanging views and experiences would be interested.

Servas was founded in 1948 as a private venture in international relations. Reasoning that person-to-person contact by people from countries around the world is a worthwhile goal, a network of volunteer hosts was put together. In addition to Japan, there are hosts in at least 70 other countries. If it is possible, travelling members are expected to act as hosts on their return to a settled life, although this is not compulsory. Many hosts have never travelled themselves, but open their doors to travellers as their contribution to world understanding, and as a way to bring a little of the outside world to them.

It is preferable to join Servas in your home country. Joining requires filling in an application form and appearing for a personal interview in order to ensure that the applicant is sincere in his interest in Servas and its ideals. Regional staff are voluntary, but there are staff and administrative expenses at the local, national and international level; for this reason a contribution of about U.S. $30 (it varies from country to country) is required. For the address of the national offices in your country, write to the international president: Mr Graham Thomas, Servas International Peace Secretary, 80 Bushwood, London E11; send an international reply coupon (or stamps if in the UK).

Those who who are unable to join Servas before reaching Japan can make contact in Tokyo. The latest contact is Mr. Inuma (tel (03) 3710-0223), though it might be better to check with the TIC to find out the current coordinator. This program would be best suited to someone who will be in Japan for a while, because an interview is necessary, and there may be other delays.

Communes

Few outsiders are aware of the existence of several communes in Japan. They have a long history; Itto-en commune in the Kansai area (near Kyoto) dates back to 1905. Several welcome foreign visitors, usually on a paying basis, although it is often possible to reduce or eliminate the charge by working at commune tasks.

To write ahead for information, contact:

Moshe Matsuba
Kibbutz Akan
Shin Shizen Juku, Nakasetsuri
Tsurui-mura, Akan-gun
Hokkaido 085-12
Japan

This is one of the communes that welcomes visitors.

If you arrive in the country without the opportunity to write ahead, telephone the head office of the Japanese Commune

Movement at (0288) 26-2038. They speak adequate English to give information, but do not correspond in any language but Japanese. For reference, the address is:

The Japanese Commune Movement
Head Office
2083 Sakae-cho
Imaichi-shi 321-12
Tochigi-ken
Japan

Various publications in English have been produced by the Movement. Contact Moshe Matsuba for details of what is currently available. Enclose a couple of U.S. dollar bills or the approximate equivalent in another convertible currency to cover their postage costs. (Do not send a bank draft, etc., for the greedy banks will take it all!)

Free Guides

In some cities, like Nara, local organizations organize a free guide service, so Japanese who can speak some English and who are interested in meeting foreigners are willing to act as unpaid guides for sightseeing in the city. Make inquiries at the TIC offices in Tokyo and Kyoto.

Teaching

One of the best ways to meet a cross section of Japanese people is by teaching English. The system of teaching English in schools is so poor in Japan that private schools are necessary to provide an opportunity to learn from native speakers. Teaching without a proper visa is not legal, of course, but it seems the Immigration bureau does not waste too much of its time tracking down illicit teachers.

The only problem with teaching is that you may get any level of student. It is difficult to carry on conversations about Japanese society and culture with beginners who have trouble just putting five words together correctly. However, in free conversation classes with advanced students it is possible to learn a great deal about Japan that doesn't appear in books. It is interesting that Japanese people will express very open and candid opinions in English (or another foreign language) that they will not say in Japanese; there are many constraints on behavior in Japanese society which are reinforced by the very structure of the language. Through teaching you also have an opportunity to experience every type of personality, from very open (and contrary to the stereotyped image of the Japanese) to girls who are so painfully shy that they refuse to answer questions for fear of making a mistake. (There is more information on teaching in the section on long-stay visas.)

Casual Meetings

During your stay in Japan, some of the most pleasant memories will probably result from meeting various Japanese people. They can give you information about the country and insights into the society, customs, etc. Many warm friendships have developed from such casual conversations. (It is interesting that a Japanese who can speak English reasonably well and who has overcome the initial fear of talking with foreigners that affects the majority of Japanese (a long story in itself) will often be more friendly and relaxed with a foreigner than with his own people because the foreigner will not expect the social niceties that Japanese are supposed to display when first meeting another Japanese.) Thus, if someone starts talking with you and the conversation seems interesting, then you will probably be rewarded by the results.

If you are busy with personal affairs, or are not free or otherwise inclined to talk at that moment, then do not feel obliged to do so. It is not uncommon for Japanese, particularly males of university age, to have the attitude that any foreigner they encounter has nothing better to do than provide them with free English practice. Some are rude enough to cut into the middle of a conversation. Many foreigners, particularly those who have been in the country only a short time, are still operating under the myth of "exquisite Japanese politeness" and feel that they would mortally insult any Japanese by refusing such a wish. Forget this brainwashing! Good manners are good manners in any country. If you do not welcome an intrusion, by a Japanese or anyone else, you need not be put upon. You may politely inform the person that you are busy, wish to carry on your conversation with the other person, etc. For the average person this should be a sufficient hint. If the interruptor then persists, you are free to be more firm as the circumstances require. This is not a recommendation to rudeness in general social situations, for most Japanese are very nice and conversations can be interesting, but you do not have to inconvenience yourself to accommodate someone else's lack of politeness and good manners.

Foreigners have a curiosity value to most Japanese. At places popular with tourists, many Japanese (especially children on a school excursion) will be outgoing and may even want your autograph. (Star for a day!) Keep this in mind if bombarded with a constant chorus of "Aro" ("Hello") and try to keep smiling. (If it happens in larger centers, you have the right to be annoyed, for they should have outgrown such behavior.) Interestingly, although Westerners are a rare sight back in the boonies (some Japanese may have never seen a foreigner), many travellers have observed that people in such areas are often more natural with foreigners than those in the cities.

THE AIDS FACTOR There is a certain element within the Japanese press that takes particular delight in finding any fault (real or otherwise) in Western products, society, behavior, culture, morals, etc. This gives them an opportunity to attack the West and, by implication, show the inherent superiority of the Japanese way. The AIDS epidemic of recent years had provided a splendid opportunity to stir up anti-foreign feeling, an aspect never too far below the surface of many Japanese anyway.

Numerous attacks against Westerners, particularly Americans (and, most particularly, American blacks) had been printed in these publications (one gives careful consideration to using the term "yellow journalism" in such cases), with the effect that some of the less-alert members of the Japanese public (they do exist, despite what has been put out about the higher IQ of the Japanese) had been induced to make the pavlovian association: foreigner = AIDS. On a TV AIDS information phone-in show, for example, one caller asked if he was at risk because he had held the train handstrap just used by a foreigner, and a black Canadian woman was temporarily banned from using a local public bath (until she protested vociferously). Another wrote that some well-dressed office types had pointed at him on the train and said very clearly "AIDS".

I write at length on this subject because such attitudes are quite likely to affect a number of foreign travellers in Japan in the form of remarks or even unkind treatment.

Public awareness of AIDS, however, is at last changing, in part due to a major HIV blood scandal uncovered in 1996. Unapproved sales of unheated blood products (imported from the US) by a Japanese drug company in the mid-1980s, despite knowing the risk of HIV infection from such products, resulted in public outrage and legal action. All this has helped to give wider support and better education about the AIDS-causing virus.

That said, there is a very good chance that any increase in the prevalence of AIDS in Japan will be due to "sex tours" made by a small portion of the male population to the fleshpots of neighboring countries, where there is too good an opportunity to become infected by local "business girls".

Dating

Any foreigner in Japan (apart from gays) is likely to date a Japanese of the opposite sex. The "picture" is quite different for western males and females, good for the former, often not for the latter.

One of the characteristics of the upbringing of Japanese women is subordination to males, beginning with her brothers. In a relationship, she generally looks after her man. (To many Western men first exposed to this coddling it seems like paradise arrived, and many are happy with this level of relationship.) Conversely, Japanese males tend to be spoiled from childhood, so the result is that Japanese men and Western women tend not to be very compatible. This is reflected by the ratio of only one marriage of a Japanese male to a Western female to every 10 of Japanese women to Western men, and a high rate of divorce by Western women who have married Japanese men (particularly those who married overseas, and found the man reverting to Japanese behavior upon their return to Japan). Many Western women living in Japan do not enjoy their lives very much.

For some Japanese men there is prestige in dating a Western woman. While this is not the general rule, some foreign women tend to wonder if they are being asked out for their company or for the prestige they bring. One American woman had this experience; her date took her to a restaurant . . .

with 10 of his male buddies (and then asked her to pay for her meal!). Fortunately, this extreme is rare. Many Japanese men have a very distorted view of western women, especially their moral standards, and expect them to leap into bed upon request. Any woman who suspects this attitude in her Japanese friend and wishes to dispel it should easily be able to give a suitable hint in conversation.

There are various ways to meet Japanese of the opposite sex. In Tokyo, there are coffee shops where people go to chat in English ("conversation lounges"), and several places where people gather for drinks and conversation; in Tokyo, *Henry Africa* and *Charleston* are well-known examples, though there is always the language problem. (Such places tend to come and go in popularity, so it is necessary to ask around and find the current "in" place.) There are also many discos in the large cities; the Roppongi area of Tokyo has several. They are not cheap, generally about ¥3000–4000 entrance charge, which includes some drinks and eats. Their main drawback as meeting places is that the sound levels are so high it is almost impossible to talk, and many discos and clubs admit only couples.

After meeting a suitably charming young woman (or man) there comes the matter of future meetings. Some families are open-minded and have no objections if their daughter or son has an *appointment* (date) with a foreigner, but others (especially wealthy and upper-class families) may object strongly. Suspicion and dislike of other races is universal. (One American friend who only delivered a message to a Japanese girl living in a university residence learned later that the keepers of the place had phoned her parents in Kyushu to inform them of this horrific occurrence.)

A problem encountered by some males

dating a Japanese girl concerns twosomes. There is the distinct possibility that a girl who meets a man casually will keep a second date, but will show up with a girlfriend in tow. On further meetings she may appear alone once she knows there is no danger, while others will continue to show up accompanied. The latter is a probable write-off.

Marriage

The following information has been true in the past, but may have been changed by recent developments. (The publication *Now You Live in Japan* was once the source of information on the subject, but with the changes in Immigration regulations, it has disappeared. A successor may have appeared by the time this edition becomes available.)

Foreign men and women marrying Japanese have, in the past, been affected differently by Japanese law. When two Japanese marry, the wife's name is removed from her family's register and transferred to that of her husband's family. Because registry is tantamount to citizenship, a foreign spouse may not be put into a family register. This has caused different treatment for foreign males and females. In principle, both sexes are now to be treated equally. The following gives an idea of the situation as it was previously to show the improvements now in effect.

A foreign wife was allowed to remain in Japan as long as her husband resided there and sent a letter to Immigration authorities whenever her period of stay was due for renewal, stating that he wanted her to remain. A foreign husband had no right of residence just because he was married to a Japanese woman; a Japanese wife was expected to reside in her husband's country. A foreign man needed an independent reason for remaining in Japan (work, study,

etc., with appropriate visa), or else he could be deported with his children, who had to take on his nationality. Anyone considering marriage to a Japanese should discuss the matter with someone from their embassy in addition to inquiring about relevant Japanese laws. (Sometimes it is advantageous to be married in the overseas country if there is the possibility of returning there to live at some time in the future.)

Children of mixed marriages often have a difficult time in Japan because their foreign blood sets them apart from the rest of the population in a society that values sameness and uniformity. They may also have difficulty deciding the society to which they belong, Japanese or foreign; it is a problem trying to be both, and such children often fail to fit in completely with either, not learning either language perfectly. (The pressure to be the same as everyone else is so severe that even Japanese children who have lived for some time overseas are often picked on after their return to Japan because they are "different".)

It is unlikely, as in some countries, that any Japanese girl would be try to find a way out of the country by marrying a foreigner, so it isn't necessary to try to figure if the girl's affection is genuine or feigned. However, one should give careful thought as to how well she would fit in back home.

Anyone considering marriage to a Japanese and remaining in Japan (particularly a foreign man marrying a Japanese woman) should have the prospective partner read the following two books (written in Japanese) if they are still available:

Sugao no Kokusai Kekkon The Japan Times (¥1200)
Kokusai Kekkon Handbook Akashi Shoten, Tokyo (¥1600)

They describe both procedures and the potential problems.

Understanding the Japanese: The Cycle of Life

To understand a country, it is helpful—if not essential—to understand the lives of the people. The following is a very abridged portrayal of the cradle-to-the-grave route travelled by a few typical Japanese.

Birth is most often in a hospital. Health standards are very high, and infant mortality is perhaps the lowest in the world. (However, the death rate up to about age 10 is the highest in the developed world, and higher than in many third-world countries, probably because of very low safety-consciousness; foreigners are horrified to see that almost every child in the front seat of a car is not restrained in any way, and thus at great risk in any sudden stop.) Interestingly, Japanese babies are said to have a 10 month gestation, not nine as in actuality, because the counting begins at the end of the last monthly cycle, not from the time of the first missed one.

Infants are carried in close contact with their mothers, and she is rarely out of sight, so the child never has anxieties about affection or care. This feeling of security is believed to have many beneficial psychological results, though the spoiling causes problems later in life.

Childhood is the happiest time in Japan, for they are allowed to do much as they please ("spoiled rotten" is a more blunt description!), rarely punished, and disciplined only mildly. It is a time of life looked back on fondly by many, especially men, for there are so many privileges with so few responsibilities.

As the children grow up, the mother trains them in the way expected by society, both as her mother did and as neighborhood mothers are similarly doing. There are differences between city and country ways, differences are developing as some of the old ways become discarded, and there are some differences based on education and class identification, but there is quite a remarkable similarity in outlook of mothers from one end of the country to the other.

City mothers generally push their children much harder in the academic direction than those in the countryside or smaller centers, and the school standards are also generally better in larger cities, so an education gap does exist. (There is not much perceived need for a highly educated farmer or fisherman, either by the educators or the people involved, although some children do "escape" the traditional life through education.)

Sex roles are clearly differentiated. Although no longer true with urban families, in rural areas, generally, boys are given pampered treatment by mothers and receive preference over female children, and the girls are expected to defer to any boys (although this—like so many other aspects of Japanese life—can vary from family to family). This pampered treatment does, however, generate a feeling of dependence (*amae* in Japanese) among boys, a feeling that lasts a lifetime for many men. It is said that many look for a wife who will spoil them in the same way that their mothers did. (The term "Peter Pan syndrome" pops up from time to time in description.) The sense of dependence is also felt toward to schoolteachers, the boss at work, or any other leader in the person's life, and is one explanation for the lack of personal exertiveness remarked on by many.

In former days, there was also a seniority role, with the eldest boy being accorded priority over any other children. (In the case of twins, the first-born was the more important.) This boy would normally inherit the family property, and was also expected to take care of the parents in their old age.

The carefree stage begins to be circumscribed early, and competition among the academic stream (though this term is not used, all students theoretically being treated as equals) begins as early as nursery school (age 3 or 4) to get the child onto the fast track that leads to the right kindergarten, to the right primary school, to the right high school, and finally to one of the top universities. Children of these "education mamas" will be urged all their formative years to study with the aim of passing the fiendishly difficult (and often tricky) entrance examinations of the top few universities. It is very common for the children to attend cram schools (*juku*) after regular school hours to have a few more facts pushed into their heads, or to have made clear what had been skimmed over rapidly in regular school. Children in regular school do not interrupt the teacher with questions or requests for elaboration (at most schools; there are some exceptions) and the teacher proceeds at the pace set by the Ministry of Education. (Every class of a given academic year is supposed to cover exactly the same material at the same time, throughout the country.) It is up to the child to find out any information not comprehended.

The system right through to university is based on cramming in facts and having the students regurgitate them. The result is excellent results in math and technical subjects, but there is little if any practice in analysis and drawing conclusions, a fact of life that becomes apparent to a foreigner after extended exposure to Japanese adults who have been through the system. The educational system and curriculum is under complete control of the national government, and there has been an intentional policy of keeping the younger ignorant of almost any aspect of Japanese history that

reflects badly on the country. The young generation knows very little, for example, about the horrors of WWII and the occupation of China, etc., that went before it.

School is generally not a happy experience for a large percentage of students, for the academic pressure is high (aimed at an academic elite), and most schools have a myriad of rules rivalling those of the military, down to specifying the allowable type of undershirts for the boys, and (at some schools) even compelling the boys to wear their hair close-cropped. Although physical punishment is nominally banned, some teachers are quite brutal physically, and almost every year one or more few students have been assaulted severely. Not all is gloom and doom, but schools are not as free and interesting as they are in many other countries.

The first six years of school are primary school, followed by three years each of junior and senior high. Successive years bring on ever-increasing study loads. Those who are not successful in passing university entrance exams may go on to a technical school, or may join the workforce in a factory, store, or other similar type of work. (Some students who were unsuccessful with the exams one year may try again several times. Such long-term triers are nicknamed *ronin*, the word for masterless samurai who used to wander around the country looking for work.

The remarkable thing about the Japanese educational system is that the most difficult part is getting *into* university, because of the very difficult entrance exams. Once in, most students have a second childhood, with very undemanding courses. Few are flunked. (These comments, seen often in the English-language press in Japan, probably refer mostly to students in the arts and humanities. One can only assume that engineers and other science-oriented students have a more demanding curriculum, if Japanese manufactured products are to be used as the criterion for judgment!)

As with everything in Japan, there is a hierarchy of universities, with Tokyo and Kyoto national universities (*Todai* and *Kyodai* respectively) being at the top of the perceived ratings. Next comes a clutch of universities led by Keio and Waseda (both private institutions in Tokyo) and several other private and national universities, then local universities. The reason for the great popularity of the first two is that their graduates are almost certain shoo-ins for offers to work with the prestigeous public service, while those from any other university rarely succeed. This ensures that the public service has the academic elite, but it also makes for a very incestuous relationship between those two universities and the government, and can produce scholastically excellent naifs.

The same type of relationship is very common within universities and within departments, so that a student normally does all his studies at one university (through to PhD) in one department (no cross-pollenation), and universities normally hire only their own graduates for teaching posts. The result is a very insular world, designed largely to maintain the *sempai-kohai* relationship of leader and protege. The protege's role is, if he wants to advance (there are relatively few women post-grads), to promote the ideas of his benefactor, not to engage in his own independent research that might upset the applecart. The result is that not all research coming out of Japanese universities is worthy of the name, and some would actually be laughed at if translated into a foreign language. However, the system has obviously produced the people needed to push the country forward, so something is working right (or has so far).

A couple of decades ago, it was pre-

dominently men who attended four-year universities, while the majority of women opted for a two-year college program. The reason was rooted in the same Confucian ideas that it is the men who should work, and that women should stay at home raising children and taking care of the man. In the past it has been the rare company that offered any senior position of any kind to a woman employee, no matter how much ability she had. This is still the general case, but slowly the barriers are coming down and women are being given more opportunities. There is an element of circularism at work here. Traditionally women have been expected to marry after a few years in the company, so the company did not give them good jobs. The women, perceiving that career possibilities were limited, never tried to move much beyond filing, writing, gopher, and tea-making activities, their role being regarded as assisting the men, the real doers. Two years at college was considered enough to give the women a final polish, a taste of higher education, a touch of exposure to foreign culture in the form of an English or French literature course (but not enough, heaven forbid, that she would become fluent in the foreign language or become really tainted by Western thinking that would make her unmarriageable or unacceptable in the still rather closed Japanese society). They had been perfect office workers, without the drawbacks of ambition, and prime candidates to be married off to the company's male employees.

Things are changing, with two-year colleges diminishing in number, and the larger and most progressive companies are making it possible for some women to move into responsible positions, and a few have even given overseas postings to top women employees, something unthinkable in the most moderrn companies just a few years ago (although it should be noted that most of these jobs are of the translation and correspondence type). It is a time of change and moderate ferment, and an interesting time to observe the country in its evolution from rigid male dominance to one of greater equality. (It isn't all that many years ago that women were kept out of responsible posts even in today's most socially progressive western countries, so credit should be given to Japanese companies for the progress made so far.) One interesting possibility of this change is that women, by not having been subjected to the rigidifying influences that have been acting on the men, may turn out to be better able to think logically and may excel in occupations like computer programming! Time will tell.

Once into a company after graduation, the new worker's world is also circumscribed. In the most rigid of companies, there may be a training program lasting up to half a year and strongly resembling military training, with living in barrack-like quarters, early morning rising with calesthenics and exercises, training, singing the company song, and being indoctrinated with the company way of doing things. Most companies will hire only new graduates, so that everyone joins at the same age. Until recently a person joined a company for life, and job-hopping was almost unknown (largely because companies would not hire workers from another company), but this rigid structure is slowly giving way and some companies now hire specialists who have worked with other companies.

The men making up this group of workers, generally found only in large companies, are known in Japanese as *sarariman* (salaryman), and are really the only people in Japan who have what was generally called "lifetime employment". They would normally advance in lock-step for several years, although the more able would have their chance to show their abilities and slowly pull ahead of the pack. If they did not do something rash or disgraceful, they could expect to remain on the payroll until retirement. However, these people made up only about 35% of the adult male population.

Factory workers do not have quite such security, although companies in Japan have done their best to find alternative work for their employees in bad times rather than just laying them off, as happens in most other countries. In large companies with ongoing prosperity, a worker would expect steady employment, although his pay might not be as high as that of the higher administrative workers.

It is in the smaller companies that things are more uncertain. By lacking the prestige that goes with size, they cannot attract the best educated people who might help them move ahead, and they cannot pay the same wages that the large companies can. In actuality, there is a two-tier or multi-tier structure in business, with a small number of very large and prestigious companies (cars, electronics, optical goods, machinery, etc.) that can afford to give the top conditions, and a large number of small companies that make the myriad of parts and sub-assemblies that go into the products of the big companies. One of these small companies may be only a single family, and the pay that they receive for making these parts is only a fraction of what the major companies pay their own employees. The five-day work week and eight-hour day are unknown to these workers, and they may get only two days a month off and work 12 hour days to make a living. These are the workers not seen during the visits by foreigners to large factories, but they are contributing in no small way to the prosperity of the country. Without them, the large companies could not give such good conditions to their own armies of workers (nor produce at such low costs), and when there is a downturn in business, it is these small companies that get squeezed first for cost reductions, etc.

The average salaryman will wait until he is in his mid-to-late twenties before marrying, while the women are around 25. (Over 28, women begin to worry, since the average man is looking for a sweet young thing who is going to pamper him as his mother did and have no strong views of her own, qualities that diminish as the woman experiences more of life and the world.)

In days gone by, marriage was as much a union between two families or clans as between two people, and it was not uncommon for the two families to get together and decide that their son and daughter were well suited to each other and would be married. The two actually involved would have had no say in the matter. Nowadays such determining of matters by parents is so rare as to raise comment the few times it occurs. What are called "arranged marriages" in many English-language publications are actually marriages resulting from arranged introductions, *omiai* in Japanese. Such introductions may be arranged by relatives, friends, business acquaintances, a boss, or professional matchmakers called *nakodo*. The parents are normally present at the first meeting if they live in the same city; independent offspring away from home may make their own arrangements. (The former are more interesting to the onlooker as the parents size each other up while the children often sit with downcast eyes hoping that the whole business will go away.) If the two young people feel that there is sufficient mutual interest, they will arrange to meet again. After only a couple of dates they might decide to marry, or they could meet several times and then call the whole thing off.

Nowadays, however, less than half the marriages in Japan are the result of arranged introductions. The others are known as "love marriages", though realistically better termed "random introduction", for couples who meet by *omiai* usually also develop a sense of affection for the prospective partner before agreeing to marry. (The arranged introduction system has the advantage that the couple will be from compatible backgrounds and serious about marriage, so they will be "primed" for acceptance with a suitable partner. It is not so different from the matchmaker in many traditional European societies.)

To Westerners, reasons for getting married in Japan sometimes seem rather trivial or shallow, more financial than romantic, somewhat more akin to arranging a corporate merger than linking two lives. Although there are many marriages based on affection as strong as Westerners know, many other couples seem content with an arrangement whereby the husband brings in an income and the wife tends the house, and bears and rears the children, with little apparent affection between them. In some cases this may be accurate, and in other cases the couple are just not demonstrative in public. Probably for many couples a feeling of mutual respect is sufficient. Marriages resulting from *omiai* appear to be just as stable as those of a seemingly more romantic origin. It is certainly more and more common to see married couples holding hands and showing affection for each other in public than was true only five to ten years ago.

If a young salaryman has shown no inclination to get married by his late 20s, it is not uncommon for his boss to start making moves to introduce him to likely wife prospects. It is considered to be an unnatural condition not to be married, and indicates a lack of stability for a man. This is not good for his career prospects. (It is not unknown for (undeclared) male and female homosexuals to marry just to stop the social pressures to get married.)

The marriage ceremony is usually Shinto, although some families prefer a Buddhist ceremony, and a growing number in the larger cities choose a Christian ceremony with white wedding gown because they like the "mood". In the case of the first two, only close family members attend the actual wedding, and all guests attend the reception banquet. Costs of weddings are generally astronomical.

When the couple marry, one of the two is taken in as a member of the other family. Usually the woman joins the man's family and takes his name, but it is not uncommon, if the girl's family has no son to carry on the name, for the man to become part of her family and to take her family name.

It has traditionally been a worry for a woman to marry the oldest son. In smaller cities and farm communities, the wife and the son live with the parents and, in the worst case, the wife may be treated virtually like a servant by the mother-in-law. (Like everything in Japan, this is case-by-case, and many mothers-in-law are gracious and helpful to the new bride.) In the cities, where housing is so cramped (except for those who can afford the exorbitant rents demanded for spacious accommodation), there is no room for the husband's family, so this occurrence is becoming less common. The nuclear family is fast becoming the norm. With the media (print and TV) bringing new ideas into even the most remote communities, women are learning that being an unpaid servant is not necessarily their lot in life.

In the early days of salaryman's marriage, the couple will probably live in a small apartment in a multi-storey building. The building is quite possibly owned by his company and apartments rented at minimal cost. The apartment would typically have three small rooms plus a bathroom, the large one about 6 mats in size (one tatami straw mat is about 1 x 2 meters), the smaller 4 1/2, and the kitchen about 2. The large room is usually actually covered with mats, while the smaller might be plain concrete. The large room serves as living room during the day, and as bedroom at night, when the bedding is taken out of a closet and unrolled on the mats. Instead of being the picture of Zen emptiness, the rooms are normally chock-a-block with a TV, video recorder, cabinets and low tables, air conditioner, a stack of magazines and photo albums, ornaments, and usually an incredible jumble of other items. (I visited a home in which the smaller room was filled with a full-size grand piano!) The lack of storage space in which to put things away and the resulting untidiness is one reason for Japanese reluctance to entertain at home. (Homes in the countryside are usually much bigger.)

As the couple becomes better established, they may buy a small house or condominium. To afford the purchase, employees of large companies are often elegible for low-interest loans, but in worst cases it has not been unknown for not only the couple work to pay off the mortgage, but their children may also be expected to continue for a number of years afterwards. Many couples have just resigned themselves to having to rent all their lives.

Life is no bed of roses for Mr. Salaryman. He typically has to commute one to two hours each way every working day, and spends long hours at the office. Although the nominal working day is eight hours, he typically works another two to three hours as a matter of routine. He may grumble (outside the office) about this extra time, for he is largely coerced into it by the fact that everyone else is doing it and he doesn't want to appear to be a shirker, since togetherness is the rule in offices. (In many companies, it is direct coercion from supervisors that generates the "everyone else is doing it" situation.) In compensation, the extra pay that he earns may buy the luxuries that might otherwise be out of reach. Whether he actually accomplishes much during his overtime is not so important; the *appearance* of working hard is often the important criterion (form being generally more important than function in Japanese society).

After work he might go out for an hour or two of drinking with his workmates. He might really enjoy this, or he might actually prefer to go home to his wife and children (for he often arrives home after thay have gone to bed), but in many companies the after-hours drinking is virtually compulsory. One subversive opinion about this practice is that the men quickly run out of outside interests to talk about and end up talking shop, to the benefit of the company.) The younger generation of salarymen more and more is putting family ahead of company, when possible. (Before he married, he went out drinking nearly every night, alcohol being an important lubricant for social coherence.)

Mr. Salaryman usually hands over his entire pay to his wife, who then pays the bills and gives him an allowance.

The average family is about two children, and the national rate of population increase is very low, less than 0.6% annually (1.57 children per woman around 1990, not enough to maintain the population longterm). Larger families would be too large for most houses, and their income is stretched if they are paying for a house. Most women are content with the role of mother to her children and comfort to her husband, although increasing numbers are

returning to work after the children are old enough to be cared for by others. (Day-care centers are almost unknown.) It has similarities to the pattern of movement out of the kitchen into the world that took place in the USA and elsewhere beginning 20 to 30 years ago.

The pattern of marriage has undergone much change since the war, with more couples doing activities together as families, rather than each partner having virtually a separate life. On the other hand, with the increased freedom offered by an independent income from a job, not a few older women are shucking off uncaring, demanding, domineering, or otherwise undesirable husbands whom they tolerated while the children were growing up. (The nickname for such men is *sodai gomi*, "bulky trash", a category for garbage collection.) Divorce at any earlier stage would have been out of the question due to the small or non-existent settlement that they would typically receive. Sometimes a woman divorces her husband just before he retires when she realizes that he would be underfoot all the time, or wait until he receives his lumpsum retirement settlement and obtains most or all of it in the divorce settlement, leaving him with nothing for his old age.

Of course there is no single pattern to marriage, but these few lines will have to suffice.

Assuming that the couple has stayed together and put their children through university or otherwise seen them on their way, retirement for the man comes early, typically 60 (increased from 55 only early in the 1990s). After this, of course he is still young, not at the end of his working life as was the case when that age became established, and the family probably needs a continuing income, so he will usually have to find another job. To an outsider this seems to be a waste of experience gained with many years, and some companies are taking note and extending the time at least until 60. The average lifespan for men is given as 75.6, that for women 81.4 (1990), which are claimed to be the longest in the world (though one wonders sometimes about the reliability of the statistics, since there are no factors of Japanese life that should increase life over that in western countries); women can expect to outlive their husbands by many years. When the end does come, most Japanese have a funeral with Buddhist rites, although a few choose Shinto. This leads to the observation that people generally look to Shinto for happy events, and to Buddhism for the sad ones. (Buddhism has beliefs about the afterlife, whereas there is no body of scriptures for Shinto.) After the ceremony, the body is cremated and, after a period of time, the ashes are buried under a headstone. The memory of each person will be preserved in the form of a small, vertical wooden tablet with the person's name written on it. These tablets are kept at the family altar (*butsudan*). At various times these people are venerated by the family, but they are not worshipped as some foreigners may believe. The veneration could be regarded as a type of on-going memorial service.

Communication with the Japanese

If time permits, it is useful to take at least an introductory course in spoken Japanese before going to Japan. Even in the big cities it can be difficult to communicate using only English, and it is that much more difficult in the boonies. It *can* be done; thousands have managed before you! If you have no time to take a course, the most valuable assistant during your travels will be the basic phrasebook the *Tourist's Handbook*, available free from the Tourist Information Centers in Tokyo and Kyoto

(and, presumably, by mail from overseas JNTO offices). It has the most often asked questions and a series of answers in both languages, so a Japanese person can point to the correct answer.

Learning the Language

For the benefit of those who plan to study Japanese, the following notes may be useful.

For self-study of the rudiments of the language, one of the best books is *Japanese For Busy People*, published by Kodansha International, and *Japanese Made Easy* by Monane, published by Tuttle. For a comprehensive study of Japanese, *Beginning Japanese* by Jorden is an old standby. It is published by Yale University Press.

The Japanese language is reputed to be difficult. The Japanese love to believe this, for they have a great psychological need to believe that everything about their ethnic make-up, society, culture, and language, are unique and related to no other. Their academics are careful to avoid any line of research that might contradict this comfortable belief. Conveniently ignored is the fact that Korean and Japanese are (to quote R.A. Brown in The Japan Times while reviewing Roy Andrew Miller's *Nihongo: In Defence of Japanese*), "as structurally isomorphic as any languages could be: for any Japanese morphological or syntactic pattern there is an identical pattern in Korean. . . ." He continues, " . . . and every educated Korean is well aware of this. Japanese tend to find it astonishing.")

However, while it is true that the *writing system* is probably the world's most convoluted, the language itself is relatively simple, at least in the earlier stages. Any language that has no gender, no singular or plural, no verb endings, no noun endings, no adjective endings, and almost no irregular verbs, has certainly eliminated many of the complications of nearly all western languages. Of course there are compensating complications, such as the lack of relative words (like "that"), and the difference of most sentence structures from those we are familiar with, but the language is by no means as difficult structurally as it is made out to be. The biggest problem much of the time is social, knowing when to use what level of politeness, and *that* requires a detailed knowledge of the structure of Japanese society.

Much is made of the supposed vagueness of Japanese. However, it is not the language itself that is vague, but rather the way it is used. Japanese can be spoken just as precisely as English, but to do so would often be considered impolite; instead, the speaker alludes to or suggests a fact, leading the listener to the information, so as not to appear superior or presumptuous in suggesting he knows something the listener doesn't. Women use this suggestive form to a greater extent than men, which makes their statements less forceful or believable than a similar statement by a man. The existence of "women's language" and "men's language" is clearly sexist by Western thinking, but is an inescapable fact. (The existence of "women's language" is a problem for foreign men who learn Japanese from their girlfriends, for they sound like gays!)

Actual meanings are traditionally conveyed as much by gesture and tone of voice as by the words themselves. Because of the circumlocutions often required to bypass a direct statement, misunderstandings can easily occur (among Japanese), with the result that the Japanese language is excellent for maintaining social distinctions but poor for imparting information and knowledge. (It is largely a disaster for writing technical materials, and it is common for one Japanese not to be able to understand what another has written.)

Younger Japanese today tend not to follow the older conventions of speech and are dropping many of the "formula" phrases, with the result that the older people are complaining that young people are losing the ability to pick up these cues, and that they have to state everything exactly if they want to get their message through!

Certainly the language is not simple, due to the multitude of verb forms and the many words needed to indicate social distinctions, but it is not difficult to learn a major proportion, perhaps 70 per cent of the language in *romaji* (the romanised form). You have to learn the written form for the rest because each character (*kanji*) has at least two pronunciations, *on* (Chinese) and *kun* (Japanese), and the pronunciation of a character may well change when it is used in combination with others. Without knowing the *kanji* and its different readings, it would be impossible to comprehend these shifts.

These multiple readings for *kanji* manifest themselves in the worst form in names of people and places, for some pronunciations may be unique to a particular name. It may sound silly, but the average Japanese cannot pronounce the names of a large number of places on a road map, particularly those in Hokkaido, where they are derived from Ainu words. As much as possible, the correct local pronunciations of place names are used in this book; these may occasionally differ from names in literature printed in Tokyo, for they may use Tokyo readings of the *kanji*.

In the written language, important words are written in *kanji* (Chinese characters) while grammatical endings are written in *hiragana*, a syllabary of all the vowel and consonant-plus-vowel sound combinations in the language. Yet another complete syllabary of exactly the same sounds is used to (try to) transliterate foreign words.

Unfortunately they use this method initially for learning the pronunciation of English, so many learn incorrect pronunciations since the syllabary is deficient in l, f, and some other sounds.

Conversing in English

Except with Japanese who have really mastered English, usually by living overseas, there will be problems with many questions requiring a "yes" or "no" answer. In Japanese a "yes" answer will mean "Yes, what you say is true", so it is essential to avoid asking negative questions, like "Aren't you going?" A Japanese will answer "yes" if he is *not* going, "no" if he *is* going. It takes a while to get into the habit of asking unambiguous questions.

Another problem is an "or" question. Even though Japanese has an exact equivalent, they seem to have insuperable difficulty recognising that there is a choice between A and B. Ask "Is it A or B?", and the answer will almost invariably be "yes". The simplest way around the problem is to say "Is it A? Is it B?".

It is surprising that young Japanese do not speak English better than they do; most of them seem unable to put together more than one or two sentences of correct English. About 300 hours of instruction is given at junior high school level, and nearly 500 hours in senior school. A further 300–600 hours at university is required to become an English teacher, yet a very large proportion of teachers at all levels cannot carry on a conversation in English; they have learned English in the same way as they are teaching it, as a field of academic study without relevance to real-life communication. Another problem is that English is initially taught using the Japanese *katakana* syllabary to represent English sounds, a purpose for which it is entirely inadequate, having no distinction between the

letters "r" and "l", and misrepresenting several other sounds, which explains the frequent interchange of these letters. (Often quoted is the banner strung across the Ginza when General MacArthur was being proposed for U.S. President: "We play for MacArthur's erection".)

Also at fault is what is termed locally (by foreign residents) as "shopping bag English", a mishmash of English words strung together using Japanese syntax (probably) and with frequent misspellings (they refuse to use dictionaries). Added to this is the fact that a seeming majority of the hundreds, or thousands, of words borrowed from English are given incorrect meanings in the Japanese usage. Probably the average person believes that anything in print is correct, and will repeat the error.

The Japanese must have a sense of humor. Why else would the car manufacturers choose names that Japanese cannot pronounce correctly, with a copious mix of r's and l's, such as "Gloria", "Corolla", "Tercel", or "Starlet".

Romanization

As a (much appreciated) courtesy to visitors to Japan, many signs are written in *romaji* (Roman letters). Unfortunately there may be difficulty in knowing how to pronounce them because there is more than one system of romanization.

The most common is the Hepburn system, devised more than a century ago and still useful as an aid to English speakers in pronouncing Japanese correctly, although it will be of negligible use to speakers of other languages. The other major system, that of the Ministry of Education, is useful in formal studies of Japanese but is not very useful for general application because it is necessary to learn the conventions of the system in order to interpret the words so written.

The Hepburn system, with few changes, is used throughout this book. Either it or the Ministry of Education system may be seen on signs in Japan, sometimes both in the same sentence.

The following is a list of the major differences between the two systems (both of which the Japanese learn); the Hepburn is pronounced like normal English.

Hepburn	Ministry of Education
shi	si
sha	sya
shu	syu
sho	syo
chi	ti
cha	tya
chu	tyu
cho	tyo
tsu	tu
fu	hu
ji	zyi
ja	zya
ju	zyu
jo	zyo

There is much carelessness (or ignorance) in the spelling of words in . One common mistake is interchanging "a" and "u", because they sound the same to the Japanese. (Compare the sounds of the vowels in "a cup".) This is almost certainly the explanation of Honda's choice of name for a motor scooter, the "Flush". (It is a pity that another company beat them to the name "Champ".) Because "n" and "m" are also interchangeable, the word "damper" (meaning a shock absorber to British) gets written "dunper". Sometimes, also, one sees "thu" instead of "tsu", or "tu"; thith ith a mithtake ath the "th" thound doethn't exthitht in Japanethe. (It seems a matter of principle not to use a dictionary to check the spelling in written work of all kinds.)

Phrase List and Vocabulary

Japanese is basically easy to pronounce. The consonants are pronounced much the same as in English (all "hard", not "soft"), and the vowels are similar to those in Italian:

a   as the English indefinite article
e   as in the "a" of ale
i   as in machine
o   as in oh
u   as in the "oo" of hoot

The "o" sound shifts when followed by "n". so the Japanese word *hon* rhymes with the English word *on*, not *own*.

Although there is a rhythm to the language, there is not nearly as much stress on individual syllables as in English, and each syllable is generally pronounced separately and with nearly equal stress. Thus, the city name *Hiroshima* is "hi ro shi ma", not "hi rosh' i ma", as one often hears overseas.

The following phrases may prove useful in daily travels. They are intended for survival, not as a language course, and have been simplified, in some cases until barely grammatical (but they should be understandable).

yes *hai*; *ee*
no *iie*; *chigau* (different); *nai/nai des* (not/it is not). All mean "no" but most books only give *iie*; it is too abrupt and rude for use with friends (except as in "No, you can't pay for this."). The other two forms are heard more often.

how much?	*i'kura?*
how many?	*ikutsu?*
where? (is)	*doko? (des'ka)*
when?	*itsu?*
which one/way?	*dochira?*
where is ...?	*... wa, doko des'ka?*
this ...(+ noun)(here)	*kono ...*
that ...(+ noun) (near you)	*sono ...*

that ...(+ noun) (over there)	*ano ...*	4	*yottsu*	*yon, shi* (*shi* is a
this (thing)	*kore*			homonym of
that (thing, near you)	*sore*			"death", so is
that (thing, yonder)	*are*			often avoided.)
here	*koko*	5	*itsutsu*	*go*
there (near you)	*soko*	6	*muttsu*	*roku*
there (yonder)	*asoko*	7	*nanatsu*	*nana, shichi*
right	*migi*	8	*yattsu*	*hachi*
left	*hidari*	9	*kokonotsu*	*kyu*
beyond	*saki*	10	*to*	*ju*
this side of	*temae*			
far, beyond	*muko*	11	*ju-ichi*	
in front of	*mae*	12	*ju-ni*	
next to	*tonari*			
straight ahead	*massugu*; *zuutto*	20	*ni-ju*	
	(or *zuuuuuuto*	30	*san-ju*	
	when spoken by	49	*yon-ju-kyu*	
	country people!)			
today	*kyo*	100	*hyaku*	
tomorrow	*ash'ta*	200	*ni-hyaku*	
day after tomorrow	*asatte*			
yesterday	*kino*	1000	*sen*	
		5000	*go-sen*	

NUMBERS For numbers up to 10, the Japanese have one set of words which can be used alone, and another for use only with a "counter". A counter is one of many words, depending on the shape or nature of the object. The with-counter numbers are used to make composite numbers above 10, and in expressions of time. There are too many counters to mention here, so use counterless numbers or write the number down.

10,000	*ichi-man* (Not *ju-sen*; Japanese count by ten-thousands.)
20,000	*ni-man*
25,000	*ni-man-go-sen*
100,000	*ju-man*
1,000,000	*hyaku-man*

TIME

o'clock (one o'clock)	*-ji* (*ichi-ji*) (Use with -counter numbers for time.)
minute (for telling time)	*- pun/fun*
second (duration)	*- byo*
hour (duration)	*- jikan*
year (date)	*- nen*
year (duration)	*- nenkan*

The number goes after the word for the things. When requesting something put "o" between the word for the object and the number; e.g., *Kore o futatsu kudasai* ("two of these, please").

TELEPHONE

hello	*moshi moshi* (The caller usually says this first.)

	counterless	with-counter
0	*zero*; *re*	
1	*hitotsu*	*ichi*
2	*futatsu*	*ni*
3	*mittsu*	*san*

may I speak with ...?	...-san onegai shimasu. (-san = Mr., Mrs., Miss etc)
isn't here	imasen
extension (e.g., ext 153)	naisen (ichi-go-san) (counter numbers are used here)

POST OFFICE

post office	yubin-kyoku
stamps	kitte
poste restante (general delivery)	kyokudome-yubin tome oki
registered	kakitome
special delivery	sokutatsu
air mail	koku bin
sea mail	funabin
aerogram	koku shokan
money order	yubingawase
stamped post card	yubinhagaki
parcel	kozutsumi
letter	tegami

TRAINS

ticket	kippu
one way	katamichi
return	ohfuku, shuyuken
express	tokkyu
limited express	kyuko
rapid (no surcharge)	kaisoku
local	kaku eki teisha shite, (seki)
reserved (seat)	
unreserved	jyuseki
What track for ... (station)?	... (eki) yuki wa, nan ban sen (des' ka)?
next train/ tram	tsugi no densha
basic charge (all trains)	unchin
limited express charge	tokkyu ryokin
green car (first class) charge	gurin ryokin
excursion ticket	shuyuken

YOUTH HOSTEL

(I am a) member
kai-in (des')
membership card
kai-in sho
Are you a member?
Kai-in des'ka?
Do you have a membership card?
Kai-in sho arimas' ka?
Do you want meals?
Shokuji wa?
evening meal
yu-shoku
breakfast
cho-shoku
Do you have a sleeping sheet?
Shiitsu arimas'ka?
I am a member.
Kai-in des'.
May I stay?
Tomare mas'ka?
full
Ippai
Is there a room available tomorrow/the day after tomorrow?
Ash'ta/asatte heya wa aitemas'ka?

PLANNING A LONG-TERM STAY

Japan is an interesting place to live, and there are many reasons why foreigners want to stay a while. Some want to study traditional Japanese arts. Some want to gain proficiency in the Japanese language. Some want to study martial arts. Some want to attend a Japanese university. Some want to teach English or make money in some other way. Others just like the mood and atmosphere, and want to partake of it a while longer, to learn more about Japan and its people. It can be a very enjoyable country in which to live, to develop, to grow. It is many things to many people, foreign and different, yet having similarities (in the big cities, anyway!) to familiar places so it is not threatening. The following notes should be of use to anyone staying in Japan longer than for a short touristic sojourn.

The information in this section gives some guidance about the types of activities possible, how to arrange them, and tips based on the experiences of myself and many others who have been through this process already.

Immigration

Information regarding immigration regulations applying to long-stay visitors is included in the section on immigration earlier in the book.

Studying

Studying in Japan can be broken into three broad categories: academic, cultural, and religious.

Academic

Studies at Japanese universities leading to undergraduate or postgraduate degrees, or studies on an exchange basis, etc., at accredited educational institutions are usually arranged between the Japanese and foreign university. With the assistance of your home institution it will be possible to obtain a student visa prior to arriving in Japan.

A very useful source of information in Japan is the Information Center, Association of International Education, 4-5-29 Komaba, Meguro-ku, Tokyo 153. Their book *ABC's of Study in Japan* probably has answers to most questions regarding study in the country.

Cultural

To study various aspects of Japanese society and culture, such as the tea ceremony, flower arrangement, the Japanese language, the game of I-go, etc., it is usually difficult to arrange a course and obtain a visa prior to arriving in Japan. As detailed in the section on visas, the normal practice is to go to

Japan and make arrangements while in the country, then to arrange the visa.

Studying the traditional arts, particularly flower arrangment and the tea ceremony, is regarded by many Japanese virtually as a way of life. (The name for the tea ceremony is *sado* or *chado*, literally "the way of tea".) Both are regarded as fit activities for women to practise to improve themselves, to introduce an element of traditional Japanese culture into their lives, and thus to make them better Japanese. Because of this, neither is intended to be something to be studied for a few weeks before moving on to another interest. A Japanese taking up one of these arts expects to take lessons for literally years, at considerable expense. In addition, the student must pass through several grades, each graduation costing large amounts of money.

(I attended one such party put on by a student advancing to a teacher's certificate; the display and demonstration that she had to give, plus a "gift" to the teacher, came to more than U.S. $20,000. Masters of tea ceremony and flower arrangement schools are very rich people and have been able to construct impressive buildings on some of the world's most expensive real estate because of the system. An outsider should not be tempted to call it a racket, but it certainly does separate the students from a great deal of money . . . although it does so *gracefully*.)

In the larger cities there are a few organizations that are prepared to give a short course in flower arrangement, in English, at costs more in line with what foreigners regard as acceptable for a course of study. It is also possible to see the tea ceremony being performed on a daily basis.

For information on any of these activities, talk with the knowledgeable personnel at the TICs in Tokyo or Kyoto.

Martial Arts

There are many martial arts being taught in Japan, and within each there are likely to be several schools, each with a different emphasis, degree of physical contact (and danger of injury), and so on. The best way to find a suitable art and school is to join the Japan Martial Arts Society, a group founded in 1983 by experienced foreign practitioners. Membership within Japan costs ¥4000, plus a ¥1000 registration fee. Overseas residents may join and receive the society's newsletter by remitting U.S. $35 (including the $5 registration fee) by cheque or international money order payable in U.S. dollars to JMAS, CPO Box 270, Tokyo 100. Members are entitled to tap the vast knowledge of the "old hands".

Zen Study and Meditation

One of the few things regarding Japan that most people outside the country seem to know about is Zen Buddhism. Contrary to popular belief, however, the general Japanese populace does not spend large amounts of time silently contemplating gardens or speculating on the sound of one hand clapping. Zen is a little esoteric even for the average Japanese.

There are two main Zen sects in Japan, Soto and Rinzai. Differences between them are minor. In "zazen", Soto practitioners face a wall, while in Rinzai they face the room; Rinzai uses more "koan" (riddles) than Soto; and Soto sessions last longer, typically 40–50 minutes against 20 or so for Rinzai.

Most Zen temples and instruction centers in Japan will accept those who speak Japanese or who are already familiar with the practices of Zen meditation. Otherwise, foreigners are generally not welcomed unless they have an introduction from a reputable Zen teacher.

The best opportunity for those who do not speak Japanese is offered by the International Zen Center of Japan, located on the outskirts of Fukuyama in western Honshu, about 50 kilometers west of Okayama. The center is a sub-temple of Shinsho-ji, which belongs to the Rinzai sect, and actually welcomes visitors of any age, nationality, or religion, male or female, for short or long stays. The contribution/fee is ¥3000/day, ¥70,000/month.

An information sheet is available giving further details and access information to the Center. Write to:

> Mirokunosato Shinsho-ji Kokusaizendo
> Numakuma-cho, Numakuma-gun
> Hiroshima-ken 720-04
> (Tel. 0849-88-1305; FAX 0849-88-1710)

It would be a courtesy to include a dollar bill or equivalent in a convertible currency to cover their mailing cost. If making a reservation, send your name, contact address, telephone number, desired length of stay, and intended date of arrival. (In Japan, send a reply-paid postcard (*ofuku hagaki*) so they can confirm accommodation.)

Another possibility is *Eihei-ji* temple, one of the two main temples of the Soto sect in Japan and famous throughout the country. It is located near Fukui, which is on the east shore of Lake Biwa, not too far from Kyoto. Its magnificent, historic, buildings, and mountainside setting make it a target of thousands of sightseers each year, along with the many who wish to study Zen. Foreigners are invited to participate in the activities of the temple and may arrange accommodation there. It is necessary to organise this well in advance of a proposed visit so arrangements can be made. Contact: Sanzenkei, Eiheiji, Eiheiji-cho, Yoshida-gun, Fukui-ken.

Jofuku-ji on Shikoku is a small, local temple that also functions as a Youth Hostel (7404 in the YH Handbook). The young priest is friendly and speaks good English. He welcomes visitors who wish to join him informally in meditation. It is a "family"-type temple and no advance arrangements are needed for Zen participation, although like any hostel it may be booked up on any given day, so it might be advisable to check first. The temple is located on the side of a valley, peaceful at any time and very pretty in November when the leaves change color. The address is: Jofuku-ji, Awafu 158, Otoyo-cho, Nagaoka-gun, Kochi-ken. Tel. (0887) 74-0301.

There are no temples in Kyoto where foreigners can receive instruction in English. Several temples used to let foreigners join in, but too many became restless and disturbed others. An introduction from another priest would probably be the only way to obtain admission to temples in Kyoto. If you have a sincere interest, contact the TIC in Kyoto; they may be able to help.

A good introduction to Zen is *Zen Mind, Beginner's Mind*, by Shunryo Suzuki, a Soto priest. You'll find a very large selection of Zen books at English bookstores in Japan, especially in Tokyo (Kinokuniya, Maruzen, Jena, etc.).

Working

With the exception of a small number of jobs that use a particular technical, financial, or other special skill (computer designer, cook, etc., most of whom are hired overseas or transferred to Japan by their companies), the work available to foreigners generally is related to English (and, to a lesser extent, other foreign languages). This includes teaching, translation, copywriting, and technical writing and rewriting (the latter two usually involving translations from Japanese). The following notes should give some useful knowledge of the situation and employment possibilities for the types of work that most foreigners do.

As detailed in the earlier section on immigration, you cannot immigrate to Japan and then look for work. You must have a job offer from an organization that is qualified to sponsor you for a working visa.

Teaching

The Japanese are eager for English lessons, and there is a continuing need for teachers. Most work at small, private "schools", the quality of which varies from dedicated to doing a good job through to being a purely money-making scheme. Since it is easy to start a school, and it can be lucrative, the average would be biased toward the latter end of the scale.

The better schools demand some credentials, such as a degree in English, a TOEFL (Teaching of English as a Foreign Language) certificate, or some other qualifications, while the worst of the latter will take anyone who walks in the door and can make themselves understood in English, no matter how bad the accent, pronunciation, or grammatical knowledge. (The latter type of school will of necessity be a short-term arrangement, for the Immigration department is now demanding that applicants for a teaching visa have university-level qualifications. Most up-market schools want only teachers of North American or British origins (and accent), so Aussies and Kiwis, for example, generally have a rough time if their accent is strong. It is also difficult for native speakers of English who are not of European appearance, even if their speech is flawless. Thus, those from Africa or the Indian-subcontinent, for example, or even North Americans of Japanese ancestry, would have much more difficulty landing a job, no matter how perfect their accent and how good their qualifications and ability.

The schools (and, presumably, the students) would really prefer the "total learning experience" of English teaching only by a Caucasian with blonde hair and blue eyes (preferably with big knockers as further qualifications).

The better schools require that teachers have a working visa, and can sponsor prospective teachers for same if the school is large enough and the teacher will be working nearly full time.

Strange things can happen in trying to do things correctly, however. In one case a few years ago, a couple of South Africans of English ancestry applied for a working visa to teach English. They were turned down because an official found in a reference book that the official language of their country was Afrikaans, so they, therefore, could not be qualified native speakers of English!

The less prestigious schools will hire anybody, no questions asked about visas or any other qualifications, and thus these organizations provide expense money for large numbers of travellers in Japan on tourist visas replenishing their coffers. (This not to knock these amateur teachers completely; many make an honest effort to try to teach their charges, and may actually be more enthusiastic and effective than the more credentialled ones.)

Although it is nothing to count on, it seems that the immigration officials do not go out of their way to find schools that are hiring non-documented foreigners. Without foreign teachers, there would be a gross insufficiency of people able to teach English authoritatively; most Japanese teachers of English in the public school system are incapable of even an elementary conversation in the language they are teaching.

Pay is commonly around ¥3000 per hour of working time at schools, but it can be difficult to get more than a couple of consecutive hours at one school, so large numbers of teachers are in continual movement by train from one school to another. Those working full-time at one school will typically be offered around ¥250,000 per month. The rate of pay has not increased (if anything, has decreased) in recent years due to the ever-larger numbers of foreigners in Japan (including even ex-Wall street yuppies). A deduction for income tax of ten per cent is usually made, although the actual rate may be higher when the tax return is filed. Pay for private lessons can be substantially higher (with payment of tax depending on the honesty of the teacher), but it takes much time (and a sponsor for some sort of long-stay visa) to become established giving private lessons.

Teaching *can* be fun, if you are fortunate enough to have an advanced student or free-conversation class able to speak in high-level English. It can be a great way to learn about Japan and the people, for the Japanese can be remarkably outspoken in a foreign language, and teachers with private students may find themselves acting also as confidant and hearing more about private Japanese matters than they ever dreamed possible. (The very way that Japanese must be spoken has an inhibiting effect in Japanese conversation, to say nothing of the restrictions imposed by social "rules".) Women in class will even discuss matters forcefully, and argue (politely) with men, much to the astonishment of the latter! Unfortunately, these jobs in advanced classes are the "plums" of the profession and the most in demand, so the veteran teachers will usually get them. Someone must lay the groundwork to get the students up to this level, and this is the "entry level" position that new teachers normally are given. Trying to coax a response out of terminally shy, downcast-eyed teenage girls (*any* response!), overcoming the insidious effect of years of exposure to "shopping bag" English and English words incorrectly borrowed into Japanese (rather than "borrowed", a better expression would be "kidnapped for immoral purposes"), or trying for the hundredth time that day to get a class to remember that a plural subject requires a plural verb, can be very trying. Most teachers earn their pay.

Finding a job is a combination of combing the want ads in the newspapers (*The Japan Times*, the Monday edition, is the best single place to look, but then everyone else is chasing the same jobs), going around to schools, being given unwanted classes by other teachers, personal introductions, self-promotion (ads on notice boards and even on utility poles), and good luck. The best time of the year would be prior to the new semesters beginning in September and January. The summer is the slackest time because many students are on vacation.

Teaching positions are more easily found in Tokyo than in other large cities because it is both the commercial and political capital of the country. They are difficult to find in Kyoto because so many foreigners want to live in that historic and cultured city that there is usually an oversupply of willing teachers. Those who do live in Kyoto often have to commute to Osaka, an hour away by train, or even Kobe, two hours away.

On the other hand, schools in smaller cities outside the metropolitan areas advertise fairly regularly. Since relatively few foreigners want to live in such places, away from the bright city lights, anyone who enjoys (or can tolerate) slower-paced provincial cities will have a much higher chance of landing a job, with the associated probability of lower living costs.

A number of schools recruit overseas, and some of these are good institutions.

However, more than a few people have arrived in Japan only to find that the school was second rate, or that they were far out in the sticks.

A few who are working in other fields regard teaching English as (pardon the borrowing) "the last refuge of the scoundrel", but there are many qualified, dedicated, and hard-working teachers in the profession.

TEACHING ASSISTANTS: NATIONAL PROGRAM (JET) In recent years, the Japan Exchange and Teaching program, a joint effort of the Home Affairs, Education, and Foreign ministries has brought sizeable numbers of young foreigners (generally, recent university graduates) to Japan to help teach English at junior and senior high schools of the national school system. Each year, several hundred people, mostly recent university graduates, are selected from the USA, Canada, Britain, Australia, and New Zealand. Pay is quite respectable, around ¥300,000/month, and positions are available in all parts of the country (although choice is not always given). No special training in teaching English was required, just a degree from a recognised university. In 1991 there were 2874 participants.

The scheme is not all gravy and easy sailing for the teachers, as conversations and letters to newspapers have revealed. It seems that most such teachers rarely see any single class more than once a month, so they are doing little more than presenting a foreign face and spouting a few sentences. It is not uncommon, moreover, for the class homeroom teacher to carefully unteach the native-speaker's correct pronunciation, even while the foreigner is still in the room! A good tolerance for frustration is recommended as one qualification for any prospective applicant. Still, the program is a brave beginning toward teaching English as a practical means of communication rather than solely as yet another subject for examinations, and should be encouraged. (The fact that high-school students have only three hours of English per week, and that nearly all of this is boring grammar and translation drill, is the discouraging side.)

On a more positive note, the program does give an excellent opportunity to live among the Japanese and experience Japanese daily life first-hand.

Required reading for any prospective JET teacher is the book *Learning How to Bow*. Refer to the Books section for further information.

An inquiry to a Japanese diplomatic mission should result in more information.

TEACHING ASSISTANT: MUNICIPAL Tokyo, and probably some of the other large cities, have English teaching programs that hire foreigners as teaching assistants. The work is similar to that described above; providing a living example of English speech. In some schools the foreigners are given wide scope to talk, teach, and motivate, while in others they may do nothing more than read a passage, one line at a time, while the teacher discusses each in turn. The pay is good, although the number of hours may be limited per day. Qualifications in the past have been a university degree, though not necessarily in education. It is necessary to inquire from the municipal board of education; these jobs are not advertised.

SCHOOL TEACHING: NON-GOVERNMENT SCHOOLS There are several international schools in the large cities, particularly Tokyo, that have been set up to teach the children of foreign residents (and Japanese children whose foresighted parents want them to be at ease internationally). Vacancies occur from time to time for qualified teachers of a regular Western school curriculum. Pay

and conditions are considered quite reasonable, and the school can be the sponsor for a visa. Qualified American teachers can also make inquiries about teaching at Department of Defence Schools at various military bases around Japan.

UNIVERSITY LECTURING There are many universities that have English programs, and most will have native-speakers on staff. Staff for such positions will likely be recruited overseas, for they will want persons with specialized qualifications (whether really needed or not). Although the pay is good, the job generally has the same frustrations of private English schools due to uninterested students.

Non-Teaching Jobs

Various opportunities arise for persons with skills in written English. The following notes introduce the most common of these jobs.

COPYWRITING Those with a bent for catch-phrases may be able to find a niche with one of the advertising agencies or smaller outfits that prepare the text for promotional literature, pamphlets, catalogs, and other publications. (The largest agencies usually fill such positions by people with a proven track record whom they bring in from overseas. They are the ones who get the perks, like an apartment as well as higher pay.) There are many small agencies, sometimes associated with translation companies, that try to get this work from large companies. These positions may be advertised in newspapers (Monday *Japan Times* especially), but it can be productive to target companies in the field for direct inquiries. Japan, particularly Tokyo, can provide opportunities for doing this sort of work that would never open up in a western country, so one can obtain experience that can be used elsewhere later.

TRANSLATION There is a crying need for competent native speakers of English to do technical translation. As I can aver from experience since late 1979 in correcting and rewriting translations of a wide variety of technical materials for large and well-known Japanese companies, there is a great scarcity of competent technical translators. Few foreigners who have technical knowledge learn Japanese to the level required for translating, and those who do study Japanese usually have no technical background. (Most translators are Japanese people with no technical knowledge, and they are working into a language that they know very imperfectly. There are other problems, as elaborated on below.)

Objectively, though, it must be said that despite the actual need, there is no guarantee that a native-speaking translator will be able to find work, for almost no Japanese working in companies requiring translation work seem able to recognize that any problem exists. All evidence points to the common attitude that, because a text has been sent to someone called a "translator", it will automatically be exactly correct. Very few Japanese are competent to judge if text in English is correct; in fact, the more that it sounds like Japanese written in English words, the better many think it is! Because of this attitude and mentality (virtually universal), the truly competent translator does not have a better chance of getting work than an abysmally bad one, especially if the latter is Japanese.

There are several frustrations that can be expected in translation work that the prospective translator should be aware of. One is the fact that the Japanese generally write their language very poorly, often with abysmally bad organization of information, and omitting incidental bits like subjects and verbs, sometimes using incorrect , and generally creating a product that can take up to ten times as long to translate as an equivalent document from a European language into English. In addition to the frustrations that this engenders, this poor writing has an even more serious side-effect, that it makes the pay per hour quite poor (especially considering the expertise and study required) due to the low throughput.

A second frustration comes from the fact that the Japanese cannot recognize good English and, moreover, believe that their few years of study at the rate of two to three hours per week has equipped them to understand any nuance of English and to write it as well as any native speaker. In the past, it was all too common for a translation by a competent native speaker to be "edited" by a junior Japanese staff member (with no special training in English) into a hopeless garble. A translator must be prepared for long hours along with the frustration since everything is always needed yesterday.

REWRITING AND TECHNICAL WRITING Japan is probably the only country where most translators work from their own language into the target language. The knowledge of any foreign language by Japanese is generally rather imperfect (a kind way to express it), with predictable results. Thus, it is standard practice for any translation to go next to a native-speaker rewriter to be put into correct English.

If the original translator has a good technical knowledge, this may require nothing more than putting the result into grammatically-correct form. This is the rare case. In addition to having problems with poor knowledge of English, many translators seem not to understand what they are reading in Japanese, either because they do not understand the technicalities of the subject, or simply because the original Japanese is so poorly written that no person other than the original writer can understand what it says.

A good rewriter must draw on a prior technical knowledge of the subject and supply missing information. The work is a combination of a crossword puzzle and a detective story. Most Japanese are not aware of this need for careful examination of the translated product, assuming that because it has come from a translator it must be correct, so the work of a good rewriter is not generally appreciated, as reflected in the pay and the expected throughput.

This type of work is a natural for someone with a technical background and who can write correct English (often mutually-incompatible abilities, unfortunately!). The work most often available best suits a background in electrical engineering or computer science because of the huge volume of computer documentation cranked out every year. There is a lesser demand for people familiar with the technology and terminology of the chemical, medical, pharmaceutical, construction, nuclear, electrical and electronic, machinery, and other technology-based industries. Some rewriters work on a freelance basis; others work full-time for one company. Each arrangement has its advantages and shortcomings.

Freelancers have to hope that they will be able to make sense out of the translation using only the words on the pages given to them, usually without even the accompanying diagrams to which the text is keyed; this is often an impossible task. The translation agencies that give out such work want only quick throughput, and few (if any) have any interest in ensuring that the rewriting work is correct. They know that the customer will usually not know the difference. (It is sad, but true.)

Full-timers working for one company (not a translation agency) have the chance for greater job satisfaction than do freelancers because they can go back to the source of the original material and straighten matters out completely. However, it may take a while on the job (and perhaps a few tantrums) before the rewriter manages to gain some authority to specify what should and should not be allowed to pass, and to be able to keep out of finished work the "little fingers" that would otherwise make "corrections" that seem (to them) required to make it into truly correct English (i.e., English that sounds like Japanese). The rewriter working full-time in a typical Japanese company is likely to find that the Japanese employees do unexplainable things, like preparing glossaries of English words that correspond to Japanese technical words used in the company and inserting "meanings" that are not correct, without ever checking the meanings with the native speaker before printing it for use as the translation "bible" (personal experience).

Working with the product of Japanese printing companies will be both amusing and frustrating. For example, a typesetter can look at a correct, typed manuscript, read an "a", and type a "u", or similarly substitute an "r" for a clearly typed "l". (There is a psychology Ph.D. here for somebody!) In fact, working in almost any Japanese company leads foreigners to wonder how the Japanese have been so successful, for they seem to do so many things in a way that defies logic and is counter to their own best interests. Every foreigner working in Japan has tales to tell. (The countless articles in foreign magazines about adopting Japanese business practices bring rueful smiles.) When problems are identified, supervisors will often want to delay any correction for fear of hurting the feelings of the person who screwed up originally.

Full-timers do well to get much over ¥2500 per hour, but there is the advantage that every working hour of the day is being paid for. Larger companies can sponsor rewriters for a working visa because they are offering full-time work, the normal requirement for a contract acceptable for a visa. Such jobs do not appear frequently, but tend to be advertised in the newspapers (Monday edition of *The Japan Times*).

Some companies may offer a contract which the company representative says will cover all income tax, so the negotiations are on a net basis. In such cases, it is wise to establish that this means payment of the full tax, not limited to the standard 10 per cent deduction from each pay. (The effective rate could be higher.)

For freelancers there is work from the many translation agencies. Sometimes they advertise in the newspapers (Monday edition of *The Japan Times*, again), but many jobs come up through word of mouth, or by finding the names of translation agencies and approaching them directly. There can be much flexibility in freelance work, and some rewriters have a nominal contract with an agency as a "full-timer" for visa purposes, but actually do work for that company only as it comes available, picking up any other assignments that come up in the meantime. This type of work is a favorite with those on cultural and similar visas because it can be done on a spare-time basis. In reality, however, anyone doing this work must take any assignment that comes along lest he/she lose future work with that agency. Since they have their names with a number of agencies, they commonly find that they have no free time at all! Pay can be on a per-page basis, or by the hour in the agency office. In an office, pay can range from ¥2500 per hour

for beginners to over ¥4000 for people who have proved their knowledge and ability, so it can prove reasonably lucrative if the person does not need to have much free time.

PUBLISHING With the increasing need for English-speakers with specialized abilities as Japan progressively becomes more "internationalized" (i.e., they realize that it is good policy to produce documentation in correct English), some companies that produce such materials require people who are adept at operating word processors and familiar with other aspects of desktop publishing. Much of this type of work is handled through specialized agencies, some of which recruit overseas as well.

Newspapers have need of persons with the ability to rewrite translations (and "translations") of news stories originating in Japanese, and openings sometimes come up. Some have recruited overseas. The pay is reputed to be quite good. A high throughput is required due to the pressure of deadlines, and the translations have the same range of quality found in general translation work, so there can be frustrations. Apart from being fortunate enough to find an advertisement overseas, the best approach here would be to contact the individual English-language newspapers directly.

Other Fields

TECHNICAL SPECIALISTS People with specialized technical knowledge, particularly related to computers, may find work with Japanese companies in their field. Due to the nature of such work it is difficult to give any guidance on job-hunting. Many positions are filled by overseas recruitment. If looking inside Japan, keep in mind that the Japanese have the reputation (deserved or otherwise) for a poor ability to write good computer software, so an expert might find an opening.

Some Americans have had good contracts with U.S. banks to maintain their "obsolete" Cobol programs. These jobs have been recruited overseas and have included perks like housing.

COOK A category that qualifies a foreigner for a working visa is as cook in a non-Japanese restaurant, although it would be necessary to show credentials, certificates, or some other evidence of qualification.

MODELLING One of the fields in which a westerner can often land more lucrative assignments than a Japanese is modelling. Western models, especially girls with blonde hair, are widely used for modelling clothes, promoting shampoo (despite the fact that all Japanese have black hair that is totally different in texture), and appearing in all manner of advertising work. (Even Japanese wedding halls have shown two Caucasians in a simulated marriage ceremony!) Judging by billboards visible everywhere in the cities, extraordinary beauty is not always necessary for such work.

There are many modelling agencies in big cities like Tokyo. Sometimes they advertise, but most prospective models find the names of the agencies and make the rounds one after another. There is strong competition for jobs, so there can be long periods without an assignment, although the pay when one does score is very good. (Some models are hired overseas, and have their fare and living expenses paid, in addition to salary, in return for a fixed and exclusive contract.)

When a job has been secured, however, there may be a long wait for pay to be received, for the agency does not get paid until at least a month later, and they may try to stall themselves. Anyone who will soon leave the country should let it be known that they expect to be paid on the spot.

FILM EXTRAS Sometimes jobs come up as extras in films. This is one place to demand cash payment at the end of the shooting, for these companies are often underfinanced and "neglect" to pay.

HOSTESSING AND RELATED ACTIVITIES Another type of work is working as a hostess in clubs or nightclubs. They can make a good income just from their "official" duties of talking with customers, but girls who have done this work uniformly remark that it is boring. They have to make small talk with men, mostly Japanese men who speak next to no English, and it is a continual battle to keep men's hands in their laps—their own, that is. A major problem with this type of work is that the famous nightclubs, like the Copacabana and the Mikado, have all closed, although many small clubs and bars do offer some opportunities.

Taxes

Income taxes are generally lower than in most Western countries, though the Japanese still think they are hard done by. In addition to income tax, there is also a ward (*ku*) tax, which is typically of the same order of magnitude as the national tax. Income tax is largely covered by a standard 10% withholding deduction, while the ward tax must be paid by the person. There is, in effect, a year of grace during which ward tax is not paid, since it is calculated from the national tax paid. Some unscrupulous individuals have been known to move to a different ward every year to escape this tax.

A further impost is for national health insurance, which will be of the same order of magnitude as the ward tax (or higher). Eligibility of full-time employees for national health insurance depends on the municipality in which they live; in some places it is impossible to join, and in others it is impossible not to! If you are eligible for this insurance plan and sign up, there is (unfortunately) also the obligation to pay into the national pension plan, about ¥30,000 per month (except those over 40). Unless you stay in Japan after retirement, you will not be able to get any benefit from this, but it is not possible to get out of paying for it once you have enrolled for health insurance. It might be worth investigating the possibility of taking out private health insurance (medical costs are high) and arranging with your employer not to do anything that would cause you to be enrolled in the national scheme. (These words are written only for guidance. Be sure to check the current situation for yourself!)

Publications

Books that may give useful guidance beyond what is written above are listed in the earlier Books section.

House Hunting

For those who plan to remain in Japan for a considerable period of time and who wish to have their own accommodation, here are some tips and general information on house hunting in Japan.

Be forewarned: Looking for accommodation is usually a sure way to see an unpleasant side of the Japanese. Many agencies have refused to deal with foreigners who walk in through their doors, even if they speak Japanese fluently, or they may speak to the house-seeker in a rude manner. If one gets past this barrier, it is similarly not uncommon for the house-owner to refuse to rent to a foreigner. (Many foreigners have reported through the years that their landladies are in a class of their own as to petty-mindedness and suspicion.) On the other hand (as in my case), the people who own the building may be very friendly and accommodating, but this type (unfortunately) is a minority. These words are put in as a forewarning of the problems that have been encountered by many who have gone before.

To avoid problems as much as possible, the best advice is to take a Japanese friend along who can act as spokesman and reassure the agent/owner that you are trustworthy, honorable, solvent, reliable, able to fit in with Japanese customs, clean, and unlikely to pee on the tatami, bring disrepute on the neighborhood, or otherwise disgrace the owner and his/her descendants. A recent development is agencies that specialise in finding housing for foreigners in the reasonable-rent range. They advertise in the *Tokyo Journal* and probably in *Kansai Time Out*.

A Japanese sympathetic to the problems of foreigners unable to find accommodation, Takajisa Oishi, offered several suggestions and observations in the letters column of the *Japan Times*, presented here in edited form with my comments.

-Landlords are in a business with risks Japanese tenants are likely to be less of a risk.

-Japanese tenants are legally required to have a guarantor. Plan to obtain same from your employer or school.

-The best seasons for house hunting are February–March and September–October.

-Ask your boss to rent a house or apartment in the company's name and rent it to you, or ask your company to issue a document indicating that you are a full-time employee with them, together with a statement of your annual income, to show to the landlord.

-The main complaints of landlords are tenants' lack of keeping the kitchen clean, and for having roommates without permission.

A stated willingness to incorporate agreements not to cause these problems into a rental agreement could also tilt the balance in your favor.

Costs

Housing in Tokyo and other metropolitan areas is very expensive; in smaller places, prices are considerably lower. In the metropolitan areas, a single room about three meters square, may be found for less than ¥20,000 a month, but any reasonable accommodation (solo) with a minimum of facilities (kitchen with sink, gas outlet, bath/shower, toilet) and close to central Tokyo, will usually cost at least ¥40,000 or more like ¥50,000–80,000. Places with a shared toilet and bath are less expensive, and there are some bargains to be found if you can spend a long time looking. These prices refer to normal "everyday Japanese" accommodation; for apartments and houses comparable in size and facilities to those found in the USA, Canada, Australia, etc., the rents are astronomical—from ¥250,000 up to ¥2 million a month.

Room sizes are measured by the number of *tatami* (reed) mats that do or could fit. There are actually at least three "standard" sizes of tatami in use in Japan, but one mat is roughly a meter wide and two meters long. A small room is three mats (*san-jo*), a medium one, 4-1/2 mats (*yo-jo han*), and a large one, six mats (*roku-jo*). Larger rooms do exist, but are not so common. Room types are listed as either Japanese-style (*wa*), with tatami; or Western-style (*yo*), with a concrete or wooden floor, probably carpeted. In Japanese language listings, it is common to see abbreviations such as 2DK, 3LDK, and 3L+DK; the digit is the number of bedrooms, "DK" indicates combined dining room and

kitchen (in addition to the bedrooms), "LDK" is combined living room-dining room-kitchen, and "L+DK" is living room plus combined dining room-kitchen.

Apartment buildings and concrete houses have higher rentals than wooden buildings because of the greater comfort (no freezing drafts in winter, common in older wooden buildings), strength, and fire and earthquake resistance.

It is usually necessary to have a bundle of money on hand before moving into your own apartment. First, there is one (or more) months' rent in advance (*maekin*); second, there is a deposit (*shikikin*) of one to four months' rent, refundable when leaving—minus the cost of any repairs; third, there is "key money" (*reikin*), which is nothing but a bribe to get the place. Reikin is commonly two months' rent, occasionally one, rarely none, and not returnable; fourth, there is the agent's commission, one month's rent; fifth, there is frequently a maintenance fee, which may vary from a reasonable ¥1000–3000 per month to ¥10,000 at the more ritzy addresses. Finally there are separate charges for gas, water, electricity, and telephone—all of which are expensive. Telephone installation charges are high compared with North American rates, and it is necessary to buy a telephone bond (which can be resold immediately for negligible loss).

Location

The major cities, like Tokyo, Yokohama, Osaka, and Kyoto are very large and, despite quick train service, commuting long distances can waste a lot of time. Remember though, that express rail service can make it possible to get to places in Tokyo from some distance outside more quickly than one can walk to a subway/train station if there is no station nearby. After settling into a job or routine and stabilizing your activities, ask others about the best or preferable residential areas. In Tokyo, for example, long-term residents (and people stationed in Tokyo for business) want to live in Roppongi/Azabu because they are close to downtown, and because Roppongi has the brightest of night lights. Consequently, there is little housing at reasonable cost in these areas. The Hiro-o and Shibuya areas are well-regarded, while Ebisu, Gotanda, and other areas can be equally convenient and less expensive, even if they're not quite as fashionable. Check access to subways, JR lines, or bus lines (but remember that many buses routes don't run after mid-evening). The farther away from a train or subway line, the lower the rent.

Types of Accommodation

STUDENT In Tokyo, the Tokyo Gakusei Kyokai (Tokyo Student Association) has advertised assistance in finding reasonably priced apartments in various areas of Tokyo. The phone number given was (03) 3295-3131.

TEMPORARY There are several places in the large cities, like Tokyo and Kyoto, where foreigners can rent a room for a few days or weeks. Most common are the "foreigner houses" detailed in the earlier Accommodation section for short-term visitors. These are usually listed in publications like *Tokyo Journal* and *Kansai Time Out*. Many of these places are small communities in their own right, and it is not uncommon for people to stay weeks on end because of the pleasant and supportive mood that they find there. Unfortunately, they are quite often full.

LONG-TERM There is more than one way to find long-term accommodation (more than a few months). One choice is to follow up advertisements in newspapers, on bulletin boards, and leads received by word of mouth, but one is then at the whim of chance as to location. The alternative is to choose one or two areas that seem interesting, and then look for listings of places available in that area via a rental agency.

Near almost every railway station, and elsewhere in most districts, are rental agencies (*fudosanya*) with listings of apartments, houses, and rooms for rent in that district. The doors and windows of their offices are usually plastered with sheets of paper describing the many places available so passers-by can read them. The agent will ask about the type of accommodation required, number and sizes of rooms, and any other feature desired, then will prepare a list of places that might be suitable, taking clients to see them until one is found that is satisfactory. His charge for each placement is usually one months' rent. Add this to all the other charges listed earlier and you may have to lay out seven months' rent before moving in. Fudosanya-san rarely speak much English, except for the ones who look like used car salesmen and specialise in the horrendously expensive rental market catering to foreign executives on large living allowances. To overcome both the language problems, and the possible difficulties described at the end of this section, it is highly advisable to go with a Japanese friend when hunting any type of accommodation.

Newspaper advertisements for accommodation are usually for high-priced executive-style places, but occasionally there are reasonably priced ones. Newspaper ads appear daily, but the *Japan Times* on Friday has the most comprehensive Tokyo listings.

Bulletin boards may have ads for apartments, houses, rooms, sublets, "housesitting" arrangements, or shared accommodation. Look for them at supermarkets in areas with a large foreign population, or at the Tokyo TIC, Com'inn and other "conversation lounges".

In large cities there are usually regular English-language publications that carry classified ads. In Tokyo, *the Tokyo Weekender* (weekly) and *Tokyo Journal* (monthly) have sizeable sections of classified ads, including accommodaion. Occasionally there are some moderately-priced apartments listed by their owners (so there is no agent's fee).

TOKYO

Tokyo is one of the most populous cities on earth, the center of government and commerce in Japan, and a major industrial city. It is difficult to put an exact number on the actual population because in the central part it varies by nearly two million between day and night. The actual Tokyo administrative area is 2031 sq km and includes many wards (*ku*), which are cities in their own right. Adjacent Kawasaki and Yokohama form one vast conurbation with Tokyo itself. Therefore, while the population of Tokyo is quoted at around 12 million, it totals 15 million or more when these areas are included, and within 50km of central Tokyo there are about 30 million persons.

Tokyo can be enjoyed for shopping and entertainment, but it has relatively little of historic sightseeing interest; what did exist was largely destroyed by the 1923 Kanto earthquake or wartime bombing. It is better to go to Kyoto, Nara, Kamakura, Nikko, etc., for sightseeing. On the other hand Tokyo is a very interesting place to live and explore slowly and in depth.

The following section describes first how to get into and out of the city, transportation within Tokyo, accommodation, sightseeing, and then shopping.

ARRIVAL AT NARITA AIRPORT

Nearly all international flights to Tokyo arrive at Narita airport (Narita-kuko), located 66 km out in the countryside east of Tokyo. A minimum of 1-1/2 hours is usually required to get from there to central Tokyo, making it one of the world's more inconveniently located airports.

A high-speed rail service was included in the "planning" stage, but less than 1% of the land required for the line was ever purchased, and until 1991 the only "system" for getting into Tokyo was cobbled up from existing rail lines plus a new bus service. In 1991 the underground station, there from the start of operations but blocked off because of the lack of tracks to the terminal, was finally put into use by JR and Keisei lines.

Narita "errport" (as it has been called) is Japan's contribution to the world's collection of vast projects started on half-vast ideas. It would have been better to enlarge the existing and infinitely more convenient Haneda airport, which would also have avoided the opposition to Narita from farmers and student radicals that still continues, with occasional sabotage and other disruptive tactics. This is the cause of the inspection on entering the airport from Tokyo and police around the airport. These security measures help account for the high airport departure tax of ¥2000.

There is one possible way to avoid all the problems of Narita airport: fly China Airlines. Their flights land at Haneda airport, so you avoid the problem completely. Unfortunately this isn't possible for everyone as CAL is usually heavily booked.

If your first destination in Japan is a city other than Tokyo, it may be preferable to try to get an international flight to a point closer to that city. However, Osaka and Nagoya are the only other major airports with large numbers of connections; the regional airports generally have flights only to nearby places such as Seoul and Hong Kong. (The situation changes yearly, so it does no harm to ask a travel agent what alternatives currently exist.)

If you are among the majority who use Narita, you'll find that the airport has well-signposted routes through quarantine/health, immigration, and customs check points. Although there are two terminals, the following information is applicable to both unless otherwise noted.

If you are planning to obtain a Shore Pass (described in the section on immigration), look for the mobile desk at the entrance to the immigration-check hall. If you have a residence-type visa (working, etc.), you are permitted (despite possible protest from Japanese in the line) to use the lines marked "Japanese". (Refer to the earlier "Customs" section for information about declaring unaccompanied baggage.)

Once clearing customs you can purchase Japanese currency at the numerous money changers in the arrival concourse (same floor) and on the departure (4th) level. The rates at these places are the same as at banks in the city. Remember that yen is the only currency that can be used in Japan; it is illegal and impossible to use anything else, including U.S. greenbacks, so buy enough.

The arrival concourse, the ground floor, is the first place where incoming passengers can be met by friends. Be sure that anyone meeting you knows your airline and flight number so they can be in the correct terminal and at the correct end of the building. (But it would be a kindness to arrange to meet them in Tokyo because of the inconvenience, time, and cost involved for them to get out to the airport.)

Before heading into Tokyo, stop at the TIC office if you want any information and JNTO pamphlets. The small office is tucked away, almost out of sight, at the junction of the central block and the south wing, on the side nearer the runway; it is sometimes omitted from airport directories. (Other "information centers" in the middle of each wing are generally useless because most of the staff don't speak English.) The TIC information that will be of immediate use is *Tourist Map of Tokyo* (405-E), *Map of Tokyo and Vicinity*, and *Tokyo* (222-E); the last is available in several languages. The *Tourist Map of Tokyo* has the best subway map available, with place names in both Japanese and Roman characters (romaji); it is very useful when faced with a fare chart written only in Japanese.

Good news is that the TIC will make reservations (up to three places) for travellers at economical *ryokan/minshuku*, for Tokyo and a large number of other places around the country. (This program is detailed in the section on accommodation.) The number of places participating in the program is limited, and not all will be rock-bottom budget type, but the TIC does also have listings of low-cost accommodation in popular places like Tokyo and Kyoto (though possibly only for reading on the premises). The TIC is open from 0900 to 2000 daily.

Counter in the concourse can arrange accommodation in one of more than 25 hotels in Tokyo. These hotels, however, begin in the moderate price range and work upward.

There are also counters for baggage delivery to any point in the Tokyo area. The cost can be worthwhile if your bags are very heavy and you would have to move them on public transportation.

Counters for car rental agencies are located in the center block of both terminals. No one in their right mind would try driving in Japan on first arrival, but you can get an idea of prices for future reference.

There are several counters, all well marked, for the various transportation services to Tokyo and nearby places, such as Omiya, Chiba, and even Disneyland, (though the Keisei counters in terminal 1 sell tickets only for their more costly Skyliner). These are detailed immediately below. Both Keisei railway and JR also have counters in the underground concourse (en route to the train tracks; escalators down from both wings are well marked) where their tickets can also be purchased; these counters are usually much less crowded than the ones on the arrivals level, and there should be someone able to speak some English at each. (Tickets for lower-cost Keisei trains are sold on this level.) Note that in terminal 2 there is no counter for railway transportation at the concourse level. You must either ask at the information desk or follow signs at the escalator directing you to the JR/Keisei trains below. The JR office (named "Plaza") in the underground concourse is where holders of vouchers for a Japan Rail Pass can obtain the pass and have it validated. However, if your travel plans are not yet firm, you can do this later in Tokyo; it does not have to be changed immediately.

Getting to Tokyo

The three most practical ways of getting into Tokyo from Narita airport are Keisei train, JR train, and buses. Any others are very expensive; a taxi would cost a small fortune, about ¥20,000, and a hire car about double that. (Both JR and Keisei are also useful for those going to the Chiba and Boso-hanto peninsula area.)

The trains leave from a station beneath each terminal building, while the buses leave from in front.

Keisei Trains

The least expensive and most frequent (up to 72/day) way into Tokyo is by one of the Keisei line trains. There are two types of service from the airport to the terminus, Keisei-Ueno (on the northeast side of Tokyo): "Skyliner" (sometimes listed as "Liner") expresses that stop only at Keisei Ueno (one hour; ¥1630; all seats reserved) and at Nippori, a few minutes earlier, and *tokkyu* ("rapid") expresses (73 minutes; ¥910), which make a few more stops. All signs advertising Keisei trains promote only the Skyliner (and obtaining reservations for same); the reserved-seats-only Skyliner trains are more posh than the ordinary *tokkyu* cars (and are rated as more comfortable than those of the competing JR NEX service), but the less-expensive (and more frequent) *tokkyu* trains are quite acceptable. There are four non-smoking cars (*kinen-sha*) on Skyliner trains, available by request; all *tokkyu* cars are non-smoking.

The type of train and terminal station (usually Ueno) for the next three trains are clearly shown by illuminated signs (alternating Japanese and English) over the ticket office in the underground concourse and at the entrance to the tracks. (A Skyliner is indicated as "Liner".) A posted timetable near this office shows all trains through the day, and a timetable pamphlet is also available at the TIC office in the airport.

Reservations are required for all Skyliner seats, and the next few trains are not infrequently sold out. In this case it is faster to take an ordinary *tokkyu* train; you will nearly always get a seat since the trains originate at the airport.

Skyliners run at 40-minute intervals through most of the day and at 30 minute intervals in late afternoon (21/day), the last leaving at 2200. There are nearly 50 *tokkyu* trains/day, the last at 2243 and reaching Ueno at 2357.

Both types of Keisei service stop at Nippori, two stations and about five minutes before Ueno. Nippori allows easy transfer to the JR Yamanote line, which circles Tokyo, as well as the JR Keihin-Tohoku line, which overlaps the former for several stations within Tokyo (but it skips some stops during the day to give faster *kaisoku* service). From Keisei-Ueno station, the terminus, it is only a short walk to JR Ueno station for the above two JR commuter lines and many JR intercity lines, as well as to the Ginza and Hibiya subway lines. From Ueno it is easy to get to Tokyo International Youth Hostel.

It is possible to get on to the Asakusa (pron. "Asak'sa") subway line at Aoto (platform 1) to go to the south and southwest of the city, and save 10–15 minutes over the time in *tokkyu* to KeiseiUeno. The only problem is that some trains from Aoto run on the Asakusa tracks only as far as Sengakuji, where they switch off and become Keikyu (Keihin-Kyuko) line trains going to Yokohama. Asakusa trains have Nishi-magome as terminal station. (There is also a chance that the train from Aoto will terminate at Oshiage, a few stations away, in which case you will have to change trains; again the train may be to Nishi-magome or to Yokohama.) This route is better for those who can cope with possible complications! The information on this route is included because for many years a number of trains from the airport ran directly to Nishi-magome; possibly this useful service will be reinstated.

The first part of the trip in from Narita is through farming country with many rice paddies and even one thatched-roof house, visible to the right of the train.

JR Narita Express (NEX)

As with the Keisei service, there are two types of JR train, one a premium-priced non-stop express (Narita Express, NEX; one hour; ¥2890; 23/day), the other a less-frequent (17/day) regular express (Sobu *kaisoku*) at lower cost (90 min; ¥1260). Also, as with the Keisei service, reservations are required for the non-stop NEX trains. These are frequently sold out for the following two or more departures, so consider using the ordinary Sobu service (but see the next paragraph). There are green cars (first class, at a surcharge), and all are nonsmoking cars.

Unless you have a particular reason for going to Tokyo station there is no advantage to using the Sobu *kaisoku* service, for it is both slower and costlier than the Keisei *tokkyu* trains. (At ¥1630, the Skyliner is not much more expensive than the slower Sobu train.) Ueno is only four stations away from Tokyo station, and Nippori station (five minutes before Keisei-Ueno and accessible by both Keisei services) is only six stations away.

In both terminals, the entrance to the JR tracks are in the underground concourse. The destination of the next few JR trains is shown on a sign at the entrance. Often the destination is shown as Shinjuku, Ikebukuro, Yokohama, Kurihama (beyond Yokohama), or some other place; all these trains go through Tokyo station en route.

There will be different entrances to the tracks for JR NEX and Keisei in the underground concourse. If you follow the signs, there shouldn't be any problem. Whether you ride NEX or Sobu, a "Liner" or *tokkyu*, tracks will be clearly designated.

Airport Bus

For many travellers, the most convenient transport (though not the cheapest) into the Tokyo area is one of the many airport buses. As detailed below, the various bus services go to Tokyo station, Shinjuku station, Tokyo City Air Terminal (TCAT), and several hotels in various parts of the city. Tickets can be bought at any of a number of well-marked counters inside the building.

There are two competing services; the larger is misleadingly identified as a "Limousine" service, the other as "Airport Shuttle". The latter goes only to hotels, while the other serves the same hotels plus other places (detailed below). Check the

Limousine Bus Routes

Palace Hotel
Imperial Hotel
Dai-Ichi Hotel Tokyo   **Ginza**
Ginza Tokyu Hotel   **Line**
Ginza Tobu Tokyo Renaissance Hotel   **Narita Airport**

Asakusa View Hotel   **Asakusa Sta.**
Hotel East 21 Tokyo

Tokyo Prince Hotel   **Shiba Line**
Hotel Okura

Koraku Garden Hotel   **Tokyo City**
Hotel Edmont   **Air Terminal**
Fairmont Hotel   **Kudan Line**   Royal Park Hotel
Hotel Kayu Kaikan
Diamond Hotel

Miyako Hotel Tokyo
Hotel Laforet Tokyo
Hotel Takanawa   **Tokyo Station**
Westin Hotel Tokyo   **Shinagawa /**
Hotel Meridien Pacific Tokyo   **Ebisu Line**
Takanawa Prince Hotel
New Takanawa Prince Hotel
                                                Tokyo
Holiday Inn Crowne   **Disneyland**
Plaza Metropolitan
Sunshine City Prince Hotel   **Ikebukuro**
Hotel Grand Palace   **Line**
Four Seasons Hotel

The New Otani
Akasaka Prince Hotel   **Akasaka**
Akasaka Tokyu Hotel   **Line**
ANA Hotel Tokyo   **Haneda Airport**

Keio Plaza Hotel   Haneda Tokyu Hotel
Century Hyatt Tokyo   **Shinjuku**
Tokyo Hilton   **Sta.**
Shinjuku Washington Hotel
Park Hyatt Tokyo

schedules of both for the minimum delay to your destination. The buses leave from the front of both wings of terminal 1 as well as terminal 2, so they offer the advantage that you do not have to carry your baggage any farther than the exit on the same level as the arrival area.

The trip to all city destinations is a nominal 2 hours or so (70–90 minutes to TCAT), but these times could be extended by an hour or more during the "rush" hour. (TCAT is reached directly by expressway and is least affected by such traffic.) The fare is ¥2700–2900, half price for children and the handicapped.

Only buses to TCAT, Tokyo station, and the Shinjuku area run throughout the day, leaving Narita as early as 0645; most services to the other areas begin in the afternoon and end around 2100. The latest buses to Tokyo station leave at 2300, to the Shinjuku area at 2230, and to TCAT at 2300.

TCAT is at Hakozaki, 2.5km from Tokyo station, and is on the Hanzomon subway line (Suitengu-mae station). From the Hanzomon line, you can easily transfer to the Ginza line at Mitsukoshi-mae (first stop), to the Tozai, Marunouchi, Chiyoda, and Mita lines at the following station, Otemachi, and to the Shinjuku line at Jimbocho (the next).

A 10- to 15-minute walk away from TCAT are two other subway stations, Ningyocho station (Asakusa and Hibiya lines) and Kayabacho (Hibiya and Tozai lines), but the lines accessed by them can be reached more easily by transferring from one of the lines reachable from the Hanzomon line (Asakusa line: by Tozai line to Nihombashi; Hibiya line: by Marunouchi line to Ginza or Kasumigaseki).

There is also a shuttle bus between TCAT and Tokyo station, but since a bus goes directly to Tokyo station from the airport, this does not offer any great benefit.

The following is a guide to frequency and destinations of services (mid-1995):

Tokyo station; 15–20-minute intervals throughout the day

Tokyo City Air Terminal (TCAT); 10- to 20-minute intervals throughout the day

Shinjuku (Shinjuku station–Keio Plaza–Hyatt); 26/day

Shinjuku (Hilton–Shinjuku station–Shinjuku Washington); 25/day

Akasaka (Tokyo Zen Nikku–New Otani–Akasaka Prince–Akasaka Tokyu); 16/day

Ginza (Palace–Imperial); 1 hour intervals from 14:10

Ginza (Tokyo Renaissance–Ginza Tokyu); 1 hour intervals from mid-afternoon

Shinagawa (Pacific–New Takanawa Prince–Takanawa Prince); 11/day, most in afternoon/evening

Ikebukuro (Grand Palace–Sunshine City Prince– Metropolitan); 12–17/day

Kudan (Koraku Garden–Edmont–Fairmont–Kayu Kaikan–Diamond); 2/day

Ebisu (Westin); 4/day

There is also service (infrequent) to Maihama and Yokohama area hotels.

Transfer to Haneda Airport

Haneda is used for nearly all domestic flights; there are only about 10 from Narita. The most convenient way to transfer from Narita to Haneda is by bus (another "limousine"). The fare is ¥2900, departures are every 20 to 50 minutes, and the trip is scheduled to take 90 minutes (except during traffic slow-downs). For safety, you should allow at least 4-1/2 hours between scheduled arrival at Narita and scheduled take-off at Haneda.

An alternative to the bus for those on a truly tight budget, is to take the Keisei line to Ueno, change there to the JR Yamanote line and go to Hamamatsucho, then take the monorail from there. This might halve the fare, but would take longer.

To Yokohama

Passengers destined for Yokohama will find that the "limousine" bus service to Yokohama City Air Terminal (YCAT, not far from Yokohama station) is by far the quickest and most convenient way, taking about two hours. Buses leave every 20 to 50 minutes. The fare is ¥3300. A cheaper, slower way is via either Keisei line to Keisei-Ueno and then walk to Ueno JR station, or by JR service to Tokyo station, and change in both cases to a Keihin-Tohoku train to Yokohama station (few stops en route).

ARRIVAL AT HANEDA AIRPORT

Because of the running contretemps between the governments of Taiwan and (mainland) China, Taiwan's national airline, China Airlines, was denied the dubious privilege of using Narita airport when Japan recognised the Peking government. China Airlines (Taiwanese) have been crying all the way to the bank ever since because they have the most convenient service into Japan of any airline. They have several flights a week from Taipei and the U.S. West coast, but advance bookings are required because of the airline's understandable popularity. All Japan's domestic flights to and from Tokyo use Haneda airport.

Haneda to Tokyo

Nearly all Japan's domestic flights to and from Tokyo use Haneda airport. This airport is connected to the JR rail system of Tokyo by the monorail. The way from the airport terminal to the monorail station is clearly marked, and tickets are available from vending machines; the machines give change. The monorail terminus is at Hama-matsucho, on the south side of Tokyo, one of the stations on the JR Yamanote and Keihin-Tohoku lines.

Haneda to Narita

Transfer between Haneda and Narita airports is simplest by "limousine" bus (¥2900). Buses operate between 0910 and 2050 pm. It is wise to allow about 4-1/2 hours for connections between flights at the two airports.

Haneda to Yokohama

The simplest way from Haneda to Yokohama is by bus to Yokohama station. Buses depart at 8 to 15 minute intervals and cost ¥540 (1 hour). The alternative is monorail to Hamamatsu-cho, and JR from there.

Haneda to Kawasaki

There is bus service between Haneda airport and Kawasaki station every 20 to 30 minutes. The trip takes about 25 minutes and costs ¥230.

DEPARTURE FROM NARITA AIRPORT

Getting to Narita from Tokyo

The most convenient ways to get out to Narita airport are airport bus, Keisei train, and JR train. Sage advice for anyone going from Tokyo is to begin your trip four hours prior to your departure time, to allow for traffic delays and missed connections plus the security checks, check-in, Immigration formalities, and so on. In addition, with the advent of the fast JR service from Tokyo station in 1991, many travellers were tending to arrive only a short while before departure time, causing delays. Also, the immigration check-out has been a mob scene at times in past years, with so many people trying to go through that the overflow extended back up to the waiting lounge.

Airport Bus

Buses to Narita airport (direct to the departures level of the terminal) leave from Tokyo station, Tokyo City Air Terminal (TCAT), and Shinjuku station frequently through the day, and large numbers also leave from the hotels listed in the section on getting in to Tokyo. The earliest buses from TCAT and the above stations are just before or after 0600. The trip is scheduled to take two hours (70–90 minutes from TCAT), but you should allow an hour or two extra during times of heaviest traffic. You can obtain up-to-date information on the exact departure times from the Tokyo TIC and any large hotel.

Bus from TCAT

Many (but not all) airlines permit complete check-in at TCAT, so you don't have to touch your bags again until your final destination. For these airlines, a bus is assigned to each flight, and the flight is held back if the bus is delayed. To allow for potential traffic problems, check-in at TCAT for these flights is typically three to four hours ahead of departure. A great advantage of checking in at TCAT is that you can then go upstairs to the Immigration office and complete your formalities there. You will be given a card indicating that this has been done and, at Narita, you bypass any crowd in the immigration hall and exit immediately to the departure lounge by the gate on the far right side.

Note that there are separate buses for passengers who have checked in at TCAT and those who are taking their luggage with them. The exits to the coaches are both on the second floor, but separate; the checked-in entrance is above the front entrance of TCAT, while the other is farther inside the building on the right-hand side.

There is also an Immigration office in the TCAT building which was originally intended (supposedly) to allow travellers to obtain a Re-entry Permit on the way out of the country, but in practice the delays encountered made this an unwise idea. In 1990, it took me more than two hours, while it was readied in 30 minutes in 1991.

TCAT can be reached easily by Suitengu-mae station of the Hanzomon subway line. The route is well signposted. There is also a shuttle bus to it from Tokyo station (Yaesu side).

Bus from Tokyo Station

The bus from Tokyo station leaves from in front of the Daiwa Bank opposite the front entrance (Yaesu side, the side remote from the Tokyo Central Post Office). If you use the Marunouchi subway line to get to Tokyo station, you will have to walk 10 to 15 minutes under the station via an underground passageway (signposted "To Yaesu side", or similar); from JR trains it will be somewhat less. (But if you're already in Tokyo station, it would make more sense to use one of the JR services to get to Narita.)

Bus from Shinjuku Station

Buses leave Shinjuku station at regular intervals throughout the day. However, a Japanese travel publication stated that these buses are typically 40 minutes later than advertised due to heavy traffic both on and off the expressway. It recommended not using the bus from the west side of the city (Shinjuku and Ikebukuro areas).

Keisei Trains

The Keisei railway offers a simple way to get to Narita airport, from either Keisei-Ueno or Keisei-Nippori stations. As for the service from the airport, there are both Skyliner (24/day; 60 min; ¥1740) and "rapid" (tokkyu) expresses (40/day; 73 min (most); ¥940), the latter being the cheapest transportation available. All Skyliner seats are reserved. (Seats can be reserved up to a month in advance at Keisei-Ueno station, at the airport when arriving, and at JTB offices.) Tickets for the next train can be bought on the spot if there are seats available, but in busy times trains are likely to be sold out. In this case, it is quicker to take a tokkyu train. There is no reservation for seating on tokkyu trains; they are ordinary commuter coaches, so you might have to stand for part of the trip in peak periods. Trains leave from Keisei-Ueno station, and all stop en route at Nippori station, about five minutes away.

Keisei-Ueno station can be reached via Ueno station of JR (Yamanote, Keihin-Tohoku, and other lines) or subway (Hibiya or Ginza lines). Using JR Ueno station, leave the train platform via the overhead passageway located at the north end (away from Tokyo stn.), walk along the passage toward track No. 1, exit, cross the road, turn left, and walk down the hill; to the right, about 50 meters along, is the entrance to the underground Keisei station. The transfer from the subway lines is well marked and should be no problem to follow, but it is rather long if you are carrying heavy baggage. Keisei-Nippori is accessible from JR Nippori station (Yamanote and Keihin-Tohoku lines).

An alternative way to get to the Keisei line is to take the Asakusa subway line through to Aoto, go to the platform for tracks 3 and 4, and catch one of the expresses coming from Keisei-Ueno bound for Narita-kuko (airport) station. (If your Asakusa train terminates at Oshiage, six stations before Aoto, simply take the next train on to Aoto and change as just described.) Note that some local trains also pass through Aoto, as do some expresses that terminate prior to the airport. Signs along the platform identify the terminus of every train, in *romaji*, so you can avoid the locals. (The color of the destination sign on a train indicates the type: black *kanji* for locals, and green or red for expresses.) The TIC normally has a timetable of Keisei trains.

There will be a security check when you leave the airport station, so have your passport or other ID ready. They may inspect your baggage, but the officials are usually more thorough with that of Japanese passengers because of the continuing series of terrorist attacks on the airport by student radicals.

JR Trains

Two types of service go from Tokyo station to Narita airport: Narita Express (NEX) and Sobu *kaisoku* express. (Many of these originate at Shinjuku, Ikebukuro, Yokohama, and other stations in the region.) Reservations are needed for the former (23/day; one hour; ¥2890), while the latter are ordinary commuter coaches (18/day; 90 min; ¥1260). The tracks are easily accessible from the Marunouchi side, and transfer from the Marunouchi subway line is quite short.

Illuminated signs by the entrance give full details on the next several trains. Make a note of the platform and time, for trains not going to the airport also start from the same tracks. The trains of interest are indicated as "Narita Express" and "Rapid Airport Narita", the latter being the Sobu *kaisoku*. (Signs inside the entrance to the tracks may be written "Yokosuka Sobu line NEX".) There are Green Cars (first class, with surcharge), double-decker cars, and non-smoking cars as options when buying your ticket. If the next NEX is sold out, it will be faster in most cases to take a Sobu kaisoku, for NEX trains run only at 30- to 60-minute intervals.

There is an escalator down all but the last level. The destination of the train on each track is marked in English.

Note that the NEX is considerably more expensive than a Keisei Skyliner but no faster (though it does leave from a more centrally located station). Skyliner coaches are also rated as more comfortable, though both have been custom designed to give more luxury than typical trains.

Getting to Narita from Yokohama

As described in greater detail in the Yokohama section, the simplest way to Narita airport is by bus from Yokohama City Air Terminal (YCAT). Buses leave every 15 to 20 minutes, the trip is scheduled for two hours, and the fare is ¥3300.

At the Airport

After check-in at Narita airport, you can shop for duty free items in the terminal buildings (though prices are high); you can also buy liquor and a smaller selection of other items after passing through Immigration. There is a ¥2000 airport departure tax. Tickets are sold by machines at the entrance to the stairs down to the immigration lounge. Turn in any certificates for tax-free purchases just before the Immigration check. (The ground won't open up and swallow you if you fail to do this. It seems largely an exercise to keep bureaucrats employed.)

DEPARTURE FROM HANEDA AIRPORT

Getting to Haneda from Tokyo

From Tokyo to Haneda airport is such a simple process that one sentence of instruction is about all you need. Go to Hamamatsucho station (JR Yamanote line), follow the signs to the monorail, buy a ticket (¥300), ride the train, and you're there.

Getting to Haneda from Yokohama

The most convenient way to reach Haneda from Yokohama is by bus from YCAT. They leave every 8 to 15 minutes, cost ¥440, and are scheduled to take about 30 minutes.

TRANSPORTATION OUT OF TOKYO

Japan's well developed and efficient transport system means that you can get to almost any part of the country from any other part with relative ease. The following describes the systems.

Air

With the exception of a very few flights out of Narita, all domestic air transport to/from Tokyo goes through Haneda airport. There are direct flights from Tokyo to about 35 different cities, while even more are accessible with a transfer at the major regional airports of Sapporo, Osaka, Nagoya, Fukuoka, and Naha (Okinawa). Sample air fares are given in the general Getting Around section.

Rail—JR

Shinkansen

There are three super-express Shinkansen lines linking Tokyo with the most important regions of the country. The Tokaido Shinkansen line runs through Nagoya and Kyoto to Osaka, at which point the name of the line changes to Sanyo Shinkansen (no change of train needed for through trains). The line continues through Okayama and Hiroshima to the terminus at Hakata (Fukuoka), in northern Kyushu. The Tohoku Shinkansen runs northeast through

Sendai to Morioka, and the Joetsu Shinkansen runs north via Takasaki to Niigata on the north coast. All Shinkansen trains leave from Tokyo station. (During holiday peak periods, extra trains of the Tohoku and Joetsu lines may also start from Ueno.)

These are the most important trunk lines in Japan, linking the majority of the largest cities. They are explained in more detail in the general Getting Around section.

Regular JR Lines

Tokaido Honsen (Main Line)

Trains of this line begin at Tokyo station, offer express service to Kawasaki and Yokohama (28 minutes), and continue some distance down the coast, generally as far as Atami, Odawara, Ito, or Mishima.

Within the Tokyo area, these trains stop only at Shimbashi and Shinagawa. This line, along with the Yokosuka line, is the quickest route to Yokohama. These are *kaisoku* expresses, which means that there is no surcharge.

Some night or overnight trains go to more distant destinations, such as Osaka, Shimonoseki, Kumamoto, and Nagasaki, but a sleeper would be extra even for a holder of a Japan Rail Pass. Most travellers to Kyushu, for example, would prefer to go by Shinkansen during the day as far as Hakata and transfer to a connecting day train. Those without a JRP would find the night buses considerably cheaper.

Yokosuka Line

Trains begin at Tokyo station, provide express service to Yokohama (28 minutes), and continue on through Kamakura (about one hour), and Yokosuka (about 80 minutes) to Kurihama, at the bottom of the Miura-hanto peninsula. All Yokosuka line trains are *kaisoku* expresses, so there is no

surcharge. Trains leave Tokyo station every five to 15 minutes. Within metro Tokyo they stop only at Shimbashi and Shinagawa stations. Most of these begin as Sobu Honsen line trains from Chiba; from Tokyo station they continue as Yokosuka line trains (and vice-versa in the opposite direction).

Chuo Line

There are two "Chuo" lines. The Chuo Honsen ("Main Line") originates at Shinjuku station and gives both "L" express service (with surcharge) westward to Matsumoto with few stops en route (Hachioji, Otsuki, Kofu), and a slower express that goes as far as Otsuki (a gateway to the Mt. Fuji area), making more stops en route. Chuo-sen commuter lines originate at Tokyo station or come from Chiba, and run as far as Mitaka or Takao, west of Tokyo.

Takasaki Line

This begins at Ueno station and runs northward through the Kanto plain to Takasaki or beyond. There are connections through the mountains to Niigata by the Joetsu line. Regular Takasaki line trains that stop at all stations are normal fare; the expresses have a surcharge.

Tohoku Honsen (Main Line)

This begins at Ueno and overlaps the Takasaki line as far as Omiya, then turns northeast. The tracks run through Sendai and Morioka to Aomori, at the far north of Honshu, but there are only a few night expresses that actually run through to Aomori and even Sapporo. To go to places like Fukushima and Sendai, more than one change of train would be required. Those with a JRP would take the Shinkansen, and those without would probably consider the bus.

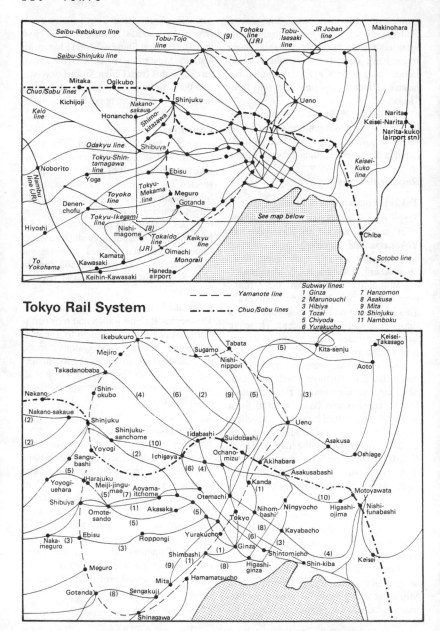

Tokyo Rail System

Subway lines:
1 Ginza
2 Marunouchi
3 Hibiya
4 Tozai
5 Chiyoda
6 Yurakucho
7 Hanzomon
8 Asakusa
9 Mita
10 Shinjuku
11 Namboku

- - - - Yamanote line
- ∙ - ∙ - Chuo/Sobu lines

Joban Line

Services run from Ueno through Mito to the east coast and follow the coast northeast to Sendai; most trains run only to Mito or Taira. Only a few expresses run direct to Sendai, including two that go as far as Aomori.

Sobu Line

As with the Chuo line, there are two types of Sobu line service, Sobu-sen and Sobu Honsen. The Sobu Honsen (main line) runs between Tokyo station and Choshi (up from the Boso Peninsula) giving express service to Chiba, Narita city, and Choshi. Express trains to Narita (terminus) operate as *kaisoku* trains (no surcharge), but expresses to Choshi have a surcharge. A large number of the Sobu Honsen trains into Tokyo continue past Tokyo station, becoming trains of the Yokosuka line, giving express (*kaisoku*) service to and beyond Yokohama. The Sobu-sen line gives local service (every station) between Chiba and Mitaka; from Ochanomizu to Mitaka, it runs parallel to the Chuo-sen (orange).

Private Railways

The private railways generally act as commuter feeder lines between Tokyo and smaller communities. Only a few run to areas of any touristic interest or are likely to be used by the average traveller. The station of each in Tokyo is near or close to a station of the JR Yamanote line, and a subway line connects with almost all of them. Many private lines act as a continuation of the subway line. The following lines are mentioned at some point in this book as being of some use to get to places of interest. Details of these services are given in the write-up for the specific attraction.

Line	From	To
Tobu	Asakusa	Nikko
Keihin-Kyuko	Shinagawa,	Miura-hanto peninsula
	Kawasaki,	
	Yokohama,	
	Yokosuka	
Toyoko	Shibuya	Yokohama
Odakyu	Shinjuku	Odawara, Hakone area, transfer for Mt. Fuji area
Tobu-Tojo	Ikebukuro	Kawagoe
Keisei	Ueno	Narita, Narita airport, Chiba

One of the maps included in the JNTO *Tourist Map of Tokyo* shows and identifies all the private lines and shows the connecting subway line without identifying the latter. However, the accompanying subway map shows the private lines as black lines, so the two maps can be used together to identify which subway line connects with which private line.

Buses

There is a growing number of expressway bus services out of Tokyo. These are described briefly in the Getting Around section. Among them are buses to Kyoto, northern Honshu, the Mt. Fuji/Hakone areas, and many other places to the west and south far into Kyushu.

Ferries

Long-distance ferries from Tokyo and vicinity offer reasonably low cost transportation to a number of distant parts of Japan, with the bonus of a "sea cruise" and the economy of saving accommodation costs for one or two nights. They are described in the general transportation section earlier in the book. There are also ferry services from nearby Kawasaki, and from Oarai, a little to the north, near Mito.

GETTING AROUND IN TOKYO

Tokyo has a comprehensive public transportation system. Although large and complex, it is easy to use once you understand it, and is the cheapest way to get around the city. Comprising the system are suburban feeder buses, 11 private railways, 10 subway lines operated as two separate systems but linked at transfer stations, JR train lines, and city buses. The major shortcoming is that there is no system of free transfers between systems; a separate fare is required for each. (An open pass is available; see below.) You must keep your ticket and surrender it at the end of the journey (except on buses).

Try to avoid the peak periods 0730–0930 and 1600–1930; there are millions of people on the move, and it will seem they are all in your coach. (The subway system carries over seven million people daily.) It is also a time that will go far toward destroying any illusions about the "exquisitely polite Japanese", as they have no compunction about squeezing past or in front of you to enter (or leave!) a train, or about putting a hand (or, more politely the back of their wrist) in your back and pushing as soon as the doors open. (It can be a game to move sideways just enough to pin a "squeezer" immobile against the doorframe without seeming obvious about it. Also, there is no law about reaching behind you and removing a pushing hand . . . politely of course.) The behavior of the Japanese getting on and off trains is analogous to that of their companies in foreign markets, pushing in relentlessly. Once on a train, always hold on to a strap or bar, for a sizable number of the other occupants will try (unsuccessfully) to get by on balance alone, and are likely to topple like dominos when the train starts and stops.

If you have trouble climbing stairs, you will be at a severe disadvantage, for many stations do not have escalators, and some of the staircases are long. This can make the difference between the subway and train system being usable and not.

Tickets

Tickets are sold by vending machines. Fares are shown on a large map over the machines, but the maps are almost invariably in *kanji* only. The JNTO *Tourist Map of Tokyo* is invaluable here for its two transportation maps. *Communications Network* shows the names of all private and JR railway lines in the greater Tokyo area in both *romaji* and *kanji*; *Subways in Tokyo* does the same for the subway lines within the city and the railway lines that continue from many of them. Each subway line has a color code that is used to identify the line on maps and on signs in stations showing the route to follow for a transfer.

Most subway and JR stations have hand-out maps of the lines for the convenience of foreigners, but they show the name only in *romaji*. To ask for a map, say "Densha no chizu-o kudasai."

One way around the fare problem is to buy the lowest fare ticket and pay the difference at the "Fare Adjustment" window at the destination (or to the ticket taker). A perplexed look when standing at the ticket machine will probably prompt some assistance.

Some ticket machines have a single large number, like "160"; they sell a single value ticket. Most machines have a row of buttons for selecting the fare (two rows actually, the bottom one for children's tickets). The machines give change, so it is safe to insert coins in excess of the fare. The most recent machines can be truly confusing, even for Japanese residents, for they have buttons for nominating the transfer station, the transfer line, the number of tickets, and other options. Fear not! You will be able to work it out!

If you put coins into the wrong machine and realize the mistake before pushing a fare button, you can get the coins back by pushing the button marked 取消し (torikeshi). If you accidentally buy a ticket for a fare higher than required, etc., take it immediately to the ticket puncher, the Fare Adjustment window (on the inside of the entrance wickets), or push the button marked 呼び出し (yobidashi) and ask for a refund. (The equivalent of "I goofed" is machigai' mash'ta.) The latter is also the button to push if the machine jams and keeps your money. You cannot get a refund of excess payment at the end of your journey.

Note that it is often quicker to get to a destination by using a combination of JR and subway than to use one system exclusively, but it will be more costly because separate tickets are required for each.

Commuter Tickets (Kaisuken)

These are also available for travel between two specific stations and give 11 rides for the price of 10. These are 11 tickets of the same value, but without start and finish stations. When you enter the station, you insert your ticket (the attendant can also do this) into a small machine on his counter; this stamps the name of the starting station. In this way, tickets can be used for any journey of the indicated (or lower) value. These tickets can be bought at larger stations at the office, or from some vending machines (instruction required!). Eidan system tickets are valid only on Eidan trains; likewise for Toei. You can also buy a prepaid SF metro card usable for both systems. This will not offer any discounts, however.

Day Passes

Special one-day unlimited-use passes are available. One type is valid on all the subway lines and another on JR commuter trains. The subway "one-day open ticket" costs ¥650 for adults, ¥330 for children. The JR pass is called a "free kippu", and is valid for unlimited travel on JR trains for one day within the bounds of the Yamanote line. A pass valid on all transportation—all ten subway lines, JR lines and buses—costs ¥1460 for adults, ¥730 for children. Subway passes are available at the subway pass office at several main stations, such as Shibuya, Shinjuku, Otemachi, Ebisu, Ochanomizu, Kasumigaseki, Ginza, Akasaka-mitsuke, and Ikebukuro. If you have to use the subway to get to the pass office, you can obtain a refund of the amount paid to get there.

Commuter Passes

Passes are available that permit an unlimited number of trips between any two stations in the Tokyo area (and all stations in between). A pass can cover a journey using two systems, for example, on a JR line and a connecting subway line. Passes are available for one, three, or six months; they will be of more interest to residents.

Timetables

There is generally a timetable for a line posted somewhere along the platform. The listings headed with the symmetrical kanji are for services from Monday to Saturday (heijitsu); the other listing is for Sundays and holidays (kyujitsu). (If there are three listings, the middle one is for Saturday.)

Subways & Private Railways

Tokyo has a good subway system. Trains are frequent and clean, and the system covers the city intensively within the Yamanote loop line and beyond it some distance (especially to the east). The system is made up of 11 lines: four municipally run Toei

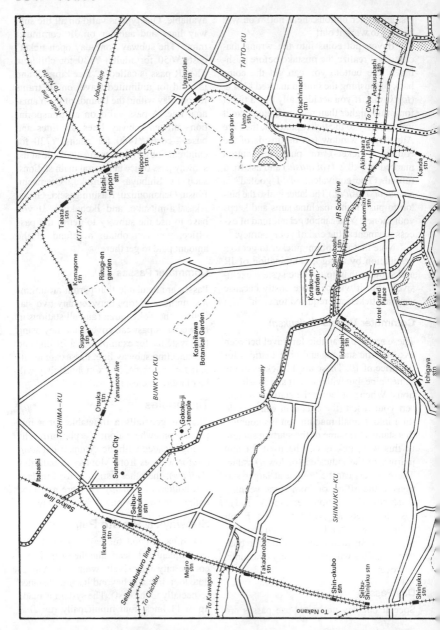

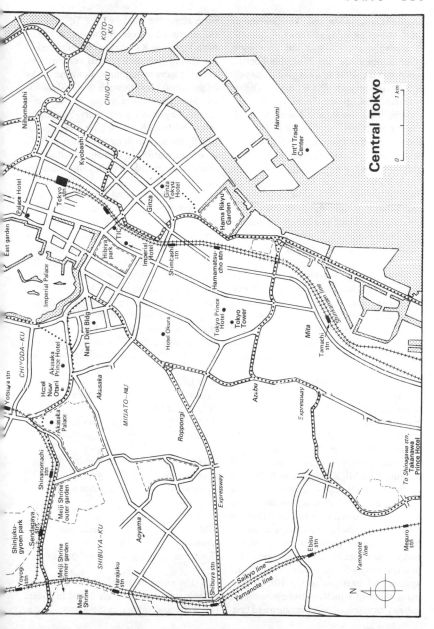

Central Tokyo

0   1 km

lines—Asakusa, Mita, and Shinjuku (sometimes shown on signs as Toei 1, 6, and 10, respectively, even though the lines were given names in the late 70's) plus Toei 12 (opened in late 1991 and not given a name), and seven private *Eidan* lines—Ginza, Marunouchi, Chiyoda, Tozai, Hibiya, Yurakucho, Hanzomon, and Namboku. Passengers can transfer among the Eidan lines and among the Toei lines without extra charge, but a transfer from one system to another requires a new fare to be paid. The vending machines sell tickets that allow a transfer and cover both systems; the total cost being less than the purchase of two separate tickets (but you may need instruction on the buttons!). Similarly, a new fare must be paid when transferring to/from the JR system, private railways, or buses.

When changing from one subway line to another, it is sometimes necessary to exit the station and re-enter another wicket some distance away. In cases like this it is useful to have a ticket valid for the full fare through to the final destination lest the ticket taker at the first station want to take your ticket when you exit.

Every subway line permits a transfer to the JR Yamanote loop line somewhere, some also to the Sobu or Chuo line, and every subway line connects with or runs onto the tracks of a JR line or one of the 11 private railway lines. In the case of a private line, it is possible that no transfer will be required at all; some subway trains will continue along the tracks of the private line and operate some distance as one of its trains. (It will usually be as a local train, so it may be worthwhile to change to an express if you are going far on the private line.) A new fare is charged as soon as the journey crosses the boundary of the second system. An example is the Hibiya line, many trains of which continue beyond the subway terminus of Naka-meguro and continue along the tracks of the Toyoko line (which runs between Shibuya and Yokohama) as far as Kikuna. At the other end of the Hibiya line, some trains continue beyond the subway terminus, along the tracks of the Isezaki line through to Kita-kasukabe. Similarly, you can get to Kawagoe (slowly) by staying on many Yurakucho trains. When a change of train *is* required, it usually requires nothing more than walking across the platform. At the most arduous, it might be necessary to walk a short distance to another platform.

At stations serving lines of both subway systems there are machines selling tickets for both, as well as for transfering to any connecting private railway line. There may be up to a dozen machines, each one with different markings (only in *kanji*). It's complicated even for the Japanese, so don't be embarrassed to ask for help. For assistance, carry your copy of the JNTO *Tourist Map of Tokyo* described above. The following is the color scheme of the cars of the various lines; the color is also used as a code to identify the various lines on maps.

EIDAN

Ginza	orange
Marunouchi	red
Chiyoda	dark green
Tozai	light blue
Hibiya	grey
Hanzomon	purple
Yurakucho	yellow
Namboku	aquamarine

TOEI

Mita	dark blue
Asakusa	pink
Shinjuku	lime green

The name of every station in the subway system is clearly identified in *romaji* on walls and pillars in the station. Signs, also labelled in *romaji* and color-coded the same as on fare maps, clearly indicate the direction to walk when transferring from one line to another.

The timetable for the line using a platform is posted over the platform. The symmetrical *kanji* identify services from Monday to Saturday (*heijitsu*); the other identify Sundays and holidays (*kyujitsu*). Some timetables have Saturday listed separately in a middle column. On private railway timetables the red, green, or blue numbers represent express services; black numbers indicate local trains.

JR Trains

JR runs several lines in the Tokyo area. Most important are the Yamanote loop line that circles the city in both directions, the Chuo line that crosses the city, and the Keihin-Tohoku line (which overlaps the Yamanote line between Shinagawa and Tabata). Other lines feed into these. Fares are a minimum ¥120, and are charged by distance.

At any JR station in Tokyo it is possible to buy a ticket to any other station in Japan, except for Shinkansen and reserved seat tickets, which must be purchased at a station with a Green window.

Every JR station in the Tokyo area (and generally throughout the country) is identified by signs over the platform in *romaji* as well as Japanese, but they are rather high and difficult to see when standing in a train. There aren't many signs, so watch carefully when entering a station. On either the overhead sign or on another sign at platform level there is normally the name of the station in large *kanji* and *romaji*, and in the lower left and right corners are the names of the next station in either direction. On each platform, hanging overhead near the edge of the platform and at right angles to the tracks will be a small sign giving the

names of major stations ahead along that line; there is usually one sign in *romaji*.

The number of signs in *romaji* indicating the route to follow to change trains, or for particular platform or station exit, varies widely. Tokyo station is well marked with illuminated and color-coded signs in English, while Shinjuku, an extremely busy station, has the illuminated color signs, but nearly everything is exclusively in Japanese.

Information on JR services anywhere in Japan, including Tokyo commuter trains, is available in English by phoning 3423-0111.

Several JR lines run within the Tokyo area and to nearby cities, so the following brief explanation may be useful. Remember *kaisoku* trains are semi-expresses, skipping several stations thereby giving faster service, but without the surcharge usually applied to express services.

Yamanote (Loop) Line

Yamanote trains are green or have green stripes.

The Yamanote line circles the central part of Tokyo. Trains run in each direction at very frequent intervals throughout the day, tapering off later at night. Like all trains in the Tokyo area, service stops soon after midnight, although these trains are usually the last public transport to stop for the night.

There are 29 stations around the loop. Making a complete circuit takes about an hour and is an often-recommended introduction to the city. Three of the stations (Tokyo, Ueno, and Shinjuku) are the starting points for JR intercity trains. Since these stations are often used by visitors, they are detailed below. All the 11 private suburban railways begin at their own stations adjacent to various stations of the Yamanote line. (Many of these lines connect directly with subway lines.)

Keihin-Tohoku Line

Keihin-Tohoku trains are blue. Trains of this line run from Ofuna (below Yokohama) into Tokyo and north to Omiya, running parallel to the Yamanote line around the east side of the city from Shinagawa (SW Tokyo) to Tabata (N Tokyo). They stop at every station en route until about 1030 and after about 1530, and either line may be used over this distance; between those times, trains stop only at Shinagawa, Tamachi, Tokyo, Akihabara, Ueno, and Tabata within Tokyo.

Chuo and Sobu Lines

Chuo trains are orange. There are two Chuo lines, but the Chuo Honsen line (originating at Shinjuku station) is an intercity express (westward-bound), so not relevant here.

Sobu yellow trains stop at every station between Mitaka (some distance west of Tokyo) and Chiba (to the east), providing local service.

Chuo orange trains begin at Tokyo station and give *kaisoku* express service to Shinjuku (and vice versa). En route they stop only at Kanda, Ochanomizu, Yotsuya, and Yoyogi. Passengers in a hurry to get to one of the intermediate stations across the city not served by the Chuo line take it to whichever of the latter three stations is closest to their destination, then take a Sobu yellow train the rest of the way. (Those going from Shinjuku to Akihabara can take the Chuo orange to Ochanomizu and change to the Sobu line just by walking across the platform.)

West of Shinjuku there are two types of Chuo orange service. "Ordinary" *kaisoku* trains make the same stops as Sobu yellow trains as far as Mitaka, but continue west to Takao. (Some branch off at Tachikawa and

run to Ome and Okutama; these are convenient for U.S. Air Force people going to Fussa for Yokota air base.) "Special" (*tokubetsu*) kaisoku make only one stop between Shinjuku and Mitaka, and skip several stations between Mitaka and Takao. There are three *tokubetsu kaisoku* trains per hour, in addition to more frequent "ordinary" *kaisoku*. Both types use the same platform, so it is necessary to refer to a timetable to select the desired type of train.

Yokosuka Line

Yokosuka trains are cream and blue. The Yokosuka (pron. "Yoh-kohs-kah", *not* "Yoh-koos-kah) line starts at Tokyo station and provides express service southwest to Yokohama (28 minutes), stopping only at Shimbashi and Shinagawa in the metro Tokyo area. They continue beyond Yokohama through Kamakura (just under one hour) and Yokosuka (home of Yokosuka U.S. Naval Base) to Kurihama on the Miura Peninsula.

Tokaido Line

Tokaido trains are orange and green. The Tokaido line starts at Tokyo station and provides express service southwest to Kawasaki (not served by the Yokosuka line) and Yokohama. Together with the Yokosuka line, it is the fastest way to Yokohama (28 minutes), stopping only at Shimbashi and Shinagawa in Tokyo. Trains continue beyond Yokohama to the Atami area.

Main JR Stations

The multitude of platforms at some stations in the Tokyo area is confusing even to residents, and overwhelming to newcomers. New lines and extensions are added every year. The following information serves only as a general guide to the visitor, valid as of mid-1996.

Tokyo Station

Modelled on Amsterdam station, Tokyo is the main station of the city. Its services include all super-express Shinkansen lines, plus ordinary and express services southwest down the coast, and trains east and southeast. It is also the starting point for some commuter trains running west past Shinjuku.

The accompanying table is useful for general orientation. Note that because the Tokaido line trains (both locals and expresses) leave from the same platforms, it is necessary to check a timetable to be sure of getting the right type of train.

Tokyo station has two sides: Yaesu is the major side, Marunouchi the minor. An underground passage links them. It is one of the best signposted stations in Japan as regards English, color coding, and illuminated signs.

Tokyo station (Yaesu side) is the point of departure for highway buses to Nagoya, Kyoto, and Osaka, as well as various night buses to Kyoto, Osaka, and various other cities, such as Yamagata and Sendai. The shuttle bus to TCAT leaves from across the road from the Yaesu side exit. Information

TOKYO STATION

Track	Line	Route
1, 2	Chuo orange	Express to Shinjuku and on to Takao.
3	Keihin-Tohoku	Local service north to Tabata, Omiya.
4	Yamanote	Loop line counter-clockwise to Ueno, Shinjuku, etc.
5	Yamanote	Loop line clockwise to Shinagawa, Gotanda, etc.
6	Keihin-Tohoku	Local service to Shinagawa, Yokohama, Ofuna.
7–10	Tokaido	Mixed local and express trains beyond Yokohama to Odawara and Atami (with connections to Shizuoka, Kyoto, Nagoya, and Osaka).
12, 13	Tohoku Yamagata/Joetsu Shinkansen	Super-express service to Sendai /Yamagata and Morioka/Takasaki and Niigata.
14–19	Tokaido/Sanyo Shinkansen	Super-express to Nagoya, Kyoto, Osaka, Hiroshima, and Hakata.

Underground (Chika) One of two underground stations

1-4	a: Yokosuka	a: Express *kaisoku* to Yokohama; local service on to Kamakura, Yokosuka, and Kurihama.
	b: Sobu Kaisoku	b: Express *kaisoku* to Chiba and Narita; express (surcharge) and local service to both and beyond.
	c: Boso Tokkyu	c: Express service to Boso Peninsula.
	d: Narita Express (NEX)	d: To Narita airport.

Underground (Chika Keiyo) The other underground station

1-4	a: Keiyo	a: Tokyo–Chiba.
	b: Musashino-sen	b: Looping outer suburban line.
	c: Boso Tokkyu	c: Express service to Boso Peninsula (beyond Chiba).

services are also on the Yaesu side.

The Marunouchi subway line is on the Marunouchi side. Signs clearly indicate the way.

The four lines from the "chika" station (see table) offer plenty of scope for confusion, for trains arrive from both directions at all platforms and depart in both directions from two of them. Consult a timetable to be sure of getting the right one. There is a large timetable (with English) at the foot of at least one of the escalators.

Ueno Station

Ueno is the station for most trains headed north and northeast. It is not difficult to get confused, but the station is fairly well signposted and with the following platform information it shouldn't be too hard to transfer trains. For orientation, the important thing to remember is that the main concourse is above the tracks at the north end (the end away from Akihabara and Tokyo stations).

Platforms 1–4 serve trains that circle Tokyo or run to points nearby, while others serve destinations farther away. As with Tokyo station, several lines depart at various times from any number of platforms, so check a timetable for the right one.

Transfers to tracks 13–18 require a little searching, for they are not in line with tracks 1–12; they are to the east side of the station, and downstairs from the overhead concourse. The way to the Ginza and Hibiya subway lines can be followed easily, as can the route to Keisei railway station.

Shinjuku Station

Shinjuku is claimed to be the busiest station in the world, with several JR lines, two subway lines, and three private railways delivering passengers to or near it. Only one long-distance JR line leaves from it, the

---

UENO STATION

In the following table, abbreviations are used for the names of the lines:
To = Tohoku Honsen line; Ta = Takasaki line; Jo = Joshinetsu line; Jb = Joban line;

Track	Line	Route
1	Keihin-Tohoku	Local service to Tabata, Omiya (terminus).
2	Yamanote	Loop line counter-clockwise to Tabata, Ikebukuro, Shinjuku, etc.
3	Yamanote	Loop line clockwise to Tokyo, Shinagawa, Gotanda, etc.
4	Keihin-Tohoku	Local service to Shinagawa, Kawasaki, Yokohama, Ofuna (terminus). (Some stations are skipped during the day.)
5–8	To, Ta, Jo.	
9	To, Ta, Jo, Jb.	
10	Jb (local).	
11, 12	Jb (local).	
13–15	To, Ta, Jo.	
16	To, Jb.	
17	To, Ta, Jo, Jb.	
18	Jb.	
19, 22	Joetsu Shinkansen/Tohoku Yamagata Shinkansen	

Chuo Honsen. It has express trains west towards Kofu and Matsumoto, as well as ordinary services terminating somewhat closer.

An underground passage on the north side of the station links east and west sides and has the entrance to Shinjuku station of the Marunouchi subway line. (Farther east in the same passageway is Shinjuku-sanchome station.)

The tracks are accessible via two tunnels from inside the JR wickets. The southernmost of these tunnels can be used to get to the Keio and Odakyu private railways (which have their stations on the west side of the JR station) by purchasing a Keio or Odakyu ticket on the east side.

Shinjuku station is probably the most bewildering on earth, an architectural disaster, with very poor planning of concourses, passages, stairs, and so on. By late 1991 it had finally achieved a useful level of signposting in English.

Buses

There is a large network of bus routes throughout the greater Tokyo area. They act mostly as feeders to railway and subway lines, often through incredibly narrow streets. Most routes run between large JR stations. Buses generally stop running after 2100.

The drawback of buses is that the destination is written only in *kanji* and the drivers rarely speak English. However, since the destination is often a station, you can check if the *kanji* on a bus correspond to the characters for one of the JR stations. At every bus stop there is a sign with the names of the destination stations (in Japanese), a route map and the schedule.

Buses are, of course, subject to the delays of Tokyo's heavy traffic, so travel is slow in the morning and afternoon peak periods. In Tokyo the fare is paid when entering the bus and the fare is marked on the cash box. Strips of tickets are also available.

SHINJUKU STATION

Track	Line	Route
1, 2	Saikyo-sen	To Shibuya, Ebisu.
3, 4	Saikyo-sen, also NEX	To Urawa, Omiya, Kawagoe. To Narita, airport.
5, 6	Chuo Honsen (long distance)	Trains to Otsuki, Kofu, Matsumoto.
7	Holiday *kaisoku*	To Okutama.
8	Chuo orange	*Kaisoku* express to Tokyo station (all day).
9	Sobu (yellow)	
10	Chuo	*Kaisoku* express to Takao.
11	Sobu	Local service east through Akihabara to Chiba: after 2210, all but one go to Tokyo station.
12	Yamanote	Loop line counter-clockwise to Shibuya, Gotanda, Shinagawa, etc.
13	Yamanote	Loop line clockwise to Ikebukuro, Tabata, Ueno, etc.
14	Sobu yellow	Local service west to Mitaka for most of day; through to Tachikawa and Takao in late evening.

Note : Trains for Shimoda (Izu Peninsula), Nikko, etc. are also available.

Buses are most useful to residents who have the time to establish what lines go where they want to go. At least one map *Great Tokyo Detailed Map* (Nippon Kokuseisha; ¥680 at bookshops), shows bus routes, but check the date of publication.

Streetcars

There is a single surviving tram line in Tokyo, running in the north of the city from Ikebukuro to Oji (on Keihin-Tohoku line), not a generally useful route.

Taxis

The drop charge (mid-1995) is ¥650 for the first 2 km, plus ¥80 for each additional 280 meters. Between 2300 and 0500, there is a 30% surcharge. It is frequently difficult to impossible to get a taxi late at night because they are looking for passengers going a long distance (which equals a large fare; foreigners usually want to go to nearby destinations) and because company employees often have vouchers and are willing to offer double or triple fares (by holding up two or three fingers). Ordinary Japanese suffer from this too.

ACCOMMODATION

There is a wide variety of accommodation available in the greater Tokyo area, ranging from hotels that match the world's best (with matching prices) to more modest and affordable.

The good news for budget travellers, especially of the backpack type, is that the number of places catering to them has increased greatly in the last few years, so the choice of places to stay is much more varied and the chances of finding a room more likely. However, the number of people travelling in Japan has also gone up, so it may still be necessary to make quite a few phone calls to find a room, especially in popular seasons.

The list in this book of places to stay is much more extensive for Tokyo than for any other city because this is where the majority of travellers land and need a roof over their heads for a night or two while getting organized. Listings of alternative sources of accommodation can be found in publications available at the TICs at Narita airport and in the city (*Japanese Inn Group*, *Hotels in Japan*, *Japan Ryokan Guide*, etc.), in *Tour Companion*, and in *Tokyo Journal*. (The latter has the most advertisements of "foreigner house" type accommodation, popular with travellers and those staying longer periods.) The "top of the line" hotels are not listed here because the people who use them are normally travelling on a pre-arranged itinerary with all accommodation reserved. If you arrive in Tokyo and wish to stay at such a place but have no reservation, there is a desk in each wing of Narita airport that can make on-the-spot bookings for more than 25 of Tokyo's top hotels.

As noted in the section on Narita airport, the TIC there can make reservations for economy *ryokan* and *minshuku* in Tokyo and elsewhere. The same service is also available at the TIC in the Ginza area. (This service is detailed in the Accommodation section.)

If phoning for reservations, note that all 8-digit numbers listed can be dialled as local calls within Tokyo. If calling from Narita, the call is long-distance, and the Tokyo numbers must be prefixed by "03".

The following listings begin with the youth hostels. Although there is private accommodation available with fewer restrictions and at no higher cost, the YH locations are quite central and they can be useful for obtaining information on the other hostels throughout the country. After the hostels come the reasonably priced private accommodation, then the *ryokan* and business hotels and other hotels at relatively moderate cost.

Youth Hostels

Tokyo Kok'sai (International) Youth Hostel. The main youth hostel of Tokyo is a bit of a showpiece and one of the best in Japan—as befits the municipally operated hostel in the nation's capital. Located on the 18th and 19th floors of a new high-rise building, it has a good view over the north of the city, "ginormous" baths, and comfortable rooms.

Hostel regulations are similar to those that will be encountered throughout Japan, possibly a bit more relaxed; the doors close at 2230 (and don't open until 0630—which is a bit awkward if you need to catch an early flight), and visitors can normally stay for only three days. The hostel is municipally owned, so you don't need to be a YH member to stay; a passport for identification is sufficient. The telephone number is (03) 3235-1107. Room charge is ¥2,650–2,890 per night, depending on the season (if heating or air conditioning is in use).

The hostel can be reached by JR and two subway lines, as follows; all stations are named Iidabashi.

The JR Chuo (yellow) line, running between Akihabara and Shinjuku is the most convenient transport to the hostel. You can transfer to this line from the Yamanote and Keihin-Tohoku lines (through Ueno) at Akihabara, and at Ochanomizu from the Chuo (orange) line. Leave the station at the front of the train (if coming from Akihabara) then turn right at the street and walk downhill about 20m. Turn right into the open plaza area and walk into the arcade covered by the arched glass roof, to the elevators (on the left); the left hand bank of elevators goes to the top floors and the 18th floor reception desk.

The Yurakucho subway line, from Yu-rakucho (near Ginza) and Ikebukuro, brings you closest to the hostel at Iidabashi station, but it has the fewest transfers from other lines. These can be made only from the JR station at Yurakucho (walking distance from Ginza and Hibiya subway stations), at Nagatacho from the Hanzomon line (from Shibuya), and at Ichigaya (one station away from Iidabashi) from the Shinjuku line. At Iidabashi station, exit from the station at the rear of the train (if coming from Ichigaya), follow signs for exit B2, and finally take exit B2a. At street level, walk uphill the short distance to the JR station, and turn left into the plaza described above.

The Tozai subway line runs between Otemachi/Nihombashi and Takadanobaba. You can transfer at Otemachi (Marunouchi, Chiyoda and Mita lines), Nihombashi (Ginza line), Kayabacho (Hibiya line), Kudanshita (Shinjuku line) and Takadanobaba (Yamanote line); both the Ginza and Hibiya lines pass through Ueno.

The other hostel is Yoyogi Youth Hostel (tel (03) 3467-9163), located in one of the dorms constructed for the Tokyo Olympics. You can get there from the Shinjuku station of the Odakyu railway (on the west side of JR Shinjuku station) by local (non-express) train to Sangubashi, the second stop. Exit the station, take the small road to the left across the tracks, take the pedestrian bridge to the other side of the large road, and continue to the right to the entrance gate of what looks like a university or school. The YH is on the grounds.

The hostel can also be reached via Harajuku JR station or Meiji-jingu-mae or Yoyogi-koen stations of the Chiyoda subway lines, but these require a longer walk. (The buildings are old and have not been well maintained, so are a distinct second-best to Tokyo Kokusai YH.)

There are also youth hostels in Chiba

city (tel. (043) 294-1850, Tateyama (tel. (0470) 28-0073), Kujukurihama (tel. (0475) 33-2254), Kofuso (tel. (0436) 36-2770), all within an hour or so of Narita airport; and at Yokohama (tel. (045) 241-6503), Kamakura (tel. (0467) 25-1238), and Takao (tel. (0426) 61-0437), all within an hour or so of Tokyo on the west side). There are others in the region that could be used if all the above are full; the TIC offices should have a YH Handbook for reference.

Private

Okubo House is in a category all its own. Although it is privately owned, it requires guests to leave by 1000, and has a midnight curfew. However, because of its singular nature and the fact that it has been a fixture for foreign travellers for years, it deserves some extra space. Okubo House was originally a workman's dormitory until it was discovered by foreigners, and it has been a mainstay since then. It has mostly dorm rooms (male only) for about ¥1800, but has some single and double rooms starting at ¥3000. (A hint; take your bath early! The Japanese workmen living there have never heard of the etiquette that requires soaping before getting into the tub. They sluice one bucket of water over themselves, then hop into the tub and methodically start rubbing off all the dirt . . . into the water.) Okubo House is near Shin-okubo station (Yama-note line); turn left from the station exit, then left again at the first side street and walk almost to the T-junction about five minutes away. Tel: (03) 3361-2348.

Foreigner Houses

In recent years numerous private homes have opened as communal-type accommodation, with shared cooking facilities, one or more common rooms with TV, etc., and dormitory and individual bedrooms (singles, doubles). There are no curfew regulations as there are with the youth hostels and Okubo House, so guests can come and go at will, and remain during the day. Most offer cheaper weekly and monthly rates, and many people who are establishing themselves long-term in Tokyo stay on for months because of the community atmosphere that develops. These "foreigner houses" are the closest equivalent to the cheap hotels found on the travellers' route through southeast Asia and India.

Unfortunately, these houses come and go, and many had to be deleted from the listing in the last edition. However, some new ones have come along and have been added. If there is no phone service when you call, just try another. And check *Tokyo Journal* for new ones. Note: Several small apartment buildings are being used for this sort of low-cost accommodation, and several in the following lists are for weekly or monthly accommodation rather than for daily stays. Please choose accordingly, for it is too dificult to separate them.

Apple House. Tel. 3962-4979; ¥2300; Oyama (Tobu-Tojo line from Ikebukuro).

Bilingual House. Tel. 3200-7082; weekly/monthly; three houses on Seibu-Shinjuku and Keio lines.

Friendship House. Tel. 3765-2288, 3327-3179; weekly/monthly; several locations.

Green Peace. Tel. 3915-2572; weekly/monthly; Kami-nakazato (out of Ueno or Shinjuku).

House California. Tel. 3209-9692; monthly; Kami-kitazawa (Keio line)/Tanashi (Seibu-Shinjuku line).

International House California. Tel. 3209-9692; Kami-kitazawa (Keio line from Shinjuku).

Magome House. Tel. 3754-3112; ¥1900;

Nishi-magome (Toei-Asakusa subway).

Maharajah Palace. Tel. 3748-0568/9; weekly/monthly; Ishikawadai (Ikegami line from Gotanda).

Mickey House. Tel. 3936-8889; two houses; ¥1300 Kami-itabashi (Tobu Tojo line NW from Ikebukuro); ¥1600 Takadanobaba (Yamanote line).

Midori House. Tel. 3754-3112; monthly; Nishi-magome (Asakusa line).

Taihei Houses. Tel. 3940-4705; Kamagome (Yamanote line)/Nishi-sugamo (Mita line).

Higashi Nakano English Center. Tel. 3360-1666; ¥2000; Higashi-nakano (JR Sobu line).

Tokyo English Center. Tel. 5370-8440; ¥2000; Fujimigaoka (Keio-Inokashira line).

Tokyo House. Tel. 3910-8808; Otsuka (Yamanote line)

Tokyo International House. Tel. 3945-1699; one week min.; several locations in central Tokyo.

Toyama House. Tel. (3303-1601); Nakashimbashi (west side of Tokyo).

Yoshida House. Tel. 3978-3964; monthly; Oizumigakuen (Seibu-Ikebukuro line) and other locations.

YTC House. Tel. 3946-5266/3576-5255; ¥1600; Nishi-sugamo (Mita line).

Listings new with this edition follow:

AAA House. Tel. 3320-3201; monthly; several locations.

Apple House (new). Tel. (0422) 51-2277; ¥1000+, monthly; 18 min. out of Shinjuku.

Cosmopolitan House. Tel. 3926-4746; monthly; 20 min from Shinjuku.

Green Forest Corp. Tel. 5272-7238; monthly; several locations

International Guest House. Tel. 3266-0979; several central locations.

Kettle House. Tel. 3645-4028; ¥1800+, monthly; central (between Tokyo and Shinjuku stns).

Kingdom House. Tel. 3382-0151; ¥2000, monthly; Ikebukuro

Manten House. Tel. 3466-2710; monthly; Sasazuka (Keio-Shinjuku line).

Marui House. Tel. 3962-4979; monthly; Ikebukuro.

Midori House. Tel. 3754-3112; ¥1900/monthly; Nishi-magome (Toei Asakusa line).

Shinnakano Guest House. Tel. 3383-0975; monthly; Shin-nakano (Marunouchi line).

Takanawa House. Tel. 3780-2611; monthly; Takanawadai (Toei-Asakusa line).

Villa Paradiso. Tel (045) 911-1184; monthly; Tama Plaza (toward Yokohama) (Shin-tamagawa line)

Yokohama Hillside House. Tel. (045) 243-3210; monthly; Yokohama

Ryokan and *Minshuku*

As mentioned in the general Places to Stay section, staying at a *ryokan* or *minshuku* is probably the best way to experience what life is like in a Japanese house. Most places have a range of prices (with and without private bath, meals, etc.) and rates may be lower by the week. An asterisk indicates a member of the Japanese Inn Group. The prices below are for the cheapest category for single/double.

Chomeikan Ryokan. Tel. 3811-7205; ¥6000; Hongo-sanchome stn. (Marunouchi subway).

Fuji Ryokan. Tel. 3657-1062; ¥5700; Koiwa stn. (JR Sobu line)/Keisei-Koiwa stn. (Keisei line).

Fujikan Ryokan. 3813-4441; ¥5000; Hongo-sanchome stn. (Marunouchi subway).

*Katsutaro Ryokan. Tel. 3821-9808; ¥4500/8400; Nezu stn. (Chiyoda subway)/Ueno stn. (JR Yamanote/Keihin-Tohoku

lines/Keisei line/Hibiya subway)

Kimi Ryokan. Tel. 3971-3766; ¥4300/7000; Ikebukuro stn. (JR Yamanote line)/Marunouchi subway).

Kikaku Ryokan. Tel. 3403-4501; ¥6000; Sendagaya stn. (JR Sobu line).

*Kikuya Ryokan. Tel. 3841-6404; ¥4700/8000; Tawaramachi stn. (Ginza subway).

Koshinkan Ryokan. Tel. 3812-5291; ¥4000; Nezu stn. (Chiyoda subway).

*Mikawaya Hotel. Tel. 3844-7757; ¥6500/12,000; Asakusa stn. (Ginza/Asakusa subway).

Nagaragawa Ryokan. Tel. 3351-5892; ¥6000/9000; Yotsuya-sanchome stn. (Marunouchi subway).

*Sansuiso Ryokan. Tel. 3441-7475; ¥5500/8600; Gotanda stn. (JR Yamanote line/Asakusa subway).

*Sawanoya Ryokan. Tel. 3822-2251; ¥4400/8200; Nezu stn. (Chiyoda subway).

Shimizu Bekkan Ryokan. Tel. 3812-6285; ¥8400; Hongo-sanchome stn. (Marunouchi subway)/Suidobashi or Kasuga stn. (Mita subway).

Shinriki Business Hotel. Tel. 3731-4706; ¥6200/10,400; Kamata stn. (east exit; JR Keihin-Tohoku line).

Shoheikan Ryokan. Tel. 3357-0551; ¥8800/14,300; Yotsuya stn. (JR Sobu line/Marunouchi subway).

*Suigetsu Hotel. (Ohgaiso bldg). Tel. 3822-4611 or 3828-3181; ¥8000/14,400; near Nezu stn. of Chiyoda subway, Ueno area.

Tsukuba Hotel. Tel. 3834-2556; ¥5000/9000; Inaricho stn. Ginza subway).

ORIENTATION

Tokyo is rather surprising. At first glance it appears to be a rather featureless jumble of uninspiring, often drab, buildings. But after a little looking around, you come to appreciate it for what it is, a huge community with many interesting places to see and things to experience; a place that grows in appeal with each day or year. There are many places in Japan with more readily identifiable "things to see" but none offers the combination of a giant metropolis with "everything" and the "local village" atmosphere that exists just under the surface.

Information

The single best source of information for travel in Japan, and a surprisingly large range of other types of information to interest overseas visitors, is the Tourist Information Center in central Tokyo, one of the three information offices operated by the Japan National Tourist Organization (JNTO). (The others are located at Narita Airport and in Kyoto.) The office is open Monday to Friday from 0900 to 1700 (unless they revert to earlier policy of closing from 1200 to 1300); on Saturdays, from 0900 to noon.

As we go to press, the Tokyo TIC is moving to its brand new office in the basement floor of the Tokyo International Forum, 3-5-1 Marunouchi, Chiyoda-ku. This lavish glass, steel, and stone structure, designed by New York-based architect Rafael Viñoly, houses a complex of exhibition, concert, and conference halls, and is Tokyo's first convention cum art center. The TIC office promises to be a treasure-mine of information as before. The Forum building is easily located by its imposing size, right next to the Shinkansen tracks and Sogo Department Store.

Access from JR trains: If travelling on the Yamanote or Keihin-Tohoku lines, get off at Yurakucho station. Walk to the end of the platform in the direction of Tokyo station and look for a sign for Tokyo International Forum or Marunouchi area. Note the Sogo Department Store on the left (it has a Youth Hostel booking office in the basement; closed Tuesday) and exit from the station on that side. (The exit is the

Forum exit.) The Forum building will be clearly visible across the street. You can also get off from Tokyo station. Walk on the Marunouchi side, where there will be a passageway dotted with trees and shrubbery all the way to the Forum. Once you enter the atrium lobby of the Glass Hall, take the escalator one floor down to the basement level where the TIC is located.

Hibiya subway line: Get off at Hibiya station and leave the platform at the end closest to Ginza station (next stop). Walk up to the exit, double back between the exits (one on each side of the passageway), and follow signs to exit A4b, which is the underground entrance to the Forum. Walk up the steps and you will be on the basement floor. Walk straight ahead and follow signs to the TIC.

Chiyoda and Mita subway lines: Get off at Hibiya station on either line. Both lines are located some distance from the Hibiya line's Hibiya station, but they are all connected by underground passages. After exiting from the platform, follow signs for the Hibiya line. This will lead to a long passage. Follow signs to Exit A4b, which is also the entrance to the Forum.

As described in the Accommodation section, the TIC will make reservations for economy *ryokan* and *minshuku* at no charge.

JNTO and Other Government Literature

The following are some of the Tokyo-related publications available from the TIC that will be useful to the visitor. (They have information for the entire country.)

Maps

Tourist Map of Tokyo is the best map of Tokyo available, showing the parts of the city of most interest to visitors, plus detailed maps of some areas like Shinjuku. It has the best subway/railway map, color coded to match the colors used to identify the actual cars (or the individual lines). Most important, station names are shown in both *kanji* and *romaji*, making it easy to figure out destinations and fares. A bonus is the map "Transportation Network—Tokyo and vicinity" which shows all railway lines, both JR and private, for a considerable distance out of the city.

Map of Tokyo and Vicinity, also a JNTO publication, shows the area around Tokyo beyond the Fuji/Hakone/Izu area to the west, Nikko to the north, and Chiba to the east. It is excellent for orientation. It also has a good map, "Transportation Network—Tokyo and vicinity".

Metropolitan Expressway is a Tokyo-region expressway map that could and should be of use to motorized travellers. (The concept of plurals is impossible to absorb for most people in charge of publications.) Unfortunately, due to a lack of thinking power on the part of those making it up, it is next-to-useless for its purpose because nearly all expressway names have been shown in their exact, literal English translation, rather than the way they are shown on signs on the spot! In addition, numerous roads and expressways are identified as a "line". Thus, the road indicated on signs as "Dai-ni Keihin expressway" is shown on the map as "Second Keihin Road", and the road signposted as "Kampachi dori" is shown on the map as "Kanjo8-Line" (sic; spacing as shown). I wrote to the authority producing the map in early 1990 advising them of these errors, but nothing had been corrected on the 1991 map. For those with some time to learn the real names of the roads, the map is excellent for understanding the road network in the Tokyo region.

Pamphlets

Tokyo is the simple title of an information

brochure on the city. It gives some history, general and sightseeing information, and has listings of some museums, galleries, and other attractions.

Walking Tour Courses in Tokyo describes what you can see in walks around the Imperial Palace, Ueno-koen park, Asakusa, a bit of the Shitamachi area, and other parts of the city.

A very useful publication is their listing of economical accommodation in the Tokyo area and all of Japan and related publications for more expensive hotels, *ryokan*, and other accommodation.

Also in their racks (behind the staff area) are other brochures for specialised aspects of Tokyo and Japan in general (summarised JR timetables, information on trains and buses to Narita airport, etc.), plus pamphlets on a large number of other cities and regions in the country. It will be worthwhile to look at the titles of these publications. You can also talk to the staff and tell them exactly where you plan to go and request relevant information.

Staff at the TIC have filing cabinets bulging with miscellaneous information on every imaginable subject, so they can give information on anything from finding a dentist to where to find some unusual handicraft.

A telephone information service operated by the TIC is available during working hours; tel (03) 3502-1461. There is also a recorded message giving information about current cultural events and festivals in the Tokyo area; tel (03) 3503-2911 (English) or (03) 3503-2926 (French).

Other Publications

Tokyo City Guide, subtitled "Tour Companion" (its former sole name), is a free twice-monthly paper aimed at tourists. It is *available at the TIC, the American Pharmacy (near the TIC), hotels, airline offices, travel agents, and some supermarkets frequented by foreigners. It is a good source of information on events for the following couple of weeks, with details of festivals and cultural/entertainment offerings, movies, gallery showings, concerts, etc., in the Tokyo area. There is also space devoted to shopping, restaurants, and night spots. It is a commercial publication, so its listings should be regarded in that light, with its advertisers expecting more favorable coverage. Single copies (¥200 plus postage) and subscriptions are available in Japan and overseas from: Tokyo News Service Ltd., Tsukiji Hamarikyu Bldg 10Fl, 5-3-3 Tsukiji, Chuo-ku, Tokyo 104.

Tokyo Journal, a monthly publication, covers a lot of ground. Its front pages have short articles on various subjects related to Japan, some of interest mainly to residents and others for anyone interested in the country. Its format has varied through the years, but it seems to have settled on presenting interesting articles on modern Japan, bringing an objective look to many facets (good and otherwise) of the country that is lacking from most sources. The larger part is devoted to information about coming events such as concerts (classical and popular music), dance, kabuki and other traditional Japanese performing arts, films, and exhibitions at museums, galleries and department stores. Its classified ads also list pubs and similar places which feature live music, a large number of restaurants and drinking places, conversation lounges, travel agencies and other services, Japanese language schools, and a number of low cost accommodation places. It also has useful maps with banks and important buildings used as landmarks. Cover price is ¥500. It is available at most bookstores (especially in large hotels), the American Pharmacy, many travel agencies, supermarkets and restaurants popular with foreigners. Single copies and subscriptions are available in Japan and overseas from: Tokyo Journal, Cross Cultural Communications, Inc., Cross Culture Communications Building, 12-2 Minami-motomachi, Shinjuku-ku, Tokyo 160.

Tokyo Weekender is a weekly free newspaper aimed at foreign residents in Tokyo. The lead article may be on any topic under the sun, but every issue has social, fashion, food, and entertainment pages. There is a weekly film review, and a listing of foreign language films at Tokyo theatres. Occasional articles deal with the Japanese and life in Japan, past and present, and give some insights rarely seen elsewhere, such as discussions of the plots and biases of Japanese films and TV shows (often anti-Western). It provides good coverage of the six annual sumo wrestling tournaments and has a classified ad section for goods, services, and accommodation of interest to foreigners. (It has been changing its format through 1991, so it may have a somewhat different emphasis from that described here.) It is released Fridays and can be picked up at the TIC, most large hotels, the American Pharmacy, many supermarkets and pubs or restaurants catering to foreign clientele (mostly in Roppongi and Akasaka). Single copies and subscriptions are available in Japan and overseas from: Tokyo Weekender, Tuttle Bldg. 2Fl, 1-2-6 Suido, Bunkyo-ku, Tokyo 112 (phone 5689-2471/3).

Tokyo Time Out has similarities to *Tokyo Journal*, but is aimed more at the entertainment-oriented reader. It has similar listings of events. Take a look and see if it suits your tastes.

There are, have been, and will be other magazines aimed at English-speakers. They tend to have a short lifespan (the above have lasted from a few to many (Weekender) years. A mid-'91 entrant was *The Japan International Journal*, which grandiosely described itself on a promotional handout as "Tho (sic) only comprehensive general monthly magazine for improving the understanding of Japan". The reaction of this cynic was, "Oh, goodie! Yet another publication to try to 'explain' the Japanese." The initial issue covered much the same ground as many before it, and it was filled with glossy ads for luxury goods of the type seen in in-flight magazines, so it will be interesting to see what format (if any) it evolves into.

The magazines mentioned in the earlier general information section on publications are available, sometimes sporadically, at a number of Tokyo bookstores.

The English-language newspapers have travel columns, such as the well-regarded "Going Places" by Anne Pepper in the *Japan Times*. Unfortunately, the columns on little-known places of interest usually don't find their way into books.

Books

Numerous publications covering specific aspects of Tokyo have come onto the market in recent years and are suggested for exploring Tokyo in greater detail.

Introducing Tokyo, by Donald Richie (Kodansha International), is a series of descriptions of interesting parts of the city.

Footloose in Tokyo, by Jean Pearce (Weatherhill; ¥1500), is a series of walking tours in the vicinity of the 29 stations of the Yamanote loop line, giving background not only on the specific area, but also on Tokyo and Japan in general.

More Footloose in Tokyo, by Jean Pearce (Weatherhill; ¥1200), covers the Shitamachi area plus Narita in a manner similar to her earlier book - a walking tour with descriptions of what you're seeing and its significance/history.

Day-Walks Near Tokyo, by Gary D'A. Walters (Kodansha International), gives a number of walking tours in the vicinity of the city.

Around Tokyo, Vol I and II by John Turrent and Jonathan Lloyd-Owen (Japan Times; ¥1200), are compilations of columns from the *Japan Times* describing a large number of well-known and obscure attractions in Tokyo and vicinity.

Tokyo Now and Then, by Paul Waley (Weatherhill; ¥5000), describes Tokyo in great detail as it is now and how it was then; with many interesting anecdotes to bring to life the things you can see.

Discover Shitamachi, by Enbutsu Sumiko (name written Japanese style, published by *The Shitamachi Times*; ¥1500), deals with Shitamachi in greater detail than Jean Pearce's book, making it somewhat heavier reading but it contains more insights and information.

Japan for Kids, by Diane Wiltshire Kanagawa and Jeanne Huey Erickson (Kodansha International; ¥1900), the first complete guide for families visiting Japan, has detailed sections on entertainment, shopping, and outings for kids in Tokyo. Even if you don't have children, this is an up-to-date informative guide.

Tokyo City Guide, by Connor and Yoshida, is (if not out of print) a well-regarded and lively aid for seeing and appreciating this giant city.

Tokyo: A Bilingual Map, (Kodansha International); shows major streets, buildings, etc., in Japanese and English.

Tokyo Metropolitan Area: A Bilingual Map, (Kodansha International); shows six prefectures neighboring Tokyo, in Japanese and English, with maps of Yokohama and Kawasaki.

Tokyo A Bilingual Atlas, (Kodansha International); a useful reference book for finding anything in the city.

Tokyo Restaurant Guide, by John Kennerdell (Tokyo Journal); a guide to a wide variety of good eating places.

Check also the general Books section for coverage of places outside the city.

WELCOME FUROSHIKI For newly arrived residents of Tokyo (i.e., transferred business people and families from overseas) there is a very useful information service called "Welcome Furoshiki". A *furoshiki* is a traditional Japanese square of cloth used to wrap and carry items; it is symbolic of a package of information that "WF" offers free. A WF member visits the homes of newcomers, gives the "bundle" containing a great deal of useful information (much of a commercial nature; this pays for the service) and answers questions about settling into this unfamiliar new land. (Please note that Welcome Furoshiki is not set up to give travel information of the type desired by travellers or anyone just passing through; that job is handled competently by the TIC.) To contact Welcome Furoshiki, phone 03-3760-8560.

Things to See

How do you begin to look around a city that is home to 12 to 14 million people? Is it even possible to explore Tokyo? Certainly not all of it, but there are ways to nibble at parts to get some idea of the whole.

Tokyo was, in the past, described as a collection of villages; except for the fact that many of these "villages" are now cities in their own right with central areas of large stores and commercial buildings, the description is still valid.

In Edo days (to about 1867) there were two major divisions of Tokyo—Shitamachi (pronounced *Sh'ta machi* meaning "downtown") for the common folk, and Yamanote ("near the mountains") for the wealthy and powerful. (The Yamanote train line largely encircles the Yamanote area, hence its name.)

Although a center of power since the early 1600s, there is little of historic interest in Tokyo. This is partly because Kyoto continued to be the imperial capital with the figurehead emperor, his court, and the elaborate structures (such as temples and palaces) that went with it through this period, while Tokyo was more a military and governing center that did not attract such grandiose construction. It is also because the great Kanto earthquake and wartime bombing destroyed most of the city.

In the following pages are some general words on modern Tokyo, followed by further detail on a few of the major areas of greater interest to visitors. This will be enough to keep anyone busy for a couple of days. For more detailed explanation it is advisable to obtain one or more of the many guide books to Tokyo that have been published in recent years; they give vastly more detail on the attractions of this city than can possibly be crammed into a general book of this sort.

For a quick introduction to the city, a long-recommended and still valid suggestion is to ride the Yamanote loop for one circuit of the city, a trip of about an hour. This will show how so much of the city is made up of low-rise houses interspersed with taller apartment and commercial buildings. Since the line passes through most of the major sub-city areas, it also gives a view of the tremendous amount of development that has taken place in these clusters.

All of Tokyo, with the exception of some small pockets in the Shitamachi area, was quite literally flattened by bombing during the last stages of World War II. Photos from that time show vast expanses where not a building was left standing. The contrast with today, only 50-odd years on, is phenomenal.

The first post-war buildings were ticky-tacky, flimsy wooden structures, a few of which still stand here and there through the city. The next generation saw these replaced by generally drab and dreary, but functional, concrete structures. With the incredible increase in wealth in Japan in the past 15 years or so, these are progressively being replaced by architectural showpieces, often of imaginative though sometimes non-functional shape. These are giving an entirely new and stylish look to many parts of the city, initially in the fashionable areas, but also in local neighborhoods. (Much of this is being protested because the new buildings destroy the homey character that existed in many of these districts.) Walking through some of these nouveau riche areas, like Harajuku, Roppongi, Shinjuku, etc., gives the realization that Tokyo (parts, anyway) is developing into a city that may rank well in the world for physical attractiveness—something unimaginable 20 years ago. Part of the enjoyment of Tokyo is just looking around at some of the more attractive, or outrageous, of its physical assets.

For a better understanding of the character of the various elements that make up this enormous city, it is worth spending the money on Jean Pearce's *Footloose in Tokyo* books.

In general, to "attack" Tokyo successfully, read the following pages, pick up a map and literature from the TIC, obtain copies of *Tokyo City Guide* and perhaps one of the books listed, pick out the places of interest, and go!

Ginza, Hibiya, and the Imperial Palace

If any part of Tokyo were to be called its "heart", it would be the Ginza district. In this one area are branches of nearly all the country's major department stores, many other high fashion shops, and the most expensive restaurants and drinking establishments—for *very* big spenders only. Close by is the Marunouchi financial district, and just a short walk away is the reason why this area first came to prominence, the Imperial Palace.

Dating from Edo days, this was the area where the higher ranks of society obtained their necessities and fineries, and the tradition has continued. The following is a brief look around.

Imperial Palace Grounds

One might expect a magnificent castle to stand in Tokyo, as they once did in Osaka and Nagoya, but Tokyo never had such huge buildings despite the quite massive walls and embankments that can be seen. It is not possible to enter the actual palace grounds except on January 2 and the Emperor's birthday. At other times visitors must be content with a stroll around the moats and a look at the fortifications and the scenic east garden.

If starting from the TIC, just turn left and go a couple of hundred meters to where a moat comes into view to the right, then continue along until the first road across the moat. This leads to a large open park area, Kokyo-mae Hiroba (Imperial Palace Plaza), and further on Kokyo Gai-en (Imperial Palace Outer Garden). The large, open pedestrian-only area to the left leads to Nijubashi bridge, which gives the only good view into the grounds. With the bridge in the foreground this is a typical Japanese castle "view"—a fortification wall with a white defensive building atop it. (A newspaper report said that Nijubashi was the most-photographed place in Japan—almost invariably as backdrop for a photo of visitors.)

A few minutes walk north (use the Tokyo map from the TIC for these explorations) brings you to the entrance of Higashi Gyoen (East Garden), which is open most days until 1500. Entry is through some of the massive stonework of the original defensive walls, and the garden has many of the attractive features of Japanese gardens. A small zig-zag bridge here is unusual, being of Chinese derivation and seldom seen in Japan. In Chinese mythology evil spirits can move only by hopping, and can turn only with great difficulty. By walking in zig-zags, as here, people being followed by the spirits step aside, and the evil spirits hop into the water and drown. (The same story explains why there is a high sill to step over when entering the gate of a temple; the evil spirits cannot hop over it.) Believe it or not, Tokyo Bay once lapped shores very near here. The land from here to the port is all landfill.

The only other sightseeing relative to the palace is to stroll at leisure along the moats around the walls. Except during the cherry blossom season there is little incentive to go beyond the Sakuradamon gate. But when the blossoms are out, the area at the top of the hill and beyond has some of the most magnificent displays of this short-lived spectacle in the country.

The path around the palace is a well-known jogging route, with distance markers. The nearby Imperial Hotel (successor to the one designed by Frank Lloyd Wright) has a jogging map.

The moats, by the way, are home to a large number of graceful swans, and in winter attract many migratory birds including some, like the mandarin duck, that are quite exotic for the center of a huge city. (To give an idea of the extent of the original fortifications, the long body of water visible from Chuo line trains between Ichigaya and Ochanomizu stations, and another near Akasaka-mitsuke subway station, are remains of the outer moats.)

The Imperial Palace can be reached from Hibiya stations of the Chiyoda, Hi-

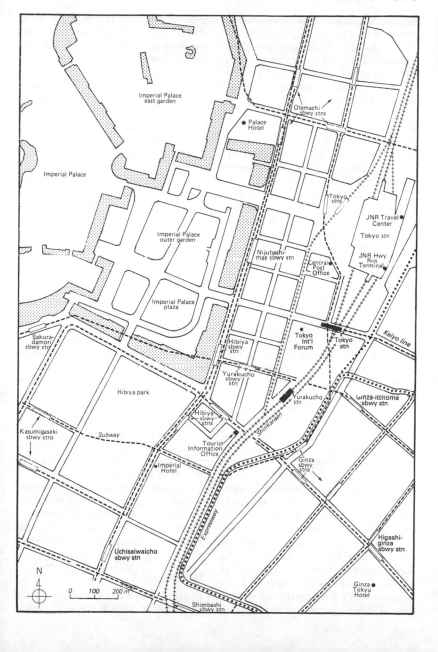

biya and Mita subway lines, Nijubashi-mae station of the Chiyoda line, Otemachi station of the Mita, Marunouchi and Tozai subway lines, Tokyo station of the Marunouchi line, and Tokyo and Yurakucho stations of the JR Yamanote and Keihin-Tohoku lines.

Ginza Area

If you follow Hibiya-dori, the road that runs along the edge of the moat that is closest to the Ginza area for about 15 minutes (past the end of Hibiya-koen park), you'll find yourself at Zojo-ji temple. The temple itself is unremarkable, being a post-war concrete structure, but one of its entrance gates, dating back to 1605, survived the war and still has its Nio guardian gods. If you will not be able to go to Kyoto or Nikko, where other such gates and gods may be seen, this is a good chance to see who kept the evil spirits at bay.

Walking along Harumi-dori (the road that passes the TIC) from the palace, soon brings you to the "bright city lights" with shops of every imaginable kind, selling cameras, pearls, cloisonne ware, etc. The shops are mostly for the Japanese, but there are several that cater to foreign visitors. One of these is the International Arcade, underneath the railway tracks. Continuing on Harumi-dori for a few hundred meters, past the large Ginza crossing, leads to the traditional-looking Kabuki-za theatre, Tokyo's major kabuki theatre.

Ginza crossing is the main landmark in this area, identified by the main Mitsukoshi Department Store on one corner and the circular San-ai building diagonally opposite. The cross street at this intersection is Chuo-dori, on which the majority of the Ginza department stores are located. One of the simple must-do's of a visit to Japan is a walk through a large department store to marvel at the range (and sometimes price!) of goods available. This may give some idea of the type of furniture and other household goods that find their way into Japanese homes, although armchairs, fancy dining-room tables, and the like, are generally bought by "untypical" (Westernized or wealthy) families. Furniture intended for tatami living, such as low tables, is often beautifully finished in flawless lacquer that would be a showpiece back home if it weren't for the size, weight, and cost. Lacquer and ceramic dishes of high quality (and matching price) may be seen here, and give a quick education in Japanese taste—useful when deciding what souvenirs to take home. The Japanese do not eat from utensils decorated with temples, dragons, Mt. Fuji, and other touristy symbols of Japan.

To the north from Ginza crossing, Chuo-dori leads to Akihabara and Ueno. The few km to Akihabara can be walked in about an hour, and you can get some idea en route of what makes modern Japan tick. In addition to the many modern buildings, banks, and other commercial establishments with their modern computer systems and other high-tech equipment, there are still some old-fashioned shops selling antiques, kimono, dolls, fans, and *zori* (the dress sandals worn with kimono).

Chuo-dori is blocked to traffic in the Ginza area on Saturday and Sunday afternoons, when shoppers stroll at will and tables are set up for eating.

Akihabara, the fantastic "electronics" district, can also be reached by train (from Yurakucho, Tokyo, or Kanda stations) or the Hibiya or Ginza subway lines. (As mentioned, it can also be reached by a long walk up Chuo dori from the Ginza.)

Akihabara

To gain a good appreciation of the state of technology in Japan it would be hard to beat a visit to Akihabara. This is the electrical wholesale and retail center of Tokyo, and by far the largest concentration of electrical and electronics stores in the world. There are literally hundreds of shops. Some are tiny hole-in-the-wall cubicles selling a single product line (transformers, electrical meters, etc.), while others are huge multistorey electrical department stores. Visitors even from countries that are well served with a variety of electronic goodies will be amazed to see so many models, and even some products that are never seen outside Japan. (For details on buying electrical goods in Japan check the general "Things to Buy" section.)

Even if you are not buying, just wandering around the area and taking the escalators inside some of the buildings is an interesting way to spend some time.

The JR Akihabara station has an exit to the side of the tracks where most of the shops are located (to the left when arriving from Tokyo station, or toward Shinjuku if arriving from that station.) It is a bit confusing getting out of the station; from the Shinjuku direction it is necessary to take the central stairs down to the next level of platforms, then find the correct exit. The Hibiya subway Akihabara station exits on the wrong side of the JR tracks, so it's necessary to find one of the cross streets to the main area. The simplest way to get to the main area from the subway is to exit from the rear of the train (when going from the Ginza direction) and find the farthest exit in that direction. Up at ground level, walk to the nearby corner and turn left. The road leads under the JR tracks to the main shopping area.

Ueno

Attractions of the Ueno area are the zoo (not one of the world's greatest), the National Science Museum (many working exhibits showing how some scientific and technological items function), Tokyo National Museum (primarily art and history), Tosho-gu shrine, and a historic five-storey pagoda.

The zoo is very popular for its pandas, over which the Japanese went ga-ga when they were first introduced (the epitome of Japanese taste is *cute*). Located at the south of Shinobazu-ike pond is Shitamachi Fuzoka Shiryokan, a small "museum" of shops and houses of the type once common in Tokyo before wartime bombing and the 1923 Kanto earthquake destroyed them.

During the brief cherry blossom season, thousands of revellers set up parties on any patch of open ground in Ueno-koen park. The object is to appreciate the beauties of the blossoms, although after consuming copious quantities of sake, many have difficulty even distinguishing light from darkness. Still, it is an object lesson for many other cultures, how a huge number of people can get absolutely pickled without becoming belligerent. Japanese usually just sing louder, if a bit more off key, the drunker they get.

An area that was the site of the postwar black market, and which has continued selling low-priced goods, is Ameyoko, across from the south exit of Ueno station. A sign over the entrance street identifies it in *romaji*.

The sub-map of the Ueno district in the JNTO map *Tourist Map of Tokyo* will be sufficient for looking around this area.

From the station area, you can walk along the broad Asakusa-dori avenue toward Senso-ji temple (described just below). It is a major thoroughfare, so local color is lacking unless you wander around the back streets. There are many shops selling Buddhist funerary items, such as large and ornately carved *butsudan* (family altars where memorial tablets are kept) and large lotus leaves, all brilliantly decorated with gold leaf.

Along Kappabashi-dori (shown clearly on the JNTO Tokyo map), just north of the crossing with Asakusa-dori, are many stores selling goods related to the restaurant business. Several shops sell the incredibly realistic plastic replicas of food of the type seen in restaurant windows everywhere in Japan. Unfortunately, they are not cheap, a single piece of sushi costing about ¥700, but they are all hand-made, and the artisans making them take up to ten years learning the craft. Anyone with the money could purchase an entire feast. Kappabashi-dori is between Inaricho and Tawaramachi subway stations, a little closer to the latter.

Shitamachi

In Edo days, Shitamachi was the area in which the common people lived and worked, and where most of the ordinary trade was carried out. The people were unrefined, spontaneous, and lacking in the reticence imposed on the general populace by the decrees of the Tokugawa rulers. The people still living in this area regard themselves as a breed apart from the rest of Tokyo's residents, and many of the old attitudes and ways of life survive, although it, like every other part of Japan, has changed much in the past decades.

There is no place marked "Shitamachi" on a map; it is an ill-defined area generally to the east of the Yamanote line, from above Ueno to the Tsukiji area. It was an artificial creation of the shogun who wanted to keep all less-desirable elements in one area where they could be watched more easily. The famous Yoshiwara pleasure district was an important part of the scene, taking care of the sexual desires of all men of Edo. Although prostitution was

made illegal in 1958, the same sorts of activities go on under a different guise, both in the old Yoshiwara district and everywhere else in Japan.

The type of establishment offering these activities was, until recently (early 1985), called a *toruko* or "turkish bath", but protests by Turks (and especially the ambassador) finally brought a change. These establishments are now called *soapland*, from the female attendants' practice of bathing the customers, often using their own bodies to apply the soap.

The heart of Shitamachi is Asakusa Kannon temple, properly known as Senso-ji. A visit can be combined with a walk through some of the back streets.

The temple is very active with worshippers praying for some sort of assistance, lighting bundles of incense and catching the smoke to rub on afflicted parts of their bodies to relieve an ache or pain, or just plain enjoying themselves. The approach is lined with shops selling every manner of tourist junk. The shopping street is often described in terms like "street of gaily decorated souvenir shops".

As a single place to visit, it leaves me quite underwhelmed. Both Senso-ji and its five-storey pagoda are only post-war concrete reproductions, and thus lack any of the features of workmanship that make historic Japanese temples so remarkable. If you are going to Kyoto later, you will see vastly finer and older temples with extraordinary woodwork. It can be interesting for people watching, and the temple very definitely *is* worth visiting during its annual festivals in March and October. The festivities feature a Chinese-style dragon; held up by numerous poles, it twists and writhes around the temple courtyard in a most remarkable way. Times will be given in *Tokyo City Guide*, but they have previously been wrong, so get there an hour or so before the listed time in order to avoid disappointment.

Senso-ji can be reached by Ginza or Asakusa subway to Asakusa subway station, or by a special double-decker bus from Ueno station (as well as regular buses, but they have no markings in English). Upon arriving at the large Kaminarimon gate, look diagonally across the main road for the ward-operated information office. They are set up to give assistance in English for sightseeing in the area.

The books *More Footloose in Tokyo* and *Discover Shitamachi* are invaluable for exploring this area in depth, giving volumes of information that cannot be presented in adequate detail in a general-coverage book.

After sightseeing near the temple, an alternative to the usual way back is to take the water taxi down the Sumida-gawa river. This trip takes about an hour and ends at Takeshiba pier, beside Shiba Rikyu and Hama Rikyu gardens (close to JR Hamamatsucho station at the edge of the harbor and near Tsukiji fish market). The starting point is just upstream and to the left of the bridge across the Sumida-gawa river, a short distance beyond the subway station. The location is shown clearly on the JNTO Tokyo map.

Fukagawa Edo Museum

This is an interesting attraction all by its lonesome in an area not noteworthy to visitors for anything else. However, it is worth seeking out, for it has a masterfully produced representation of the appearance of the Fukugawa district of Tokyo (then Edo) around 1840. In a large, specially-constructed building are replicas of shops, houses, stalls and storehouses, exactly as they would have appeared at that time, a total of eight "complete" buildings and three "fronts". (Although all new, the mate-rials have been realistically weathered to look genuinely aged, and every detail of construction is authentic, even where not visible.) The lighting changes regularly to give a sense of changing time of day, and sound effects reinforce the impression of being in a real community, from the crowing rooster to the sound of peddlers. A sense of humor is evident, including a dog beside the fire watch-tower with raised hind leg. Admittance costs ¥300, and the English booklet (¥500) is a worthwhile investment. Professionally produced in perfect and enjoyable English, it describes the many features of the buildings that would not be self-evident, and tells the story of such a community from the point of view of the people who would have lived there (while unobtrusively slipping in the history of the area and the country).

The museum is reached by first going to Kiyosumi-koen garden (on the JNTO Tokyo map); across from it are two old fashioned lanterns on each side of a narrow road. The museum is a couple of hundred meters down this road, on the left. The easiest way to get to Kiyosumi-koen is to go to Monzen-nakacho station (Tozai subway line), take exit 3, and catch a 33 bus from in front of the pachinko parlor. Get off at the fourth stop, "Kiyosumi-koen". You can also walk north along Kiyosumi-dori (near the station) for about 15 minutes, or south the same amount of time along the same street from Morishita station of the Shinjuku subway line.

Shinjuku

Shinjuku is the up-and-coming sub-city of Tokyo. Due to its geological stability (an important factor in earthquake-prone Japan), it has Tokyo's only collection of high rise buildings, including the very costly new city hall. It is also the place to go for the best camera shopping and good general shopping, and has a large percentage of the entertainment establishments of the city.

The high-rises are all located on the west, or "new city", side of Shinjuku station (which is reputed to be the busiest in the world, and a good contender for the title of "most confusingly laid out"). On this side, down the small side streets, are the main stores of Yodobashi and Doi camera stores, as well as any number of other shops specializing in computers, watches, and just about anything else you can think of.

The Highway Bus Terminal for buses to the Mt. Fuji and Hakone areas is close to the main Yodobashi store, and is clearly shown on the TIC map. This part of Shinjuku has also attracted a number of large hotels; in one small area there is the new Hilton, the Century Hyatt, the Keio Plaza, and the Shinjuku Washington, plus many others. Adjacent to Shinjuku station are two major department stores, Odakyu and Keio; trains of the same name leave from stations in their basements.

The east side of the station has most of the major department stores and many fashion-oriented shops. The two largest camera stores, Yodobashi and Sakuraya, have their showpiece branches side by side facing the small square overlooked by a giant TV-like screen made up of thousands of light bulbs. The Takano building next door, by the way, is on the most valuable piece of real estate in Japan. Nearby, the Kinokuniya bookstore has large numbers of foreign-language books (mostly English), and its ground level entrance is a popular meeting place because of the shelter it offers.

Nearby are hundreds, if not thousands, of restaurants and drinking places, many catering to the university senior/recent graduate age through to early thirties/unmarried office worker type, although sections of Shinjuku still have attractions of interest only to males, such as strip shows, pink salons, gay bars, no-pants coffee shops, peep shows, and the like.

Until a new law came into effect concerning operating hours in February 1985, the sex scene was almost wide open, particularly in the area known as Kabukicho on the east side and north of the major shopping streets. Live sex shows and activities that would be surprising even in Bangkok, were commonplace prior to the new law, but police can now enter any establishment without a warrant, all such businesses must close by midnight, and touts are prohibited. So much went on so blatantly in the past and was ignored by the police that many people wondered if money was exchanging hands. Future events will either weaken or strengthen these suspicions. One thing that will not have changed is the large involvement of yakuza gangsters in the operation of many, if not all, of the sex-oriented (or even regular drinking) establishments, and there is still the risk of being stuck with a horrendous bill for a single drink. If you walk or are enticed into a place with large numbers of hostesses sitting with customers, it is advisable not to sit down unless you have established in advance what it will cost you. The ¥18,000 glass of beer was invented in places like these.

Although the new law has had little more than a temporary effect on "the business", and the large number of love hotels in the area, which are exempt from the midnight curfew, doubtless continue to be busy, the character of Kabukicho has changed. It is now filled with bars and karaoke pubs, frequented by young office workers and students in search of inexpensive entertainment. By the way, if patronizing one of these love hotels, note the price schedule on the wall; sometimes the first hour is comparatively cheap but the second hour jumps considerably in price.

Meiji-jingu

Meiji-jingu is probably the finest Shinto shrine in Japan and well worth a visit. It was built early this century to honor Emperor Meiji, who reigned during the eventful period 1867–1912, when Japan changed from a self-isolated feudal country to a world power, largely under the guidance of this emperor and his advisors. The shrine was destroyed during the war and rebuilt afterwards in the original style.

The shrine grounds are extensive and heavily wooded, offering a respite from the bustle of the city. Its broad paths lead to the main shrine building, a simple structure of traditional style and the finest of materials and craftsmanship. Because of its exalted status among the shrines of Japan, it is a popular place for blessings for various events, and you can often see such ceremonies being performed by priests in traditional Shinto costumes.

Visiting the shrine is particularly worthwhile on January 15, "Coming of Age Day", when countless young women in beautiful kimono attend Meiji-jingu as part of the customary celebrations. It is very crowded but a wonderful opportunity to take many colorful photos. Another good time to visit is the Shichi-go-san festival on November 15, when young children dressed in very ornate kimono are taken there. New Year's Day, although a customary time to visit the shrine, is not recommended, as the grounds are incredibly packed.

The entrance to the shrine is close to Harajuku station (Yamanote line) or Meiji-jingu-mae station of the Chiyoda line.

Yoyogi-koen and Harajuku

Close to Meiji-jingu are Yoyogi-koen park and Omote-sando boulevard, as well as the youth fashion shopping district of Harajuku.

Omote-sando ("main approach to a shrine") is a high fashion shopping district. Being one of Tokyo's few tree-lined streets (short though it may be), it has some of the flavor of a Paris boulevard. Any day of the week is a good day for fashion window shopping/buying, and there are some tourist oriented shops with reasonable prices, such as the long-established Oriental Bazaar..

Harajuku, while a mecca for crazy youth fashions, is also a venue for high-fashion and high-price clothing, and some very high-style eating places. Anyone young at heart can enjoy a stroll and will see evidence that Japan has become one of the world's wealthiest nations.

Shibuya

Shibuya, one stop by the Yamanote line south of Harajuku, is another popular shopping and entertainment area. Like Harajuku and Shinjuku, the area appeals to a particular age group, in this case those of about senior high school age. For this reason there are plenty of fast food and generally moderately priced restaurants. It is also a high fashion area, with many modern and interesting buildings, and imaginative window displays.

The most famous landmark in Tokyo is the statue of the dog Hachiko; just look for a few hundred people standing around in an open area on the north-west corner of the station, waiting for their friends to show up, and you'll find it. The real Hachiko was an Akita dog that waited faithfully at this station for months for his master to return home, not knowing that he had died at work. We do not know if the story is completely true, or if it was exaggerated by the pre-war military-run government to instill in the people a similar sense of devotion to duty.

The main area of greatest activity is diagonally across the large intersection from Hachiko. The mall continuing the diagonal leads past many of the most popular restaurants, with sidestreets holding many more, along with amusement arcades and other teen attractions.

There are shops of all kinds along both main roads of this intersection. To reach one that is out of the ordinary, follow the road running parallel to the tracks in the direction toward Harajuku, and take the left fork up the hill. This very fashionable street, with British-style phone booths, trees, buildings with imaginative fronts, and department stores, leads to the Olympic Stadium (dating from the 1964 Olympics). At one intersection partway up the hill is a Parco department store. Turning left at this corner leads to Tokyu Hands, a store that would be out of the ordinary in any country. It must surely be the ultimate leisure craft emporium in the world, with supplies for nearly every imaginable handicraft available on its multiple levels. Do you want a traditional Japanese saw or plane that cuts on the pull stroke, an ultra-accurate micrometer or miniature lathe, a model boat kit, interior decoration supplies, art materials, the makings of metal or lapidary jewellery, electrical-electronic hobby equipment, a computer, or you-name-it? It's all here, and more!

Roppongi

Roppongi has become the main playground of the people of the modelling, TV, and advertising world, with numerous discos and bars as well as many restaurants for a colorful nightlife. Prices cover a wide range, to cover budgets from student's to millionaire's. There are several Western franchise fast-food restaurants and countless of other types. (Few of the latter will fit into a traveller's budget, unfortunately, as is the case in most of Japan.)

Roppongi is most easily reached by Hibiya subway line. The exits at the front of the train when travelling toward Ginza lead to Roppongi crossing, the main intersection. On one corner is the best-known landmark and rendezvous point, the Almond coffee shop. The majority of the favorite entertainment places are on this side of the expressway, on both sides of the major cross road and in the many side streets running off it. It could take a lifetime to explore this territory. Some of the establishments offer country music and other entertainment aimed at Westerners living in Japan (and to Japanese who have acquired the taste); these are often advertised in *Tokyo Weekender*, and may also be listed in *Tokyo Journal*.

Gardens and Parks

Tokyo, like most Japanese cities, has only a small fraction of the park area per citizen considered usual in western countries. Cities in Japan are for commerce and housing, and little else. Tokyo does have a few sizeable parks that make for pleasant strolls, but they would be of more interest to foreign residents than those on a short visit looking for a garden with the traditional Japanese characteristics. (The best of these in the Tokyo vicinity is Sankei-en, in Yokohama.)

The best parks in Tokyo are probably Koraku-en garden, Rikugi-en garden, the Shizen Kyoiku-en, and Shinjuku Gyoen park. All are shown on the TIC map. Others are Hama Rikyu Garden and Koishikawa Botanical Garden. The parks are enjoyable in summer when the shrill sound of the *semi* (cicada) may be heard; indeed they may be loud enough to make conversation difficult. Their "me-me-me-me" or chirring sound is one of the memories of Japan.

Museums and Galleries

Tokyo has a large number of interesting museums and galleries. Visitors to Ueno park can visit both the Tokyo Metropolitan Art Museum and the Tokyo National Museum.

The TIC pamphlet *Tokyo* lists the main museums that would be of interest to visitors. The *Tokyo Journal* lists the major museums, galleries (art and photo), and department store exhibits (a major type of gallery in Japan), and the displays/themes of each for the coming month, along with the prices and special features. *Tokyo City Guide* has a similar listing, updated biweekly. The Saturday or Sunday issues of the English-language newspapers give details of the displays for the coming week; the page from the *Japan Times* is usually posted at the TIC.

Lookouts

Several tall structures around the city offer views of the huge expanse of Tokyo. In the clear weather of winter the view may extend to Mt. Fuji.

Tokyo is a very flat city, built at the edge of the Kanto Plain, and lacks any features of particular note other than other buildings, so one of the free viewpoints (below) would probably give as good a view as anyone would want.

The two bargains, which are the 52-storey Sumitomo Building in Shinjuku, to the west of the station (observation level on 51st floor), and Top of Yebisu at Ebisu Garden Place, near Ebisu station (observation levels on 38th and 39th floors). There is no charge at either of these, and both buildings have several restaurants of not-unreasonable prices (by Tokyo standards) offering a good view along with pleasant dining.

Tokyo Tower, 333 meters tall, is a slightly enlarged copy of the Eiffel Tower and has an observation lounge at the top, along with a wax museum and restaurants. Access to the first level costs ¥800 and it costs an extra ¥600 to get to the 250m level.

The World Trade Center building has an observatory on its 40th floor; access costs ¥600.

Tokyo Disneyland

In April 1983 Tokyo gained the first Disneyland outside the U.S.A. Built at a cost of hundreds of millions of dollars, to strict Disney standards, it offers the same type of attractions as the U.S. original, including "theme lands" (Westernland, Adventureland, Fantasyland, Tomorrowland, and World Bazaar), plus a number of rides (such as a Mississippi paddlewheeler and the Western River Railroad), and a variety of other forms of entertainment. The 51-meter Cinderella Castle is the focal point and symbol of the park.

Tokyo Disneyland is open every day during summer (April through August); closed on Tuesdays from September to November; and closed Tuesdays and Wednesdays from December through February (except during holidays). In summer the hours are 0900 to 2200; and in winter, 1000 to 1800. Admittance-only tickets cost ¥3400/3100/2300 for adults/high school students/children, but there is then a separate charge for each attraction. A "passport", entitling you to enter all attractions as many times as you like, for one day, costs ¥4800/4400/3300 (weekdays only); and a "Big Ten" book of tickets gets you into 10 attractions.

There are two simple ways to get to Disneyland. The first is by Tozai subway to Urayasu station, from where a shuttle bus (from the nearby terminus) runs to the entrance about 20 minutes away. The bus costs ¥220 for adults and ¥110 for children. The second is by a 35-minute shuttle bus ride from Tokyo station, which costs ¥600. The shuttle buses leave from the Yaesu (east) side of the station; on the Yaesu side, take the north exit (kita guchi) and follow the tracks to the left. There are also buses directly to Disneyland from several tourist hotels nearby and from Narita airport, and some of the overnight buses described elsewhere start from Disneyland.

Festivals

There are festivals in Tokyo or nearby nearly every month. The TIC has free information sheets that list all festivals in Tokyo and all over Japan. The bi-weekly handout *Tokyo City Guide* also gives information on major events of this kind. A major festival is often the front page feature, and others during the week are also described. Festivals are least frequent in winter, begin in spring (rice planting time), are very numerous in late summer (*obon* season), and climax in autumn with the harvest-related festivals.

Tours

There is a variety of guided tours for seeing Tokyo. They cannot be recommended to the budget traveller as the same attractions can be seen by using public transport, this book, and other tourist literature and maps, for a fraction of the cost. However, for those who find climbing the seemingly endless stairs of the subway and train stations a bit tiring, or who have only a limited amount of time and no worries about watching their yen, a bus tour certainly offers convenience. There are daily tours of the high spots of Tokyo for ¥9,000–10,000, and a tour of some industrial factories for ¥10,000. Night tours take in a glimpse (extremely brief and not really worth the high price) of a stage show, a geisha show, and

the Kabuki theatre, plus a *sukiyaki* dinner, for ¥12,000–13,000. (Reports have stated that the stage show was abbreviated, the geisha show similarly short, and the dinner rather skimpy.) One can go to the Kabuki for as little as about ¥1000 on one's own. There are other tours to Kamakura, Hakone, Nikko, etc., but again they are very expensive compared with what it would cost using public transport. Information about all available tours is given in *Tokyo City Guide* and in pamphlets given out at all major hotels and the TIC.

Personally guided tours of central Tokyo and Shitamachi, using public transport for economy, are given by Mr. Oka, who advertises regularly in Tokyo Journal and elsewhere. Phone (0422) 51-7673 for details.

Places to Visit Near Tokyo

There are many places of interest within easy travelling distance of Tokyo. They can generally be visited as day trips out of Tokyo, though an overnight away from the city will give a better appreciation of the more distant ones.

Kamakura is the home of the great Buddha statue, one of the most famous sights of Japan, and has several noteworthy temples.

Yokohama has Sankei-en garden, one of the best in Japan, and a famous Chinatown.

Kawasaki has an interesting park with numerous old thatched-roof farm houses that have been moved here from various parts of Japan. It offers the simplest way to glimpse what life was like a century or two ago.

Hakone offers a scenic mountain and lake; in good weather you can get a magnificent view of Mt. Fuji.

Mt. Fuji is surrounded by many scenic lakes, and you can climb the mountain during July and August.

Kawagoe has a large number of well-preserved century-old shops and houses, and gives some idea of the appearance of a city of those days.

Matsumoto has the only surviving authentic traditional-style castle within comfortable traveling distance by train from Tokyo (about 3 hours).

Nikko has the incomparable splendor of the Toshogu and Daiyuin mausolea, plus lake and waterfall scenery.

Mashiko is the town closest to Tokyo where pottery is made in notable quantities.

SHOPPING

Tokyo is probably the best place in Japan to shop for Japanese antiques and handicrafts, as well as modern optical, electronic, and other high-tech goodies. (It is advisable to refer to the general "Things to Buy" section earlier in the book, before setting out.)

If buying a camera or lens, first check prices at the discount stores in Shinjuku before laying out any money. Some stores in and near Ginza do give reasonable prices but others count on the fact that many well-off foreigners are not aware of the lower prices that are available in other parts of the city. Three companies in Shinjuku are in intense competition: Sakuraya, Yodobashi (the original camera discounter), and Doi. (There are other camera stores as well, so it might be worth checking out what they are offering.)

All three stores have tax-free (*menzei*) departments that should be able to offer the lowest price, but it never hurts to check the with-tax (*kazei*) price, as strange things in the distribution system sometimes allow these to be lower. It's also wise to check prices of camera and lens separately; sometimes it's cheaper to buy each piece at a different shop.

Generally, the lowest prices in the country and the greatest selection of lenses and accessories will be found in the Shinjuku shops. Also, the main offices of the major manufacturers are in Tokyo, and special-order items would be easier to obtain. Never buy a foreign-made camera in Japan, for the prices are outrageous.

The Akihabara area is the place for the greatest variety of electrical and electronic goods at their lowest prices. (Many stores also sell the more popular models of cameras, and are worth checking if you have the time to shop around.) Several stores have departments or floors to display models specially designed for use overseas (correct voltage, frequency, and other specifications, etc.). Another source of such models, though their prices may be higher and the variety more limited, is the shopping arcades in large hotels and the International Arcade, which is more or less under the railway tracks in the Yurakucho area, close to the TIC.

Japanese dolls are available in the department stores, as well as in other shops. There are several types (faces and hands, in addition to costumes and prices). I have found that Takashimaya in Nihombashi had the best selection of good-quality dolls whenever I wanted to buy one.

The department stores are also a good source of items used by the Japanese in their homes (though of the more elegant type), such as lacquerware, pottery, and other ceramic goods. Department stores are generally not the bargain centers they are in western countries, but typically have a name for up-market goods, in both quality and price.

There are several flea markets held in Tokyo on an irregular and regular basis. It is best to contact the TIC for details because of the changeable date, time, and venue.

ENTERTAINMENT

Visitors to Japan have the chance to see a variety of traditional Japanese performing arts, while foreign residents need not worry about being cut off from Western varieties of entertainment.

Kabuki

There are several theaters in Tokyo where the colorful Kabuki is performed. Kabuki-za and Kokuritsu Gekijo theaters are well set up for English-speaking audiences, having radio earphone commentaries on the play as it progresses. The earphone devices rent for ¥600 plus a refundable deposit. (These may not be available for use in the lowest price seats.) Program notes in English may also be available at the theater, giving a detailed description of the action, act by act. Prices are lower for matinees, and there is sometimes a reduction for foreign visitors with their passport. Prices start in the ¥2000 range. There are performances much of the time, but some weeks there will be none. For listings of performances, with a summary of the stories, look at *Tokyo Journal*, *Tokyo City Guide*, and the Saturday *Japan Times*. The TIC will also be able to give such information.

Noh

Performances of this traditional type of drama are given at a variety of theaters. Up-to-date information is available from the same sources listed for Kabuki.

Bunraku

Performances of these puppet plays are occasionally presented in theaters such as Kokuritsu Gekijo. Information is available from the same sources as for noh and kabuki.

Music

In addition to the traditional Japanese performing arts, there is a surprising variety of Western-type entertainment. Road shows of western pop and rock performers regularly appear in Tokyo. (Some now-well-known Western singers have actually springboarded to fame beginning in Tokyo.) Stage shows are popular. One of the best known is the Takarazuka Revue, in which all parts are filled by women. There are several symphony orchestras and smaller chamber groups of high quality. Concerts are given regularly. The best listing of these events will be in the *Tokyo Journal*, *Tokyo Time Out*, and *Tokyo City Guide*, as well as the weekend newspapers. Prices are high, typically ¥3000 to ¥5000 per ticket.

Films

Foreign movies are shown with their original soundtracks and Japanese subtitles. They are often screened in Japan soon after their release overseas, with runs lasting between a few days and several weeks. Typical admittance price for first run films is ¥1800–2000. The best listings of films are in *Tokyo Weekender* and *Tokyo Journal*. There are also "cheap movies", reruns at lower prices, listed in the former. Also check *Tokyo City Guide* and *Tokyo Time Out*.

PLACES TO EAT

Tokyo has an incredible range of eating places, ranging from modest stand-up *soba* (noodle) shops to posh restaurants and nightclubs serving international cuisine at international prices. Although out of the price range of the average reader of this book, French cooking second only to the best offered in France is available in Tokyo, as is Italian and other top-rated international cooking. A guide to the higher-level places and a few moderately priced ones as well, is the Kodansha International book *Good Tokyo Restaurants* by Rick Kennedy. There are extensive listings and advertisements for various kinds of restaurants in the *Tokyo Journal*, *Tokyo City Guide*, and *Tokyo Weekender*; the first two give some indication of the price range.

Japanese office workers and students depend on the countless restaurants in the vicinity of the major stations for the majority of their "bought" meals, so the prices there are about as reasonable as can be expected in Japan. All the popular entertainment areas, like Shinjuku, Harajuku, Shibuya, and even Ginza, have many reasonably priced restaurants and beer halls. They usually have wax replicas of the food, with prices, in the window so it's easy to order and there are no surprises when the bill arrives.

There are many Shakey's Pizza and Pizza Hut shops throughout the city with a Monday through Saturday special from 1100 to 1500 of all the pizza you can eat for about ¥600. There are also other well-known American fast food outlets like Kentucky Fried Chicken, McDonald's, Wendy's, and Arbie's. The young Japanese have taken to these with a passion, so there will only be more and more as time goes by. (They also seem to be the places where teenage girls go to smoke.) There is an outlet of at least one of them near every main train or subway station, and they probably offer the greatest bargains in

terms of value for money (with the bonus of being familiar names offering familiar food). There are also some branches of American restaurant chains like Victoria Station and Red Lobster, though these are not budget eateries, and the menu of the former seems to have shrunk in recent years. If you look around you'll find there is no problem finding virtually any kind of food in Tokyo. Residents travelling by road in the suburbs and edge of the city will encounter many of what is known as "family restaurants", with names like "Sunday Sun". These have a good selection of Western-type food at reasonable prices, and they have menus with beautiful color photos of every item so there can be no problem with identifying what is on offer.

IMMIGRATION OFFICE

The main office for any immigration purpose is located in central Tokyo. It can be reached most easily by Chiyoda subway line to Otemachi station and exiting at the head of the train when going away from Hibiya. Leave by exit C2, walk to the corner, cross the street, and turn left. It is the "government-looking" building adjacent to the corner building. There is also an office in the Tokyo City Air Terminal building, but for any function other than issuing a re-entry permit it might not be very useful.

FOREIGN EMBASSIES

The following are the telephone numbers of the Tokyo offices of some foreign embassies. When calling from outside of Tokyo, numbers must be dialed with the area code 03.

Australia	5232-4111
Austria	3451-8281
Belgium	3262-0191
Canada	3408-2101

China	3403-3380
Denmark	3496-3001
Finland	3442-2231
France	5420-8800
Germany	3473-0151
Greece	3403-0871
India	3262-2391
Indonesia	3441-4201
Ireland	3263-0695
Italy	3453-5291
Korea	3452-7611
Malaysia	3476-3840
Netherlands	5401-0411
New Zealand	3467-2271
Norway	3440-2611
Pakistan	3454-4862
Philippines	3496-2731
Russia	3583-4224
Singapore	3586-9111
Spain	3583-8531
Sri Lanka	3585-7431
Sweden	5562-5050
Switzerland	3473-0121
Taiwan *	3280-7811
Thailand	3441-7352
UK	3265-5511
USA	3224-5000

* See following notes

Taiwan

Since Japan recognised the People's Republic of China, Taiwan has been doing business in Tokyo under the name "Association of East Asian Relations"; tel (03) 3280-7811. For visas it functions exactly as a consular office. To reach it, take the Hibiya subway to Kamiyacho, exit, then walk uphill along the major road (Sakurada-dori) in the direction of Tokyo Tower. Go straight across the large intersection at the top (keeping the Tower to your left) and continue downhill, on the left-hand side of the road. Look for the sign "39 Mori Building" on the front of a modern building with a glass-and-chrome theme and circular au-

tomatic doors. Office hours are 0900–1100 and 1300–1600 Monday through Friday. The postal address is: 5-20-2 Shiroganedai, Minato-ku, Tokyo (tel. 03-3280-7811).

Korea

Many travellers go to Korea from Japan, both for sightseeing and for obtaining Japanese visas. Korean diplomatic representatives are located in the following cities.

Tokyo	(03) 3452-7611
Sapporo	(011) 621-0288
Sendai	(0222) 21-2751
Niigata	(025) 230-3411
Yokohama	(045) 621-4531
Nagoya	(052) 935-9221
Osaka	(06) 213-1401
Kobe	(078) 221-4853
Fukuoka	(092) 771-0461
Shimonoseki	(0832) 66-5341
Naha	(0988) 55-3381

In Tokyo, visas are not issued at the embassy, but at a separate building about 10 minutes away on foot. (Telephone: 3452-7611.) The easiest way to reach it is by bus. In all cases, get off at Ni-no-hashi bus stop; it has the same name on both sides of the road. Of the following buses, the first four let off passengers on the same side as the consulate building, the other three on the far side. The building is a tall white structure, about 100 m along in the direction taken by the first four buses after leaving the stop.

The following listing gives the bus number and the names of the starting and terminal JR railway stations.

85 Shimbashi	Shibuya
10 Tokyo (S exit)	Meguro
91 Tokyo (N exit)	Shinagawa
70 Shinjuku (W exit)	Tamachi
10 Meguro	Tokyo (S exit)

| 85 | Shibuya | Shimbashi |
| 99 | Gotanda | Shimbashi |

Visas are granted on the spot within an hour except to Japanese who have to wait several days. Cost is the yen equivalent of U.S. $1.50. One photo is required, nominally 6 x 6 cm (but smaller accepted).

MEETING THE JAPANESE AND OTHER RESIDENTS

Visiting a country without meeting some of the people is wasting half the cost of getting there, especially in Japan where it is so easy to find Japanese people who are interested in talking with foreign visitors. Tokyo, being so cosmopolitan (by Japanese standards) is the best city to meet the locals, exchange ideas, and talk about your respective countries. Of course, not all Japanese have an overwhelming desire to meet foreigners, and some would probably prefer that we all stayed at home, but the following is a guide to meeting the ones who do.

HOME VISIT An admirable program organised by various authorities throughout the country is the Home Visit plan. A number of Japanese families have agreed to host foreign visitors in their homes for a couple of hours in the evening. (Further details are given in the general information section earlier in the book.) The TIC office makes the arrangements for such visits in Tokyo. Although they can possibly make arrangements for a same-day visit (if absolutely necessary) they are much more comfortable with a couple of days notice. There are host families who speak English, French, German, Italian and Chinese.

INTERNATIONAL 3F CLUB One of the most useful organisations in Tokyo to know about for more than a decade was the International 3F Club, "3F" for short. It provided the opportunity to meet a large number of English-speaking Japanese in congenial and informal surroundings, and had other programs, such as excursions and parties. Unfortunately, financial incompetence around 1987 resulted in its belly-upping. However, it appears that its founder is doing a phoenix, and a successor has been organized. In addition, others are continuing the original activities of the original 3F Club. Inquire at the TIC to find out what the current programs of this type are.

Conversation Lounges

A popular institution in Tokyo is the conversation lounge. The basic format is a coffee shop or similar that offers various diversions such as magazines, videotapes, games, etc., and the opportunity to chat informally with Japanese customers (usually relatively young). There is no organised program, and the type of people there can vary from one day to the next, but visiting one can be a good way to learn a lot about contemporary Japanese in an informal manner. The best listing of such places is in the *Tokyo Journal*. Two such are Cornpopper (tel. (03) 3715-4473) and Howdy Howdy (tel. (03) 5467-4757).

Groups and associations advertise regularly in the *Tokyo Journal*. Check the ads for compatible groups.

There are several other organizations that may be of interest to visiting or resident foreigners.

THE SOCIETY OF WRITERS, EDITORS AND TRANSLATORS (SWET) The written English word is the theme. It would be of interest to anyone involved with any aspect of writing English (editing, technical writing, rewriting, translating, advertising, etc.). It has practical seminars and other get-togethers, and the bimonthly newsletter is very literate and interesting. For more information, write to: SWET, PO Box 8, Komae Yubinkyoku, Komae-shi, Tokyo 201. Membership brings listing in the Directory, a copy of which is sent upon registration and payment of membership dues.

THE FORUM FOR CORPORATE COMMUNICATIONS This is an association of people involved in public relations and related activities. They have luncheons with guest speakers. Notices of forthcoming events are listed in the Announcements section on the back page of the *Japan Times*.

INTERNATIONAL FRIENDS Formerly the Tokyo Gay Support Group, can give information on the gay scene in Tokyo and has a list and map of gay bars and other meeting spots. The group can be contacted by phone at (03) 5693-4569 or by mail: CPO Box 180, Tokyo 100-91.

THE INTERNATIONAL FEMINISTS OF JAPAN This group may be contacted by telephone: (03) 3792-4110 (Anne Blassing). By mail, it is: IFJ, CPO Box 1780, Tokyo 100-91. The IFJ Newsletter is published monthly and is available overseas by subscription. Notices of meetings appear in the English-language dailies and in the *Tokyo Journal*.

Other organizations that might interest visitors or residents are listed in the *Tokyo Journal* monthly, and irregularly in the *Japan Times*.

RELIGIOUS

Christian

There are numerous churches in the greater Tokyo area, representing virtually all the major denominations. For listings, refer to a Saturday issue of the *Japan Times*, *Tokyo Weekender* or the *Tokyo Journal*.

Jewish

The Jewish Community Center (near Hiroo subway station of Hibiya line), has Friday, Saturday, and holiday services, Talmud classes, and provides other services and support to the Jewish community. Tel: (03) 3400-2559.

Muslim

The Islamic Center in Setagaya-ku provides a place for prayer and other activities. Tel: (03) 3460-6169.

TOKYO REGION

The region around Tokyo offers some of Japan's most interesting places to visit, including Kamakura, Mt. Fuji, and the Hakone area. Nearly all can be visited in day-trips, though some might be more enjoyable if spread over two or more days. This chapter follows an arc around Tokyo from the south-west to the south-east.

WEST FROM TOKYO

There are several individual attractions and interesting areas to the west of Tokyo. Many can be visited as day trips or weekend outings, or en route to Kyoto and other destinations in western Japan.

Although generally industrial/commercial in nature, Kawasaki and Yokohama both have some points of interest, and the many sights of the historic city of Kamakura are only a short distance beyond Yokohama. South of Kamakura is the Miura-hanto peninsula, and west of the city lies Odawara, gateway to the Izu-hanto peninsula, the Hakone area, and Mt. Fuji. Going west from the Hakone/Fuji area takes you along the south coast (generally heavily urbanized and uninteresting); going north leads inland via Matsumoto (site of the only historic castle in the Tokyo region) through much more interesting and less-travelled regions. The following section describes each in turn, with optional routes.

Kawasaki

Kawasaki is a typical Japanese industrial city with virtually nothing of interest to visitors, with one notable exception that makes a visit very worthwhile—a museum of traditional Japanese farmhouses.

Nihon Minka-en

Nihon Minka-en means "Japan Farmhouse Park". It is a collection of traditional thatched-roof buildings that have been moved to this peaceful forested site from many places around Japan. The museum offers a very convenient way to get a glimpse of how Japan looked in centuries past; the oldest building dates from 1688. A pamphlet in English, given at the entrance, explains the origin, use, and unusual points of each building, and there are many descriptive signs in English around the grounds for further information. Visitors are free to wander through the interiors of many. The second floor of one building is a museum of traditional farming implements, utensils, and tools plus some armor and weaponry. It is closed on Mondays; no entry after 1600.

Access from Tokyo is by Odakyu line from Shinjuku station to Mukogaoka-yuen station; the express from track 5 takes about 30 minutes. From the south exit (minami guchi), look for the monorail and follow along to its right; continue straight on at the main road where the monorail turns left. The museum is a 15 minute walk from the station.

With an early start it should be possible to take in Nihon Minka-en and Yokohama's Sankei-en garden in one day. To get to Yokohama from Mukogaoka-yuen station, backtrack one stop toward Tokyo to Noborito and change to the JR Nambu line

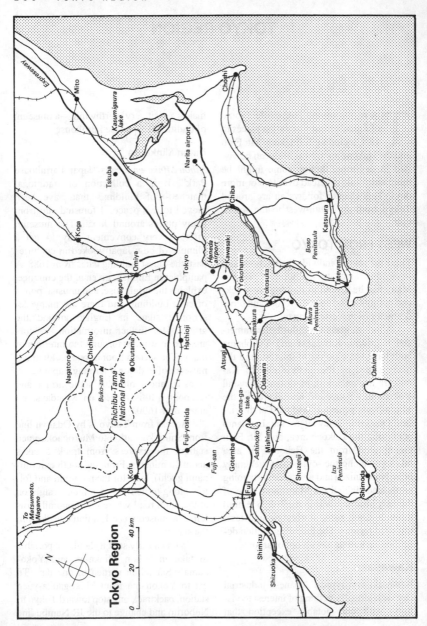

Tokyo Region

N

0　20　40 km

going south. At Kawasaki, change to a train to Yokohama. (At Mukogaoka-yuen you can get a single ticket that permits the transfer to the JR line; tickets are issued from the left-most of the vending machines—buy a low-priced ticket and pay the difference later.)

Other Attractions

Kawasaki is known for its "soapland" red light district (named Horinouchi), and its many love hotels; it is one of the three or four best-known such places in Japan.

Kawasaki has one other attraction, the interesting annual festival, Jibeta Matsuri. This festival honors Kanamara-sama—deities of the metal phallus. It is based on a fable of a maiden (beautiful and rich, of course) who had an unusual and terrible affliction. She was "inhabited" by a sharp-toothed demon that bit off the phallus of two successive grooms who tried to perform their wedding night duty. A divinely inspired blacksmith took the girl with the aid of an iron phallus that de-toothed the demon while de-flowering the maiden. And everyone lived happily ever after, especially the Kawasaki businessmen who have revived the festival, which also honors the gods of businesses, growth, prosperity, reproduction, etc., all of which are various forms of fertility. Whatever the motives, everyone has a good time during the festival, when phalluses are carried in procession and local smiths re-enact the forging operation. The whole thing is a good humored celebration of the joys of sex.

The festival is held on April 15, near Kawasaki Taishi station, beginning with music in the early afternoon, a parade of the sacred palanquin and masked people carrying phallic offerings (1600–1700), followed by the forging (1700–1800), then an outdoor banquet.

From Tokyo (Shinagawa station) take the Keikyu line to Keihin Kawasaki station, then transfer to the Kawasaki Taishi line downstairs. Taishi station is about 10 minutes away. From the station (there is only one exit) cross the street outside, turn right and walk about 50 meters.

Getting There

From Tokyo, Kawasaki can be reached by train by the JR Tokaido line (from Tokyo, Shimbashi, or Shinagawa stations only). This runs non-stop from Shinagawa to Kawasaki. (The JR alternative is the Keihin-Tohoku line, but it stops at every station.) Both these lines continue to Yokohama (the next stop for a Tokaido train). You can also use the Keikyu line from Shinagawa station (or from Sengakuji station on the Asakusa subway line).

There is a daily ferry service between Kawasaki and Hyuga in eastern Kyushu. There is also a car-and-passenger service from Kawasaki across the bay (Tokyo-wan) to Kisarazu on the Boso-hanto peninsula.

Yokohama

Yokohama is a port and business city about 20 km from Tokyo. It has become the second largest city in Japan (nearly three million people), but both Tokyo and Yokohama have expanded toward each other (along with Kawasaki) and now form one vast conurbation. Being a commercial city, it offers little for the sightseer; its large office buildings are much the same as those anywhere.

The city has a short history by Japanese standards. Before 1850 it was only a sleepy fishing village. With the signing of the treaty forcing Japan to open its doors after 250 years of seclusion, Yokohama became one of six ports open to the world and was the port for Tokyo. At the time it was an ugly expanse of mud, and

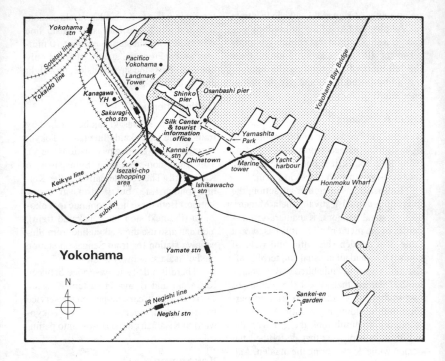

Yokohama

was chosen by the Japanese officials to keep unwanted and unclean foreigners as far from the capital as possible, in conditions less than pleasant. It has improved somewhat since then. (It is a pleasant enough place to live in, but doesn't have huge amounts of things to see.)

Information

Beside the Silk Center Building (facing the harbor) is the Kanagawa Prefectural Tourist Information Center. It has a good selection of useful information on Yokohama and for travel elsewhere in Japan. Tel (045) 681-0506.

There is usually a free handout map, but it may be of the all-too-typical Japanese type with distorted scales, incorrect loca-

tions, and "north" off in a strange direction and not indicated.

Home Visit

If you wish to visit a Japanese home in Yokohama for a couple of hours in the evening, arrangements can be made at the Tourist Information Center, at the Yokohama International Welcome Association (ground floor, Silk Center Building, tel (045) 641-5824), or at the Silk Center Hotel (tel (045) 641-0961).

Things to See

The attractions of Yokohama are limited and most are located quite close to each other: Yamashita Park (along the harbor front), Marine Tower, Port Viewing Park,

Chinatown, and the Silk Center Building. The premier destination, Sankei-en Park, is a convenient bus ride away.

Silk Center Building

This houses a permanent display of all aspects of the silk industry, from raw cocoon to beautiful fabric. The simplest way to get there from Yokohama station is by bus from the depot beside the Sky Building, opposite the East Exit. Bus 26 passes in front of the Silk Center; buses 8 and 58 pass nearby (get off at the Post Office).

Marine Tower

From the Silk Center it is a simple walk along Yamashita Park to the very visible Marine Tower. On a clear day it is possible to see distant Mt. Fuji; this is more likely in the cooler months or following a day of strong winds. From Yokohama station buses 8, 26, and 58 pass nearby.

Port Viewing Park

This park is an alternative to Marine Tower for viewing the harbor (though not Mt. Fuji). The road up to it can be found easily from the vicinity of the Tower. This area is known as the Bluffs and has been the prestige residential area, especially for foreigners, since Yokohama was opened to the outside world.

Chukagai

Near the tower is Chinatown (*Chukagai* in Japanese), the only one in Japan. It is known for its restaurants and shops selling Chinese products and curios.

Sankei-en Garden

After the Tower, catch a No. 8 bus to Sankei-en garden. This is one of the most beautiful garden parks in Japan—in my opinion far more attractive than the "Big Three" at Mito, Kanazawa, and Okayama.

It dates only from the late 19th century and was built by Tomitaro Hara, a wealthy silk merchant. It is laid out around a large pond, with walking paths circling it and branching off to other places. Wooded hillsides totally obscure the ugly reality of the surrounding 20th century. One of the side paths leads to the Inner Garden, which is laid out in the traditional Japanese style, and is an excellent example of the landscape gardener's work. Within the Inner Park are several historic buildings, including the traditional-style mansion Rinshun-kaku; these were moved here from other parts of Japan.

Elsewhere in the park, on the highest hill, is an old three-storey pagoda in excellent condition. It was built in the 15th century and moved to the park in 1914. A nearby lookout gives a good view of the harbor, and on a clear day you can see Mt. Fuji, though the view is spoiled by a tall smokestack.

Near the pagoda is another noteworthy building, the Yonohara farmhouse, a huge thatched-roof building. It dates from 1750 and is held together only by straw ropes—there are no nails in it whatsoever. This one was moved here in 1960 when the opening of a new dam flooded the valley where it was located. The only other similar buildings are in the Shirakawago area of Gifuken, so take this opportunity if you will not be able to see others in their native surroundings.

To return to Yokohama station, or the vicinity of the Tower or Chinatown, take a No. 8 bus going in the same direction as the one that took you to the park. Get off anywhere near the Tower. The closest railway station is Ishikawacho on the Negishi (Keihin-Tohoku) line.

Places to Stay

Kanagawa Youth Hostel (tel (045) 241-6503) is about 10 minutes from Sakuragi-cho station. From the station, in the direction of Yokohama station, you can see the "Golden Center" Building (that's the name in Japanese if you have to ask someone); there is a wide street on the far side of it. Walk to the right along that street, keeping the elevated railway tracks to the right until you reach a short, steep incline leading up to a steep cobblestoned street to the left and a traffic bridge to the right. Turn left up the hill and the hostel is on the right about 100 meters along.

There are hotels of a variety of price ranges to choose from. If you want to stay overnight in a typical Japanese lodging (*ryokan* or minshuku), the Tourist Information Center can help with bookings. There is also an office for minshuku reservations and information located on the balcony beside the Sky Building, at the end of the elevated passageway from Yokohama station to one of the bus stations.

Note that Kamakura is about half an hour away from Yokohama (or an hour from Tokyo) and may be a preferable place to stay. Nihon Gakusei-kaikan Youth Hostel (tel (0467) 25-1234) in Kamakura has 400 beds.

Getting There

Air

If you are going to Yokohama direct from Narita or Haneda airports, the most convenient service is by airport bus. It connects with Yokohama City Air Terminal (YCAT), a few minutes from Yokohama station. Refer to the Narita and Haneda airport sections for details of cost and frequency. Travel time from Narita is scheduled at two hours, but extra time should be allowed for traffic tie-ups.

When flying out of Narita on many airlines, luggage may be checked in at YCAT and not touched again until the destination. These planes are held back for passengers if the bus is delayed. (See below for details on how to get to YCAT from the station.)

A cheaper but more time-consuming way to get to Narita airport from Yokohama is by JR Yokosuka or Tokaido train to Shimbashi, and change there to a Yamanote train to either: 1: Ueno station, and take the Keisei line to Narita, or 2: Tokyo station, and take the NEX or the Narita Kaisoku train to Narita.

Sea

Yokohama is a port of call for cruise ships, and is served by regular sailings to and from Nakhodka (Russia) at the eastern extremity of the Trans-Siberian Railway. Passenger ships arrive at the modern International Port Terminal located at Osambashi Pier.

To get to Yokohama station from Osambashi Pier you can walk, catch a bus, or go by train from the nearest station.

After clearing Immigration and Customs, passengers walk along the pier to the mainland. At the entrance to the pier is a small square; on the right side is a map of Yokohama and the first of many indicators pointing the way to Sakuragicho station (from which trains can be caught to Tokyo); on the left is the nine-storey Silk Center Building. It is a simple 20–30 minute walk to Sakuragicho. If you follow the signs to a tree-lined avenue you can walk along that to Yokohama Park and through there to Kannai station. Both stations are on the Negishi (JR) line, a local line with trains to Yokohama station; Sakuragicho station is the starting point for the Toyoko line, a lower-cost alternative into Tokyo (to Shibuya).

Buses No. 8, 20, 58, and 1 go to Yokohama station via Sakuragicho station; buses 11, 21, and 22 terminate at the latter. To get to the bus stop from the pier, walk straight ahead past the Silk Center Building (on the left) to the first major cross street (the Post Office is to the right). The bus stop is a little farther along the street from the far right hand corner.

Train

To reach Yokohama from Tokyo or Narita Airport, there are five rail services—three JR and two private lines, Toyoko and Keihin-Kyuko (Keikyu).

From Tokyo station there are two express services, both taking 28 minutes to Yokohama. Both the Yokosuka and Tokaido lines stop only at Shimbashi and Shinagawa in the metropolitan Tokyo area, and each makes one more stop before Yokohama, the Yokosuka line at Shin-kawasaki, and the Tokaido line at Kawasaki. Trains of both lines depart at five to 15 minute intervals through the day. Trains on the Keihin-Tohoku line stop at all 12 stations from Tokyo to Yokohama.

From points near Eidan (private) subway lines, the most convenient and cheapest way to go is probably by the Toyoko line which starts from Shibuya (which can be reached via Ginza or Hanzomon subway or JR Yamanote lines, but a separate ticket must be bought for the Toyoko line in any case.) A direct transfer to the Toyoko line (without changing platforms) can be made from the Hibiya subway line at Naka-meguro; a new fare zone begins here because of the change to the Toyoko line.

From stations on the Toei (Asakusa and Mita) subway lines, go to Sengakuji and transfer there to the Keikyu line to Yokohama.

Getting Around

Yokohama station is a busy communications center, being served by JR, three private railway lines, a subway, and many buses. The station has undergone extensive remodelling in recent years and there are now

relatively good markings in English, sufficient at least to find most connections.

The above-ground facilities over the station include a hotel and a department store, and the actual station section is basically a broad underground passageway leading to most of the lines. The main entrance is the west exit (nishi guchi) and is the loading zone for most of the buses. The east exit (higashi guchi) is connected to another bus loading zone by a passage over a major expressway. The train platforms are numbered from the east exit end.

Tracks 1 and 2 are for Keikyu trains (private line). Track 1 trains go west to Yokosuka and the Miura-hanto peninsula. Trains from track 2 run to Kawasaki and Shinagawa (Tokyo). Some of these continue past Shinagawa to Sengakuji station, on the Mita subway line; the train may terminate here or continue some distance along these tracks towards Oshiage. Keikyu expresses are marked with green or red *kanji* on the front and side of the trains, and locals are marked in black.

Tracks 3 to 10 are JR services.

Track 3 is the Keihin-Tohoku line, providing local service as far as Ofuna (also a stop on the Yokosuka line). It becomes the Negishi line one stop out of Yokohama.

Track 4 is the Keihin-Tohoku line, providing local service to Tokyo and as far north as Omiya. It stops at all 12 stations along the way to Tokyo and is no cheaper than the much faster Yokosuka and Tokaido lines; in the Tokyo area it runs parallel to the Yamanote line for many stops. This is the line to take for connections with the Shinkansen at Shin-yokohama station; go one stop to Higashi-kanagawa station and transfer to a Yokohama-sen line train bound for Hachioji; the third stop is Shin-yokohama. Keihin-Tohoku trains are light blue.

Tracks 5 and 6 are Tokaido line services west to Odawara, Atami and Nagoya. Many of these are expresses, for which there is a surcharge. (It is necessary to consult a timetable to distinguish them in advance; the trains have red *kanji* destination signs for expresses, black for locals.)

Tracks 7 and 8 are Tokaido line services to Tokyo, stopping en route only at Kawasaki, Shinagawa, and Shimbashi, the latter two being stations in the metro Tokyo area. This is one of the two fastest services to Tokyo. Tokaido line trains are orange and green.

Track 9 is Yokosuka line (pronounced Yoh-kohs-kah) service west to Kamakura, Zushi, Yokosuka, and Kurihama, at the south-east side of the Miura-hanto peninsula. Some of these are expresses with a surcharge; refer to the notes for Tokaido line trains.

Track 10 is Yokosuka line express service to Tokyo, stopping only at Shin-kawasaki, Shinagawa, and Shimbashi en route; beyond Tokyo, many of these trains continue to or toward Chiba as the Sobu line. Yokosuka line trains are cream and blue.

Tickets for all JR as well as Keikyu trains can be purchased from vending machines in the underground passageway. If you are not sure of the fare to your destination, buy the cheapest ticket and pay the difference at the other end. (Keep your ticket.) JR services to Tokyo are more expensive than either the Keikyu or the Toyoko lines.

The tracks of the second private line, the Toyoko (Tokyo-Yokohama) line are on the west side of the station. It runs from Sakuragicho (two stops beyond Yokohama) to Shibuya, on the west side of central Tokyo. It offers convenient transfer to the Hibiya subway line at Naka-meguro, and to the JR Yamanote line and the Ginza and Hanzomon subway lines at Shibuya.

The entrance to the Toyoko line tracks is to the left when entering Yokohama station through the west exit; ticket machines are nearby. (The tracks can also be reached via an entrance directly from JR tracks.)

Track 1 of the Toyoko line serves trains that go only two stops, to Sakuragi-cho.

Track 2 serves trains bound for Shibuya (Tokyo).

Trains with the destination marked in red are expresses (*kyuko*) and reach Shibuya 10 minutes faster than those marked in black. These colors are also used on timetables.

To get to the Yokohama subway, follow the passage toward the west exit, climb up the stairs, and turn left. Continuing down the passage to the end leads to an open area and exit to the right; the subway entrance is just outside and is identified in English.

Straight ahead at this exit is the entrance to the Sotetsu line that runs west and intersects the Odakyu line to the Odawara area.

Yokohama City Air Terminal (YCAT) is easily reached from the east exit of the station. A shuttle bus runs from stop No. 1 about three to five times an hour. Fare is ¥180 and the trip takes only a few minutes. Look for dark blue minibuses identified by the letters YCAT on the side. If you don't have to carry luggage it is about a 15 minute walk. Turn left from the front of the station and walk until you see New Japan Motors (a Ford dealer) across the wide road. YCAT is across the road and down the side street.

Kamakura

Now a resort town for day-tripping Tokyoites and residence for many fortunate citizens, Kamakura was effectively the capital of Japan from 1192 to 1333 when the *bakufu* military government of the Minamoto family gained the upper hand in Japan. During that period it became very prosperous, but it subsequently declined to a regional government center. It finally lost all special status in 1603 and became a quiet backwater.

Kamakura, the most interesting single place in the Tokyo area to visit for historic remains, should be on everyone's "must see" list. The best-known attraction is the famous Kamakura *Daibutsu* (Great Buddha), but there are other sights as well.

Information

Two useful leaflets, *Kamakura* and *Fuji-Hakone-Izu-Kamakura*, are available from the Tokyo TIC.

There is a program of volunteer student guides who show visitors around Kamakura at no charge in return for the opportunity to practice English. To fit in with the students' free time, the tours are given only on weekends. The Tokyo TIC has more information and can make arrangements.

Things to See

Kamakura station is a good starting point for sightseeing in the area as it's a terminus for buses as well as the Enoden railway line to Fujisawa and on to the beach resort town of Enoshima. A day pass *(furii kippu)* for unlimited travel on city buses is available for about ¥750, but most visitors will not use it enough to make it a bargain. Passes are sold at the ticket office close to the police post, to the left when leaving the bus terminal side of the station.

Finding your way around Kamakura on foot is very simple because of the large number of signposts in English that give the distance to the next place to see (usually a temple or shrine). Every point of interest has a plaque at its entrance giving its history in English. The following route takes in the major attractions.

Daibutsu

The most famous single sight in Kamakura is the great bronze figure of Buddha *(Amitabha)*. It sits in the open, having looked for more than seven centuries with half-closed eyes on the rise and fall of Kamakura as a seat of power. The seated figure is more than 11 meters tall, plus pedestal, and weighs nearly 100 tonnes. The pose and position of the hands represents the Buddhist symbolism for steadfast faith, and the expression on the face is one of great serenity. It is a work of art far superior to the larger Buddha figure at Nara.

The statue was cast in 1252 and was originally protected by a temple, but a tidal wave in 1495 swept this away and the figure has been in the open ever since. That tidal wave must have been monumental, as the Buddha is nearly one km inland! (The temple has a welcome facility—clean toilets, including a western-style one *with* toilet paper!)

Access is by bus No. 3 or 7 to Daibutsu-mae stop, bus No. 8 to nearby Hase Kannon temple, or the Enoden train to Hase station.

Hase Kannon Temple

This is an interesting temple to visit before or after Daibutsu. It is famous for a huge nine-meter figure of Kannon, the Buddhist Goddess of Mercy (after whom Canon cameras were originally named). It was carved from a single camphor log, reputedly in 721 AD. A similar figure, said to have been carved from the same log, may be seen in Hase-dera, near Nara.

The building housing the figure is a new concrete structure styled to blend with the older parts of the temple while still protecting the figure from fire and displaying it with well-placed lighting (no photos,

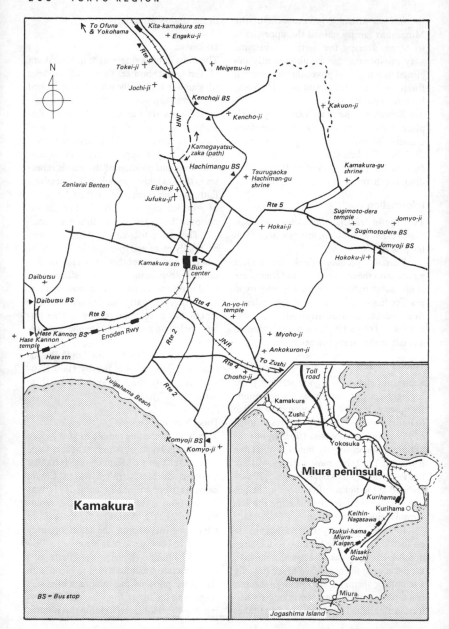

N

To Ofuna & Yokohama
Kita-kamakura stn
Engaku-ji
Rte 9
Tokei-ji
Meigetsu-in
Jochi-ji
Kenchoji BS
Kakuon-ji
Kencho-ji
JNR
Kamegayatsu-zaka (path)
Hachimangu BS
Tsurugaoka Hachiman-gu shrine
Kamakura-gu shrine
Zeniarai Benten
Eisho-ji
Jufuku-ji
Rte 5
Sugimoto-dera temple
Jomyo-ji
Hokai-ji
Sugimotodera BS
Jomyoji BS
Hokoku-ji
Kamakura stn
Bus center
An-yo-in temple
Rte 4
Daibutsu
Daibutsu BS
Rte 8
Myoho-ji
Hase Kannon BS
Enoden Rwy
Rte 2
JNR
Ankokuron-ji
Hase Kannon temple
Hase stn
Rte 4
To Zushi
Chosho-ji
Yuigahama Beach
Rte 2
Komyoji BS
Komyo-ji

Kamakura

BS = Bus stop

Toll road
Kamakura
Zushi
Yokosuka
Miura peninsula
Kurihama
Kurihama
Keihin-Nagasawa
Tsukui-hama
Miura-Kaigan
Misaki-Guchi
Aburatsubo
Miura
Jogashima Island

TOKYO REGION **269**

unfortunately). This piece of religious art is accompanied by many smaller, carved wooden figures of Kannon and other Buddhist personages.

The grounds of the temple are also interesting. On the climb up to the main building you see hundreds of small figures of Jizo, patron deity of children, pregnant women, and travellers; many are dressed with little bibs and hats. At ground level there is a small grotto with a number of figures carved in the stone walls of the circular chamber.

Hase Kannon is about 200 meters from Daibutsu. It can be reached from Kamakura station by bus No. 3, 7, or 8 to Hase Kannon stop, or you can take the Enoden railway to Hase station.

From here, you can continue to Enoshima by Enoden or by bus No. 8; or go on foot or by taxi to Zeniarai Benten.

Zeniarai Benten Shrine

The name means "money-washing" shrine, from the belief that any money washed here will be returned two or three times over. While some search for ¥10,000 notes, the sceptics limit themselves to loose change. The money is placed in little wicker baskets and then swished around in the pool in the small cave on the ground. The washing is supposed to be efficacious only on days related to the zodiacal sign of the snake, but this doesn't stop anybody, no matter what the day.

Many wooden *torii* have been donated to the shrine and arranged in picturesque rows like short tunnels. After a steep uphill walk, the temple is finally reached through a tunnel cut through the rock.

Zeniarai Benten can be reached by walking from Hase Kannon or from Hase station; the route is adequately signposted. There is no bus, but you can catch a taxi.

Kencho-ji Area

From Zeniarai Benten you can either return to the station or follow the roads to the Kencho-ji area. There are a few temples along the way, and the final leg is along an unpaved road over a ridge and down the curiously-named Kame-ga-saka dani— "Turtle Slope Valley". From Zeniarai shrine it is about 1.5 km as the crow flies, but it is definitely a much longer hike; the slope is nicely wooded though, and you pass an interesting *ryokan* which is reached, like Zeniarai shrine, by a tunnel cut through solid rock. From the station, the Kencho-ji area is quickly reached by bus No. 9 or 10; get off at Kenchoji stop.

Kencho-ji Temple

The greatest and most picturesque of the temples of Kamakura, Kencho-ji was founded in 1253. The main hall dates from 1646 and has the appearance of well-preserved age. The great sanmon gate and nearby belfry are equally picturesque. Other glimpses of buildings set in pretty gardens or other artistic settings can be found by wandering along the paths of the grounds.

Meigetsu-in Temple

Close to Kencho-ji, this little temple is really worth visiting only in June, when the huge number of hydrangea are in bloom.

Engaku-ji Temple

Close to Kita-kamakura station, this temple dates from 1282, but virtually all the old buildings have been destroyed, many by the 1923 Kanto earthquake. The great *sanmon* main gate is impressive, and one of the buildings is reached through a wooden gate with intricate carvings of lions and dragons. There are glimpses of beauty here and there, but the effect is not maintained, and the main building is made of unromantic concrete. Superficially it resembles Ken-cho-ji in layout, but has less to offer.

There are other temples nearby that may be explored if time allows but all are low-key. Downhill from Kencho-ji is a side entrance to Tsurugaoka Hachiman-gu shrine.

Tsurugaoka Hachiman-gu Shrine

Occupying the place of honor in Kamakura, the shrine is built on a hillside overlooking the city and a long boulevard that leads to the sea. The boulevard is divided by twin rows of cherry trees that attract throngs of people in spring.

Hachiman is the god of war, so it was natural for the military government (the *bakufu*) to dedicate the shrine to him. The present site was first used from 1191, the successor to an earlier one founded elsewhere in 1063. The present colorful orange buildings date from 1828. The small museum in the main building houses armor, swords, masks, and other historic items.

At the foot of the staircase leading down from the shrine is a Noh stage, from which a long stone-paved walkway leads to the front entrance; it is always crowded on weekends and holidays. To the left is the Kamakura Kokuho-kan (municipal museum) which displays a number of treasures of the Kamakura and Muromachi periods (1192–1573) that belong to various shrines and temples in the area. Near the main entrance to the grounds, to the right, is the Prefectural Modern Art Gallery. Also near the entrance is the steep *taiko-bashi* (Drum Bridge) a sort of practical joke in stone, as it is so steep that you cannot walk up and over; a running start is required to carry you across. Getting to the other side is reputed to grant a wish. The shrine is unbelievably crowded on New Year's Day.

Hokoku-ji Temple

Access is across Hanano-bashi bridge, an ordinary concrete structure, but look out for the colorful carp in the stream below. The temple is not noted for its buildings, but for the beautiful bamboo grove behind, which is interspersed with numerous historic gravestones. At the teahouse in one corner you can sit and contemplate the small but attractive garden behind the grove.

Hokoku-ji is a Zen temple, and zazen meditation is held in the garden before 0800 every Sunday; anyone may participate.

Hokoku-ji can be reached from Hachiman shrine or the station by No. 5 bus to Jomyoji stop.

There are several other temples and shrines along the same road, including thatch-roofed Sugimoto-dera, which is the oldest temple in Kamakura. Most of these temples are of historical interest only, however, and have little visual appeal unless you are familiar with Japanese history.

Komyo-ji Temple

This temple is usually nearly deserted, yet for visual appeal it is one of the most worthwhile destinations in Kamakura. The temple dates from 1243, although the main building is a modern concrete structure (but of traditional appearance). What sets it apart from other temples in Kamakura is its *karesansui* garden of rock, gravel, and greenery at one side of the temple, and another garden consisting of a lotus pond (best from late summer) and other picturesque elements arranged in front of an attractive building. Unlike most other temples, there is no charge to see either.

Other attractions of the temple include a large and old-looking *sanmon* gate, a bell tower with some of the finest wood carvings in Kamakura, and a number of interesting tombs. Although many other temples in the city have extensive burial areas, this is the only one with a memorial for pet animals; look for a large monument on the right with food dishes left out.

To get there, take a No. 2 bus from the station.

Getting There

Kamakura is easily reached in just under an hour by Yokosuka line from Tokyo, Shimbashi, and Shinagawa stations in metro Tokyo, or from Kawasaki or Yokohama (track 9). From Yokosuka it is the fourth station.

Enoshima

This is a popular beach resort town west of Kamakura. Because it is close to Tokyo it gets extremely crowded on summer weekends.

The main beach is Higashi-hama (higashi = east); on the Katase side of the Katase River is Nishi-hama beach (nishi = west), accessible by Katase-bashi bridge. Also on the Katase side is an aquarium and Enoshima Marineland.

In the harbor is Enoshima, the island that gives its name to the area. It offers the hillside Enoshima shrine (reached by steps or escalator), various recreation facilities, and scenic views at Chigogafuchi, including two nearby caves. Enoshima-jinja shrine has a nude statue of Benten, the Indian goddess of beauty and the only female among the seven Japanese deities of good luck. There is an observation tower that gives a good view of Mt. Fuji in one direction and Oshima Island in the other. The latter (described later in this chapter) can be reached by ferry from Shonan Harbor, on the north side of the island. Enoshima island is easily reached by a footbridge.

The beach here will, like most Japanese beaches, be mostly of interest for residents only. Nearly every beach in the country is crowded and very littered in summer, and lifesaving facilities are not to be depended on. (Like most beaches, it will be nearly empty after the first of September.)

Getting There

To get to Enoshima from Kamakura, you can go by Enoden train or bus No. 8 from Kamakura station. There is also the monorail from Ofuna on the JR Yokosuka line.

To continue from Enoshima to the Hakone/Izu/Fuji area, take the Enoden line to Fujisawa and transfer to the JR to go to Odawara or Atami (described later in this section).

Miura-hanto Peninsula

This peninsula projects into Sagami-wan bay between Yokohama and Kamakura. The east side is mainly industrial and commercial, and includes Yokosuka Naval Base, the largest U.S. naval base in Japan. The west side and southeast coast is largely beach and resort territory.

A bus from Zushi station runs down the west coast to Misaki station; it passes beaches, the Emperor's walled-in villa at Hayama, and several good views of the sea and pleasure craft. During clear weather (winter, late autumn) Mt. Fuji is clearly visible.

Aburatsubo

Aburatsubo has a large aquarium—praised by some, a disappointment to others. It is named Sakana-no-kuni ("Fish World"). As well as displays of live fish, it has a dome onto which films are projected to give the impression of being underwater. Buses run between Misakiguchi station and the aquarium; the trip takes about 15 minutes. Loudspeakers, the bane of Japan, disturb the peace for a long distance in all directions around the aquarium.

Jogashima Island

Located at the far southwest tip of the

peninsula, Jogashima has preserved a picturesque cape as parkland, sparing it from "development" and the encroachment of urban sprawl. The shore is made of strangely twisted rocks, obviously volcanic lava. There are several small pools, some with colorful little fish. Anyone wanting a peaceful place for a picnic or just for relaxing by the sea would enjoy it, and it's a good destination for a day-trip (or longer if you have the time) to escape Tokyo. It was almost deserted during my late-September visit, but it might be more crowded in summer. There is a youth hostel nearby.

Buses run to Jogashima from Misakiguchi station; the trip takes about 30 minutes.

Miura-kaigan Coast

Above the "bulge" at the bottom of the peninsula is Miura-kaigan (coast), known for the very long Shonan-hama beach, with good white sand and temperate water (crowded in July and August, but good off-season). Access is by Keikyu railway to any of the three stations: Miura-kaigan, Tsukui-hama, and Keihin-nagasawa; local buses run along the coast. There are many *minshuku* and *ryokan* along the beach.

From Kurihama, a ferry crosses to Kanaya on the Boso-hanto peninsula (on the opposite side of Tokyo-wan bay); service is approximately every 35 minutes through the daylight hours.

FUJI-HAKONE-IZU AREA

Some of the finest scenery in Japan is located close to Tokyo, and is easily reached. The centerpiece is Mt. Fuji, while the other areas offer views of Fuji and attractions of their own. This section begins with a description of the Odawara area, followed by the Izu-hanto peninsula, continues to the Hakone area, and finishes with the area around Mt. Fuji.

Kozu

Kozu is the transfer point for JR train lines between the Tokaido Honsen line down the coast and the Gotemba-sen line to Gotemba, a major gateway for the Mt. Fuji area. These services are described in detail in the section on Mt. Fuji.

Odawara

Odawara's main attraction is a reconstruction (1960) of Odawara-jo castle. It preserves the outward appearance of the ancient castle but is not "authentic". With a genuine 17th century castle at Matsumoto (just north of the Mt. Fuji area) there is not much incentive to visit this one.

Odawara can be considered a gateway to the Izu-hanto peninsula to the southwest, and the Hakone area and Mt. Fuji to the east and northeast.

Odawara can be reached by the JR Tokaido Honsen line (one hour from Tokyo by the fastest express; 1-1/2 hours by local train—¥1240.) You can also use the Kodama services of the Tokaido Shinkansen (40 minutes, ¥3240), and the Odakyu (Odawara *Kyuko*) express line. Odakyu services are detailed in the section on Hakone because more travellers would use them for going there than to Odawara.

IZU-HANTO PENINSULA

The Izu-hanto peninsula is probably the most popular seaside recreation area for Tokyoites. There are some interesting historical sites and some nice scenery, but it is low key and the resorts are crowded during the summer season. It is better regarded as an excursion destination for Tokyo residents and of secondary interest to short-term visitors.

For additional information, the Tokyo TIC has a pamphlet *Fuji-Hakone-Izu-Kamakura* and an information sheet *The Izu Peninsula*.

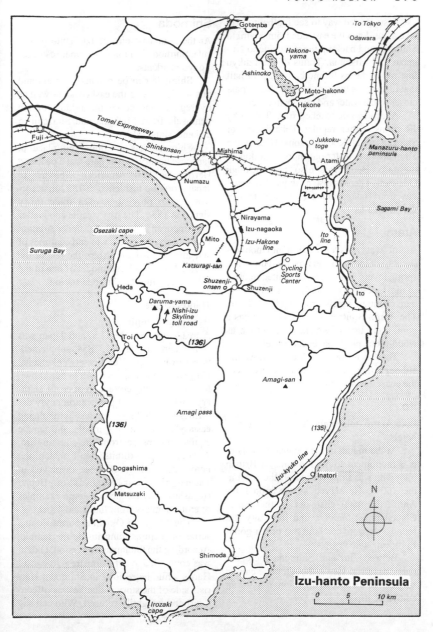

To Tokyo

Odawara

Gotemba

Hakone-yama

Ashinoko

Moto-hakone

Hakone

Tomei Expressway

Fuji

Shinkansen

Mishima

Jukkoku-toge

Atami

Manazuru-hanto peninsula

Numazu

Sagami Bay

Osezaki cape

Nirayama

Izu-nagaoka

Mito

Izu-Hakone line

Ito line

Suruga Bay

Katsuragi-san

Shuzenji-onsen

Shuzenji

Cycling Sports Center

Ito

Heda

Daruma-yama

Nishi-izu Skyline toll road

(136)

Toi

Amagi-san

Amagi pass

(136)

(135)

Dogashima

Izu-kyuko line

Inatori

Matsuzaki

N

Shimoda

Izu-hanto Peninsula

0   5   10 km

Irozaki cape

A suggested way to see Izu-hanto is to take a bus down the east side from Atami to Shimoda and back up the west side to Numazu and Mishima. Trains of the Izukyu line run as far as Shimoda, but about half that distance is through tunnels; buses pass closer to the water and give better views.

Atami can be reached from Tokyo by JR trains, either regular Tokaido-sen or Shinkansen (all Kodama, some Hikari); the Shinkansen is faster but more than double the fare. Both lines also pass through Odawara. There is also a frequent bus service from Hakone along a scenic route over the mountains.

Atami

Atami was a favorite of honeymooners (largely of the weekend type) and other hot spring lovers, but will be of limited interest to most western visitors as it is little more than countless hotels strung up the hillside. The Atami Bijutsukan (art museum) has a good collection of Japanese arts, such as wood-block prints, lacquerware, etc.

There is no swimming beach at Atami, although there are swimming areas down the coast towards Ito.

Ito

Like Atami, this is another town of resort hotels.

At the mouth of the Okawa river there is a monument to Will Adams, a British pilot who was shipwrecked off the coast in the 1600s. He served as the model for Anjin, the main character in the James Clavell novel *Shogun*, and in reality did found a shipyard that built two ocean-going European style vessels.

Between Ito and Shimoda there are many beautiful views, though none can be singled out for special attention; it's just an enjoyable trip.

Shimoda

At the southeast end of Izu-hanto peninsula, Shimoda is a major summer resort for Tokyo residents.

Shimoda can be reached by train and bus services along the east coast, as well as by regular bus down the middle of the peninsula from Mishima and Shuzenji to Toi and Matsuzaki.

Shimoda has an important place in Japanese history. It was here that Townsend Harris, the first American diplomat to Japan, took up residence in 1857 in accordance with provisions of a trade treaty signed in 1854. The treaty came about after the American "Black Ships" under Admiral Perry forced the country to end centuries of self-imposed isolation from the rest of the world. There is a large model of one of the side-wheel ships at Shimoda station.

Things to see

Ryosen-ji Temple

A treaty between the U.S. and Japan was signed here on May 25, 1854, supplementary to one signed earlier at Yokohama. However the temple is much better known for its interesting collection of erotic statuary—which a JNTO publication coyly describes as "Buddhist images symbolising ecstasy". The phallic symbols, and female equivalents, range from life-size upward. Although the exhibits don't match the heroic proportions of those displayed at Tagata-jinja (near Nagoya) or Beppu (Kyushu), they do include some examples of erotic statuary from India and Tibet.

The "story" of Okichi is portrayed in a series of pictures hung inside the temple. According the the Japanese version, Okichi was compelled to act as mistress to consul Harris while he resided in Shimoda; Harris's side of the story is that he was offered a girl and haughtily refused. Who can say which version is true? (The Japanese have a long history of slanderously maligning foreigners, so their version may be more suspect.) Elsewhere in Shimoda is Hofuku-ji temple, built for the repose of the soul of Okichi.

Ryosen-ji is a 10–15 minute walk from Shimoda station. A rather vague map of the town is available from the station.

Gyokusen-ji Temple

This was the residence of Harris and the first foreign consulate in 1857; he lived here for about 1-1/2 years. It is about two km from the station on the east side of Shimoda at Kakisaki village (accessible by bus from the station). Of curiosity value on the grounds is a monument erected by Tokyo butchers to the first cow slaughtered in Japan for food. The temple is well identified in English by a roadside sign on the sea side of the road. Monuments and plaques on the site give all necessary information.

At the edge of the sea, opposite the road leading to the temple, is a tiny shrine set at the bottom of a large, picturesque wind-sculpted rock.

Yumiga-hama Beach

This is probably the best beach in the Shimoda area, accessible from Shimoda by bus in 20 minutes. There are also other beach areas closer to town, on the way to Kakisaki. The beaches are all jam-packed in July and August (parking lots full by 0600!), but they are almost empty just a few days into September.

Places to Stay

There are countless *minshuku*, *ryokan*, and hotels around Shimoda, but the town is very crowded during the summer and asking for a room at one after another can be a waste of time. There is an accommodation center at the station and another across the road from it. Both will phone and arrange a room.

Irozaki Cape

The southern-most tip of the peninsula is noted for its high perpendicular cliffs. You can get there from Shimoda by bus in 40 minutes, but a boat ride from Shimoda, or an excursion out of Irozaki port, gives a better view. Boat information is available from the station.

Dogashima

The single most scenic place along the west coast is Dogashima.

The geological structure of the area around this town (at the lower end of the west coast) is sedimentary rock that is banded in distinct layers. Erosion or physical separation has resulted in a large number of huge rocks that jut out of the sea. It is scenic from the shore, but can be seen much better from a cruise boat out of Dogashima.

WEST COAST

The west coast above Dogashima has fewer resort towns than the east coast, and there are many lovely sea views most of the way up, making the travelling more enjoyable than along the east coast. Buses run north as far as Heda, then turn east inland towards Shuzenji, so anyone wishing to continue around the coast to Mito would have to hitch across the gap between Heda and Ose-zaki cape.

NORTHWEST CORNER

The northwest corner of the Izu peninsula offers excellent views of Mt. Fuji over Suruga-wan bay in clear weather (generally late autumn and winter).

Suggested places are:

The top of Katsuragi-san, easily reached by cable car from Izu-nagaoka town (accessible from Mishima via Nagaoka station).

The beach at Mitohama (near Mito).

Along the coast between Mitohama and Ose-zaki cape.

The top of Daruma-yama, accessible by Nishi-izu Skyline toll road.

By hiking from Shuzenji-onsen via Heda-toge pass, one of the best hiking trails on the peninsula.

An unusual sight along the coast between Mito and Ose is the old Swedish luxury passenger ship *Stella Polaris*, permanently berthed and serving as a floating hotel.

There is boat service several times a day between Numazu and Matsuzaki, halfway down the west coast, stopping at Heda and Toi; other boats from there enable a trip the rest of the way down the coast. There is also a boat service between Matsuzaki and Shimizu. (These are mostly summer services.)

Mito

Of interest here is a natural aquarium formed by nets stretched between rocks. Dolphins and great turtles may be seen.

NORTH CENTRAL AREA

Shuzenji-onsen

This town takes its name from Shuzen-ji temple, which was founded in the ninth century. It is a typical hot spring resort town with many hotels and *ryokan* using the hot water.

Unusual is a hot spring, Tokkonoyu, that bubbles forth at the edge of the small river that passes through the town. A roofed, slatted-wall bathhouse has been

built around a pool of comfortably warm water. For those not too shy to disrobe and hop in (no one can see in from outside) there is no charge.

There is a youth hostel on the hill behind the town.

Shuzenji-onsen is reached by bus from Shuzenji station, the terminus of Izu-Hakone Tetsudo railway from Mishima. Shuzenji is the transfer point for bus travel though the middle of the peninsula from Mishima to Shimoda. There is also service to Ito and other points on the peninsula from Shuzenji; further information is available in *jikokuhyo* or from tourist information sources.

Cycle Sports Center

Less than half an hour from Shuzenji by bus is one of the two cycle centers in Japan. There are several courses and tracks of various types and lengths, and hundreds of bicycles for rent. It is well suited for people who want to try a variety of bikes before purchasing, and is also a weekend recreation center with reasonable-cost accommodation.

Nirayama

Egawake, the oldest private house in Japan, is located near this town. The 700-year-old building was the residence of the hereditary administrators of the Izu area, so it is large and has a pretty garden, canopied by a number of tall old trees.

Access is by bus from Nirayama station of the Izu-Hakone railway line between Mishima and Shuzenji.

Mishima

Rakuju-en landscape garden, which dates from late last century, is the main attraction of this town. Mishima is on the Tokaido Honsen line, and is the starting point of the Izu railway line to Shuzenji, which runs partway down the middle of the peninsula. It can also be reached by boat in summer from Matsuzaki.

There are many buses through the day (more than 20 in summer) from Mishima to Kawaguchi-ko (north of Mt. Fuji), via Gotemba and Fuji-yoshida. The trip takes 2-1/4 hours and costs about ¥1700. There are also up to 10 buses a day to Shingogome, on the south flank of Mt. Fuji, probably the most popular starting point for climbing the mountain.

WEST & SOUTH OF IZU/FUJI

West and south from the Izu-hanto/Fuji area, the road and train lines run very close to the coast; the inland area is inhospitable mountains with very few settlements. Apart from a couple of places around Shizuoka and Shimizu, there is little of interest to anyone except students of Japanese industrialization. Unless you want to go directly to Kyoto, there is little incentive to go this way by road, as Route 1 is incredibly busy, and very slow to travel on, a continuous conurbation with countless stop lights and dirty air. Only trains and vehicles on the Tomei expressway move quickly.

To see some of the "real" Japan with rural areas and some historic remains, including one of the nation's finest castles, it is better to consider travelling through the Hakone and Fuji areas to Matsumoto (via Kofu).

However for those who wish to take the coastal route, the following describes the few attractions along the way.

Okitsu

This was the 17th stage on the old Tokaido highway from Edo (Tokyo) to Kyoto. There is still a *honjin* (inn) that was designed to accommodate *daimyo* (feudal lords) during their periodic travels between Kyoto and Tokyo. The *honjin* still functions as a *ryokan* .

Seiken-ji temple has a very pretty landscape garden; it is about one km west of the station.

Fuji

The name of this city sounds inviting, but the place isn't. The only attractions are paper mills and other industries. On a clear day there is a good view of Mt. Fuji from trains and motor vehicles passing the city.

Fuji is a junction of the Tokaido Honsen line and the Minobu line to Kofu and on to Matsumoto. For getting around to the scenic areas north of Mt. Fuji, however, trains cannot be recommended, for travel time can be as long as five hours. The best way to reach the Kawaguchi-ko area is by bus from Fuji or Fujinomiya stations and clockwise around the mountain. In summer, up to three buses a day run out of Fuji along this route; out of season it may be necessary to take a train to Fujinomiya and go from there by bus.

Shizuoka and Shimizu

Tosho-gu Shrine

On the south side of Kuno-zan hill (near the coast), and between Shimizu and Shizuoka (accessible from both cities by bus), is Tosho-gu shrine. Ieyasu Tokugawa was interred here before finally being laid to rest at the magnificent and famous Tosho-gu shrine at Nikko. The shrine, accessible after a climbing more than 1100 steps, is very colorfully decorated, with much gold leaf.

Nihondaira

This is a plateau atop Udo hill, one valley away from Kuno-zan hill. You can get to the top by a cable car that begins near Tosho-gu. Also, buses run across it via Nihondaira Parkway between Shizuoka and Shimizu stations. From the top there is an excellent view of Mt. Fuji in one direction (in clear weather) and the bay and Miho-no-matsubara (a narrow strip of pine forest along the water) in another.

Rinzai-ji Temple
A couple of km to the north of Shimizu station is this temple best known for its beautiful garden. Nearby is Sengen-jinja shrine. Its festival is April 1–5.

Toro
In 1943 the remains of a settlement about 1800 years old were discovered in this area (in the vicinity of Rinzai-ji). Excavations have revealed a lot about life in those days, including the living places of its people. The term "pit dwelling" given to the homes gives the impression of living in squalor, but they were actually built on ground level and earth walls about a meter or so high were built around the base to keep out water. The dwellings were round, with thatched walls built on a wooden framework. Reproductions of such dwellings (and some elevated store houses) can be seen at the park in Toro; the houses were actually quite cosy. The museum has displays of implements excavated from the 16 ha site.

Oi-gawa Valley

One of the only two steam-powered train lines left in Japan, the Oi-gawa Honsen private line, runs through this valley. (The other steam line, the JR Yamaguchi-sen in the far west of Honshu, reverted to special steam runs after being completely dieselized.) In past summers there have been up to four runs in each direction between Kanaya and Senzu, leaving Kanaya at various times between 0955 and 1415, Senzu between 1442 and 1658, taking about 1-1/4 hours each way. Be sure to check the current schedule ahead of time.

The journey through the Oi River val-

ley from Kanaya is pretty, and at Senzu you can continue on a different line where the cars are pulled by a miniature diesel loco. This one really twists and turns, passing over deep chasms and climbing ever higher. Its terminus, Ikawa, is a popular starting place for climbing in the South Japan Alps.

There is a small youth hostel a short distance from Kanaya.

There is little of interest west of this area along the coast until Nagoya, where the narrative picks up again. (See also descriptions of the Kiso and Tenryu-gawa valleys in the Chubu section, both of which lead to the coast near or above Nagoya.)

HAKONE AREA

Hakone, and its nearby attractions, is the closest resort to Tokyo, and is therefore very popular with Japanese holiday makers. Because of its attractiveness to the local population, it is also heavily promoted for visiting foreigners—perhaps too much so in view of the differences in interests between Japanese and visitors.

The major attractions of the Hakone area are good views of Mt. Fuji, Ashinoko lake, some interesting historic remains, and other views of the volcanic terrain. Be warned, though, that much of the beauty and interest of the area comes from having Mt. Fuji as a backdrop, and this mountain is notoriously bashful in spring, summer, and early autumn, often totally obscured by cloud even from close up. Because of this, the later in the season (late-autumn and winter) you visit, the better the chance of seeing the undeniably superb form of Mt. Fuji. Japanese visitors may not be too concerned with missing the view, but foreigners who may only have a short time in Japan should plan their itinerary accordingly.

The following describes a vaguely circular route through the Hakone area that minimizes backtracking. The starting point is Odawara or Yumoto-onsen. Access is by JR and Odakyu train from Tokyo.

Transportation to the Hakone Area

JR

JR services to Odawara were described in the Odawara section, early in the Fuji–Hakone–Izu section. At Odawara station take the Tozan railway (platform 11 or 12) for the trip up the mountain. (It stops en route at Yumoto-onsen, the terminus for Odakyu Romance Car trains.)

Odakyu Line

The Odakyu (Odawara-kyuko) line, running from Shinjuku (Tokyo) Odakyu station, is the most convenient way to start a Hakone trip. Any of its trains can be taken as far as Odawara: 70 minutes for the *Romance Car* train (¥1250), while the local and express Odakyu trains (¥630 and ¥870) take 110 and 75 minutes. The Romance Car trains are the preferred way to go, however, for (in addition to being substantially faster) they continue past Odawara to Hakone-yumoto (¥1280), where the transfer to the Tozan line (see below) is more convenient. The Romance Car train, though more expensive, is considerably more luxurious than the ordinary trains, and this is one case when I can suggest that it is worth spending the extra money for first class. Passengers in the front car can look out through the panorama window at the front of the car.

A good buy for economy and convenience (no need to stand in line for tickets during busy times) is a "Hakone Free Pass". Sold by Odakyu railway, the pass covers the standard Odakyu rail fare (Romance Car or express is extra), plus cable cars, boats, etc., in the area for four days.

An alternative starting point for sightseeing in this region is Togendai, accessible by bus from Tokyo (Shinjuku Highway Bus Center), Gotemba, and Odawara.

Tozan Railway

This one- or two-car train, which resembles a municipal tram, starts from Odawara station. The "little train that could", once into the mountains, struggles valiantly against the steep gradient, groaning all the while. It makes a number of stops along the way to the terminus at Gora, and its route includes three switchbacks. Trains depart Odawara every 20–40 minutes.

The following describes the stops en route and on connecting cable cars, etc., going over the mountain and down the other side to the shore of Ashinoko lake.

Things to See

Miyanoshita

The only (low key) attraction here is the Fujiya Hotel, a five minute walk uphill from the station. It was the first western-style building to be constructed in the Hakone district (1878), and has since had wings added that are more modern, giving an interesting blend of American colonial and Japanese architecture. The main building has the mustiness of age, rather like a dowager who has known better days. It will appeal mostly to those of a nostalgic frame of mind who wish to see how expatriates once spent their summers. The library and its old books are still there, as is one billiard table.

You can have coffee in the first floor lounge overlooking the pond and garden; prices are reasonable. In the lobby there is a display case with a large number of miniature figures playing "native" instruments. (But they are native to Indonesia and Malaysia! They are leftovers from the days when officers from the British colonies vacationed in the cooler Japan mountains to escape the tropical heat.) At basement level

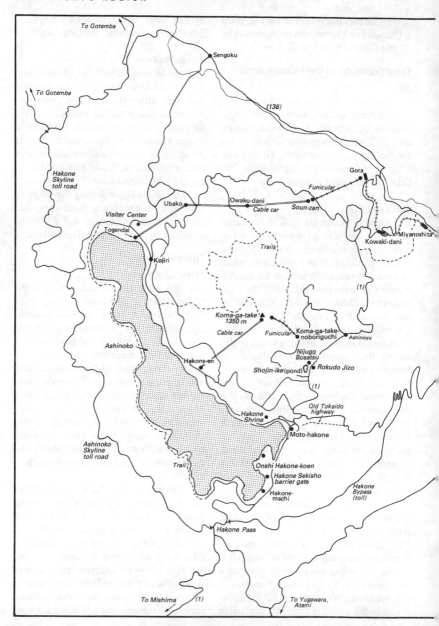

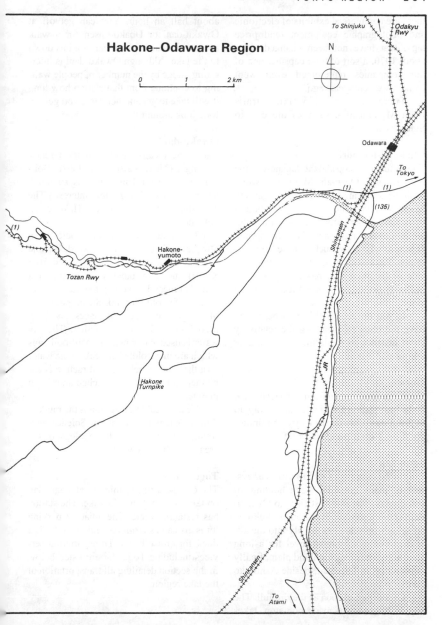

Hakone–Odawara Region

there are commercial exhibits of electronic and photographic equipment (and price tags) that have not been changed since about 1970, a sort of time capsule; one of the companies represented even went bankrupt several years ago.

There are several walking trails from Miyanoshita, such as the one to Sengen-san.

Chokoku-no-mori

This is the train stop and the Japanese name for "Hakone Open-air Museum" where sculptures are arranged around a garden. Many western visitors have spoken highly of it, though the garden and several other attractions are largely aimed at day-tripping Japanese who enjoy such "exotic" western things. Parts of it can be seen from the right side of the train as it passes, so you can probably decide for yourself if it's worth a visit.

If you do get off the train here, you have the choice of walking the relatively short distance to the terminus at Gora or taking a later train.

Gora

Gora, the upper terminus of the Tozan line, is the base station for a funicular railway up to Soun-zan. Cars depart every 15 minutes for the 1.2 km trip and cost ¥280.

Soun-zan

This is the base for a four km cable car system of many gondolas, each holding 10 passengers. The line first rises to Owaku-dani station, passing over Souen-jigoku en route, where steam jets noisily into the air. It then continues almost level for a long span across a rolling highland plain, finally descending to Togendai, beside Ashinoko lake.

Cars depart as soon as they're full. The trip to Togendai, if made non-stop, takes about half an hour. You can get off at Owaku-dani or Ubako-onsen for a walk around and catch a later car or a bus down to the lake. Although Owaku-dani is interesting, judge by the number of people waiting to continue from that station how long it will take to get another car if you get out for a look around.

Owaku-dani

The name means "Valley of the Greater Boiling". (There is also one of Lesser Boiling, the Kowaki-dani, but it is so much lesser that it is of negligible interest.) The "Greater" is the crater of old Hakone-san volcano.

The road and walking route from Owaku-dani station lead upward; on one side is the bus stop (for the bus to and from Kojiri), and on the other is the entrance to a path that meanders among the traces of activity of the old volcano. Steam pours out of the ground in several places, and grey mud boils endlessly at another. The hot water is used at one place to hard-boil eggs which are then sold; chemicals in the water turn the shells black. Each attraction is explained in English on an etched aluminum plaque.

Near the cable car station is the modern Shizen Kagakukan (Natural Science Museum), which explains the geology of the area, as well as the wildlife.

Togendai

The cable-car line terminates at Togendai, on the shore of Ashinoko lake. The station has restaurants, etc. The adjacent parking lot is also a bus terminal, and behind it is a dock for cruise boats. Transportation services including Togendai are listed below in the section detailing all transportation of the lake region.

Hakone-en

The main attraction of Hakone-en is the recreation center with its bowling alleys, swimming pools, golf course, etc. It also has camping facilities. An "International Village" has reproductions of houses from 29 nations, each containing arts and crafts of the country. The recreation center will probably be of very limited interest to short-term visitors (except for the camping) as it is intended primarily for the Japanese, to give them a break from Tokyo with a touch of the exotic west.

Koma-ga-take

Hakone-en is the base station of a cable car (¥610/1030 one way/return) to the top of Koma-ga-take mountain (1327 meters). If the weather is clear, the summit offers a superb view of Mt. Fuji and Ashinoko lake. From the top of Koma-ga-take you can take the funicular railway down to Komagatake-nobori-guchi (¥360/620 one way/return).

Shojin-ike Lake

This lake is almost directly below the base station of the funicular. You can take a bus from nearby Ashinoyu to the lake and the historic stone carvings of the Buddhist deity Jizo. Get off the bus when several carved stone monuments, about the height of a person, come into view; Shojin-ike lake is just around the corner.

Rock Carvings

At the end of the lake closer to Ashinoyu, where the road bends, a path leads down a few meters to a large rock covered with 25 carvings of Buddha; this is called Niju-go Bosatsu. Some are very artistically executed and all are in remarkably fine condition considering their exposure to the elements from the time of the Kamakura era (1192–1333).

About 100 meters along the road (toward Moto-hakone) is a large and benevolent figure of Jizo (*Jizo-sama*), the Buddhist patron of travellers, children, and pregnant women. The figure is about two meters tall and was carved primarily for the benefit of foot travellers in this very difficult mountain terrain. (This was on the Tokaido, one of the main roads from Tokyo to Kyoto and Osaka.) There are several smaller and less interesting figures nearby; together they are known as Rokudo Jizo.

From here, take a bus (or hitch or walk) from the stop on the side nearer Jizo-sama, down to lake level; get off at Sekisho bus stop at the entrance to Hakone-machi town (at the top of a downgrade) and walk along the short street running off the main road toward the lake. This leads to Sekisho barrier gate.

Hakone-machi

Sekisho Barrier Gate

During the Edo era, under the rule of the Tokugawa military government (1600–1868), travel was tightly controlled to prevent the movement of arms and men. Local *daimyo* were compelled to spend part of each year in Edo (Tokyo), effectively as hostages, so there was frequent movement of daimyo and their entourages along this road.

The main checkpoint on the Tokaido highway between Edo and Kyoto was Hakone Sekisho, built in 1619; all travellers had to produce "passports" at this point. The barrier stood until 1869. An exact reproduction was built in 1965 across the road from the original site. Wax figures dressed in period costume show how things looked at the time.

Nearby is the dock for the regular cruise boats to Kojiri and Hakone-en.

Hakone Shiryokan

A short distance up the road (or along the lake shore) from the barrier gate is this small museum housing materials related to the gate. Most are unintelligible to foreigners and of little interest, but there are some firearms and armor, etc. The same ticket allows admittance to both the museum and the barrier display.

Onshi-Hakone-koen

This is a park next to the museum, with peaceful walking paths through a small forest. During clear weather this area offers a good view of the upper part of Mt. Fuji, complete with reflection in the lake.

During my last visit there I was amused to see beautiful paintings of the lake, the opposite shore, and Mt. Fuji, on the easels of a school class. The children had obviously been well prepared for their trip and were determined to portray the beauty of the area, despite the fact that they actually couldn't see more than 50 meters in front of them due to fog over the lake!

Sugi-namiki

Just a short distance beyond the garden is the entrance to a section of the old Tokaido highway that runs parallel to the modern road for half a km between Hakone-machi and Moto-hakone. It is lined with majestic cryptomeria (cedar) trees that were planted in 1618 to provide shade for travellers. The trees make the walk to Moto-hakone town most enjoyable. From the shore at Moto-hakone, near the bus station, you get the best shoreside view of Mt. Fuji in the area.

Moto-hakone

Hakone-jinja Shrine

A short walk from Moto-hakone (and about two km from Hakone-en and the Koma-ga-take base station) is Hakone-jinja. The present main building dates from 1667, though the shrine is believed to date from the eighth century. The buildings are not particularly noteworthy as shrines go, but the mysterious atmosphere of the place is. The path is lined with venerable cedars, and the shrine is set among equally huge trees, dating from the 17th century.

There is a picturesque red torii gate in the lake just offshore. Be satisfied looking at it from a distance as it is made of practical but unromantic concrete.

The shrine festival takes place on August 31 when lanterns are set adrift on the lake as part of the *obon* ceremonies.

Old Tokaido Highway

A short distance up the hillside road from the lakeside bus terminal of Moto-hakone (by the large torii) is the beginning of a stretch of the original Tokaido road. A pedestrian overpass leads up to it. Because of the hill, the road was paved with stones for a considerable distance to make walking easier and to prevent rain from destroying the path.

Most people will be content with a look and a photo at the beginning, but a walk of about 20 minutes takes you to a coffee shop and restaurant in a traditional-style building that also houses Edo era exhibits. Buses return to Moto-hakone and also go to Odawara (opposite direction), but service is not frequent, about two an hour until mid-afternoon.

Places to Stay

There are many hotels, *ryokan* , and *minshuku* of all price ranges in the many hot-spring resort towns and other centers in the area. The most famous is the Fujiya at Miyanoshita, the oldest hotel in the area, while the most luxurious might be the Prince beside the lake. As for all accommodation in Japan, reservations may be made in advance through any travel agent in the country (and would be recommended due to the great numbers going to this area).

There is a youth hostel at Soun-zan, very close to the base station of the cable car to Owaku-dani, (tel. (0460) 2-3827).

Transportation Beyond Hakone

From the Hakone-machi/Moto-hakone area there is a variety of ways to continue.

The following summarizes transportation services around the lake and between the lake and "the outside world". Some of these are seasonal, and may not run during the colder months. Prices go up yearly, so these are only a guide.

Togendai

Buses run between Togendai and Odawara (¥970; 60 minutes) at 10 to 20 minute intervals through the day (until about 2045 in summer from Togendai), following a route over the mountain via Sengoku and Miyanoshita (roughly parallel to the Tozan railway).

About nine buses per day run between Togendai and Gotemba station (¥780; 45 minutes) via Sengoku, but the last one from Togendai is not much after 1600.

Boats run at about 40 minute intervals through the day (final sailing: 1730 pm from Togendai) along the lake following the route Togendai-(50 minutes)–Hakone-machi–(10 minutes)–Moto-hakone. The fare to either from Togendai is ¥850; between Hakone-machi and Moto-hakone it is ¥250.

Check for local buses running along the shore to connect to the other towns along the shore (Moto-hakone, etc.).

Kojiri

Another boat service runs from Kojiri to Hakone-en, Moto-hakone and Hakone-sekisho-ato (¥600, ¥800 and ¥800).

About 23 buses per day run between Kojiri and Odawara over the mountain via Owaku-dani, Miyanoshita, and Hakone-yumoto. About 10 of these buses start/finish at Hakone-en (toward Moto-hakone from Kojiri). The fare Odawara–Kojiri (55 minutes) is ¥900; Odawara–Hakone-en (65 minutes) is ¥1000. To/from Hakone-yumoto will be somewhat less.

Hakone-machi/Moto-hakone

There are two bus services between these two places and Odawara (via Hakone-yumoto), both going over the mountain, but following slightly different routes; the station for Koma-ga-take is listed for one (but only a single bus per day is shown as stopping there), and some of the buses start from the barrier gate, Sekisho). Service is every 15 to 30 minutes until after 2000. The fare to Odawara is ¥920 (60 min; 40 min to Hakone-yumoto).

Buses also go from the Ashinoko area south to Atami via two routes. From Moto-hakone/Sekisho there are regular buses south (about 12/day) via a route over the mountains, passing through Jukkoku-toge pass with its good views of Mt. Fuji (in clear weather). One of the stops is Jukkoku-toge-nobori-guchi, the base station for a funicular railway up to a scenic viewpoint. The bus trip takes an hour and costs ¥900.

The alternative route is the bus from Moto-hakone/Hakone-machi via Yugawara (one hour, ¥1000) to Atami (85 minutes, ¥1150).

About 8 buses a day run from Moto-hakone/Hakone-machi to Mishima (50 minutes) and Numazu (75 minutes); the highest fare is Moto-hakone–Numazu (¥1050), and is less to/from Hakone-machi and/or Mishima.

MT. FUJI AREA

Every visitor to Japan wants to see Mt. Fuji, or Fuji-san as the Japanese call it (*never* Fuji-yama!). It is the symbol of Japan recognised universally and is truly one of the world's most beautiful mountains. It was revered, understandably, for centuries as a sacred peak, and is a spectacular sight no matter how many times you see it.

Almost the ideal of what a volcano should look like, the now dormant Fuji-san last erupted in 1707, covering the streets of Tokyo 100 km away with a thick layer of black volcanic soot. Its symmetrical, snow-capped cone rises 3776 meters from an almost perfectly round base. Around its north side are five lakes, Fuji-go-ko, that add their own beauty.

Several places offer superb views of the mountain: from the Shinkansen as it passes near Fuji city; from the Tomei expressway; from Nihondaira, near Shizuoka; from several places in the north-west corner of the Izu-hanto peninsula; from several places in the Hakone area; from Nagao-toge pass, between Hakone and Gotemba.

There are also clear views from many points along the roads that nearly encircle the mountain, chiefly beside Yamanaka-ko, and between Yamanaka-ko and Sai-ko lakes. West of Sai-ko the view is not as good because of a "shoulder" at the base of the cone which diminishes the symmetry seen from other directions.

Visitors should be forewarned, however, that the famous volcano is very bashful for most of the year. In spring, summer, and early autumn, Fuji-san is usually partly or totally obscured by clouds, even from close up.

Access

From the Tokyo area, the two major access routes to the Mt. Fuji area are Fuji-yoshida/Kawaguchi-ko, and Gotemba. The former can be considered the main one of the two

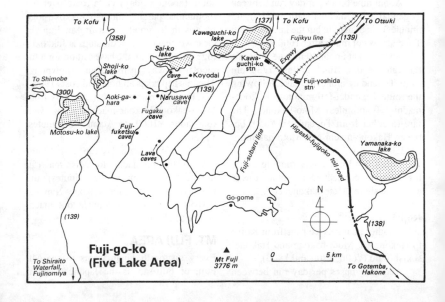

for sightseeing if you don't plan to climb Mt. Fuji. Refer to the end of the section for information on transportation to the places mentioned.

Gotemba

Gotemba is a typical, rather nondescript, Japanese city, with no particular attraction apart from providing a bus connection to Shin-go-gome ("New Fifth Station"), which has become the favorite starting point for the ascent of Fuji-san. (Bus services to Shin-go-gome and the older Go-gome are detailed in the section on climbing the mountain.) Going by road, views of Mt. Fuji are negligible or unexciting almost anywhere in the vicinity of Gotemba itself. From the city, the road climbs for several km to the tableland (Gotemba-kogen) that surrounds much of the mountain, which finally comes into clear view near Yamanaka-ko lake.

Travellers with a limited amount of time to see Mt. Fuji and the lake area would probably be best advised to go directly to Fuji-yoshida from Tokyo, but if time permits a route from Gotemba past Yamanaka-ko will give a more complete view. There are about 24 buses a day between Gotemba and Fuji-yoshida; most of these go farther in each direction—to/from Mishima (1-1/2 hours south of Gotemba) and to/from Kawaguchi-ko (10 minutes west of Fuji-yoshida).

Yamanaka-ko

This lake, and the resort town on its shore, is a popular recreation area, offering swimming, boating, coffee shops, and other kinds of sports (tennis, for example) and other entertainment that appeals to young Japanese. Rental boats and water-skiing are available by the hour. There are many *minshuku*, pension, etc., in the area, but reservations will likely be necessary due to its popularity with young people.

Fuji-yoshida

The only role of this city is as a transportation center, other than its annual festival on August 31. The many bus services to/from it for travel around the north side of Mt. Fuji are described later in this section.

Fujikyu Highland Amusement Park

This park is more of interest to residents than to visitors (except perhaps those with children). It is close to both the bus station and Fujikyu Highland station of the train line between Otsuki and Kawaguchi-ko (which is understandable since the Fujikyu railway built the amusement park to attract money).

Kawaguchi-ko Lake

This is the second largest of Fuji-go-ko (Fuji five lakes) and is a popular resort with Tokyo residents.

Kawaguchiko-machi Town

The largest town on the lake is Kawaguchi-ko. Close to Kawaguchi-ko station, the terminus of the Fuji-Kyuko railway line, is a cable car providing access to the top of Tenjo-san mountain, where a lookout offers a superb view of Mt. Fuji and the lake.

Also of interest in the town are two museums. Fuji Hakubutsukan, in front of Fuji Lake Hotel, has exhibitions related to the people, geology, etc., of the area. It is noted for the Amano collection of erotic items from bygone days. This is a good opportunity to see some aspects of the large role that fertility symbols played in the lives of the Japanese not so long ago. Such symbols of this very earthy element in Japanese society are not commonly seen these days, though its physical expression remains very popular and supports a large industry. The museum is a 10 minute

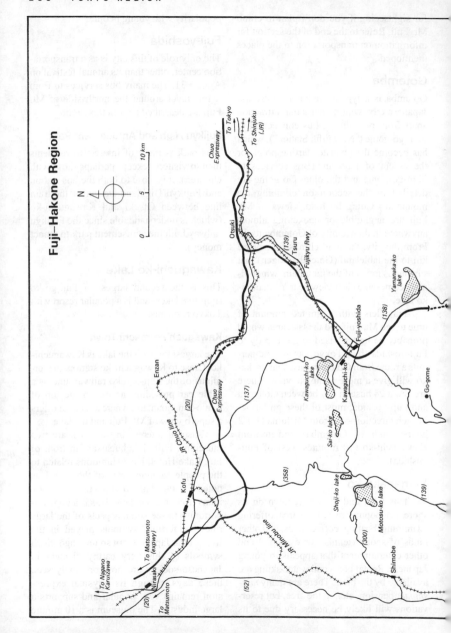

Fuji–Hakone Region

N

0   5   10 km

To Tokyo

To Shinjuku (JR)

Chuo Expressway

Otsuki

Tsuru

(139)

Fujikyu Rwy

Fuji-yoshida

(138)

Yamanaka-ko lake

Enzan

Chuo Expressway

(137)

Kawaguchi-ko lake

Kawaguchi-ko

Sai-ko lake

Go-gome

JR Chuo line

(20)

Kofu

(358)

Shoji-ko lake

Motosu-ko lake

(300)

(139)

JR Minobu line

(52)

Shimobe

To Matsumoto (expwy)

To Nagano Karuizawa

Nirasaki

(20)

To Matsumoto

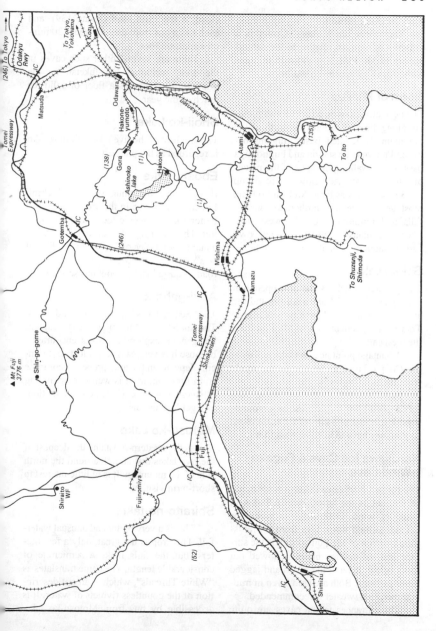

walk from the station.

Yamanashi-ken Visitors' Center is a museum of material relating to the natural history of Mt. Fuji. It is about 15 minutes walk from Kawaguchi-ko station.

North of Mt. Fuji

The next attractions lie west of Kawaguchi-ko, along the road around the north of the mountain. Scheduled buses running between Fuji-yoshida station and Fujinomiya pass within walking distance of the places of interest mentioned below. There are up to 13 buses a day as far as Motosu-ko lake; most go considerably farther, to Shiraito falls and Fujinomiya on the west side. There are many sightseers in their own cars, so hitching should be no problem.

Sai-ko Lake

This picturesque lake is less developed than Kawaguchi-ko and Yamanaka-ko, and the area around it is still largely wilderness. There is an excellent view of Mt. Fuji from the west end.

A vantage point near the lake is Koyodai (Maple Hill), along one of the roads from the main highway.

Saiko Youth Hostel is close by and offers a good view in picturesque surroundings. It is about two km off the main road, so you may have to hitch or walk to it.

Narusawa Ice Cave & Fugaku Wind Cave

The former, Narusawa Fuketsu is not made of ice, nor is the latter, Fugaku Fuketsu, made of wind. Both are lava tubes (or caves), formed when lava from a prehistoric eruption of Mt. Fuji cooled on the surface and still-molten material flowed out from below, leaving the rough and jagged inner surfaces. Both are cold, even in midsummer, so a sweater is recommended.

The entrances to the caves are quite close to the main road (Route 139), and each has a bus stop; they are about 20 minutes apart on foot.

There are several other such caves in the area, including Fuji-fuketsu on the Shoji trail, which has a floor of solid ice much of the year.

Shoji-ko Lake

The smallest of the five lakes of Fuji-go-ko is regarded as the prettiest.

Eboshi-dake

If you have the time, you could climb Eboshi-san to take in the view from Shoji Panorama, the scenic lookout at the summit. There is a superb view over the Aoki-gahara Jukai ("Sea of Trees") to Mt. Fuji. It is a climb of 60 to 90 minutes from the road. Inquire locally about bus services.

Aoki-gahara

The "Sea of Trees" is an area of wild forest. The Shoji trail to Mt. Fuji passes through it, but general exploration is not encouraged because it is very easy to get lost, and mineral deposits in the area prevent a compass from functioning. It is well known among Japanese as a place where people intentionally get lost and die.

Motosu-ko Lake

This is the western-most and the deepest of the five lakes that stretch around the north side of the mountain. It is of little interest to short-term visitors.

Shiraito-no-taki

This is a very pretty and unusual waterfall. The drop is not great, only a few meters, but the falls make a semicircle of considerable length. The name translates as "White Threads", which is an apt description of the countless rivulets of water. It is accessible by bus from Motosu-ko lake.

Nearby is another waterfall, Otodome-no-taki.

Fujinomiya

This city is of no inherent interest other than as a starting point for buses to Shingo-gome.

GETTING THERE & GETTING AROUND

Gotemba and Fuji-yoshida/Kawaguchi-ko can be reached by both train and bus from Tokyo.

Gotemba

ODAKYU TRAINS Though few in number, the most convenient services to Gotemba are the four daily expresses from Shinjuku (Tokyo) which, instead of veering south to Odawara at Shin-matsuda, switch to the JR tracks at Matsuda and run directly to Gotemba. These take about 1-1/2 hours and cost about ¥2000.

Other Odakyu trains can be taken as far as Shin-matsuda, from where you need to change to the JR Gotemba-sen line at adjacent Matsuda station.

JR By JR to Gotemba the most convenient service is one of the two daily expresses from Tokyo station or one of the four from Shinjuku station. There are also ordinary Tokaido Honsen line trains from Tokyo to Kozu, with a change to the Gotemba line. There are about 15 local trains a day from Kozu to Gotemba via Matsuda, which take about one hour.

BUS Gotemba can be reached by the highway bus that runs along the Tomei expressway from Tokyo to Nagoya. The buses do not go into Gotemba, but stop at a turn-off on the expressway, from where passengers can walk a short distance to the local road and local transportation. Gotemba station is about one km from Tomei-Gotemba bus stop.

Fuji-yoshida and Kawaguchi-ko

TRAIN
The simplest way of reaching the area is by one of the four direct JR expresses from Shinjuku (Tokyo). If you take one of these trains note that the train is separated into two parts at Otsuki, so be sure that you are in the correct end.

There is also the JR Chuo Honsen line to Otsuki, where you change to the Fuji-Kyuko (Fujikyu) line for the rest of the trip.

BUS During the summer there is very good service from the Shinjuku Bus Terminal to Fujikyu Highland bus terminal. Many of these continue on to Kawaguchi-ko and Yamanaka-ko, lesser numbers to Motosu-ko. One or more go to "old" Go-gome on the north side of Mt. Fuji. The fare to Kawaguchi-ko is ¥1450, to Yamanaka-ko is ¥1700 and to Go-gome is ¥2100. (There are many extra runs on some days, so it is necessary to consult a detailed timetable to determine how many there on a given day.)

Between Kofu (to the north of Kawaguchi-ko) and Fuji-yoshida/Kawaguchi-ko there are about 17 buses a day (90 minutes, ¥1200). Kofu is a major stop on the way to Matsumoto.

CLIMBING MT. FUJI

The Japanese have a saying to the effect "He who climbs Mt. Fuji once is a wise man. He who climbs it more than once is a fool".

Those foreigners who believe they are wise will be pleased to know the ascent of Fuji-san is not too difficult.

There are two major starting points, (old) Go-gome ("fifth station") on the north flank, and Shin-go-gome ("new fifth station") on the south flank. From these places the climb is little more than five km, takes just over five hours, and is mostly a matter of putting one foot in front of the other.

The "official" climbing season is through July and August, when the weather is predictable and the conditions not hazardous to climbers wearing normal cool weather clothes. There are no restrictions on climbers, and people do climb throughout the year. Out of season, however, the high altitude can cause very rapid changes in the weather, and the temperatures can plunge rapidly. There is a definite risk of strong snowfall, blizzards, etc. If you do decide to climb in winter, make sure that you take all the necessary precautions; every year climbers die on the mountain because of insufficient preparation.

Anyone in reasonably good health can make the climb, and there is no danger of getting lost, for there is a continual stream of climbers.

Most people used to make the climb during the day, but increasing numbers now begin climbing well after dark and continue through the night, planning/hoping to watch the sunrise from the top or flank of the mountain. There are huts at various places along the upper reaches of the major trails, but they are crowded, do not have a good reputation for cleanliness, and everyone gets turfed out at a very early hour anyway. (One foreign visitor wrote to the Japan Times complaining that the hut-keeper had very rudely blocked him from entering because he was a foreigner.) By starting around midnight or a bit earlier, you may avoid the need to stop for a sleep.

The major aim of climbing Fuji-san is to witness the experience of *goraiko*, the sunrise. But, although the sunrise is so often spoken of, the fact is that in early morning the top is often enshrouded in mist and visibility is not good until later in the

morning. One guide who has made the climb several times (from the north side) recommends watching the sunrise from Hachigome, the eighth station.

The descent can be made more quickly on the north side than the south because a large patch of the mountain side is covered with volcanic sand and you can slide down it very quickly. This is called *sunabashiri* ("sliding on sand").

In olden times before buses went to points high up on the sides, it was customary to walk the distance from the railway stations and then climb to the top. Several trails still exist, but these days they would be better regarded as hiking paths for a day's outing (without climbing). The best known such trails are the Yoshida trail from Fuji-yoshida station, the Kawaguchi trail from the town of that name (it joins the Yoshida trail at the sixth station), the Shoji trail from the Shoji-ko lake area (which passes Fuji-fuketsu cave along the way), and Gotemba trail from Gotemba. There is also a circular trail around the mountain about half way up.

The following description of climbing Mt. Fuji is reprinted with kind permission of Jean Pearce who writes a regular column in the *Japan Times* and has produced well-regarded guides for exploring Tokyo on foot.

I know what I should have been doing a year ago. I should have been jogging every morning, doing deep knee bends and running up the subway steps in preparation for what everyone should do once but never twice—climb Mt. Fuji. But I know now how to answer this question: What should I take along on the climb?

You don't need much of anything, but you must be a stoic if that is your choice. We climbed in the heat of late July but it was freezing after the sun went down. You can have a year's variety of weather—it rains, the sun beats down, you'll be groping in the mists. Be sure to have a cover-all plastic raincoat. After the storm, you can put it between the layers of your clothing when you get cold to seal in your body warmth, if you have any. And beware of the sun. Have a hat to shade your face and wear long sleeves. Even on a hazy day, Fuji-san's sun can inflict a painful burn.

You can buy lemons, hard boiled eggs, soft drinks, beer and sake, and such standard foods as soba and oden. Prices are high but remember, you didn't have to carry them. Take along foods that don't spoil easily such as cheese, cucumbers, nuts, chocolate and sliced meat, and a bottle of water. Toilet facilities are adequate, but don't expect them to be clean or to flush.

Take gloves. Climbing Fuji is not a stroll; you'll be pulling yourself along with a chain over some rocky areas. You'll want them if you come down by way of the lava slide in case you fall. Cinders can leave scars with the persistence of a tattoo. Have a backpack so your hands will be free, and outer clothing with plenty of pockets for immediate necessities like tissue and money. For your feet, sturdy hiking boots and two or three pairs of wool sox.

Accommodations are cozy, your own futon on your own tatami mat in friendly proximity with a hundred or so other hikers. If you don't have reservations at the top, stop early to be sure of space, and don't necessarily believe the resthouse keeper who tells you there is room at the next station. He does not know. Some like to sleep a few hours along the way and finish the climb the next morning before dawn. Since dawn usually arrives about 4:30 a.m., it seems easier to me to do it all in one piece.

Be prepared for an early morning at the summit as well. Someone will likely be pulling off your covers at, say, 3 a.m.

(that's morning?) and if you don't get up then, attendants will be back for your futon some 10 minutes later. The room must be readied for breakfast service for the morning climbers who are just arriving.

There are 10 stations but don't be lulled by that statistic as you look up and count. You can't see the top from the bottom, and there are a number of resthouses between each official station that can delude the unwary.

Climbing the mountain on the same day I did—I climbed with a group from the Press Club and recommend that you find companions—were four blind men, two boys with their bicycles (later I saw them riding around the summit), a one-legged man, an 88-year-old lady and a gentleman of 93. Not everyone gets to the top, but it is worth all the exertion you can extend to make it.

I don't believe there is a mirror on all of Fuji-san, except perhaps a sacred one in the shrine at the top. But it doesn't matter. You won't care after a while. At one stop I saw a woman powdering her nose. It looked pretty silly.

The best season to climb Mt. Fuji? There isn't one. Climb it early in the official season (it begins on July 1 and ends on August 31) and it's bitterly cold; later you'll likely have rain, perhaps a typhoon and pathways lined with discards of earlier climbers, though it wasn't the huge garbage heap that I expected, thanks in part to the tractors that, unseen, ply the back slopes carrying up supplies and returning at least some of the empty bottles. You will still marvel at the old men who jog up the mountains with three cases of beer and a dozen liter-bottles of sake on their backs for their resthouse concession; their sons, if they stay on the mountain, hire the tractor.

Oh yes, on the way back, it took us 4-1/2 hours by bus from the fifth station to the highway at the foot of the mountain, nor-

*mally a 20 minute drive. Sturdy climbers
make the summit in less. When you climb
Mt. Fuji be prepared for anything. Gan-
batte!*

Getting There

There is direct access to Mt. Fuji's base stations from Tokyo, and regular bus services
from the nearby towns.

Note: These bus frequencies are representative of mid-summer schedules, and
buses are likely to be much less frequent at
other times of the year. Be sure to check
with *jikokuhyo* or a source of travel information.

To Go-gome (North Side)

From Kawaguchiko station there are 14
buses a day (¥1560). The latest of these
during the peak climbing season arrives
shortly before 2200, obviating the need to
sleep at any of the huts.

From Hamamatsucho Bus Terminal
and Shinjuku Highway Bus Terminal (both
in Tokyo), buses go directly to Go-gome
(¥2160/2340) in three hours or less. There
are many other buses from the Shinjuku
terminal (and a few from Hamamatsucho)
to a number of locations, mainly the various lakes, in the vicinity of the mountain.

To Shin-go-gome

From Gotemba station there are two different services via different routes to Shin-go-
gome. One takes 45 minutes and costs
¥1300, the other 70 minutes and ¥2380.
The last of these arrives in the late afternoon.

From Mishima station there are several
buses a day (numbers depending on the
week and day) to Shin-go-gome, the last
one arriving as late as 2005 (two hours,
¥2300).

From Fujinomiya station there are also
several buses a day (again, numbers depending on the day) to Shin-go-gome
(western entrance) the last arriving as late
as 1940 (about 95 minutes, ¥2380).

CONTINUING NORTHWEST FROM MT. FUJI

From the Mt. Fuji area there are many further destinations. Those to the east, south
and southwest have been described. It is
easy to continue northwest through Kofu to
Matsumoto and the many other interesting
places described later in the Central Honshu chapter.

Kofu

Near Kofu is a scenic gorge, Shosen-kyo.
The most scenic part begins at Sen-ga-taki
waterfall and continues for four km through
the rocky gorge. Access to the entrance is
by bus from Kofu station. Kofu can be
reached from the Mt. Fuji area by bus (up
to 17 a day; ¥1350) from Fuji-yoshida/Fuji
Highland/Kawaguchiko. It is also served by
many daily buses from Shinjuku Bus Terminal and JR trains.

SAITAMA-KEN

This section covers the Chichibu-Tama
National Park, Kawagoe, and Sakitama
Kofun-koen. Other attractions of Saitama-
ken are included in descriptions of the
Nagano-ken and Tochigi-ken (Nikko) areas
in later chapters.

Chichibu-Tama National Park

This large national park is located northeast of Kofu and Yamanashi. It is divided
into two sections, Chichibu and Okutama,
in parallel valleys. Both offer enjoyable nature walks and are especially popular with
day-tripping Tokyo residents. A hiking trail
extends between the two sections of the
park.

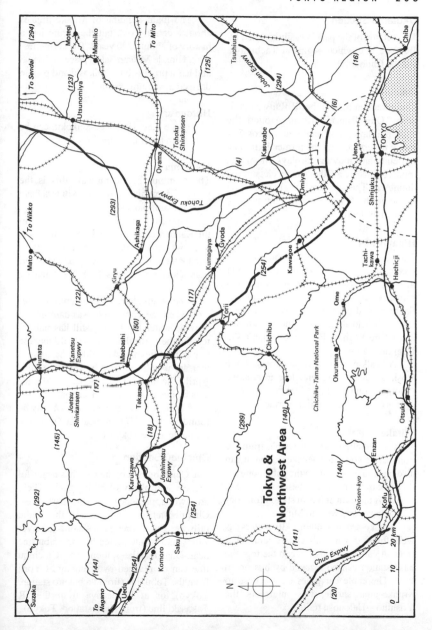

Tokyo & Northwest Area

Chichibu-Tama National Park

Shōsen-kyo

Shinkansen

Tohoku Shinkansen

Tohoku Expwy

Kanetsu Expwy

Joetsu Shinkansen

Joshinetsu Expwy

Chuo Expwy

Joban Expwy

To Sendai
To Nikko
To Mito
To Nagano

Motegi
Mashiko
Utsunomiya
Oyama
Tsuchiura
Chiba
TOKYO
Ueno
Shinjuku
Kasukabe
Omiya
Ashikaga
Mato
Kiryu
Kumagaya
Gyoda
Kawagoe
Tachi-kawa
Hachioji
Maebashi
Toni
Chichibu
Ome
Okutama
Numata
Takasaki
Karuizawa
Enzan
Otsuki
Kofu
Suzaka
Ueda
Komoro
Saku

(294)
(123)
(125)
(294)
(16)
(6)
(293)
(4)
(254)
(122)
(17)
(50)
(171)
(145)
(18)
(299)
(140)
(254)
(141)
(140)
(292)
(144)
(254)
(20)

N

0   10   20 km

Okutama Section

This section of the park is easily reached by JR Ome line which begins at Tachikawa (on the Chuo line).

Ome

The attraction here is the JR Railway Museum, Ome Tetsudo Koen. Around the main building are several steam locos formerly in service with the former JNR. The museum has moving displays of model trains. Meals are available in an elegant old dining car. The museum is in Hikawa-koen to the north of the city, a 15 minute walk from Ome station.

Hinatawada

The general appearance of the town is scenic, with a low mountain looming over it. The town is famed for its plum blossoms, which attract many visitors in late February and early March. An interesting festival is held at this time. The best known groves are Yoshino Bai-en, less than a km from the station.

A walking trail extends beyond the Yoshino area via several low mountains (Sampo, Hinode, and Mitake). The trail passes close to Mitake-jinja shrine.

Mitake

Mitake-keikoku (gorge) is visible from the train before you reach Mitake station; it can also be seen on foot from the path along either side of the river. The best way to see is to get off the train at Sawai station (one before Mitake) and walk to Mitake.

Mitake-san mountain (930 meters) is well forested with tall cedars and other trees. A cable car runs close to the top; the base station can be reached by bus or on foot. The cable car gives easy access to Mitake-jinja shrine; this intersects the Yoshino—Hatonosu trail.

The main building of Mitake-jinja is about a century old, but the shrine has a history of about 1200 years. The shrine festival, Hinode Matsuri, takes place on May 8 and has a procession of mikoshi and people dressed in samurai armor.

Hatonosu

The gorge here, Hatonosu-keikoku, can be seen from the train or on foot.

Okutama

The terminus of the railway, this is the point of departure by bus for Nippara cave and Okutama-ko lake.

Nippara shonyudo is the largest cave in the Kanto area; it is lit for about 280 meters to allow exploration. The area is pretty in late October when the leaves change color. It is about 40 minutes from Okutama by bus.

The south shore of Okutama-ko, created when the Tama river was dammed to provide water for Tokyo, still has natural terrain; the north shore has typical Japanese tourist facilities and about 6000 cherry trees that are usually at their best around mid-April. The lake can be reached in 20 minutes by bus from Okutama station.

Further information on the area may be found in the JNTO publication *Okutama*, available at the Tokyo TIC.

Chichibu Section

The Chichibu part of the park has beautiful scenery and plenty of hiking trails. There are two approaches into the park area: Chichibu-tetsudo railway and the Seibu railway. The former passes along the river valley and is intersected by the Seibu line near Ohanabatake station. The Chichibu line can be reached by changing at Yorii from the Tobu line (from Ikebukuro station, Tokyo), or at Kumagaya from the JR Takasaki line (from Ueno station, Tokyo).

By Seibu line from Shinjuku station (Tokyo) the trip takes 1-1/2 hours by limited express, longer by local train. By JR it takes about two hours, and slightly less by the Tobu line.

The Chichibu line route (described below) takes in more and is the only way to reach Mitsumine-guchi, the innermost station.

Nagatoro

Several attractions are accessible from stations near Nagatoro. Near Nogami station is Nagatoro Sogo Hakubutsukan, a small museum of rocks and fossils. A similar museum is Chichibu Shizen Kagakukan (Natural History Museum), five minutes from Kami-nagatoro station.

Nagatoro is well known for its nearby scenery, which features sheer rock faces and interestingly-shaped rocks, including a "rock garden"—a famous rock formation near the river. It is about five minutes from Nagatoro station. The area is beautiful in spring when blossoms deck a line of cherry trees that stretch 1-1/2 km from Nagatoro to Kami-nagatoro, in summer when the azaleas are in full bloom, and in autumn when the leaves turn amazing colors.

An excellent view of the area may be had from Hodo-san. A cable car goes to the top of the mountain; its base station is easily reached by bus from Nagatoro station. Hodo-jinja shrine is close to the upper station.

Kami-nagatoro

A boat ride through the rapids of the Arakawa river is available from either end of the Oyabana-bashi bridge, taking 25–30 minutes. The terminus is Takasago-bashi bridge.

Chichibu

The main attraction of the city is Chichibu-jinja, 200 meters west of the station, one of the three most famous shrines of the area (along with Hodo-jinja at Nagatoro and Mitsumine-jinja). It is noted for large buildings and its tall, old trees. Its night festival of December 3 is well-known throughout Japan for the procession of lantern-lit *dashi*, ornate historic festival wagons.

Chichibu Shiyakusho Minzoku Hakubutsukan, the Municipal Folk Museum, has good displays of articles traditionally used by people of the area in their daily life. It can be reached quickly by taxi or on foot in 40 minutes.

There are two good hiking trails, a relatively short one near Buko-zan, and another that joins the Chichibu and Okutama areas.

The starting point of the shorter trail is Yokoze station of the Seibu line. It climbs to the top of Buko-zan (1336 meters), passes Mitake-jinja and the entrance to Hashidate stalactite cavern, then descends to Urayama-guchi station (Seibu line). In addition to picturesque mountain scenery, the area around the cavern has a Karst-type topography with large outcroppings of limestone that resemble sheep or tombstones when seen from a distance. (Similar terrain can be found in west Honshu and northern Kyushu.) The cavern may be explored.

The hiking trail to Okutama, called Okuchichibu Ginza, stretches between the two sections of the park. From the Chichibu end it begins at Mitsumine-guchi station (the terminus of the Chichibu line). You can climb to Mitsumine-san on foot or take the cable car. Mitsumine-jinja can be visited along the way; it has a history of about 2000 years. When Buddhism and Shinto were intertwined, it was the center for ascetic *yamabushi* pilgrims and priests of the Tendai sect of Buddhism; some may be seen today, and halls on the grounds serve priests and pilgrims as well as climbers and hikers.

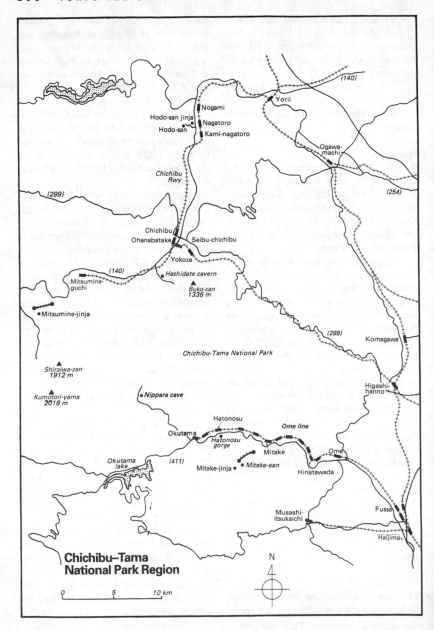

Chichibu–Tama
National Park Region

0   5   10 km

N

The trail is about 10 km long, and passes along the ridges that stretch between mountains. The trail splits between Shira-iwa-zan and Kumotori-yama, one fork going to Nippara, the other toward Oku-tama-ko lake. The trail is well signposted and there are several lodges and huts along the way.

Points along the route are listed in detail in the JNTO publication *Chichibu*, available at the Tokyo TIC. Many areas like this that offer good hiking are covered by detailed maps that may be purchased at map specialists in large cities. They are often only in Japanese, but the general features can be readily understood.

Hikes in this and other areas in the Tokyo area are described in publications listed in the Books section.

Kawagoe

Kawagoe is notable for a number of heavily-walled, tiled-roof shop buildings on and near the main street that are more than a century old. For a glimpse of "old Japan", a visit to Kawagoe can be recommended. The old buildings are shops of various kinds and can be inspected from inside.

In addition to walking around the town looking at the charming old buildings, Kita-in temple is worth a visit to see its attractive main building and garden, visible from an elevated corridor. On the grounds is the garden of Go-hyaku rakan with 500 statues of people, about 40 cm tall, in a variety of poses. They represent people who had suffered through famine, and are a little unusual. A hand-out publication gives the history.

A new municipal museum has exhibits ranging from prehistory through the modern times of Kawagoe. The building is interesting architecturally, and has a nice (if small) garden.

Kawagoe has an interesting annual festival on November 15 and 16. On display around the city on those days are 23 or so *dashi*—incredibly ornate festival wagons, some of which are prefectural treasures about 200 years old. On the second night of the festival the wagons are pulled through the streets, some in each direction of the route so that they pass each other. At every encounter, the costumed dancer on each wagon tries to out-perform the other. Each wagon carries its own musicians and supply of sake, so these performances become increasingly enthusiastic as the night wears on.

The festival dates back to 1648 and is typical of several that used to be held in the area, including in Tokyo. The dashi in Tokyo were destroyed during the war, however, so the Kawagoe festival is the only survivor.

Getting There

From Tokyo, the most convenient way to get to Kawagoe is by the Seibu line from Shinjuku, as its terminus (Hon-kawagoe) is closest to the center of the city. Alternatives are the Tobu railway (Tojo line) from Ike-bukuro (Tokyo) to Kawagoe station, or by JR from Ueno station (Tokyo) to Omiya, with a change of train to the Kawagoe line, to Kawagoe or Kawagoe-shi stations. (Many trains of the Yurakucho subway line continue to Kawagoe on the Tobu tracks, but stopping at every station; it would be faster to change to an express at Ike-bukuro.)

Sakitama Kofun-koen

The Kanto plain has been settled for more than 2000 years, as shown by excavations of ancient relics throughout the region. One of the three largest clusters of ancient tomb mounds in Japan (a custom for several centuries from the third) can be found near Gyoda, consisting of eight burial mounds plus a museum of artefacts dug up in the area.

Getting There

Sakitama Kofun-koen (Sakitama Tomb Park) is reached by taking a JR train (Takasaki-sen line) from Ueno station to Fukiage station, then changing to a bus bound for Gyoda via Sama. The stop is Sangyo-doro; from there the park is a 15 minute walk.

CHIBA-KEN ▬▬▬▬▬

Curving around Tokyo Bay to the east of Tokyo is Chiba-ken. The areas adjacent to Tokyo (Chiba-shi city and beyond) are largely residential suburbs. Much of the rest of the peninsula is used for market gardening of vegetables and flowers. There are excellent beaches on the south-east and east coasts, but attractions for tourists are otherwise quite thin on the ground and the area is of interest mainly to Tokyo residents looking for a weekend excursion.

Chiba

Chiba city is noted for its many "soaplands", which offer the ultimate service of brothels but with a greater element of fantasy fulfillment. They can't be wholeheartedly recommended to foreigners because of the language problem which might result in refused admission or apparent overcharging for special favors. With suitable male Japanese companions, however, it might be an interesting (but pricey) way for a foreign man to delve into other aspects of Japanese society. (Such places are also tending to refuse entry to foreigners because AIDS is generally regarded in Japan as exclusively a "foreigner's disease". There is an element of xenophobia at work here.)

Sakura

The city of Sakura is the site of an excellent place to visit for those interested in Japanese history. The National History Museum is very large and has a wide range of exhibits, many of which visitors are free to touch. Also featured is a very large number of samurai houses, possibly the largest number in a single place in Japan. The location is the grounds of the former castle, Sakura-jo. The most convenient access is from Keisei-Sakura station. (This is the same line that goes to Narita airport from Ueno; the station is the fifth from Narita.) The book *Weekend Adventures* has further details.

Narita

The city of Narita, after which the nearby airport is named, is famous among the Japanese for Naritasan temple (properly Shinsho-ji). It has stood on the present site since 1705, but succeeded another elsewhere dating from 940. Its pagoda dates from 1711 and Niomon gate from 1838, but the large main building is a recent (1968) concrete structure fashioned to resemble the traditional wood. It is a temple of the unusual Shingon sect of esoteric Buddhism which is known for ascetic practices. It is possible that you may see pilgrims bathing in icy water in winter, or walking endlessly around the temple chanting sutras.

Visitors have a good chance of seeing the interesting ceremony of blessing a car for safety. Results are not guaranteed, but any help is useful for driving in Japan.

Behind the temple, occupying much of the 20 hectares of the grounds, is the very attractive Naritasan-koen, a landscape garden of traditional design with ponds and artfully formed and arranged "hills". Also nearby is Naritasan historical museum.

Naritasan is easily reached by taxi or bus from the stations of both JR and the Keisei line.

Only a couple of km away is Boso Fu-doki-no-oka (Ancient Cultural Park) which comprises ancient tomb mounds approximately 1500 years old, and a modern museum housing relics excavated in the area.

Boso-hanto Peninsula

The main attraction of the Boso-hanto peninsula is the seaside. Popular resorts are Shirahama, Tateyama, Hota, and Katsuyama. In the area of the latter two is Pearl Island, where pearls were once cultured.

Farther north is a very long beach named Kujukurihama—which means 99 Ri Beach, a *ri* being a measure of length.

Note that some of the beaches are hazardous due to strong undertows. Further information about this area, including a good map and booklet, can be obtained from the Tokyo TIC.

IZU ISLANDS

Within the bounds of Tokyo are, among other things, two live volcanoes. They present no danger because they are located on two of several small islands south of Tokyo that are included in the Tokyo-to administrative area. The islands, part of the Fuji volcanic chain, are called Izu Shichi-to, meaning Izu Seven Islands. There are in fact more than seven, but some are very small.

Until recently the islands were relatively isolated, and some were used during the Edo period as a place of exile. They have now become popular as a holiday resort, especially among young Japanese. The islands can be reached by boat and by air. Schedules change by season, so it is best to get up-to-date information on reaching any of the islands from the TIC in Tokyo.

Oshima

This is the largest of the islands (91 sq km);

the name means "Big Island". Its high point, literally and figuratively, is Mihara-yama (758 meters), which last erupted in 1986, and forced evacuation of the island for several days.

Activities on the island include swimming at several beautiful beaches, climbing the volcano (on foot or by bus from Okata or Motomachi), and visiting the "Hawaiian" Botanical Garden of tropical and subtropical plants that can be grown in the mild climate.

The town of Sashikiji and the nearby area are known for old houses and customs which differ from those on the mainland. There is a distinct dialect on Oshima and the other islands in the group. The dark traditional costume with a white pattern is unlike a kimono; an "apron" substitutes for the obi (sash), and the headdress indicates if a woman is single or married.

For places to stay there are about 120 *minshuku* , 70 *ryokan* , two youth hostels, and five campsites to choose from, but advance reservations are suggested.

Bus service makes travel simple. There are two tour buses each day at 0700 and 0900 from both Okata and Motomachi.

The island is crowded during summer because it is close to Tokyo and easily accessible by boat from Tokyo, Atami, Ito, and Inatori (near Shimoda), and perhaps Shimoda in season, and by air from Tokyo.

Toshima

This tiny island (4.2 sq km) is the smallest of the group. It is round and of volcanic origin, but the fires have gone out. There is almost no flat land on the entire island, 60 per cent of which is given over to growing camellias, from which fragrant oil is extracted. They bloom in late January and February. There is one concentration of people in the north, a few

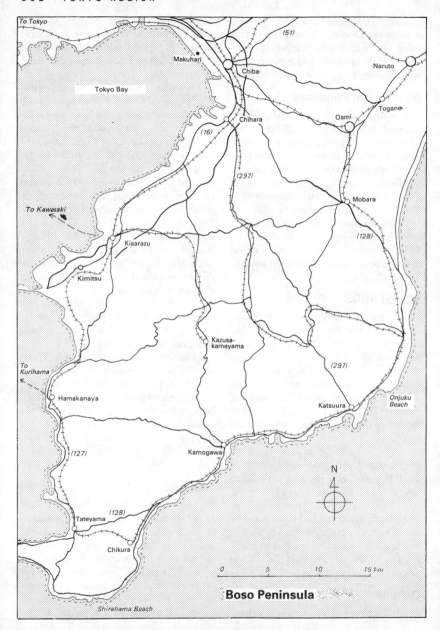

To Tokyo

Makuhari

Tokyo Bay

Chiba

Naruto

(51)

Chihara

Oami

Togane

(16)

(297)

Mobara

To Kawasaki

(128)

Kisarazu

Kimitsu

Kazusa-
kameyama

(297)

To Kurihama

Hamakanaya

Katsuura

Onjuku
Beach

(127)

Kamogawa

N

Tateyama

(128)

Chikura

0   5   10   15 km

Boso Peninsula

Shiraihama Beach

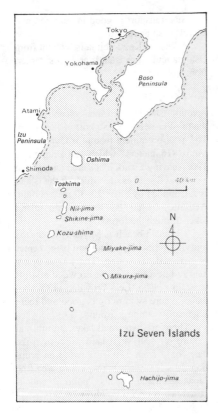

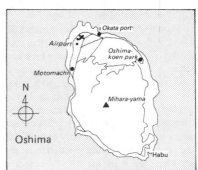

cemetery from the days of the exiles. Habuse-ura beach has very high cliffs (up to 250 meters), but it is better for surfing than swimming. Another beach is Awai-ura.

The main town, Honmura, is reached by boat from Oshima and Tokyo.

The houses on the south of the island are interesting because they are constructed of lightweight volcanic rock that is mined in the area; they are known for their unusual architecture. Objects carved of the rock are on sale, as is locally-distilled shochu.

There are plenty of places to stay with about 235 *minshuku* and seven *ryokan*, but reservations are recommended in the summer because the island has become very popular in recent years among young Japanese.

Shikine-jima

Despite its diminutive size (3.8 sq km), this island offers more than its share of interesting attractions. The scenery along the rugged shore is spectacular, with 10–30 meter cliffs encircling the island; inland it is mostly flat. Most of the population is found in fishing communities to the northeast, like Nobuse and Kohama.

Shikine-jima and Nii-jima were once the same landmass, but tidal waves in 1688

hundred people who make their living from the camellia oil business. Accommodation is limited, four *minshuku* and one *ryokan*. Access is by boat from Oshima.

Nii-jima

This island (23.4 sq km) is rather elongated, with a volcanic peak at each end and long beaches on each side. Swimming is excellent at several places. Maehama (on the west) offers the best swimming and white sand, but is very crowded in season. There is a campsite to the north. In the area is a museum, hotspring, temple, and a and 1704 separated them.

There are several beaches around the island, with a variety of surfaces, from rock to sand. There are two beaches where hot-spring water gushes out to form a natural (and free) onsen. The water of both is too hot to enter directly, but at Ashi-tsuki you can bathe at the seashore, where the 60°C water mixes with the sea. At Jinata the sea mixes with the hot water only at high tide and cools the 80°C water enough to be enjoyable. Play it by ear as to whether a swimsuit is needed.

This was one of the penal/exile colonies, and some traces of those days still remain.

A festival is held around January 24 for the return of the souls of sailors lost at sea. In mid-June there is a sea festival.

On the island there are about 100 *minshuku* and five *ryokan*, so there are plenty of places to stay, but reservations are suggested in summer because it is also popular with young people.

Bicycles can be rented at shops, but the island is small enough to walk around easily.

Shikine-jima can be reached by boat from Nii-jima.

Kozu-shima

This gourd-shaped island (18.5 sq km) has a dead volcano in the center. Most of the population lives on the west side; fishing, farming and catering to tourists are the main activities. The island is an excellent place for fishing from the rocks, swimming is good at Tako-wan (a white sand beach), and you can also climb the central peak.

There is a boat festival on January 5, "Juria" matsuri on the third Sunday in May, Bon odori from July 13–16, and a shrine festival on August 1–2.

There are about 200 *minshuku* and five *ryokan*.

Bus transport is good in summer, and bicycles can be rented.

Access to Kozu-shima is by boat from Oshima and other islands and, in summer, from Tokyo as well.

Miyake-jima

A round island with a live volcano, this is the third largest (55.1 sq km) of the group. The most prominent feature is Oyama volcano (815 meters) which last erupted in 1962, leaving a stark black area resembling a collapsed sand castle. Much of the island is surrounded by cliffs 20–30 meters high. Activities include swimming and inland hikes through the forests.

The main beach is Miyake-hama; it is unusual for its black sand and is the center of seaweed harvesting. There is camping nearby but it tends to be crowded and littered in season. Less crowded is Okubo-hama, where swimming is good and there is a nearby camping ground.

There are two small lakes, an unusual feature on such an island. Shin-myo-ike dates only from 1763 following an eruption. It is less than one sq km in area (the Japanese name means "pond"), and is largely surrounded by cliffs 70–80 meters high. The water is salty and mysteriously takes on seven different colors through the day. You can climb to the rim and look down on the water. The other lake, Tairo-

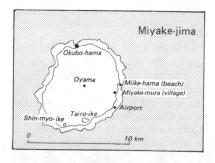

ike, is only a smidgen bigger (1.2 sq km) but much older, 2000 years or so. It contains fresh water and is used as a water supply reservoir, so swimming and camping, etc., are banned. Although the island has a nearly tropical climate, the lake has many qualities of a mountain lake, an interesting contrast on such a small island.

There is a boat festival on January 2, a shrine festival on January 8, and the *ajisai* (hydrangea) festival in mid-June.

There are plenty of places to stay, as on the other islands: 130 *minshuku* , 12 *ryokan* and a youth hostel.

Access is by boat from Oshima or Hachijo-jima, or by air from Tokyo.

Mikura-jima

Although this smallish (20 sq km) circular island is only 20 km from Miyake-jima (an hour by boat) there is only infrequent service, six or seven times a month. It is rugged, with cliffs 100–300 meters high round the periphery, a 100-meter waterfall on the west side, and a dead volcano in the middle. There is not a single stretch of level road on the island, there is no public transport, and the entire population lives on the north side.

There are 12 *ryokan* , adequate for the few who can wait out the period between boats; camping is not allowed.

Hachijo-jima

The most southerly of the Izu group, this is the second largest (71 sq km). It is characterised by two volcanic peaks, Higashi-yama (Mihara-yama) in the southeast and Nishi-yama in the northwest, and cliffs along most of the rugged coast. It has a mild and wet climate year-round.

Hachijo-jima was the outermost of the islands used for exile, and some relics may be seen, such as the ruins of large houses.

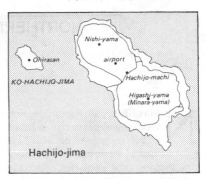

Tourism is a relative newcomer to the island and some old customs may still be found. A local type of cloth, ki-hachijo, is still woven and colored with vegetable dyes from local sources. It is one of the souvenirs of the island; others are sake, and shell and coral products.

The scenery can be seen by bus tour beginning at Hachijo shiyakusho (city hall) daily at 0930, or by rented bicycle. Another attraction is Jiyugaoka-yuen park, where bullfights are held. Like those on Shikoku, Okinawa, and some other islands of Japan, and as far away as Indonesia, the fights are not between man and beast, but are a test of strength between two bulls; the winner pushes the other out of the ring.

The Exiles Festival is held on August 28.

There are nearly 100 *minshuku* and 22 hotels or *ryokan* on the island.

There are boats from Tokyo and flights from Tokyo and Nagoya.

N orth of Tokyo are some of the most interesting places to visit in Japan. A few are man-made relics, but most are natural scenic beauties or curiosities. Perhaps most interesting, especially for the traveller with time to spare and an interest in the "real Japan", is the legacy of folkways. The northern part of Honshu, called nothern Honshu ("east-north"), was late in being developed, and in this respect it still lags behind other parts of the country. This is to the disadvantage of the people who live there (though conditions are now quite modernized) but to the distinct advantage of foreign visitors who want to see at least some aspects of Japan as it used to be. (There are modern amenities, of course, so there is no hardship involved when travelling in the area.) I would rank the northern Honshu area with the Noto Peninsula/Chubu areas as the best in Japan for independent exploration. More folklore, dances, and tradition survive, concentrated in these areas, than in most other parts of the country.

This chapter describes a route northward along the east coast and through some of the center, and a southbound route along the west coast and other parts of the center. This covers the maximum of territory with a minimum of backtracking, and also allows description prefecture by prefecture, as their boundaries follow the same geographical features used for laying out this itinerary. You can also go to Hokkaido from the northern tip of Tohoku and then resume the route without missing anything.

INFORMATION

Travellers starting from Tokyo should visit the TIC and obtain information sheets on the areas in which they plan to travel. Tell them of your proposed itinerary and request their suggestions. Several information sheets are now available, and others are added yearly. Sample titles are: *Towada-Hachimantai National Park* (MG-31), *Morioka and Rikuchu Kaigan* (*coast*) *National Park* (MG-38), and *Sendai, Matsushima and Hiraizumi* (MG-023). These sheets have up-to-date transportation schedules and fares and list several hotels, as well as giving sketchy sightseeing information of the "official" variety.

A very detailed guide book covering only Tohoku appeared in 1982 and has become very popular with travellers. *Exploring Tohoku* by Jan Brown (Weatherhill) is almost of the "telling too much" type, but its plenitude of information has something for everyone and will certainly be invaluable for foreign residents in the area. It has been updated, and should remain a good info source, especially if its information is combined with that of this book.

TRANSPORTATION

The following times and frequency of trains and buses are provided as samples of services available at the time of writing. Although there is a large degree of repetitiveness of schedules from year to year, there is no guarantee that any particular service will be as listed, so be sure to check travel plans with an up-to-date *jikokuhyo* (book of

Northern Honshu

timetables). Because of lack of demand, or roads impassible due to snow, many of the services described are suspended from early November to late April.

Trains

There is a good network of JR lines in northern Japan: a line along both east and west coasts, two roughly parallel lines up through most of the middle, and several crosswise linking lines.

In addition, there are two Shinkansen super express lines (up to 240 km/hr) linking Tokyo with cities in the region covered in this chapter.

TOHOKU SHINKANSEN This line was originally intended to go to Aomori and then through a tunnel under the Tsugaru strait to Hokkaido. However, economic reality struck hard, and the line was terminated at Morioka, a considerable distance above Sendai and about 80 per cent of the way to Aomori (at the northern end of Honshu); in 1991 there is talk of completing it as far as Aomori. Via the quickest express, the time from Tokyo to Sendai, the largest city in the region, will be one hour 44 minutes; to Morioka, 2 hours 36 minutes.

JOETSU SHINKANSEN This line links Niigata (almost directly north of Tokyo) with Tokyo. Via the fastest train, the distance can be covered in 108 minutes.

Buses

There are several long-distance bus services, both overnight and by day, from Tokyo and vicinity to Sendai, Yamagata, Hirosaki, Aomori, Morioka, and several other places in the Tohoku region, as well as within the region. The ones from Tokyo are detailed in the earlier Transportation section, but it is necessary to look at *jikokuhyo* (particularly the map specifically

showing the long-distance bus routes) for information on all of them.

In addition to these long-distance buses, there are many other bus routes within the region to places not served by railways, or between large centers via mountainous routes where railways would be difficult to build. These are shown in *jikokuhyo* as thin double blue and double red lines (JR services on which a Japan Rail Pass may be used), and a single thin blue line (others).

IBARAKI-KEN ■■■■■■■■

Tokyo is on the edge of the Kanto plain, one of the largest areas of flat terrain in Japan, which is why it was one of the most prized fiefs in feudal times. The plain is intensively populated in all directions outside Tokyo.

Tsuchiura

An interesting festival, Hanabi Matsuri, is held here the first Saturday in October each year. Hanabi means "flowers of fire" and this is, in effect, a trade show of fireworks manufacturers, who show off their best products in one of the most colorful fireworks displays of the year. Tsuchiura is on the Joban line, which runs to Mito.

Mito

The main drawcard of this city is Kairaku-en, a garden traditionally rated by the Japanese as one of the three finest in Japan. I have visited it on two occasions and had the same reaction both times—a feeling of acute disappointment. The garden is, for the most part, little more than open lawn, with clusters of trees or bushes. It seems ironic that two of the most celebrated gardens in Japan (the other is Koraku-en in Okayama) are noteworthy primarily for their vast expanses of lawn; perhaps it is this novelty that reaps such a rating. There are many other gardens in the country that would be better examples of what foreign visitors are looking for in Japanese gardens—those at Yokohama, Hikone, Takamatsu, and Kagoshima, to name just a handfull.

The Kairaku-en garden was completed in 1843. Of interest within its grounds is Kobuntei, a building (reproduction) where Nariaki—one of the lords of Mito—used to meet learned men, relax, and compose poetry. (The town was formerly the home of an important branch of the Tokugawa family.) The building is well made of fine materials and is a good example of the simplicity and refined restraint of traditional Japanese architecture. (Some of the modern variety is a bit strange.) It is surrounded by tall trees and the atmosphere is very peaceful. Even the shrilling of *semi* (cicadas) in summer adds a rural note, in contrast with the commercial appearance of the surrounding city. The garden is close to Kairaku-en station, one stop from Mito station.

TOCHIGI-KEN ▬▬▬▬▬

The main attractions of Tochigi-ken are the pottery town of Mashiko, ancient Buddha statues at Oya, the incomparably beautiful and ornate Tosho-gu shrine at Nikko, mountain scenery, and the start of the valley with the most thatched-roof houses in Japan.

Mashiko

Of the several historic pottery centers of Japan, the most accessible from Tokyo is Mashiko, a couple of hours to the northeast. A visit to Mashiko can also be conveniently combined with a trip to Nikko, as they are in the same general area.

The pottery of Mashiko is made entirely from local materials—from clays to glazes. They do not lend themselves to

elaborate techniques, so the results are rather simple and seem to me (who professes neither deep knowledge nor interest in pottery) a trifle crude. However to ceramic freaks this equals native charm, and the sometimes rough surfaces, simple designs, and frequent asymmetry are all to be treasured. The properties of the clay could be improved with additives, but the potters prefer to use only natural materials. If you like pottery, you will enjoy a visit to Mashiko. It is also interesting for those who would like to learn something about traditional Japanese methods of making and firing pottery, as there is a large number of "climbing kilns" and a visit to one is easy to arrange (though they are fired but occasionally).

The town of Mashiko owes its fame to Shoji Hamada, who found here a town of potters who had been turning out serviceable but simple and repetitive designs since 1852. He settled in the town, absorbed their traditions and then built on them, establishing his own kiln in 1930. As his fame spread, it reflected back to the town that had nurtured him. Adding to the fame of the town and the name of Shoji Hamada was the English potter, Bernard Leach, who lived and studied here for several years before returning to his homeland to spread the Mashiko influence.

Things to See

The town is filled with shops selling the local wares, so it could take a week to examine all its products thoroughly. There is a free handout map available at most shops in town. A good starting place is the Hamada "home".

The Hamada Home

The "home" is made up of thatched-roof houses moved from elsewhere in the area, plus two stone *kura* (storehouses) of the

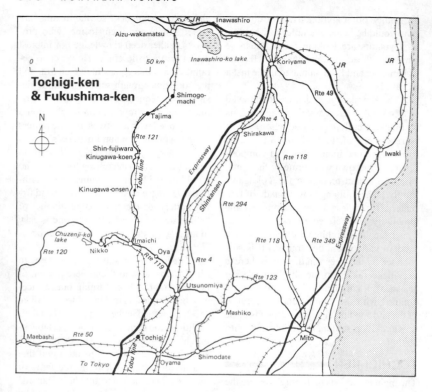

**Tochigi-ken
& Fukushima-ken**

N

0   50 km

Inawashiro
Aizu-wakamatsu
Inawashiro-ko lake
Koriyama
JR
JR
Rte 49
Shimogo-machi
Tajima
Rte 4
Shirakawa
Rte 121
Shin-fujiwara
Kinugawa-koen
Rte 118
Iwaki
Tobu line
Kinugawa-onsen
Expressway
Shinkansen
Rte 294
Rte 118
Rte 349
Chuzenji-ko lake
Rte 120   Nikko   Imaichi
Oya
Rte 4
Expressway
Rte 119
Rte 123
Utsunomiya
Maebashi   Rte 50
Mashiko
Mito
Tochigi
Tobu line
Shimodate
To Tokyo   Oyama

type found throughout the region. The kura houses the Mashiko Sankokan (Reference Collection Museum), a collection of odds and ends that Shoji Hamada gathered during his travels outside Japan. There are few treasures, and little of his own work. I found the place more interesting for the old farmhouses that Hamada had brought to this place in 1943. The largest one was built in 1850, and houses furniture and other things brought back from abroad. Although visitors cannot enter the house, you can look in through the doors and windows and admire the massive pillars and crossbeams of the building itself, which is a fine example of a traditional house of this era.

There are no nails used in the construction of these houses, so they can easily be dismantled and moved. The roof is unusual because the bamboo poles are used at the peak to anchor it in place (again typical of the region). There are other buildings of the same type elsewhere in the grounds, one lived in by Hamada's widow.

Shimaoka Pottery
Adjacent to the Hamada grounds is the Shimaoka pottery, also well worth visiting. While many of the kilns used here are small oil or gas fired units, the famous kilns of Mashiko are the traditional *nobori-gama* wood-fired climbing kilns, two of which

are in the grounds of the Shimaoka pottery.

There are always some foreign students working in the village and they are often willing to give a guided tour or direct you to other kilns. The kilns have several chambers arranged up a hillside. Firing begins in the lowest chamber, with the gases climbing and preheating the other chambers. When the first chamber has been thoroughly fired, fuel is then added to the second chamber and the first allowed to burn out. This sequence is repeated until all chambers have been fired. Because of the size of the kilns and the fuel consumption, many of the large kilns are fired only three or four times a year. It is an awesome sight as the flames and sparks shoot high over the stacks at the top of the hill.

There are many of these kilns scattered around the hillsides and they can be found easily enough, but the distances become appreciable. A look at the Shimaoka kilns will probably be adequate.

If you are able to arrange a visit, try to look at the carpentry of the new Shimaoka building as well, as it is a fine example of the best traditional Japanese woodworking skill. A crossbeam of untrimmed tree trunk is supported on two poles, each of which has its end shaped to match the shape of the crossbeam, and vertical supports for shelves are keystoned into notches so that they support without nails. The new house took more than a year to build, all the work being done by one family of carpenters.

As for finding pottery to buy, there is no problem whatsoever. There must be few towns in the world with so many shops selling the stuff—some by recognised potters (at high prices) and much at very reasonable prices, turned out by the large number of anonymous workers who make the bulk of the output. Everything, however is handmade. Those interested in weaving should look for the Higeta Workshop.

Getting There

There are two ways to get to Mashiko. The most convenient way is to go first to Utsunomiya station, which is on both the Tohoku Shinkansen and the ordinary Tohoku Honsen lines (the latter starting from Ueno station in Tokyo), then transfer to a bus for Mashiko. The bus trip takes one hour and costs ¥1000 each way. There are more than 20 buses a day in each direction.

Those who wish to go entirely by JR train should go from Tokyo to Oyama (same JR lines), transfer to the Mito-sen line (32 a day) and go as far as Shimodate (the fifth station, or fourth by express), then change to the Moka-sen line (eight per day), which goes through Mashiko (seventh station). The train travel alone by this route totals nearly an hour, and there will be waits between trains; the stop at Shimodate ranges from two to 30 minutes, for example.

Oya

At Oya, near the city of Utsunomiya, there are 10 Buddha images carved in relief in the rock wall of the protective overhang. The temple building of Oya-ji extends back into the shallow cavern, protecting the images. It is believed that they date from the early Heian period (794-897 AD) and are the oldest stone statues of Buddha in Japan. Near the temple is an unmissable (27 meters) concrete statue of Kannon, the goddess of mercy, finished in 1954.

Visible in the surrounding countryside are the quarries and nibbled-away hills that are the source of the soft stone (tuff) used in structures such as the granaries (*kura*) throughout the region and beyond Nikko. Many small workshops can be seen where the stone is cut into building blocks.

Getting There

The easiest way to reach Oya is by bus

from Utsunomiya station; the trip takes about 25 minutes.

Nikko

Nikko is one of the "must-sees" of Japan, to be included in even the shortest visit. Adjacent to the town are some of the most beautiful buildings in the world, ornately colored and covered with gold leaf. The surrounding area is also famed for its natural scenery—waterfalls, a lake resort, forests, and volcanic mountain peaks.

Information

The trip to Nikko is so popular that the Tokyo TIC has prepared free notes that give useful and up-to-date information on trains, accommodation, and sightseeing. Be sure to get them before leaving Tokyo.

Things to See

The term "sensory overload" was invented just for Nikko, particularly the Tosho-gu and Taiyuin shrines, as well as for lesser shrines in the area. Superlatives become exhausted before the sightseeing does; you should allow a full day to absorb it all. The best way, if time permits, is to spend a night in Nikko and stretch your sightseeing over two days. Keep in mind that during the summer it may rain heavily for an hour or two from about midday, so try to get an early start.

Rinno-ji Temple

At the top of the hilly main street stands Shin-kyo, the Sacred Bridge, an orange structure blocked to traffic. Follow the road

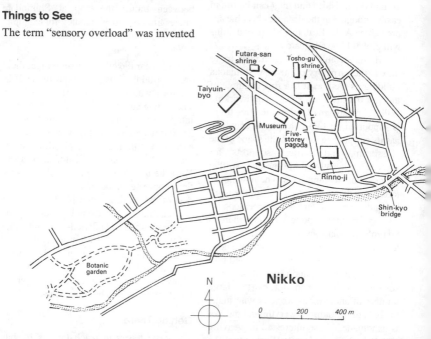

Nikko

around to the left of the hill, to the footpath up the hill. This leads to one corner of the compound of Rinno-ji temple. The major point of interest of this temple is Sambutsudo, Temple of the Three Buddhas, the largest in the Nikko mountains. It houses three gilded wooden statues (five meters tall) of Kannon (a Buddhist saint with 11 faces and 1000 arms), Amida-Nyorai, and the Bato-Kannon (believed to be the incarnation of animal spirits).

The large avenue at the left side of Rinno-ji is named *omote-sando* ("main approach") and it leads to Toshogu shrine, the most important single structure in Nikko. To the left of the path is a five-storey pagoda, 32 meters tall, built in 1818 and redecorated in recent years. At the entrance to the shrine is a tall granite torii gate.

There is a basic fee of ¥230 for admittance to the Toshogu shrine, Rinno-ji temple, and Futaara-san shrine.

Tosho-gu Shrine

Entry to this shrine is through *omote-mon* (also called *Nio-mon*) gate, with its statues of the guardian Nio-sama—Deva kings. The decorations are but a hint of what is to come. From the gate, the path bends to the left. The decorated buildings encountered on the right are the lower, middle, and upper storehouses. On the upper storehouse are noted relief carvings of elephants created by a sculptor who had seen only drawings of the animal. To the left of the path, opposite the middle storehouse, is the sacred stable, the only unlacquered building in the compound. Overhead are various

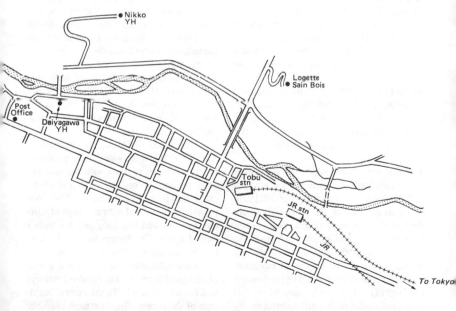

carvings of monkeys; second from the left is a famous panel featuring the three monkeys in the "see, speak, hear no evil" poses. Carvings of monkeys were reputed to fend of diseases in horses. Visitors can feed the sacred horse (which is only too happy with its role) by purchasing a small dish of carrot slices.

Facing the upper storehouse, and to the left of the bronze *torii*, is the Kyozo (Sutra Library), which houses nearly 7000 volumes of Buddhist sutras (sacred writings). Beside it is the sacred fountain where Japanese visitors rinse out their mouths to purify themselves before proceeding farther. The water is safe to drink.

YAKUSHIDO TEMPLE The next flight of stairs leads to the middle court. The similar buildings on each side are the belfry and the drum tower. Beyond the drum tower is Yakushido, the only Buddhist-style structure in the shrine. Yakushido is famous for its Crying Dragon, Naki-ryu, a ceiling painting in an inner chamber. Admittance to this inner shrine requires a separate ticket, which may be paid for when first entering Toshogu. Visitors stand on a marked spot, clap their hands together, and the echo sounds like the reverberating roar of the dragon. The painting is quite recent, as the roof was destroyed in a fire in 1961.

Yomei-mon (GATE OF SUNLIGHT) Returning to the courtyard and climbing the next set of steps leads you to the most beautiful gate in Japan and one of the most elaborately decorated structures on earth. Yomei-mon contains a wealth of intricate carvings, gilt, and lacquer work, any detail of which would be worthy of display in isolation. The Japanese nickname is Higurashi-mon (Twilight Gate), the implication being that you could admire it until overtaken by night. You'll understand the sentiment when you have seen it.

Among the 12 supporting columns are two seated figures, and on the beams atop the columns are the white figures of stylized lions. From these beams, a complex and attractive branching of brackets spreads out to support the balcony that surrounds the second storey. On the ends of the beams are carved *kirin* (mythical Chinese animals), and between the black and gilded brackets are carvings of a Chinese prince, sages, and immortals of Chinese mythology. The balcony surrounding the second storey incorporates panels depicting Chinese children. The beam ends are decorated by white dragon heads, and a dragon cavorts on the central beam. Above that, the rafter ends are detailed with lacquered and gilded dragon heads.

A low fence, also decorated, runs from either side of the gate and surrounds the courtyard. On the inside of the gate, back to back with the seated figures, are colorful *koma-inu* (guardian lions or dogs). Through the gate and to the left is the *mikoshi-gura*, where the *mikoshi* (portable shrines) are stored. These shrines are carried in the two annual festivals (May 17–18 and October 17). *Kaguraden*, in the courtyard, is the stage used for performances of *kagura* (sacred shrine dances).

The closed gate facing the courtyard is Kara-mon (Chinese gate). It is predominately white, in contrast with the fantastically brilliant colors and gold leaf of the other buildings and structures. The door panels are decorated with carvings of various flowers and bamboo, and the pillars with dragons. The figures around the support beams depict Chinese celebrities.

Kara-mon gate and the Sacred Fence (Tamagaki) surround the *Haiden* (oratory) and *Honden* (main hall), the central buildings of the shrine. The innermost chamber of the Honden (the *Gokuden*), with its splendid interior (the supply of superlatives is becoming exhausted!) is where the spirit of Ieyasu Tokugawa is enshrined. (His body is buried in a simple tomb on the hill behind the shrine.) It is a Shinto custom for illustrious historical figures to be considered *kami* (gods or spirits) so it is natural for the shrine of his spirit to be the more magnificent. The spirits of Hideyoshi Toyotomi and Yoritomo Minamoto are enshrined in the same hall. You can visit the innermost chamber, but is forbidden to take photos, which is unfortunate because the interiors are brilliant.

The last area of interest at this shrine is the tomb of Ieyasu Tokugawa, reached through the doorway to the right of the Sacred Fence. Over the doorway is the famous carving Nemuri-neko—the sleeping cat. There are said to be no mice or rats in the building because of its presence. The tomb is reached by climbing about 200 steps, among immense cedar trees. The tomb itself is severely simple, and resembles a small bronze pagoda.

Back on Omote-sando, around the corner from the pagoda, there is an avenue through the trees. On the left, close to the pagoda, is the shrine museum, which houses a good collection of armor and other relics. It has exhibits showing how the buildings are constructed, how the wooden beams are protected by multiple layers of lacquered cloth, and so on.

Futara-san Shrine

Farther along the path, away from Omote-sando, is Futara-san shrine. It is of lesser interest, and is best left to see at the end (if you have any energy or interest left).

Taiyuin-byo

Visitors to Nikko are guided to Toshogu by every tourist publication. What is often left out of the literature completely is another shrine nearby that is only a little bit less spectacular than Tosho-gu, and which would be worth visiting anywhere else if it were the sole attraction. That is Taiyuin-byo.

Taiyuin-byo is the shrine dedicated to Iemitsu (1604–51) who constructed Tosho-gu in honor of his father, Ieyasu. It is somewhat smaller than Tosho-gu, but almost up to its standards in beauty. (I think that the Haiden and Honden are even more beautiful than the equivalent buildings of Tosho-gu.) In addition, it is possible to stand back some distance to take in their beauty and gain some perspective, as well as to photograph them. (The buildings of Tosho-gu are closely surrounded by a wall, and photography is prohibited.)

Approaching Taiyuin-byo, you first walk through *Nio-mon* (Deva king gate) with its guardian statues. You then pass a small garden and can see the sacred fountain ahead and to the right. Turning left, you climb the stairs to *Niten-mon* (Two Heavens Gate), named for the two Buddhist deities Komokuten and Jikokuten. On the other side of the gate are the Gods of Wind and Thunder; the former is holding shut the opening of the bag of winds.

After climbing more stairs, you pass through *Yasha-mon* (named for its four figures of Yasha, a Buddhist deity), and arrive at the middle court with its belfry and drum tower. Between the middle court and the inner shrine is a Chinese gate, beautifully decorated and flanked by the sacred fence. Time and weather—it snows profusely in Nikko—take their toll of the decorations, and they must be continually repaired or repainted. The intricate carvings of birds were retouched in 1978, and possibly since then, so they should stay colorful for several years.

Inside the inner shrine is the oratory (Haiden), from which a passageway leads to the inner main hall (Honden), both interiors being richly decorated with carvings and gold leaf. To the right of, and behind, the main buildings is a walkway that leads to the tomb itself, a simple structure by comparison.

AESTHETICS ALERT: The aesthetes look down their noses at Nikko because it is not "typically Japanese", claiming it is too gaudy, unrepresentative, etc. True, it *is* atypical, but it is quite in the flamboyant Momoyama style. Certainly it should not be missed, both for the tremendous amount of work that has gone into it and for the sheer visual splendor.

Before being brainwashed about Japanese "restraint" in art and taste, realize that a considerable amount of misunderstanding by modern art historians is floating around regarding the aesthetic tastes in ancient times in Japan. Many statues as we see them now are plain and undecorated, just the natural wood or other material, but when they were new they were often, if not usually, decorated with gold leaf, and quite spectacular to behold.

Nikko Museum and Botanical Garden

Beside Hanaishi bus stop (en route from Nikko station to Chuzenji), is Nikko Botanical Garden. A short distance back toward town is Tamozawa villa, a former imperial residence, now a museum. Set in a quiet garden, the building was constructed of the finest materials and is a good example of good Japanese architecture, though it is larger than most wooden buildings in Japan.

Festivals

Nikko is noted for several annual festivals. On October 17 and May 18, there is a great procession of hundreds of people dressed in samurai armor and other costumes of the Tokugawa era. *Mikoshi* (portable shrines) carry the enshrined spirits of Ieyasu, Hideyoshi, and Yoritomo. This is a big event and always crowded, but worth seeing for both the glimpse of pageantry and the feel of bygone days. On May 17, the Ennen-no-mai (Longevity Dance) is also held in front of Sambutsudo, with two priests in elaborate costume performing ancient dances.

On August 5–6 there are very popular (Waruku-Odori) folk dances during the *obon* season, which honors the souls of ancestors. Similar dances are held in communities throughout Japan at this time, but the Nikko dance is particularly famous.

Other days with festivals are May 17 (at Sambutsudo), and April 14 and 17 at Futara-san jinja shrine.

Places to Stay

As befits one of the most popular tourist destinations in Japan, there is no shortage of places to stay in Nikko, but it is wise to book ahead through a travel agent (e.g., JTB or the minshuku association, or through one of the TICs) to be sure of a room. Much available accommodation is of the high-quality, high-cost type. However, there are two youth hostels. Nikko Youth Hostel (tel. (0288) 54-1013; 70 beds), once infamous for its surly, officious staff, has been transformed by new management into one of the best in Japan, with a relaxed, open house atmosphere. Nikko Daiyagawa Youth Hostel (tel. 0288) 54-1974; 26 beds), is an alternative. Not far away by train is Shinko-en Youth Hostel (tel. (0288) 26-0951/0817; 33 beds) at Imaichi. It is near Shimozuke-osawa station, two stops out of Nikko on the JR line.

Getting There

From Tokyo there are two train lines, JR and Tobu. The latter is the more convenient, as there are many more trains each day, they are quicker, and the fare is lower. Tobu trains leave from Tobu station in Matsuya department store in Asakusa, not far from Asakusa station of the Ginza subway line.

There are about 21 *tokkyu* expresses (¥2000), a couple of *kyuko* expresses (¥1500), and about 11 *kaisoku* expresses (¥1000). The first seven *tokkyu* trains of the day (the last leaving at 1000) take just over 100 minutes to get to Nikko, and no change of train is required. The other *tokkyu* take between 107 and 118 minutes, and require a change at Imaichi (one station before Nikko). The *kaisoku* take between 119 and 130 minutes, and no change of train is required (except for two in the afternoon).

There are local trains, but they take an eternity and cost the same as the *kaisoku*.

Nikko to Chuzenji

Regular buses from Nikko run several kilometers up the twisting Iroha highway to Chuzenji-ko lake, a popular summer resort. One of the bus stops along the way is Akechi-daira, a lookout and the base station for a 300m cable car that leads up to a higher lookout (*tembodai*; three minutes, ¥600 round trip). This lookout has a much better view (in clear weather), taking in Kegon-no-taki waterfall. The source of the water is Chuzenji-ko lake, which can be seen clearly (in good weather, anyway), backdropped by the conical peak of Nantai-san (2844 meters). From the tembodai there is a trail (for those who wish to take the cable car only one way) that leads to a ridge surrounding the lake (possibly the rim of an old volcano). A 30-minute walk leads to Chanoki-daira, the top station for a one km cable car that leads down to a point close to Kegon falls (¥320/600 one-way/return). A handout map/brochure of the area is available from the Nikko Youth Hostel (and possibly elsewhere in town). On the many walks in this area you will find enough points of interest to last for several days.

In uncrowded times the bus trip takes about 50 minutes, but on weekends in the summer when the cooler weather is an attraction, and in the autumn when the colored leaves are beautiful, the road is clogged, and the time for the trip can easily be doubled, trebled, or more. (It would not be worth the aggravation at those times.)

Chuzenji-onsen

This is an extremely popular and very crowded resort town. The lake can be toured by regular excursion boat from various points, either by circling the lake (55 minutes, ¥700), or crossing it from the town to Shobugahama (20 minutes, ¥400). South from the town, on the shore of the lake, is Chuzen-ji temple, which is worth a visit. The principal attraction is a 1000-year-old, tall wooden statue of Kannon-bosatsu. The carving, made from a single tree, has far fewer than 1000 arms, and the 11 faces are worked into a crown on a single benevolent visage. The present temple dates only from 1902, when it was moved from a point west of Chugu-shi shrine after the buildings were washed away. A booklet in good English explains other details of the temple.

Chugushi-jinja Shrine

This is the middle shrine of the three that make up Futara-san. (The first is at Toshogu.) A museum here has a reasonably good collection of armor and swords, as well as portable shrines. The collection is similar to those of many Japanese museums. A trail begins in the shrine grounds and leads to the peak of Nantai-san, a four-hour climb.

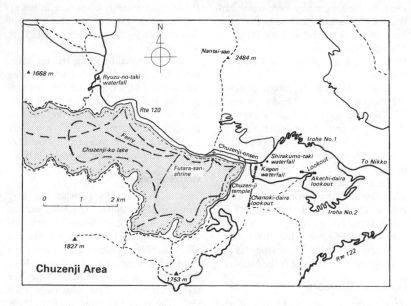

Chuzenji Area

Kegon-no-taki

Kegon waterfall drops 100 meters from an escarpment into a wide basin below. The falls are not visible from the surrounding cliffs; the best view is from the tembodai lookout (as described earlier). An elevator takes you to the foot of the falls, where the full power of the plummeting torrent can best be appreciated.

Shirakumo-taki ("White Cloud") Falls

This waterfall, one of the many in the area, is located a short distance from Kegon falls. The best vantage point is Kasasagi-bashi bridge, which crosses the ravine near the midpoint of the plunge.

Imaichi

Travellers going to Nikko from the Utsu-nomiya or Tokyo direction by train might wish to consider getting off at Imaichi first,

then taking a bus to Nikko (13 km) instead of going all the way by train. The reason is that the road is lined for much of the distance with thousands of tall, straight cedar trees. They were planted by a feudal lord over a period of years. He lacked the money to contribute a sumptuous structure when the shrine was being built, so he had the trees planted instead. About 13,000 trees still stand, and although the narrow avenue is crowded with traffic during the summer season (especially on weekends), it still retains its stately dignity. Check with the TIC in Tokyo about schedules and bus connections to ensure there won't be a long wait in Imaichi. Remember that noon rain!

Thatched-Roof houses

Route 121 runs north from Imaichi to Aizu-wakamatsu (in Fukushima-ken). Along this road is the largest concentration of thatched-roof houses that I encountered during more than 60,000 km of road travel around Japan. The road follows a river valley for much of the journey; the scenery is nearly always beautiful and often rustic, with many old houses. Many changes have taken place in the last 10 years though, and it is much a part of modern Japan.

There is a bus service the full length of the valley from Imaichi through Kinugawa-koen and Tajima to Aizu-wakamatsu. There are enough buses to guarantee connections, but there may be waits of an hour or more. It is also possible to make the first leg to Kinugawa-onsen or Kinugawa-koen by Tobu line train and the last leg from Tajima to Aizu-wakamatsu by JR. But because the houses of interest are along the road, the bus will be more interesting (at least until it reaches the start of the flat and open country around Kami-miyori, and that place is so close to Aizu-wakamatsu that there is no reason to change to a train).

Ozenuma

A little farther into the hinterland beyond Nikko (westward) is the very popular swamp of Ozenuma. Swamps don't usually sound exciting but this one is a bit special, and very popular with the Japanese. It is set on a plateau 1400 meters high, with a generous amount of pretty scenery, wildflowers, and unspoiled nature, including a lake that reflects nearby low mountains that have patches of snow into late spring.

Trails of logs are laid out as hiking tracks through the swamp, but they're usually wet and slippery, so take appropriate footwear.

The entry road branches from Route 120 at Kamata, about 50 km from Nikko, and from there it is another 25 km or so. The Ozenuma area can be reached by public transportation. There are up to nine buses a day from Tobu-Nikko station to Yumoto-onsen (about 1-1/2 hours), where you change to one of the three daily buses as far as Kamata (about 1-1/2 hours). From Kamata, nine buses a day go to Oshimizu (40 minutes) and another 10 run between Numata and Kamata.

Ozenuma can also be approached from the north. Up to three buses a day (2-1/2 hours) run from Aizu-tajima station, in the thatched-roof valley. There is a youth hostel at Tokura and other accommodation facilities in the area.

GUMMA-KEN

From Nikko you can travel on through Gumma-ken to Numata. (Gumma-ken is described in the chapter on Central Honshu.)

Numata

One route through this part of Japan is between Nikko and Nagano via Numata and Kusatsu. Numata, in addition to being the gateway for visits to Ozenuma, also has one historic relic that might be worth a look. It is the house of a wealthy merchant, built two and a half centuries ago, and believed to be the oldest in eastern Japan. It is located in Numata-koen (park).

FUKUSHIMA-KEN

Tajima

A little more than halfway up the valley lies the town of Tajima. It has a museum of folk craft, housing items that were used in daily life. One traveller rated it better than the similar but more famous museum at Kurashiki in Okayama-ken. Ask for the Mingei Hakubutsukan.

Shimogo-machi

In this region of thatched-roof houses, this small town is noteworthy for a street with more than a dozen such houses, side by side. The appearance of this area must be

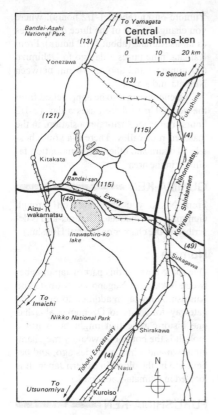

almost as it was one or two centuries ago.

Aizu-wakamatsu

This city was the site of the strongest castle in Tohoku (northeast Japan) at the end of the feudal era. At the time of the Meiji Restoration, the local lord resisted in favor of the Tokugawa who had ruled Japan for about three centuries. Imperial troops battled the garrison for a month, and the castle was destroyed. There is a realistic replica of the castle in the city today, but there are still authentic castles extant elsewhere, so this is not of great interest. There are, how-

ever, several attractions nearby.

Aizu Buke-yashiki

This is a reconstruction of samurai housing as it looked at the time of the civil war. (Most of the city was destroyed by fire in 1868.) Museums on the grounds show various aspects of Aizu-region culture and history.

Iimori-yama

During the civil war fighting of 1868, between the forces of the Tokugawa shogunate and those seeking to restore the emperor Meiji, a detachment of teenage army cadets was facing defeat on this hill. Rather than surrender, they ritually killed themselves. The hill, with its graves and monuments, can be climbed on foot or by long mobile sidewalks. A museum, Byakkotai Kinnenkan, has exhibits from this time.

Sazaedo

This is an interesting and unusual structure, a sort of Buddhist shrine that is probably unique in Japan. Although the roof over the entrance is of the traditional shape found at many temples and shrines, the main building is a tall, octagonal, wooden structure. Inside, ramps spiral upward both clockwise and anti-clockwise, meeting at the top after two complete revolutions. The "bridge" at the top, joining the two ramps passes over 33 figures of Kannon (goddess of mercy).

Inawashiro-ko Lake

The lake area is a popular resort destination in summer and winter, for swimming and skiing, so there are many *minshuku* and *ryokan* in the vicinity. The land around the lake is flat and there are few vantage points for a good view. Probably the best point is at Okinashima (take a bus from Inawashiro station). The popular Okinashima-so koku-min-shukusha is located on a hill above the road; it's a good place to stay, almost as large as a hotel, but an advance booking is usually necessary. There is an excellent view over the lake from the grounds and, when the atmospheric conditions are right, a superb view of of the volcanic peaks of Bandai-san.

Next door to Okinashima-so is a bit of a curiosity. It is a very large house of turn-of-the-century western style, named Tenkyokaku. The characters translate as "heavenly mirror house" and refer to the fine view of both the lake and Bandai-san (although trees obscure much of the Bandai view now). The villa was built early in the century by Prince Takamatsu, and Emperor Hirohito spent his honeymoon here in 1924. It is open to the public and is still richly furnished and decorated with its orig-inal fittings.

Kitakata

Kitakata is located a short distance north of Aizu-wakamatsu and is noted for the very large number of old *kura* (storehouses) scattered around the town. Walking or cy-cling (bicycles are available for rent) around the streets is an enjoyable way to spend a few hours. There are also horse-drawn carriages, structured like miniature kura, that carry passengers throughout the town.

Making *geta* is one of the cottage in-dustries of the townspeople. Pieces of wood in various stages of being made into these characteristic Japanese clogs can be seen outside houses. The wood is seasoned sev-eral times during the cutting and shaping operations.

There is a large map posted near the station showing the location of the gura, and handout maps may be available from the information center there. To the west of

Kitakata, both road and rail lead to Niigata.

Sugiyama

The main street of the tiny and very rural hamlet of Sugiyama, about nine km north of Kitakata, is made up almost entirely of kura.

Bandai Area

The area of Bandai-Azuma National Park, near Aizu-wakamatsu, includes some of the prettiest, most interesting, and accessi-ble mountain scenery in Japan. There are several volcanic peaks in the area, mostly dormant or extinct. In 1888, a series of colossal explosions literally blew off the top of Bandai mountain, hurling the rock in a general northward direction over an area of 70 sq km. The "instant excavation" changed the topography of the entire area, burying 11 villages and killing nearly 500 people. The rock blocked the former course of the Hibara and Nagase rivers, creating dozens of lakes, ponds, and swamps, each one said to be a different color. The colors range from deep emerald to jade and turquoise, probably due to dis-solved minerals, for this was once copper-mining country.

Bandai-san, now a group of peaks, is much like part of the rim of a crater. Its northern side still has the vivid, jagged scar of its eruption, as there was no lava flow to change the appearance. The explosions were caused by steam or gas pressure, and it was the first volcanic activity there in over a 1000 years.

Things to See

The main center for sightseeing is amidst the heads of several lakes, the three largest being Hibara-ko, Onogawa-ko, and Akimoto-ko. During the summer there are boat cruises on Hibara-ko lake, either back and forth be-tween Bandai-kogen and Yama-no-ie, or in

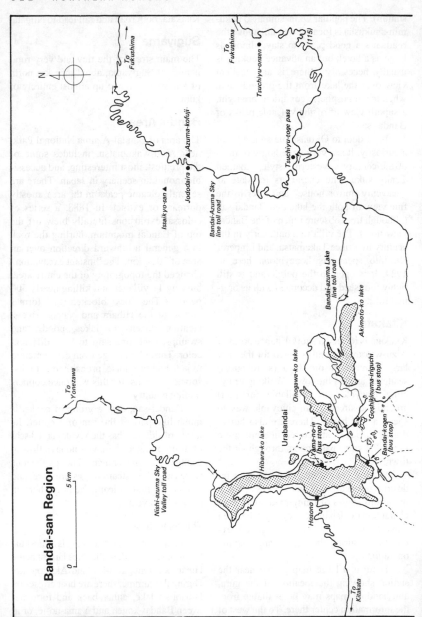

Bandai-san Region

To Fukushima

To Fukushima

N

Tsuchiyu-onsen ● (1115)

Tsuchiyu-toge pass

Azuma-kofuji ▲

Jododaira ●

Issaikyo-san ▲

Bandai-Azuma Sky line toll road

Bandai-azuma Lake line toll road

Akimoto-ko lake

Onogawa-ko lake

Goshikinuma-iriguchi (bus stop)

Bandai-kogen (bus stop)

Hibara-ko lake

Urabandai

Tama-no-ie (bus stop)

Hosono

Nishi-azuma Sky Valley toll road

To Yonezawa

To Kitakata

5 km

0

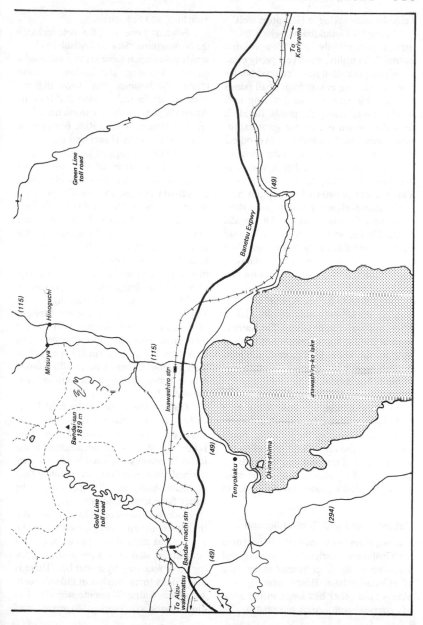

a circular route taking in Hosono as well.

Nearby is Goshikinuma, which translates unromantically as "five colored swamps". In reality, it is a very pretty cluster of more than 200 multi-colored bodies of water, varying in size from small ponds to a sizeable lake. A four km long trail wends its way among the ponds. Beside it lie rocks thrown out by the great explosion—some small enough to move, others as large as trucks. It is one of the most enjoyable nature walks in Japan, and relatively little known by foreign visitors. The hiking course (*haikingu kosu*), begins near Goshikinuma-iriguchi bus stop, just a short walk from the very pleasant Ura-bandai Youth Hostel, and meets the main road again at Bandai-kogen, a fancy name for a collection of shops and tourist accommodation. At the nearby docks are boats for rent and cruise boats.

Very close to the youth hostel is Bishamon-ike, the largest pond (actually a lake), where rowboats can be rented. The water is so clear that the boats appear to be floating on green air. In the background, glimpsed through breaks in the thick forest, is the stump of Mt. Bandai.

A little beyond the end of the trail at Bandai-kogen there is a road that runs a short distance toward Bandai-san and a network of trails covering the mountain. Some lead around the rim; others extend to the southern foot of the peak near Inawashiro-ko lake. This is certainly one of the most enjoyable walking and hiking areas in Japan.

Getting There and Getting Around

The two main bus stops in the Bandai area are Goshikinuma-iriguchi (entrance) and Yama-no-ie, the latter located at the edge of Hibara-ko lake. Buses connect these places (and other bus stops in the area, of course) with Aizu-wakamatsu, In-awashiro, and Fukushima.

Towards Yonezawa, the route includes the Nishi-azuma "Sky Valley" toll road; towards Fukushima, there are two toll roads, the 13 km-long Bandai-Azuma Rine ("line"; the Japanese don't know that the word is only for train tracks), and Bandai-Azuma Skyline, definitely worth travelling on. The Bandai-Azuma Rine begins near Ura-Bandai Youth Hostel and passes between the lakes Onogawa-ko and Akimoto-ko, providing views of Bandai-san and Hibara-ko lake. It intersects route 115, which goes from Ura-bandai to Fukushima, either directly or via the Bandai-Azuma Skyline. The Skyline road, nearly 30 km long, runs mostly along ridges and the crests of the mountain range, passing through the collection of peaks known as Azuma. The most interesting of these are Azuma-kofuji (Azuma-Little Fuji), and Issaikyo-san, its neighbor. Both are moderately high (1705 and 1949 meters), but the space between them has filled in considerably so that the road passes very close to the northern rim of Azuma-kofuji. You can climb up in less than 10 minutes and look or climb down into its crater—probably the most accessible one in Japan.

On the other side of the road is *Issaikyo-san*, an active volcano that jets steam with a continuous roar. Anyone who is the least bit energetic can scramble to the top in 30 minutes or so, and be rewarded by a superb view over the conical-cratered top of Azuma-kofuji and the rapid drop to the valley floor and Fukushima city.

Jododaira bus stop is located between the two mountains, and buses between the Bandai area and Fukushima can be used to get there. A stop-over is possible, continuing on or returning by a later bus. There is also a daily round trip out of Fukushima to Jododaira, with a 50 minute stop. The bus circles back via Tsuchiyu-toge pass and

Tsuchiyu-onsen. The trip takes 3-3/4 hours and leaves at 1300. The area is very popular with sightseers, so hitching should be good.

MIYAGI-KEN

Sendai

The largest city in northern Honshu, Sendai was flattened during the war and has been rebuilt like any typical Japanese commercial city, with many large buildings and straight streets in the central area. One of the main streets, Aoba dori (Green Leaf Avenue), is very attractive in the stretch where the trees are growing. It is rather high fashion, with many shops and good hotels, and has the feeling of a European city street. The rest of Sendai is unexceptional, however, though foreigners there say it's a good place to live, for the mountains are an hour in one direction and the sea an hour in the other. Short-term visitors will find only a small number of attractions, namely Osaki-Hachiman shrine, Rinno-ji garden, Zuihoden mausoleum, and possibly the grounds of the former castle, Aoba-jo.

Information

Useful maps and information in English, for sightseeing in the city, are available from the information center in the station.

A guide book prepared by foreign residents gives good sightseeing and other info on Sendai and vicinity. Simply titled *Sendai*, it should be available at Maruzen bookstore, Sendai station, and downtown hotels for about ¥1300. Either the same book retitled, or a new guide, is *In and Around Sendai*, by Vardaman, Garner and Brown. (Refer to the Books section.)

Things to See

Aoba-jo Castle & Grounds

Aoba-jo (Green-leaf Castle) stood on this hill until 1872. Now only the fortification walls remain, and the grounds have been made into a municipal park. A museum in the grounds has art and objects related to the history of the city and castle.

Sendai was founded, and Aoba-jo built, by Masamune Date in 1600, after he had defeated opponents of Shogun Toyo-tomi and become the third greatest feudal lord in the country. He was buried in an elaborate mausoleum, Zuihoden, on Kengamine hill, a short distance from the castle. The original stood until destroyed by bombing in July 1945. A five-year reconstruction project began in 1974, during which the vault underneath the structure was excavated, revealing the well-preserved bones of the lord plus several items buried with him. Masamune Date's remains were reinterred after construction of the building, but the funerary items have been put on display in the small museum adjacent to the memo-

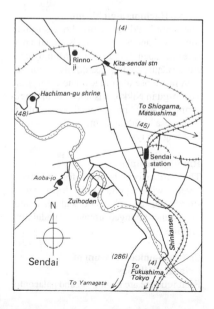

rial. Also shown there is a videotape of the excavation and reinterment with appropriate Shinto ritual.

A path leads from Zuihoden to two other mausoleums, Kansenden and Zennoden, which mark the tombs of the second and third lords, Tadamune Date and Tsunamune Date. All three memorial buildings sharing Kengamine hill are excellent postwar reconstructions. Although made of concrete, they have been decorated in the brilliantly colorful Momoyama style, and look very impressive. There are figures of people, animals, and flowers all in natural colors, elaborate and colorful roof supports, and much gold leaf. The buildings cost in excess of ¥800 million to rebuild.

Kengamine can be reached from Sendai station on bus 25; the name of the stop is Tamaya-bashi. The road from the bridge leads past Zuiho-ji temple, which was built by the second lord Tadamune in honour of his father.

Osaki-Hachiman-gu Shrine

The main building of this shrine survives from 1607 and is one of the National Treasures of Japan. It is a genuine Momoyama-era structure and is beautifully decorated with much use of gold leaf and color. Like Tosho-gu in Nikko, it is not at all in the restrained style normally thought of as "Japanese", although the outlines of the building are typical.

Rinno-ji Temple

The garden here is noted for its artistic layout, with a pond as the focus, and a stream, clusters of bamboo, and other natural beauties arranged around the undulating grounds.

Saito Ho-onkai Museum of Natural History

Featured here are geological and palaeonto-logical specimens of the area, including some dinosaur skeletons. However, the museum is rather small, as is the number of exhibits in relation to the ¥300 admittance charge (a typical sum in Japan).

Festival

To the Japanese, one of the most famous and favorite festivals in the country is Tanabata (Star Festival) August 6–8. It is based on an old Chinese story of the princess and the peasant shepherd who could meet only once a year. During the festival the city is hung with elaborate paper decorations, but there is almost no action worthy of note and the average westerner would find it about as exciting as a submarine race.

Places to Stay

There are many hotels and ryokan in Sendai, as well as four youth hostels.

Long-Distance Ferries

From Sendai, long-distance ferries ply daily to and from Tomakomai (Hokkaido) and Nagoya. The terminal is on the coast at Tagajo, which can be reached by JR train or bus from Sendai station.

Sakunami-onsen

This resort town, 28 km from Sendai, grew up around a hot spring occurring at the edge of a small river. The spring, at the bottom of the gorge that runs parallel to the road, can be reached via the lobby of the Iwamatsu Hotel. The baths, or *rotemburo*, are five small pools sheltered from rain and snow by a simple wooden roof. The only "wall" is the gorge face; the other three sides are open to nature, and a favorite winter pastime is to sit in the hot water and drink sake while admiring the snow.

Access is by JR Senzan line to Sakunami station; the line runs between Sendai and Yamagata. There is also a regular bus service from Sendai that runs directly to Sakunami-onsen.

Shiogama

This is the port for Sendai, and of limited interest. The main feature is Shiogama-jinja (shrine), a large structure mostly painted orange and white, although inner buildings are built in a traditional manner with very simple lines and natural wood. In the grounds is a museum of historic relics and exhibits related to whaling, which used to be carried out here. The shrine is on a wooded hill near Shiogama station.

Boats run regularly between Shiogama and both Matsushima-kaigan and Otakamori, passing by many of the little islands for which Matsushima Bay is famous. Details on boat services is given in the following section on Matsushima.

Matsushima

About 40 minutes by train (JR Senseki line) from Sendai lies famed Matsushima Bay, which is dotted with more than 250 small islands of strange shapes, covered with twisted pine trees. Some of the islands are inhabited, while others are little more than dots in the water. (Matsushima means "pine islands".) The area is regarded as one of the traditional "big three" of Japanese natural scenery (along with Amano-hashidate, north of Kyoto, and Itsukushima, near Hiroshima). It is certainly pretty and worth seeing both by regular cruise boat from Matsushima or Shiogama and on foot around Matsushima.

One of the best places to view Matsushima Bay is Tamonzan hill. To get there, take a bus from Shiogama station to Tamonzan stop (the road continues on to a couple of inviting ocean beaches) and walk along the little road to the left of the electric power station (you can't miss it). After a

couple of hundred meters there is a concrete staircase which leads up Tamonzan to a little shrine and a good view over the water to the white-shored, tree-covered islands and the small boats passing through the narrow channels between them. Around the shrine, which is likely to be totally deserted, are many figurines of foxes, the messenger of Inari shrines, plus little shrine-shaped "houses", 30–40 cm tall, to shelter them.

Things to See

Oshima Island

The red-lacquered Togetsukyo bridge connects the mainland (near Matsushima-kaigan station) with this small scenic island. In former times Oshima was the site of ascetic practices by the Buddhist faithful. The only evidence of those days are the many interesting niches and small caves cut in the rocks, and many carved stone memorials and Buddhist figures. The island offers good views over Matsushima Bay.

Kanrantei

The "Wave Viewing Pavilion", or Kanrantei, is one of the best places for viewing the bay, and is just a short walk from the station past the large park. Kanrantei is a teahouse dating from the early 1600s, and was originally part of Momoyama-jo castle in Kyoto. It was "given" to Masamune Date and moved here when the castle was demolished and its major buildings scattered around Japan.

Matsushima Hakubutsukan

This museum, located next to Kanrantei, has an excellent collection of Japanese suits of armor, swords, pikes (used by foot soldiers to fight cavalrymen), and a number of pieces of high quality lacquerware, all of the Date clan.

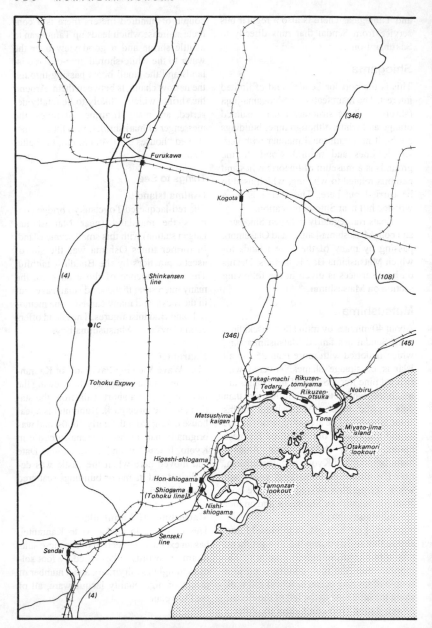

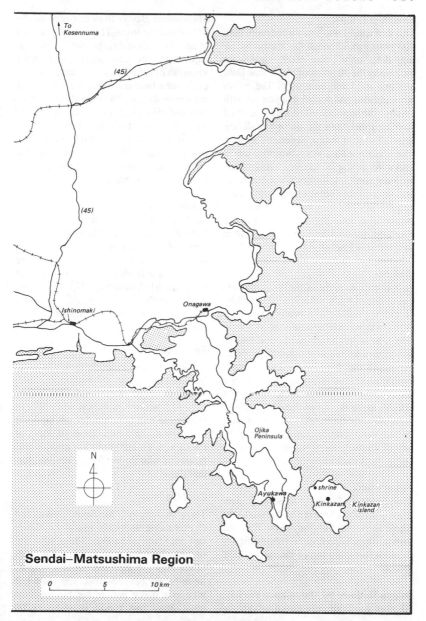

*To
Kesennuma*

(45)

(45)

Ishinomaki

Onagawa

*Ojika
Peninsula*

N

Ayukawa

• *shrine*
Kinkazan

*Kinkazan
island*

Sendai–Matsushima Region

0   5   10 km

Zuigan-ji Temple

This Zen temple was established more than 700 years ago, although the present buildings date "only" from 1609. They were built under the direction of Masamune Date and are of Momoyama style. The paintwork is faded and peeled, but you can still admire the myriad of ornately carved wooden panels and the decorated sliding doors. The temple is a National Treasure, which is surprising since this area was a backwater until quite recently. The grounds are very restful; tall trees shade the large area, and you can see the rooms carved out of solid rock that were once the quarters of monks. The temple is located across the road from the dock area, down a sidestreet signposted in English.

Godaido

At the left extremity of the dock area are two short red bridges that lead to Godaido, on the tiny island of Godaido-jima. Godaido, which could be described as a worship hall, is part of Zuigan-ji, and houses five statues of Buddhist figures. The color that might once have existed on the building has weathered away, but the wood has survived the centuries well and the carved animals under the eaves, the complex supports of the roof, and other details are worthy of note. The interior is said to be beautifully decorated, but the building is opened only once every 33 years.

Fukura-jima

The entrance to Fukura-jima is easily identified because the long red bridge out to the island is visible from anywhere near the harbor. There is no historic significance to the island but it is a sort of natural botanical garden.

Saigyo Modoshi no Matsu-koen Park

Another good, all-encompassing view of Matsushima Bay is from this park on the hill behind the town. The view is beautiful at any time of the day, but the best way to enjoy it is to spend the late afternoon on the verandah of the Panorama restaurant with a coffee or a beer and watch the last rays of the sun on the bay. There are also two lookouts that afford views of other parts of the bay. The simplest way to get to the park is by taxi; you can go on foot if you feel like a two km climb. (The only problem is that tall trees are growing up and blocking the view more each year.)

Festivals

On August 15 the Matsushima Toro-nagashi festival is held at Matsushima-kaigan. Thousands of tiny lanterns are set adrift from the beach (at about 1900), after which there is a fireworks display. The festival is part of the Buddhist observances of *obon*, the Festival of the Dead, which is held throughout Japan. There is also a lesser festival the following day.

Places to Stay

There are more than 40 ryokan around Matsushima-kaigan. Matsushima Youth Hostel is on Miyato Island, and can be reached from Nobiru station, or by boat to Otakamori and then bus (or on foot) the three km to the hostel. From the dock at Otakamori, go left past Otakamori-kanko Hotel and take the left fork in the road further along.

Boat Cruises

There are both scheduled public boats and charter cruises available around the islands that dot Matsushima Bay. These offer one of the most pleasant ways to see the sights of the area.   Scheduled one hour cruises leave hourly between 1000 and 1600 and take in a major part of the bay's scenic areas. Seats cost ¥1800; standing; ¥1200 for adults, ¥600 for children, with a discount for groups of 15 or more.

Charter boats also cruise the bay at a fixed price (regardless of the number of passengers) determined by the route taken. This can be ¥3000, ¥4000, ¥6000, or ¥15000.

In addition to round trip cruises, there are up to 16 boats per day in each direction between Matsushima-kaigan and Shiogama (¥1400; 60 minutes).

Between Shiogama and Otakamori (Miyato-jima island) there are three boats daily in each direction; between Matsushima-kaigan and Otakamori there are two boats daily in each direction (¥1200 minimum; 60 minutes).

At Matsushima-kaigan the boats dock at the central pier, which is easily reached from Matsushima-kaigan station. At Shiogama, boats leave from Shiogama-ko port, a five minute walk from Hon-Shiogama station (Senseki line).

Continuing from Matsushima

By road above Matsushima, you have the choice of continuing on Route 45 along the coast, with the option of a sidetrip down the scenic Ojika-hanto peninsula, or following Route 346 and 108 to Route 4 inland. Description begins with the inland route; the coastal way is described following the section on Morioka.

Ojika-hanto

A trip down the beautiful south coast of this peninsula can be recommended, especially if you have your own transport and can stop at the many lookouts. The coastal views include a succession of bays, interesting rock formations, little fishing villages, many fishing boats, and of course the ocean itself. This is not good territory for cyclists, as there are many steep hills.

There are seven buses a day (1-3/4 hours, ¥1400) from Ishinomaki to Ayukawa near the southern tip, and a daily boat (in each direction) that leaves Ishinomaki at 0940 and Ayukawa at 0730.

Beyond Ayukawa (no public transport listed) the road leads around the top of the peninsula to a fine view of Kinkazan Island, just a short distance off the coast. You can sit and admire the view from the restaurant close to the entrance to the toll road.

Ayukawa is a whaling port and the museum (near the dock for the Kinkazan boat) has an exhibit about whales and the industry.

Kinkazan

A "mysterious" atmosphere seems to surround this island which is just off the coast of Ojika-hanto peninsula. Various visitors have mentioned the peace at night, especially when staying at the youth hostel located at Koganeyama-jinja (shrine). The name Kinkazan means "Gold Flower Mountain", which seems to be in reference to the sparkle of mica in rocks on the island.

Koganeyama-jinja is one of the main attractions of the island, and is surprisingly large for such a remote place. There may be an early morning (at about 0630) service, featuring sacred dances by shrine maidens, with traditional music and chanting by priests. The island is covered with dense bamboo groves and forests, and monkeys and deer roam free. Behind the shrine a two km path leads to the top of the mountain where there is another shrine. The walk to the top takes an hour or so.

Getting There

Up to 10 ferries a day run between Ayukawa-ko port and Kinkazan (¥750); the single boat between Ishinomaki and Ayukawa is one of these. In addition there are up to five ferries a day between

Kinkazan and Onagawa, which is the terminus of a JR line (¥1600 minimum: 85 minutes).

Continuing Northward

Above the Matsushima-Ojika Peninsula area you can go inland along Route 4 to Miyagi-ken and Iwate-ken, or along the east coast. There are several roads and railway lines linking Route 4 with the coast, so it is possible to criss-cross to take in nearly all the places of interest without backtracking.

Inland route Route 4 is slow, crowded, and not very interesting but *shi kata ga nai*—it can't be helped. To get to Narugo and its nearby geyser turn off onto Route 47 at Furukawa, or take the train.

Narugo

This town, actually the collective name for a series of hot-spring resorts, has numerous ryokan and hotels catering to the hot-spring crowd, as well as an unmemorable (but adequate) youth hostel. The town is not particularly noteworthy—basically a string of buildings up the sides of a hill—but some very attractive lacquerware is produced here, and the town is famous for its Narugo-kokeshi dolls. *Kokeshi* are very simple, with a cylindrical (lathe-turned) body, round head and simple, painted features. The Narugo dolls "cry" when the head is turned, one explanation (veracity not guaranteed) being that families made them years ago to honor the souls of girl babies that had been abandoned in the open to die because there was not enough food to support them (being less-useful females). Many dolls are made in shops along the main street, and you can watch the process.

Onikobe-onsen

One of Japan's few geysers, and probably the highest spurting, is located at Onikobe-onsen (a collective name for several onsen, meaning "ogre's head"). About 14 km above Narugo, the geyser can be reached by bus from Narugo station; just ask to be let off at Onikobe kanketsu-sen-onsen. From the stop, the small park surrounding the geyser is down a side road.

The geyser is "artificial" to the extent that a hole was bored to tap the underground pool, but the eruption, every 30 minutes or so, is entirely natural. Water shoots at least 15 meters into the air for several minutes. Close by is a warm water swimming-pool that can be used by those who have already paid to see the geyser.

Narugo-kyo Gorge

About three km outside Narugo, near Nakayama-daira-guchi, this gorge is an enjoyable place to walk, though it is more enjoyable with a companion. It follows a small river for about four km. To get there, take a bus from Narugo station.

The Tsuruoka area of the west coast is easily reached from this point.

IWATE-KEN ▬▬▬▬▬▬

Hiraizumi

Taking the inland route you come to this ordinary looking town, once the cultural center of the area, which contains the most historic temple in northern Japan. Nearby are two interesting gorges and beautiful views of typical farmland with some of the largest and finest farmhouses in the country.

Things to See

Chuson-ji

This temple was founded in 1105 to accompany a fortress in Hiraizumi built by the Fujiwara family. Of the more than 40 buildings then standing, only two have survived. One, Kyozo, is not particularly note-

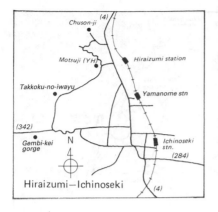

Hiraizumi—Ichinoseki

worthy, but the other, Konjiki-do, is a marvel of finely executed, ornate decoration. Konjiki-do ("golden hall") was originally protected by an outer structure, but recently a new concrete building was put up around it to provide a climate-controlled environment. At the same time, it was restored to its original splendor, using authentic materials from the same sources as the ones used initially. The exterior is lacquered black, and there are large panels of mother-of-pearl and gold leaf. Inside are three altars, each with 11 Buddhist deities (three Amida, six of Jizo and two of Ten). The building is small (only 5.5 meters square) but you can stand for a long time admiring it through the protective plate glass. The remains of three of the Fujiwara rulers lie under the central altar.

The grounds of the temple are very restful, set at the top of a large hill that overlooks fertile farming country. An avenue of tall trees lines the stone-paved road up from the entrance. The entry fee also covers the nearby Sankozo museum.

There are many buses to the temple from the station throughout the day, and the entrance is a drop-off point for the bus that runs between Hiraizumi station and Ichi-noseki station (the next large town).

Motsu-ji

During the era of the Fujiwara, this was the largest and greatest temple in northern Honshu. All the buildings from that time have been destroyed over the years and nothing but foundation stones and Oizumi-ga-ike pond and garden remain, although there are some picturesque buildings of more recent vintage around the grounds.

The temple grounds would be very peaceful if it weren't for several PA systems with different recorded messages, two of which can usually be heard at any one time.

The youth hostel is in the temple grounds, and guests are allowed to walk around without paying the admittance charge.

The temple is about half a km from Hiraizumi station. You can get there by bus or by walking out of the station and across the main road (Route 4), then continuing along the road on the other side of Route 4.

Takkoku-no-iwayu

A few km further along the road that curves past Motsu-ji, is a small interesting temple in the mouth of a cave. It is built on pillars, like a small scale Kiyomizu-dera (Kyoto). The temple is a 1946 reproduction of a much more ancient structure. Faintly visible in the large rock near the temple is an image of Dainichi-Nyorai, believed to date from the late 11th century.

Gembi-kei Gorge

This gorge is only about one km long and never more than a few meters deep, but the river has carved the solid rock into a most picturesque and intricate natural sculpture. You can walk its full length along the banks where there are many Jacob's wells (circular holes bored into the rock by the

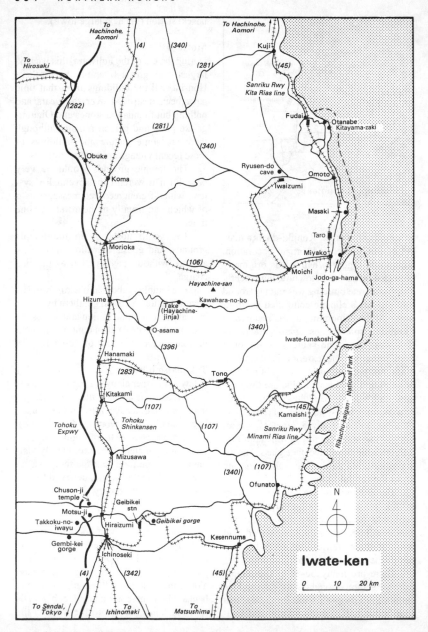

Iwate-ken

0   10   20 km

action of rock-bearing water). It is a very pretty place and well worth a visit.

The gorge, which is past Motsu-ji and Takkoku-no-iwayu, is easily accessible by bus from Hiraizumi station. The trip there passes through pretty countryside and by large prosperous-looking farmhouses.

Geibi-kei Gorge

Near Hiraizumi is another gorge, but this one is of heroic proportions and is one of the great bargains of Japan. For about ¥1000 you can take a truly memorable 90 minute boat trip up the river and back. The flat-bottomed boat is poled by two boatmen up the slow moving Satetsu-gawa river between grey and blue streaked cliffs and large rocks. On the way upstream the only sounds are the splash of the boatmen's poles, the ever-present cicadas (in summer), plus wheeling, raucous crows (which by the way, have a Japanese accent, and say "haw" instead of "caw"!). The ride ends at Daigeibi-kei, a cliff that rises straight and flat for about 100 meters. It is a fitting climax to the ascent.

On the way down, the boatmen serenade their 50 or so passengers with plaintive, traditional songs that echo off the rock walls. This was one of the most beautiful, peaceful, relaxing, "Japanese" moments of my travels in Japan. (A late-season traveller wrote that the boatmen were not unwilling to take him alone in a boat, and that he enjoyed the trip immensely.)

It can be reached by JR from Ichinoseki; it is the sixth station (Geibi-kei) on the way to Kesennuma, on the coast. (Ichinoseki is a stop on the Tohoku Shinkansen, two stops from Hiraizumi.) Geibi-kei can also be reached by bus from Hiraizumi station.

Mizusawa

Anyone interested in an unusual souvenir of Japan should look for a little shop that sells fish traps. These are the simple type, centuries old in design, that funnel water through the trap so the fish is caught in an inner chamber. I spotted it along the main street as I rode through, but don't know if it still exists.

Kitakami

Though it is not one of the famous Tohoku festivals, Kitakami's annual extravaganza is quite interesting. Its history goes back only 30-odd years, but the format varies from year to year as dancers, floats, etc., from other festivals in Japan are invited to participate. There are usually lion dances, kagura dance displays, sword dances, drumming, and fireworks. The festival is held from August 7–9. It is best to inquire locally to determine the best day to visit.

Tono

Tono is a large town situated in a long agricultural valley east of Kitakami on the road toward Kamaishi and the coast. Its relative isolation until the turn of the century has meant that many of the old legends and folk tales have remained more a part of people's lives here than in most other parts of Japan. And that's the way the people of Tono want to keep it. They have rejected industrialization and are endeavoring to retain as much of the atmosphere of the past as is practicable. The town itself is unremarkable, like almost any other in the country, but there are still several *magariya* (traditional thatched-roof L-shaped farmhouses) in the valley, either lived in or used for storage or animals, and some of the old waterwheels are still in use.

Information

To the right when leaving Tono station is the combined information and accommodation booking office. They have two maps

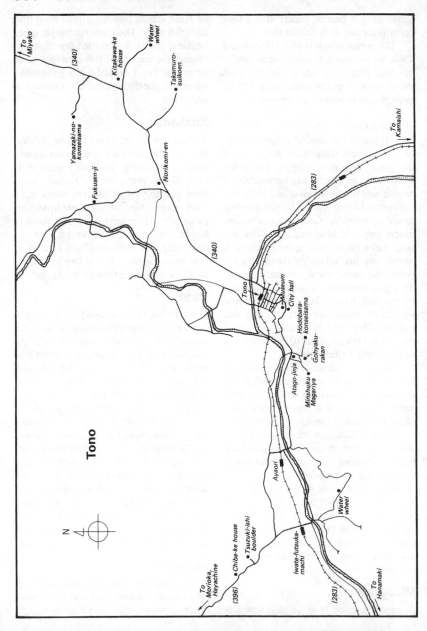

NORTHERN HONSHU   3 3 7

of Tono: one is an all-too-typical Japanese color pamphlet with cute little pictorial representations of the local sights which give absolutely no indication of where they really are; the other is a "proper" map. When the two are used together, the first is handy for finding the *kanji* name for the place, while the second can be used for actually getting there.

The various attractions around Tono and the roads to them are conveniently signposted.

Things to See

Chiba-ke

This imposing structure, sited on a hill about nine km from Tono (along Route 396), was the home of the Chiba family, very wealthy farmers. It dates back about two centuries and was restored recently because it is regarded as one of the ten most important historic farmhouses in Japan.

Waterwheel

One of the few functioning waterwheels (not decorative) in the area can be found along the road that runs south from Iwate-futsukamachi station (the second east of Tono station). The word for water wheel is *suisha*.

Gohyaku-rakan

Carved in relief on boulders in a shallow ravine and on the hillside are several hundred images of faces, the 500 *rakan* (disciples) of Buddha. They were carved in the mid 1700s by a priest to console the spirits of the hundreds who died of starvation following two years of crop failures. A few of the images can be found easily; the rest of the nearly 400 known to survive could take quite a while to locate.

The Gohyaku-rakan can be found by first locating Atago-jinja shrine, which is near Route 283, across from a major bridge

west of the bus terminal. The stone carvings are about 300 meters up the hill in a peaceful wooded area behind the shrine.

Fukusen-ji

There are several shrines and temples in Tono itself, but perhaps the most interesting to visit is Fukusen-ji, about six km from the station. There is a large Ming-style gate at the entrance, but its main feature is a very tall statue of Kannon, the goddess of mercy. It is, it must be said, more impressive for its 17 meter height than for the artistry of the woodcarving, even though it was carved from a single piece of 1200 year old wood.

Norikomi-en

The main attraction here is an old *magariya* house with authentic furnishings to give an idea of what life was like in days gone by. Both in the house and in an adjacent building there are demonstrations of old crafts, such as weaving and straw sandal making. Another building houses hundreds of Oshira-sama dolls—simple figures that are little more than a 30 cm stick with a crude face, dressed in a square of brightly colored cloth. There are also other displays and an old steam locomotive in the grounds of Norikomi-en, which is located just past the turn-off for Fukusen-ji

Places to Stay

Near Gohyaku-rakan is Minshuku Magariya, a typical L-shaped thatched-roof house, about 80 years old, that offers accommodation. The owner is friendly, and the warm welcome is a good way to get the feel for old Japan. To make a reservation you can ring 01986-2-4564. There are numerous other *minshuku* and *ryokan* in Tono, and bookings can be made at the office near the station.

Transportation in the Area

The train line serving Tono (JR) runs between Kitakami (on the Tohoku Shinkansen) and Kamaishi, a nondescript industrial city on the east coast, from where a JR line runs north to Miyako and beyond. The Sanriku railway Minami Rias-sen line runs south from Kamaishi to Ofunato, where JR services resume.

Hayachine-san

The mountain, Hayachine-san, has been regarded as a sacred place for centuries. These days it has become a popular destination for walkers, and on July 31 and August 1 every year, a very interesting festival is held in the little village of Take, on the flank of the mountain.

Take

The festival of Hayachine-jinja shrine in Take (pronounced Tah-kay) begins on the night of July 31 with performances of a very rare type of theater unique to this part of Japan. *Yamabushi-kagura* is a collection of stories acted out in dance. Prior to the war, farmers in Tohoku used to regularly act out these very energetic masked dance-dramas in their farmhouses during the winter nights, a tradition hundreds of years old. Since the arrival of television, however, the performances are limited to this annual festival and others on January 3, December 17, and the second Sunday of June.

Performances are given on the stage in the courtyard of Hayachine-jinja on the night of the 31st. (Take is tiny, so it's not hard to locate the shrine). The music, drumming, and cymbals are quite primitive, somewhat reminiscent of Balinese music.

The next morning (try to get there by 0900), there is a procession from the main shrine to a smaller shrine nearby. The preliminaries include the blessing of *mikoshi* (portable shrines), a time-honored Shinto

ritual. Then out comes the most fascinating attraction of the festival, the *shishi*. Twenty or more *shishi*—townspeople dressed in lion costumes that are topped with very large and magnificent wooden masks of lion heads—parade along the road, the heads held high overhead so that the "animals" are much taller than a man. The masks have glossy black lacquered faces, fiery eyes, and gold teeth outlined in red. The mane is made of white tassles of paper, and the lower jaw is hinged so it can open and shut to make a resounding "clack".

The procession, which includes many children dressed in white, is led by long-nosed, red-faced *tengu*. The *shishi* stop periodically to give dance demonstrations, accompanied by musicians on drums, flutes, and gongs. The jaws of the lions clack resonantly in unison with the music, producing an effect that can only be described as truly eerie. But for the other onlookers, you would think that you had been dropped into a surreal world.

There are further performances of yamabushi-kagura at the shrine following the procession. At the same time, amateur sumo wrestlers perform in a ring in a nearby field.

Places to Stay

Because Take is a base camp for walking in the mountains, there are several places in the town that offer accommodation, nearly all in the form of very large open rooms with one or more tatami mat per person. The rooms are big enough to hold 60 or more people. There is an information service for the festival (tel 0198-48-5864); they may also be able to help with reservations for accommodation.

Getting There

Take is part of the town of Oazama, from which there are up to eight buses a day;

three of these originate at Hanamaki station and a fourth at Kitakami station. Two buses continue on through Take to Kawahara-nobo, a high point along the road used as a starting point for walking on Hayachine-san.

Morioka

Morioka is the northern terminus of the Tohoku Shinkansen from Tokyo. The centerpiece of the city is Iwate-koen, a park, on the former site of Morioka-jo castle, but now just a respite from the crowds. It can be reached from Morioka station via Saien-dori, one of the two main shopping streets (the other is O-dori). Across the river and to the left is the Gozaku area, a series of old shops looking much as they did a hundred years ago.

The Tazawa-ko lake area is a relatively short distance to the west of Morioka, easily accessible by train and bus, as are Akita, Mt Iwate, and the Oga Peninsula, also to the west (described in the Akita-ken section), and Miyako, Kuji, Hachinohe, and Towada-ko lake to the east and north (below).

Coastal Route from Matsushima

Northward from the Matsushima area you can continue along Route 45. The road runs close to the sea for much of the way, but except for near Ofunato there is little in the way of coastal sights until Miyako. At Kesennuma you reach the beginning of Rikuchu-kaigan National Park.

Ofunato Area

Scarcely worth the name "peninsula", the little extension of land below Hosoura has enough natural attractions to interest the traveller who is not in a hurry. The first place of interest, almost at the tip, is Go-ishi-hama, which means "Go stone beach". *Go* is a popular board game played with

black and white stones; the stones found on the beach here are round and black, and in the past provided many "pieces" of the right size for the game. (Visitors are requested not to take any.)

The beach is less than a km before the Goishi-kaigan bus terminus, where there is a booking office for the many *minshuku* in the area, a restaurant, and a delightful wooded park.

Back toward town is Anadoshi, another sight definitely worth seeing if you're into seascapes. Anadoshi is a triple arch of rock formed from centuries of erosion.

Getting There

There are regular buses from Ofunato bus terminal or station, via Hosoura, to Goishi-kaigan, some of which go on to Anadoshi. From Kamaishi, Route 283 leads inland to Tono, Hayachine, and the attractions along Route 4.

Miyako

The city of Miyako is a major gateway for travel up the Sanriku-kaigan coast and, with the opening of the Sanriku railway Kita Rias line, travel in the region is now faster and more reliable than on the local buses. The main problem with the line, however, is that more than half its length is

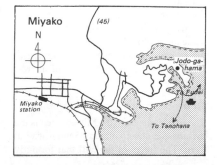

though tunnels, cutting into the sightseeing en route.

There are two youth hostels in Miyako, both near the station, and there is an accommodation office at the station that can help you find a *ryokan*. (Initially they told me there were no rooms, but a Japanese companion persisted and got us one in the end.)

The coastal attraction nearest to Miyako is Jodo-ga-hama—"Paradise Beach". A finger of the cliff reaches out and descends into the water, forming a sheltered cove for swimmers. Walking trails stretch along the coast north of Jodo-ga-hama and are marked on the handout map given out at Miyako station.

Sanriku-kaigan Coast

In summer there is a daily cruise boat that goes from Jodo-ga-hama to Otanabe, leaving at 0830 and arriving at 1125 (¥2900; return departure: 1320). This boat passes the most spectacular sight, the cliffs of Kitayamazaki, which are well over 100 meters high. From Otanabe it is possible to go back by bus to Kitayamazaki-tembodai, an excellent viewpoint built specifically to overlook the cliffs, then continue on by another bus to the next train station and use it either to return to Miyako or continue on to Kuji. There are also five other boats in each direction from Jodo-ga-hama to Taro (¥1200; 40 minutes) and Masaki (¥1300; 60 minutes), both much closer to Miyako. From any of these boats you can see at least some of the cliffs for which this coast is famous, and the boat goes close enough to shore to see the specific points of interest clearly.

Taro

The first sight above the Miyako area is the picturesque stone column "Sanno-iwa" at Taro. The finger of the cliff that formerly stretched into the ocean has been eroded away from both sides, leaving this solitary tower about 50 meters tall and 10 meters across the base.

There are three buses a day from Miyako, and the cruise boats from Jodogahama stop at Taro harbor.

The rest of the coast north to Fudai is a succession of spectacular headlands, wave-washed rocks, eroded arches, sheer cliffs, interesting rock formations and, of course, the blue ocean itself.

Ryusendo Cave

This is one of the three major caves in Japan. Visitors are permitted 300 meters into it, passing stalagmites and stalactites. Ryusendo can be reached by bus from Iwaizumi (which is served by JR via Moichi). Buses also run directly from Morioka and from Komoto, on the coast. There are *ryokan* and *minshuku* at Iwaizumi and at other tourist spots in the area.

AOMORI-KEN ▬▬▬▬

This is the northernmost part of Honshu and is of interest mainly for access to Hokkaido. If you are travelling up the east coast, Hachinohe is the first ferry port; others are Aomori, Noheji, and Oma.

Hachinohe

This coastal city is most noteworthy as the port for regular daily boats to Tomakomai, on Hokkaido. Using this route to Hokkaido allows you to bypass the relatively uninteresting northern tip of Honshu.

Those interested in archaeology can visit Kokokan, a small museum in Hachinohe, which houses several thousand Jomon era relics dug up in the area.

Another attraction of Hachinohe is the city's annual festival (one of many in the region during the first week of August). The festival is a lengthy procession of

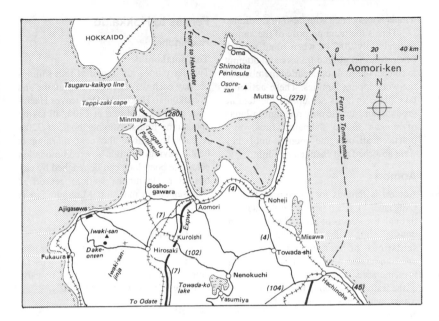

floats depicting a theme from Japanese or Chinese history or mythology—castles, lucky gods, demons, warriors, dragons and, of course, beautiful maidens—and each float is accompanied by a large *taiko* (drum) beaten tirelessly by a relay of young men. Each float is a group effort of a neighborhood of the city. It seems that foreigners are still a rarity here even during the festival; I saw no others, and was kindly invited to stay in the home of a local family.

Misawa

Travellers through Misawa with time to kill while waiting for a train, etc., could venture into the amazingly kitsch Komaki-onsen. This large Japanese-style resort complex includes a large bath of several pools, a park area with reconstructions of famous historic structures, and a lake for boating. Komaki-onsen is about five min-

utes walk from Misawa station. Admittance is ¥800.

Shimokita-hanto Peninsula

The eastern horn of northern Honshu is quite flat and rather bland. There are beaches all along the inner coast, but they collect all the floating debris of the area, so are not good for swimming. With the exception of festival time at Osore-san, most visitors only come here to take the ferry from Oma to Hokkaido.

Osore-zan

This mountain has been regarded as sacred since at least the 9th century. Entsu-ji temple was built on its flank on the north shore of the small lake Osore-zan. The landscape around the lake is desolate, stark and white, the result of underground minerals deposited on the surface by hot springs. The temple is associated with *itako* or mediums.

This is the main purpose of the annual festival (July 20-24), when blind women (the mediums) go into trances and attempt to contact the souls of departed members of the worshipping families. These activities take place in tents set up on the temple grounds, and are the only remnant in Japan of *minkan shinko* shamanist rites, once practiced all over the country until they were absorbed and changed by Shinto.

Aomori

Aomori is famous for its Nebuta festival (August 3–7), when very large floats move through the streets at night. The floats are unusual, huge three-dimensional representations of men and animals that are illuminated from the inside. The sight is memorable. An explanation of the origin of the festival is given in the section on Hirosaki, which has a similar festival called Neputa.

Places to Stay

The youth hostel can be reached from Aomori station by bus No. 1; get off at Sakaimachi-itchome. It is associated with a temple, and a faint drumming may be heard in the morning.

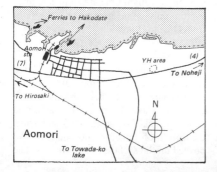

Aomori

Ferries to Hokkaido

Hachinohe

To Tomakomai

Two ferry lines run a total of four sailings per day each way between Hachinohe and Tomakomai, Hokkaido. One leaves Hachinohe at 0845, and two at 1300, all taking about nine hours. Another boat, at 2200, reaches Hachinohe the next morning at 0630, saving a night's accommodation cost. The boat dock can be reached by city bus from Hachinohe station; get off at Shin-sankaikan-mae stop. Minimum fare is ¥3900.

To Muroran

There are two boats/day to/from Muroran. One in each direction arrives at a useful time of the day, the other two in early morning. Minimum fare is ¥3900.

Aomori

To Hakodate

Until 1988 Aomori was the port used by most travellers for getting to and from Hakodate by ferry. With the opening of the Seikan tunnel, however, JR train service from Aomori station under the sea to Hokkaido does the job.

To Muroran

There is a ferry service from Aomori to Muroran on Hokkaido. Muroran is very convenient for reaching the popular Shikotsu-Toya area of Hokkaido, but the arrival times in Muroran are very awkward. Departure/arrival times are 1445/2130 and 2130/0430; minimum fare is ¥3400.

Noheji

To Hakodate

Three ferries a day sail in each direction between this town and Hakodate at a minimum cost of ¥1400. Sailing times are 1230,

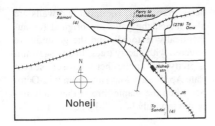

Noheji

1700, and 0035; transit time is about 4 1/2 hours. The terminal is a couple of km west of town, and can be reached by bus from Noheji station. On the Hokkaido side, the ferries dock some distance from the center of Hakodate, making it more awkward for foot travellers.

Oma

To Hakodate
Up to five ferries per day cross each way between Oma and Hakodate (¥1000). However, the boat docks at the same previously mentioned awkward-to-reach terminal in Hakodate.

To Muroran
In the summer there is one sailing per day between Oma and Muroran, leaving Oma at 1500, and Muroran at 0930 (¥1400). In summer there is an extra sailing each way at the reverse of the above times.

Tsugaru Peninsula

The western pincer of Mutsu Bay, at the top of Honshu, is the Tsugaru-hanto peninsula. A spine of low mountains up the middle and a west coast of small lakes and marshes limits the habitability. Only the east coast is very populated and is, in fact, one endless fishing village squeezed between the water and the hills almost immediately behind. Nets can be seen drying everywhere. By road it is slow going; the

JR line runs along this coast and would doubtlessly be faster and more relaxing.

The most notable scenic view is from the northern tip, Tappi-zakicape, with its semi-circular bay, rocky shoreline, and green-covered cliffs that slope into the sea.

Few visitors come here, as the previous major attraction of a ferry connection between Minmaya and Hokkaido has stopped. To reach the cape, take one of the six daily trains (95 minutes) from Aomori to Minmaya, then a bus from the station to the Tappi-zaki lookout (*tembodai*).

The Seikan tunnel under the strait to Hokkaido plunges underground near here.

Northwest Coast

A train trip down the west coast from the base of the Tsugaru Peninsula is an enjoyable way to see this section of Honshu. The JR line (five per day) between Hirosaki and Higashi-noshiro (between Akita and Odate) runs as close to the water as practicable and offers excellent vistas over the ocean and rocky coastline for nearly its full length.

Juni-ko Lakes

Those who like walking, or nature, or both, should consider a stop at Juni-ko. Juni-ko means "Twelve Lakes", and takes its name from the many bodies of water dammed by a landslide caused by an earthquake. All are quite small, some big enough for an enjoyable row around, others almost small enough to jump over. There are walking trails through the forest and around the larger ponds; a circuit takes a couple of hours. An engraved wooden sign at the bus terminal shows the routes.

Juniko can be reached from Juni-ko station by bus. Buses are scheduled to meet all five trains from Noshiro (to the south), and three of the five from the Hirosaki direction. They remain at Juni-ko for 50 to

100 minutes before returning to the station. Four of the five make good connections with trains bound for Hirosaki, and three connect well with trains for Noshiro.

Aomori to Towada-ko

The shortest route to the area around Lake Towada, recommended if you're in a hurry, is the direct road south through scenic woodland areas. An enjoyable stop en route is Suiren-numa, a small pond backdropped by four mountain peaks, still snow patched in late July. The area is at its best in autumn. There are at least 11 buses a day.

For those in less of a hurry, the route south via Hirosaki is more interesting.

Hirosaki

The information office at Hirosaki station may have a copy of the city-produced brochure *Hirosaki* showing a couple of temples that might be of interest—Chosho-ji and Seigan-ji.

Things to See
Hirosaki-jo Castle
This lovely original castle (not a replica)

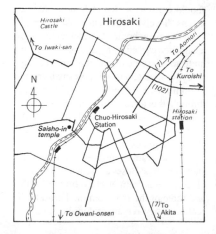

dates from 1610. The moat and walls are also intact, the gates are original (or authentically restored), and the grounds are covered with cherry trees. In any season it is pretty; during the cherry blossom season (late April–early May) and from mid-October when the maples are at their autumn-best it is a truly beautiful place to visit.

Saisho-in Temple
Standing in the temple grounds is a five-storey pagoda dating from 1672. Although many people believe that Japan is full of such pagodas, they are in fact relatively rare and therefore worth a visit.

Festivals
Hirosaki is famous throughout Japan for its Neputa festival, August 1–7, which is very similar to the Nebuta festival of Aomori.

The floats of the festival are smaller than those of Aomori and of a different format—rather like a three-dimensional fan, with scenes from Japanese or Chinese mythology painted on the two faces and the edges. Lights inside them, either candles or electric, illuminate the scenes beautifully.

The numerous *dashi* (carts carrying the floats) parade through the streets on a different route each night, accompanied by drummers and other musicians. A map showing the route-of-the-day is available from the information office at the station.

The origin of the Neputa (and Nebuta) festival is unknown. One version is that a Japanese military commander used giant figures similar to those carved in the floats to terrify the Ainu (whom he was fighting at Hirosaki), and that he celebrated his victory on reaching Aomori. The *Official Guide* indicates that a military commander, Sakanoue, used such figures in the late 9th century to subjugate rebels (who might well have been Ainu or other tribesmen fighting against the southern Japanese who were advancing into their territory).

These two festivals, along with ones at Hayachine-san (July 31–August 1), Yamagata (August 6–8) and Akita (August 5–7), make early August an excellent time to visit this part of Japan, especially as its climate is less hot and humid than that of the southern regions.

Buses are available from Hirosaki or Kuroishi to Nenokuchi and Yasumiya on Towada-ko lake (described later).

Iwaki-san

The cone of this 1625-meter dormant volcano dominates the flat countryside west of Hirosaki. It can be climbed in about four hours (7.3 km) from Hyakuzawa-onsen, or can be approached the easy way by bus and chairlift. Five buses a day go from Hirosaki station to the top of the mountain (*sancho*) from where the chairlift begins. On the mountain, you may see white-garbed pilgrims wending their way up the paths. They are members of the *yamabushi* sect, an offshoot of Buddhism that includes many elements of Shinto. If considering a trip to the top, observe the weather carefully; if clouds can be seen near the summit, the view from there may be totally obscured by fog.

Iwaki-san-jinja Shrine

Situated on the southeast flank of Iwaki-san, this shrine is surrounded by a large grove of tall, ancient trees. The buildings are painted a reddish-brown, and some doorways and other details have elaborate carvings overhead. According to a previous *Official Guide*, the shrine is often called "Nikko shrine of northwest Honshu". Well, the shrine is pleasing in appearance, but bears no resemblance to *Tosho-gu* (Nikko) and is not worth a special trip for its beauties. It is popular with pilgrims, and busloads of them may be seen being guided through the rites of the shrine by the priests, to the sound of drumming.

Similarly, Iwaki-san's description was: "The mountain is often called Tsugaru-fuji because of its remarkable resemblance to Mt Fuji". Most mountains will resemble Fuji if they are volcanic cones, and Iwaki-san is one of at least 12 in Japan so described!

Towada-ko Lake

One of the most popular destinations in northern Honshu is the Towada-ko area. Its main appeal is its natural scenery and the chance to escape from the built-up city areas. The lake is the third deepest in Japan, 334 meters, and is located in an old volcanic crater. The sides of the crater rise sharply, as you'll see if you arrive by bus from Tawada-minami; the road snakes down 'round countless twists and switchbacks on its way to water level.

The area invites exploration on foot, but there is a road around the entire circumference of the lake and buses pass over all parts of it at some time during the day.

The main centers of population around the lake (all small) are Yasumiya, Utarube, and Nenokuchi. Most of the shore has been left in its natural state, without the rows of souvenir shops, etc., that characterise too many resorts in Japan.

Things to See

Oirase Valley

The most popular walk in the area is through the Oirase valley, which stretches 14 km northeast from Nenokuchi. The Oirase-kawa river originates at the lake and flows through the only break in the crater wall. Along the way its character varies between shallow and placid to a narrow torrent rushing around rocks and plunging over falls. A tree-canopied path follows the

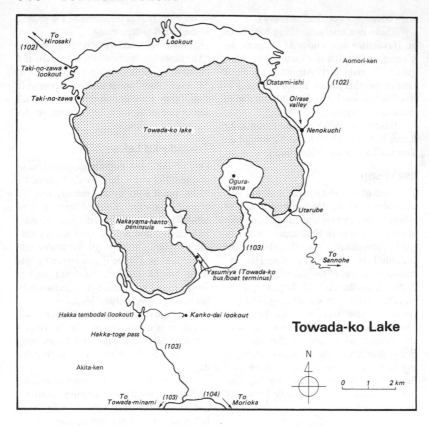

Towada-ko Lake

To Hirosaki (102)
Lookout
Taki-no-zawa lookout
Taki-no-zawa
Aomori-ken
Otatami-ishi (102)
Oirase valley
Towada-ko lake
Nenokuchi
Ogura-yama
Utarube
Nakayama-hanto peninsula
To Sannohe
(103)
Yasumiya (Towada-ko bus/boat terminus)
Hakka tembodai (lookout)
Kanko-dai lookout
Hakka-toge pass
(103)
N
Akita-ken
0   1   2 km
To Towada-minami (103)   (104)   To Morioka

river, and in October the leaves are amazingly colorful.

From Nenokuchi you have the option of returning to Yasumiya by bus or boat. Boats run every 30 minutes until mid-afternoon between Nenokuchi and Towadako town. The trip takes one hour, costs ¥1130, and passes by the most scenic parts of the lake. These include the volcanic cone of Ogura-san, which bulges into the lake, and Nakayama-hanto, the peninsula on which Yasumiya is located.

AKITA-KEN

Oyu-onsen

Between Towadako town and Towada-minami (20 minutes from the latter) is Oyu-onsen. Anyone interested in archaeology should stop here to see the mysterious stone circle Oyu-iseki, which is about 20 minutes by local bus into the countryside. It is not so spectacular for itself, but for what it represents. It is an arrangement of stones in a circle about 46 meters across, with a central group of stones and an upright rock; the origin is unknown but it is believed to be

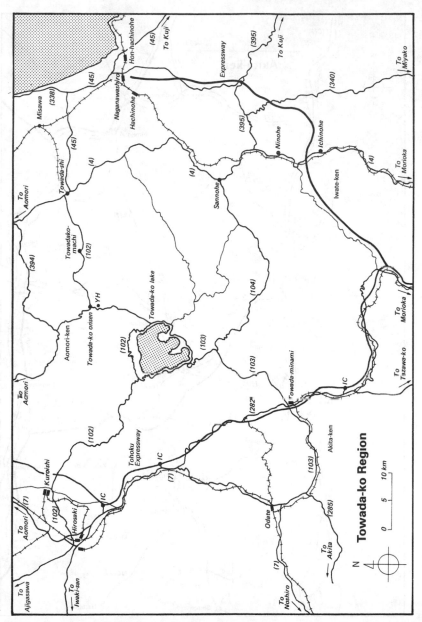

Towada-ko Region

N

0   5   10 km

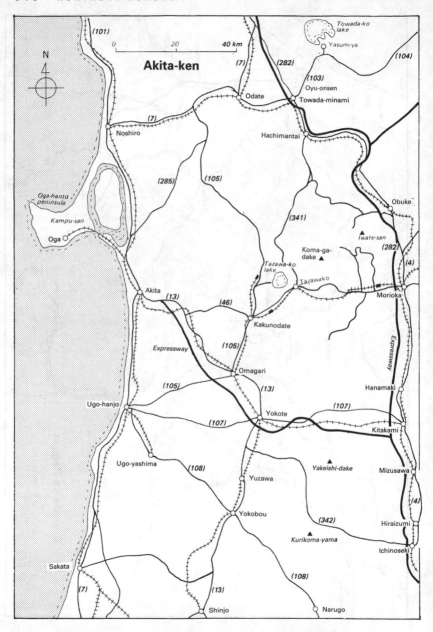

about 4000 years old. It was discovered in the early 1930s and excavated 20 years later. Of the 30 or so stone circles known to exist in Hokkaido and Tohoku, this is the largest and finest.

There are plenty of buses every day that pass through Oyu between Towada-minami and Towadako or run direct to Oyu-onsen so it is quite easy to make this a day trip. There is also a youth hostel in Oyu about 100 meters from the bus station.

Places to Stay

There are many hotels, ryokan, and minshuku, in addition to the youth hostels. It is possible to inquire about accommodation in Yasumiya, but because of the popularity of the area it is risky to turn up without a reservation (particularly during the October school excursion season). Yasumiya, on the south shore, is the transportation center of the lake area; the name of the bus stop is "Towada-ko". Hakubutsukan Youth Hostel (Museum YH) is quite close; Towada YH is between Yasumiya and Wainai, on the lake near Hotel Hakka. The other nearby hostels are at Towadako machi, Nishitowada, and Oyu.

Getting Around

Starting from Yasumiya, any of the 17 daily buses to Odate or Morioka can be taken a few km along the mountain road up the south rim to Hakka-toge tembodai (Hakka pass lookout), which gives an excellent view of the lake. Another lookout nearby is Kogakudai. From Wanai, on the lake, there are four daily buses running clockwise around the lake (toward Hirosaki) to Taki-no-zawa-tembodai, for probably the best view of the lake. After that it is possible to get a bus coming from Hirosaki and take it as far as Nenokuchi to have a look round the Oirase-dani valley.

There are also 'round-the-lake cruises

out of Towada-ko (up to seven per day) that last one hour and cost ¥1130.

Noshiro

This small city has an interesting festival during the same period as the other main Tohoku festivals. On the night of August 6 there is a parade of lantern-lit festival wagons similar to those featured in the festivals of Takayama, Furukawa, Kyoto, etc. For up-to-date info you can ring (in Japanese only) 0185-52-2111.

Oga-hanto Peninsula

This promontory, formed by submarine volcanic activity long ago, has an indented coastline with many unusual and scenic rock formations and reefs.

A good starting point for seeing the peninsula is Monzen (reached by bus from

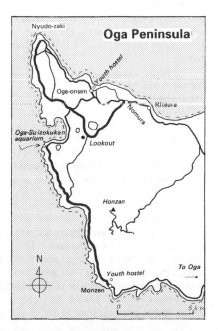

Oga Peninsula

JR Oga station; up to 14 through the day). Between late April and the end of October boats cruise along the coast from Monzen to Oga-Suizokukan aquarium. About six buses per day make the trip between the aquarium and Oga station.

(It should be easy to hitch back if desired.) The boat schedule is posted at the Monzen bus terminal, and both it and the bus schedule are also printed in *jikokuhyo*.

Things to See

Oga-Suizokukan

This aquarium is definitely worth visiting. In addition to commonplace ocean fish, it has some truly weird and wonderful creations of nature that outdo anything that a Walt Disney cartoonist could dream up— some incredibly beautiful, others equally ugly. There are also several alligators, crocodiles, and large turtles.

A very unusual sight here, and at Monzen, are dugout boats still in everyday use (with outboard motors!). The availability of large trees in the area makes them possible.

Nyudo-zaki Cape

From Oga-Suizokukan, you can continue by bus to Nyudo-zaki cape via Oga-onsen. From the cape, a toll road runs along another stretch of cliff and between two small green lakes, ending at Nomura. At the cape, and elsewhere, you are likely to see masks and costumes of *namahage* (ogres) as part of tourist promotion advertising. In a traditional festival at New Year, groups of young men in similar ogre costumes visit homes of the town, where they are formally received by the master of the house. They pause to honor the family shrine, then walk around the house shouting "Any good-for-nothing loafers here?" Because this festival has become so well known throughout Japan, many outsiders want to see it, so there is a "special" on New Year's Eve for their benefit. The "real" festival is held later among only the residents.

Places to Stay

There is accommodation available at several centers on the coast, including Oga city and Monzen. Oga Choraku-ji Youth hostel at Monzen is better than usual. It is part of a 1200 year old temple; an alarm clock is unnecessary because drumming, which is part of the religious ceremony, begins at 0630.

At Oga-onsen there are several ryokan and minshuku, plus another youth hostel.

Akita

This city is noteworthy only for its famed annual Kanto festival (August 5–7), when young men balance tall bamboo poles that support as many as 50 lighted paper lanterns on cross-bars.

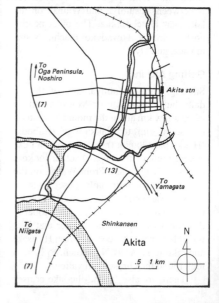

Tamagawa-onsen

South of Towadako and below Kazuno, the road splits into Route 282 (to Morioka) and Route 341, which passes through the Hachimantai plateau (Towada-Hachimantai National Park). There are several hot-spring resort towns in the area. Just a little off Route 341 lies Tamagawa-onsen, one of the most typical of these traditional resorts. Nearly all the buildings are old and simple wooden structures built close to the springs. Typical is the large old bathhouse which you pass to reach the ravine that is the source of the hot water. It has several pools, and mixed bathing is still the practice. However, like many such hot-spring towns, it is more of a health clinic than a resort, and the bathers are mostly geriatrics. In the ravine, there is one stream that has some of the most unusual water you're likely to see—it is brilliant orange. Further upstream, a violent bubbling and boiling marks the emergence of many gushers of hot water, one of which boils two meters high in winter.

Water from the different streams is sluiced separately to various pools, each of which is believed to provide a cure or effective relief for specific ailments. Some streams are laden with yellow minerals and this water is led into settling chambers, where it is cooled so the minerals can be collected for sale.

A common sight up in the ravine is one or more people lying on straw mats. The earth is hot (potatoes cook if buried a short distance underground), and people believe the heat is healthy. Nearby is a small concrete pool in the open air filled with hot water and free to the public.

Getting There

Tamagawa-onsen is linked by eight buses a day to and from Hachimantai station, and seven a day to Tazawa-ko station. There is a reasonable amount of traffic for hitching.

A toll road, the Aspite Line (Japanese name), leads across the mountain range from Route 341 toward Routes 282 and 284, past several peaks. It's enjoyable if you happen to be going that way, but not worth a special trip.

Tazawa-ko Area

Besides Tazawa-ko lake, there are several interesting places to visit, such as the nearby mountains and plateaus, Kakunodate town, Dakikaeri gorge, and the general countryside. It sticks in my mind as one of the most enjoyable areas I visited in Japan while researching this book.

Tazawa-ko Lake

This is a classic caldera lake, and the round shape of the old crater is apparent. The swimming is good and the water shallow for some distance off shore—before it plunges to 425 meters, the deepest in Japan.

Tazawako-kogen Plateau

Located a few km from the lake, the plateau offers some of the most interesting and scenic nature walks in Japan. The scenery ranges from highland scrub (low trees and bushes) to a dormant volcano. There are several trails, the most interesting of which takes in Koma-ga-dake mountain and vicinity. The scenery is quite outstanding (if the highland area is not fog-bound) and the walking and climbing are within the range of anyone except cardiac patients.

Koma-ga-dake erupted in October 1970—a fascinating event I was lucky enough to see. Following an explosion, gases shrieked from the earth like the exhaust of a hundred jet engines, then molten rock from underground slowly clogged the vent and finally sealed it. For many min-

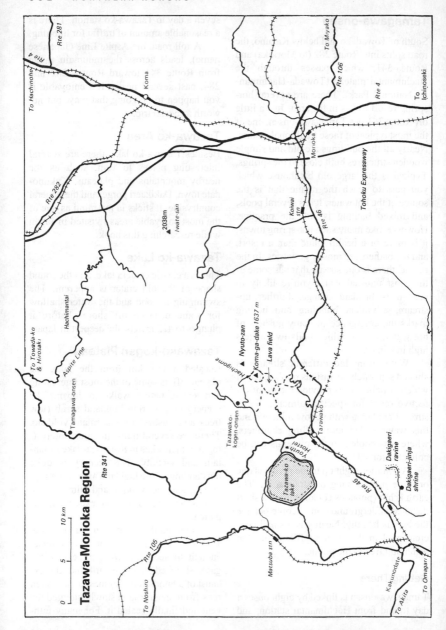

Tazawa-Morioka Region

To Hachinohe
Rte 281
Rte 4
Koma
To Hachinohe
Rte 282
▲ 2038m
Iwate-san
To Towada-ko & Hirosaki
Hachimantai
Aspite Line
Tamagawa-onsen
Rte 341
0 1 5 10 km
Rte 105
To Noshiro
Matsuba stn
Tazawako-kogen onsen
Nyuto-zan ▲
Hachigome ▲ ▲ Koma-ga-dake 1637 m
Lava field
Tazawako
Youth Hostel
Tazawa-ko lake
Rte 46
Kakunodate
To Akita
To Omagari
Dakigaeri ravine
Dakigaeri-jinja shrine
Morioka
Rte 46
Koiwai stn
Tohoku Expressway
To Miyako
Rte 106
Rte 4
To Ichinoseki

utes the air was silent until, as amazed on-lookers watched, a dome began to form and smoke rose over it. Finally, when it had reached a height of about four meters and a diameter of perhaps 10, the pressure became too much and the dome shattered, hurling fragments high into the air. Toward dusk, the red glow of rock chunks could be seen as they traced arcs in the air. The cycle repeated itself again and again.

The tens of thousands of tons of rock hurled out then now lie in a "river" of rough-textured boulders that stretches down one side of the hill. It is quite fascinating to explore this area to see the amazing forms and shapes of the lava. Some of the boulders have a rippled surface caused by the hot gases that blasted past them. Others rocks were torn asunder while hot and taffy-like and the strings of then-sticky rock can still be seen, looking like stretched bread dough.

The easiest way to reach the top is by bus from Tazawa-ko station (three per day) to Koma-ga-dake-Hachigome ("Eighth Station") and then a 40 minute walk up a clearly marked trail. Two other trails start lower down, one beginning at the road near the Seishonen Sports Center, the other at the top of a string of three ski lifts. The base of the bottom lift is called Mizusawa Daburu Rifuto (double lift). There is some road traffic and hitching is possible, but you might have to wait a while.

The first route takes you to the rim of a bowl that looks down on a couple of mini-cones and the high "bump" of Me-dake (the peak that erupted in 1970). Its black top, and to the right, the river of boulders ejected at that time, shouldn't be missed. On the rim of the bowl is a small hill, on the left side of which is a path that leads down to the foot of Me-dake and the floor of the small, green valley, as well as the mini-peaks. On the other side of the hill is a

long trail down to the lava river and Me-dake. ("Me-dake" means "female peak"; there is also an Odake—"male peak"; by pre-Shinto custom, all natural features came in matched pairs, or a male and female aspect was found when there was only a single feature.)

The last bus leaves Hachigome at 1545, which restricts extended walks in the area if you intend to take the bus back down. There are two other trails down, but to find them it is better to have used them to climb up as well, as there are unmarked forks that can lead you astray (as I can certify). It is advisable to carry food and a lot of water, as there are no sources on the mountain, and the climbing generates a healthy thirst.

The region around Tazawa-ko is ideal for exploration by those with their own transport, although buses do cover several routes. The farmland is good and the people prosperous, so the houses (some with thatched roofs) are large and handsome. Residents take pride in their homes and the surroundings, and one of the delights is the sight of long stretches of flowerbeds along the roadside. There is a youth hostel at Matsuba that looks nicer than usual (it is a private home), but it was full when I visited the town.

Places to Stay

There are several ryokan, hotels, and min-shuku around the lake, so accommodation is plentiful, although reservations would be advisable in summer. There is a good youth hostel near the lake. The evening meal when I visited was sukiyaki, and the large dining room usually was like a big party. Definitely light years ahead of most hostels and worth a trip to enjoy. (Reports are that this dinner is not every day.)

Kakunodate

This town is very unusual and offers a good chance to see daily life in picturesque surroundings. Although located in the far north, almost a cultural backwater, it preserves a number of 350-year-old samurai houses in surroundings of tall, old trees, quite unlike almost any other place in Japan. The old houses stand mostly on a single street, not far from the station, where a large map is posted as a guide. The houses are open to the public for a reasonable fee and provide an interesting glimpse into the past. Most have simple but elegant tree-shaded gardens, and are built with the best materials.

A guide for sightseeing in the samurai area can be obtained (for a reasonable fee) by calling the Municipal Shoko-kankoka (tel (01875) 4-1111). The Denshokan hall, in the samurai area, serves as a museum and training center for making articles of cherry bark and has a tour information center as well.

Many cherry trees have been planted along the Hinokinai-gawa river which flows through the town, so the area is especially beautiful in spring.

Dakikaeri-keikoku Ravine

A few km outside Kakunodate is this small gorge, near Jindai station, accessible by train or bus. While offering no spectacular vistas, it provides an enjoyable hour's walk through relaxing surroundings to the upper reaches. The most memorable impression is the intense turquoise color of the water. The swimming is good in several places.

Iwate-san (Iwate-ken)

This mountain (2038 meters), which dominates the area north-west of Morioka, is conical when viewed from the east, but in fact has two peaks. (Naturally it is called "Iwate-fuji".) It is quite easily climbed; two popular starting points are Yanagisawa and Amihari-onsen, both accessible by bus from Morioka.

Yokote

On February 15–16 each year, this town is the scene of an interesting festival that emphasises the snowy nature of this part of Japan. The people build *kamakura*, igloo-like snow houses, in which the local children, by custom, play games and serve tea. (It has become a tourist attraction.) The station has information on their locations.

YAMAGATA-KEN ▬▬▬

The Mogami-gawa river flows through the valley between Shinjo and Tsuruoka. From May to November, boat rides are available to shoot the rapids. The trip takes one hour, costs ¥1500, starts at Furukuchi and fin-

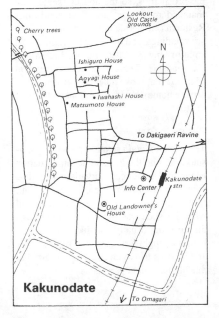

Kakunodate

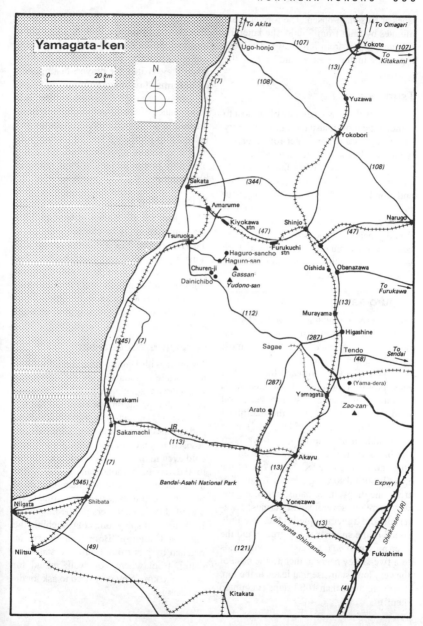

Yamagata-ken

0   20 km

N

ishes at Kusanagi-onsen. The former is 20 minutes by train from Shinjo, the latter 10 minutes by bus from Kiyokawa. The boat trip takes in the most scenic part of the river.

Tsuruoka

This out-of-the-way small city plays host to some of the most unusual religious activity in Japan. It is a major center for *shugendo* which combines Buddhist and Shinto beliefs. In the city itself is the famous temple Zenpo-ji, which has a picturesque pagoda and a building with hundreds of images in every imaginable pose lining its walls. It can be reached by bus from the station. The friendly people at the station information center can put you on the right bus and are well prepared with any other info or assistance you might need.

Haguro-san

Of the three mountains of Dewa (Dewa-sanzan), Haguro-san is the closest to Tsuruoka, the most accessible and the most interesting to most people.

There two ways to reach the top. The most prosaic (but quickest and easiest) is by bus from Tsuruoka station via a toll road. The "scenic route" is the traditional way, starting from the village of Haguro (accessible from Tsuruoka by bus). Near the bus station is a gateway that leads to steps down to a wooded gorge, one of the most beautiful forest glades in Japan. Tall trees line the walking paths, and along the way there are several small shrines, a waterfall, and a picturesque bridge. The only sound in the summer is the breeze and the ever-present *semi* (cicadas). The path leads to a five-storey pagoda, then to the base of the very long staircase that leads to the top. There are more than 1000 steps (I counted them!).

At the top is Haguro-san-jinja, a large thatched-roof structure looking like a combination of a shrine and temple. Near it you can still see the tiny huts used by pilgrims when they visited for prayer, fasting, and other forms of religious penance.

Anywhere on the mountain there is a good chance of seeing *yamabushi* pilgrims, dressed in white and carrying rosaries and bells. During the day you can sometimes hear the sound of a conch shell being blown by priests as part of their religious observances.

Places to Stay

Many temples and homes at Haguro offer accommodation. Help can be obtained at the Haguro (bus) or Tsuruoka (train) stations if you wish to stay pilgrim-style. The youth hostel is several km down the coast from Tsuruoka and can be reached by train. The information center at the station can help with other minshuku, ryokan or hotel accommodation.

Gassan & Yudono-san

Together with Haguro-san, these form the three sacred mountains of the Shugendo sect. Gassan is the main peak, and Yudono is an outcropping on one flank. At the top of Gassan is Gassan-jinja, to which pilgrims and others climb in summer. Climbers are advised to take warm clothing as it gets cold even in mid-summer. A toll road runs to the top of Yudono-san. Probably the most fascinating sights are the mummies of two ascetic priests who were voluntarily buried alive in chambers on the mountain. Both are on display, one at Dainichibo, the other at Churen-ji. Both temples can be reached by bus from Tsuru-oka station to Oami, from where you walk inland for about one km. (You may need to ask for directions.)

Dainichibo

The mummy here is always on display in a passageway that encircles the temple. Photos are permitted and some light enters by windows. The *miirabutsu* (mummy) is that of a man who ate no meat or grain, living (if that is the word) on nuts, root vegetables, and seeds. His purpose was to remove from his body all substances (like fats) that could rot. When he reached the age of 96 (in 1783) he was buried by his disciples. They dug him up after three years and three months, dried his body, and put him on display. His wish was for people to look on his body and be inspired to understand Buddhist ideas.

Churen-ji

Only a kilometer or so away from Dainichibo, at Churen-ji, is the second mummy. However, this one is kept in a glass case in the main hall, and special arrangements must be made to have the drape removed. This man was an itinerant preacher who travelled round Tohoku and Kanto. In 1821, during an epidemic in Tokyo that was causing blindness, he went there, prayed and, as an act of atonement, tore out one eye and threw it into the Sumida river. He was known as the "priest of the eye". In 1829, at the age of 62, he was buried at Churen-ji, and dug up after his death.

Yamagata

Anyone interested in studying traditional Japanese society would find this town a good place to visit or live for a while. Each section of the town has its own traditional industry or craft, and many crafts are still performed as daily work. The father of one of my friends makes his living by hand-forging and polishing agricultural shears. He makes one or two pairs a day and sells them for ¥20,000 each.

Festivals

The city's main festival is Hanagasa Matsuri (Floral Sedge Hat Festival), on August 6–8, when thousands of townspeople in costume dance through the streets at night.

Zao-zan

This mountain is best known for its winter skiing. In addition, Zao is famous for its *juhyo*, or tree monsters. The monsters are not demons that live in trees, but actually the trees themselves that get coated so thickly with ice in winter that they become cylinders of white, creating a weird and wondrous scene. The *juhyo* are not a coating of snow, but the result of freak atmospheric conditions in the area that produce supercooled water vapor in the air that turns to ice the instant that it touches anything, in this case the trees.

The tree monsters can be seen (even if you don't ski) by taking the "ropeway", a cable car starting at Zao-sanroku base station. The 1734 meter climb takes 15 minutes and costs ¥550/1100 (one-way/return), and goes up to Juhyo-kogen, the lower extremity of the *juhyo*. A second "ropeway" rises a further 1839 meters through the *juhyo* zone to the top, Zao-jizo-sancho. The combined cost of the two cable cars to the top is ¥1100 one way, ¥1800 return.

The Zao area has a large number of ski trails for varying levels of skill, and plenty of ski lifts. The "ropeway" to the summit can also be used repeatedly for skiing through the juhyo zone and costs ¥500 per trip.

A year-round attraction of the Zao area is Zao Okama, a caldera lake about 300 meters across. The scenery here is desolate and interesting for the shapes and colors of the rocks.

Places to Stay

There are many hotels, ryokan, and min-shuku scattered around the mountain, many at onsen (hot spring sites). The largest concentration is along the Zao Echo Line toll road that passes along the southern flank. There are also some lodges on the upper levels, including Juhyogen Lodge at the peak. Almost any travel agent can provide information and make reservations.

Getting There

The simplest access to the Zao area is from Yamagata station by the hourly bus to Zao-onsen (45 minutes). An alternative is to take the less frequent bus from Kaminoyama station to Zao-bo-daira and Karita-chushajo, or from Yamagata station to the same two places via Zao-onsen. As with other popular ski areas, there are direct bus services in winter from locations in Tokyo; buses for Zao leave from Ueno station.

Yamadera

The main attraction of the Yamagata area lies several km out of town. Yamadera ("mountain temple") is properly known as Risshaku-ji. The buildings are scattered around the heavily wooded mountainside. Some are perched at the edge of precipices and look as if they will topple at any time. It takes two to three hours of climbing on foot to visit the various temples. The place is best visited with a friend as the exploration can become a bit boring on your own. Access is from Yamadera station, which is reached by bus or train from Yamagata or Sendai.

Yonezawa

Formerly a castle town of the Uesugi family, the small town is now noted for the tombs of 12 generations of the family. They resemble 12 small wooden shrines

laid out in a row beneath tall trees. A bus runs from Yonezawa station.

From Yonezawa, a local road connects with Nishi-azuma Skyline toll road, which leads to the Bandai-san area (described in the northward section). Route 121, which goes over a mountain range from Yonezawa to Kitakata and Aizu-waka-matsu, is a twisty gravel road in parts, with no buses listed and little traffic. The west coast is also easily accessible from the Yonezawa area, and from Kitakata and Aizu-wakamatsu Route, 49 takes you the 120 km westward to Niigata, a gateway to Sado Island.

NIIGATA-KEN ■■■■■■■■

Niigata

Located on the Japan Sea almost due north of Tokyo, Niigata is an international port of entry and one of the ports for sailing to nearby Sado-ga-shima island.

Tsuruoka (Yamagata-ken) is straight up the coast, but the terrain is not terribly interesting along that route as Niigata lies on a large plain that is flat right to the water. The area produces more rice than any other prefecture in Japan. Travellers planning a journey in that direction can make a trip to Sado Island, then return to Honshu at Naoetsu (thus bypassing part of

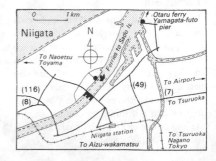

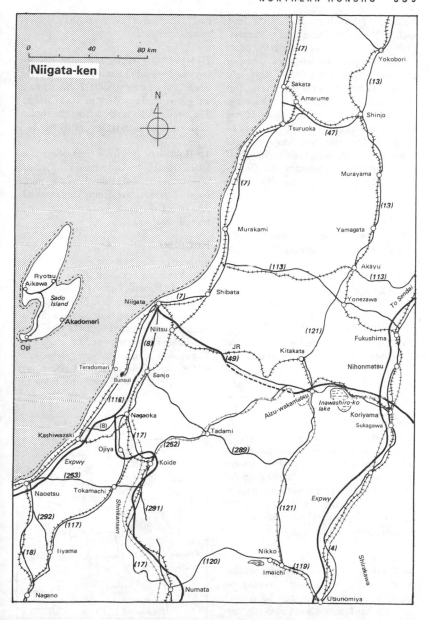

Niigata-ken

the coast), from where road and rail lead south to Nagano and Matsumoto (Nagano-ken). The road southwest along the coast toward the Noto Peninsula (a gateway area for the Northern Japan Alps and northern Gifu-ken) is not so exciting, but the destinations at the end are worth seeing.

There is little to see in Niigata. If you have a few hours to kill, pick up a copy of the glossy brochure *Sight Seeing Niigata* (trilingual—in Russian even!) and see if there's anything that interests you. Copies are available at the information office at the station.

Festivals

April 12–18: Hakusan-jinja Matsuri. One feature is masked dances by shrine maidens.
August 20–23: Niigata Matsuri. On the last day of the festival there is a spectacular display of fireworks near Bandai-bashi bridge.

Places to Stay

There are hotels and other accommodation in Niigata. Assistance may be obtained at the information office in the station. There is a youth hostel on the outskirts of town (tel (0252) 29-0935).

Transportation

International: Russia

Niigata airport receives international flights from Khabarovsk (Russia). Many passengers on the Trans-Siberian Railway use this service as there are not enough ferries to Yokohama. The airport is a few km northeast of the city center; buses connect with Niigata station.

Domestic

To Tokyo Niigata is the northern terminus of the Joetsu Shinkansen superexpress train. By the fastest service (the Asahi), Tokyo is less than two hours away. By reg-

ular (and cheaper) expresses, the trip takes about four hours.

To Sado Island Niigata is the main port for ferry and hydrofoil services to Sado Island (there is also an air service). Further details are given in the section on Sado Island. The dock can be reached from the station in about 20 minutes on foot, or by bus 14.

To Hokkaido The ferry from Niigata to Otaru (Hokkaido) is the most economical way to reach Hokkaido from the north coast. Ferries leave from Yamanoshita-futo (pier), which can be reached by bus 7 from the station.

Naoetsu

Situated on the coast southwest of Niigata, Naoetu's main attraction is the ferry service from Naoetsu Port to Ogi on Sado Island. If you're travelling south by road (along Route 18) through Naoetsu toward Nagano keep your eyes open for the many old-fashioned prewar wooden buildings. These old wooden houses and shops have sliding wood and glass front doors, and canopies that extend over the sidewalk from the buildings. They aren't worth a

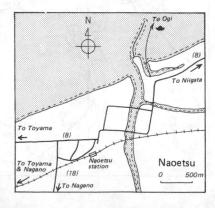

special trip, but do provide a glimpse of something that has vanished almost everywhere else in the country in the rush to plate glass and brick.

SADO ISLAND

Sado-ga-shima Island is the fifth largest of the islands of Japan. The main attraction is its remoteness. Despite the large number of sightseers annually (about one million), the people of Sado continue much as they have done for decades or even centuries. It is like most island communities—the people are more friendly and the pace of life is slower. These, of course, are not things a visitor can actually see, but if you have a feeling for atmosphere you should enjoy a visit.

The island is made up of two long, oval-shaped mountain ranges with a fertile valley sandwiched between them.

Ryotsu

The main town on Sado is Ryotsu, a small-townish port city at the northeast end of the valley. Starting from here, one route (along the south side of the valley) first passes Honma-ke Noh theater, where performances of local dances and folk theater are given during the summer. Check locally about these performances.

Konpon-ji Temple

This temple is located in a forest setting, 30 minutes from Ryotsu by bus.

Myosen-ji Temple

Set in a forest, this temple has a 21-meter tall pagoda.

Ogi

This town lies near the southwest corner of the island, and is the other major port for boats to Honshu.

In Ogi harbor there is a chance of see-

ing "washtub" boats—perfectly circular, flat-bottomed boats made in the manner of staved barrels. They were once a common sight around the island, and were originally used for harvesting seaweed and shellfish. Their main use these days is as a tourist attraction. If you see one, you can hire a ride.

Other routes to Ogi are by circling southwest along the coast from Ryotsu, or by crossing the hilly spine of the southern range by one of three small roads. One source indicates a bus service on all, while another shows buses only on the western route across to Akadomari and around the eastern tip. Inquire locally. There is defi-

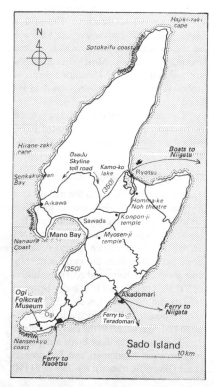

Sado Island

nitely a section of the south coast without buses.

Past Ogi, toward Nansenkyo, there are many old houses built over 200 years ago. Along the way is the Ogi Mingei Hakubutsu-kan (folkcraft museum). The coast becomes rugged around the Nansenkyo–Sawazaki area, then becomes quite gentle until the far side of Mano-wan bay, past Sawada. Sado is of volcanic origin and the rock outcroppings have the weird shapes typical of once-molten lava, aided by the erosion of the sea. There are many beautiful views.

Aikawa

This was formerly the major gold mining center of Japan, once the largest producer in the Orient. Its miners were often prisoners, many of whom died here. The gold is nearly gone now but visitors can tour one of the mines, Sodayu-ko, which started about 360 years ago. Most of its passages are low and narrow. Mechanised displays (robots) show how the mining was done by hand.

Continuing up the coast, you pass more pretty coastal scenery and indented bays, with the Sotokaifu-kaigan coast the most attractive.

Getting There & Getting Around

The main port for boats to the mainland is Ryotsu. During the peak season there are up to 10 hydrofoils a day to and from Niigata. The trip takes one hour and costs ¥5300. There are also up to nine ordinary boats per day to/from the same port; they take about 2-1/2 hours and cost a minimum of ¥1730. There is one boat a day between Niigata and Akadomari; it costs ¥1550 and takes 3 hours, leaving Niigata in the afternoon and Akadomari in the early morning.

There are up to three boats a day each way between Akadomari and Teradomari (near Okozu JR station); the fare is ¥1190

and the trip takes two hours. Between Ogi and Naoetsu there are up to five boats a day that take 2-1/2 hours and cost ¥1910. There is also an airport near Ryotsu.

Buses run between the major centers on the island, so there is no problem getting around. There are also tour buses offering tours lasting four to eight hours. They leave from Ryotsu and Ogi.

HOKKAIDO

okkaido is the northernmost major island of Japan. Although it was settled quite late in Japanese history and, visibly at least, has little of historic interest, it is the home of an aboriginal people who are not related to the Yamato Japanese (who comprise almost the entire population of Japan). There is evidence that the island has been occupied for about 23,000 years.

Hokkaido's strong suit is natural beauty and outdoor activities, with features that interestingly combine the flavor of broad, rolling river valleys flanked by low wooded hills like those of eastern North America, with high and volcanic mountains. Much of the island is empty and wild, with most of the population in the river valleys. Because the climate of Hokkaido is colder than that of the south islands, traditional farming methods and crops did not succeed, so foreign experts (mostly American) were brought in as advisors in the late 19th century. With them came large farms, dry-land crops, barns, silos, and cows (a rarity elsewhere). These are very exotic to the Japanese but of limited interest to foreign visitors. Most travellers will prefer the coastal, mountain, and lake regions where the characteristic Hokkaido scenery, mostly of volcanic origin, can be enjoyed.

Hokkaido was long a frontier region of little interest to the central governments in the south of Japan. The major groups of inhabitants were native peoples of various origins (mostly unknown), including the Ainu, Gilyak, and Oroke.

Not much is known about the Ainu, who also live on Sakhalin Island. It is generally believed that they are a Caucasian race, but next to nothing is known about their origins, It seems their languages have no known relatives elsewhere in the world, although there are tribes in Siberia with similar shamanist forms of worship based on a cult of the bear, and it has been observed that Ainu and Navajo music is similar.

It has also become known that they are recent arrivals on Hokkaido, having settled only about 800 years ago, displacing an even more mysterious people who seem to have occupied the island for much longer. Ainu used to live on Honshu as well, and possibly as far south as Kyushu, but they were a peaceful people and no match for the more aggressive Yamato Japanese, so they were slowly pushed back into the remoteness of Hokkaido.

Ainu men are very hirsute, and the large number of Japanese men (compared to Chinese and Korean) with a heavy beard is probably a legacy of intermarriage early in Japanese history.

Up to the end of the last century, the Ainu lived a life of hunting and fishing, and engaged in small-scale agriculture of dry-field crops (no rice). By the last decade of the century the encroaching settlements of the southern Japanese had almost destroyed the Ainus' way of life, and they were a dispirited people seemingly on the way to extinction. The central government adopted a policy of forcibly assimilating the Ainu into the mainstream of Japanese life. They were made to take Japanese names, and forbidden to use their own languages. As a

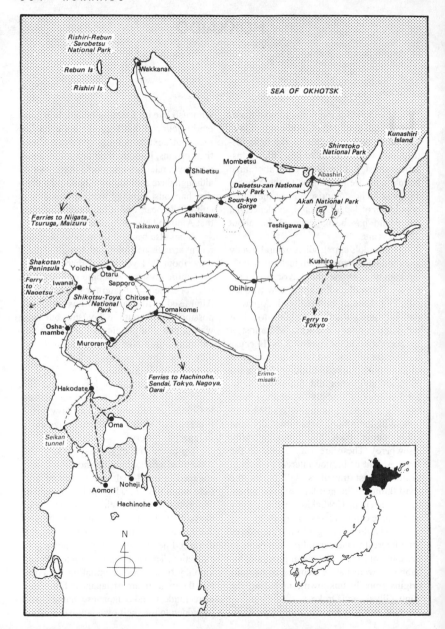

result they have adopted Japanese names, language, and customs, and would be difficult to identify by sight. In Japan there is discrimination against those who are "different", so most Ainu do not advertise their racial heritage. There are perhaps only 15,000 full-blooded Ainu left in Hokkaido. The only Ainu wearing traditional garments do so for the benefit of visiting tourists. They may be seen at Shiraoi, Noboribetsu-onsen, Asahikawa, in the area around Akan-ko and Kutcharo-ko, and wherever tourists gather. A feeling of ethnic pride is developing among them these days.

No one speaks any of the Ainu languages fluently, but many place names are of Ainu origin. This can cause problems because nearly all are written in kanji, and southern Japanese are unable to read many place names correctly because of their unique pronunciation. Many of the pronunciations do not even appear in kanji dictionaries.

The Gilyak were a hunting and fishing people like the Ainu and were largely found in Sakhalin. They also lived along the lower Amur River on the mainland, and are a Mongolian race.

The Oroke lived on Sakhalin and were nomads who lived off their reindeer herds. They are a Tungas people and are related to the Orochi of the Amur River delta region. They were not originally inhabitants of Hokkaido, but the takeover of Sakhalin by the USSR after World War II caused several Oroke to move to Hokkaido. There are about 30 Oroke scattered around the island, one of whom has opened a small museum at Abashiri.

INFORMATION

If you are in Tokyo prior to going to Hokkaido, visit the TIC and request any literature they would suggest for the areas in which you plan to travel. Also pick up a copy of their listing of festivals of the month and check it for Hokkaido events.

A useful book describing 23 festivals unique to the island (some Ainu), with articles from a local English-language newspaper, may be available from some newsstands. It can also be obtained by mail (price ¥980) from:

> Tast Corp.
> Tokan Bldg.
> Kita 7, Nishi 4
> Kita-ku
> Sapporo.

GETTING THERE

This island is connected to the main island by the Seikan tunnel under Tsugaru Strait served by trains. The Hokutosei is a *tokkyu* overnight train leaving Ueno station (Tokyo) in the afternoon or evening and arriving in Sapporo morning or noon the next day, taking about 17 hours. The Shinkansen line reaches only Morioka, in northern Honshu, may reach Aomori when the railroad building project stops, but will probably never go to Sapporo. The tunnel is used by ordinary trains, about 15/day from Aomori, some of which originate in Morioka, most arriving in Hakodate.

Air

The main airport is at Chitose, serving Sapporo. There are also local airports around the island fed via Chitose.

Ferries

Listed below are several ferry routes between Hokkaido and ports on Honshu.

Hakodate

There is service to this major port of entry from Aomori, Noheji (east of Aomori), and Oma (near the northern tip of the Shimokita Peninsula).

Hakodate–Aomori

For speed freaks, there is a hydrofoil (known as the "Jet Ferry") service three times a day during the warmer months (100 minutes; ¥6300). To find the dock, ask for the "Jet Ferry noriba". A conventional ferry also runs, up to 14 times a day, taking four hours (¥1400). At both Hakodate and Aomori, the ferry terminal is some distance to the west of the city and is inconvenient to reach. Unless the terminal at Hakodate moves, you can reach the JR station from it by following the road from the terminal, turning right at the first T-junction, left at the next corner, and continuing until you intersect with a major road. The bus stop is across the road and to the right. The name of the stop (written only in Japanese) is Hokudai (Hokkaido University). Take bus 1 to the station.

Hakodate–Noheji

There are three boats a day on this run (4 hr 40 min; ¥1400). The terminus is a few km to the west of JR Noheji station; a bus service makes the connection.

Hakodate–Oma

Up to five boats a day make the crossing to Oma (100 min; ¥1000).

Muroran

There are ferries to Muroran from Aomori, Oma, Hachinohe, Oarai (north of Tokyo), and Naoetsu (on the north coast of Honshu, approximately halfway between Niigata and Toyama). The second-last is quite a distance down the east coast of Honshu. Muroran can be useful for visitors with only a few days for Hokkaido, for it is very close to the Toya-ko and Shikotsu-ko area, one of the two most popular and interesting regions for travellers in Hokkaido. The ferry terminus ("Ferry noriba") at Muroran is easy to find, one km from the JR station.

Buses connect terminus and station.

Muroran–Aomori

There are two ferries a day in each direction (about 7 hours; ¥3400). One of the arrival times each way is inconveniently early in the morning, however.

Muroran–Oma

Up to two boats per day make this crossing (5 hr; ¥1400).

Muroran–Hachinohe

There are two boats daily on this run (8 hr; ¥3900). This port saves quite a bit of travelling to the north of Honshu, but either the departure or the arrival time may be early in the morning for all sailings.

Muroran–Oarai

There is one overnight boat in each direction (about 18 hours; ¥9570).

Muroran–Naoetsu

There is a midnight boat once a week each way between Muroran and Naoetsu (about 17 hours; ¥5150).

Tomakomai

There are ferries between here and Hachinohe, Sendai, Tokyo, Oarai, and Nagoya. Tomakomai is quite close to Sapporo, and is not far from Noboribetsu nor that much farther away from the Toya-ko and Shikotsu-ko area than Muroran.

Tomakomai–Hachinohe

Boats of two lines sail a total of three times a day each way (nine hours; ¥3900).

Tomakomai–Sendai

Two different lines have daily services to/from Sendai (14–17 hours; ¥8850). All sail overnight, with reasonable departure/arrival times. (One of these is the boat between Nagoya and Tomakomai.)

Tomakomai–Oarai

There is one overnight boat in each direction (20 hr; ¥9570).

Tomakomai–Tokyo

There is a daily service in each direction. The trip takes 31 hours (¥11,840), and requires one overnight southbound and two northbound.

Tomakomai–Nagoya

One boat runs daily in each direction, stopping en route each way at Sendai. The trip takes about 39 hours total (¥15,450), and requires two nights.

Kushiro

This port gives easy access to Akan National Park and the popular parts of SE Hokkaido, the other main area of major touristic interest.

Kushiro–Tokyo

There is a ferry every one to two days in each direction. The trip takes 33 hours (¥14,420), and requires one overnight southbound and two northbound.

Otaru

There are services from here to three points along the northern coast of Honshu, the latter two quite close to Kyoto: Niigata, Tsuruga, and Maizuru.

Otaru–Niigata

There is a daily boat of one line in each direction, and one a week (southbound only) by another (about 20 hr; ¥5150).

Otaru–Tsuruga

There are four sailings a week in each direction (31–34 hours southbound, about 3 hours less northbound; ¥6590). South-

bound, three take one overnight and one take two overnights; northbound, all take two overnights.

Otaru–Maizuru

There are four sailings a week in each direction (30 hours southbound, 28 northbound; ¥6590). The trip takes one overnight southbound, two northbound.

Iwanai

From this small and relatively remote port on the west coast, at the western base of the Shakotan Peninsula, there is a service to Naoetsu.

Iwanai–Naoetsu

Twice a week there is a midnight ferry in each direction between Iwanai and Naoetsu (about 18 hours; ¥5150).

GETTING AROUND

For long-distance travel, there are JR lines around nearly all parts of the island, as well as a number of long-distance bus routes. In addition, there are many other bus routes through the more mountainous or unpopulated regions. *Jikokuhyo* is the source of information on these services, with particular note of the map of long-distance bus services (in addition to the regular map of all other services). A peculiarity of the bus services here (and in other similarly isolated parts of the country) is that the summer is often considered to end in mid-August— after which services may be reduced or even non-existent.

ON THE ROAD

Hakodate

Hakodate is the primary port of entry to Hokkaido from Honshu. For a long time access was by train ferries from Aomori (Honshu); with the Seikan tunnel under the strait, access is by several trains a day now run from Aomori to Hakodate. Many terminate at Hakodate, but a few continue to Sapporo. By train to Sapporo, there are several L expresses via Tomakomai (about 3-1/2 hours) but no locals, while there are almost no direct services via Otaru; one or two changes of train will be necessary.

There is an information office at the JR railway station. It should have maps of the city detailing the old section of the city and be able to help in finding accommodation.

Things to See

Hakodate-yama

The city of Hakodate is dominated by Hakodate-yama (335 meters), a large hill of volcanic origin at the end of a small peninsula that forms a natural shelter for ships. The view of Hakodate at night from this hill is considered the finest night view in Japan; a carpet of colored lights stretches into the distance.

It is possible to walk up, but it is easier to take the cable car ("ropeway") that runs to the top from a base station part-way up the hill (¥600 up; ¥1100 return). The base station is easily reached from tram stops Horaicho on line 2, or Jujigai on lines 3 or 5. From the latter, go one street west, then uphill.

Motomachi (Old Section)

The first impression of Hakodate is that it is an unattractive city, but its appeal grows. It has character—something that most Japanese cities lack. In the port area and on the hillside at the base of Hakodate-san, the Motomachi district has many old and decrepit buildings, distinguishable because they are American or European in style. They date from the Meiji and Taisho eras (late 1800s and early 1900s) and have been

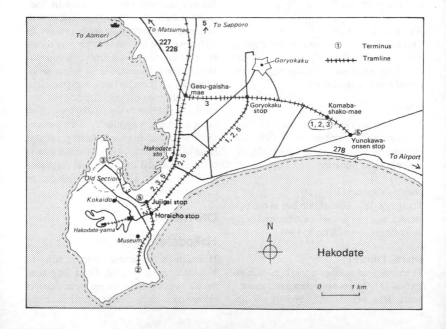

recognized by the authorities as comprising an area of historic architecture. The area is charmingly seedy for the most part, but it seems the buildings will be preserved and maintained, and probably restored in part.

There is no particular street to see; each one has its quota. It is interesting just to wander around. Tram 3 passes by a number of such buildings near the harbor terminus, and the streets of nearby hillsides are a good area to explore. One place to look for is an old public hall, Kokaido, a large, ageing, and sagging wooden building that resembles a Civil War era mansion from the American south.

In the same area is the Japan Orthodox Hakodate Resurrection Church, a Byzantine-style building dating from 1916 and starting to show its age. It's especially pretty at night when lit up. Nearby is the Hakodate branch of the Higashi-honganji temple. An amusing sign post, one of many directing the on-foot explorer to places of interest in the area, shows a sweating priest frantically beating a *mokugyo* (wooden gong), a feature of prayers of that sect.

Like some of the old buildings, the trams in Hakodate are also a trifle decrepit and all the more charming for the nostalgia they engender. Only wooden cars (dating from 1949) are in use—the modern metal ones rusted away in the salt air.

Hakodate Museum

On the other side of the hill is Hakodate-koen (park), an attractive wooded area noted for its cherry blossoms in late April. In the park is Hakodate Hakubutsukan (museum) which has a good collection and modern display of artefacts of the aboriginal races that inhabit(ed) Hokkaido. If you have time to see only one museum in Hokkaido, this would be the best choice. It is close to the last two stops on tram line 2,

and not too far from the Horaicho stop.

Goryokaku

This is an interesting fort, the only one in Japan built in a European style (finished in 1864). It is shaped like a five-pointed star, a design which allows defenders to rake all approaches with gunfire. It was the scene of a siege in 1868 when supporters of the Tokugawa shogunate resisted the Meiji Restoration for more than a month. A small museum inside the walls has relics of the battle, and a small tower allows a view over the area. The walls themselves are low, perhaps five meters high, and there is no superstructure, only the walls and moats. It is now a park, and cherry trees in the grounds make it pretty in late April and early May. The fort is close to Goryokaku-gyoen-mae tram stop, which is the common point for all tram lines in the city.

Trappist Convent and Monastery

The convent is located five minutes from Yunokawa station by bus. It is famous in Japan for its butter and candy, and is the only Trappist convent in Japan. The Trappist monastery is located at Oshima-Tobetsu, 26 km from Hakodate.

Places to Stay

There is one youth hostel in Hakodate, Hokusei-so (tel. (0138) 57-3212); it is several kilometers from the station in the hot-spring town of Yunokawa ("hot water river"), a suburb of Hakodate. From the station take a tram 5 and get off at Yunokawa-onsen (the second-last stop on the line). Be sure to get a 5 going the right way. (Trams 1, 2, and 3 go as far as the car barn, one stop before Yunokawa-onsen, which would add over half a kilometer to the distance to the hostel.)

The hostel is located amidst resort hotels, and its bath is fed with the same naturally hot (and *very* hard) water, so you can enjoy the privilege without the cost of a resort hotel. The hostel tends to be quite full on weekends. If you arrive early in the day, consider staying in the scenic Onuma area, about 25 km away.

Getting Around

There is an all day tram-and-bus ticket for about ¥600 and a 10-tickets for ¥1000 special at both the train station and the bus station.

Hitching Out of Hakodate

If you wish to hitch to Sapporo and elsewhere immediately, it is necessary to get to Route 5. If arriving by car ferry from Honshu, get off the bus at Gasu-gaisha-mae, which is near a large gas holder. Just before reaching it, the road from the ferry terminal follows an overpass that curves to the left and intersects a major road at right angles; that is Route 5. Gasu-gaisha-mae can also be reached by bus from Hakodate station.

WEST OF HAKODATE

Matsumae

This was the capital of Hokkaido from the 16th century, when the island was known as Ezo. It was the site of the last feudal castle to be built in Japan (and the only one in Hokkaido), but a fire destroyed the original buildings. A concrete reproduction shows the former appearance and about 5000 cherry trees make the place one of beauty from late April.

EAST OF HAKODATE

Mt. Esan

This is an active volcano (618 meters) with steaming vents at the summit and an oval crater. It can be climbed in about an hour. Access to the base takes about 2-1/4 hours by bus from Hakodate.

NORTH FROM HAKODATE

The view from either the train or the road (Route 5) leaving Hakodate is typical of the valley scenery anywhere in Hokkaido—broad rolling farm land interspersed with numerous towns. After 25 km or so, road and rail pass through a tunnel and the scenery changes abruptly. You are suddenly confronted with the very scenic Konuma-ko lake, which reflects the squat volcano Koma-ga-take. This is the entrance to Onuma Kokuritsu-koen (Quasi National Park), a very enjoyable place to spend a day or two. Travellers arriving at Hakodate might consider making their way here for the first night in Hokkaido instead of Hakodate.

Koma-ga-take

Visible for the next 20 km or so, Koma-ga-take consists of three peaks—Sawara, Kengamine and Sumidamori. It is an ugly brown ulcer on the green countryside, but is nevertheless picturesque in its own way. Originally conical, it has lost its top through explosions, and now has an elongated flat and sloping top.

Mt. Higure

As well as the view over Lake Konuma, the best outlook is considered to be Konuma Hill; another is the top of Mt. Higure (313 meters). It is an easy walk to the top, where there are three smaller craters within the large horseshoe-shaped outer rim; the rim is two km east-west and 1.5 km north-south, sloping towards the sea. Any of the three youth hostels in the area will have information on the best routes. It is also possible to circle the mountain by train. From the sea side you can see distant Mt. Yotei across the bay (weather permitting).

Hakodate to Oshamambe

As Koma-ga-take falls behind, the road and railway run parallel to the shore of Uchiura Bay for the next 70 km or so, to a point slightly beyond Oshamambe. They are seldom far from the water, and travellers with the time to stop will find beachcombing in this area probably the best in Japan because the bay seems to act as a collection point for anything floating in the area. Stop anywhere distant from habitation and the beach is almost sure to be littered with hand-blown glass fishing floats that have been washed ashore. I stopped at random three times and each time found more than 20 floats within half a kilometer of where I started; carrying them all became a problem! It appears they are replenished regularly because one beach I picked over on the way north had another 25 or so by the

time I returned just a month later.

The road passes through many fishing villages; draped everywhere are fishing nets, with fishermen making repairs. On flat areas you can often see large pieces of *kombu*, an edible seaweed, laid out to dry.

Oshamambe to Sapporo

There are two suggested routes between these cities. One follows the railway and Route 5 inland in a northward loop, while the other continues around the bay, then cuts inland and touches on the Lake Toya-ko area before continuing through mountainous terrain to Sapporo. The first passes mostly through river valleys and, near Sapporo, a dismal succession of unappealing towns, but it offers the option of a looping sidetrip through Shakotan-hanto (peninsula). The second route passes through much more attractive scenery for most of its length.

The traveller who has adequate time and who plans to circle back to the Toya-ko area can combine the best of both these routes by taking the first to Yoichi, circling the Shakotan Peninsula to Iwanai, then cutting over to Kutchan and Kimobetsu and carrying on from there by the second route to Sapporo.

Oshamambe to Kutchan

Both road and rail run parallel through this region of river-valley farmland. Between Niseko and Kutchan it skirts Mt. Yotei (1893 meters), now extinct. The top is mostly lava-covered, but the lower sections are wooded. Climbing Mt. Yotei is popular with the Japanese and is not particularly difficult. (Most "mountain climbing" in Japan is simply a matter of putting one foot in front of the other for a long enough period.) One popular route is via Hirafu station by bus to Nangetsu-ko lake, from where you begin the climb. The walk up

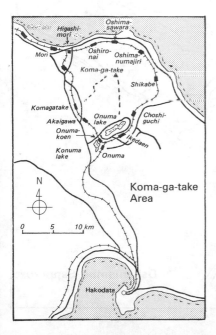

Koma-ga-take Area

N

0   5   10 km

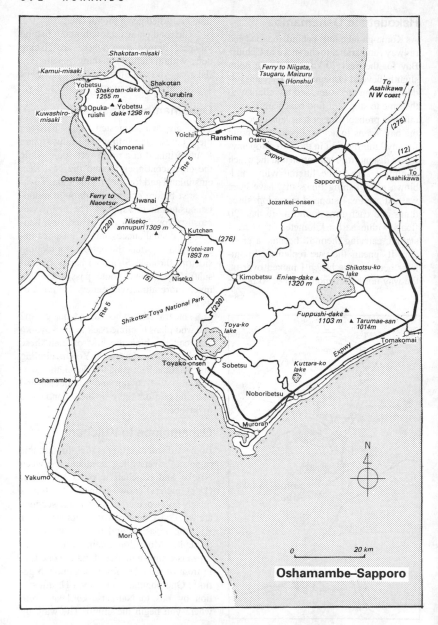

Oshamambe–Sapporo

takes about four hours, plus an hour at the top to walk around the three calderas. For up-to-date information try the Niseko Youth Hostel in Kutchan.

Niseko-annupuri Mt. (1309 meters), also near Kutchan, is rated as one of the four best ski areas in Hokkaido. There are nearby onsen for relaxing in afterward. Kombu-onsen is noted for its autumn leaves.)

Kutchan to Yoichi

Yoichi is best regarded as the gateway to the Shakotan Peninsula. The town has an aquarium, and offers tours of the Nikka Distillery, near Yoichi station (Monday to Saturday).

Shakotan Peninsula

The Shakotan Peninsula is noted for its rugged scenery—cliffs rising out of the sea as high as 250 meters, and the peaks of two mountains, Yobetsu (1298 meters) and Shakotan (1255 meters). Two capes mark the tip of the peninsula, Kamui and Shakotan; the former has a huge rock rising abruptly about 40 meters from the sea. Buses run from Yoichi as far as Yobestu.

Yoichi to Sapporo

The short distance between these two cities includes the best sand beach on Hokkaido (at Ranshima), as well as shorter stretches of beach at irregular intervals. There are several prehistoric relics in the area. Oshoro Stone Circle is a rough circle of large stones about one meter tall, located on Ranshima-Kawa river, southeast of Ranshima station. Other indications of early settlement have been found in the area, such as traces of a dwelling, pottery, tools, Oyachi Shell Mound, a fort, and a cave with more than 200 pictographs on the walls (both in the Fugoppe area, estimated to be about 1500 years old).

Tengu-yama, three km southwest of Otaru station, offers good skiing.

Otaru is a ferry port with services to and from Niigata, Tsuruga and Maizuru. There is also an overnight boat from Otaru to Rishiri Island off the far north coast of Hokkaido. More details on that are given later.

To Sapporo via Toya-ko Lake

This route continues around the shores of Uchiura Bay, then turns inland to Toya-ko

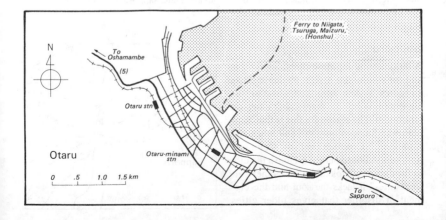

lake and continues through highland scenery to Sapporo. It is by far the more scenic route and is recommended for travellers in a hurry or for those who will be going in this direction only once. From Toya station (on the bay) there is a regular bus service to Toya-ko onsen on Toya-ko lake. (The many attractions of the Toya-ko area are described in detail in the section on Shikotsu-Toya National Park).

From Toya-ko, Route 230 climbs to a plateau, passing areas of forest land with broken-top trees, smashed by rock ejected in the 1977 eruption of Usu-zan. As the road climbs beside the lake, you get a superb view of Nakajima, a cluster of small volcanic islands poking up in the middle of Shikotsu-ko lake (Nakajima means middle island(s)). Other points of interest are Usu-zan, probably steaming profusely, and Showa-shinzan. Once on the plateau, the road leaves the lake and the view of Yotei-zan begins to dominate the landscape. From there to Sapporo the road passes through a very pretty mountain and farming region with few built-up areas.

The road passes through Jozankei-onsen, one of the best known spas in Japan. (Mixed bathing, formerly the custom here, has gone the way of the auk.) Autumn is the best time for a look around, as the leaves are beautiful at that time.

Sapporo

A rarity among Japanese cities, Sapporo is laid out with streets at right angles and has an address system that makes sense to foreigners (as is true for many other cities on Hokkaido). The reason for this is that Sapporo was founded only in 1869 when the *Kaitakushi* (Commissioner of Colonisation) was stationed here to establish the city as the capital of Hokkaido. Like other "instant cities" it lacks the soul and the element of disorder that gives older cities

their character. The somewhat sterile atmosphere is, however, offset partly by many parks and gardens. Foreigners find it a pleasant place to live, but as a tourist goal it is rather low-ranking. It is at its best when the bright lights of the Susukino district give it a magical touch. Those with a larger budget will find it has the best night life north of Tokyo with more than 3500 bars and cabarets.

The main street, O-dori, is famed for its great width (105 meters), but this is a deceptive statistic because most of the space is occupied by a park-like boulevard. This is a popular place in summer when visitors sit around, usually huddled under the inadequate number of trees. (Why do city planners seem to love huge open spaces which become intolerably hot under the summer sun?) At the east end of the boulevard is the TV tower (147 meters) which gives a good view over the entire city.

Information

The first move is to pick up a map and pamphlet from the tourist information center in the station. The map shows the points of interest and subway and other transportation lines. The JNTO map of Japan also has an adequate Sapporo map on the back.

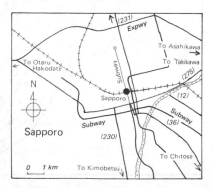

Things to See

The Botanical Garden

The Botanical Garden has about 5000 species of plants from Hokkaido and the rest of the world. It is an attractive setting for a stroll or picnic.

Museums

The Batchelor Museum of Ainu artefacts, closed at last report, occupied one of the old western style buildings in the gardens. It takes its name from an English minister who lived in Sapporo for 40 years. The house was moved to its present location after his death and displays his collection of items of daily use. If the artefacts are on display elsewhere, they are worth seeing.

The Clock Tower Building

This is the only Russian-style structure left on Hokkaido, the clock of which has been a Sapporo landmark since 1881.

Maruyama Park and Maruyama Natural Forest

Remnants of natural forest that provide recreation grounds and ski slopes in winter.

Moiwa-yama

This mountain provides a lookout over the city. It is accessible by cable car from near Ropeway Iriguchi-mae subway station.

Kaitaku-no-mura Historical Village

Located in Nopporo Forest Park, about 12km outside Sapporo, this Village contains many buildings and representations from Hokkaido's early days, and gives a feel for the colonization period. Access is easiest by subway (Kaitaku-kinenkan Iriguchi), and alternatively by a Kaitaku-no-mura bus from Shin-Sapporo station.

Festivals

Sapporo is best known for its Snow Festival, the first weekend of February, when O-dori boulevard (and other open areas) are built up with huge snow and ice sculptures of people, famous buildings, and mythological figures. These sculptures are probably the most impressive of any winter carnival in the world.

Shopping

The main shopping area is Tanuki-koji (Badger Alley), an eight-block long arcade. Also well known is the shopping arcade that stretches underground from the TV tower under the boulevard and then turns to run to Susukino, a reflection of the cold winter climate.

Places to Stay

There are three youth hostels in the Sapporo area. By far the most convenient to reach is the one near the station.

Getting There

In addition to the JR and road connections, Sapporo is easily reached by air from other parts of Japan. The actual airport is at Chitose, about an hour away by bus. (The JR bus terminal is beside the station.) The city of Tomakomai is only a short distance beyond Chitose; it is the port of entry for ferries connecting with Nagoya, Tokyo, Oarai, Sendai, and Hachinohe in Honshu, as detailed at the beginning of the Hokkaido section.

Getting Around

Sapporo has the nicest subway in Japan. Like those in Montreal and Paris, it runs on rubber tires and is therefore very quiet. Stations are marked in *romaji* at the station, but next and previous stations are labelled only only in Japanese, as are trains, maps, etc.

Asahikawa

In the Chikabumi district of Asahikawa, the

Ainu Kinenkan (memorial hall) combines a reasonably good museum with a large number of souvenir stands that sell Ainu handicrafts—mostly identical wooden bears and statuettes of Ainu people. Many Ainu live in the area. One or two (usually elderly) people may be dressed in traditional costume and delegated to satisfy tourists' cameras. Dances are performed—when a tour bus turns up. If you are going to Noboribetsu, Akan, or Shiraoi, it is not worth seeking out Chikabumi.

From Asahikawa you can make a side-trip north to Wakkanai or proceed east to the major attractions of that area.

Places to Stay

The youth hostel is quite good, has a ski tow in the back yard, and you can get information on buses to Wakkanai or elsewhere. But if you arrive early in the day and are not going to Wakkanai, consider pressing on to Soun-kyo, where two youth hostels sit in the midst of beautiful gorge scenery, near good hiking territory.

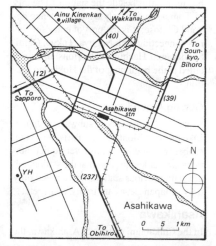

Rishiri-Rebun-Sarobetsu National Park

The islands of Rebun and Rishiri are combined with a part of the mainland to form the Rishiri-Rebun-Sarobetsu National Park. The islands are described below.

Wakkanai

Wakkanai is as far north in Japan as it is possible to go. It is 250 km from Asahikawa, and the road passes mostly through flat land where the scenery consists of spreading farms, barns, and silos. Modern farming machinery is the rule here, so if you see a farmer on horseback, he will be riding for pleasure.

Wakkanai is reminiscent of Reykjavik in Iceland. The houses are low, with brightly colored roofs in red, green, and blue. The landscape around Wakkanai is quite different from that of most of Japan—it is windswept, with low scrub and few trees along the coast. In late summer the grass is a picturesque golden color and there is a feeling of splendid isolation, obtainable in so few places in Japan. Those who like the romance of the Hebrides (not a gay novel) will enjoy the ambiance of the coast near Wakkanai, especially to the north and west around Noshappu-misaki cape. In late summer the light has a particular "northern" quality, giving a characteristic atmosphere. The main industry of the district is fishing, which also adds to the local atmosphere.

Rishiri & Rebun Islands

A very popular excursion with the Japanese is the boat trip from Wakkanai to the islands of Rishiri and Rebun. Although close together, the two islands have a totally different history. Rebun has been there for millions of years and was formed by an upthrust of the earth's crust. Rishiri, on the other hand, is a comparative "youngster", only a few hundred thousand years old, formed when a submarine volcano built itself above the ocean surface. The picturesque cone of Rishiri-zan (1719 meters), now gullied by eons of rain, remains as a reminder of the eruption. The magnificent isolation, unspoiled environment, beautiful scenery, seabirds, wildflowers in profusion, and little fishing villages, are the main drawcards to these islands.

An almost circular road runs around Rishiri, and bus transport is available (six per day, each way). Hiking trails are set out and connect the major points of interest around the island. Scenic spots include the view of Rishiri-zan over the small lakes Hime-numa and Otadomari-numa, and many seascapes including capes that jut into the sea.

Rebun is very low, but nonetheless offers scenic views near Nishi-uedomari, the view of Todo-shima island from Sukotonmisaki cape, and the towering rock, Jizo-iwa.

Places to Stay

There are three youth hostels on Rebun and one on Rishiri.

Getting There

Access from Wakkanai is by Higashi Nihonkai ferry; two boats a day go to Oshidomari (Rishiri) and to Kafuka (Rebun), and there is one a day to Funadomari (Rebun) and to Kutsugata (Rishiri). Other ferries of the same line run from Kutsugata to Kafuka (one per day) and from Oshidomari to Kafuka (two per day). There is a similar number of sailings in the opposite direction. There is also an overnight boat from Otaru (near Sapporo) to Kutsugata

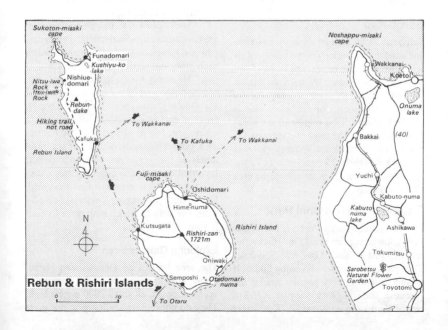

and Kafuka (¥7500), returning to Otaru in the evening. It could be of interest to those who wish to see the northern islands and the tip of Hokkaido but don't relish the return trip by land from Wakkanai, since it is not the most exciting scenery.

More information on the boat connections is available at the TIC in Tokyo, the information center at Sapporo station, and in Wakkanai.

Getting Around

Roads and transport facilities are not overly developed on either island, but are adequate. Hiking is enjoyable and, since the islands are small, it is a good way to look around. On Rebun you can take the bus one way and hike back in one day. There are sure to be young Japanese people doing this, and they're usually happy to have an extra person tag along. Many will be camping.

Sarobetsu

Sarobetsu is an area of swampy coastline and sand dunes known for the beauty of its wildflowers. It can be reached by bus from Wakkanai to Bakkai, by train to Bakkai (the northern most point of entry), or by going to Toyotomi, from where a bus is available (through the middle of the park) to Wakasakanai. The most important part is Sarobetsu Gensei-kaen (Natural Flower Garden); it is about 15 minutes from Toyotomi station. Forget it in the spring; the area floods annually.

Daisetsu-zan National Park

Daisetsu-zan Kokuritsu-koen is one of the best-known scenic areas in Hokkaido, ranking just behind Akan and Shikotsu-Toya parks. For those who enjoy hiking it is superb, and is very popular among the Japanese. The entrance to the park is 16 km east of Kamikawa on Route 39. (Kamikawa is about 45 km east of Asahikawa.)

From Kamikawa onward you get occasional glimpses (to the right) of a group of volcanic peaks known collectively as Daisetsu-zan. The most pronounced peak is the sloping cone of Asahi-dake ("Sunrise Mountain", 2290 meters), the highest mountain on Hokkaido. Climbing and hiking in summer and skiing in winter are popular activities in this area.

Soun-kyo Gorge

The single most scenic attraction of the park is Soun-kyo (gorge), a canyon on the Ishikari river extending 24 km from the entrance to the park. Rock walls rise sharply on both sides of the road, and outcroppings of jagged rock jut from cliff faces. In the middle of the gorge is the hot-spring resort town of Soun-kyo-onsen, with a number of resort hotels and two youth hostels. It is a base for climbing and hiking through the Daisetsu-zan area.

About three km farther along the gorge are two picturesque waterfalls, Ryusei-no-taki and Ginga-no-taki, which are close to each other but separated by huge Tensho-iwa ("Heavenly Castle Rock").

Near the end of the gorge are Kobako and Obako ("small box" and "large box"), closely enclosed sections of the gorge where you feel as if you're at the bottom of a box. The walls of the "boxes" and much of the gorge are columnar basalt, lava that cooled into large crystals. Australians from Victoria will find the gorge like a hundred Hanging Rocks laid side by side. The way in which both were formed is similar.

Exploring Daisetsu-zan

The area known as Daisetsu-zan (Great Snow Mountain) consists of a number of volcanic peaks, all about 2000 meters high. They do not require scaling gear nor great

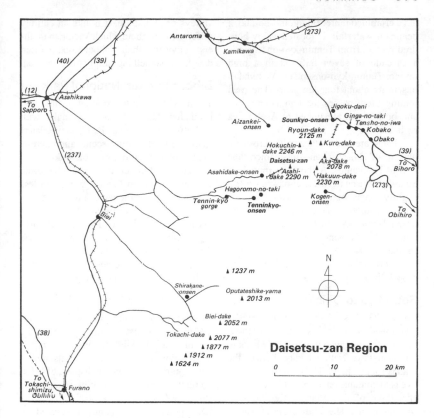

Daisetsu-zan Region

skill, but instead invite exploration because of the ease of walking through the terrain. It is basically an undulating plateau that fills in the area between the various peaks that make up the mountain. The view is one of small craters (some steaming), wildflowers, the crater of Daisetsu-zan, and open spaces with no signs of civilisation. A network of trails makes walking easy.

The best-known trail runs from Soun-kyo-onsen to Yukomambetsu-onsen; it can be walked in a day with little effort. From Soun-kyo-onsen, a cable car runs a good part of the way up the side of Kuro-dake

("Black Mountain", 1984 meters). From there the path is easy to follow past Ryoun-dake (2125 meters), Hokuchin-dake (2246 meters) and Asahi-dake (2290 meters), to the upper station of the "Daisetsu-zan Asahi-dake ropeway" (cable car) that leads down to Asahidake-onsen. This resort has a good youth hostel, with a view of Asahi-dake, as well as other accommodation.

Continuing along the path you come to Hagoromo waterfall, Tennin-kyo-onsen, and Tennin-kyo gorge. Tennin-kyo ("Heavenly Maiden") gorge is similar to Soun-kyo, but its sides are less steep and the cliff faces have crumbled more. Hagoromo-no-taki, a beautiful waterfall, is located a few hundred meters from Tennin-kyo-onsen; it is a cascade of seven falls set in a high ravine. Tennin-kyo-onsen and Asahidake-onsen are about four km apart. The road joining them passes through Tennin-kyo and both onsen are linked to Asahikawa by bus.

There are many other trails across the plateau of Daisetsu-zan—nicknamed "the roof of Hokkaido". A short one runs from Soun-kyo-onsen to Aizankei-onsen, while a slightly longer one goes to Kogen-onsen; both are shorter than the hike to Asahidake-onsen/Tennin-kyo-onsen. A bus service is indicated to Kogen-onsen, but not to the former.

More information is available locally, especially at youth hostels.

Soun-kyo to Obihiro

Route 273 runs south to Obihiro and is mentioned only as a shortcut for those pressed for time who wish to circle back to Shikotsu-Toya National Park. Part of the road is rough gravel. The preferred alternative is to continue on toward Bihoro and the attractions of the Akan-ko–Kutcharo-ko–Mashu-ko area. The following brief section details only the route to that, and other nearby areas.

Soun-kyo to Shiretoko Peninsula

After leaving Soun-kyo, Route 39 continues eastward through Onneyu-onsen, Rubeshibe, Kitami, and Bihoro. The fields around Kitami are planted with peppermint (claimed to be the world's best, naturally), and at Rubeshibe Youth Hostel there is a well-preserved steam engine of the type used in Hokkaido up till the early 1970's. Otherwise there is little of interest along the way. Like many roads that pass through the valleys of Hokkaido, it is like an entirely different topic about which Victorian mothers advised their about-to-be-married daughters, something simply to be endured.

Bihoro to Akan National Park

Those with a limited amount of time will head for Akan at once; it ranks with Shikotsu-Toya National Park (detailed later) as one of the two most scenic and interesting travel destinations on Hokkaido.

The most direct route would be Route 243, which goes to Teshikaga, more or less in the middle of the park. You could turn off it at Lake Kutcharo-ko. This gives an excellent view over the lake from Bihoro-toge (mountain pass). Another way is via Route 240 to the west entrance of National Park, but it would probably cause a considerable amount of backtracking.

Bihoro to Abashiri

Abashiri is a fishing port with some remains from prehistoric times as well as the recent past. The slightly musty but enjoyable Municipal Museum in Katsuraoka-koen (park) has a good display of Ainu artefacts from the area, plus pottery and stone tools (relics of aboriginal dwellers who predated the Ainu) excavated at nearby Moyoro Shell Mound. The museum is one km southeast of the station, and the Shell Mound is northeast of the station on the left bank of the Abashiri river.

Late in the summer of 1978, Daahen-nieni Gendaanu, one of the few Oroke people who moved to Hokkaido from Sakhalin Island, opened a museum to keep alive the memory of his people, nomads who lived by herding reindeer. (There are still Oroke living on Sakhalin Island.) The Oroke word for the museum is *Jakkadohuni*; it may be known in Japanese as Oroke Kinenkan. It would be worth visiting and the curator is friendly.

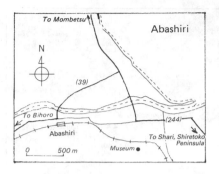

North of Abashiri are two lagoons, Notoro and Saroma. In this area and noted on the map in the TIC brochure on Northern Japan (older editions, anyway) is the intriguing "Coral Grass Gregarious Spot" but, alas!, there is no further explanation. (It might refer to an unusual red plant that grows on swampy ground; in September the fields are quite bright red.)

The nearest youth hostel is at Genseikaen (next section) or go slightly farther north or south to one of the others.

Abashiri to Akan National Park

There are two suggested routes to follow: one is direct, while the other circles around the Shiretoko Peninsula. Both offer better scenery than the route back through Bihoro.

East of Abashiri along Route 244, the first attraction is Gensei-kaen (Natural Flower Garden). This is a strip of coastal sand dune that is heavily overgrown by wildflowers (the result of a dune stabilization program) which bloom in late June and early July. It begins at Kitahama, and continues along the road for about 30 km to Shari. It is always the target for swarms of Japanese photographers.

At Hokuto, before Shari and about 25 km out of Abashiri, the road turns off to Koshimizu and then goes on to Kawayu and Teshikaga. Kawayu is the center of many of the attractions of Akan National Park.

Instead of turning off for Koshimizu, you can continue along Route 244 to Shari and beyond (on Route 334) to Utoro on the untamed Shiretoko Peninsula. Beyond Shari, you can look inland and see the jagged cone of Shari-dake (1545 meters), and later, the rounded outline of Unabetsu-dake (1419 meters). Shari-dake is also visible along much of the length of the direct route.

Shiretoko Peninsula

Shiretoko is an Ainu word meaning "end of the Earth", and it lives up to its name. The end of the peninsula is a national park, the most "primitive" in Japan. There is a small number of hiking trails, and roads go along both the northwest and southeast coasts, but not to the tip. A single road crosses it, from Utoro to Rausu.

From the middle to the tip there are three major mountains, Rausu-dake (1661 meters), Io-zan (1563 meters), and Shiretoko-dake (1254 meters). At the base of the peninsula is Unabetsu-dake, and between it and Rausu-dake is a smaller peak. Io-zan is one of the most unusual volcanoes on earth—when it erupts, it emits pure sulfur. During its most recent eruption, in 1936, more than 15,000 tons of this yellow element poured out. The volcanoes (all but Io-san are extinct) are a continuation of the chain that extends through the Kuril chain to Alaska; on Hokkaido, this is the Chishima volcanic zone.

It is almost impossible, however, to see the mountains while travelling along the road, for it passes close to their base, and in many places the road has been hacked out of the hillside rock. The best way to see the beauty and splendor of the peninsula is by boat (detailed later).

The cape is famous for its rugged cliffs that rise as much as 200 meters from the

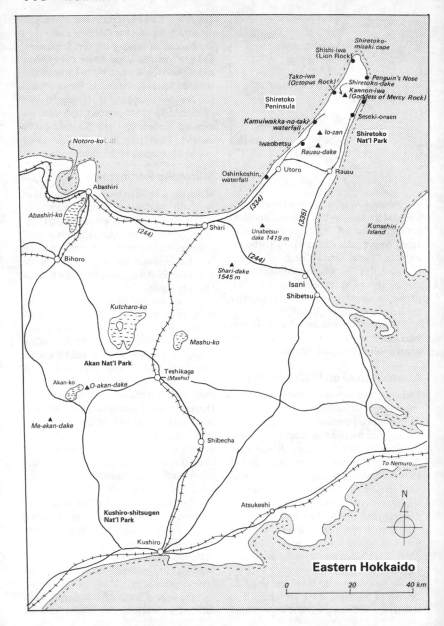

Shiretoko-misaki cape

Shishi-iwa (Lion Rock)

Tako-iwa (Octopus Rock)

Penguin's Nose

Shiretoko-dake

Kannon-iwa (Goddess of Mercy Rock)

Shiretoko Peninsula

Seseki-onsen

Kamuiwakka-no-taki waterfall

Shiretoko Nat'l Park

Io-zan

Iwaobetsu

Rausu-dake

Notoro-ko

Oshinkoshin waterfall

Utoro

Rausu

(334)

(335)

Abashiri

Kunashin Island

Abashiri-ko

(244)

Shari

Unabetsu-dake 1419 m

Bihoro

(244)

Shari-dake 1545 m

Isani

Shibetsu

Kutcharo-ko

Mashu-ko

Akan Nat'l Park

Teshikaga (Mashu)

Akan-ko

O-akan-dake

Me-akan-dake

Shibecha

To Nemuro

Kushiro-shitsugen Nat'l Park

Atsukeshi

N

Kushiro

Eastern Hokkaido

0   20   40 km

sea and stretch up to 10 km without a break. The cliffs are noted for their black-and-white stripes, layers of volcanic rock alternating with sedimentary rock. Time, wind, and water have sculpted them into many fanciful shapes that resemble real objects and beings.

Hot Springs

There are several places along the shores where hot-spring waters collect in pools near the water's edge, making natural *rotemburo* (open-air pools). One is located near Kamuiwakka-no-taki waterfall. These are popular, especially with young vacationers. There's no charge; just peel off and hop in.

Walks

One place that rewards hiking is the Shiretoko-go-ko (five lakes) area near Iwaobetsu. Another destination is Io-zan and its two large craters and fuming vents. The four-hour hike begins near Kamuiwakka waterfall. Visible on the sea-bottom near here is yellow sulfur from the 1936 eruption. Information on other trails can be obtained locally; youth hostels are usually invaluable for such help.

Places to Stay

There are five hostels on the peninsula, three near Utoro (Utoro, Utoro-onsen, and Iwaobetsu), and two near Rausu. There is also one each near the north and south bases of the peninsula, Shibetsu, and Shari. The former has a Genghis Khan supper similar to that described later for the Shikotsu-ko hostel.

Getting There

During the milder months there are boat excursions out of Utoro to or toward the tip, Shiretoko-misaki cape. One lasts 3-3/4 hour (lv 1210; ¥6000), the others 90 minutes (up to five per day; ¥2400).

Kunashiri-to Island

This, along with the islands of Etorofu, Shikotan, and the Habomai group, was seized by the former USSR two weeks after the end of World War II. This was contrary to the Yalta Agreement, and there is no legal basis for the occupation because the islands had always been indisputably part of Japanese territory. The issue is very much alive in Hokkaido and you are likely to see numerous signs that show the map of Hokkaido and the occupied islands, a reminder of the Soviet action. Residents of the peninsula would like to have access to the rich fishing grounds around the islands. With the incredible changes that have taken place since 1990, there is a good chance that some settlement may be reached during the life of this edition. Kunashiri can be seen from a boat or from parts of the southeast coast of the peninsula.

Akan National Park

This is one of the two major scenic regions of Hokkaido. The attractions can be divided into two areas, those centered around Kutcharo-ko lake, and those around Akankohan town.

Kutcharo-ko Area

The main attraction of this area is the remnant of a gigantic volcanic crater, the bounds of which are now difficult to discern. The present body of water is only a small part of the former huge lake. Over time the level of land has changed and new smaller volcanoes have popped up. A good landmark for sightseeing in the area is Kawayu railway station.

Kawayu-onsen

About three km from Kawayu station, Kawayu-onsen is a typical hot-spring re-

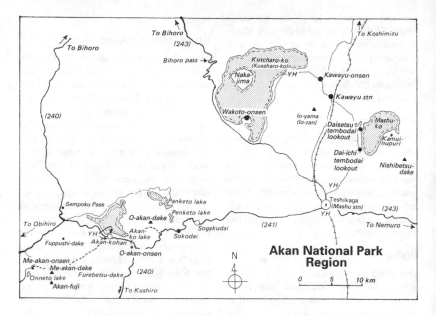

sort, full of hotels (most rather costly) and streets lined with souvenir shops—most of which have captive bear cubs or Ainu wood carvers as the attraction. There is a youth hostel in the town.

Kutcharo-ko

This is a caldera lake, but its circular shape has been changed beyond recognition by the intrusion of later volcanoes. Due to the high mineral content the water is a very unusual green, but the nearby terrain is nearly the same level as the water, so vantage points high enough to see the color of the lake are not conveniently located. The best view can be obtained from high ground like Bihoro-toge (pass) on the road from Bihoro. The lake is an enjoyable place to relax. Because the youth hostel on its shore uses the baths of the neighboring hotel, you have the advantage of a visit to a resort without the painful cost. The bath is quite

memorable, with continually overflowing hot water in a pool four meters square and about knee-deep; smooth flat pebbles on the bottom give an unusual feeling underfoot. Large windows give a view out over the lake toward Mokoto-yama (1000 meters). On my first visit to this hostel (in 1970) hostellers were accommodated in the resort itself, but I'm not sure if travellers late in the season still get this treatment.

Wakoto-hanto

A small bump on the map at the south end of the lake indicates this mini-peninsula, little higher than water level. Hot-spring water rises from below and feeds two open-air baths at Wakoto-onsen, (both are free and mixed); at Sunayu it warms the sand of the beach (Sunayu means "hot sand"). There is a camping ground on the peninsula as well as others along the shore. There may be performances of Ainu dances at

Sunayu during the summer.

Mashu-ko

Nearby is the remarkable and beautiful lake, Mashu-ko. Situated partway up the side of a sprawling mountain, its water is claimed to be the clearest in the world. In 1978 it was clear to a depth of 34.8 meters (41.6 meters in 1911). However, it would be extremely difficult and dangerous to try to reach the water's edge to try to see for yourself. Like many other calderas, the walls of the old volcano that encloses it rise very steeply, giving negligible foothold. It is better to be content admiring the incredible blue of the water from the two observatories, or to walk around the rim. Dai-ichi Tembodai, the look-out spot nearer the town of Teshikaga, gives the better view, showing part of the crater in the peak of Kamuinupuri, on the far side of the lake. Both observatories (the other is called Dai-san Tembodai) give a good view of the entire lake, which appears to fill two separate craters that have linked. On a sunny day, when the color of the water is most intense, the view is quite unforgettable—one of the most memorable in Japan.

Dai-san Tembodai is 14 km from Kawayu station; the other is a little farther on. There is a regular bus service in the area linking Kawayu station to Mashu station via Mashu-ko. Depending on the month there are five to eight buses a day. Hitching should be easy and would get around the problem of inflexible bus schedules.

Io-zan

This active volcano emits volumes of steam that can be seen 10 km away on the road from Koshimizu. From two ravines in the side of the earth-brown mountain, sulfurous (smelly!) steam issues forth, gently wafting from some vents, violently jetting with a great roar from others. Around these holes,

vivid yellow needles of sulfur have crystallized out of the steam. Io-zan means "sulfur mountain".

For the ultimate in natural foods, you can buy eggs cooked by the heat of the earth in one of the little saucepan-size pools that boil endlessly. Look for the old women near the base of the ravines.

Akan-ko Area

The area around Lake Akan (Akan-ko) is noted for scenic beauties, mountains, Ainu people, and a weed that behaves like a submarine. Like Kutcharo, Akan-ko is located in the remnants of a huge volcanic crater, the shape of which has also been changed beyond recognition by subsidence and the incursion of the smaller volcanic peaks, O-akan dake and Me-akan-dake. The size of Akan-ko was originally much greater, but the intrusion of O-akan-dake broke it into the present Akan-ko and two smaller lakes, Panketo and Penketo. On the east shore is an area of bubbling mud called Bokke—which describes the plurp sound of the bursting bubbles (to Japanese ears, at least).

Akan-kohan

The focal point of the lake is the hot-spring resort town of Akan-kohan. Within the town is an Ainu *kotan* (village) where Ainu people can be seen living their "ordinary daily life"—amidst the countless souvenir shops. As mentioned earlier, the Ainu have largely been absorbed culturally by the ethnic Japanese, and almost no one knows more than a few words of the original Ainu languages. However this is at least a chance to obtain a small idea of the old ways. They may also be seen at shops in town, carving an endless succession of wooden bears.

Marimo Weed

Another attraction is this curious weed. Not

just any old garden-variety weed, mind you, but one that acts like a submarine, with the ability to rise and sink in the water. Marimo is actually an intertwined mass of hair-like green algae that has formed into spongy spheres up to 15 cm in diameter. Other species live in Lake Sakyo (in Aomori-ken), Lake Yamanaka near Mt. Fuji , and in some lakes in Siberia, Switzerland, and North America, but it is quite rare elsewhere. The Akan variety is the largest and is considered the most attractive. In the past so many people were taking marimo home as a souvenir that there was a danger they would be wiped out, but they are now under government protection.

All excursion boats on the lake stop at a small island on which a marimo "sanctuary" has been built, and visitors can see them lying on the bottom of concrete tanks, doing their thing. There is also a glass tank containing many marimo at the Akankohan town information office located beside the police station on the short street across the road from the Akan Kanko Hotel.

On October 10 each year there is a "traditional" Ainu festival in honor of the marimo. It supposedly celebrates Ainu legends about the marimo, but publicity photos show Ainu elders carrying a type of tray used only in Shinto observations. Since Shinto is foreign to the original Ainu culture and worship, one may question the authenticity of the festival.

O-akan & Me-akan

The most prominent peaks in the vicinity of the lake are easily climbed and offer beautiful views as a reward. Closer to the town is O-akan-dake, the trail to which begins at O-akan-onsen; ask for the "O-akan Hiking Course". The summit is 10.7 km from the onsen. Me-akan-dake probably offers the more beautiful and unusual scenery from its summit—a weird view of extinct and active volcanic cones, steam jets, and the overall impression of being on the moon. It can be climbed from either Akan-kohanonsen or from Me-akan-onsen, which is 20 km west of Akan-kohan. From the former the summit is 10.7 km, but from the latter is only 2.2 km.

Lookouts

There are two well-known scenic lookouts on the road (Route 241) between Teshikaga and Akan-kohan. Sogakudai ("Two Mountains Lookout") gives a good view of Meakan-dake and O-akan-dake, while Sokodai ("Two Lakes Outlook") overlooks (need it be said?) two pretty lakes, Penketo and Panketo. The whole area is at its finest in autumn when the leaves turn into masses of reds, oranges, and yellows.

Places to Stay

There are three youth hostels near the lake, as well as others in the general area, plus many hotels of varying prices (tending toward the high, this being a resort town).

Getting There & Getting Around

Akan National Park is readily accessible from Kushiro (due south on the coast) by JR via Mashu and Kawayu-onsen stations (in the Kutcharo-ko lake area), and from Abashiri and the Shiretoko Peninsula areas (on the coast to the north).

There are also several bus services. The most picturesque run goes from Bihoro (inland to the north) via Bihoro-toge pass, the lower shore of Kutcharo-ko lake, Kawayu-onsen, Mashu-ko lake, and thence to Akan-kohan. This service is by a sightseeing excursion bus, and can also be used to get up to Mashu-ko lake. Another bus service goes to Kawayu-onsen from Abashiri, but this does not run through to Kawayuonsen at all out of season. There is also a bus service from Kushiro to Kawayu-onsen.

Direct to the Akan-ko lake area (Akan-kohan), there is bus service from Bihoro and Kitami (to the north), Kushiro (to the south), and Ashoro and Obihiro (to the southwest), all of which are on JR lines.

The area is very popular with Japanese tourists, so there will be no trouble arranging transport to the various attractions, either by tagging along with other travellers using public transportation, or by hitching with one of the many passing motorists.

Kushiro

Kushiro, on the south coast, and the coast itself in this area, are of no particular interest, but Kushiro is connected with Tokyo by regular ferry service. (For more details, see the beginning of the Hokkaido section.)

The main attraction of this largely industrial city is the sanctuary for rare red-crested white cranes at Tsuruoka (20 km west of Kushiro station). The number of resident cranes is small, but several hundred come to feed in the winter.

The other attraction that the local authorities promote is Harutori-koen (park), with its lake and an Ainu "village". These would be best regarded as something to see while waiting for a train or boat connection.

Akan to Tomakomai

This route west from Akan National Park includes some of the prettiest countryside in Hokkaido. Tomakomai is a port for ferries to Honshu, and gateway to Lake Shikotsu and Shikotsu-Toya National Park.

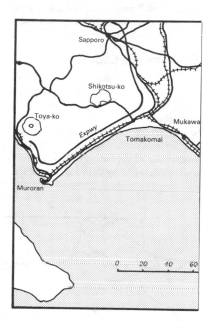

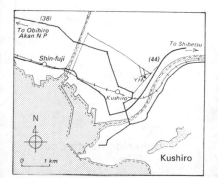

Obihiro

The first destination along Route 241 is Obihiro, an unexceptional town with a nice youth hostel very close to the station; if the custom continues, you'll find that the staff rush out with banners to greet and send off hostellers.

From Obihiro there is a choice of routes, through the mountains directly to Tomakomai, or down the large peninsula below it, around the tip of Cape Erimo, and up the other side, ending also at Tomakomai.

Coastal Route to Tomakomai

There is a bus from Obihiro station to Hiro-o (14/day), and another (4/day) from there to and around the tip, then some distance up to Samani, which is the final station on a JR line from Tomakomai. There are four direct trains each way between Samani and Tomakomai, and another one or two runs with a break of up to an hour partway along.

Erimo-misaki Cape

At the bottom of the peninsula is Cape Erimo and Erimo Quasi National Park. The tip of the cape is noted for 60-meter cliffs that become a line of rocks and reef protruding several km out into the ocean like a line of sentinels. The cape is desolate, swept clear of vegetation by winds, and is usually blanketed by thick fog in summer.

Inland Route to Tomakomai

Beyond Obihiro, Route 38 leads to Tokachi-Shimizu; from there you branch onto Route 274 as far as Hidaka and then to Route 237 to Tomikawa on the coast. From Hidaka you have the option of switching to JR train to Tomakomai.

The road from Tokachi-Shimizu to Hidaka (Nissho Highway) passes through almost total wilderness and offers many lovely views of the Hidaka mountains as the road snakes up and down over crests. There are also glimpses of the green Saru river as you near the coast. It contrasts with most roads on Hokkaido, which follow valley floors.

About 15 km before Tomikawa is the town of Biratori, known for its large Ainu population, but similar in appearance to any other Hokkaido town. From Tomikawa, it is another 45 km to Tomakomai.

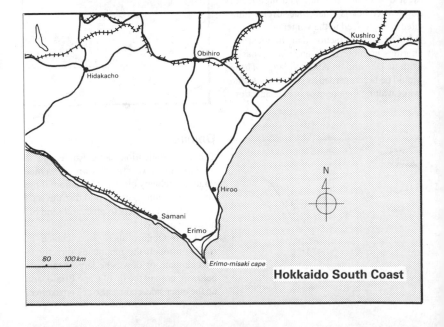

Hokkaido South Coast

Tomakomai

This port and industrial city is the gateway to the attractions of nearby Shikotsu-Toya National Park. It is close to Chitose airport (which also serves Sapporo, 65 km away), and is connected to Hachinohe, Sendai, Tokyo, O-arai (above Tokyo), and Nagoya by regular ferry service. (For more details, see the beginning of the Hokkaido section.)

From Tomakomai ferry terminal, bus 41 runs to the station, from where you can make bus and train connections to other parts of Hokkaido. The same bus goes to the ferry terminal, but service is infrequent, so a taxi may be necessary if you are rushing to catch a boat.

It is possible to reach Cape Erimo (described above) by train and bus from Tomakomai.

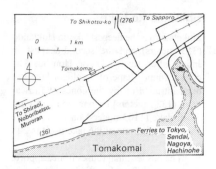

Shikotsu-Toya National Park

If you had time to visit only one part of Hokkaido, the area of Shikotsu-Toya should be it. The major attractions are around the lakes Shikotsu and Toya, plus the town of Noboribetsu. Some might want to add the town of Shiraoi. Attractions are both natural and human.

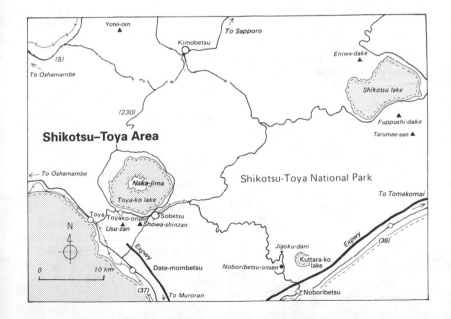

Shikotsu-ko Lake

Shikotsu-ko is the deepest lake on Hokkaido (363 meters) and the second-deepest in Japan, after Tazawa-ko on Honshu. The classic round shape of a caldera lake has been intruded on by the cones of Eniwa-dake (1320 meters) on one side and Fup-pushi-dake (1103 meters) on the opposite shore. The altitude of the lake itself is 248 meters.

The bus terminal (buses from Sapporo, Chitose, and Tomakomai) is at Shikotsu-kohan. Boat cruises are available on the lake from a point near the bus terminal. Swimmers should take note that the bottom slopes gently for the first 10 or so meters from the shore, then plummets sharply.

Eniwa-dake

The low cone of this volcano is the most prominent feature of the lakeshore. It is steep, but can be climbed easily, and makes a good day's excursion. The starting point is Poropinai, accessible by a toll road (beginning near the bus terminal) along the lake. The climb to the crater top takes about three hours, and on a clear day you can see as far as Sapporo, as well as Lake Okotampeko on the far side and the other

mountains around the lake.

Fuppushi-dake

The outline of this low mountain is visible across the lake from Shikotsu-kohan.

Tarumae-san

Behind Fuppushi is this unusual volcano. During its 1909 eruption, a dome of lava 450 meters across and 100 meters high formed in the central crater. It varies in its activities these days; sometimes it shows few signs of life, most of the time it sends plumes of steam into the sky, and it erupted in May 1978 and February 1979. The rim of the crater can be reached from the town of Morappu (part-way round the lake from Shikotsu-kohan).

Places to Stay

The Shikotsu-ko Youth Hostel is very close to the bus terminal, as are quite a few more expensive resort hotels. The hostel is noted for its evening meal, which is vastly superior to the usual hostel fare. It is a Genghis Khan, a filling and tasty Hokkaido specialty of mutton and vegetables cooked at the table on special domed burners. This is a very inexpensive way to try the dish; in summer it is prepared on tables outdoors under a row of tall pines, and the mood is one of a giant party. The hostel is famous throughout Japan for this and for its later entertainment, when the dynamic house-mother leads everyone in dancing. Staff can also advise on getting to the various attractions.

Shikotsu-ko Lake

Getting There

Shikotsu-ko is easily accessible from Sapporo, Tomakomai, and Chitose; in all cases buses run from the railway station. The trip takes about 45 minutes from the latter two, and about 80 minutes from Sapporo.

Noboribetsu-onsen

If you could sample only one hot-spring resort in Japan, this would be a good choice. It is one of the few that a foreigner can enjoy fully, for *onsen* can usually be sampled only by staying at an expensive resort hotel. In Noboribetsu, however, the famous baths are open to the public and are among the most magnificent and largest in Japan. There are also other attractions in and around the town to add to its interest.

The town is a few km inland from the coastal town (and railway station) of Noboribetsu-shi. It is built on the slope of a hill, with the bus stations part-way up. Akashiya-so Youth Hostel is a short distance down the hill from them; other youth hostels are located in the town.

Going up the hill, you pass numerous hotels and streets lined with souvenir stalls patronized by large numbers of Japanese tourists, many dressed in the *yukata* (light, cotton "bathrobe") of their hotels. The souvenir stalls all sell wood carvings of bears and representations of Ainu people (some

of fancifully beautiful maidens). The only glimpses of originality are a few anomalies like a Vishnu-on-Garuda, as seen everywhere in Bali, or a large and incongruous Polynesian-like figure—both carved by a Japanese who read many books on folk-art. Some of the carvings are well done and would be classed as sculpture if they were not all so nearly identical.

The Baths

Continuing up the hill, the road levels off. Where it branches to the left there is a large brown hotel; this is the Dai-ichi Takimoto Hotel, famous for its enormous bath room—and one experience a visitor should not miss.

The entrance for non-guests of the hotel is to the left of the building. After undressing (take your own towel), you enter the cavernous bath room, at least 100 meters long and half that in width. There are nearly 20 large pools in the main section, plus a small number in the women-only section, all of differing size and shape, with water of varying mineral content and temperature. At the far end is a shallow wading pool that has the only cool water in the place—which is worth remembering!

There are numerous fonts where you can sit and wash before taking the waters. The little squirrels gush drinking water; drink frequently to avoid exhaustion from dehydration.

This was, until comparatively recently, one of the few major hotels where mixed bathing remained, but prudery (and resultant peeping at the women who did continue to go into the mixed section) led the hotel to change its policy to one of separating the sexes.

The bath closes to non-guests at 1700, though you may be able to stay on after that time; it seems possible to go in the evening if you get permission from the front desk.

Noboribetsu-onsen Area

To Toya-ko lake

0   1 km

Oyu-numa

Kuttara-ko lake

Dai-ichi Takimoto Hotel

Jigoku-dani

Noboribetsu Onsen

Kuma-yama (Bear Mt)

Expwy

To Shiraoi, Tomakomai

(36)

Noboribetsu stn

To Muroran

The only problem with the baths is the high cost, ¥2000.

Jigoku-dani

Beyond the baths, a further 150 meters or so up the hill, is the unusual and scenic Jigoku-dani (Valley of Hell), so named for the evil smell and noise of steam and boiling water that pours forth from the earth. The colorful valley is a ravine with small hills and gullies where the yellow earth has been stained in bands and patches by the minerals deposited by the water over the centuries. The valley is the source of the hot water used in the baths of the town, and different pools have different kinds of water. At maximum flow, it can exceed 75,000 liters per minute—a householder's dream.

The path through the valley (the dangerous areas are roped off) begins above the car park at the end of the main street through the town. There is no admission charge. The name "hell" is very appropriate—if you broke through the crust, you could be scalded to death before being rescued. Pleasant thought! Down in the valley is a Buddhist shrine to ward off evil.

Oyu-numa

The path through Jigokudani hooks sharply to the left; at that point is a small gravel path, labelled in Japanese only as leading to Oyu-numa. It leads up to a gravel road, across which is the observation point which overlooks the boiling pond. Oyu-numa ("hot water pond") is an intriguing large pool of muddy water that boils continuously. It sits in what is believed to be the crater of an extinct volcano. It is simultaneously scenic and ugly.

Beside the path are some small stone statues with cloth bibs and a sad story. These are figures of Jizo, the protector of children (as well as travellers and pregnant women). One of his responsibilities is the souls of dead children and sewn to each bib is the name of the dead child whose soul is to be helped into the underworld. Areas of subterranean activity like Jigokudani are obviously entrances to hell.

The road that is crossed while walking to the lookout leads to Kuttara lake (to the right); to the left it leads back down to the car park at Jigokudani.

Kuttara-ko

This is a classic caldera lake—almost perfectly round, with the surrounding shore rising steeply to an almost level rim. On a crystal-clear sunny day, the water is an intense sapphire blue, said to be even in deeper in color than that of famed Mashuko. On a hazy day (judge from conditions over Noboribetsu) only the outline of the lake will be visible, and the water will be a characterless grey, making the trip to the lake a disappointment.

From the lookout over Oyu-numa it is about three km to a lookout over Kuttara-ko. It is a further 2.5 km down to the bus terminus/rowboat rental/restaurant at the edge of the lake. Buses leave Noboribetsu-onsen at 0930, 1100, and 1350, take 40 minutes to reach the lake, and return 20 minutes later (¥320 each way). Check the schedule locally or in Jikokuhyo, for it changes year to year. Taxi, hitching, and walking are alternative ways of getting there.

Kuma-yama

Overlooking Noboribetsu-onsen is a high hill, Kuma-yama (Bear Mountain). A trip up could be suggested if it weren't for the extortionate ¥2100 return fare for the cable car (10 per cent discount with a youth hostel voucher). Back in 1970 it was possible to walk to the top quite easily, but the trails have been blocked to ensure revenue.

The main attraction (to foreigners) is a

reproduction of an Ainu settlement, with five or six buildings built in the traditional Ainu style—grass thatch over a wooden framework. The bottom building houses a small museum. Four times a day, a number of elderly Ainu re-enact several of their traditional dances, chants, and ceremonies—centered on the bear. Traditionally, a bear was raised from a cub, then ceremoniously killed, thus releasing the soul of the dead Ainu believed to be trapped within. Nowadays a bewildered bear cub is "shot" with a blunt arrow that does it no harm. Yes, the whole thing is for the tourists, but it is the only way to get a first-hand idea of their former customs. The participants in the ceremonies are mostly in their 70's, so even this remnant of Ainu culture may not be around for long. (In 1970 there were still some aged women with tattooed faces, but it is doubtful that any survive.)

The performances, at 1030, 1530, 1930, and 2010, are held in the second building from the bottom of the slope. No photos may be taken during the ceremonies, and it is unlikely that anyone will pose afterward. To guarantee a good seat, be at the base station of the cable car more than half an hour before a performance (especially in the busy summer season) to be sure of getting a car up the mountain in time.

Another "attraction" of the mountain is a large enclosure full of very large and dangerous Hokkaido bears. They are obviously bored by a life of sitting around on unyielding concrete and have devised many tricks to cadge biscuits from visitors. Although these bears lead a much better life than those in cages at Shiraoi, both places exemplify a definite shortcoming of the Japanese—a total disregard for animals and their basic welfare. Another building houses a Bear Museum that shows and tells you everything you ever wanted to know

about bears—but the text is in Japanese.

Minor entertainment at the top of the mountain may include goose races.

The view from the top over the sea, neighboring mountains, and Kuttaro-ko is very good on a clear day.

The base station of the cable car is reached by walking up a short sidestreet off the main drag of Noboribetsu and either walking up a flight of steep steps (past a number of souvenir shops) and following the path, or taking a chair lift that runs parallel to it (but the distance is so short that the latter is only for the very tired). The base station is a just a short distance away in the large building.

Noboribetsu to Toya-ko

During the summer months there are six buses a day over the mountains from Noboribetsu-onsen to Toya-ko-onsen. The trip takes 1-3/4 hours (¥1900) and is much quicker and more scenic than by train around the bottom of the peninsula. Several of the buses also include Chitose airport.

Shiraoi

About 3000 Ainu have settled in this town, which is about 20 km from Noboribetsu on the way to Tomakomai. It was originally known for its reproduction of a small Ainu *kotan* (village), but is now more famous for its commercialism. To get in to see five or so Ainu-style buildings, the bored, frustrated, and pitiable bears in tiny cages, and a five-minute performance of chants and dances by a few Ainu women who look as if they'd rather be elsewhere, you first have to pass through a very large and modern building full of stall after stall of Ainu souvenirs—all staffed by ethnic Japanese.

The redeeming features of the place are a well-presented modern museum of Ainu artefacts and life-size reproductions of daily activities in traditional times, plus an excellent booklet, *Shiraoi & Ainu*. This gives a great deal of information about the traditional way of life, far more than is available from sources other than scholarly journals, and is presented from the Ainu point of view—which is often quite different from that appearing in official Japanese publications.

Compared with this village, however, the "settlement" on Kuma-yama is much less commercialized, gives a better view of Ainu customs and, comparing costs, is not much more expensive to visit (if starting from Noboribetsu-onsen). Kuma-yama would normally get the nod as the better place to visit but for Shiraoi's good, modern museum and the excellent publication already mentioned.

Shiraoi can be reached easily from Tomakomai or Noboribetsu (on the coast) by train or bus. The bus stop (Shiraoi-kotan) is right in front of the village; from the train station, you walk along the road for about 20 minutes until you see a large archway over a side road.

Muroran

At the tip of the peninsula is the city of Muroran. Apart from the annual festival

Muroran

To Oshamambe, Hakodate

0   1 km

To Sapporo, Noboribetsu, Tomakomai

Higashi-muroran stn

Ferry to Aomori, Hachinohe, Oarai

Muroran stn

N

Chikyu-misaki cape

(July 28–30), and the cliffs of Chikyu-mi-saki, the sole attraction of this dark steel-producing city is that it is the terminus for ferries to Aomori and Hachinohe (northern Honshu). These give the option (when coming from Honshu) of skipping Hakodate and the not-so-interesting 150 km from there to Shikotsu-Toya National Park. From Muroran to Toya-ko-onsen (Toya station) it is no more than 50 km by bus (eight per day) or train, and Noboribetsu-onsen (Noboribetsu station) is only about 25 km away by bus (eight per day) or train. The train goes to Noboribetsu town on the coast (from where buses go the short distance up to Noboribetsu-onsen) and on to Tomakomai and Sapporo. All trains for Toya, and about half of those for Noboribetsu/Tomakomai/Sapporo leave from Higashi-muroran station, three stops from Muroran station.

Toya-ko Area

The remaining area of interest in the Shikotsu-Toya National Park is found around Lake Toya. In addition to the beauty of the lake and its central islands, there is much evidence of past and ongoing volcanic activity. Toya-ko lake is another circular caldera, much larger than Kuttaro-ko. In its center are the islets that collectively comprise Nakajima (middle island); they are the remains of the volcano whose crater forms the basin of the lake.

Lookouts

An excellent view of the lake, Toyako-onsen, and Usu-zan mountain can be had from the lookout at Abuta, beside the road to the coast. From the T-junction near the bus station and police station, the lookout is 1.6 km up the hill.

Other good views can be found by following the road clockwise around the lake (Route 230 to Kimobetsu). From the same

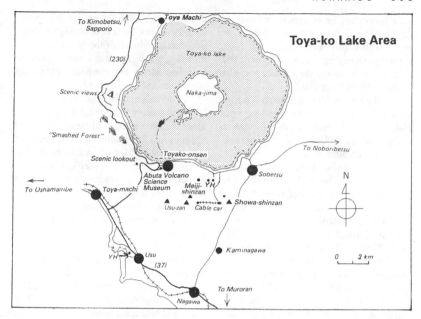

T-junction, the road goes at lake-level for a short distance before beginning to climb to a broad plateau. Just over six km up the hill (one km above the entrance to the Toya Country Club) there is an excellent view over the lake. On the plateau, there are other good views of the lake and its islands, and visible inland is the tall cone of Mt. Yotei. Beyond the red barn-like restaurant/bus stop, the road goes inland and the lake is lost to sight.

There is a road down to Toya-machi (the town of Toya), at lake level, and from there a road circles the lake, back to the youth hostels and hotels. (The road down is loose gravel and not recommended to those on two wheels, and the view from the lower road only so-so.)

Showa-shinzan

"New Mountain of the Showa Era" is one of the most remarkable pieces of rock on Earth. On December 28, 1943, earthquakes hit the area around Toya-ko. Near Sobetsu, to the southeast of the lake, the formerly flat farmland began to rise and, during the next two months, formed a hill nearly 25 meters high. Between late June and late October, many volcanic eruptions took place and the hill continued to grow. By November it had reached a diameter of 800 meters. The climax came when a tower of hardened lava started to rise through the crust of the earth. By September 1945 it had reached a respectable 150 to 200 meters above the surrounding terrain. There it sits today, a chunk of colorful yellows and browns, bare of vegetation, and issuing steam from many crevices.

A friend once said that he feels a sort of affection for sharks, tidal waves, and volcanoes, for they remind man just how powerless he is against nature. A realization of the immense forces at work lifting this huge chunk of rock should push any ego back into place; the rock showing above the surface weighs at least 100 million tons!

At the base of Showa-shinzan is a museum relating to the volcano (nothing special; about ¥500), and the Ainu Kinenkan (Ainu Memorial Hall), which contains some memorabilia of the native peoples. Also here is the base station of the cable car to the top of neighboring Usu-zan (¥1350), an active volcano (described below).

The road to the "instant mountain" turns off the Sobetsu highway about four km out of Toyako-onsen, just beyond the youth hostels. There are buses from Toyako-onsen to Showa-shinzan.

Where this road skirts the east side of Usu-zan, the surface has subsided or been raised more than half a meter. It seems that Usu-san is rising at a rate of 15–30 cm each year.

Usu-zan

This volcanic mountain overlooking the town of Toyako-onsen is the mother of all recent geological disturbances south of Toya-ko lake, and is known for its frequent eruptions. Showa Shinzan is one of its offspring; another was Meiji-shinzan in 1910, a much less spectacular production. To maintain its reputation, Usu erupted in August 1977, and for more than a year afterward there were a dozen or so perceptible earthquakes a day (of short duration) plus about 200 measurable by seismograph. This was its most spectacular eruption, as photos on sale around Toyako-onsen clearly show. An immense cloud of black ash and soot was blown about 10,000 meters skyward, and 30 cm of fine ash fell on Toyako-onsen, causing some buildings to collapse, burying crops, forcing the evacuation of the populace, and causing a giant headache for those who had to clean up the mess. Chunks of rock hurled out during the eruption damaged much of the forest land near the town, and broken tree tops and stripped branches along the roadside remain as silent witnesses to the event.

Usu-zan's activity since then has been confined mainly to blowing out great volumes of steam and gas, although it erupted again in July 1978, sending more clouds of ash and dust high into the air, to the delight of visitors (including myself), and the annoyance of the townspeople who had to clean up the many cm of fine dust. At that time, supposedly more than 80 per cent of the volcanic energy had been dissipated, so it is unlikely that activities will be as spectacular in the future.

The cablecar from Showa-shinzan mentioned earlier runs to the top of Usu-zan. Several of its towers were wrecked by the 1977 eruptions, but were repaired when it became safe again to venture near the top, and new hiking trails have been set out.

Museum

Near the bus station is the Abuta Volcano Science Museum (ask for Abuta Kazan Kagakukan), identifiable by a small wooden fishing boat in the car park in front; it is visible as you descend the hill from Toya station on the coast. This is a museum that should not be missed. It has videotapes of the 1977 eruption and the aftermath, a car damaged by ejected rock, a seismograph recording earth tremors as they happen, and most interesting of all, a room with a model of the volcano, complete with "pillar of smoke". To the accompaniment of actual recordings of the eruption, "lightning" flashes through the plume, and the floor shakes with terrifying realism, simulating the earth tremors and explosions that actually took place. The museum also has an excellent display of relics from the area and an exhibit of items used until recent times by people in their daily work. The museum is open late April to mid-November.

Places to Stay

The shore of the lake has been heavily built up with tourist hotels, and is a popular summer retreat from the heat of Honshu. Swimming and boating (commercial cruises available) are popular activities. The town of Toyako-onsen is the largest center on the lake, and has several deluxe resort hotels.

The two youth hostels are about four km out of town on the road to Sobetsu. When I was at Toya Kankokan Youth Hostel in 1978, all the window frames and doorways had been pushed out of square, walls were cracked, and the bath pool had a distinct tilt.

Getting There

Toyako-onsen is linked eight times a day by bus with Muroran and Noboribetsu-onsen, the latter by a scenic mountain pass. The JR station on the coast is called Toya, but the actual town of Toya (Toya-machi) is on the lake, several km inland, and it is necessary to take a bus from the station. The main touristic center is Toyako-onsen. (Toya-machi is on the opposite side of the lake from Toyako-onsen.)

Getting Around

There is a regular bus service around the lake and surrounding area. Bicycles can be rented near the bus station and are a very convenient means of getting around.

Toya-ko to Noboribetsu

Refer to the Noboribetsu-onsen write-up for information on the bus service between the two places.

CENTRAL HONSHU

This section covers much of what is traditionally regarded as Chubu, or central Japan, plus Hokuriku, the coastal region. For the traveller who wants a feel for the "real" Japan, this is one of the two or three best regions of the country to visit (along with parts of Tohoku, for example). Until only a few years ago much of the area was quite isolated and, except for boats on narrow rivers, some places were completely cut off during winter. As a result, many folk traditions that have disappeared elsewhere still survive quite strongly here. The region also offers much natural beauty, historic remains (including a fine authentic castle), and some of the most interesting festivals in Japan.

The areas covered here are parts of Gumma-ken, Nagano-ken, northern Gifu-ken, Fukui-ken, Ishikawa-ken, Toyama-ken, and northern Aichi-ken. The route followed begins north of Tokyo, as a continuation of the description of the Northern Honshu section. It begins with a journey through Kusatsu, Karuizawa, and Matsumoto, and from there by alternative routes, one through scenic valleys partway to the south coast area, the other into the heart of the Chubu area (the northern alps mountains and Takayama region) and the Tateyama region.

CHUBU REGION

Transportation

The Chubu region is mountainous, and there are few people and fewer roads in the Southern Japan Alps part of the region. In the other parts there are many public transportation services. A brief summary would be useful.

From Tokyo, there is good rail service up one valley to Shiojiri and on to Nagoya. Another line from Tokyo goes via Takasaki (near the top of the Kanto plain) to Nagano and on to Naoetsu, on the north coast. A line from Shiojiri leads through Matsumoto to Nagano. From Shiojiri, another line runs down the Tenryu valley to the coast, below Nagoya. Apart from some lesser lines (some mentioned in the text), transportation is by bus on the many roads through the valleys and over mountain ranges. A copy of *jikokuhyo* is essential if you are travelling with public transportation.

Kusatsu (Gumma-ken)

This is one of the best-known hot-spring towns in Japan, with more than 130 *ryokan* in the central part of town. Yuba (Hot Water Field) is the origin of the hot water, which gushes, boiling, from the ground. Sulfur residue is left behind as the water cools, is collected, and sold as *yunohana* (hot spring flowers), a home remedy.

Netsunoyu (Heat Bath) is the main public bath, and is famous for its exceedingly high temperature. It is so hot that (reputedly) a "drill master" has to enforce discipline to ensure that bathers stay in for the prescribed time. Anyone who stays in accommodation with Japanese people knows that they can withstand water that would boil a lobster, so this must really be hot!

Kusatsu is also a ski resort and has several pleasant walking paths nearby.

Central Honshu

0 20 40 60 80 100 km

NORTHERN NAGANO-KEN ▬

Karuizawa

Much touted in tourist literature as the "ideal" resort, Karuizawa is in fact a place of high-fashion for the summer, more of interest to residents of Japan who are seeking an escape from the heat of Tokyo. It is largely for the rich, as indicated by the fact that more than 250 shops based in Tokyo and Yokohama have branches here, so it has aspects of a shrunken, transposed Tokyo. In summer it is extremely crowded. The city is divided into several parts, the main area being Kyu-karuizawa ("Old K."). The station is two km away. Most places likely to interest the economy traveller lie outside the town.

Information

More information on Karuizawa is available in the JNTO pamphlet *Karuizawa-kogen*, available at the Tokyo TIC (and possibly at Kyoto).

Asama-yama

The backdrop of Karuizawa is Asama-yama, a conical volcano that is still active. Its last major eruption was in 1783, when awesome amounts of lava poured forth. This lava field, Onino-oshidashi, can be seen easily by taking a bus (55 minutes) from either Karuizawa or Naka-karuizawa stations. Asama-yama can be climbed quite easily from several starting points, the favorite two being the above stations. It is advisable to check before climbing, because the volcano still erupts from time to time and climbing is banned when it is active.

There is a good view of Asama-yama, as well as the surrounding countryside, from Usui-toge (pass), which can be reached on foot in 30 minutes. Kumano-jinja shrine is nearby. The pass itself was part of the old Nakasendo highway between Kyoto and

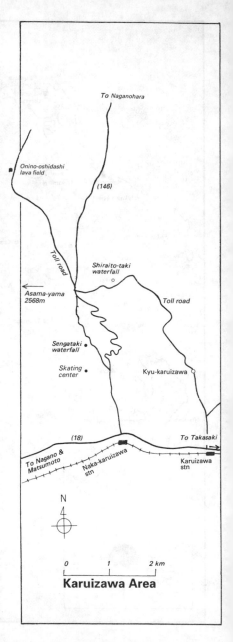

To Naganohara

Onino-oshidashi lava field

(146)

Toll road

Shiraito-taki waterfall

Asama-yama 2568m

Toll road

Sengataki waterfall

Skating center

Kyu-karuizawa

(18)

To Takasaki

To Nagano & Matsumoto

Naka-karuizawa stn

Karuizawa stn

N

0   1   2 km

Karuizawa Area

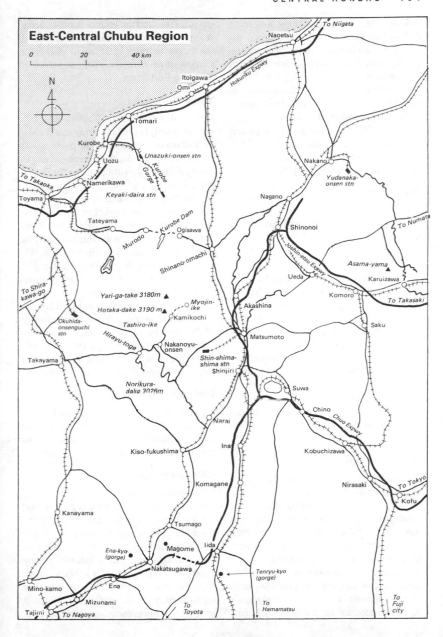

East-Central Chubu Region

0   20   40 km

N

To Niigata

Naoetsu

Itoigawa
Omi

Hokuriku Expwy

Tomari

Kurobe

Unazuki-onsen stn

Uozu

Kurobe Gorge

Namerikawa

Keyaki-daira stn

Nakano

Yudanaka-onsen stn

To Takaoka

Toyama

Nagano

To Numata

Tateyama

Murodo   Kurobe Dam

Ogisawa

Shinonoi

Joshin-etsu Expwy

Asama-yama

To Shira-kawa-go

Shinano-omachi

Ueda

Karuizawa

Yari-ga-take 3180m

Myojin-ike

Komoro

To Takasaki

Hotaka-dake 3190 m

Kamikochi

Akashina

Saku

Okuhida-onsenguchi stn

Tashiro-ike

Hirayu-toge

Nakanoyu-onsen

Matsumoto

Takayama

Norikura-dake 3026m

Shin-shima-shima stn

Shiojiri

Suwa

Chino

Chuo Expwy

Narai

Kiso-fukushima

Ina

Kobuchizawa

Komagane

Nirasaki

To Tokyo

Kofu

Kanayama

Tsumago

Ena-kyo (gorge)

Magome

Iida

Tenryu-kyo (gorge)

Mino-kamo

Nakatsugawa

Ena

Mizunami

To Fuji city

Tajimi   To Nagoya   To Toyota   To Hamamatsu

Tokyo. Some old towns along this route that still retain much of their original appearance are described in the later section covering the Kiso River Valley (southern Nagano-ken).

A 30-minute walk from Karuizawa station leads to Shiraito falls, three meters high and spread along a width of 70 meters.

About 300 species of wild birds inhabit the sanctuary near Hoshino-onsen. They can be watched from two observation huts or from the 2.4 km walking path.

Places to Stay

There are many hotels, *ryokan, minshuku*, villas, camping grounds, and two youth hostels around Karuizawa.

Nagano

The city of Nagano lies in a valley hemmed in by mountain ridges on two sides. Nearby are the best skiing areas in the Tokyo region, such as Shiga Heights; snowfalls in the mountains can reach as much as 15 meters over a winter. It was an area near here, in neighboring Niigata-ken, that Nobel Prize winner Kawabata wrote about in *Snow Country*.

Nagano will be the site of the 1998 winter Olympics, and a shinkansen line is scheduled to be built through to it via Karuizawa.

Zenko-ji Temple

The main attraction of Nagano is Zenko-ji, a temple which draws several million visitors a year. It houses historic statues that are shown only every seven years (the next showing is 1994); the rest of the time they are concealed. A totally dark tunnel passes beneath the altar, along which people grope their way hoping to touch the "key of Paradise" that is supposed to guarantee easy entry to Heaven. There is nearly always a service in progress for the benefit of visit-ing pilgrims, and the interior is richly decorated with Buddhist motifs. It is one of the better temples in Japan to visit for a glimpse of the ceremonies of one branch of Japanese Buddhism.

Yudanaka-onsen

Into the mountains from Nagano (about 25 km northeast) is the hot-spring resort town of Yudanaka. It has open-air pools which are famous from the photographs of snow-covered monkeys sitting in them keeping warm in winter.

Beyond Yudanaka, you can continue by the Shiga-kusatsu-kogen toll road to Kusatsu, then cross to Nikko and Oze-numa via Numata. Since there are so few individual attractions in Gumma-ken, this route description is split between the present section (as far as Numata) and the part of the section on Northern Honshu that covers Tochigi-ken (Numata to Nikko).

The following write-up continues to Matsumoto. From there, routes are first described southward through two river valleys, then others westward to Takayama and to points north and south from there.

Matsumoto

The city of Matsumoto is situated in the basin of mountain ranges. It possesses one of the finest castles in Japan, and this alone makes it worth visiting.

Matsumoto Castle

Matsumoto-jo (castle) is the most easily reached feudal castle in the region around Tokyo. The trip can be made in four hours from Shinjuku station (Tokyo). The castle stands an imposing six storeys above its surrounding moat, and is unusual among Japanese castles because it is black, rather than the usual white. The original, and much smaller, castle on this site was built in 1504, but the present structure was built

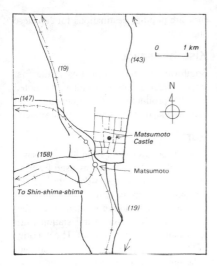

between 1592 and 1614. It is important enough to rate as a National Treasure. It has two main towers, the taller having six storeys. The moon-viewing turret on one corner was added when the defensive character of the castle was no longer important. Swans swimming in the moat add a gracious note to its beauty. In the compound of the castle is the Minzokukan (folklore museum) which houses an exhibit of 60,000 artifacts of history, archaeology, folklore, and geography.

The castle is a little over one km northeast of Matsumoto station and even closer to Kita-matsumoto station. Streets near the castle are narrow and winding, typical of castle towns.

The TIC in Tokyo has an information sheet that gives more details on transport, sightseeing, and accommodation in Matsumoto.

Getting There

From Tokyo, the least expensive way to get to Matsumoto is by bus from the Shinjuku bus terminal (10/day; ¥3400; 3 hr 10 min) and Tokyo station (2/day; ¥3400; 3 hr 40 min).

By train, there are several departures through the day by JR train from Shinjuku station (tracks 5, 6, 8, and 9; consult a timetable!). Nearly all trains are "L" *tokkyu* expresses (just a bit under or over three hours; ¥5900). There is one *kyuko* limited express very early in the morning (3 hr 50 min) and a clutch that leave Shinjuku in the late evening. The two closest to midnight (before and after) reach Matsumoto between 0430 and 0500; these could permit saving a night's accommodation, at the cost of a probable stiff neck. *Kyuko* trains are ¥4900.

The only local trains from the Tokyo area leave from Takao, some distance out the Chuo line from Shinjuku, and would require about five hours.

The TIC information sheet has updated fare and schedule information.

The main train line (from the Shiojiri direction) continues to Nagano and beyond through to Naoetsu on the north coast, while a lesser line goes to Itoigawa, also on the north coast (to the east of Naoetsu). From Naoetsu there is ferry service to two ports on Hokkaido, as well as to Sado island.

Continuing from Matsumoto

Most travellers will likely continue from Matsumoto to Takayama (a very recommendable journey). Description of that route will be given immediately after the following sections describing alternative routes from Matsumoto that go southwest down a pair of river valleys, the Kiso River (via Shiojiri), or the Tenryu River (via Okaya, below Shiojiri). Followed to their ends, the rivers lead to the south coast and to near Nagoya. However, it is possible to see the best of one river valley using train for access and bus/boat for sightseeing, cut cross-country through the mountains to the other valley by bus, then return to Matsumoto via another group of attractions, again using the train, after which you can finally continue to Takayama, all without the need of backtracking. The route described below will be down the Kiso River valley and back up the Tenryu River Valley.

South from Matsumoto

Kiso River Valley

Along with very enjoyable scenery, the Kiso River Valley (southwest of Matsumoto) is worth visiting to see three villages that have remained relatively unchanged for nearly two centuries. Narai, Tsumago, and Magome were located along the old Nakasen-do ("Middle Way") highway between Kyoto and Edo (Tokyo). Every year there were grand processions of *daimyo* along this road between the two cities. Their retinues often numbered in the thousands (at least one of 30,000 was recorded), a measure of the power and wealth of the baron. Because the distance between the cities was great, there were post stations where travellers could rest overnight. To meet the exalted demands of their guests, the *ryokan* (inns) had to be of high standard; some of these fine buildings are still standing.

A visit to one or all of these towns is highly recommended. Apart from a few collections of old buildings that have been gathered from other parts of the country, there are relatively few places in Japan where you can see more than one or two old buildings in any one place. In these three towns, however, you can see a large number side by side, with only a few newer buildings interspersed. The towns retain their old appearance mainly because they were bypassed when the railways were built late in the last century. Their future is assured because of the interest (rather belated) by the Japanese in their past, and

they are popular destinations for Japanese sightseers.

Kiso-hirasawa

Southward from Shiojiri, this is the first town of interest along the valley. It is noted for the production of lacquerware, and there is a lacquer museum near the station.

Narai

One station (JR) away from Kiso-hirasawa is one of the 62 post towns used by travellers along the Nakasen-do highway. The old buildings are easy to find as they line the main street and are located only a few minutes on foot from Narai station (turn left when leaving the station). The majority of the buildings fronting the street are old, although there is a larger proportion of newer structures than in the other two towns. However, Narai is less accessible, so there are fewer fellow sightseers to contend with, and you can enjoy the atmosphere a little better.

There are several buildings open to the public, and money would be well spent visiting a few.

Kiso-fukushima

During the Tokugawa era this was the most important barrier gate of the Nakasendo road. Here the documents of travellers were inspected to verify that they had permission to travel. Life was very strictly regulated in those days (down to such details as to what kind of clothes one might wear and even the position in which one had to sleep!), and most people were not allowed to leave their appointed work or home village. Some mementos of those days survive in the form of old buildings and exhibits in museums.

Yamamura Daikan Yashiki

This was formerly the residence of the

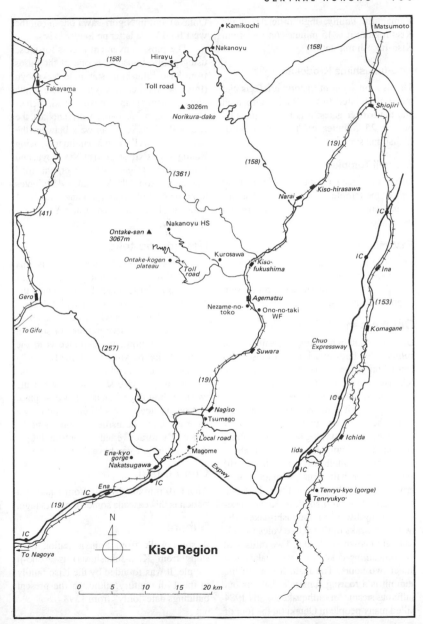

Kiso Region

0   5   10   15   20 km

Yamamura family, high officials in the Kiso region; it is 15 minutes on foot from Kiso-fukushima station.

Kiso-fukushima Kyodokan

This is a museum of historic artefacts and materials related to the Nakasen-do road and the barrier gates; it is five minutes by bus or 25 minutes on foot from Kiso-fukushima station.

Kozen-ji Temple

One of the three largest temples in the Kiso region, the temple is known for its Kanun-tei garden. It is close to both of the places listed above.

Festivals

July 21–August 16: Kiso Odori—folk dances of the Kiso region.
July 22–23: Mikoshi Matsuri—procession of portable shrines.

Ontake-san

Ontake mountain is a popular destination in summer for both pilgrims and those who enjoy hiking. There are many shrines on it (Ontake ranks second only to Mt. Fuji in sacredness), so man's presence cannot be forgotten, but it is the natural environment that is the main attraction.

One popular starting point for climbing is Nakanoyu, from where a climb of about 1-1/2 hours through forest (mostly uphill) and a further half hour on mainly open ground leads to the plateau. From there you can walk and climb south to Kengamine-dake or northward to Tsugushi-dake—the two main peaks of this active volcano, collectively known as Ontake. Two trails lead to Kengamine-dake; the walk takes just under two hours. The main feature of the summit is a roaring fumerole that jets out sulfurous steam. An earthquake in early 1984 killed many people in Ohtaki (at the foot of

Ontake) and in Nigori-kawa onsen (on the west flank); the latter no longer exists.

The most convenient access for those using public transport is one of the buses from Kiso-fukushima station to Nakanoyu (three per day, each way), or to one of the higher starting points above Ohtaki, such as Ontake-kogen, Hakkai-zan, or Tanohara, the end of the line. You can walk between the two roads, well-known landmarks being Rokugome (sixth station) at Nakanoyu, and Hachi-gome (eighth station) on the road leading up from Ohtaki. It takes 45 minutes to get from Fukushima to Otaki and 1-3/4 hours to Tanohara—¥840 and ¥1750 respectively.

Nezame-no-toko

Some distance below road level is this small but pretty "miniature" gorge, an outcropping of large rocks through which the river has carved its way through the ages. There is a large area where buses can park (the place is only five minutes or so from Agematsu station); the entrance is to the north of the parking lot. I inadvertently avoided paying the admittance fee by walking down a service stairway between the two large buildings. The name means "place that opens sleepy eyes", but I suppose we have to allow the namers some poetic licence; it's attractive but not outstanding—worth visiting if you have the time.

Ono-no-taki

About 10 minutes by bus from Agematsu station is this cascade some 10 meters high.

Suhara

A short walk from Suhara station (two stops from Kiso-fukushima) is Josho-ji temple. It was founded by the Kiso family in the 14th century, although the present buildings date "only" from 1598.

Tsumago & Magome

Both these post towns have preserved much of their original appearance. It would be difficult to choose between them, so why not visit both? The walk between them takes about three hours and passes along the old Nakasen-do road, although there is a fair amount of uphill walking in either direction. Tsumago is laid out almost on the level (there is a bit of a gap between two sections of the town), while Magome is strung out down the side of a steep hill. In Magome, the Wakihonjin Okuya, a building shaped like a castle (built in 1877) has an exhibition of material regarding the old post towns.

Festival

November 23: Tsumago Matsuri takes the form of a procession of townspeople dressed in the style of ancient times re-enacting one of the processions of the daimyo who travelled along the Nakasen-do road in feudal times.

Places to Stay

There are buildings open to the public in both towns, and many have been converted to *minshuku* so travellers can stay overnight. The towns are very popular with tourists and the accommodation is usually fully booked in season, so it would be advisable to make reservations if possible. Refer to the section on *Minshuku* for information on bookings from Tokyo.

Getting There

Both Tsumago and Magome are linked with the city of Nakatsugawa by regular bus service (Meitetsu line). From Nakatsugawa station, it takes about 30 minutes to Magome and a bit over an hour to Tsumago. There is also a direct bus connection to Magome from Nagoya; the trip takes about two hours. If you are coming from Matsumoto or Shiojiri, Nagiso is the closest station to Tsumago. More information can be obtained from the TIC in Tokyo, which has sheets on the Kiso region, including transportation.

Nakatsugawa (Eastern Gifu-ken)

Nakatsugawa is the JR station closest to Tsumago and Magome on the line (Chuo Honsen) between Nagoya and Shiojiri), and also affords access to nearby Ena-kyo gorge.

There is a road between Nakatsugawa, in the Kiso River valley and Iida, in the Tenryu River valley, the gateway to Tenryu-kyo gorge. The Meitetsu bus from Nagoya takes this road (Nagoya–Nakatsugawa–Iida), enabling making a loop out of Matsumoto.

Ena (Eastern Gifu-ken)

This city, served by the same JR line as Nakatsugawa, is the gateway to Ena-kyo gorge.

Ena-kyo Gorge

This scenic gorge near Ena city is about 12 km long. Several boats a day cruise up the gorge and back, a 30 minute trip (¥1230). The boat dock is reached by bus from Ena station; destination name: Ena-kyo (several buses daily at 20–40 minute intervals; ¥260).

Tenryu River Valley

Another route from Matsumoto southward (branching off at Shiojiri) is through the Tenryu (Heavenly Dragon) River valley to Iida by JR or along Route 153. The scenery is pleasant enough to make the trip enjoyable, and there are a few points of special note.

Ina

The grounds of the former castle Takato-jo are very pretty in the cherry blossom season (probably a couple of weeks later than in Kyoto and Tokyo).

Tenryu-kyo

The major attraction of the river valley is the scenic Tenryu-kyo gorge, accessible from Iida. Tenryukyo station (JR) is near the gorge, but the most enjoyable way to see this and other parts of the Ina valley is by boat. One route runs through the Tenryu rapids, starting at Benten, 10 minutes by bus from Iida station (¥3000; one hour; up to 8/day). These terminate near Tenryukyo JR station. Another boat trip leaves from the latter location and goes to Karakasa (¥2570; one hour; up to seven per day). Karakasa, Tenryu-kyo, and Iida are all close by on the same JR line and there are more than 20 trains/day (several only between Iida and Tenryu-kyo), so it is easy to get from one to the other. There are many *ryokan* and *minshuku* at Tenryu-kyo (with a booking office near the station); it is a pleasant place, with some walks along the river in addition to the boats.

In addition to JR train, Iida can be reached from Tokyo (Shinjuku Bus Terminal) by 15 buses through the day (4 hr 15 min; ¥4120). It can also be reached by one of the 13 daily buses (2-1/2 hr; ¥2310) from Nagoya (Meitetsu Bus Center). The latter buses come via Nakatsugawa (gateway to Tsumago, etc.) in the Kiso River Valley, and can be used to travel between Nakatsugawa and Iida on route 256. This permits a trip down one valley from the Matsumoto area, crossing to the other valley via route 256, and returning along that valley to the Matsumoto area.

Continuing Southward from the Iida/Nakatsugawa Areas

The route south from Iida ends at Toyohashi, an industrial city on the coast of no particular interest. For details of the two peninsulas in that area, refer to the short section *Southeast from Nagoya*, following the write-up on Nagoya in the next chapter (Kinki region).

The valley in which Nakatsugawa is located leads to Nagoya. The area around Nagoya (which includes Gifu, Inuyama, and Seki) is also covered in the Kinki chapter, along with Kyoto, Nara, etc.

Continuing Westward from Matsumoto

The following description continues the route that most travellers in this area will likely take onward from Matsumoto: westward through the scenic mountain and farmland terrain of the northern alps to Takayama and beyond.

Matsumoto to Takayama

The trip from Matsumoto to Takayama via Kamikochi can be recommended as a chance to see an area of relatively unspoiled rural Japan. The route is definitely off the beaten track for most foreign tourists (although I suspect that you may encounter some others holding this book!), but the route uses well-established scheduled transportation and takes you through a scenic region of mountains, beautiful valleys, and picturesque little farms.

The first leg of the trip is by Matsumoto Denki-Tetsudo private railway from Matsumoto to Shin-shima-shima (22 minutes; ¥670; about 25 trains per day with the first at 0350 - for the early birds). Do not mistake this stop with Shimojima, which is three stops before Shin-shima-shima. The next leg is by bus from the terminus across

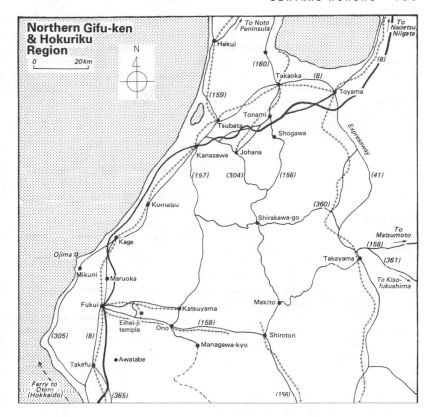

Northern Gifu-ken & Hokuriku Region

the road from the railway station. You can either go as far as Nakanoyu and transfer directly for Takayama (55 minutes; ¥1500; up to 14 per day), or go to the end of the run, to the scenic delights of Kamikochi (another 20 minutes; ¥1950 total), and return to Nakanoyu after looking around for a few hours. There are many *minshuku* and *ryokan* in Nakanoyu and a booking office for finding accommodation. (In the opposite direction, some buses go beyond Shinshima-shima to Matsumoto Bus Terminal.)

From Kamikochi and Nakanoyu there are up to ten buses a day to Hirayu-onsen

(55 minutes from Nakanoyu, 70 from Kamikochi; ¥1400 from both). Several of these continue to Norikura (1-3/4 hours from Nakanoyu), described below.

From Hirayu-onsen it is only an hour to Takayama (¥1330; many buses through the day). The phrase "up to" indicates that services are more frequent in summer and on weekends.

Schedules are such that you can begin at Kamikochi/Nakanoyu, go to Norikura and spend a couple of hours walking around, then return to Hirayu-onsen and either stay the night or continue on to Takayama. (The same type of connections are, of course, available in the opposite direction.) The climb to Norikura and approach to it across the highland plateau in the bus is probably the most scenic part of the trip.

If you don't want to go all the way to Takayama, an alternative is to travel to Norikura from Matsumoto (as described) then return to Shin-shima-shima directly by bus (¥3000; up to five a day). The schedules for all these trains and buses are given in *jikokuhyo*, so it is possible to schedule your travels through the region with military precision.

Kamikochi

Some people believe that this highland basin west of Matsumoto is the most beautiful area in the northern alps. The most impressive single view is the one seen during the last few minutes of the trip in from Nakanoyu, just before reaching the cluster of lodges and inns and the parking area. The valley opens up on to a broad flood plain with the wall of mountains behind forming an impressive backdrop. This view alone justifies the trip, though there are some very pleasant walks through wooded paths beside the river. There is no lack of company, and it is interesting

to observe how the normally reserved Japanese greet each other while enjoying the natural surroundings. The number of previous hikers can be judged by the height of the cairns—piles of stones built up one at a time by people leaving a marker of their passing.

Several trails begin at Kamikochi. The main trail from the car park leads to Kappa-bashi, a famed suspension bridge across the Azusa-gawa river. From the bridge there is a beautiful view of Mt. Hotaka, and nearby is a rock sculpture of Walter Weston, a Briton who was the first alpinist to explore the Japan alps in the last century. Prior to this the alps were regarded as sacred or inhabited by evil spirits, and were avoided. Other attractions, apart from the general pleasant mood, fresh air, and scenic views, are Tashiro-ike and Taisho-ike ponds and Myojin lake. A three-hour walk from Kamikochi passes Myojin lake, Tokusawa, and Yokowao. Trails continue beyond here to nearby high peaks, such as Yari-ga-take (Spear Mountain—the "Matterhorn" of Japan), but scaling them is for the experienced only. Every year dozens of Japanese are killed in falls from slopes.

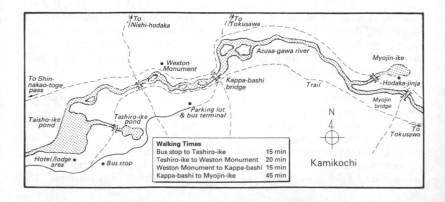

Walking Times

Bus stop to Tashiro-ike	15 min
Teshiro-ike to Weston Monument	20 min
Weston Monument to Kappa-bashi	15 min
Kappa-bashi to Myojin-ike	45 min

Norikura-dake

This is the most accessible peak in these alps, despite its 3026 meter height, for a toll road runs most of the way to the top, crossing an alpine plateau en route. Buses via the Norikura Skyline go as far as Tatamidaira (2-1/2 hours from Kamikochi; less from Nakanoyu or Hirayu-toge), from where a three km hike (90 minutes) leads to the top. It is high enough that a few patches of snow can be found as late as August.

As mentioned above, there are regular bus services from the Norikura area to Takayama.

GIFU-KEN (NORTHERN) ▬▬▬

Takayama

The city of Takayama ("High Mountain"), often called Hida-takayama, has been a prosperous area for several centuries, and there is a tradition of cultured living that you would not expect to find in an isolated river valley. Several fine old houses and other buildings survive in the city; these and other attractions make wandering around the city interesting and pleasurable, and make Takayama one of the most worthwhile places in Japan to visit.

Information

Your first stop should be at the information booth in front of Takayama station to pick up a copy of their English-language booklet *Hida-Takayama*. It lists all the places of interest to visitors, with a brief description of each, and locates them on a map. (Ignore the reference to the "pubic gym"; despite the well developed sex industry in Japan, this is sure to be a disappointment.) If you are starting from Tokyo, you should also obtain from the TIC a copy of the information sheet on Takayama; it has up-to-date details on train connections, accommodation, days when attractions are closed, and other valuable information.

Things to See

Hida Kokubun-ji Temple

This is the oldest temple in the Hida region, originally founded in 746. The main hall is about 500 years old.

Kusakabe Folkcraft Museum (Kusakabe Mingeikan)

The house itself, dating from 1880, is a fine example of the residence of a wealthy merchant (Kusakabe family) of that era. The interior features heavy beams of polished wood; these enhance the overall elegance of the rest of the building. There is also a collection of folkcraft items from the region. It is closed Wednesdays from December to February.

Yoshijima House

A neighbor of the Kusakabe house, this building was the residence of the Yoshijima family, also wealthy merchants. The two are among the finest houses in Takayama. Yoshijima House is closed on Tuesdays from November to February.

Shishi Kaikan

This is an exhibition of the elaborately carved and ornately lacquered wooden lion-heads used for dances during processions.

Hachiman Shrine

The shrine is the site of the autumn festival (described below). In the grounds is Takayama Yatai-kaikan, an exhibition hall containing four of the 23 elaborately decorated *yatai* festival wagons, arranged as you would see them in an autumn or spring procession. This gives at least an impression of the magnificence of the festival for those who are unable to see the real thing.

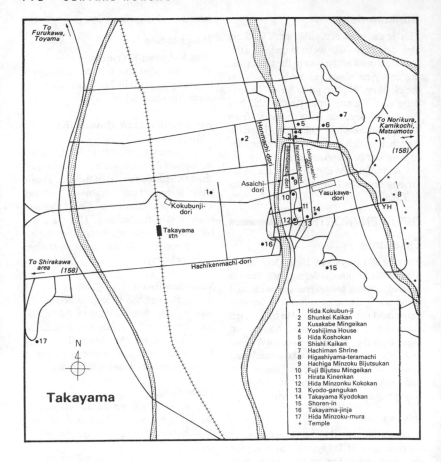

1 Hida Kokubun-ji
2 Shunkei Kaikan
3 Kusakabe Mingeikan
4 Yoshijima House
5 Hida Koshokan
6 Shishi Kaikan
7 Hachiman Shrine
8 Higashiyama-teramachi
9 Hachiga Minzoku Bijutsukan
10 Fuji Bijutsu Mingeikan
11 Hirata Kinenkan
12 Hida Minzonku Kokokan
13 Kyodo-gangukan
14 Takayama Kyodokan
15 Shoren-in
16 Takayama-jinja
17 Hida Minzoku-mura
• Temple

Takayama

Higashiyama Teramachi
Teramachi means "temple town". The name comes from the row of 10 temples at the foot of Higashi-yama (East Mountain). (The youth hostel, at Tensho-ji temple, is in this area.)

Hida Fubutsukan
This is a museum showing artefacts related to the way of life in the Hida region.

Hachiga Folk Art Gallery (Hachiga Minzoku Bijutsukan)
The folk-art collection of the Hachiga family is housed in this building.

Hirata Memorial Hall (Hirata Kinen-kan)
Art objects belonging to the Hirata family, descendants of a wealthy merchant, are displayed in this museum.

Kyodo Gangukan

This museum houses about 2000 traditional toys from different regions of Japan.

Municipal History Museum (Takayama Kyodokan)

Built in 1876 and formerly a storehouse, this building belonged to the Nagata family and now houses many items of local history as well as a famous Enku statue. The latter is one of many well-known statues roughly sculpted with a hatchet by the itinerant priest Enku.

Shoren-ji Temple

Shoren-ji temple (main building dating from 1504) is built in a unique ancient style, and is famous for the elegant curved shape of its roof. It was moved here from Shirakawa-go (described later) when the Miboro dam was built in 1961.

Furui-machinami

Step back in time with a stroll down *furui-machinami* where old houses and shops line both sides of the street. Many of the buildings are restaurants, coffee shops or souvenir shops (the owners have to make a living too), but the overall impression is that of a century or so ago. The buildings with the large spongy- looking "ball" hanging from the eaves are old sake warehouses, where various kinds of sake are still on sale. For more than a millennium, Takayama has been known for its carpenters and woodworkers, so have a look at the small chests, trays, bowls and chopping blocks on sale in the shops. Some of Japan's most tasteful souvenirs, such as woodblock prints, papier mache figures, and special sake flasks are made and sold in Takayama.

Takayama Jinya

This imposing building was the residence of the local governor in the Tokugawa era, and was originally the heart of a large complex of buildings. Now most are gone except for eight samurai barracks and a garden behind the main building. Closed Wednesdays.

Hida Folklore Village (Hida Minzoku-mura)

With the mountains that surround Takayama as a backdrop, and the interesting setting of the park itself, the first impression here is that of a functioning ancient village. It is probably the best park of its kind in Japan, with many traditional farmhouses (mostly thatched) and other buildings (up to 500 years old) set up around a pond. The "village" includes houses from a number of districts in the mountains around Takayama, including the Shirakawa-go area. Because the buildings were held together with ropes and not nails, they could be dismantled and reassembled without damage. A pamphlet in English describes the salient points of the various buildings. The park is a couple of kilometers from the station, and can be reached by bus (half hourly; ¥200), taxi, or on foot. It is especially beautiful in autumn. (Parks on a similar theme can be found in Kawasaki, Kanazawa, and on Shikoku.)

Other Sights

There is also a number of museums and exhibitions worth visiting. They include the following: the Shunkei Lacquerware Hall (Shunkei-kaikan), Fujii Folkcraft Museum (Fujii Bijutsu Mingeikan), and the Hida Archaeology Museum (Hida Minzoku Kokokan).

There is also a pair of delightfully grotesque statues of pot-bellied goblins with long arms in the middle of the main river bridge.

Festivals

Takayama is justly famous throughout Japan for its spring and autumn festivals, two of the most magnificent and interesting in the country. Huge, incredibly ornate festive wagons, *yatai*, are put on display for most of the day, and later pulled through the streets. The tradition of building *yatai* began a couple of centuries ago as a supplication to the gods to protect the inhabitants of the city from a plague that was ravaging the country. Their prayers seemed to be successful so the custom continued (a sort of preventive medicine) and the carts became more magnificent each time as a spirit of competition developed among wealthy merchants. As Takayama was a wealthy town, the best materials and construction could be afforded. To duplicate one today would cost about half a million dollars! A booklet is available giving the history of each *yatai*—some are nearly 300 years old. During the rest of the year the wagons are stored in *yatai-gura*, tall concrete (fireproof) storehouses with no windows, and *very* tall doors. As mentioned earlier, there is a permanent display of four *yatai* during the rest of the year at Yatai-kaikan, in the grounds of Hachiman shrine.

The wagons (which are hard to describe as they resemble nothing known in western countries) include intricate wood carvings that form panels and pillars of the structure, antique tapestries of European origin, and other embellishments. In addition, a few of the *yatai* have mechanical "dolls" that perform amazing movements and tricks, all controlled by wires and pushrods; the ingenuity of their designers deserves greater recognition. A typical doll "walks" out along a beam, rotates and bows to the audience, pivots around completely a couple of times, then releases a shower of flower petals. One *yatai* even has a couple of acrobats that swing from perch to perch.

The performance times of the dolls during the display of the *yatai* is indicated on a board near the wagons. It pays to arrive early for a performance to get a good place, as the crowds are very heavy.

The spring Sanno Matsuri is held on April 14–15 near Hie-jinja (shrine), the autumn Yahata Matsuri on October 9–10 in the grounds of Hachiman-jingu. There is a total of 23 *yatai*; 12 are shown at the spring festival and the other 11 in the autumn. There are also parades of people in various feudal costumes. An interesting feature is one of the musical instruments, a circular metal pan that is struck with a wooden mallet to produce a peculiar "ging" sound; it seems to be found only in this district.

Places to Stay

There is a youth hostel in Takayama at Tensho-ji temple (tel (0577 32-6345). When I visited, the house-mother was having a love affair with the PA which, like most PA systems, had only one setting—full blast. At 2200 (lights-out) she prattled on for 15 minutes to tell her charges to go to sleep . . . while they were all lying in the darkness waiting for her to keep quiet! (A later traveller reports more normal conditions.)

As might be expected in a town that is very popular with Japanese sightseers, Takayama has plenty of *minshuku* and *ryokan*. Reservations may be made at offices set up for the purpose, located near the station. One is at the information booth in front of the station; another is down the street to the left, and a third is at the far side of the department store opposite and to the right. They are signposted only in Japanese, but the *kanji* for "*minshuku*" are prominent and can be recognised easily.

The phone number of the Takayama *Minshuku* Association is (0577) 33-8501/2;

the Takayama *Ryokan* Association is (0577) 33-1181. Have someone call in Japanese, as it is unlikely that anyone will understand English. There is also a Kokumin-shukusha (Peoples' Lodge), tel (0577) 32-2400. The cheapest hotel is the Meiboku (tel (0577) 33-5510) which has double rooms for ¥8000. The Hida and Green hotels are more expensive, tel (0577) 33-4600 and 33-5500 respectively.

Getting There

From the south, Takayama is easily reached by JR train from Nagoya, etc., via Gifu. There is also a year-round bus service to and from Gifu. From mid-May to mid-October there is the combination of buses and a train via Shin-shima-shima from Matsumoto, as described earlier in this chapter. From the north, there is JR service to and from Toyama and possibly a bus service. Highway 41 is a major road linking Nagoya with Toyama and there is quite heavy traffic, so hitching should be no problem.

Getting Around

Since the city is laid out with streets at right-angles (a rarity in Japan) it is easy to find your way around Takayama, and it is small enough that the energetic can see it on foot or by bicycle. The latter can be rented from at least two shops on the main street (to the left when leaving the station, on the opposite side of the street) at ¥1500 per day.

There is a regular bus service that goes to or near most of the attractions of the city and circles back to the station. A "free pass" (the "Japlish" term) costing around ¥900 is available; it gives unlimited travel for two days and can be bought at the station. Buses run every 20 minutes between 0900 and 1640.

Furukawa

About 15 km above Takayama is the small city of Furukawa ("Old River"). It has a number of old houses and the appearance of some of its streets is, overall, perhaps more traditional than that of Takayama. It is a pleasant place to walk around, and there is a chance that a rickshaw will be available for short rides.

Festival

Furukawa is probably best-known for its annual festival, which is well worth trying to see. Furukawa Matsuri is held on April 19–20. The feature is a night procession of a huge drum on which two men sit back-to-back and swing their hammers down to strike the two ends in unison. The festival dates back 1500 years, so I was told, to the time when drums were used to scare boars away from the crops.

The festival lasts two days, and it is worth trying to see all of it. During the day there are processions of the nine *yatai* (festive wagons similar to those at Takayama and Kyoto). The wagons are elaborately decorated, though they are not as large or imposing as those in the other two cities. Two of them also have ingenious mechanical dolls which are on display on the second day of the festival. Times for their performances are posted beside the *yatai-gura* (the concrete buildings where they are stored the rest of the year). Unless there have been any changes, the times for the *kirintai yatai* (a kirin is a mythical dragon) are 1330 and 1530, while the *seyutai yatai* could be seen at 1000 and 1500. The dolls are at least 170 years old (ca 1820) and are marvels of design skill, similar to those described for the Takayama festivals. Such dolls can also be seen at one of Nagoya's festivals.

During the processions of the first day,

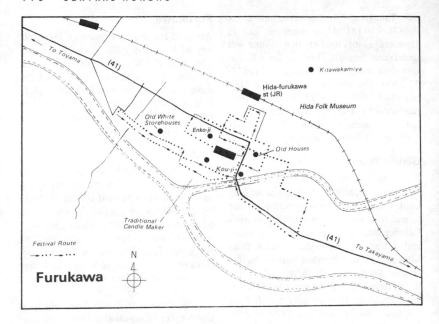

Festival Route
- - ·· - ·· -

N

Furukawa

To Toyama

(41)

● *Kitawakamiya*

Hida-furukawa
st (JR)

Hida Folk Museum

*Old White
Storehouses*

Enko-ji

Old Houses

Kou-ji

*Traditional
Candle Maker*

(41)

To Takayama

many townspeople in old costumes accompany the wagons. Children are dressed at their best (as they are for the more crowded Takayama Matsuri), so it is a splendid chance to photograph them dressed in very beautiful kimono. Many boys play the unusual "ging" instrument described in the section on the Takayama festival.

Throughout the festival young men go from door to door performing a *shishi-mai* (lion dance). The *shishi* has a magnificently carved wooden head with jaws that clack shut in a most amusing way. If there are children nearby, the dancer operating the head may get right down to the ground to try to scare the child—usually he or she laughs with delight. Two assistants manipulate the lion's body and the dancers are accompanied by a small troupe of flute players and a drummer who keeps rhythm with healthy wallops on a wheeled drum.

After dark on the first night, bonfires are lit at several intersections of the town, and at about 2200 the lids of the sake casks are broken open and the contents liberally distributed to the young men carrying the drum, as well as to any passers-by who wish to indulge. Any foreigners present (usually few) receive special attention, and it becomes a problem keeping sober enough to see the rest of the festivities, let alone take pictures. The fires and sake help to keep the young men warm, for the nights are still cold (nearby ski-grounds still have large patches of snow on them) and they wear nothing but *haramaki* around their middles and a loincloth. After they have become sufficiently soused, one after another demonstrates his balancing skills by scaling a bamboo pole and lying on it, all his weight held by the small circle of the pole pressing into his belly.

Not long afterward, the procession with the large drum begins. The drum (at least 1.5 meters in diameter), the two drummers, and at least 10 other people carrying lanterns, are supported on a large structure of bamboo poles and beams that is carried through the streets on the strong shoulders of many (usually inebriated) young men. The drum is preceded by a large number of people in costume who carry lighted paper lanterns; the effect is beautiful. Most houses, *ryokan*, and *minshuku* along the parade route (it circles through the town several times through the night) have upper-storey windows that can be removed completely to give a good view of the parade—by far the best vantage point to watch it. The celebration and inebriation are, by the way, historically part of Japanese festivals, and have been for the last 2000 years.

During the festival there is a special table set up at the station to help people find rooms. However, many of the rooms are at ski lodges many kilometers out of town, accessible only by taxi, so it would be worth trying to arrange accommodation in advance. There is a youth hostel at Takayama, but the drum procession takes place too late at night to allow time to see it and get back in time for lights-out.

48 Waterfalls

Between Takayama and Furukawa there is a turn-off (signposted in Japanese) pointing the way to 48 Waterfalls (*Yonju-hachi taki*), about eight km off the main road. They are a pleasant low-key bit of scenery—the water flow and the drops are moderate—but they provide a peaceful walk relatively remote from humanity (most of it, anyway).

SOUTH FROM TAKAYAMA

Gero

Though not an attraction to draw a traveller, someone may be hitching and get dropped off here and want to look around. Gero is a typical hot-spring resort, basically a collection of concrete hotels that feature the mineral-laden water, mostly for therapeutic benefits. There are no attractions for the casual visitor, except that travellers with time to spare could check out one travel publication's mention of a village of *gassho-zukuri* houses (explained a couple of pages later in the section on the Shogawa valley area) transplanted here from Shirakawa-go when it was flooded by the waters of the Miboro dam. (I cannot guarantee its existence.) Those in a hurry can rely on the existence of houses still at Shirakawa-go, and a "village" of houses transported to Takayama.

Another attraction of Gero is the Chubu Sangaku Kokogaku Hakubutsukan (Archaeological Museum).

Zenshoji

One stop above Gero is Zenshoji station; nearby is Zensho-ji temple, the largest in the Hida region. Hida is the name given to the region roughly from above Gero to beyond Takayama.

SHOGAWA VALLEY AREA

Not far west of Takayama is a very interesting region, the Shogawa river valley. (It is also accessible from the south from the Gifu area, and from the north from Takaoka.)

The area was settled in the 12th century by survivors of the Heike (Taira) clan who were defeated by the Genji (Minamoto) clan in the great battle of Dan-no-ura (near Shimonoseki) for control of Japan. The Taira fled to this and other remote areas to escape slaughter by their foes.

The area was still considered remote as late as 1961, when construction of the Miboro dam brought it to greater attention. Even until 1978, the only communication during winter was by boat along the river. Nowadays there is a year-round bus service. The description of this region overlaps Gifu and Toyama prefectures, which has made it difficult to obtain information on the area as a whole because prefecturally-prepared travel literature tends to studiously ignore places even a kilometer outside its own boundaries.

Gassho-zukuri (Thatched-Roof Houses)

The outstanding feature of the region is its characteristic large three- or four-storey thatched-roof *gassho-zukuri* houses. These are the largest traditional farmhouses in Japan; many are 200–300 years old. Surrounded as they are by hills and mountains, and remote from most influences of the late 20th century, they make the region one of the most charming and traditional in Japan. A visit to such an area (there are relatively few left) should be on the itinerary of any visitor who wishes to get a feel for "old" Japan.

Gassho-zukuri means "hands held in prayer" (i.e., Buddhist-style, with palms together and fingers stretched straight up). In former times, a single house accommodation 30 to 100 people on the ground floor; upper storeys were used for the production of handicrafts (utilitarian in those days, not for sale to tourists) or for raising silkworms, and the attic was used as a storehouse.

The area is increasingly popular with Japanese tourists seeking what remains of the traditional Japan. As a result, a large number of the houses function as *minshuku* and take in guests, thus producing an income and ensuring their survival.

Shirakawa-go

This village is made of several *buraku* (hamlets), each containing some of the thatched houses. Ogimachi is by far the most interesting, as it has the lion's share of *gassho-zukuri* clustered together (11 of which are now *minshuku*). Other nearby *buraku* are Hatogoya and Iijima, both of which have only a few. The original village of Shirakawa was inundated when the Miboro dam filled in 1961, so its buildings were moved elsewhere. Some can be seen at Takayama's Hida Folklore Village, Yokohama's Sankei-en garden, and at Kawasaki's Nihon Minka-en.

The present village of Shirakawa is small, and the main activity for visitors is just to look around and savor the atmosphere. All the houses are within walking distance of each other and there are rice paddies in the immediate vicinity, so the mood is certainly rural. Many of the houses have old farm implements hung outside as an open-air museum display. A good vantage point can be reached by walking (or taxiing) a couple of km up the Supa Rindo highway, which links the village with Kanazawa. Another is from the foundations of a former castle.

Information

All the *minshuku* give out copies of a sketch map that is quite adequate for sightseeing. The largest house in Ogimachi, formerly the chief's residence, is a museum.

Places to Stay

One of the most memorable experiences of a visit to Japan would be a night spent in one of the many *gassho-zukuri minshuku*. Although modern amenities have been added, the traditional appearance of the exterior has been retained in all cases and the

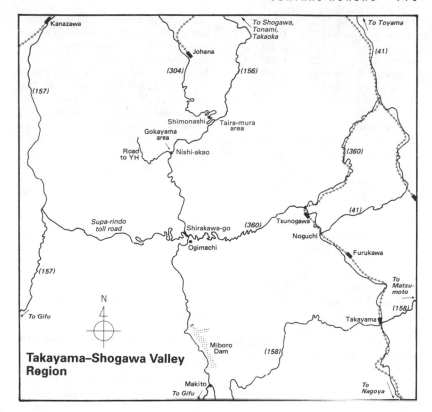

Takayama–Shogawa Valley Region

common-rooms often have the original hearth over which is suspended a pot-hook. All guests eat together and, if my experience at the Juemon was typical, the lady of the house keeps everyone company, pours beers and sake for them (paid for separately), and even sings folksongs of the region and performs local folk dances.

Listed below are the names and phone numbers of almost all the *minshuku* in Ogimachi. In the July–August season this area is very popular, and it is advisable to phone ahead to be sure of having a place to stay.

None of the proprietors speaks English, so you will need a Japanese person to phone for you. It might be possible to book through an agency in Tokyo or other large city, or at the station in Toyama or Gifu. The number in brackets is the approximate age of the house. The charge per night is uniform for all *minshuku*. The area code for Ogimachi in Shirakawa-go is: (05769).

Juemon	6-1053	(300)
Yosobe	6-1172	(230)
Nodaniya	6-1011	

Kidoya	6-1077	(200)
Gensaku	6-1176	(170)
Magoemon	6-1167	(280)
Iicha	6-1422	(200)
Koemon	6-1446	(200)
Furusato	6-1033	(150)
Yoshiro	6-1175	

The hostess at Yosobe seemed extra-pleasant and friendly, but the people in charge of the last two *minshuku* did not seem very interested or helpful to me, although a Japanese friend recommended the Yoshiro highly.

While it is not a *gassho* house (only a country farmhouse), some travellers have had only the highest praise for a *minshuku* they stayed in near Shirakawa-go; it is Minshuku Osugi (address: Okubo Shirakawa-mura, tel (05769) 6-1345).

A few km above the village of Shirakawa-go is another small cluster of *gassho* houses to the west of the road and down near the valley floor. There is a *minshuku* advertised on a sign at road level (Toichin-so: tel (07637) 3632), but the surroundings are not as picturesque as at Shirakawa-go.

Getting There

The Shirakawa-go area can be reached by public transport from Gifu, Nagoya, etc., to the south, from Takaoka to the north, and from Takayama to the east. From Nagoya, a simple way is by JR train to Mino-ota (nine per day; one hour), and from there to Mino-shirotori (also nine per day but generally not connecting; two hours); from Shirotori there are five buses a day (two hours) to Ogimachi (via Makito), which terminate at Hatogaya, a short distance beyond Ogimachi. There is also a single bus from Nagoya station to Ogimachi (5-1/4 hours) and Hatogaya. From Gifu, not far from Nagoya, there are many JR trains to Mino-ota (40 minutes), plus many buses through the day from Shin-Gifu station through to Shirotori (just over two hours). From Takaoka, JR runs as far south as Johana (20 per day) from where two buses a day run south to Hatogaya (one hour). Two buses a day also go from Takaoka station to Shimonashi (bypassing Johana; 1-1/2 hours) where you can transfer to a Johana–Hatogaya bus. From Takayama, you can go by bus to Makito (six per day; 1-1/2 hours) and then change to a Shirotori-Ogimachi bus.

There are two routes to and from Kanazawa. The old one is via Route 304 to Taira-mura, where it meets Route 156; buses run on this route. The new Supa Rindo ("Hakusan Super Forest Pathway") toll road runs much more directly through the mountains and links Shirakawa-go with Route 157 straight to Kanazawa, but there is no bus service. Two-wheeled vehicles are not, unfortunately, allowed on this road.

TOYAMA-KEN ▰▰▰▰

Gokayama

A little farther north, across the boundary into Toyama-ken, are the *gassho* houses of Gokayama (which is technically part of Kami-taira, or "upper Taira village"), beginning at Nishi-akao. There are so few that they can be identified by name. First comes the Iwase family; a little farther on, at Suganuma (Kami-taira) you find the houses that make up the Gokayama Seishonen Ryoko Mura (Youth Tourist Village) which offers accommodation. Near the Tourist Village is a road that turns off and runs inland to the west. This leads to Etchu Gokayama Youth Hostel, itself a *gassho* house (tel 07636 7-3331). Another house (Murakami family) can be found at Kaminashi (Upper Nashi), a hot spring town. At Shimo-nashi (Lower Nashi) you can see traditional Japanese paper (*washi*) being made at Goka-shi Kyodo-kumiai (Goka Paper Producers' Cooperative).

Toga

The inveterate *gassho-zukuri* can also find some in the Kami-momose section of Toga village. I haven't been there, but photographs indicate that there are five thatched houses close to each other. Being not at all well known and very more remote, it would be guaranteed not to be touristy. There should be at least one *minshuku* in the area. You would need your own vehicle. One map shows a good road direct to the village from just above Furukawa/Takayama, with a minor road linking that road to Inokuchi, a little above Taira. Another major map gives no hint of such a road.

Going north from this area along Route 156 leads to Takaoka and Toyama. JR trains can be taken from Tonami. (Branching off 156 onto route 304 first leads onto twisty gravel road, but then passes through some pretty scenery.) The route north leads to Johana (soon after the road reaches flat land), where a JR line begins; the road goes through to Kanazawa.

Tateyama/Kurobe Gorge

Another interesting part of the northern Japan alps is the Tateyama area. Although it is not so far from Kamikochi and area as the crow flies, the earth-bound human must circle far around to the coast in order to reach both the Tateyama mountain area and Kurobe gorge. Both are easily reached from Toyama.

Toyama

Toyama has little in the way of attractions, but is the starting point for two good excursions into the northern Japan alps (no need of climbing). One is an excursion to nearby Kurobe-kyo gorge, the other to Tateyama mountain (and through the mountains to Nagano-ken, if desired. In addition to access from the Shogawa valley area as just described, it is also easily reached from Kanazawa and Takaoka to the west, and from Niigata and Naoetsu, farther up the north coast.

Tateyama

A popular excursion is to the Tateyama mountain group, which is centered around Tateyama itself (3015 meters). For most sightseers, a day trip out of Toyama will take in the scenic high points of the area (more than a pun there!). It is possible, however, to continue on the Tateyama-Kurobe Alpine Route through to Shinano-omachi, in Nagano-ken. The full trip is rather costly, and the best scenery is in the first part, up to Murodo; from Toyama, Murodo is an easy day trip.

The route from Toyama starts at Dentetsu-Toyama station, from where the Toyama-chiho Tetsudo line runs frequently to Tateyama station (about 60 minutes and ¥1010 ordinary/about 50 minutes and ¥1160 by the few expresses; about 25/day total). The route passes through pleasant countryside en route, and the sheer cliffs of the mountain range come into view some time before Tateyama station is reached.

From Tateyama, a funicular train climbs for seven minutes to Bijo-daira (¥620). An exceptionally twisty, low-gear-all-the-way, 55-minute bus ride through scenic mountain vistas follows, terminating at Murodo (¥1630). En route it passes scenic, 2-km-away Shomyo-taki waterfall (Japan's longest, including a drop down a sheer 126 meter cliff face), and offers a view at Midagahara over the surrounding area. The route is open from May 15 to November 5; if you travel soon after it opens, you may find yourself at times in a canyon cut through snow up to 10 meters deep.

Murodo is a base for walking to Mikura-ga-ike pond or Jigoku-dani ("Hell Valley")—an area of steaming solfataras (volcanic vents), or for climbing Tateyama Oyama or Tsurugi-dake peaks. The climb from Murodo to Oyama is steep and is nearly five km long; the view from the top takes in a number of surrounding peaks and valleys.

After walking around the sights in the Murodo, you can take the bus back to Bijo-daira and return to Toyama, or you can continue on to Shinano-omachi by the rest of the Tateyama-Kurobe Alpine Route. (The trip up this point has covered most of the best scenery in the region; the rest of the Alpine Route is costly.)

NOTE: Check the weather before embarking from Toyama on this trip. If it is cloudy in Toyama, and especially at Tateyama sta-

tion, there is little sense in continuing. It was cloudy the day I went, and I could rarely see more than 10 meters from the bus during the entire ride to Morodo; the trip was a complete waste of time and money.

Tateyama-Kurobe Alpine Route

This route passes through territory that was the province only of alpinists until 1971. From Murodo the route continues by a 10-minute LPG bus ride (18 per day) through a tunnel to Daikanho (¥2060; oh, to have that franchise!). From here the route takes a cable-car across a wide valley, and a funic-ular train down to Kurobe-ko lake, behind Kurobe dam, the largest arch dam in the Orient; the first (seven minutes) costs ¥1240, the second (five minutes), ¥820. From the end of the dam there is the option of going up to Kurobe-daira, a lookout over the dam, before going to the station for the

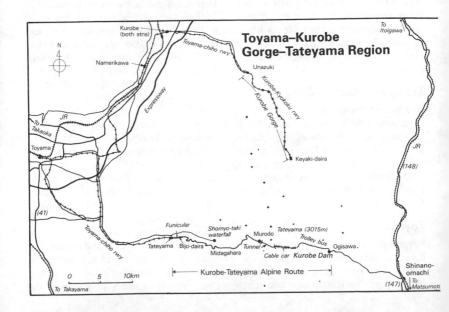

trolley bus. The only such line left in Japan, it takes travellers to Ogisawa (16 minutes; ¥1240) for an almost-immediate connection with a regular bus that runs to Shinano-Omachi (40 minutes; ¥1200). There are 11 trips a day in each direction by the trolley bus and the connecting bus. The cable-car and funiculars run more frequently, and generally dovetail for minimum delay, so you can take some time to look around and continue by a later departure without a long wait, or continue almost at once.

The Tokyo TIC has an information sheet with up-to-date prices and times.

Omachi (Nagano-ken)

Omachi is in Nagano-ken, and is located on a JR line and Route 148, both of which run through a river valley north to Itoigawa (on the north coast) and south to Matsumoto. Nagano and its nearby attractions are situated in another parallel valley separated by a chain of mountains. There are two small local roads across to Nagano, but no bus service; it is necessary to go down to Matsumoto before being able to take public transportation up to Nagano.

Kurobe-kyo Gorge

The least complicated trip into the alps (and one of the most enjoyable) is a train ride through Kurobe-kyokoku, the Kurobe Gorge. (The line was built to carry supplies to the construction site of the Kurobe dam.) The starting point for the 20-km run by the Kurobe-kyokoku railway is Unazuki-onsen. This is easily reached by the Toyama-chiho Tetsudo railway from Toyama (Dentetsu Toyama station; separate from JR station), by transfer from the JR stations at Namerikawa, Higashi-namerikawa, or Uozu, or at Kurobe (separate station); there are up to 26 trains a day (¥1550 from Toyama ordinary, ¥1800 express). It can also be reached by road.

From Unazuki-onsen the narrow-gauge train runs through deep gorges to Keyaki-daira, taking about 90 minutes (16 trips daily during the May 1–November 30 season; ¥1300 each way). For maximum view, the train is made up of open-sided carriages consisting of little more than seats and a roof. (One train a day has closed-in carriages (called "Panorama sha"); this train has a surcharge of ¥600 each way.)

It is not possible to go on past the end of the gorge; you must return to the coast or Toyama. There are several stations along the way through the gorge, so it is possible to walk part of the way. It would be best to ride all the way in, then decide which sectors would be most enjoyable on foot.

HOKURIKU REGION

The Hokuriku area is north and west of the northern alps. It takes in the coast west from Toyama (including the Noto peninsula), curving around through Kanazawa and Fukui, down to the strip of land north of Biwa-ko lake.

Takaoka

Near the eastern base of the Noto Peninsula is Takaoka. The city is noted for its lacquerware, as well as copper and iron products, and is the main source in Japan of large cast bells. If you are interested in artistic foundry work, you might be able to arrange a visit to a workshop; try the town hall (shiyakusho) for contacts.

Sightseeing potential in the city is limited. It does have the third largest Daibutsu (statue of Buddha) in Japan but, although it is described as being of bronze, it looks more like green-painted concrete and cannot be compared with the serene beauty of the famous Daibutsu at Kamakura near Tokyo.

castle grounds have been used for the buildings of the civic center, etc., and are not otherwise interesting.

Festivals

There are festivals on January 14 and June 2–3 as well as the following:

May 1: procession of *dashi* (large carved and decorated wagons). The dashi used in this procession are old but not as fantastically elaborate as those of Takayama or Kyoto.
May 15: night processions of at least seven large floats lit by lanterns.
August 3–7: Tanabata, with pretty paper decorations on the streets—but not much action.
September 23: Daibutsu festival.

Takaoka Region

As well as using Takaoka as the starting point for trips around the Noto Peninsula, you can go south to the very interesting Shogawa River valley and the old houses of Shirakawa-go area described earlier. There are buses from Takaoka station along Route 156 through the valley. There is also a JR line as far as Johana, from which another road links up with 156 at Taira-mura, the northern extremity of the area of old houses mentioned above. The attractions of the Japan alps, southeast of Takaoka, are described in the Chubu section covering the Nagano area, the route from Matsumoto to Takayama, plus the section covering the Tateyama area.

Things to See

Zuiryu-ji

The best place in Takaoka to visit is, in fact, the youth hostel (3207; tel. 0766-22-0179), because it is actually a large and venerable temple about 350 years old. Zuiryu-ji is a Zen temple of the Soto sect. The main building and the ceremonial entry gate are large, and the spacious grounds are surrounded by a traditional wall. It is unusual to find such a splendid structure in such a remote area as this. There is a peaceful feeling because there are no hordes of tourists. It is not worth a special trip, but for anyone who plans to stay overnight in the area it can be highly recommended. As a bonus, the wife of the priest speaks good English and can tell you a bit about the place.

Temples

Other temples in Takaoka are Kokutai-ji and Shoko-ji. Shrines include Imisu and Keta. The foundations of the old castle and its moats still stand, and are rather pretty during the cherry blossom season, but the

ISHIKAWA-KEN ▬▬▬▬

Kanazawa

A favorite of Japanese tourists, Kanazawa has much to recommend it to foreign visitors as well. This part of Japan has undergone relatively little industrialization, so there has been less of the tear-down-and-rebuild activity that has destroyed so much of the heritage of Japan. It also escaped bombing during the war, the only large city other than Kyoto to do so. Many old buildings have survived and old neighborhoods are almost unchanged from their appearance of decades or a century ago.

Strangely, being so far from cultural influences like Kyoto (the area is heavily covered with snow in winter, making transport in former times very difficult for much of the year), the city has historically been a center of culture and learning. A major factor is that it is one of the richest rice-growing areas, and it was the largest feudal land tenure in Japan. Another is that the Maeda clan who controlled the city and region, beginning with Maeda Toshiie (who captured the city in 1583), valued education and a cultured life. They spent the wealth wisely and promoted such crafts as lacquerware and weaving, encouraged artisans to settle, and established fine buildings and traditions that survive to this day.

A large proportion of the attractions of Kanazawa are located near Kanazawa-jo (castle), mostly around an irregular loop encircling Kenroku-en garden, and can be seen on foot. The castle can be reached by bus in 15 minutes from Kanazawa JR station (about 2.5 km away); the stop is pronounced "Kenroku-en-sh'ta".

Information

The photocopied information sheets provided by the Tokyo TIC give useful additional details on accommodation, etc. In Kanazawa there is a large guide map and an information office in front of the station (to the left when leaving), as well as a small office at the handicrafts center (Kanko Bussankan). If you do get lost, you will probably have no trouble getting assistance; I have never experienced so many offers of help as in Kanazawa when I stopped to consult my maps.

If you really want to experience all that Kanazawa has to offer, use a copy of Ruth Steven's guide book *Kanazawa*. It is a labor of love, and describes everything in the city that is worth seeing, in a lighthearted and informative manner. Its first printing sold exceptionally well (Kanazawa residents bought thousands!), but it has been reprinted and updated and should be available in Kanazawa. It is normally stocked in the foreign-language bookstores in Tokyo.

Home Visits

To arrange a visit to a private home in Kanazawa, ring 20-2075.

Things to See

Kanazawa-jo

Little remains of the former imposing castle because of a series of fires in the last century. The fire of 1881 destroyed all the major buildings except Ishikawa-mon gate, parts of the walls, moats and the armory. The site of the castle has been used as the campus of Kanazawa National University, but this should have moved out by now. In one corner of the grounds is Oyama-jinja shrine.

Oyama-jinja

The gate of this shrine is very unusual in design and history, and is unlike that of almost any other in Japan. It was designed in 1870 by a Dutchman, a scientist who was teaching in the city during the westernisa-

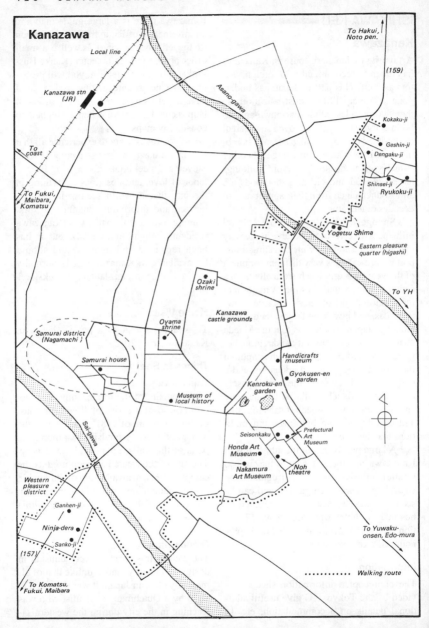

Kanazawa

Local line

Kanazawa stn (JR)

To coast

To Fukui, Maibara, Komatsu

Asano-gawa

To Hakui, Noto pen.

(159)

Kokaku-ji

Geshin-ji

Dengaku-ji

Shinsei-ji

Ryukoku-ji

Yogetsu Shima

Eastern pleasure quarter (higashi)

To YH

Ozaki shrine

Kanazawa castle grounds

Oyama shrine

Samurai district (Nagamachi)

Samurai house

Sai-gawa

Handicrafts museum

Gyokusen-en garden

Kenroku-en garden

Museum of local history

Seisonkaku

Prefectural Art Museum

Honda Art Museum

Noh theatre

Nakamura Art Museum

Western pleasure district

Gannen-ji

Ninja-dera

Sanko-ji

(157)

To Komatsu, Fukui, Maibara

To Yuwaku-onsen, Edo-mura

•••••••••• Walking route

tion period. The top two storeys of the gate strongly suggest two squared arches, one atop the other, of traditional Chinese design. Filling the top arch is a stained glass window that was originally used as a lighthouse for ships on the Sea of Japan. The shrine itself dates from 1599 and was built to honor Toshiie Maeda, the founder of the Maeda clan; it was moved to its present site in 1873.

Other arches similar to those of this gate may be found on the Karamon (Chinese gate) of the innermost buildings of Toshogu shrine in Nikko, and in Nagasaki at Kofuku-ji (nicknamed the "Chinese" temple).

Gyokusen-en Garden

This was the garden of the Nishida family and is laid out in a circular style around a pond.

Ishikawa-ken Kanko Bussankan

Ishikawa-ken is famous for several handicrafts, including some of Japan's finest lacquerware, cloth weaving and dyeing, pottery making, wood carving and others. This museum makes it possible for visitors to see some of the crafts being produced. Master craftsmen give daily demonstrations in lacquerware, carving of wooden heads for *shishi* (lion dolls), gold beating, *kaga yuzen* (fabric dyeing), and *kutani* (pottery-making). An excellent pamphlet in English gives sufficient explanation of the crafts to understand the processes. Demonstrations are given on the third floor. There are restaurants and shops selling a wide variety of handicrafts native to the area. In addition, there is a tourist information office at the entrance, but beware of their map of Kanazawa; it may still be an all-too-typical Japanese handout map, very stylised, not to scale, and with north off to the left. (Closed Wednesdays in winter.)

Kenroku-en Garden

Considered by the Japanese to be one of the three finest landscape gardens in the country, Kenroku-en dates from 1819. It is quite extensive, covering 10 hectares. Roku means "six", and Kenroku-en combines the six features considered essential to fine gardens: vastness, solemnity, careful arrangement, coolness (water), age, and pleasing appearance.

The garden is spacious and encloses two ponds, and has many attractive aspects. It is, to me, by far the most attractive of the "Big Three" gardens. However, although Kenroku-en is certainly worth seeing, my feeling was that it did not quite live up to its advance billing. One reason for this is that because it is among the "Big Three" (the Japanese *love* to rank everything), so it is a "must-see" for Japanese sightseers, and the garden will almost invariably be noisy and bustling with people from countless tour buses and lacking the tranquility required to appreciate it. The mood is not aided by the constant blare of loudspeakers extolling its virtues.

The north entrance to the garden is across the road from Ishikawa-mon gate of the old castle grounds, but there are also other entrances.

Seisonkaku

On the southern edge of Kenroku-en is Seisonkaku, a beautiful two-storey mansion built by one of the *daimyo* for his mother. It is a fine example of *shoin-zukuri* architecture. In addition to the design and workmanship of the house and garden, there is also an exhibit of many items used by the Maedas. (Closed Wednesdays.)

Ishikawaken Bijutsukan (Prefectural Art Museum)

A very short distance from Seisonkaku, this museum is most worthy of note for its collection of *kutani* pottery.

Nohgaku Bunka Kaikan (Prefectural Noh Theater)

Noh plays are performed here frequently, mostly by amateur groups, but there is a regular professional performance on the first Sunday of every month. (Some sources claim the third Sunday, so be sure to check!) Performances last from 0900 to 1700. The theater dates from 1972 and includes the stage that was salvaged from the old Noh theater that stood beside the town hall. The theater is just a short distance south of Seisonkaku. (Closed Mondays.)

Honda Zohinkan (Memorial Art Museum)

Also located near Seisonkaku, at the top of the hill, this museum houses a collection of items used by the Honda family, the chief retainers under the Maeda.

Nakamura Kinen Bijutsukan (Memorial Art Museum)

Close to the Honda Museum, this is a large Japanese-style house that belonged to a wealthy sake dealer named Nakamura. He donated the house and his collection of Oriental art (including fine lacquerware and utensils for the tea ceremony) to the city. (Closed on Tuesdays and the day after national holidays.)

Kyodo Shiryokan (Museum of Local History)

This museum has a variety of exhibits of local archaeology, folklore, and history, including one relating to the processions required of local daimyo to Edo (Tokyo) in feudal times (which often involved thousands of people). The building looks incongruous, as it is a western-style red-brick structure built as a high school in 1891, at the time when westernization was in full swing. Note that on the map included with the information sheets available at the Tokyo TIC, this is labelled "History Museum". (Closed Mondays.)

Samurai District

Walking through the little lanes of the old samurai town of Nagamachi gives at least an impression of olden times. There are several typical narrow crooked streets lined with packed-earth, tile-topped walls that keep out curious eyes. Most of the houses, however, are actually from the Meiji era (1868–1910), rather than genuine samurai-built houses. One authentic samurai house which has been restored and is open to the public as a museum is Buke Yashiki Ato (closed Wednesdays). Another old house, Saihitsuan, is used for demonstrating *yuzen*, the traditional method of hand-painting patterns on silk for kimono (closed Thursdays in winter). For a look over two former samurai gardens, have a coffee at either Kaga-no-niwa or Nokore (both closed Thursdays).

After visiting the samurai area and shopping in the many stores along the nearby main street, you can return full-circle to Oyama shrine or leave it until last along with a more leisurely look at the handicraft-making displays at the handicrafts center.

Higashi (Geisha) District

Higashi is one of Kanazawa's two "old" districts, most popular with visitors because they preserve much of the atmosphere of former times. According to one story, the Maedas decreed that geisha areas and temples be placed on the banks of both the Asano and Sai Rivers, so that invaders would be distracted by one or the other. More likely it was a way to minimise their effect on daily life, just as Tokyo had the Yoshiwara area set aside for its geisha houses. The main attraction is just wandering along the back streets among the old houses and temples. Visitors are allowed into one of the still functioning geisha houses, the Shima (usually open 0900 to 1700; closed Mondays). Another, the Yogetsu, has been turned into a *minshuku*.

Teramachi

This is the second of the "old" districts. The geisha houses are no longer mentioned but the temples still remain, including Myoryu-ji, one of the most unusual in Japan.

Myoryu-ji

Dubbed *Ninja-dera* (Ninja temple) this is not merely a temple but a type of fortress with labyrinthine secret passages, hidden traps, and exits, to hold off attackers while the *daimyo* escaped. Myoryu-ji was the Maeda family temple. There are tours lasting 20 minutes, but the temple is so popular that it is generally necessary to make reservations (tel 41-2877, in Japanese); on Sundays and holidays it may be impossible. The best time to go is mid-afternoon. If there are not many people scheduled for a tour, it may be possible to squeeze in without a reservation. Some of the guides may speak English. (Closed first and 13th of each month and New Year.)

Edo-mura

Of interest to many will be Edo-mura, a "village" of Edo-era (17–19th century) buildings that were moved here from different parts of Japan. Some of the buildings are luxurious mansions and houses, while others give an idea of the less-exalted conditions of the ordinary people. The village is well done, but the number of buildings is rather small (about 20) in view of the rather high admittance charge (¥650).

Included in the price, however, is entry to nearby Danpuen, a small village concentrating on crafts; a minibus goes every 20 minutes between the two villages. The village rather suffers in comparison with the similar park in Takayama, but it is worth seeing if you don't have to pinch pennies. Access is by Hokuriku Railway bus 12 from Kanazawa station to Yuwaku-onsen; Edo-mura is a short walk uphill.

Festivals

There are many festivals through the year. Most are small neighborhood affairs, but there are some very large and well-known ones as well.

February 10–16: Performances of *dekumawashi* (a kind of puppet theater unique to the area) at the community center of Oguchi. Performances are at night, so it is advisable to make prior arrangements for accommodation in the village.

April 19–20: Gokoku-jinja Spring Festival featuring dances by shrine maidens.

May 15: Shinji Noh performance, given outdoors at Ono-minato-jinja (in Kanaiwa); a 370-year-old ritual.

June 13–15: Hyaku-man-goku Matsuri celebrates the entry into Kanazawa, in 1583, of Toshiie Maeda, first lord of the Maeda clan. (Other sources say June 12–14, so check in advance.) Features include a procession of people in colorful feudal costumes (on the last day), folk dancing in the evening, geisha show at Kanko Kaikan, tea ceremony at Kenroku-en and Seisonkaku, and martial arts displays.

July 24–25: At Ono, three mountain demons (villagers in bright costume) spend two days going from house to house exorcising demons with flutes and drums. Ono can be reached by bus from Musashi.

August 1–3: Ono-minato-jinja Matsuri, held in Kanaiwa town, is famous for its carved wooden floats.

August 15: *Obon* dances at Hatta village

(night); its Sakata Odori is one of the few in Japan in which old costumes are worn and music is live, not recorded.

October: Through the month there are local shrine festivals.

October 19–20: Dances by shrine maidens at Gokoku-jinja shrine.

November 15: Shichi-go-san (7-5-3) festival, celebrated everywhere in Japan. Go to Ishiura-jinja to see children dressed in beautiful kimono.

Places to Stay

There are two youth hostels in Kanazawa. There are many hotels, *ryokan*, and *minshuku* (especially in Higashi); bookings can be made at the station. There is a very interesting inn/restaurant in a 150-year-old farmhouse, Zenigame, a few km out of town toward Edo-mura (tel 35-1426).

Getting There

Kanazawa is easily reached by train from Tokyo, Nagoya, Kyoto, Osaka, etc., via Maibara (on the Shinkansen), or by plane to nearby Komatsu airport. There are also several buses each day from Nagoya and Kyoto stations.

From Kanazawa to the Noto Peninsula

Between Kanazawa and Hakui are two large and venerable houses, Okabe-ke and Kita-ke, the homes of local governors in the Tokugawa era. In addition to administering the law, these officials collected taxes in the form of rice. Okabe-ke is somewhat larger, but both houses (which are about 10 km apart) have collections of relics from that age. Okabe-ke is accessible by bus from Kanazawa station and is close to Menden station (JR); Kita-ke is near Minami-hakui station, and there may be a bus service as well.

Keta-jinja

There is nothing of interest at Hakui itself, but just a few km north is Keta-jinja (shrine), which faces the sea and is set in a picturesque grove of trees.

Myoji-ji Temple

Only a short distance north and a little inland of Keta shrine is Myoji-ji, one of the great temples of the region. Its five-storey pagoda looks out over the surrounding flat countryside, and the view of the temple at the top of a long flight of stone steps is quite beautiful and memorable (except for the inevitable wires draped right across the middle of the scene, which will appear in any photo). The temple was established in the 13th century, although most of the present buildings date "only" from the 1600s. There is a handout pamphlet, in perfect English (hurrah!), that explains the history of the temple and each of the main buildings.

Noto-hanto Peninsula

The Noto-hanto peninsula contains some of the most picturesque scenery in Japan. There are still large rice paddies, farmers working diligently, and typical rural scenes that have remained almost unchanged for decades. Cyclists will particularly enjoy this area as there are relatively few hills, a continuation of the pleasant cycling of the Echizen coast from Fukui northward. The outer coast of the peninsula is much more rugged and scenic than the calm inner shore. The finest scenery begins just above Kanazawa and continues around to the eastern tip at Cape Rokugo, while there are beautiful, though less dramatic, views past the cape down to Nanao on the east coast.

Information

The information sheets from the TIC in Tokyo are very useful for train, bus, and boat schedules, and should be picked up for up-to-date information.

Noto-kongo

About 15 minutes north of Myojiji, a small roads turns off Route 249 to Fukuura and the shore. Between Fukuura and Togi is a 14 km stretch of coast known as Noto-kongo, noted for its scenic formations of eroded rock. Most memorable are Gammon, a grotto 54 meters deep and 15 meters wide, and Taka-no-su (Hawk's Nest), a rock that rises 27 meters and projects far over the sea. Buses run along this coast, leaving from Hakui (50 minutes away), or Sammyo (30 minutes). Boat cruises lasting about 20 minutes (¥500) leave from Fukuura.

Seki-no-hana

Above Togi, a small road turns off Route 249 and runs to and along the coast, rejoining the main road farther along. The scenery is attractive most of the way, especially around Seki-no-hana. This road is part of the regular tourist route between Togi and Monzen.

Monzen

Near Monzen is Soji-ji temple. Strangely located in this remote area, it was the national headquarters of the Soto sect of Zen Buddhism (founded in 1321) until 1818, when most of the buildings were destroyed in a fire. After that, the headquarters was moved to Soji-ji in Yokohama. The present buildings are attractive, especially in summer when the cicadas are chirring loudly. Soji-ji and Monzen are accessible by bus from Anamizu (on the uchi coast) as well as being on the regular bus run around the soto coast. The temple is a five-minute walk from Monzen bus station.

Soji-ji is a functioning Zen temple, and visitors may obtain accommodation and participate in meditation. It is best to make reservations in advance by writing to: Soji-ji, Monzen-machi, Fugeshi-gun, Ishikawa-ken. Tel (07684) 2-0005. It is apparently not possible to obtain accommodation on the spot. Costs range from ¥3500 to ¥5000.

Monzen to Wajima

Inveterate sea-coast buffs armed with a sufficiently detailed map can find roads along parts of the coast between Monzen and Wajima, but the area isn't generally famous for scenery. Your own transport would be useful, though there are buses along the main roads. There is a 5.5 km hiking trail along the coast (no road, so it is still quite primitive) between Minazuki and Kamiozawa. The former can be reached by bus from Monzen, the latter from Wajima.

Wajima

This small city on the northern coast is noted for its large-scale production of good quality lacquerware (on sale everywhere in town). About one person in every four of Wajima's population is engaged in some aspect of the craft.

There are several places where you can see the process of lacquerware making. In the area near the harbor, countless little shops turn out chopsticks with interesting patterns, the result of repeated dipping. The best single demonstration of the whole process can be seen at the main store of Inuchu (daily except Sunday). It can involve 18 or more steps, from forming the wood to the addition of layer after layer of lacquer, interspersed with careful polishing to make the finished product gleaming-smooth. Good lacquerware is a true work of art and requires more demanding detail than the better-known craft of pottery making. Somewhat directed to the tour-bus trade (but also good) is Wajima Shikki Kaikan (which also has a small museum of lacquerware on the second floor). Wajimaya store also has demonstrations.

Things to See

Omatsuri-kan

In the grounds of Sumiyoshi-jinja is this interesting museum, containing local folk art and objects related to the major Wajima festivals.

Kiriko-kaikan

An exhibition of floats used in festivals around the peninsula.

Sode-ga-hama

This is a pleasant beach near Wajima.

Markets

Every day (except the 10th and 25th of the month) there is both a morning market (*asa-ichi*) and an evening market (*yu-ichi*). The former is from 0800 am to midday at Honcho-dori of Kawai-cho, the latter on the grounds of Sumiyoshi-jinja from 1600 to 1900. Goods sold include handicrafts and other tourist items as well as food.

Divers

In the winter months, women divers operate off the coast looking for shell-fish and edible seaweed. (In the warmer weather they migrate to nearby Hegura Island.) The days are long gone when the women dived wearing only a loincloth, so the photos of lovely, shapely, topless, smiling divers are fakes. The true *ama* are older, stocky, and bashful (or camera-haters).

Festivals

There are annual festivals on April 4–5 and August 23–25.

Places to Stay

Wajima is an extremely popular destination, but there is generally no shortage of accommodation, except in July-August. In addition to youth hostels, there is a large number of *minshuku*. Near Sodegahama beach, there is a Kokumin-shukusha.

Getting There

Wajima is the terminal station for the JR line from Kanazawa and farther south (Maibara). It is also served by the bus service that circles the peninsula.

Wajima to Sosogi

About 10 km inland on the road to Anamizu is a very picturesque village of farmhouses built on the hills surrounding the rice fields. From all reports it is worth going out of the way to see.

Continuing along the coast east toward Sosogi, the coastline is very pretty. There are two places you should especially look out for. One is Senmaida (1000 terraces), a suitably poetic description for a broad ravine in which paddies have been built in terraces from sea level high up the side of the tall hill. Just before harvest time (late August-early September) would be the most colorful of all times to see this, as the rice then takes on a rich green-gold hue. (The same is true of all rice fields, of course, but few are as beautifully located as Senmaida.)

A little farther on is a fine view of the kind that is comparatively rare in Japan these days as modernization continues to take over. Terraced rice fields drop down to the sea, surrounding a small Shinto shrine. Its *torii* gate stands before the tiny building, and behind the shrine is a small, thick grove of trees. It is the epitome of traditional Japan.

Sosogi

At this town, a road branches inland from Route 249 toward Ushitsu. About 400 meters from the junction stand two of the

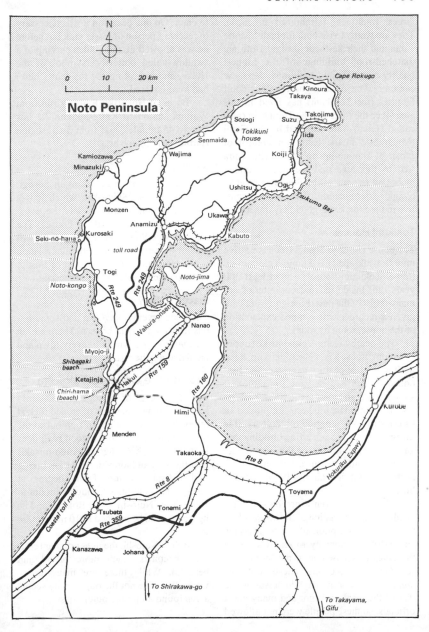

N

0   10   20 km

Noto Peninsula

Cape Rokugo

Kinoura
Takaya
Takojima
Suzu
Iida
Sosogi
Tokikuni
house
Senmaida
Koiji
Wajima
Kamiozawa
Minazuki
Ushitsu
Ogi
Tsukumo Bay
Monzen
Ukawa
Anamizu
Kabuto
Seki-no-hana
Kurosaki
toll road
Togi
Noto-jima
Noto-kongo
Rte 249
Rte 249
Wakura-onsen
Nanao
Myojo-ji
Shibagaki
beach
Rte 159
Ketajinja
Hakui
Rte 160
Chiri-hama
(beach)
Himi
Kurobe
Menden
Takaoka
Rte 8
Rte 8
Toyama
Hokuriku Expwy
Coastal toll road
Tsubata
Tonami
Rte 359
Kanazawa
Johana

↓ To Shirakawa-go

To Takayama,
Gifu

largest traditional farmhouses in Japan. They are worth a visit both for their historic value and their aesthetic design. Both are thatched-roof buildings of the highest quality materials and traditional Japanese carpentry. One of the highest ranking court families (the Tokikuni) has lived in this area since the forces of the Taira clan (also called Heike) were defeated by the Genji (Minamoto) in the battle for control of Japan at Dan-no-ura in 1185. The Taira fled to this area and the nearby inland mountain regions of the Shogawa river to escape extermination. Their descendants live in the Shirakawa-go/Gokayama area.

Tokikuni Houses

The house closer to Sosogi (they are a five minute walk apart) is Shimo-Tokikuni-ke (lower Tokikuni house); it is at least 300 years old. Inside its spacious interior are many relics of the past. Foreign visitors are given a recorder with a taped explanation of the house, room by room.

The nearby Kami-Tokikuni-ke (upper Tokikuni house) is newer, having been built in the last century to replace the first house (which had become unusable). It shows few signs of age; the finest materials and workmanship were employed in its construction, a period of 28 years. It is intriguing to find such a fine building and garden in such an out of the way place, but it was built to suit a person of very high rank, a descendant of the Kyoto nobility.

Visitors are given a notebook with a handwritten explanation of the house's history and a description of the high points and exhibits, room by room. A story in the notes tells how one of the rooms was reserved for receiving guests only of *dainagon* rank or higher, which was above that of the local governor and many court officials, so these people were not allowed to enter. On one occasion it was necessary to receive a person of lesser rank but before he was allowed in, the golden carving of a swallow-tailed butterfly (symbol of the Heike, and indicating the resident's rank) had to be covered.

Buses of Hokuriku Railway run from Wajima station to Kami-tokikuni-ke bus stop in 45 minutes, and from Suzu station (farther east) in one hour.

Museums

There are two other museums in Sosogi. Wajima Minzoku Shiryokan, which houses local folk art and items of daily use, is located between the Tokikuni houses. The other is Noto Shukokan and is a more general art museum with no particular relation to the Noto area. It is southeast of Sosogi and separate from the other attractions.

Places to Stay

There are several *minshuku* and some hotels near the two old houses. There are, in fact, *minshuku* in virtually every town and hamlet along the coast.

Around the Coast to Takaoka

The coast east of Sosogi is pleasantly scenic, with outcroppings of eroded rock at intervals. Route 249 doesn't go out to the tip of the peninsula, but a good road does lead out to Cape Rokugo (Rokugo-misaki) near the town of Noroshi. An 11 km hiking trail (Misaki Nature Trail) begins at Takaya and continues through Kinoura to Noroshi. At Noroshi, Cape Rokugo and its lighthouse can be reached in 10 minutes on foot.

Below Noroshi, the *uchi* or inner (east) coast becomes much more placid and peaceful. While there are many pretty views, there are not the outstanding scenic areas found along the outer coast.

Suzu

The main attraction of this hot-spring and port town is a large house (Kiheidon) which serves as a museum for local artefacts.

Koiji

There is a nice white beach here, 10 minutes walk from Koiji station or six minutes by bus.

Tsukumo

The name means "99 indentations" and indicates the scenic attraction of this bay. It can be seen from any of the sightseeing boats that leave from Ogi (Noto Ogi station).

Ushitsu

Ushitsu's Toshimayama Park affords an excellent view of the bay. The park, which incorporates two old houses that act as local museums, is 10 minutes by bus from Ushitsu station. The town's annual festival is from July 7–8.

Noto-jima

Little fishing villages and outdoor activities (swimming, hiking, and camping) are the main attractions of this island. Inquire locally if boat service is still available. (In past years it was, and the trip took 30 minutes.) There is a festival on the island on July 31.

Wakura-onsen

This is a typical, rather expensive, hot-spring resort of hotels and *ryokan*.

Anamizu

This town is also of negligible interest but it has a festival on July 22–23.

Nanao to Hakui

Along Route 159 between Nanao and Hakui there are many beautiful old wooden houses, particularly between Nanao and Kue.

Places to Stay—Noto-hanto Peninsula

There are 12 youth hostels around the peninsula, nine peoples' lodges, and probably hundreds of *minshuku*, as well as hotels and *ryokan*. The hostels are listed in the Youth Hostel Handbook and on the information sheet *Noto Peninsula* given out by the Tokyo TIC. One hostel I found very pleasant was the Noto-katsu-razaki Youth Hostel, right beside the water near Kabuto station.

Getting Around—Noto-hanto Peninsula

There is a frequent and convenient bus service to all places of interest around the Noto Peninsula, making it the recommended means of transport. In brief, there are special sightseeing buses around the north east end of the peninsula between Wajima and Anamizu/Ushitsu, plus regular buses that cover the following steps: Kanazawa–Togi; Togi–Monzen; Monzen–Wajima; Wajima–Ushitsu; and Monzen–Anamizu.

Trains run Hakui–Nanao–Wajima, and Nanao–Takojima. There is a JR service to Wajima and Takoshima (a little east of Suzu), but for the loop around the peninsula there are only buses. Since Wajima is more or less in the middle, it is not a useful starting point.

As there are many places to see and visit, and because the land is relatively level all around the peninsula, it is one of the best areas of Japan to explore by bicycle. Cyclists and other independent travellers should have detailed maps to enable them to follow little roads closer to the coast. The preferred direction of travel is clockwise, the Kanazawa area being a good starting point, so the sun will be to your left or behind you through the most scenic parts.

The Coast Below Kanazawa

The entire coast from (and including) the Noto-hanto peninsula, down past Kanazawa, and around Wakasa Bay has good scenery over most of its length, with numerous beaches. Nearly the entire coast, from above the Noto Peninsula, around Wakasa Bay, all the way to the western end of Honshu (Shimonoseki) is ideally suited to cyclists because it is quite flat terrain. The beaches were largely empty in mid-August when I went through last time, and there are numerous *minshuku* in all areas with touristic attractions. Most *minshuku* are close to, or even overlooking, the water, and offer cool night breezes and the sound of waves on the beach. Being by the sea, they also have a daily supply of fresh seafood; the Japanese go wild with the great variety of sushi and sashimi. (One place where I stayed served not only that, but also put together a hamburger steak in case the fish wasn't suitable to my palate.)

FUKUI-KEN

Fukui

The city of Fukui, while of little intrinsic interest, can be used as a base for visiting several nearby attractions.

Eihei-ji Temple

Beautifully located at the foot of a mountain amongst ancient trees, Eihei-ji is one of the most famous temples in Japan. As well as being a large, functioning Zen temple, with shaven-headed monks silently medi-

tating, the natural beauty of the setting makes it well worth a visit. Founded in 1244, it is one of two head temples of the Soto sect of Zen Buddhism (the other is Soji-ji in Yokohama, near Tokyo). Set on 33 sq km of grounds, the temple buildings (about 70 of them) climb up the hillside surrounded by trees as old as 600 years. An English pamphlet is given at the entrance and gives a good description of the main buildings.

The temple authorities allow foreign visitors to stay at the temple and participate in Zen meditation. (Refer to the notes on Zen meditation earlier in the book.) At Eihei-ji, visitors are expected to follow the same discipline as Japanese participants, starting with meditation at 3.30 in the wee-smalls. Arrangements should be made in advance by writing to: Sanzenkei, Eihei-ji, Eiheiji-cho, Yoshida-gun, Fukui-ken.

The temple (less than 20 km southeast of Fukui) is easily reached by Keifuku Dentetsu railway or by bus. The train is most easily caught from the east side of Fukui station (behind the building). A bike path between Fukui and Eihei-ji runs mostly along scenic river banks.

Kuzuryu-kyo/Managawa-kyo Gorges

Both of these gorges, noted for their scenery, are in the vicinity of Ono. The former is close to Echizen-shimoyama station (JR), and it is likely that buses run to the latter from Ono station (JR). Ono is on the road to Shirotori, the junction for going north to Shirakawa-go.

Tojimbo

The coastline of Tojimbo is a small-scale version of Britain's Land's End—an outcropping of volcanic rock that cooled in a pattern of roughly hexagonal pillars rising

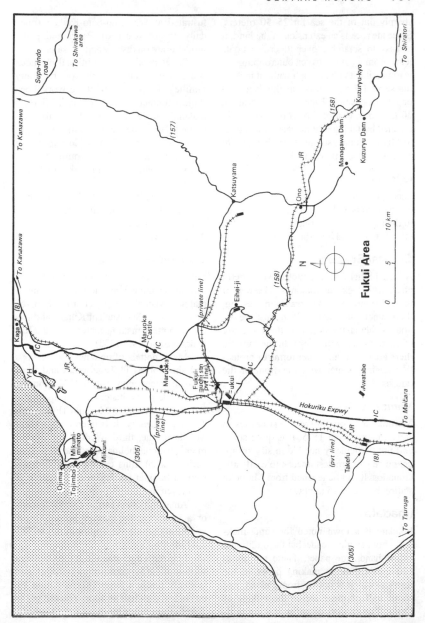

Fukui Area

sharply out of the sea for 25–30 meters. Since the rock is an extension of the land, it is easy to scramble over it; cruise boats leave from a cove between outcroppings. It is impossible to photograph without including several dozen tourists as this is a very popular destination. Tojimbo (which is about 30 km north east of Fukui) is most easily reached by taking a tram-train from Fukui to Mikuni-minato station, then changing to a bus for the last two km.

Ojima Island

A couple of km up the coast is a small forest-covered island called Ojima. It is joined to the mainland by a bridge. Visitors to the island are greeted by a shrine and torii gate.

Coastal Scenery

A little farther up is a stretch of very pretty coast with rock outcroppings. The rest of the coast up to Kanazawa is interesting, though not outstanding. Of interest are the houses facing the coast, as the roofs are often weighted with rocks. In the autumn there are boards and other forms of protection against winter winds in front of the houses.

Maruoka Castle

Maruoka-jo is one of the oldest castles in Japan, dating from 1575. It is quite small and not particularly notable in size or appearance—of greatest interest to castle aficionados. It can be reached from Maruoka station by bus in 15 minutes.

Imadate

Imadate is a town noted for paper-making—not machine-made, but the traditional *washi* handmade paper. There are about 120 establishments making paper in the district (which is not far from Fukui), and about half of these are in the village of Otaki. The process of paper-making is il-

lustrated at Washi-no-Sato-Kaikan (open daily except year-end). Paper and paper products are on display and for sale.

Paper-making by traditional methods is a cottage industry carried out by many families. To see one of these workshops (kojo), contact the Washi Kumiai (Papermakers' Cooperative) which will then arrange a visit. The Kumiai also sells paper of the area. These handmade papers are not cheap but, as they require a large amount of hand labor, the asking price is justified.

Access is from Takefu (18 km south of Fukui by JR) by a local line, the Nan-etsu-sen. The destination is the final station, Awatabe, which is in Imadate.

Echizen Togei-mura

Echizen Pottery Village was set up to preserve and continue the tradition of ceramics that has existed here for centuries. Echizen is one of the "Six Ancient Kilns", and has been a pottery making center since the Kamakura Era (1192–1333).

Many potters of note have workshops and showrooms in Togei-mura and most have no objection to visitors. Other pottery, both modern and historic, is on display at Fukui-ken Ceramics Museum (Fukui-ken Togeikan) nearby. It is open daily except Mondays, the third Wednesday of the month, national holidays and the New Year period. Local kilns can be tracked down using a booklet (in Japanese) available at the museum.

Amateur potters can take single lessons or a course at the pottery school (*togei kyoshitsu*) beside the Togeikan (tel 07783 2-2174).

Echizen Togei-mura is in the Ozowara section of the Miyazaki-mura (village), and is easily reached from Takefu station by bus in less than half an hour. You can get to Takefu from Fukui by JR, or from Maibara,

55 minutes to the south, also by JR. There is also a direct JR service from Kyoto/Osaka.

Tsuruga

On the coast facing Wakasa Bay, near the northern point of Lake Biwa, Tsuruga is one of the two ports in the area (along with Maizuru) with a ferry service direct to Otaru, Hokkaido.

Wakasa Bay

Continuing west along Route 27 or by rail from Tsuruga carries you along Wakasa Bay. Though not spectacular, the scenery is pleasant much of the way. This area is generally flat and recommendable to cyclists. One of the views along the way is the Mikata Five Lakes. They can all be seen from the top of Baijo Hill, near Lake Suigetsu.

Obama

The city of Obama is noted for Wakasa lacquerware. Obama is on the coast, and the terrain is one of a number of parallel valleys, all opening to the bay. It seems that there is one or more old temples in each valley (signposted in Japanese). With a bicycle, one could spend a pleasant day riding the few km in and out of each valley, past picturesque rice paddies, to visit each in turn. To a foreigner, probably Mantoku-ji and its landscaped garden of raked gravel and hill as backdrop would be of greatest interest. A cruise boat from Obama takes in the nearby scenic coast, Sotomo.

Wakasa-takahama

Another good view is available at Wakasa-takahama, especially at Shiroyama-koen park, 1.6 km from the station. Stretching for two km northwest of the city are the Otomi cliffs, rising almost vertical in places, sometimes more than 250 meters. Boat cruises lasting about two hours are available from Takahama.

Maizuru (Northern Kyoto-fu)

This is an industrial city of no touristic interest, but it is (like nearby Tsuruga) the port of departure for a ferry service to Otaru on Hokkaido (four boats a week). The terminal is located a short distance north of Nishi-maizuru station.

Continuing Travels

The next chapter covers first the Kinki district (which includes Kyoto, Nara, and as far east as Nagoya and Gifu), then a route around the western end of Honshu and back to a point near Maizuru, in the section on the Chugoku region. It is simple to get to Kyoto from here via the west shore of Lake Biwa, or by an alternative route through the mountains.

KINKI DISTRICT

The Kinki district, one of the traditional divisions of Japan, strictly speaking comprises the region from around Biwa-ko lake west through Kyoto to Hyogo-ken (Himeji), and from the north of Lake Biwa to the bottom of the Kii Peninsula. This write-up, however, stretches the definition somewhat in order to describe as a lump all the places of interest that can be reached easily while in the Kyoto area, for most visitors to Japan are likely to have Kyoto on their itinerary. For this reason, the Nagoya region, including the nearby areas to its north (Gifu, Inuyama, etc.) are covered here; this latter part takes up the route left off at the south of the Shogawa River Valley in the Chubu region.

The Kinki region, together with eastern Kyushu, is the part of Japan longest settled by the present-day Japanese. The original inhabitants of Japan, about whom little is known, were swamped by later arrivals who settled first in Kyushu, then established a series of military outposts along the south coast of Japan up to the Tokyo area.

The exact meaning of the name "Kinki" is lost, but the character "ki" means capital where emperors live.

Within the Kinki region are many of the prime attractions of Japan: Kyoto, the imperial capital for over 1000 years and a repository of temples, palaces, and gardens, as well as historic arts and crafts; Nara, the capital before Kyoto, with even more ancient temples and other remains from the past; Toba, with its cultured pearl industry and nearby coastal scenery; Himeji and Hikone with historic and picturesque castles, plus many other historic and natural attractions.

There are two international airports in the region, Nagoya and Kansai International. The latter serves the Osaka–Kyoto–Kobe area. Regular boat service connects Osaka with Korea and China.

Within the country the Shinkansen passes through all the major cities, and there is also air service through the same airports.

TRANSPORTATION

The Kinki district, particularly the region between Nagoya and Osaka, is intensively blanketed by railway services. Since there are many destinations of interest to foreign visitors in this area, and many places can be visited on a day trip (such as to Nara or Toba from Kyoto, or Kyoto from Kobe, etc.), it is useful to have a general idea of the frequency of train services, routing, and the travel time between one place and another. The following is a summary of the lines likely to be of most interest to visitors. There are others, some of which will be described in the chapter, but they are of limited interest and of no use for intercity travel, only to specific tourist destinations. All descriptions are from east to west, north to south, so look for the details of services between Nagoya and Osaka under Nagoya, not Osaka, etc.

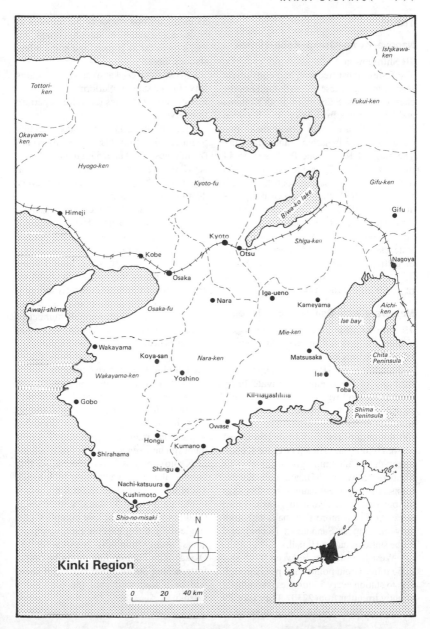

Kinki Region

Trains

Nagoya–Kyoto–Osaka–Kobe–Himeji

JR Shinkansen

The fastest, most frequent, and convenient service through these cities (though not the cheapest!) is the Shinkansen. Both Kodama and Hikari trains from Tokyo run between Nagoya and Osaka; the former make two extra stops (Gifu–hashima and Maibara). The Nagoya–Kyoto time for Hikari is 44 minutes, and for Kodama, one hour (18 minutes more to Osaka by both). Charges are the same for both. Beyond Osaka, trains are mostly Hikari, but there are several different services (e.g., some stop only at Himeji, and some even bypass Kobe) so it is necessary to check in advance to be sure of getting a suitable train beyond Osaka. Trains are very frequent—usually eight or more per hour through Nagoya.

Maibara–Kyoto–Osaka–Kobe–Himeji

JR Shin-kaisoku

Within the reduced distance Maibara to Himeji, JR runs the Shin-kaisoku service. Although it is a *tokkyu* express, and faster than any of the competing private lines, there is no surcharge over the regular fare, so its price is very reasonable. The extremities of the Shin-kaisoku are Maibara (on the eastern shore of Lake Biwa, just above Hikone) and Himeji (west of Kobe), although not all trains go as far east as Maibara. Between Maibara and Kyoto, trains skip only a few stations, but they skip all but one from Kyoto to Osaka. From there they skip more than half, although they all stop at Sannomiya (Kobe) and Kobe stations, and at Himeji.

West from Kyoto: Between 0715 and 2050 trains (from points east) pass through Kyoto station every 15 minutes (three/hour slightly irregular from 2230). They take 29 minutes to reach Osaka, 49/52 minutes to

Sannomiya/Kobe stations), 59 minutes to Nishi-akashi, and 90 minutes to Himeji. All trains go as far as Himeji, and some a few stations more.

West from Osaka: West-bound trains leave Osaka station (platform 3, 4, or 5) 30 minutes after the times listed for departure from Kyoto.

East from Osaka: Shin-kaisoku trains begin running from Osaka toward Kyoto (29 minutes away) at 0753, but begin regular 15 minute service at 0800, through the day until 2100, after which they run every 20 minutes until 2300.

Many trains continue east as far as Maibara (80 minutes from Kyoto), although some terminate at Kusatsu, about a third of the way to Maibara.

East from Himeji: Trains from Himeji are scheduled so they can leave Osaka on an exact quarter hour (except early morning trains, some of which go only as far as Osaka). Because of the variable number of stops en route to Osaka, the departure times are not as neat as for Osaka and Kyoto.

JR Tokaido Line/Sanyo Line

In addition to the many Shinkansen and Shin-kaisoku trains through this area several times an hour, there are regular (*futsu*) trains of the Tokaido and Sanyo lines that stop at every station along the way. Tokaido trains run between Maibara or Nagoya (east of Kyoto) to Osaka, and the Sanyo line from Osaka to Okayama (west of Himeji). These services are slow, and it is necessary to change trains at Maibara, sometimes at Ogaki as well (with the sole exception of a single daily direct express each way (two hours twenty minutes) Nagoya–Kyoto–Osaka). The Tokaido line might be useful for reaching stations like Hikone if there will be a long wait until the next Shin-kaisoku.

NOTE: With the exception of the fast services just described, railway connections in the Kinki district are usually more convenient, faster, and/or cheaper by private railways. The only other JR services between Nagoya and Kyoto, for example, require two or more changes of train, and the changes are not always coordinated; by one route, it is necessary to change at Kaneyama, Kamo, and Nara; by another route changes are required at Kaneyama, Tsuge, and Kusatsu. Despite these repeated changes, travel time is not inordinately longer than by Kintetsu to Nara and Kyoto.

Nagoya–Osaka

Kintetsu

The only direct (non-Shinkansen) service between these two cities is via the Kintetsu private railway. Every day on the hour, between 0700 and 1900, an express leaves Kintetsu-Nagoya and Kintetsu-Namba (Osaka) stations, arriving at the other station a bit over two hours later. The fare is ¥3350, including the express surcharge. Also, every hour on the half hour, from 0630 (Nagoya)/0730 (Osaka) until 2030 (Nagoya)/2130 (Osaka) there are other expresses from the same stations that make a few intermediate stops and take an extra 20 minutes or so, but the fare is the same so there is no advantage to it unless the faster expresses are full or one wants to make an intermediate stop, as to visit Iga-ueno. For travelling from Nagoya to Kyoto or Nara by Kintetsu, it is necessary to use the slower trains, for only they stop at Yamato-yagi to allow changing trains. (This procedure is described under Nagoya–Kyoto. From Osaka there is direct service to Nara by a different line, so there is no need to use this line.)

It is also possible to travel cheaper (and slower) between Nagoya and Osaka by non-express Kintetsu trains (same tracks) by

using the Nagoya–Yamada line to Ise-nakagawa and changing there to the Yamada–Osaka line. Time on the trains by this route would be about 3-1/2 hours plus the wait for the connecting train (¥2120 total). You could also go from one city to Ise/Toba for sightseeing and then continue to the other city by this route. Refer to the later section on services to Ise for more details.

JR

Services by JR between Nagoya and Osaka are not as convenient nor as quick. From Nagoya, it is necessary to change trains at Kamayama, and often at Kamo as well. Travel time by this route is typically 3-1/2 hours.

Nagoya–Kyoto

Kintetsu

Kyoto can be reached from Nagoya quite conveniently using Kintetsu trains by taking the Nagoya–Osaka train (slower express) to Yamato-yagi (just under two hours), and then transferring to the Kyoto–Ise line going toward Kyoto. Total travel time between Nagoya and Kyoto is about 2-3/4 hours and the cost about ¥4210. There is a Yagi–Kyoto train waiting at Yagi for almost all trains coming from Nagoya. The Kyoto–Nagoya trip is just the reverse.

JR

As discussed above, there are no direct JR Nagoya–Kyoto trains (apart from the Shinkansen and one daily express); it is necessary to change trains one or more times.

Nagoya–Nara

Kintetsu

Nara can also be reached conveniently from Nagoya by the same lines described above for Nagoya–Kyoto, but taking the

Yagi–Kyoto train only to Yamato-saidaiji (20 minutes), then taking the Osaka–Nara line to Nara (five minutes; there is a train every five to 15 minutes). The Nara–Nagoya trip is just the reverse.

JR

There is a single direct express per day between Nagoya and Nara (73 minutes). All other trains require at least one change at Kameyama, and usually another change at Kamo. There are several trains through the day. The Nagoya–Nara trip can be made in as little as just over three hours.

Nagoya–Ise/Toba

Kintetsu

The Kintetsu line offers convenient service between Nagoya (Kintetsu-Nagoya station) and Ise, Toba, and Kashikojima (on the Shima-hanto peninsula). In both directions there are *kyuko* expresses every five to 30 minutes and *futsu* (regular) trains every 15 to 30 minutes, plus about 32 *tokkyu* special expresses (the fastest) daily. *Tokkyu* trains take about 1-1/2 hours from Nagoya to Toba (¥1330), while ordinary *kyuko* and *junkyu* expresses take about 8 minutes longer and cost ¥930 (Nagoya-Toba).

NOTE: the less expensive *kyuko* and *junkyu* trains can be used for travel between Nagoya and Osaka by taking a Nagoya–Ise train to Ise-nakagawa and changing on an Ise–Osaka line train. This will be slower than the *tokkyu* Nagoya–Osaka trains (about three hours) but is cheaper. The route can also be used for a visit to Ise/Toba en route between the two large cities.

JR

JR has four expresses directly from Nagoya through to Toba, taking just over two hours. All other JR trains require a change

at Kameyama. There is usually a connecting train, and the time to Toba is typically a bit over three hours. There are several trains through the day.

Nagoya–Kii-hanto Peninsula–Osaka

A JR line runs around the periphery of the Kii-hanto peninsula. The links of this route are Nagoya–Kameyama–Matsusaka–Shingu–Wakayama–Osaka.

Nara–Osaka

Kintetsu

Between Kintetsu-Nara and Kintetsu-Namba (Osaka) stations there are 11–16 daily *tokkyu* expresses at approximately hourly intervals (depending on the direction) taking about 30 minutes (¥870), plus slower (40–50 minutes) semi-expresses every seven to 15 minutes through the day (¥410).

JR

There are nearly 90 trains a day between Nara and Osaka (each direction) via two routes. Trains of the Kansai Honsen line take 49 minutes to each of the terminus stations in Osaka–Osaka station (in the north of the city, 27 a day) and Minato-machi station (in the south of the city, 31 a day). Trains of the Kata-machi-sen line take 51 minutes (30 a day) and also terminate at Namba station. Fare for both is ¥570.

Nara–Ise/Toba Area

Kintetsu

There are no direct services from Nara but the trip can be made very conveniently by taking a local train from Kintetsu-Nara station to Yamato-saidaiji (five minutes) and catching a Kyoto–Ise *tokkyu* train; they leave Yamato-saidaiji station 30 minutes after the times listed for leaving Kyoto.

JR

It is necessary to take the Kansai Honsen

line (Nagoya bound) as far as Kameyama (about two hours), transfer to a Shingu-bound train as far as Taki, then take an Ise-bound train from there. There are generally connecting trains at Kameyama and Taki for minimum wait, but these should be checked in advance.

Kyoto–Nara

Kintetsu

The fastest Kyoto–Nara services are the 26 daily Kintetsu *tokkyu* expresses that run between Kyoto and Kintetsu-Nara stations with only a single stop (Yamato-saidaiji). Most leave every 30 to 60 minutes, on the hour or half-hour, although there are also some jokers in the pack at odd times. The earliest is 0619 from Nara, 0830 from Kyoto. Travel time is 33 minutes and the fare is ¥900.

Other expresses with the same fare but a few minutes slower and requiring a change at Yamato-saidaiji are the Kyoto–Ise *tokkyu* expresses (detailed below) and *tokkyu* expresses bound for Kashihara-jingu-mae; these generally leave Kyoto on the quarter-hour and three-quarter-hour, respectively, through the day. Travel time to Yamato-saidaiji is about 30 minutes; from that station, Kintetsu-Nara station is only a five-minute ride away.

Through the day at 10 to 30 minute intervals there are many *kyuko* expresses (somewhat slower) and *futsu* (local) trains that take 39 to 54 minutes but cost only ¥410. With these it is necessary to change trains at Yamato-saidaiji.

For the journey from Nara to Kyoto, the reverse trains can be used, so if there is no convenient train listed for Kyoto, you can take any train listed for anywhere (generally Osaka) and transfer at Yamato-saidaiji to the first train passing through to Kyoto.

JR

Through the day there are more than 50 trains running direct between Kyoto and Nara. The quickest are the eight *kaisoku* expresses (no surcharge) taking 45 minutes; the rest are locals that take 62 minutes.

Kyoto–Ise/Toba/Shima-Hanto

Kintetsu

The most convenient and fastest service between Kyoto and the Ise/Toba area is the Kintetsu *tokkyu* expresses that leave Kyoto hourly on the quarter-hour from 0715 to 1815, all of which run to Kashikojima (Shima-hanto) except the second-last which terminate at Toba. In the return direction there are 11 trains a day every hour between 0820 and 1820. The fare from Kyoto to Ise is ¥2830, and to Toba, ¥3050. (Non-express (*futsu*) trains are ¥1180 to both.)

JR

To use JR trains to the Ise/Toba area, a train from Kyoto bound for Nara can be used to connect with a train originating in Nara that will lead to the Ise area. (As detailed in the section Nara–Ise, this trip requires more than one change of train.) The quickest connection to the Nara–Ise train is at Kizu, one stop before Nara, the junction of the lines. (Many trains from Kyoto do not reach Nara in time for the earliest connection with a train to the Ise area.)

Kyoto–Osaka/Kobe

The least expensive way to travel between Kyoto and Osaka is on one of two private lines, Hankyu and Keihan. The fastest is by JR *Shin-kaisoku*. To Kobe, the less expensive Hankyu line may be used with a transfer at Osaka; the JR service is direct and faster.

Hankyu

Kyuko expresses of the Hankyu ("Osaka–

Kyoto") line take 47 minutes, *tokkyu* expresses a little less, and ordinary (*futsu*) trains take 64 minutes between the two cities. Trains of the various services are interspersed through the day and can be identified on the timetable on the platforms by color code: white on solid red for *tokkyu* (4 per hour), red in a red box is the next fastest, red for the next and black for *futsu*.

The four stations in Kyoto of the Hankyu line are conveniently located underground along Shijo-dori, and the line functions as an east-west subway line along this street, connecting with the north-south subway line at Karasuma station, although separate fares are charged for the two services. At Osaka, the terminus is Hankyu-Umeda, very close to JR Osaka station, at the north of the city. The fare is ¥330.

The Hankyu line can also be used for convenient transport to and from Kobe by taking it as far as Juso, one station from Osaka terminus (Hankyu-Umeda), and transferring to the Hankyu-Kobe line. (This line is detailed in the section Osaka–Kobe.)

Keihan

Trains of the Keihan ("Kyoto–Osaka") line take 86, 59, and 49 minutes for slowest to fastest. The main Kyoto station (Keihan-Sanjo) may be less conveniently located for many travellers, a few blocks east of Karasuma-dori, the main street of Kyoto. (Trains of the Keihan line also go to Otsu, to the east.) The Osaka terminus is Yodoyabashi, somewhat closer to the center of Osaka, and the line intersects the JR Osaka loop line at Kyobashi. (There is no convenient transfer to a Kobe-bound train.) The fare is ¥330.

JR

JR services were covered at the beginning of this section.

Osaka–Ise/Toba

Kintetsu

From 0710 to 1950 there is a *kyuko* express train leaving Ue-honmachi station at 10 after and 10 to the hour for Ise (1 hour 47 minutes) and Toba (just over two hours). (One train at 0650 goes only to Uji-yamada (one station after Ise).

Tokkyu express trains at 20 past the hour from 0720 through 1620 (except 0820) start from Kintetsu-Namba station (from Ue-honmachi three minutes later) and run non-stop through to Uji-yamada (no stop at Uji) in one hour 43 minutes, to Toba in 14 more minutes, and through to Kashikojima in 2-1/2 hours, the only direct trains there. (It is otherwise necessary to use local trains from Ise, Toba, etc.)

Fares by expresses are: Ise ¥2420, Toba ¥2880, and Kashikojima ¥3100. As well as the expresses, there are local trains at five to 20 minute intervals through the day from Ue-honmachi. The fare to Ise is ¥930.

JR

Using JR from Osaka to Ise/Toba is the same as that from Kyoto to Ise/Toba–you go to Nara first then through a succession of train changes from there.

Osaka–Kobe/Himeji

In addition to the JR Shinkansen, Shin-Kaisoku and regular services already described, there are also two private lines that can be used between Osaka and Kobe and one to Himeji.

Hankyu

The Hankyu-Kobe line runs from Hankyu-Umeda station (near Osaka station) to Hankyu-Sannomiya (central Kobe). There are expresses and locals every 10 minutes (the latter take 42 minutes, the fastest expresses, 26 minutes) and the fare is ¥260. Juso, one stop out of Umeda, is the transfer point between the Kobe line and the Kyoto line, so Hankyu trains can be used between Kyoto and Kobe. Using a *kyuko* express from Kyoto to Juso (44 minutes) it should be possible to travel Kyoto–Kobe in not much more than 70 minutes for about ¥500. The Hankyu line can also be used beyond Kobe to Himeji; this is detailed in the section Kobe–Himeji.

Hanshin

Also giving Osaka–Kobe service is the Hanshin line from Hanshin-Umeda station (also close to Osaka station) to Hanshin-Sannomiya and Hanshin-Motomachi stations, both in central Kobe. The fare to both is ¥260, and it takes about one hour to Sannomiya.

Osaka–Himeji

The alternative to the JR services detailed previously is the Hanshin Kosoku-tetsudo line from Kobe, first from Hankyu-Sannomiya to Nishi-shiro (17 minutes, ¥110), then the Sanyo-denki line to Dentetsu-Himeji station (95 minutes by local, 50 minutes by *kyuko* express, though it may be necessary to go to the next station to catch a *kyuko*; ¥720). Trains leave every 10 to 15 minutes.

Long Distance Buses

To/From Tokyo

There is long-distance bus service between Tokyo and Nagoya/Kyoto/Osaka. The buses run along the Tomei (Tokyo– Nagoya) and Meishin (Nagoya–Kobe) expressways. Day buses do not go into the many cities along the road; they stop only at shelters by the expressway from where passengers can walk a short distance to transfer to local transport.

Day Buses

Buses run frequently through the day between Osaka/Kyoto and Nagoya, and between Nagoya and Tokyo. All passengers must change at Nagoya when travelling between Tokyo and Kyoto/Osaka during the day.

Buses that make every stop in the Nagoya–Kyoto run take nearly three hours, while the few super expresses take about 2-1/2 hours. There are about 30 buses/day to Kyoto, and 10/day to Osaka, Travel time is about 3-1/2 hours. Between Nagoya and Tokyo, buses take about 6-1/4 hours. The fares are: Tokyo–Nagoya ¥5000; Nagoya–Kyoto ¥2200; Nagoya–Osaka ¥2600.

Night Buses

Every night buses run nonstop between the Keihanshin area (Kyoto–Osaka–Kobe) plus Nara and several points in the Tokyo and greater Tokyo area. At one time, when all buses started only from Tokyo station and ran to Kyoto and/or Osaka station, it was practical to list departure/arrival times, but there are now too many services.

Buses leave late enough and drive slowly enough that they reach their destination at a reasonable hour in the morning. Seats recline so sleeping is relatively comfortable, and if you're lucky you can get a seat at the back where there is slightly more leg room. The advantages of taking the night bus are the saving of a night's accommodation and an enforced early start to the day's sightseeing.

The following is a guide to services available; with rare exception, buses leave after 2200.

Tokyo area–Kyoto (¥7800–8500) (Tokyo area = Tokyo stn, Shinjuku stn., Shinjuku bus terminal, Chiba, Disneyland, Hachioji, Yokohama)

Tokyo area–Osaka (¥8100–8800) (Tokyo

area = Tokyo stn, Shinjuku stn, Omiya, Yokohama, Hachioji)
Tokyo stn–Nara (¥8240)
Tokyo area–Kobe (¥8200–8600) (Tokyo area = Tokyo stn, Yokohama)
Tokyo (Shibuya)–Himeji (¥9300)

The buses are popular and heavily used so reservations are often a necessary extra cost. Check with the TIC if a reservation is recommended.

To/From Western Japan

There are night buses along the Chugoku expressway from the Kyoto–Osaka area, including:

Kyoto–Hiroshima (¥5500)
Osaka–Shimonoseki (¥8000)
Kobe/Osaka/Nara–Hakata (¥9000/9500)
Kobe/Osaka/Kyoto–Nagasaki (¥10,300–11,100)

Other Highway Buses

There are overnight non-stop buses to Kochi and Matsuyama on Shikoku, and to Nagano, Takayama, and Niigata in the Chubu area. During the day, buses go as far as Miyako or Tsuyama, almost due north of Okayama and about midway between the coasts; these make a number of stops.

ON THE ROAD

The following description of the Kinki district moves from east to west to south, covering in turn the areas around Nagoya, Lake Biwa, Kyoto, Nara, Osaka, Kobe, Himeji, Ise/Toba, and the Kii Peninsula.

GIFU-KEN ▬▬▬▬▬

The attractions of Gifu-ken can be divided into two general groups. The first are found in several cities in the south that have always been in the mainstream of Japanese life. Some attractions of bordering prefec-

tures are also included here, either because access is easier from Gifu-ken, or because there are no neighboring attractions that would otherwise draw you to that area. The others are found in a number of locations in the northern mountain highlands, where historic isolation has preserved many traces of "old" Japan; these have already been covered in the descriptions of Takayama, Shirakawa-go, etc., in the Chubu section. The following short section will describe routes from the southern part of Gifu-ken northward, then will continue with the attractions of the southern part.

To Northern Gifu-ken

Because of the isolation of this highland area until very recently, many customs and other historical remnants have survived which makes it one of the most interesting areas of Japan to visit. There are two major river valleys, both of which have many places of interest. One extends northward from Seki along Route 156 to the isolated Shirakawa/Gokayama area of the Shogawa River Valley, famous for large thatched-roof houses. The other runs north from Mino-kamo along Route 41 (or from Nakatsugawa along Route 257) to the very interesting and historic city of Takayama. There are sufficient road links in the northern region to allow you to travel across from one valley to the next, through pretty mountain scenery.

Seki to the Shogawa Valley

The scenery along this road is pleasant for most of the journey, with typical small farms and farmhouses, few towns, and few signs of rampant modernization. The only town of note is Gujo-hachiman.

Gujo-hachiman

There isn't much to see here, but the town is renowned for its celebrations of the Obon festival, when large numbers of townspeople dance in the streets every night throughout August. This "madness" is known as *Gujo Odori* and is famous throughout Japan. The peak nights are around August 13–16, but any night from late July to early September would be equally good for a visit.

SOUTHERN GIFU-KEN ▬▬

Gifu

The city of Gifu is most famous among foreign travellers for *ukai* (catching fish by the use of trained cormorants), paper lanterns, and paper umbrellas. Among Japanese males, it is additionally famous for a large number of *soapland* (formerly known as *toruko* (bathhouse/brothels)). Gifu is located beside the large Nagara river, at the northern edge of a large rice-growing plain. It is a typical commercial city with few places of historic interest, as the city was flattened by an earthquake in 1891 and by bombs during the war. The one exception (of low-key interest) is Shoho-ji temple.

Things to See

Shoho-ji Temple

A very unusual Daibutsu (statue of Buddha) is housed in the large orange-and-white building visible from the road. The statue is made of 1000 kg of paper sutras (prayers) pasted to a bamboo frame, which was then covered with clay and stucco, lacquered and gilded. The hall is very dim and the artistry not the ultimate, but it is interesting and worth a look if you are in Gifu anyway. The statue is 13.7 meters tall and each ear (elongated very much as a symbol of wisdom) is over two meters long. It was finished in 1747, after 38 years of work, and was constructed to console people who had lost relatives in earthquakes and famines.

Jozai-ji Temple

The original temple dates from 1450 but the present one (not far from Gifu Youth Hostel) is quite recent. Visitors should regard the large structure simply as a neighborhood temple and can watch daily life go on around it. It is popular as a playground for toddlers and their ever-watchful mothers.

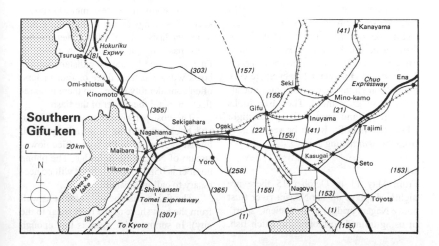

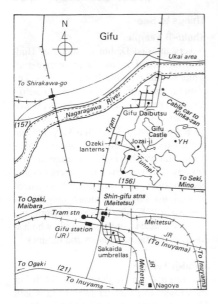

Kinkazan

The backdrop to Gifu is Kinkazan (Gold Flower Mountain). On it are located Gifu Youth Hostel and a concrete reproduction of the castle that stood at the peak until the earthquake of 1891. The new castle (1956) houses a small prefectural museum. Exercise freaks can walk up from the city or from the hostel; the lazy can take the cable-car ("ropeway") from Gifu-koen (park). The castle and mountain, however, are very much "something else to do" and not attractions of great merit. The castle looks very pretty (and *very* high up) at night when it is floodlit. It can be seen clearly from the *ukai* fishing area.

Ukai

From May 11 to October 15 there are nightly displays on the Nagara river (just above Nagara bridge) of the ancient "sport" of using trained cormorants to catch fish.

The birds are kept on a leash, and a ring around their neck prevents them from swallowing any but the smallest fish. The action takes place at night when the *ayu* (river smelt or sweetfish) can be attracted to the surface by torches blazing over the bow of each boat. One *usho*, (fisherman) in each boat, dressed in medieval grass-skirted costume, controls several birds, pulling in each one as it makes a catch, taking the fish, and putting the bird back in the water for another dive.

A large number of people can see the spectacle at one time as there are more than 130 covered boats of different sizes (capacity of 10 to 30 people). Tourists usually go out an hour or two before the fishing starts and dine (meals by prior arrangement), drink, sing, and set off fireworks. It becomes a grand party and probably more than a few revellers are unable to focus by the time the boats and birds appear. The sightseeing boats are usually lined up, and a "showboat" of women dressed as geisha performing traditional songs and dances moves up and down past them. After a suitable period of time the fishing boats make their passes up and down.

People wishing to take pictures should keep a few things in mind. The fishing performance lasts only 20–30 minutes, and the boats pass by quite quickly. A powerful flash is needed because the distance to the boats will be at least three or four meters, often considerably more, and there is no reflection to aid the power of the flash.

The cost per person is around ¥2500, and bookings can be made at any hotel, tourist agency, or at the boat office downstream of Nagara-bashi bridge. The phone number is 0582 62-0104, but it will be necessary to call in Japanese.

The fishing can be seen almost as well from the east shore of the river (near to the city). In summer the water is low enough

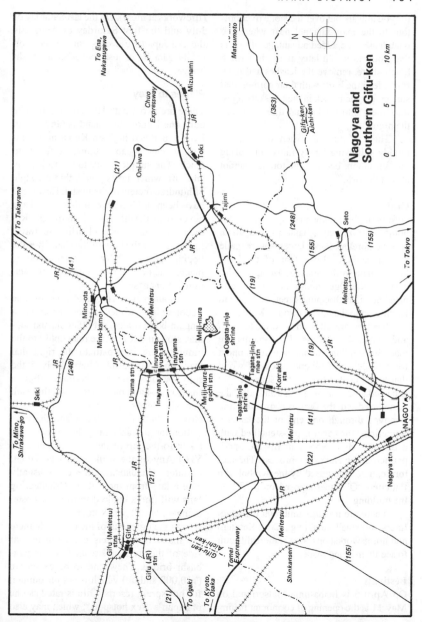

Nagoya and Southern Gifu-ken

for you to walk out over the stone river bottom to the main channel near where the boats pass. The added advantage of this is that you can watch later as the fishermen touch shore, remove the leashes and neck rings, feed the birds with their hard-earned supper, put them back in their basket-cages, load them into trucks, and disappear into the night.

There is no *ukai* when the river is muddy following heavy rains nor during the full moon, because the torches cannot attract the fish.

Crafts

Gifu is the best-known center in Japan for both *chochin*, paper lanterns and *kasa*, paper umbrellas. Paper lanterns were made here as early as 1597. One of the best-known lantern factories is Ozeki; it is located in the Oguma-cho area of the city near the main shopping street, on the road leading up to the tunnel through Kinkazan.

Visitors are allowed to walk through and watch the process. The lanterns are made by winding bamboo or wire around a form made up of several pieces of wood that lock together to give the shape. Paper is pasted to the bamboo strips and, after the paste has dried, the form is dismantled and removed through one end of the lantern. Sometimes the paper is pre-stencilled with a design, while other lanterns are hand-painted at the end of the process. The factory can be recognised by the symbol of a flattened "O" superimposed on a "Z" on the building.

There are no large umbrella manufacturers, just small shops (e.g., Kaida Kasaten) and home workshops, so it is more difficult to see them being made.

Festivals

On April 5 is Inaba-jinja Matsuri and on May 11 is the opening of cormorant fishing (fireworks at night). On the last Saturday of July and the first Saturday of August is the All-Japan Fireworks contest, held on the Nagara River just above Nagara-bashi bridge.

Places to Stay

There are two Youth Hostels in Gifu. The only one I know first-hand is Gifu Youth Hostel, perched high on Kinkazan mountain, a good location though difficult to reach. The simplest way to get to it is by chairlift, which takes you within a couple of hundred meters of the hostel. However I have been in Gifu several times and have never seen the lift actually moving. (Remember it is only a chairlift, so travel lightly.) Near the base of the chairlift is the beginning of a path leading up to the same place. The nearest tram stop from the station is Yanagase.

An alternative is to take a picturesque "Toonerville" trolley in the direction of Nagara-bashi bridge, get off at Shiyakusho-mae stop, and follow the road uphill to the tunnel; there is a path to the right that leads up to the hostel. Alternatively, at the stop beyond Shiyakusho-mae, after a sharp right-hand turn, there is another path that also leads up the hill. This stop is close to both the Daibutsu and the base station for the cable-car (which can also be taken to the top of the mountain and the YH.) Any of the walks will take 20–30 minutes. The Japanese hostellers usually take a taxi from the station. Orienteering fans will find a kindred spirit if the hostel manager is still Mr. Nomura.

At the other end of the cost scale there are many resort hotels bordering the far side of the river, upstream from Nagara-bashi bridge. They tend to be expensive (¥10,000 and up) which is not uncommon for hot-spring resorts. Gifu is rated as one of Japan's "sex hotspots", which may also affect room rates. There are also several business hotels in Gifu.

Getting There

Gifu is linked to Nagoya by JR (gifu station) and Meitetsu line (Shin-Gifu station), as well as to Gifu-hashima by bus. (Both Nagoya and Gifu-hashima are on the Shinkansen). Gifu is linked to Ogaki and Maibara by JR, and to Inuyama by both JR and the Meitetsu line (which originates at Shin-nagoya station). A railway that begins as a tram service on the major cross-road in the city (Route 156) leads to Seki and Mino.

Yoro-no-taki

Yoro waterfall is a 32-meter high cascade located in a scenic little tree-lined ravine. The nearby area has been made into a nature park with picnic facilities. The water plummets into a natural pool and visitors may, it is said, take a natural shower. (Take your own soap.)

The name Yoro translates as "filial piety", and has an interesting history. A woodcutter was extremely faithful to his aged father, even spending his hard-earned money on sake to keep the old man happy. On one occasion the water near the waterfall is said to have come out tasting like sake, a reward for his filial piety, so that he would not have to spend all his money on the bottled type. The story is said to date from the 700s (the supply ran out long ago). Access is from Ogaki via the Kinki-Nippon railway (25 minutes from Ogaki station) to Yoro station from where a bus (seven minutes) leads to the park. This is the type of attraction likely to be of greater interest to residents than to travellers.

Maibara (Eastern Shiga-ken)

West of Gifu and Ogaki is Maibara, a major railway junction for trains to Kyoto/Osaka, north to Fukui/Kanazawa/Noto Peninsula, and to the nearby centers of Hikone and Nagahama in neighboring Shiga-ken.

Inuyama (Aichi-ken)

Inuyama (Dog Mountain), on the Kiso River, is known for its historic castle, river scenery, shooting the rapids, and cormorant fishing.

Things to See

Inuyama Castle

Inuyama-jo is the oldest castle in Japan, dating from 1440. It is a pretty white structure, scenically located on top of a cliff overlooking the Kiso River. It is open to the public. Close to the entrance is the small Haritsuna shrine, where worshippers (usually older people) come, clap their hands to get the attention of the gods, make their prayer, and leave.

The castle and shrine are a short walk downstream from Inuyama-yuen station of the Meitetsu line.

Jo-an

One of the three finest teahouses in Japan, Jo-an is located in Inuyama close to Inuyama-jo. A teahouse is supposed to be the ultimate in restrained refinement, so you may concentrate on the elegant simplicity of the utensils used and the grace of the person preparing and serving the tea. Jo-an is thus a rather austere, low-key building, set in pleasant surroundings. With this background information, it can be appreciated for its inherent worth and purpose, but as a sightseeing attraction it is not everyone's cup of tea (so to speak).

Kiso River

Kiso-gawa has several scenic spots along its banks in the Inuyama area, especially where the castle overlooks the river and where a mysterious rock looms out of the

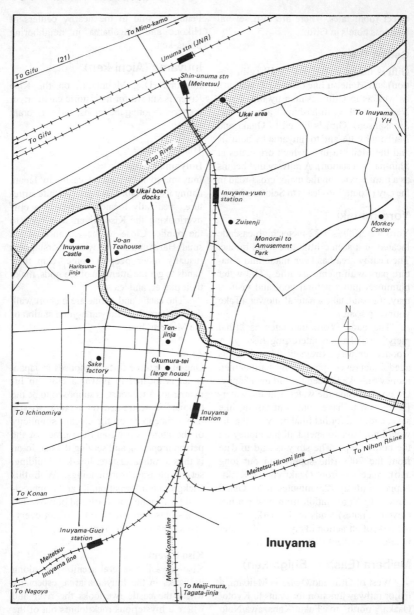

To Mino-kamo

To Gifu (21)

Unuma stn (JNR)

Shin-unuma stn (Meitetsu)

To Gifu

Ukai area

To Inuyama YH

Kiso River

Ukai boat docks

Inuyama-yuen station

Zuisenji

Monkey Center

Inuyama Castle

Jo-an Teahouse

Haritsuna-jinja

Monorail to Amusement Park

N

Ten-jinja

Sake factory

Okumura-tei (large house)

To Ichinomiya

Inuyama station

To Nihon Rhine

Meitetsu-Hiromi line

To Konan

Inuyama

Inuyama-Guchi station

Meitetsu-Komaki line

Meitetsu-Inuyama line

To Nagoya

To Meiji-mura, Tagata-jinja

water just upstream of Inuyama-bashi and Inuyama-yuen station. This area of the Kiso River has been dubbed "Nihon Rhine" (the Rhine of Japan), but only the strange rock fulfills this impression. (It would be a perfect home for water nymphs or Lorelei.) It's a pity the effect has been spoilt by some garish buildings that have been stuck on its flank, but such is the way things are done here. Nevertheless, the general area is very attractive, for the banks have been preserved as a nature park, thus being spared the "benefit" of development with hotels, restaurants, and other tacky construction seen in so many parts of Japan. Rocks along the shoreline make a walk upstream from Inuyama-yuen station an enjoyable excursion—forested hill on one side and the river on the other.

Ukai

Inuyama is another of the several places in this region that features cormorant fishing (described in detail under Gifu). At Inuyama, boats carrying spectators to the fishing area leave from the bank of the river downstream from Inuyama-yuen station, at the row of hotels. Most boats leave an hour or two before the fishing begins (soon after dark), which is rarely later than 1900, even in mid-summer (just about the only benefit of the refusal of authorities to introduce daylight saving time).

The overall scene can be viewed quite well from the shore on the Unuma side upstream of the bridge, but the boats anchor off-shore and the row of spectator boats is between the shore and the fishing boats. (You can get a better view from the shore at Gifu, and probably at Uji, near Kyoto.)

The cost for boat rental will be about ¥2500. Reservations can be made by phone ((0568) 61-0057) or through hotels and travel agencies in the area.

Places to Stay

There are many hotels and *ryokan* in Inuyama, including a number just downstream of Inuyama-yuen station. The youth hostel is about 800 meters upstream of this station and a further 400 meters uphill. It is quite pleasant (bar the noisy PA system) and one of the least expensive youth hostels in Japan.

Getting There

Meitetsu line trains run to Inuyama from both Gifu and Nagoya. From the Nagoya area, the Inuyama line runs from Meitetsu station, adjacent to the JR station, and the Komaki line runs from Kami-iida station, in the northeast of the city. Inuyama station is near the edge of the city; the next stop, Inu-yama-yuen, is the station closest to Inuyama-jo castle. The Inuyama and Kami-iida lines join at Inuyama. Shin-unuma is the terminus for trains from Nagoya and from Gifu

The name of the JR station for Inuyama is Unuma; it is on the line from Gifu to Takayama and Toyama. Inuyama-bashi, the bridge between the main part of the city and the Unuma railway stations, is the only place where I have ever seen a train caught in a traffic jam; both cars and trains use the same bridge.

Shooting the Rapids

A popular activity in this area is shooting rapids on the Kiso River for about 13 km from Mino-kamo down to Inuyama. It is a perfectly safe and enjoyable trip, possible through much of the year. This is probably the best place in Japan to try it. Long, flat-bottomed *Kisogawa-kudari* boats, guided by two or more boatmen with poles, are the traditional means of transportation although, in recent years, engine-powered boats have made an appearance. Choose the type that appeals to you.

There are two starting points in the vicinity of Mino-kamo city, one on each side of the river. One is at Mino-ota city (part of Mino-kamo) on the north bank, accessible from Gifu by JR. On the south bank, the starting point is Imawatari, accessible by Meitetsu-Hirome line from Inuyama station. Buses from Nagoya go only to the south docks. A bridge joins the two sides.

There are several companies offering tours, so check to be sure of getting the type of boat you want; more of the traditional boats leave from the south docks. There are boat trips all year at 1000, 1300, and 1400. More trips are added from March 15 through November 30 at 0930, 1030, 1130, and 1230 and 1500. One additional trip is added from May 1 through October 31 at 0900, and there is yet one more between July 1 and August 31 at 1600. The fare is around ¥3000 (children half price), and the trip takes 60 minutes.

Highpoints of the trip are at Kaniai, the rocks at Sekiheki, Rhine-yuen, and the park area along the shore at Inuyama.

Rhine-yuen is another starting point for boat rides. It can be reached from Sakahogi station on the Meitetsu line from Gifu. (The starting points near Mino-kamo, however, are probably better.)

Meiji-mura (Aichi-ken)

Within the boundaries of Inuyama is an open-air museum of more than 50 buildings and other memorabilia of the era of Emperor Meiji (1868–1910). By the Meiji Restoration he was restored to the position of an actual reigning monarch, rather than the mere figurehead that his predecessors had been reduced to during the 300-odd years of the Tokugawa. (During that period, a majority of Japanese were unaware even that an emperor existed.) He pushed Japan into the modern age after three centuries of almost total isolation from the rest of the world. The innovations of his rule ran the gamut of every aspect of Japanese life and, within 10 years of his taking power, there was a railroad operating in Japan—quite an advance on horses and hand-carried palanquins. This period is called the "Meiji Restoration", though "Meiji Revolution" would be more accurate, both for the many changes in Japanese life during that time, and the many military battles required to secure his rule.

To most Westerners, the items in the museum have symbolic rather than inherent interest. Most of the buildings for example are of 19th century Western style and rather commonplace in appearance—though to the Japanese they are somewhat exotic. Of world renown is the lobby of the old Imperial Hotel (Tokyo), a famed design of Frank Lloyd Wright.

Depending on the starting point, Meiji-mura can be reached conveniently from Inuyama or Nagoya. From Inuyama, the bus takes 20 minutes and costs ¥350. There are four per hour from 0940 until late in the afternoon. From Nagoya, the bus from Meitetsu bus center (near Nagoya station) takes one hour and costs ¥1120. There are several in the morning, but the last one leaves in the late morning.

Fertility Shrines (Aichi-ken)

The second and third stations out of Inuyama along the Komaki line toward Nagoya (don't take an express!) are located near two shrines devoted to fertility, both for crops in this rich rice-growing valley, and for humans. There are shrines of this sort scattered around Japan, but these are among the best-known and the most accessible in the country.

Oagata-jinja

This is the female shrine, and houses several natural phenomena, such as a cleft rock that resembles the female genitalia. It is a popular place of veneration for women about to marry and those who want children. The shrine is reached from Oagata station by turning right when leaving the station and walking across the tracks and up the road for about 15 minutes toward the forested hills.

Tagata-jinja

This is the male shrine. In the small building to the left of the main building is a quite amazing collection of phallus carvings ranging in size from a few centimeters to about two meters—all donated by grateful parents. The shrine is close to Tagata-jinja-mae station, the next after Oagata. Souvenirs are on sale at both shrines.

Shrine Festivals

Tagata-jinja has a very interesting festival each year on March 15. A carved wooden phallus, about three meters long, is carried in happy procession from another shrine about one km away, accompanied by Tengu (a Shinto deity with a very long nose, also of phallic significance) and several women carrying smaller carvings similar to the main attraction. The procession moves slowly along the small road behind Tagata-jinja, starting early in the afternoon. In the morning, sake casks are broken open and the contents distributed. The people carrying the *mikoshi* (portable shrine) make frequent stops during the procession to partake of the sake, and the owners of every field they pass also give them libations, so by the time they reach the shrine (about 1500 or later) and carry the mikoshi into the main building, the bearers are thoroughly sloshed and have to be guided in the right direction.

There is usually a sign at the shrine indicating the parade route. The procession used to pass along the main road, but has now been relegated to the back road for safety and better control, so its format will likely remain unchanged unless the puritanism of the police increases.

Oagata-jinja also has a festival, but its format has been changing. Up to 1978 it took place on the morning of March 15, but it has since been changed to the following weekend. In 1978 the procession featured a number of pretty young women (brides-to-be?) on decorated floats, as well as the shrine's *mikoshi*, a discreetly covered tree-root that serves as a female symbol. If you are interested in this festival it might be possible to get more information from the TIC in Tokyo or Kyoto.

Mizunami

Palaeontologists passing through this town might find the Fossils Museum of interest.

Tajimi

About 80 per cent of the porcelain for the Japanese market, and more than half of the porcelain exports, are produced in Tajimi's pottery plants. Those interested in pottery could probably arrange to visit one of the 1300 or so plants. Those interested in

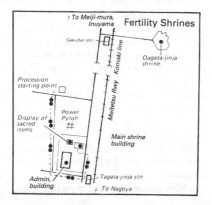

To Meiji-mura, Inuyama
Fertility Shrines
Gakuden stn
Komaki line
Oagata-jinja shrine
Procession starting point
Meitetsu Rwy
Power Pylon
Display of sacred items
Main shrine building
Admin. building
Tagata-jinja stn
To Nagoya

studying pottery should refer to the notes on Pottery in the General Section.

Oni-iwa (Ogre Rock)

Travellers between Toki and Mino-kamo might wish to stop to look at this interesting gigantic granite formation rising from the edge of the river near Oni-iwa-onsen (hot spring resort).

Seki

The small city of Seki has been known for centuries as the center of production for many of the finest swords in Japan. To this day there are still many people in the city who make their living solely from this craft, including 12 swordsmiths, plus polishers and other assistants. There is little, if any other, point of interest in Seki besides the swordsmiths, so it is worth taking a little space to describe the fascinating process by which the swords are made.

Seki Swordsmiths

The Japanese sword is the finest weapon of its kind ever created anywhere in the world; it is the ultimate expression of the swordsmith's art. It is unfortunate that their only *raison d'etre* is killing, as they could truly be described as "jewels in steel". When making a sword, a balance must be struck between hardness (for cutting) and resiliency (so that it doesn't snap in service). To accomplish these conflicting goals, Japanese swordsmiths use two processes together; they combine high carbon steel (hard) and low carbon steel (soft) in the same blade, and the tempering (heating and cooling the steel quickly to bring it to the correct degree of hardness) is varied over the width of the blade so that the back remains soft while the cutting edge is hard. This process takes a long time. A swordsmith is permitted by law to make only two swords per month, though it is not likely he could make more swords of quality in much less time than this anyway.

It is generally very difficult to see the process of making swords, for the smiths are busy and do not relish a continual stream of sightseers. Fortunately, however, demonstrations (open to the public) are given six times a year at Seki city, on the first Saturday of each of the odd-numbered months. They are given in a corner of the grounds of Kasuga-jinja (shrine), where a workshop has been set up duplicating the equipment found in a traditional smithy. Kasuga shrine is straight down the street leading from the town hall. If you are seriously interested in sword making and are not in Seki at demonstration time, there is a city official (Mr. Shigeru Matsui) who speaks a little English and *might* be able to arrange an introduction to a practising swordsmith. (Modern smithies, however, are equipped with power-operated machinery, unlike the demonstration smithy.) Mr. Matsui's phone number is (05752) 2-3131; it might be advisable to have a Japanese-speaking friend make the call.

At the Kasuga-jinja demonstration, a master dressed in traditional costume is accompanied by several apprentices (also in costume). The first striking is the most spectacular. The spongy mass of steel, after being heated in the fire by the master smith, is mashed into a cohesive blob by the hammer blows of the apprentices, a process which sends out a spray of sparks in all directions. The process of heating and beating is repeated a couple of times until the metal has become a small bar about 60 x 200 mm and 20 mm thick. Water is poured onto the anvil, and the red-hot bar is placed on it when struck; the water prevents the metal from oxidizing. This slab is next scored with a chisel and then folded back on itself.

Now follows the most important stage.

The smith rolls the glowing metal block in a small pile of black, carbonized rice husks. When the metal is completely smothered in black, he pours a brown liquid over both sides and returns the metal to the fire. The liquid is a type of clay, and the coating protects the carbon from burning in the fire. When the metal reaches red-hot temperatures again inside its "blanket", the carbon is actually absorbed into the surface of the metal.

The block of metal and clay is placed on the anvil and the metal again bashed into an elongated bar. The rest of the process is a repetition of the steps described above. The number of times this is repeated determines the carbon content of the finished steel, and thus its potential hardness. For the hardest steel, to be used for the edge of the blade, the metal is folded 20 to 25 times. The result of this folding is an incredible number of layers of alternating high-carbon (hard) and pure (soft) steel. After 20 folds there will be more than a million layers; after 25, more than 33 million! Softer steel for the inner structure of the blade may have only 10 to 12 doublings, and steel for the side plates (and back, if one is used) might have 12 to 15 foldings. The layered structure imparts a measure of resilience and flexibility that a blade of uniform composition would not have.

During the demonstration (from 1000 to 1600) there is time to make only a couple of the required pieces of steel. When all the pieces are available, they are forged together into a single mass, which is then beaten out into the rough shape of a sword. The individual pieces made for the edge, core, sides, etc., keep their relative positions through the beating stage, and the boundaries can be seen when the sword is polished. The final stages (shaping and straightening a previously made sword) are usually also shown during the demonstration.

After the sword has the proper shape, two stages remain—tempering and polishing. To enable the edge to be tempered to a high degree of hardness while keeping the back relatively soft, the blade is covered with clay so that only the edge is exposed. The clay is often made wavy so that varying widths of the edge are exposed. After heating, plunging the blade into water, and polishing, this pattern can be seen, and is one of the signs of beauty looked for in a sword. (The parts of the sword protected by the clay do not cool so abruptly, so they remain softer and more flexible.)

An interesting finale to the demonstration is a display of the use of some of the finished swords. Bamboo poles are set up, and swordsmen, dressed in traditional costume, show how effortlessly the swords can cut through pieces of bamboo. In olden times it was customary to demonstrate the sharpness of a new sword by testing how many condemned criminals it could cut through, one lying atop another.

Other craftsmen in Seki make the elaborately decorated handles, hand guards, etc., while most factories in the city make everyday knives and other cutting utensils.

If you're thinking of picking up a sword while in town, you may want to know the price so you can save up—a sword of the type being made and demonstrated would sell for about ¥6,000,000. They are only for well-heeled collectors. In Japan, they must be registered, as handguns are in most countries.

Ukai

During the season mid-May to mid-October there is cormorant fishing at Seki, as well as the better-known centers of Gifu and Inuyama.

Places to Stay

There are several *ryokan* and *minshuku* around the city, including at least two that are operated by cormorant fishermen. It is therefore possible to stay at one of the houses and have dinner on a boat for an all-inclusive price of ¥7000 to ¥8000 (which is rather high by *minshuku* standards, even including ¥1800 or so for the performance). Two such fishermen are Mr. Adachi (tel (05752) 2-0799) and Mr. Iwasa (tel (05752) 2-1862).

Getting There

Seki is easily reached from Gifu by the train that begins service in Gifu as a tram but continues far into the country parallel to the road to Seki and Mino. By JR, you could go from Nagoya, Inuyama, Minokamo, or Takayama.

AICHI-KEN ━━━━━━━━

Nagoya

Nagoya, Japan's fifth largest city, is best regarded as just a transportation center, a place to go through. It has several direct international flights, and could be a convenient place to first set foot in Japan, as there are several attractions in the general region. The city itself is of very limited interest because, due to its concentration of industries, it was a prime target during the war and was flattened. As a result, virtually all historic relics, such as the castle and Atsuta shrine, were destroyed.

After the war, Nagoya was rebuilt as a city planner's dream. Streets run broad and straight, and everything is neat and tidy— and totally lacking in soul. It is as exciting as any commercial and industrial city. On the other hand, foreign residents say it is quite a pleasant, though dull, city to live in.

Nagoya is close to Gifu, Inuyama, etc.,

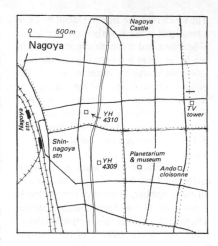

and could be used as a base of operations to those places and as far away as Tsumago/ Magome because of convenient transportation. By Shinkansen train it is only 46 minutes to Kyoto.

Information

Before setting off on the limited sightseeing of the city, stop at Nagoya City Tourist Information Office at the JR station and pick up a copy of the city map and other brochures. These give more information on the city. A full-color 32-page booklet *Nagoya* gives greater information than space allows in these pages. The information center is located inside the station, to the left of the building when walking out (tel (052) 541-4301). It is open daily 0830 to 1900. The JNTO map of Japan has a usable Nagoya map on the back.

Home Visits

A visit to a Japanese home in Nagoya can be arranged through the Home Visit Programme. You can apply at the city information office (tel 961-1111 ext. 2245), Nagoya

Tourist Information Office (tel 541-4301), JTB offices and major hotels. There is no charge for the service, but a day is usually required to make arrangements.

Things to See

Nagoya Castle

Formerly one of the greatest castles of Japan in both size and importance, Nagoya-jo was destroyed during the war. The present building retains the original stone foundations and moats, but the building is a concrete reproduction completed in 1959. It preserves the grand external appearance of the original structure, but its interior is laid out as a museum instead of the original residential arrangement.

From late September to late November, there is an interesting display of "dolls" made of chrysanthemum bushes that have been shaped so that the flowers form "faces" and "hands". They are dressed in costumes and set out in tableaux of famous historic events. The building in which they are displayed is in the central castle grounds.

Visitors are given a brochure when entering the castle describing its history and structural details extremely well. It is also available from the information center at the station.

The castle is most easily reached (seven minutes) by city bus 5 or 17 from the station. The stop is "Nagoya-jo-minami".

Tokugawa Art Museum (Tokugawa Bijutsukan)

This is a highly-rated museum containing historical treasures that formerly belonged to the Tokugawa family.

Literature about the museum usually has wording like "it contains nearly 10,000 items. . . " like armor, swords, scrolls, etc. But, while the museum may *house* so many treasures, only a disappointingly small portion is on display at any one time. The ¥500 admittance charge could be better spent at several other museums.

The museum is accessible from the castle by bus No. 16 from bus stop 6 at Shiyakusho subway station. The stop is Shindeki-machi. The same number bus can be caught for the return trip from across the street going the opposite way. The museum is on a back street and a little tricky to find. It is closed on Mondays.

Atsuta Shrine

This 2000 year-old shrine (site) ranks with the greatest shrines in the country, second only to those at Ise. It is dedicated to the sacred sword, one of the three imperial regalia. The original buildings were destroyed in the war and the present structures, which are made of concrete, are not as attractive. However the shrine is still revered, and worshippers come in large numbers. The day that I visited, mothers in beautiful kimono were taking their newly-born babies to the shrine for blessing. The shrine is easily reached by subway; the stop is Jingu-nishi ("Shrine west").

Nagoya-shi Hakubutsukan (Nagoya City Museum)

Opened in 1977, this large building houses items related to the history and folklore of the Nagoya area. (Closed Mondays.)

Municipal Science Museum

Along with general scientific exhibits, this museum has a planetarium.

Nagoya TV Tower

The tower not far from the station is promoted as a tourist attraction. Considering that the city is laid out at the edge of a vast plain, the streets are rectangular-regular, and it is industrial/commercial by nature, I never felt it necessary to look over the city from the tower's 180 meter height. (Sorry, city fathers.)

Higashi-yama-koen (East Mountain Park)

The park (84 hectares) is one of the few areas of greenery in the city. It houses one of the largest zoos in the orient, along with a botanical garden and a conservatory with many species of flowers.

Temples

There are four temples in the Nagoya area that might be worth visiting (but only in the case of people who have no chance to go to Kyoto). Kosho-ji has a five-storey pagoda, built in 1808. Nittai-ji was built in 1904 to house a relic of the Buddha, a gift of the King of Siam; the name means "Japan-Thailand temple". Near the temple is Gohyaku Rakan hall. It takes its name from the 500 statues of Rakan, disciples of the Buddha. Each face and pose is said to be different. Kenchu-ji has a historic two-storey gate at the entrance, dating from 1651. Ryusen-ji also has a large, picturesque gate at its entrance, though it is not historically noted.

Crafts

World famous Noritake china is made in Nagoya, and visitors may tour the factory at 1000 and 1400 daily (except Sundays and holidays). English-speaking guides are provided.

Visitors can watch the process of hand-painting cloisonne ware daily from 1000 to noon and 1300 to 1700 (except Sundays and holidays) at Ando Cloisonne. The workshop can be reached by subway to Sakae station. Ando is 10 minutes walk along Otaumachi-dori avenue.

Festivals

There are several festivals in the Nagoya area that would be worth seeing if you are in the area.

January 1: New Year's rites at Atsuta shrine.
January 13: (lunar) Naked Men's festival at Konomiya. (They wear loincloths.)
Early April: Cherry Blossom festival at Nagoya castle.
April 16–17: Toshogu-jinja Matsuri—this is a small local shrine festival, but interesting nevertheless. On the 16th there are performances of Kagura, ancient sacred masked dances with equally ancient and strange gagaku court music.
May 18: Toyokuni-jinja Matsuri yagumo koto and dances.
June 1: (lunar) Tenno Matsuri of Tsutsui-cho area (but celebrated throughout the city).
June 5: Atsuta shrine festival.
July 20–21: Port festival (fireworks, etc.).
July 26: Shimono-ishiki-kawa (river) festival of Sengen-jinja.
Late September to late November: Chrysanthemum Doll show (Nagoya castle).
Mid-October: Nagoya Matsuri—music, dancing, tea ceremony, folk songs/dances, kagura sacred dances/music are scheduled for the second Saturday and Sunday of the month. The high points are the procession of the Three Feudal Lords (both days), and the parade of eight *dashi*, elaborate wooden festival wagons of the type seen at the famous festivals at Kyoto, Takayama and Furukawa. A very interesting feature of these dashi is the display of mechanical dolls that are associated with some of the carts. These ingenious dolls, well over a century old, perform an amazing number of tricks and movements, all controlled by wires. Similar ones can be seen at Takayama and Furukawa (Nagano-ken).

Places to Stay

There are two youth hostels and many hotels and business hotels in Nagoya. The hostels in the city area are Aichi-ken Seinen-kaikan (tel 221-6001) and Nagoya Youth Hostel (tel 781-9845).

The information office at the station can help find accommodation. It is also possible to stay at nearby places like Inuyama YH (tel: (0568) 62-3910) and Gifu.

Getting There—International

Travellers from nearly 20 cities in Asia, Australia, New Zealand, and North America can fly direct to Nagoya. As the airport is only 30 minutes away from Nagoya station by bus (every 15 minutes), it is very convenient, especially when compared with the transportation mess at Tokyo. Processing is quick, as there are few such international flights.

The airport is not far from Kasugai station of the Meitetsu-Komaki line that goes to Inuyama/Gifu, passing the shrines of Tagata and Oagata on the way.

Buses to the airport leave from Nagoya Bus Terminal, which is located in the Meitetsu Department Store, to the right when leaving the JR Nagoya station.

Getting There—Domestic

Trains

Nagoya is a stop for all Shinkansen trains, and is also served by regular JR trains and several private lines. All connections to other points in the Kinki district are detailed in the transportation section early in this chapter. Shinkansen services are given in the general "Transportation" section early in the book. Private lines to other nearby destinations are outlined below.

There are regular bus services west to Kyoto/Osaka and east to Tokyo; these are also detailed at the beginning of this chapter. Other buses go to Takayama, Ina (Tenryu-gawa valley), Matsumoto, and Nagano, all in the Chubu region.

All JR lines use Nagoya station. Kintetsu trains leave from Kintetsu-Nagoya station, which is attached to Nagoya station. Trains of the Meitetsu line (north to Inuyama, Gifu, etc., and south to the Chita Peninsula) leave from Shin-nagoya station in the basement of the Meitetsu department store, to the right when leaving Nagoya station.

There is a second Meitetsu station at Kami-iida, within the city limits but some distance from Nagoya station; it can be reached by bus No. 1 from the latter. But it is simpler for passengers headed for to Meiji-mura or Tagata/Oagata shrines to go to Inuyama from Shin-nagoya station, change trains at Inuyama and backtrack slightly along the other line.

Ferries

There is a daily ferry in each direction linking Nagoya with Sendai (northern Honshu) and Tomakomai (Hokkaido). The boat leaves Nagoya in the early evening, reaches Sendai the next morning, and Tomakomai the morning of the third day. More details are given in the general "Transportation" section early in the book and in the section on Hokkaido. Ferries leave from Nagoya Ferry Terminal, which can be reached by city bus from the station. It is not too far from Nagoya-ko subway station.

Hitching

To hitch out of Nagoya along the Tomei expressway (to Tokyo or Kyoto/Osaka), take the subway from Nagoya station (platform 1) to Hongo. About half the trains terminate before Hongo at Hoshigaoka; if yours does, wait for the next one, which will terminate at Fujigaoka. Trains bound for Fujigaoka are shown in red on the timetable in stations. On ticket machines, the line is shown in yellow.

The entrance to the expressway is close to Hongo station. See the section on Hitching for more information.

Getting Around

Nagoya has a subway system of five lines. It is easy to use and has stations marked in *romaji* (although the station names on maps may not be). The free handout map from the information center shows the stations.

Southeast from Nagoya

To the southeast of Nagoya are the two peninsulas of Chita and Atsumi, looking like pincers poised to close on Mikawa Bay. Their attraction for Nagoya residents is a glimpse of nature, especially wild flowers in season, but they are of limited interest to foreigners.

The Chita Peninsula can be reached by Meitetsu train from Shin-nagoya station. From the terminal stations (it branches near the end) buses run from both places to Morozaki at the tip. The most exciting attraction here is the sight of buildings and other park facilities covered with sea shells. (One train terminus is Kowa, a beach resort.)

From Morozaki, ferries cross eight times daily in both directions to Irago: the fare is about ¥500. Ferries also cross Ise Bay to Toba five times a day and there is a service (14 each day) to Toba from Irako. The fare is the same for both, about ¥750. There is a service to Toba from Gamagori as well, but at about ¥3000, it is much more expensive. There are also island-hopping services in the Mikawa Bay area, along the route Kowa (noted for beaches)–Himaka-jima–Shinojima–(considered the most attractive)–Gamagori. Morozaki is another starting point to Himaka-jima to pick up the route.

At Irago, bicycles can be rented at the service center of the Toyotetsu railway (near the port) and at Irago Kokuminkyuka-mura (vacation village). The Toyotetsu line itself does not begin until half-way along the peninsula, so it is just as easy to go by bus from Irago all the way to Toyohashi station.

Those wishing to hitch on the Tomei expressway to Tokyo or Kyoto/Osaka would find it easiest to take JR from Toyohashi to Mikawa-ichinomiya and backtrack a couple of km to the Toyohashi interchange ("inta" in Japanese). Route 1 passes through Toyohashi, but this road is very congested, slow to travel on, and the scenery is depressing nearly all the way to the Mt. Fuji area.

Southwest from Nagoya

To the southwest are the attractions of the Toba area and the Kii-hanto peninsula. Toba and surrounding areas are described after the write-ups on Kyoto and Nara. The following entries are the major places encountered between Nagoya and Toba, and are located to the east of the mountain range dividing them from the Nara area. Transportation between Nagoya and the southwest area is described at the end of this chapter.

Yokkaichi (Northern Mie-ken)

There is nothing but industries in the city itself, except for its annual festival on September 26–27—a procession of a feudal lord and townspeople in costumes of that era. Inland about 20 km is Yunoyama-onsen ("Hot Water Mountain Hotspring"), at the foot of Gozaisho-yama.

Yokkaichi is a transfer point for travellers to the Toba area using JR trains.

Gozaisho-yama/Yunoyama-onsen

The main attraction (apart from the hot springs of the town, which are sufficient inducement for Japanese) is the mountain Gozaisho-yama, 1210 meters. Its upper reaches rank among the three most famous among Japanese mountaineers. However,

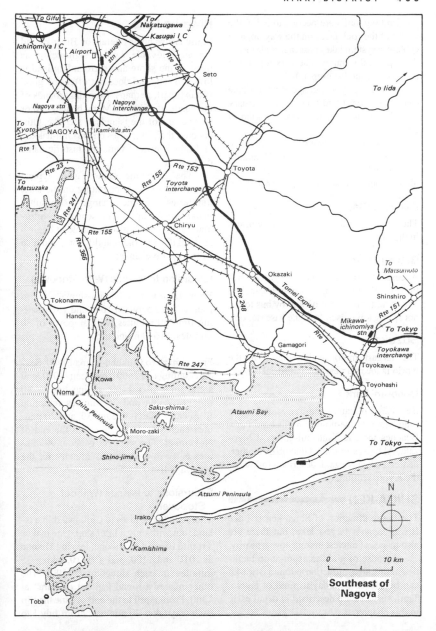

Southeast of Nagoya

no climbing skills are needed to enjoy the views of the rock faces on the way up, as a cable-car system takes passengers almost to the top in 20 minutes. The very top of the peak is reached by a separate lift.

At the top, you can see Biwa-ko lake (on a clear day) and there is a sanctuary near the top for Japanese serow, a kind of antelope.

There are three waterfalls in the area, Kugurido-no-taki, Ao-taki and Hyakken-taki. Ao-taki is the most easily reached, by hiking from the base station of the cable-car.

Places to Stay

There are about 30 hotels of varying prices in the onsen.

Getting There

Access is from Kintetsu-Yokkaichi station, by Kintetsu-Yunoyama-sen (line) to Yunoyama-onsen station and by bus to the hot spring town itself (and the base station).

Suzuka

The largest motor racing circuit in the world is located near this industrial city.

Isenoumi Park

Between Yokkaichi and Tsu stretches the long beach of Ise-no-umi prefectural Park. Beaches include Tsutsumi-ga-ura, Chiyo-zaki, Akogi-ga-ura, and Gotemba. Another, nearer Tsu, is Niezaki, described following the Kyoto section.

SHIGA-KEN ■■■■■■

The main attraction of Shiga-ken is Lake Biwa, Japan's largest lake, but there are also places of interest in some towns nearby.

Because of good transportation facilities in this area, attractions around Biwa-ko can be visited as a day trip out of Kyoto. Train services are described in detail early in this chapter.

Biwa-ko Lake

Many cruise boats operate on Biwa-ko and are an enjoyable way of sightseeing, as most of the shore and surrounding land is low and flat, and does not offer any good vistas (apart, perhaps, from the grounds of the castle at Hikone). Many boats go to or around one of the islands in the lake. Others base their itineraries on the Omi-hakkei, or Eight Views of Omi, the historic name of the area.

The following section gives typical schedules for boats operating on the lake; itineraries and times change, so consult a *jikokuhyo* for up-to-date schedules. Information on boats is also available in English at the TICs in Tokyo and Kyoto, and also from any travel agent.

Excursion to Islands (With Stopover)

From Hikone to Chikubu-shima*: Up to four sailings between 1000 and 1510; sailing time 30 minutes, with stopover of 30 minutes. ¥1660 round trip.

From Imazu to Chikubu-shima island: Several sailings (¥2300) between 1010 and some time after 1400; sailing time is 40 minutes going and 35 minutes returning from early March to June 30, and 20 minutes each way from July 1 to the end of November. The stopover is about 90 minutes early in the year, 65 minutes for the second half.

Excursions to Islands (Without Stopover)

There are two cruises to Chikubu-shima island, but with only a brief stop. One makes a round trip out of Hikone, leaving Hikone at 1010 and 1100, and at 1310, taking 35 minutes in each direction (¥3100). The other makes a round trip out of Iiura* at 1300. From April to the end of June the trip each way takes 40 minutes. From July 1 to

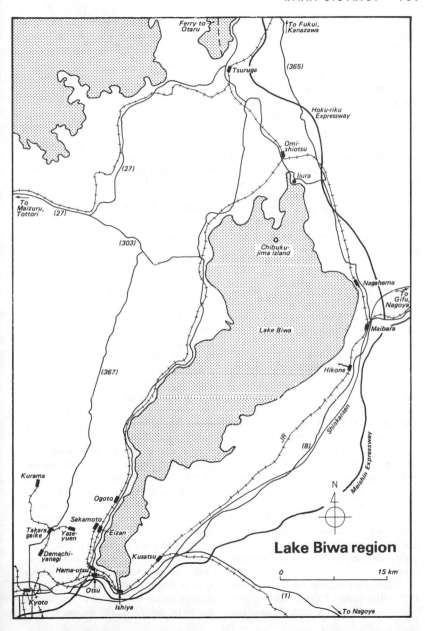

Lake Biwa region

0   15 km

the end of November, the trip going is extended to 85 minutes, with a 25 minute return (¥1430).

There are also cruises to Chikubu-shima with only a brief stop. Three leave from Nagahama (1045, 1315 and 1545 pm; 65 minutes total; ¥3100), ending at Hikone, and one leaves from Imazu (1140; 40 minutes; ¥2840), also ending at Hikone.

*These place names provide perfect proof of the absurdity of using *kanji* for place names. Of several persons queried in Tokyo, no one knew how to say them. (Jikokuhyu gives no pronunciation guide except for JR stations.) The "best effort" is given here. Locals should recognize the names, even if not correct.

Omi-hakkei Cruises

There are cruises around the lake to take in the Omi-hakkei. The most convenient of these would be those starting from Hama-otsu lasting 2-3/4 hours (up to four per day; ¥2790).

Cruises on the "Michigan"

Totally non-Japanese, but worth considering as an attraction nonetheless, the Michigan is a 900 ton stern-wheeler (paddle-wheel ship), ideal for the shallow lake with its one meter draft. The ship is 59 meters long and 11.7 meters wide, and was outfitted virtually on a cost-no-object basis. (Its ¥1.7 billion cost could have purchased a 20,000 ton cargo ship.)

There are four decks, the first three with dining facilities of increasingly higher quality (all with a foreign theme). On the third level is a stage where Dixieland music is played during the "Showboat" evening cruise.

Hama-otsu round trip: 1000, 1150, 1340, 1530 (90 minutes) ¥2000–4500. "Showboat" cruise (round trip from Hama-otsu):

1830 (2-3/4 hours); ¥4100 and up. Note that reservations are essential for the Michigan (tel. 0775-24-5000 in Japanese, or use a travel agent).

EASTERN SHORE

Nagahama

The name means "Long Beach". This town is of no special interest except during the Nagahama Matsuri (festival), April 14–15, and possibly during another festival in October.

Nagahama Matsuri

This festival is one of the more interesting in Japan and is worth trying to see. The festival features 12 *yatai* (festival wagons) which are used as portable stages on which children in costume present *Hikiyama-kyogen* (a type of comic drama). The stages are covered with miniature roofs of the same graceful shape and construction as those on temples. The wagons are decorated with elaborate carvings, gilt, and even Gobelin tapestries showing European soldiers, which are believed to have been brought from Belgium in the 16th century.

On the evening of April 14, the *yatai* are gathered in lantern-light at Hachiman shrine. The next day the *yatai* are moved from the shrine into positions on the city's streets and performances of the kyogen are given, each one lasting 20–30 minutes. Then the wagons are moved ahead to a new position (replacing the wagon that had been standing there) and another performance begins. The process is repeated throughout the day.

Watching the moving of the wagons is as interesting as the plays themselves, as each yatai weighs many tons and is only a little narrower than the small streets through which they advance. The wheels cannot be steered, so the wagons must be man-handled sideways with the use of long levers. More than one protruding advertising sign gets knocked off each year, even at the second-storey level, as the carts are at least five to six meters tall.

Hachiman-jinja is a 10–15 minute walk from the east exit of the JR Nagahama station. On festival days it is easy to follow the crowds, but there are also usually signs near the station indicating the location of the shrine and the parade route.

Other Festivals

September 2–5: Kehi-jinja, a procession of men dressed as warriors of feudal days.
October 15: Hachiman-jinja (similar to the April festival).

Kanagasakigu-jinja

In cherry-blossom season (early to mid-April), the 2000 trees in the grounds of this shrine are very beautiful.

Daitsu-ji Temple

(Nagahama Betsuin)
This temple, about 500 meters east of the station, is designed in the rather flamboyant Momoyama style, and dates from 1586.

Getting There

Nagahama is three stations north of Maibara, a major junction on the JR Tokaido main line and Tokaido Shinkansen.

Hikone

Little mentioned in tourist literature, this small city can be reached from Kyoto or Gifu in an hour, and is worth a visit to admire its pretty feudal castle overlooking Lake Biwa, and one of the loveliest gardens in Japan. Both can be reached by a 10-minute walk along the road leading from the front of Hikone station.

Other attractions in the Hikone area include Taga-jinja (shrine) and its garden,

nearby Konomiya shrine and garden, Ryotan-ji temple and its highly regarded Zen-type rock garden, Seiryo-ji temple, Daido Benzaiten temple, and Tenneiji temple. These are all described in the city office publication mentioned under Hikone-jo castle.

Things to See

Hikone-jo Castle

The castle, perched scenically atop the only sizeable hill in the area and close to the waters of Biwa-ko, was finished in 1622 and is one of relatively few original castles remaining in Japan. The main building is a National Treasure, and several of the towers and gates are rated almost as high. One of the towers functions as an art gallery and displays many art works and arms of the Ii family, the owners. (Tall people, watch your head on the beams!)

Two of the original three moats remain, and their banks give good views of the walls and the castle itself. Cherry trees line the banks and during the cherry-blossom season (usually early to mid-April) the castle and grounds are one of the most beau-

Hikone

To Fukui, Kanazawa

Daido Benzaiten

Ii-jinja

Seiryo-ji

N

Hikone-jo castle

To Maibara Nagoya

Hikone stn

1 Rakuraku-en (park) and Ii Museum
2 Genkyu-en (garden)
3 Tower
4 Taiko-mon (drum gate)

To Kyoto (JR)

Tennen-ji

(8)

To Taga-jinja, Komiya-jinja (local)

tiful places in Japan. Graceful swans swimming in the moat add a note of serene beauty.

A booklet in English is usually available (free) when entering the castle; it gives a good description of the various features of the castle and other attractions of Hikone. If the booklet *How to See Hikone in Japan* is not available at the castle or Genkyu-en garden, ask at the *shi-yaku-sho* (city office).

Genkyu-en Garden

Located just north of the castle moats is Genkyu-en, a landscape garden dating from 1678, patterned on the garden of the same name in China. Although it is not as famous as the "Big Three" gardens, I consider it far more attractive than any of them and one of the loveliest in Japan. This view was shared by a Japanese garden lover I met while strolling around the central pond; according to her it is beautiful in all four seasons. If you take bread you can feed the colourful carp in the pond. The admittance ticket for the castle also includes the garden.

Festivals

Early April: Sakura Matsuri (Cherry Blossom Festival).
April 22: Taga-jinja Matsuri.
August 1: Fireworks display.
August 8: Hikone Bayashi (dance) in the center of the city.
Autumn: Shiro Matsuri (castle festival), a procession of children in costumes of feudal days.

Getting There

Hikone is on the JR Tokaido (main) line through Kyoto, one stop before Maibara. It can be seen easily in a day trip, for it can be reached from Kyoto in a little over 50 minutes (from Osaka, about 80 minutes) by one of the many no-surcharge *Shin-kaisoku* expresses (detailed early in this chapter).

From 0900 until 2030, every *Shin-kaisoku* train on the hour and half hour out of Kyoto goes to Hikone (and Maibara), and return service is just about as regular. Holders of a Japan Rail Pass (or those not counting pennies) can also use the Shinkansen to go to Maibara (only Kodama trains, not Hikari; 28 minutes from Kyoto, 45 from Osaka) and backtrack one stop to Hikone (six minutes), but check in advance with a *jikokuhyo* to ensure that you wouldn't lose time waiting for a train in Maibara.

North of Biwa-ko

Not too far north of this area are two ports from which the long-distance ferries sail for Otaru on Hokkaido, the northern main island. Both Tsuruga and Maizuru are covered at the end of the Hokuriku section.

WESTERN SHORE

Hiei-zan and Enryaku-ji Temple

One of the four routes to the top of Mt. Hiei (on the edge of Kyoto) and to Enryaku-ji, is via Sakamoto station of the Keihan line (from Kyoto; a change at Hama-otsu station is required), or from Eizan station of the JR, both of which are close to the base station of a cable railway up the east side of Hiei-zan. The mountain and temple are described in the Kyoto section.

KYOTO ▬▬▬▬▬▬

If there is one city in Japan that every foreign visitor should experience, it is Kyoto. As it was the imperial capital for more than 1000 years, from 794, it has the finest temples, palaces, villas, and gardens in Japan, as well as the most refined culture and lifestyle.

Some over-enthusiastic writers have described Kyoto as one of the most beautiful cities in the world. It isn't. Kyoto is a modern Japanese metropolis, with its full share of Japanese urban ugly. However, dotted through the city and clustered around the edges are oases of tranquility and beauty, exemplifying the best that is/ was Japan.

The name is pronounced, by the way, so that the "y" is a consonant (as in "yet"), not a vowel; the first syllable is "Kyo", and does not rhyme with "pie". The last syllable sounds like the English word "toe". Some foreigners in Japan have been heard to garble the name into "Kyota" (or worse). The name Kyoto simply means "capital city". (Tokyo, the successor capital, means "east capital".)

Information

There is no shortage of information on what to see in Kyoto. It is the only city other than Tokyo with a government-operated tourist information center (TIC). Staff speak English well (plus other languages) and are absolute goldmines of information about any place, activity, art, or craft in the Kyoto area and elsewhere in Japan. For this reason, the section on Kyoto places more emphasis on how-to-see and what-to-see than on detailed descriptions. (Also, most places of interest have handouts or signs in English giving the history and other data.) Unless you arrive Saturday afternoon or Sunday, your first stop should be the TIC to pick up one of the excellent maps of Kyoto and the booklet *Kyoto Nara* (also available at the Tokyo TIC), and to ask any specific questions you may have about travel-related topics. They have a great deal of other information on photocopied sheets and in printed booklets; particularly useful is *Walking Tours in Kyoto*, and some rail maps.

The bulletin board in the office lists all the cultural and other performances and activities for the following several weeks, and is the most up-to-date source of information about such events.

The TIC has information about accommodation in various price ranges, and will call to make reservations at all sorts of accommodation. They also participate in the *Welcome Inn* program described in the part of the Tokyo section dealing with the TIC there. Low cost places are listed later in this section, mostly for the benefit of those who arrive after 1700 on weekdays, or on Saturday afternoon or Sunday. The Tokyo TIC also has a hand-out list of accommodation that may be useful for making advance reservations, but it has occasionally omitted popular places (like Mrs Uno's house).

A very handy booklet is *Monthly Guide Kyoto*, which lists events of the month in good detail and has descriptions of a large number of temples, shrines, and palaces. (Much of the book may be in Japanese, but the English section is excellent.) It also lists the better hotels (with prices), tours, and other useful information. The booklet is not available at the TIC, but may be obtained at the large hotels that cater to foreign visitors. It is also available in Japan by mail for a total of ¥600 from:

Monthly Guide Kyoto
30-5 Chajiri-cho
Arashiyama
Nishikyo
Kyoto

The above should not be confused with another publication, *Kyoto Monthly Guide*, which is produced by the Kyoto city government. This one is much more detailed regarding events for the month. It is available at the TIC or by mail in Japan on receipt of a ¥80 stamp, from:

Tourist Section
Dept of Cultural Affairs and Tourism
Kyoto City Government
c/o Kyoto Kaikan

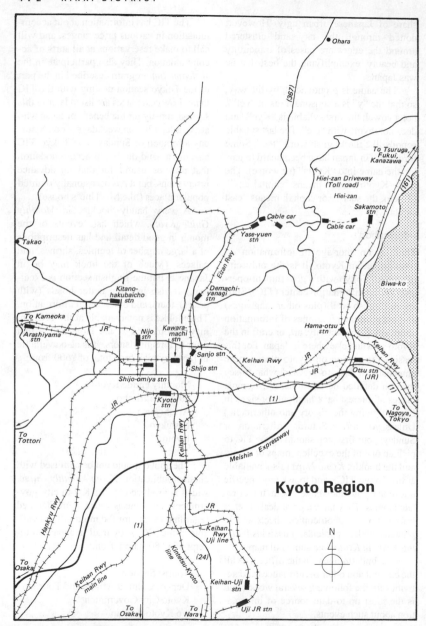

Kyoto Region

Sakyo-ku
Kyoto

Both publications are very useful.

The Kyoto City Tourist Association publishes a worthwhile guide book simply called *Kyoto*. It contains useful information such as airline phone numbers, etc., and is a steal at ¥300. For a very good explanation of many of the attractions of the city and their significance in history, purchase a copy of *Kyoto, A Contemplative Guide*, by Gouverneur Mosher.

A useful "freebie" aimed at the tourist is the monthly information paper *Discover Kinki*. It has tidbits about festivals and other events.

A useful publication for residents of and visitors to the Keihanshin region (Osaka–Kyoto–Kobe) is the monthly publication *Kansai Time Out*, which has evolved from a several-page newspaper format into a well-produced glossy magazine with interesting articles plus coverage of social, cultural, and other events of interest to foreigners, including festivals and films. It should be on sale at bookstores selling English-language publications. It can be ordered by subscription at ¥3000 per year (in Japan or sea mail anywhere) from:

Kansai Time Out
1-1-13 Ikuta-cho
Chuo-ku
Kobe 651

It might be possible to arrange single copies by phoning (078) 232-4516/7.

Another publication, more of interest to those staying long-term, is *A Resident's Guide to Kyoto*, a compilation of nearly every bit of information that one needs when arriving to stay in Kyoto for a while. It can be purchased at the YWCA (tel 431-0352) for about ¥500, by domestic mail for ¥1000, or by foreign mail for ¥1500, from:

YWCA Thrift Shop
44 Konoe-cho,
Muro-machi-dori, Demizu-agaru
Kamigyo-ku
Kyoto 602

There is a thrift sale at the YWCA on the first and third Saturday of every month (11:00–14:00), a good place for bargains, exchanging information with other foreign residents, and even homemade Western-style munchies and crunchies. (The YWCA is shown on the TIC map.)

Tickets and any other travel bookings are available from the JTB offices near the north entrance of Kyoto station, and on Sanjo, east of Kawaramachi. There is generally English-speaking staff on duty.

Post Office

The Post Office offers basic services 24 hours a day, including mail pick-up from Poste Restante. A passport or other identification will be required. Postal rates are conveniently noted in English in the main section.

Home Visit

It is possible to visit a private home in Kyoto for a couple of hours in the evening to see what Japanese home life is like. Members of the participating families speak English or other foreign languages. Arrangements should be made as far in advance as possible. (Usually this can be done in a day, but more time should be allowed.) Travel agencies and large hotels can make arrangements; you can also contact the Kyoto City information office at Kyoto station (tel 371-2108). General information on the program is given in the introductory section of this book.

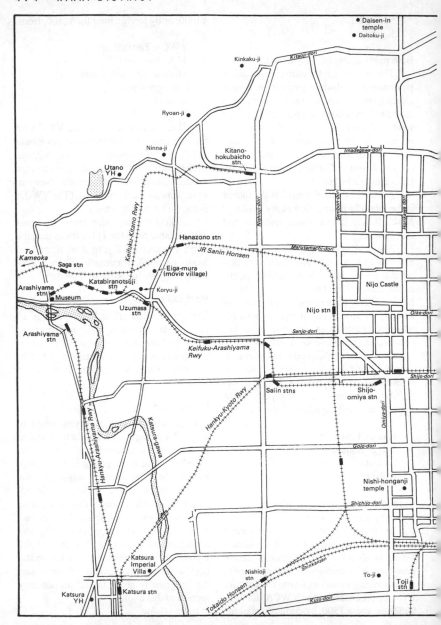

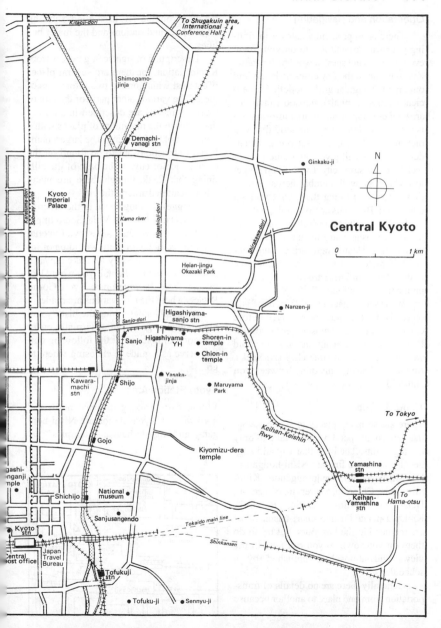

Orientation and Navigating

There is no problem whatever in finding your way around Kyoto on your own, even if you do not speak a word of Japanese. Kyoto is one of the few cities in Japan laid out on a rectangular grid (modelled on ancient Chinese capitals), transport facilities are well developed, and tourist information is readily available. I recommend that you pick up a TIC map and set out independently, as this will give you a much better feel for this historic city. Even if you do get lost you may well stumble across something more interesting than what you set out to find. Bus tours are available, but virtually all go to the same destinations: Nijo-jo, Kyoto Gosho, and Kinkaku-ji temple in the morning; Heian-jingu shrine, Sanjusan-gendo temple, and Kiyomizu-dera temple in the afternoon. These are easy to reach by public transportation.

Wear shoes that can be slipped off and on easily, for they must be removed before entering temples and most other buildings. If you are sightseeing in cool or cold weather, be sure to wear thick, warm socks, for they will be the only thing between you and cold wood floors.

Things to See

There are so many places to see in Kyoto that one could spend weeks to take in only the highlights. The ones that I would suggest trying to see first are Nishi-hongan-ji, Higashi-hongan-ji, Sanjusangendo, Kiyomizu-dera, Chion-in, Shoren-in, Nanzen-ji, Heian-jingu, Nijo-jo castle, Ryoan-ji, Kinkaku-ji, and Fushimi-inari-taisha. Most are included in the bus tours, but try to do them on your own so you can take in the views and atmosphere unrushed by a schedule.

Generally there are no details of transportation from one place to another because the map from the TIC is so good, showing all rail lines and stations and the major bus lines.

Description of sightseeing begins from Kyoto station, for there are several places of interest within one to two kilometers of there. The various other parts of the city of touristic interest are described in an order that takes in the maximum of places with a minimum of backtracking. The largest numbers of attractions are to be found on the eastern side of city, at the base of the hills lining that flank, though there are many others scattered around the city.

I suggest reading ahead to the description of Katsura Imperial Villa, Sento Imperial Palace, and Shugaku-in Rikyu Imperial Villa to see if any of them would be of interest, for it is necessary to make advance reservations to visit them; if you would like to go, refer to the write-up on Kyoto Gosho Palace, where the reservations are made.

A pamphlet describing the history and high-points is given out at virtually every attraction of note, so let the following outline serve as a guide in choosing where to go.

Kyoto Station Area

Within easy walking distance north and northwest of Kyoto station are Nishi-hongan-ji and Higashi-hongan-ji temples.

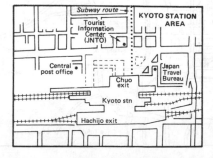

Nishi-hongan-ji

This is regarded by many as the finest example of Japanese Buddhist architecture. The temple date from 1592, but the original buildings were destroyed in 1617. The present Boei-do was rebuilt in 1636, and the *Amida-do* in 1760; the former is the northernmost of the large main buildings.

The Shoin building was originally part of the old Fushimi Castle and was moved here when the castle was dismantled. Not to be missed is the very colorful Karamon gate in the south wall (viewed from inside the grounds). Of typically flamboyant Momoyama style, it has much gold inlay on the metal fittings and brightly colored carved figures of animals and humans, many obviously of Chinese derivation.

There are four tours a day, at 1000 and 1100, 1330 and 1430. Though lengthy (if the explanation is being given only to Japanese visitors), this is the only way to see the interior buildings, the two Noh stages, Komei-no-en (a pretty garden of rocks, gravel and greenery), and other glimpses of beauty such as wide verandas made of a single plank of wood. Not open to the public, unfortunately, is the more beautiful Hyakka-en garden.

Costume Museum

Close to Nishi-hongan-ji is an interesting museum with costumes, both original and replicas, worn in Japan over the past 2000 years. It is on the fifth floor of the Izutsu Building. There is an English-language pamphlet, and the costumes are also labelled in English.

Higashi-hongan-ji

This temple has the largest wooden structure in Kyoto. The temple was founded in 1602 but the present buildings date from 1895. It is worth a look around.

Kikokutei Garden

This large strolling-type garden is/was a villa of the abbot of Higashi-hongan-ji temple. Unfortunately it has been neglected and allowed to run down, but it is little visited and provides a haven of relative peace. An interesting scandal has been hovering around it, as the abbot transferred ownership to a private individual without consulting the 10,000 or so temples affiliated with Higashi-hongan-ji.

To-ji

To-ji temple is a slightly longer distance Southwest of the station than the Hongan-ji temples are North, and is accessible on foot or from JR To-ji station. To-ji is set on extensive park-like grounds, and has the tallest pagoda in Japan (55 meters). The *kodo* (lecture hall) is a simple building containing only a few large, gilded, carved wooden figures. This was the first temple I ever visited in Kyoto, and in the late afternoon, with the sun shining in the doorway and reflecting off the floor, the effect was quite mystical (for lack of a better word). The first Europeans here must have been similarly impressed by the unfamiliar symbolism. The pagoda dates from 1644, the lecture hall from 1598, and the main hall from more recent times.

Unfortunately, To-ji is a bit off by itself, and it is necessary to backtrack to the station or catch a bus east to the Tofuku-ji area (described immediately below) after visiting it.

Southeast Area

The well-known Fushimi-inari shrine, with its many torii gates winding up the hillside, is in this area, along with several other places of interest. The TIC has a small photocopied map that is useful for general orientation in this area (as far south as Nara).

Tofuku-ji

This temple is at its best in November, when the maples in the ravine (crossed by picturesque Tsuten-kyo bridge) are at their best. Some of the architectural details of the buildings are noticeably different from those of most temples, and the *karesansui* garden of mixed greenery and raked sand has a beauty of its own.

Access is from Tofukuji stations of both JR Nara line and Keihan Honsen (main line).

Fushimi-inari Taisha Shrine

This is the largest of the 32,000 Inari shrines found throughout Japan. They honor the patron deities of agriculture and business, two of the most important activities in the country, which ensures their continued popularity. For this reason, you are likely to come across a family or members of a small business praying for success in a new venture. The fox is the messenger of the shrine deities, which explains the large number of fox statues on the grounds.

The shrine is famous for the huge number of orange-painted *torii* erected over some of the paths that wind up the mountainside. There are somewhat more than 1000 of them, so close together that they form a tunnel. They have been donated by worshippers whose supplications were answered. (You may read reports that there are 10,000 or more . . . but I counted them.)

At various shrines along the route you may see hundreds of miniature *torii* (sold at the entrance) that have been left by worshippers—they can be seen stacked like firewood at the end of the season.

Those energetic enough to climb to the top—there are many paths branching off, many leading considerable distances away—may find a stone monument engraved with the profile of Charles Bronson! He is used as the symbol of virility by a line

of male cosmetics called "Mandom".

There is a good chance of seeing some sort of ceremony at the main building; there may also be performances of the slow and graceful sacred *kagura* dances by shrine maidens. (This may depend on whether someone has paid for a performance for religious purposes.)

The shrine is reached easily from Inari station of the JR Nara line, or Fushimi-inari station of Keihan Honsen line. It is one of very few in Kyoto with no admittance charge.

Daigo-ji

This temple is located far from the others, in the far southeast of the city, and access is time-consuming. The attraction is that it has the oldest structure in Kyoto, its five-storey pagoda dating from 951. Nearby Sambon-in has one of the finest landscape gardens in Japan. There is no nearby train station; ask the TIC for access information.

Fushimi-momoyama Castle

This is marked on the TIC map and you may be tempted to see it. The original castle that once stood here was torn down centuries ago and many of its parts given to other temples and palaces. (Some are at Nijo-jo, Nishi-hongan-ji and other Kyoto temples, and can be found as far away as Matsushima, in the northern part of Honshu.) However, the present structure is only a modern concrete reproduction, and offers nothing that can't be seen better elsewhere (such as Himeji or Hikone, both easily reached from Kyoto, which have genuine historic castles).

Manpuku-ji

This is the head temple of the Obaku sect of Zen, probably the least-known of the three Zen "schools" in Japan. It was introduced from China in the mid-17th century and, until the mid-1700s, was headed by a Chinese monk. Every attempt is still made to preserve Chinese traditions. The buildings are of Chinese architectural style, which makes them unique in Kyoto.

Access is from Obaku stations of the JR Nara line or Keihan main line. (The former is closer.)

East Area

On the east side of the city are located the largest number of places of interest to visitors.

Sanjusangendo

The name means "33 bays" and refers to spaces between the pillars of this long, narrow structure which dates from 1266. The spaces are filled with a huge and intriguing collection of 1001 life-sized statues of Kannon, Goddess of Mercy. (If they look small, remember that the Japanese were once very short; many old people in the countryside are no taller than these figures.) Some of the statues wear "necklaces". The face of each statue is different; if a visitors sees one that resembles himself, it is customary for him to donate such a decoration. The central figure is a seated 3.3 meter statue of 1000-handed Kannon (from 1254) and her 28 helpers. Also take time to look at the large (but dusty) sculpted wooden statues in the back corridor. Signs in English explain all features briefly. The temple is famous for its archery festival on January 15 when arrows are shot along the long verandah.

National Museum

The National Museum is just across the road from Sanjusangendo, and is worth a visit for its large collection of Japanese artefacts from prehistoric to recent vintage. The pottery from about 2000 BC shows how little this craft has advanced since "primitive" times.

Although the museum is conveniently reached from Sanjusangendo, it might be worth saving (literally) for a rainy day. Admission is free on the 15th of each month (closed Mondays and at year-end).

Kawai Kanjiro Pottery

This is the house and workshop of the late Kawai *Kanji*ro, a noted potter. Those interested will find displays of his work, the workshop, and a climbing kiln. (Closed Mondays, mid-August and year-end.)

Chishaku-in

Of somewhat less interest, but pleasant to visit during a long Kyoto stay, this temple has an attractive garden with an unusual pond that extends under the porch of the main building. A special building is used to exhibit wall and door paintings from the 16th century that survived fires in the main building. They are considered masterpieces of their type, but may not be of great interest to non-Japanese. An English-language pamphlet gives further details.

Kiyomizu-dera

This temple is very popular with visitors, and is included on every tour. It is unusual, for the *honden* (main hall) is built out on pillars over a hillside. The grounds are especially lovely during the cherry blossom season and autumn. The present buildings date from 1633, and include a picturesque Sanmon gate at the entrance and a three-storey pagoda, as well as the famous pillar-supported verandah.

Access from the south is by walking up the long hill from Gojozaka bus stop, either through the cemetery (southernmost road) or up the shop-lined road. These shops and those along the other approaches, have a large variety of pottery and other crafts, as well as countless souvenirs and Kyoto-type nibbles.

Exploring the Back Streets

Several little streets near Kiyomizu-dera make this possibly the most enjoyable area of Kyoto for strolling. When leaving Kiyomizu-dera, take the right-hand road of the two downhill and note the first street that branches off to the right, down a set of stone steps. This is Sannen-zaka. Explore the main road as desired (also the road off to the left when leaving the temple), but return to and go down Sannen-zaka.

Like the main road, Sannen-zaka has numerous little shops selling a variety of knick-knacks. (If you see something of interest in any of the shops in the area, I suggest you buy it there, as some shops have goods that can't be found anywhere else.)

A short distance along Sannen-zaka, to the right, you will see the entrance to Sakaguchi, a lovely little garden teahouse with a pond. For a few hundred yen you can order soba (noodles) or tea and have them while enjoying the view. Pleasant, tinkly koto music provides the background and guarantees one of the most "Japanese" experiences available.

A little farther along is a coffee shop that I enjoyed, the Boga-tei. The front and interior are modern and European in appearance, but there is a pleasant courtyard at the rear with the incongruous combination of traditional Japanese garden, with stone lanterns, and sculpted trees, and a Mediterranean-style patio; for contrast, the adjoining gift shop is in a traditional house. The coffee shop can be easily identified by the decorative little Japanese shelter (to the right) over the pay phone.

A little beyond here, Sannen-zaka curves off to the left and Ninen-zaka branches off to the right, down another set of steps. There are more knick-knack shops, teahouses, and coffee shops along the way, some in garden settings. In the latter case you can look through the entrance gates to see if the attraction is appealing.

Sannen-zaka, by the way, continues on to a pagoda, the five-storey Yasaka Gojunoto, all that remains of a once-grand temple. The grounds are closed, however, so it is not worth a walk to see. Photographers will find that the view along the road is ruined by numerous power lines, but the little uphill road to the east shortly before the T-junction gives a good silhouette of the top four storeys. (A telephoto lens will be needed to cut out foreground clutter.)

The road forming the T-junction at the end of Ninen-zaka leads up to Ryozen-kannon, a large concrete seated figure of Kannon. The figure is of no historic importance, but the appearance of the statue is peaceful and reassuring. It is surrounded by a wall, but you can see through the gate without paying the entry fee if you don't want to go in.

Continuing on the road that runs along the foot of the grounds of Ryozen-kannon (reached by zig-zagging left from the end of Ninen-zaka) you pass another couple of tea gardens, temples, etc., which can be looked into. The roads ends in a T-junction at Kodai-ji temple, which can be identified easily by the strange looking spire "growing" out of the roof.

Just before the end of the road, on the right hand side, is Rakusho coffee shop. At first it appears to be like any of the other countless coffee shops in Japan, but this one has an interesting feature all its own—a charming little garden with a long narrow pond. (The garden is actually a century old, and earlier was the centerpiece of a more classical tea garden, but it has moved with the times.)

Around the pond are typical Japanese decorative motifs, like a stone slab across the water to serve as a bridge, many colorful flowers, tastefully positioned moss, etc. The most interesting sight is the large num-

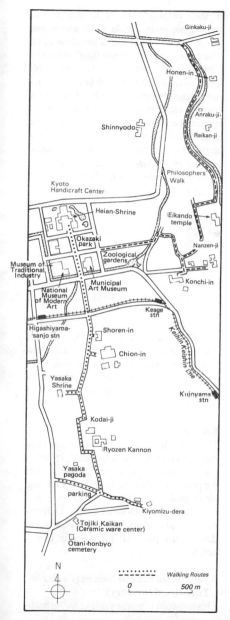

ber of huge decorative carp in the pond. They have won the Kinki district championship for several years and are the pride and joy of the distinguished-looking owner who potters around carrying out maintenance. It is not necessary to buy anything as visitors are allowed to enter just to look, but it is a good place to take a break. Prices are no higher than those at typical Japanese coffee shops, and the owner's daughter-in-law speaks English.

This area around Kiyomizu-dera (also described in the pamphlet on walks in Kyoto) is, more than any other area in Kyoto, conducive to a relaxing stroll rather than a rushed attempt to see everything in a day. Not all visitors will have the luxury of time, but those who do are sure to enjoy it, as the area has a mood difficult to find elsewhere in Japan.

Yasaka-jinja

Not far away is Yasaka shrine. It has several photogenic brilliant-orange buildings as well as one of the largest granite torii gates in Japan (on the south side), dating from 1646. It is one of the best places in Japan to see people "waking the gods"; shaking and whipping a thick rope attached to a rattly gong at the eaves, then putting their hands together in prayer. It is said to be a favorite of geisha from the nearby Gion entertainment area.

Adjacent Maruyama-koen park has a pleasant little pond and Japanese-style garden arranged around it. It is as much of interest to see how Japanese enjoy their leisure as for its own merits. In cherry-blossom time there are parties everywhere, with much happy imbibing and singing. It serves as a path to nearby Chion-in temple.

Chion-in Temple

The huge *sammon* gate at the south (main) entrance to this hillside temple is the largest in Japan, and dates from 1619. It also has the largest bell in the country. The main building is impressively large, and is best viewed in its entirety from the large open area in front. The interior is equally large, and is an excellent place to examine the great range of Buddhist symbols and other ornate gilded decorations; it is a feast for the eyes. The temple is active, not just a type of museum (as is the case with many temples), and there is a good chance of observing priests chanting prayers for deceased members of visiting families.

The garden and large building behind the main temple are also worth visiting. Although there are always other visitors around, the temple is rarely overcrowded. An English-language pamphlet gives the history of the temple, and serves as a primer on the Jodo sect, of which it is the head temple.

Shoren-in

This is one of my favorite temples. It is off the beaten path enough for it not to be overrun with hordes of sightseers, so you can enjoy its lovely little garden, the peace, and the blending of the buildings (and their architectural details) with the setting at the foot of a hill. Birds can be heard in nearby trees. It is delightful in the late afternoon, especially in autumn when the trees are beautiful; 1400–1530 is good in November, later in summer when the sun is higher. After exploring the buildings and the views from there, return to the entrance, don shoes, and walk around the garden, which is entered by a tunnel under one of the corridors (to the right when leaving the building). An English-language handout gives the history of the temple.

Nanzen-ji

Another highly recommended temple to visit, especially when the autumn leaves are at their colorful best, is Nanzen-ji. This temple began as a villa for a retired emperor, and was made into a temple in 1291. The present buildings date from post-1600. The grounds have many tall, venerable cedar trees, so the approach to the entrance is canopied by nature. The buildings of the temple feature the finest construction techniques, rooms with exquisite details (some opening onto to lovely little gardens), sliding doors with fine, treasured paintings, and several rock-and-sand Zen gardens. Nanzen-ji means "south Zen temple". A leisurely walk will be rewarding.

To the right inside the main entrance is a simple room where you can sip tea (*ocha*) for ¥200 extra. It is a good chance to appreciate the beauty of the tea ceremony (the spirit of it, anyway), sitting in the simple room on tatami mats and looking out at the little waterfall. An English-language pamphlet gives the history of the temple.

Toriyasu

Another peaceful and beautiful place for rest and refreshments is Toriyasu, a teahouse/restaurant/garden just across from the right-hand corner of the grounds of Nanzen-ji. Koto music provides the background, and tall trees the shade.

Eikando

The grounds of this temple are gorgeous during autumn, and enjoyable at other times. A graceful stone bridge arches over the pond, and the temple buildings enclose small gardens, including one of rocks and sand raked into elaborate patterns. Unfortunately, loudspeakers babble incessantly and destroy any potential for peaceful exploration.

Kyoto Dento Sangyo-kaikan (Center of Traditional Industry)

This museum is worth visiting for its beautiful lacquerware, masks, and robes for bugaku dances. (Interestingly, one mask with a small dragon atop the head of the mask is very similar to masks used in festivals in Bolivia.) It also has a reproduction of a typical, traditional Kyoto house with its long corridors (nicknamed *unagi-no-nedoko*, "bedrooms for eels") as well as exhibitions of hand-forging of knives, and other traditional crafts. The museum is located to the right of the National Museum of Modern Art and can be recognised by its unusual architecture, with a curved wall up to the second floor and a traditional square form for the upper storey. The TIC map has only the English name, which no Japanese would understand to give help with directions. The Kyoto Municipal Art Museum and the zoo are nearby.

National Museum of Modern Art

This has many large and attractive works. Note that "modern" refers to the past century or so.

Heian-jingu Shrine

A Johnny-come-lately among Kyoto's shrines and temples, Heian-jingu was built in 1895 to mark the 1100th anniversary of the founding of Kyoto as the capital of Japan. It is a three-fifths scale reproduction of the palace built in 794; the present buildings are large, so the imagination runs overtime picturing the originals. Actually, the present buildings do not even date to the last century; a mysterious fire in 1976 caused extensive damage, resulting in the reconstruction of the main hall and several other buildings.

The shrine has an extensive and pretty garden, known especially for cherry blossoms in the spring. It is a popular place for wedding parties, so keep your eyes open for brides in beautiful wedding kimono. Also, take bread crusts to feed the carp in the pond. The huge torii at the front entrance is the largest in Japan (23 meters high).

Kyoto Handicraft Center

Although a commercial establishment, this is still worth a visit. On its several floors, craftsmen may be seen using their traditional skills in damascene, wood-block print making (carving the plates and actually making the prints), pottery (making and painting), doll making, and several other crafts. Work is in progress every day of the week, but some of the people take Sunday off. For a convenient one-stop look at a number of traditional crafts, it can't be beaten. Like Heian-jingu, it is on the route of almost every tour, although a visit on your own would be more enjoyable, allowing you to move at your own pace. The products being made are sold on the premises, along with a large variety of other good-quality souvenirs (plus some tourist rubbish).

Ginkaku-ji

This temple was originally built in 1489 as a hillside retreat of a shogun, and was converted into a temple after his death. The intention was to cover the walls of the main building with silver foil; although this was never done, the name *Ginkaku* (Silver Pavilion) was given to it anyway. (In Japan, intention can count as much as performance, a tradition carried on into many aspects of modern life . . . for better or worse.)

The effect of the buildings, the rock-and-sand garden (including some unusually shaped piles of gravel), and careful use of greenery, is one of restrained elegance. It should perhaps be visited before the more flamboyant and spectacular Kinkaku-ji (Gold Pavilion Temple) for it may seem to suffer by comparison, although it is probably a better expression of Japanese taste (at least that of educated people).

Ginkaku-ji is about two km from Heian-jingu and the other attractions around it, so a bus or taxi to it will save time. A plaque at the entrance gives the history in English.

North and Northeast Area

The following five destinations are quite some distance out of the city, and most visitors will plan to see them separately after "doing" the more easily accessible places.

Shugakuin Imperial Villa

This villa dates from 1629. The upper garden is built around a pond and is considered the most scenic part of the grounds. The landscape is mostly lawn and rolling hills, and I regard it as not worth a special trip to see, at least not until after you have seen a good number of the other places described in these pages. It is at its best in autumn. Advance permission must be obtained from the Imperial Household Agency. (Refer to the Kyoto Gosho details at the beginning of the Kyoto section.) Access is conveniently from Shugakuin station of the Eizan line of the Keifuku railway.

Kyoto International Conference Hall (Kokusai Kaigi-jo)

A source of civic pride, the Conference Hall is a six-storey building constructed in 1966 beside the Takara-ga-ike pond and used for many international gatherings. It can be reached from Kyoto station by bus 5, 36, or 65; it is about one km from Takaragaike station of the Keifuku line out of Demachi-yanagi station (to the northeast of the city). The fastest access is by subway north to Karasuma-shako-mae, which is linked to the hall by bus 36. (Those attending meetings at the Hall will use the reverse of this route for getting into the city for sightseeing.) The Ohara area can be reached easily from the Hall because the

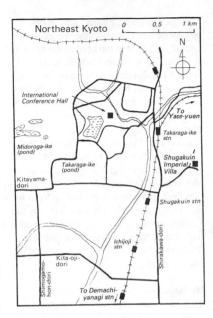

Northeast Kyoto

Conference Hall is close to the bus and rail connections to Yase-yuen and Ohara.

Enryaku-ji

This is a very large temple complex on Hiei-zan mountain, the highest point in the ridge that separates Kyoto from Lake Biwa. Temples have stood here since 788, when Emperor Kammu (who founded Kyoto as the capital) ordered its construction to guard against "evil spirits" from the north-east. One theory suggests that the "spirits" were actually Ainu or another people who predated the ethnic Japanese (Yamato).

Enryaku-ji grew to an astounding 3000 temples, and its private army of several thousand armed monks was more powerful than any government force. They terrorised other Buddhist sects and often attacked Kyoto itself if their wishes were not met. In 1571 Nobunaga Oda, who began the unification of Japan after the civil war, killed or dispersed the monks and destroyed every temple. After this, Enryaku-ji was limited to one-twentieth of its former size. Today there are still 130 temples on the mountain. The main building is the huge Kompon-cho-do.

There are four possible routes to Enryaku-ji. The first two are either by Keifuku private railway from Demachi-yanagi station, or by bus from Kyoto station, to Yaseyuen station, and then cable railway to the top. The third route is by train to the west shore of Biwa-ko lake, then a cable railway to the top of Hiei-zan. There are two stations near the base station: Sakamoto station of the Keihan line (from Sanjo-keihan station in Kyoto, with a change of trains at Hama-Otsu), and Eizan station (JR), which is on the Osaka/Kyoto–Nagahara/Omi-Shiotsu line. Fourth, there are also at least 10 buses a day from Kyoto station to the temple. The third is the most scenic route.

Ohara

Ohara is several kilometers into the country NE above the Yase area (from which the Hiei area can be visited). This small village is well known for Sanzen-in and Jakko-in temples. The women of Ohara have long been famous for their characteristic costume and customs. Unusual in Japan, they carry loads on their heads (as women in Korea do still). They may be seen on occasion in Kyoto selling produce from Ohara; in Ohara itself they may be working at souvenir stalls.

Access to Ohara is by bus that originates at Kyoto station and passes by Sanjo-keihan and Yase-yuen stations on the way, or by Keifuku railway Eizan-sen line to Yase-yuen (the base station for the cable railway to Mt. Hiei) and then by bus to Ohara. During the leaf-viewing season the buses are packed, so a start from Kyoto sta-

tion is advisable to guarantee a seat (or even managing to get onto a bus!).

Sanzen-in

This temple has, like most other temples, images of historical interest which become rather repetitive to westerners who know little of Buddhism and its art. However, the main temple has a setting of lush green, and the grounds are extremely beautiful in late October–early November when the leaves change color. It is, naturally, very crowded at that time, but still well worth going to see. An English-language pamphlet gives historical information.

Kurama

Kurama is another attraction several kilometers into the mountains, this one up another valley and almost due north of the city. The identifiable "target" is Kurama-dera temple.

Kurama-dera

Another temple known for fiery fall leaves is Kurama-dera. Although the temple dates from 770, the present main hall is only from 1971, so it is of little architectural interest. However the grounds are very pretty in late October–early November, so the temple is well worth a visit at that time. There is also an interesting festival on June 20. Access is by Keifuku railway from Demachi-yanagi station on the Eizan line and continuing from Takaraga-ike station on the Kurama-sen line.

There is a good hiking trail between Kurama-dera and Kibune-jinja shrine; it also is most recommended during autumn.

Central Area

Kyoto Gosho Palace

This is the Imperial Palace in Kyoto; it is considered to be the center of the city, from where you go "up" or "down". The palace itself is of only moderate interest, but the office of the Imperial Household Agency is located at the entrance. You apply here for permission to visit some other places associated with the Imperial family.

Kyoto Gosho was the residence of the emperor in the days when he lived in Kyoto. The present building dates from 1855, replacing one destroyed in a fire. Although the capital was Kyoto from 794, this site was not used until 1788 when a palace was built to replace an older one that was also destroyed by fire. The main buildings are replicas of the former structures and are quite simple in design, though made with the finest materials and construction methods. A guide accompanies all visitors, so the details are explained.

To enter you must fill in an application and show your passport, so arrive about 20 minutes before the tour at 1000 or 1400. (There are no tours on Saturday afternoon or Sunday.)

The palace is one of the most peaceful places in Kyoto because Japanese must wait for months to get permission to enter, and few do. Any Japanese accompanying you will have to wait at the entrance. It is a privilege for foreigners to be able to enter so easily.

Before or after the tour, file your application to visit Katsura Imperial Villa, Sento Imperial Palace, and Shugaku-in if you plan to see any of them. Permission will be given for a specific date and hour, usually within a day if requested, but you should apply soon after arriving in Kyoto to allow for delays.

Go-jinja

This little shrine, across from the west side of the Gosho, is not noteworthy except that instead of the usual *koma-inu* guardian dogs/lions at the entrance, it has two pigs.

Sento Imperial Palace

There is another palace on the southeast side of the same grounds. In addition to the buildings (which have been rebuilt many times), there is a garden completed in 1630 and designed by Kobori Enshu, possibly the most famous of all landscape-garden designers. As mentioned above, advance permission is required to enter.

Nijo-jo Castle

Although called a castle, the main building here (Ninomaru) was used as a luxurious residential palace, with extensive grounds and minimal defences (primarily the moat, walls and watch towers). A more defensive building once existed but was destroyed by fire.

The castle was built in 1603 by Tokugawa Ieyasu, the founder of the Tokugawa shogunate. Features to watch for are the architectural details of the huge Ninomaru palace, including the famous nightingale floor that "chirps" when a person's weight activates mechanisms under the floorboards (installed to warn of potential assassins). To hear the chirp clearly, fall to the rear of the group so the stomping herd passes ahead.

The garden is one of the finer landscape gardens in Japan, and makes for a pleasant stroll. The grounds hold no other great surprises but you are free to wander around the moat and walls as you wish, or leave to go on to other places.

The castle is extremely popular with visitors and is overrun with bus loads (literally by the dozen) during the peak morning and afternoon periods. The best visiting times are early in the morning, during lunch-time, and later in the afternoon; the first and last are better for taking photos, avoiding the featureless noon sun.

The beautiful Karamon gate, passed through on the way to Ninomaru palace, was originally part of Fushimi Castle. When the castle was dismantled, parts were distributed to a number of temples and shrines around Kyoto and many other parts of Japan.

Separate tickets are available for the garden alone or for the palace and garden; the latter is recommended. Like many of the major attractions of Kyoto, a large plaque at the entrance gives detailed information about the castle in English.

Shinsen-en Garden
To the south of Nijo Castle lies this small and unpretentious garden, all that remains of the 700-year-old pleasure gardens of the palace. It can be seen while walking through to Nijo-jinya. There is at least one traditional-style restaurant overlooking the garden, with sliding doors opening onto the view; the reflection in the pond and Japanese food would make a memorable experience. (But be prepared for a little language difficulty!)

Nijo-jinya
This building looks like any ordinary house, but was actually a fortress-residence for a person of rank approximately equal to baron. The interior has as ingenious collection of concealed traps, escapes and places for ambush that would allow the resident to escape any attempt at capture.

The drawback is that there is no explanation in English, and foreigners are not admitted without a Japanese-speaking escort. This would be an ideal place to visit with one of the volunteer guides described elsewhere. Gouverneur Mosher's guide book on Kyoto gives a detailed explanation of the purpose of the house and the action of the defences. An advance appointment is necessary. Obtain further details from the TIC.

Northwest Area
This description follows a route from east to west.

Kitano-tenman-gu Shrine
Quite the opposite of the flamboyant Heian shrine, Kitano is old (1607) and of a restrained Japanese style in natural wood. Its size, and the beautifully colored details and carvings, set this apart from most shrines.

Daitoku-ji
Daitoku-ji is a functioning Zen temple made up of 22 separate temples, of which eight are open to visitors. Each one is explained on the ticket (payment is separate for each, so a visit becomes expensive, and the temple has been criticised for the commercialism). Three of the best-known are Daisen-in, Zuiho-in, and Koto-in.

Kinkaku-ji
This is probably the best-known temple in Kyoto (if not Japan) because its pavilion is covered with gold leaf. The pavilion, set beside a large pond in which it is reflected, is very beautiful and worth a visit. (It is on the itinerary of virtually every full tour of Kyoto.) The present building dates only from 1955, replacing the previous structure (1397) that was destroyed in 1950 when it was set on fire by a student-monk with deranged metaphysical notions. (Mishima based his well-known *Kinkaku-ji* on this story.) The building was completely recovered in gold foil in 1987, so it should retain its beauty for many years. (The foil is much thicker than that applied originally, which was during times before Japan had become the wealthy country that it is today.)

Even though it is popular with every visitor to Kyoto and therefore crowded, a visit is recommended for the lovely views around the pond and the wooded grounds.

It is especially beautiful when the leaves change color in November. An English language pamphlet tells the history of the temple and its high points. Access from other parts of Kyoto is convenient by bus or taxi.

Ryoan-ji

This temple houses the most famous rock-and-sand *sekitei* garden in Japan. It is an enigmatic arrangement of 15 rocks in groups of various sizes in a sea of grey-white gravel that is re-raked daily into set patterns. A tile-topped earthen wall surrounds it on three sides; the fourth is a verandah of the temple where viewers may sit and admire it. The unknown designer in the 1470s left no explanation of the meaning of the garden (if any), so numerous interpretations have been concocted (any one of which is as valid as the next).

There's more to the temple than just the garden—small groves of trees, a pond, a giant *mokugyo* (wooden gong that makes a "tonk" sound when struck), a carved stone well in the shape of a coin (the water is safe to drink), the paintings on the interior sliding doors, and many details of the buildings. Ryoan-ji is in walking distance from Kinkaku-ji. (Pronounce the "Ryo" of Ryoan-ji as one syllable if you want Japanese to understand you.)

Ninna-ji

The great gate of this temple fronts onto the street, and at each side of the entrance is a huge, fearsome Nio-sama guardian god. One has an open mouth, the other closed, like Koma-inu. These are some of the finer Nio-sama in Japan, and they are better lit than most (good for photos). The grounds are large and at their best when the cherry blossoms are out; at other times the temple is only of moderate interest.

The area between Kinkaku-ji and Ninna-ji is covered by the TIC publication "Walking Courses in Kyoto".

Takao

Accessible from here, but several kilometers up a mountain valley road, is the Takao area, possibly the supreme locale in the Kyoto area for maple-viewing in the fall. There are three temples to visit while admiring the foliage, Jingo-ji (at Takao), Saimyo-ji (at Makino-o), and Kozan-ji (at Togano-o); all are within walking distance of each other.

On the approach up to Jingo-ji, tables and mat-covered areas are set up on level patches of ground and on platforms so visitors may lunch beneath the canopy of brilliant colors. The view of a Japanese family, with one or two of the women dressed in kimono, eating amidst such beauty is a memorable picture of Japanese civilization at its best.

Visitors may find a speciality of the season on sale, maple-leaf tempura; the batter tastes good but the leaf is terrible.

Buses run from Keihan-sanjo station to Takao, and pass along a road not far from Ninna-ji; check with the TIC for details and schedules. They will be extremely crowded during the leaf-viewing season.

West Area

Arashiyama

This area is on the western edge of the city, where the Hozu river emerges from a gorge and tree-covered hills spring up. Though it is often promoted as a tourist attraction, most of it will be of limited interest to short-term visitors unless nature walks are of particular appeal. (It *is* of great appeal to the Japanese, who are city-bound much of the time.) Arashiyama-koen (park) is a pleasant area at the end of a picturesque footbridge across the river from Arashiyama station (Keifuku railway); it is at its prettiest in spring because of the many cherry trees on the grounds.

The area north and west of Arashi-yama is shown on the TIC's *Walking Tour Courses in Kyoto*, but it does not detail east of the museum, so you will need to rely on the TIC Kyoto-Nara map or the one in this book.

Arashiyama Museum

One of the better museums in Japan, this is located at the north end of the bridge near the station. Kyoto-Arashiyama Hakubutsu-kan, to give it its proper name, will be of greatest interest to war buffs, but also has general appeal. It has one of the best collections in Japan of ancient armor, helmets, swords, halberds, and other weapons, as well as incredibly ornate and fine lacquer-ware. What sets the museum apart from others, however, is its display of World War II weapons, including the only Zero fighter left in Japan (all were destroyed by American authorities, but this one was fished out of Lake Biwa in 1978), a midget suicide submarine (raised from off Izu Peninsula), and an enormous gun barrel from the sunken battleship *Mutsu*. This immense piece of steel is 19.3 meters long and about two meters wide at the breech end; it fired a shell weighing over 1000 kg up to 40 km.

Tenryu-ji

The landscape garden behind the abbot's quarters is well known, although the buildings are of recent vintage (about 1900).

Nison-in

The grounds of this temple, northwest of Tenryu-ji, are planted with maples that are famous for their autumn color.

Ukai

Every night between July 1 and August 31 (except on nights of full moon or after heavy rains when the river is muddy), there is a performance near Arashiyama bridge of fishing using cormorants as the divers. (Details of this activity are given in the Gifu section.) The best view and the most fun is on a boat, but the river is not too wide, so the action can also be seen from shore or the bridge.

Koryu-ji

One of Kyoto's oldest buildings and a very large number of exceptionally old Buddhist images are found in this out-of-the-way temple. The original temple was said to have been constructed in 603 AD by Prince Shotoku. The Lecture Hall (*kodo*) was built in 1165, while the Hakkakudo building dates from 1251. The new fireproof Rei-hokan (treasure museum) has on display a large number of historic carved wooden statues, including the famous Miroku-bosatsu, which was crafted in the Asuka period (552-645) and is still in remarkably good condition. There are many other figures nearly as old. Even if you don't understand any of the significance of the figures, you can still appreciate their workmanship and marvel how well these wooden figures have survived the years.

Although the temple is close to Uzu-masa station of the JR Sanin line, trains are rather infrequent compared with buses, so most visitors will prefer to take a bus (71, 72, or 73 from in front of Wimpy's, to the left when leaving Kyoto station).

Eiga-mura

The name means "Movie Village", and is a studio used for making films that require a traditional Japanese setting. There are streets of buildings of the style of the samurai era, and others of later eras. Visitors are welcome to watch "filming", when a camera, dolly, and crew show up at some spot on the set, actors go through their lines with action, and the camera rolls. One suspects there is no film in the camera because only a single take is made of each scene, but movies are an illusion anyway, aren't they? It's all good entertainment.

There are also exhibitions explaining some of the special effects used in films. The studio is within walking distance of Koryu-ji temple, so refer to that section for access information. Many people can usually be seen walking to it, so there's a good chance you can follow the crowd. If not, ask "Eiga-mura dochira?" Everyone seems to enjoy it.

Saiho-ji

Saiho-ji was long very popular with visitors because of the unusual beauty of the 200 or so varieties of moss that have been planted in the garden. However, the hordes of sightseers caused neighbors of the temple to protest, with the result that the garden has been closed to general admittance since July 1977. Entry is still possible, but only to those who write for an appointment and are willing to pay ¥3000 as well as fulfill some other obligations. I visited the garden several times before the closure and found it nice but not special, and consider the fee exorbitant. If you really wish to see it, send a reply-paid postcard, giving your name, address, age, occupation, and desired date of visit to:

Saiho-ji
56 Kamigatani
Matsuo
Nishi-kyo-ku, Kyoto

Southwest Area

Katsura Rikyu Imperial Villa

This villa was built for the brother of an emperor and was finished in 1624. It was painstakingly repaired and restored over several years up to 1982. The buildings are of very simple design, but are made of the finest materials by the best craftsmen available. It is considered the zenith of restrained elegance, the highest point in purely Japanese architecture.

The villa is under the control of the Imperial Household Agency, and it is necessary to make an appointment in advance. (Details are given under Kyoto Gosho at the beginning of this section.) Although there may be a wait of two to three days, it is sometimes possible to go the same day. The villa is closed Saturday afternoons, Sundays, national holidays, and from December 25 to January 5.

It can be reached by bus or from Katsura station of the Hankyu Kyoto line, accessible from the Arashiyama/Saihoji area and from central Kyoto (Shijo-dori area).

South of Kyoto

Uji

For centuries the Uji area, several kilometers south, has been a summer escape from the heat of Kyoto. It is best-known for Byodo-in temple and *ukai*.

Byodo-in

This temple is unusual for its elongated structure dating from 1053. It is meant to portray a phoenix-like bird of Chinese mythology, and is the building seen on the ¥10 coin; it is considered the finest structure of the Heian period. However, most of the painted details inside the main building have disappeared with time, and you may be somewhat let down by the temple and grounds.

Ukai

A suggestion is to see Byodo-in late in the afternoon, have an evening meal or a snack, and then watch the cormorant fishing on the river at Tonoshima Island (very close to the temple). Ukai is held every night from June 11 to August 31, except during full moon or after heavy rains. You can rent a boat only, or arrange for a party/supper with food and drink. (A person who speaks Japanese would be helpful for this; the TIC might be able to offer suggestions.) The actual fishing lasts only 20 to 30 minutes, so the Japanese watchers make a party lasting the evening out of it. The fishing takes place close to shore and can be seen quite well without taking a boat, but the boat is more fun if the moderate cost is not a problem.

Access to Uji is by the JR Nara line, or the Keihan line, for which Uji is the terminus. Byodo-in is on the same side of the river as the JR station; from the Keihan station you cross the bridge and turn left.

Day Trips and Excursions

Shooting the Rapids (Kameoka)

An enjoyable excursion, especially during the heat of the summer, is to shoot the Hozu rapids. The starting point is Kameoka, accessible by JR Sanin-sen line or bus from Kyoto station. The dock is at Hozu-ohashi bridge. The trip lasts about two hours and is exciting without being dangerous. It finishes at Arashiyama. The "season" is March 11 to November 30. Boats leave six times a day (¥3000), so inquire at the TIC to be sure of getting a seat.

Kyoto is close to much of the other really interesting sightseeing territory in Japan, and many places can be visited in a day trip, or you can go out on circling routes and return after a few days. Suggested day trips include Nara, Hikone, Himeji, Ise, and Yoshino (in cherry-blossom time), all of which are described in this chapter (Kinki). Osaka can also be visited, though it can't be regarded as a tourist Mecca. Extended trips would be to the area around Nara and around the Kii-hanto peninsula. (Information on train services in the region is given early in this chapter.)

Other Things to See and Do

Museums

There are many museums other than the few detailed here. If the following sound interesting, inquire at the TIC for more information. Japan Historical Museum (Nippon Rekishikan); Kiyotaki Folkcraft Museum (Kiyotaki Mingeikan); Kyoto Ceramic Hall (Kyoto Tojiki-kaikan); Kyoto Folkcraft Museum (Kyoto Minzokukan); Kyoto Municipal Museum of Art; Kyoto National Museum of Modern Art; Kodai Yuzen (has old yuzen-dyed items); and the Steam Locomotive Museum (Umekoji Joki-kikanshakan).

Markets

There have been two monthly flea markets, one at Kitano-jinja on the 5th of every month, the other at Toji on the 21st. Be sure to check with the TIC if these dates are still valid.

For the best selection, be sure to arrive early in the morning. Don't expect any valuable antiques, as these people know the worth of their goods. (*Warning*: Don't pick up any antiques; some unscrupulous dealers carefully assemble already broken items so they "break" when touched, obliging payment.)

Arts & Crafts

Kyoto is famous for a number of handicrafts of the highest quality. These are a legacy of its past as the capital for more than 1000 years, a period when there was a continual demand for fine fabrics and lacquerware, etc. Many of these goods are still produced by the traditional methods evolved centuries ago, and you can see several types of craftsmen at work. As well as the crafts mentioned here, it is possible to arrange an introduction to other specialists through the TIC or City Information Office.

KYOTO HANDICRAFT CENTER Described earlier, this is well worth a visit to watch a variety of crafts in action. Goods may be purchased on the spot.

TATSUMARA SILK Fine silks are on display here and demonstrations are given on fingernail weaving. Inquire at the TIC for more details.

INABA CLOISONNE Demonstrations are given of making cloisonne ware. Inquire at the TIC.

MUNICIPAL MUSEUM OF TRADITIONAL INDUSTRY Described earlier, this has displays of many handicrafts of the very highest quality, along with live demonstrations of some crafts.

YUZEN An interesting and quite extensive live display here shows the historic process for producing the incredibly beautiful material used for one kind of (very expensive) kimono. Yuzen Bunka Kaikan (Yuzen culture center) is on the west side of the city near Nishi-kyogoku station (Hankyu railway Kyoto-sen line). A leaflet and more information are available at the TIC

POTTERY There are several potteries in the area, but they do not encourage visitors because of the interruption to their work. An exception is Kotobuki Toshun, which has set up special facilities in the Kiyomizu-yaki-danchi building so that visitors can see how pottery is made, and even make some for themselves. This is usually only for group tours, so inquire at the TIC if you are interested.

Shopping

Kyoto probably offers the largest variety of traditional Japanese handicrafts of any city in the country. There are many shops near the station and near many of the major temples and other tourist attractions. There are also several department stores and the Kyoto Handicraft center. A commercial map, "Shopping Guide Map of Kyoto", is useful for locating specialty shops. It should be available at the TIC and hotels. The TIC staff can also help you find anything out of the ordinary.

I found that the tax-free shops along Kawaramachi-dori gave somewhat less discount on photographic equipment than the lowest-priced shops in Tokyo, but the difference wasn't enough to worry about. If Kyoto is your first stop in Japan it is better to spend the extra yen and have it available to photograph the beauties of Kyoto rather than saving a small sum and having no photo souvenirs.

Seasonal Attractions

Cherry Blossoms

The exact time of the blossoms varies over a range of several weeks from year to year, but is generally around early–mid April. The best places to see blossoms are Kiyomizu-dera, Heian-jingu, Daigo-ji, Maruyama-koen park, Arashiyama-koen park, and Nanzen-ji. Yoshino (Nara-ken) is a mountainside planted with thousands of trees and can be seen as a day trip from Kyoto. Also highly recommended is Hikone; its castle grounds are covered with cherry trees, and the moats are lined with them.

Maple Leaves

The temples of Kyoto are among the most beautiful places in the world in autumn. The temple founders planted the grounds, which are generally located in the hills around the city, with maples. The leaves of these trees change color in a fiery display of reds and oranges rarely matched anywhere else in the world (a difficult admission for someone who comes from eastern Canada!) and their beauty underscores the fine lines of the walls and roofs of the buildings. The peak period is usually early-mid November. Temples noted for their foliage are Eikan-do, Nanzen-ji, Kiyomizu-dera, Tofuku-ji, Sekiya-zen-in, Kinkaku-ji, and Ryoan-ji. Areas close to the city include Arashiyama, Sugino, Kiyotani valley, Yase, Ohara (Sanzen-in and Jakko-in), Mt. Kurama and Kibune, and Takao (Jingo-ji and Kozan-ji).

Festivals

There are many festivals in Kyoto, but because information is so easy to obtain there is no need to list them all here. The JNTO pamphlet on Kyoto/Nara has a good listing, as do the monthly booklets listed earlier. The most famous festivals, worth making a point to see, include the following:

May 15: Aoi Matsuri. A procession of people in costumes of centuries ago passes through the streets from Kyoto Gosho Palace to Shimogamo and Kamigamo shrines.

July 16-17: Gion Matsuri. Probably the supreme Japanese festival. Huge festival carts (*yatai*) are pulled through streets on the 17th. There are 29 in all, of various sizes, all several tonnes in weight and built like miniature temples, small boats, etc., with the finest lacquer covering, gilded ornamentation, and some with European tapestries—they are a fantastic sight. The night before, they are on display in little sidestreets; many may be entered on the payment of a fee. Also open are some of the old nearby houses where families display their treasures, such as suits of armor. The TIC can give information on the route and display sites. Accommodation is hard

to find at this time, so it is necessary to book ahead or to commute from a nearby city or town.

August 16: Daimonji-yaki. Five huge bonfires that trace out one Chinese character each light up five mountains surrounding Kyoto. City lights are doused to add to the effect. It is the culmination of the Bon season when the spirits of the dead are believed to return to earth. During this season you may find neighborhood dances with hundreds of people in kimono moving in great circles and performing the slow and graceful movements of the dance. The best vantage points are Shogun-zaka hill (Hagashi-yama) and Yoshida-yama hill, near Kyoto University.

October 22: Jidai Matsuri. The name means Festival of the Ages, and it is a procession of people in historical costumes of the 13 main periods of Kyoto's history.

Entertainment in Kyoto

If you aren't worn out after a day's sightseeing, or if you want a break during the day from a seemingly endless round of temples and shrines, what else is there to do in Kyoto? There are many events that would fit into the "cultural" category, performing arts that have been passed down through the centuries and represent some of the highest levels of achievement in these fields in the world. Naturally these are not going to be everyone's cup of *o-cha*, but it would be a pity to ignore this side of Japanese life. Those looking for something less highbrow will discover that Japanese popular taste can be as earthy as that anywhere.

Performances of Traditional Dances & Arts

Through the year, at various times and theaters, there are performances of the traditional arts Noh, Kabuki, Bunraku, Kyogen, and others. As Osaka is less than an hour away by train, performances of Kabuki and Bunraku (puppet theater which originated in Osaka) given there are also in easy reach. These performing arts are explained in greater detail elsewhere in the book.

A highly recommended condensed version of all the major Japanese arts—dances by geisha, traditional *bugaku* dances, koto music, Bunraku, flower arrangement—can be seen between March 1 and November 29 twice daily at Gion Kaburenjo Theater. The show is called Gion Corner and lasts an hour; performances begin at 1940 and 2040. Each "act" is long enough to give a feel for the skill, but short enough not to be dull (most seem too short). Tickets can be bought at the door, but bookings or advance purchase may be advisable during busy seasons.

There are many performances of traditional dances at certain times of the year. Examples are Miyako-odori (Cherry Blossom Dance) throughout April, when numbers of beautifully dressed maiko (apprentice geisha) perform traditional dances, and Kamogawa-odori in May, when geisha of the Ponto-cho area perform.

To check on what is happening, obtain the booklets mentioned earlier, and be sure to stop in at the TIC where the bulletin board lists all the events of that month and the staff can give further details of anything of interest.

Coffee Shops

For other innocent entertainment there are many coffee shops. Some are only places to sit and chat; a coffee shop "date" is a common boy-girl activity, which helps explain the high prices—you're not paying for the coffee, but for the space. Many shops offer music, recorded or live; the latter is usually jazz, while recorded music may be jazz, classical, or in-between. Because such shops

come and go it is pointless to list them here; the TIC people can give suggestions. It is possible to meet people at such places, but it's all the luck of the draw.

Bars & Clubs

There is a huge number of places for drinking, as is true of any large city in Japan. Some are reasonable in cost and quite enjoyable to visit, but beware of what would be called "clip joints" in any other country—these are accepted in Japan because of generous expense accounts. It is not unknown to be billed well over ¥10,000 for a beer! There are many little pubs and "stand-bars" (Japanese term), many of which are run by companies that make or distribute whisky. These reasonably-priced places can be identified after a little practice. Don't be embarrassed to ask prices—remember the possible consequences! Avoid any place that has touts in front enticing customers in, and places with hostesses, unless you are able to check prices for all services. Hostess charges can skyrocket. The TIC may be able to give suggestions.

Bars in international hotels will be safe from gouging (though not cheap), but will generally have an international atmosphere, not the Japanese one that visitors presumably have paid a lot of money to enjoy.

There are many lower-class clubs where strippers and similar entertainment may be found. Finding them on your own may be difficult, if not impossible, so a Japanese friend would be invaluable in locating one; also a lone foreigner might well be refused entry. The cost of such a place would not be cheap; if a girl can earn ¥10,000–30,000 for an "all-nighter", she's going to expect a fair proportion of this for playing around in a club. (Do not expect the nice people at the TIC to give advice on this subject! They would doubtless prefer that foreigners know nothing about this side of Japanese society.)

Food

To help with the search for a good restaurant, the Kyoto Restaurant Association has printed a pamphlet, *Kyoto Gourmet Guide*, available at the TIC. Staff at the TIC would also probably be willing to suggest a good restaurant and perhaps even a sample menu if your visit was not at one of their busy times.

For budget diners there are many little restaurants with realistic wax displays that show you the available dishes. A former student of Kyoto University recommended Nakajima for economical food (open Monday to Saturday). The restaurants of the Shakey's Pizza chain have the bargain of all-the-pizza-you-can-eat between 1100 and 1500, Monday to Saturday, for around ¥600. If Trecca Pizza has re-opened, it will have the same deal. As in other Japanese cities, there are McDonald's, Kentucky Fried Chicken, and other familiar American fast food shops; they provide more food for the yen than just about any Japanese type of restaurant.

Places to Stay

A large number of places offer reasonably-priced accommodation in Kyoto, along with hotels of the international luxury class, plus some *ryokan* that are even more costly.

For the full listing of cheap places to stay it is best to obtain the photcopied sheets "Moderately-priced Accommodation in Kyoto" from the TIC in either Kyoto or Tokyo.

There are several youth hostels in and around Kyoto. Nearest Kyoto station is Higashiyama (tel (075) 761-8135). Because of the proximity to the station it is more likely to be fully booked. Both Utano Youth Hostel ((075) 462-2288/9) and Ki-

tayama ((075) 492-5345) are about 50 minutes by bus to the north of the city (a little less if you take the north-south subway line and go by bus from there); the latter is more out of the way. Some distance into the country (more than an hour by bus) is Kyoto Ohara YH ((075) 744-2528). Also worth considering is Otsu Youth Hostel Center in Otsu ((0775) 22-8009); it can be reached in 30 minutes to an hour. The simplest ways to get to it are by JR Kosei line to Nishi-otsu station (12 min), followed by a 13 minute walk, or by the Keihan-Keishin line from Keihan-sanjo station to Hama-otsu station (26 min), transferring there to the Keihan-Nishizaka line to Ojiyama station (9 min), followed by an 8 minute walk. Because of its distance from Kyoto and its size (308 beds), there is a good chance it will have a vacancy when the Kyoto hostels arc full. (These times and access information are from a JNTO brochure.) The hostels described in the Osaka section can also be considered as possibilities.

Favorites with travellers who don't care for the restrictions of youth hostels are two private homes, Tani House and Uno House. (075) 231-7763

Tani House ((075) 492-5489) is a spacious, traditional-style house with several rooms, one each set aside for males and females, plus several smaller rooms suitable for couples or whoever happens to get there first. The only disadvantage is that it is a considerable distance from Kyoto station. Access is by subway to the north terminus, then a westbound bus 214, 204, or 222 to Funaoka-koen stop, where a small road can be seen across the main road from a tailor shop. Follow this and turn right at the third little side-street. (It faces an earthen wall inset with tiles.)

Uno House is conveniently located not far from the southeast corner of the Kyoto Gosho. Access from Kyoto station is by bus 4, 14, 54, 200, or 215 to Kawaramachi-Marutomachi stop. From the large intersection, walk west to the second small street on the south side and turn left (there's a bank on the corner). The house is on the east side; a very small sign anounces "Uno". Travellers arriving in Kyoto by bus from Osaka airport should get off at Kyoto Hotel (on Kawaramachi-dori), a 20 minute walk to the south of Uno House. The house is something of a wonder and quite untypically Japanese, with so many added-on rooms and wings that it is a bit of a rabbit warren. Uno house has the convenience of offering simple cooking facilities for economical eating, and closeness to the city. Occasionally a room is available for long-term occupancy.

One of the benefits of staying at these two places is that the other travellers you meet there often have useful information and interesting stories.

There is another private home run by another family named Tani. It is to the south of the city ((075) 681-7437).

The least expensive *ryokan* are Yuhara (tel (075) 371-9583).

Others in increasing order of cost are given below. Prices are for the lowest-priced room (and are likely to have gone up from these shown).

Ryokan: Rakutsuso (tel (075) 761-6336, ¥8000 for two), near Heian-jingu.

YWCA: Kyoto YWCA (tel (075) 431-0351, ¥3500, women only).

Western-style hotels: Pension Utano (tel (075) 463-1118, ¥9000); Traveller's Inn Honkan (tel (075) 771-0225, ¥5500), near Heian-jingu; Traveller's Inn Hotel Sun Shine (tel (075) 771-0225, ¥5500); Hokke Club (tel (075) 361-1251, ¥9000); Kyoto Business Hotel ¥4000); Kyoto Central Inn (tel (075) 211-1666, ¥7000); New Ginkaku Inn (tel (075) 341-2884, ¥7210); Tokyu Inn (tel (075) 593-0109, ¥8300); Pension Shi-

mogamo (tel (075) 711-0180, ¥6500).

Those on large budgets who wish to sample a really fine *ryokan* in beautiful surroundings should enjoy Rankyokan, which is on a hillside above the Hozu river, just above Arashiyama and set among tall trees. The price is over ¥10,000 per person.

Temple Accommodation

Many people wish to stay in a temple in Kyoto. Unfortunately, as with Zen meditation, previous foreign guests have not conformed with customs and rules of the temples and soured any desire of temple staff to have foreign visitors. Anyone sincerely interested in staying at a temple and able to demonstrate both some genuine interest in the religious aspects and a willingness to conform to custom should contact the TIC for further information.

Getting There

Train and bus services were described at the beginning of this chapter.

Air

You can reach Kyoto easily by air from overseas and places all over Japan using Osaka's airports, Kansai International and Itami. The former is used for all international flights and about a third of domestic connections, while Itami handles the rest of the domestic flights. Information on getting from Kansai International is given in the Osaka section. For Itami, buses run every 20 minutes through the day in each direction, making the rounds of several of the better-known hotels (the Miyako, Kyoto, JAL, International, and Grand) as well as Kyoto station.

Hitching

To hitch out of Kyoto east to Nagoya or Tokyo or west to Hiroshima and Shimonoseki, take bus 19 or 20 from the station until signs for the entrance of the Meishin Expressway (marked in English) come into view. Find the entrance for the direction you want and hold up a sign (in Japanese) showing your destination. If going to a point beyond Osaka, such as Hiroshima, it is vastly preferable to pick up a car going directly that way (at least beyond Osaka) because there are several expressways in the Osaka area and, if your drive turns onto one, you could have much difficulty getting back in motion. (It is illegal to hitch beside the expressways; the only way to change vehicles is to get off at a rest stop and poll other drivers.)

Osaka is so close that it is not worth hitching to; take the train.

To hitch toward Tottori (north coast) it is simplest to take the train to Kameoka and start there (according to one source) but you could also take one of several buses (or Hankyu train) to the Katsura area and hitch on Route 9.

It seems the authorities are trying to discourage hitchhikers out of Kyoto (possibly too many are doing it), so ask among other travellers for an update.

Getting Around

Kyoto is covered by an extensive network of bus routes. The major ones are shown on a sub-map on the TIC Kyoto map. A much more detailed map (in Japanese only) is available at the bus center in front of Kyoto station. If possible, however, it is advisable to chat to the TIC staff because some of the buses are infrequent. In briefest terms, there are two loop bus lines, 206 and 214. The former goes along Higashi-oji, Kita-oji, and Karasuma streets on the way to and from the station, while the latter uses Kawaramachi, Kita-oji, and Nishi-oji streets. The character following the number tells the direction. A one-day pass for unlimited travel on city buses is available but you might not use it enough to justify the cost. There is also an "11 tickets for the price of 10" deal (ask for *kaisuken*). Both are available at the bus center, and further information can be obtained at the TIC.

Kyoto has a modern subway line running from Kyoto station north along Karasuma-dori (dori = street) to Kita-yama in the north of the city, and south four stops. (The stop before Kita-yama, Kita-oji-dori, is on the northernmost major east-west road.) The Hankyu private railway line (Kyoto–Osaka) intersects it at Shijo-karasuma and provides east-west service via four stations along Shijo-dori. Several JR and private rail lines can be used for transport within Kyoto. These are shown on the TIC map.

Taxis are plentiful. Don't worry about telling the driver your destination; if he doesn't understand your pronunciation, he can read it in Japanese on the TIC map.

Bicycles may be rented at the Bridgestone bike shop on the corner of Muromachi and Shimochoja-machi streets and from a couple of shops near Sanjo station. The TIC will know if any other shops now offer them. The bikes are single-speed clunkers, but most of Kyoto is flat so this is no great problem. A bike is probably best regarded as convenient, rather than economical, for the savings in bus fares might be negligible.

NARA-KEN

The Nara plain was one of the most important areas in the early history of Japan, and the city of Nara was the imperial capital for several years, predating Kyoto. Some structures surviving from that time, plus many relics, make the city a popular destination for visitors. There are also other attractions in the southern parts of the prefecture and the adjoining Kii-hanto peninsula (Mie-ken and Wakayama-ken).

Nara

Usually mentioned in the same breath as Kyoto, Nara is another ancient capital of Japan, only 42 km from Kyoto, and usually included in any tour of the country. It was the first permanent capital of Japan, from 710 to 784, previous to which the capital was moved after the death of each emperor. Nara witnessed the introduction of Buddhism into Japan, with the resulting far-reaching effects on culture and the arts. Amazingly, some of the temples and other structures from that period still stand. Although they were then within the city of Nara, the present city is considerably smaller, and many of them are now some distance out in the country.

Information

The TIC in Kyoto and Kyoto have a useful JNTO pamphlet *Kyoto Nara* that has some sightseeing information to complement the following pages. The JNTO Kyoto-Nara map is quite adequate for sightseeing in Nara city. Ask also for a printed sheet *Walking Tour Courses in Nara*. Finally, the Nara City tourist Information Office is located on the first floor of the Kintetsu-Nara station.

Voluntary Guides

To make your visit more interesting and enjoyable, the Nara YMCA will introduce you to one or more English-speaking Japanese who will act as unpaid guides for sightseeing around Nara. (As in Kyoto, it is reasonably expected that you pay their transport, admittance charges, etc.) A program like this is a superb way to meet everyday Japanese, as distinct from those in the tourist business. During working hours the phone number is (0742) 45-0221; Monday through Saturday. You can also check with the Kyoto TIC.

Things to See

Many of the attractions of Nara are conveniently concentrated in Nara-koen park, and can be seen on foot in less than a day. The following itinerary starts from Kintetsu-Nara station, which is located at the west extremity of the park.

Kofuku-ji

The first temple on this site was built in 710. At one time there were 175 buildings, all of which were subsequently destroyed by fire. The present *kondo* (main hall) dates from 1819. The five-storey pagoda (*gojunoto*) dates from 1426 and is the second-tallest in Japan (about 50 meters). (The smaller, graceful three-storey pagoda nearby to the south, overlooking Sarusawa-no-ike pond, is older, from 1143.) While in the vicinity of Kofuku-ji, look for the stone figures that regularly get doused with water by visiting worshippers. There is also a treasure house (built of nontraditional but safe concrete) on the grounds that has displays of the temple's treasures, mostly Buddhist images.

Here, and elsewhere throughout Nara-koen park, you can see some of the 1000 or so deer that roam at will under government protection. They are adept at cadging handouts and are not shy about pilfering picnic lunches. They are, however, somewhat skittish and shy away if touched. (There are signs in picturesque English warning about danger from bucks in the mating season, and from does with fawns.)

Nara Kokuritsu Hakubutsukan

The Nara National Museum is to the west, on the other side of a wide road and set in some distance among trees. It has a good collection of statues, smaller figures, and other treasures from various temples and other historic sites in the area.

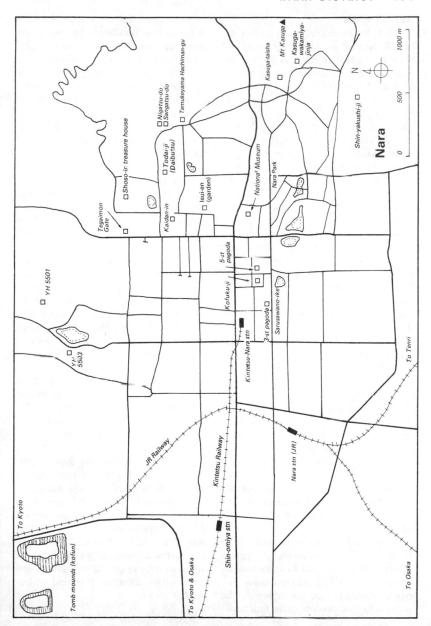

Nara

1000 m

500

0

N

Mt Kasuga ▲

Kasuga-wakamiya-jinja

Kasuga-taisha

Shin-yakushi-ji

Nigatsu-do
Sangatsu-do

Tamukeyama Hachiman-gu

Shoso-in treasure house

Todai-ji (Daibutsu)

National Museum

Nara Park

Isui-en (garden)

Kaidan-in

Tegaimon Gate

YH 5501

YH 5503

5-st pagoda

Kofuku-ji

3-st pagoda

Sarusawano-ike

Kintetsu-Nara stn

To Tenri

JR Railway

Kintetsu Railway

Nara stn (JR)

To Kyoto

Tomb mounds (kofun)

To Kyoto & Osaka

Shin-omiya stn

To Osaka

Isui-en Garden

This is a pleasant and refreshing garden, especially on a hot day when its greenery and water have a cooling effect. A private museum on the grounds exhibits a number of antique art objects of China and Korea.

Todai-ji

This is at the top of the list of places to visit in Nara. The main temple building, Daibutsu-den, houses Japan's largest bronze statue of Buddha. The building itself is the largest wooden structure in the world, even though it is one-third smaller than the original. At the entrance to the temple is Nandaimon (South Great Gate) dating from 1199. The eight-meter tall *Nio-sama* (Deva kings, guardians of Buddhism) are national treasures (like the gate), and among the finest such carvings in Japan. The *koma-inu* (normally symbols found only at Shinto shrines) in the rear niches are also highly regarded. Special biscuits for the deer are on sale in this area—no fools, the deer are also to be found here in the greatest numbers.

Daibutsu-den was built in 1709, the latest in a series from 752; it has recently had extensive renovations. The Daibutsu (Great Buddha) statue in its incense-filled interior was first cast in 749, but subsequent damage in fires has required replacing the head (at least twice), the right hand, and other parts. Possibly as a result of this later work, the statue lacks the artistry and serenity of the Daibutsu at Kamakura (near Tokyo). The statue is 16 meters tall and weighs 437 tonnes. (Further statistics are given on the admittance ticket.)

The two large statues in front of the Daibutsu are Nyoirin-kannon, who grants prayers and wishes, and Kokuzo-bosatsu, who possesses wisdom and happiness. The figure in the left-hand corner behind the statue is Komokuten, one of the four heavenly guardians who destroy all obstacles in the path of Buddhism. Another of the guardians, Tamonten, is found in the right-hand corner—he is trampling a demon.

Kaidan-in is a separate temple west of the Daibutsu-den; it contains clay images of the four heavenly guardians (all national treasures).

Sangatsu-do is the oldest structure of Todai-ji, dating from 733. Many statues of national treasure merit are displayed.

Kasuga-taisha Shrine

One of the best-known places in Nara, Kasuga-taisha is famous for its forested setting and lanterns. There are approximately 3000 lanterns, some of stone and standing as tall as a man, others of bronze and hung from the eaves of the various buildings that make up the shrine. The combination of the lanterns with the bright orange and white of the buildings is very photogenic. Lanterns line nearly all the paths of the shrine grounds, and this is within the area roamed by deer, so one is quite likely to poke its head out between two of them for a very cute picture.

The lanterns are all lit twice a year, on the day of the Setsubun festival (variable: February 2 or 3), and on August 15. The annual festival of the shrine, Kasuga Matsuri, is held on March 13 and features a colorful procession.

In addition to the four shrines (surrounded by a gallery) that make up the main shrine, there is also Kasuga-wakamiya-jinja to the south. Here it may be possible to see kagura (sacred dances) in the Kagura-den, the southern-most of the three buildings. The annual festival of this shrine is the greatest in Nara, and is a procession of large numbers of people in costumes and armor of ancient times. It is held on December 16–17.

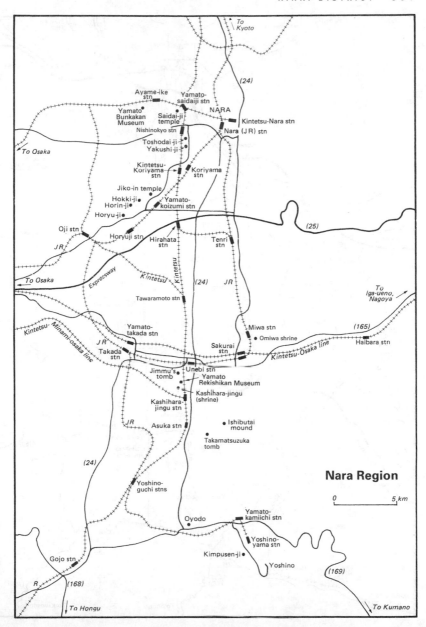

Nara Region

0   5 km

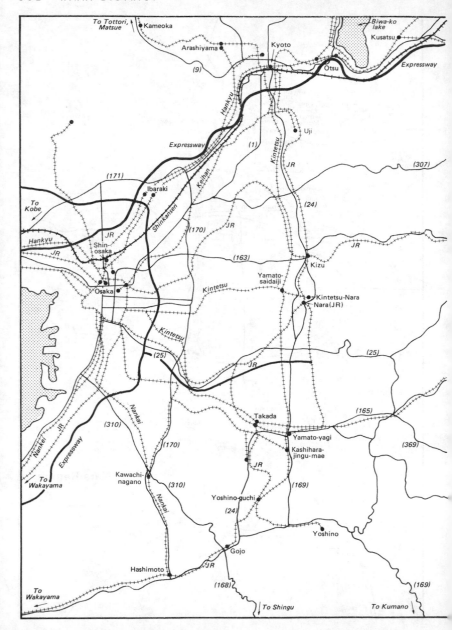

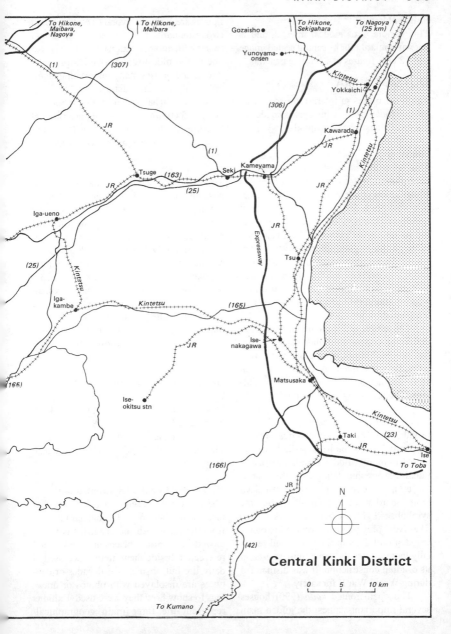

Central Kinki District

Shin-yakushi-ji

This temple is of modest interest, and is known primarily for its central seated image and 12 clay figures of 12 divine generals.

OUTSIDE NARA

The other places of interest are somewhat outside today's city, which gives an idea of the great size of the old capital.

Horyu-ji

This is one of the most important temples in Japanese history, art, and culture. Its construction began in 607 under the direction of Prince Shotoku, one of the great builders of the Japanese state (formerly depicted on the ¥10,000 note). Amazingly, some of the original structures still stand; others were added or rebuilt in later eras. Easiest access is by bus from Kintetsu-Nara station, either directly to Horyu-ji-mae stop, or after a visit to Yakushi-ji and other temples (described below).

The temple is divided into Sai-in Garan and To-in Garan (west and east minsters). Sai-in is now larger, since more of its structures have survived. A leaflet given on entry has a map that identifies the buildings. The following is a brief description.

SAI-IN GARAN Entry is via Nandaimon (South Great Gate), a national treasure dating from 1438 (rebuilt), a walled avenue, then Chumon (Middle Gate), also a national treasure and dating from the year of the temple's construction. The red deva king (guardian of Buddhism) in the gate symbolises light; the black king, darkness. The five-storey pagoda is one of the oldest wooden buildings in the world and reputedly incorporates the same timbers used in its original construction. It was dismantled during World War II for safety.

The open-fronted *kodo* (990) houses several important statues: the gilded main figures are Yakushi-nyorai (2.6 meters) and two attendants (1.7 meters). The *kondo* (main hall, another national treasure) is also one of the oldest wooden buildings in the world, and houses many important images, both sculptures and castings.

Shoryo-in has a statue of Prince Shotoku at age 45 (figure and building are national treasures), while Dai-hozo-den (two concrete buildings) have displays of many treasures of the temple.

TO-IN GARAN Leaving the Sai-in area and passing through Chumon and Todaimon (Middle and East Great Gates), you come to the To-in Garan precincts. The octagonal building in the central rectangle is Yumedono (Hall of Dreams, used by Shotoku for meditation), rated the most beautiful rectangular building in Japan. Dating from 739, it also contains a number of fine images, including several national treasures. There are several other buildings in the grounds, many of which also house historic images. Chugu-ji temple is a former nunnery attached to To-in Garan.

Horin & Hokki Temples

In the vicinity of Horyu-ji are two other historic temples, Horin-ji and Hokki-ji. They date from 621 and 638 respectively, and also house several treasured images. The pagoda at Hokki is believed to date from 685.

Nara-ken Minzoku Hakubutsukan

The Nara-ken Museum of Ethnology features a number of traditional farmhouses from the early 18th century that have been moved from various places in Nara-ken and re-erected. Inside them, items once used in daily life but obsolete for decades or centuries are displayed with photos or drawings to show how they were used. Exhibits represent the three main geographical/

cultural areas of Nara-ken: Nara plain, the Yamato highlands, and the mountains of the Yoshino area. Most interesting are the full-size scenes with life-like models of farmers, lumberjacks, teapickers, and others, all dressed in authentic garb. Some of the dummies were actually dressed by people who still make their living in the way portrayed, so even the underwear is correct!

Access is from Kintetsu-Koriyama station, from where you take a bus to Yoda-higashiyama (15 minutes). It might be possible to go by bus directly from Horyu-ji or Toshidai-ji/Yakushi-ji, so inquire locally.

Yakushi-ji

Constructed on this site in 718 after being moved from elsewhere, this temple has a considerable number of treasured figures, including the first bronze Buddha image made in Japan—the Yakushi-nyorai.

The unusual 34-meter pagoda looks like a six-storey structure, but such buildings always have an odd number of levels; this one has a sub-roof between each "real" roof, and is the only one of its kind in Japan. The pagoda is the only structure of the temple that has survived in its original form; all other buildings are later reconstructions. An excellent English-language booklet is given out on entry and explains the salient points of the temple.

Yakushi-ji may be reached by the bus that goes to Horyu-ji, or from Nishino-kyo station of Kintetsu railway (reached with a change at Yamato-saidai-ji station).

Toshodai-ji

This temple is highly regarded for its architecture and harmonious arrangement of structures. Like the other major temples of Nara, Toshodai-ji also has a number of figures that rate as national treasures. The temple is less than one km north of Yakushi-ji; you can walk or go by bus, but

walking is likely to be quicker.

Places to Stay

Most foreign visitors to Nara probably make it a day trip out of Kyoto. However, anyone wishing to explore the area in greater detail will find a good range of accommodation available, including hotels and *ryokan*. Accommodation can be booked in advance through the TIC in Kyoto or any travel agent in the country (though JTB is the biggest), and help is available at the railway stations in Nara.

There are two youth hostels in Nara, Nara Youth Hostel (tel (0742) 22-1334), and Nara-ken Seishonen-Kaikan Youth Hostel (tel (0742) 22-5540). My experience with the latter was vastly better than the first (a JYH hostel), though time may have removed the officiousness and insistance that both meals be taken there without option that formerly characterized Nara YH.

The latter hostel can be reached by following the main road that passes the Kintetsu station downhill to the north-south road that begins north of where the overpass road ends. Follow it north for a little over a km, turn left, and walk uphill for about five minutes; it will probably be necessary to ask along the way, as there are no clear landmarks. Nara YH is not too far from Kintetsu station.

Getting There

Train service is good between Nara and Kyoto, Osaka, Nagoya, and the Ise/Toba area. Refer to the transportation section at the beginning of this chapter.

Nara Plain Area

Nara city is located near the northern end of the Nara plain, an area that was settled early in the history of the northward movement of the Yamato people from Kyushu on their way to control of the Japanese islands. One legacy of this period (shared with Osaka, which was also an important city in this era), is a large number of tomb mounds or tumuli (*kofun*), possibly showing an ancestral link between the Yamato people and Korea, where tumulus building has long been a tradition. (There are actually nearly 3000 such tombs in Japan, scattered from Kyushu to the Tokyo region, most of them near formerly important defensive settlements.)

These mounds are easily seen beside Route 24 out of Nara en route to Kyoto (tombs of Uwanabe and Konabe, as indicated on the JNTO map, plus an unlabelled one). Others at Asuka kofun, believed to date from the 7th century, were opened only in 1972, and have a number of very colorful murals of Korean and Chinese style. At Unebi, near Kashihara, the Archaeology Museum displays many relics of the late Stone Age and other prehistoric items from the area.

Omiwa-jinja

This is believed to be one of the oldest shrines in Japan. The buildings are scenically located amidst tall trees. It is near Sakurai and accessible from Miwa station.

Koya-san (Northeast Wakayama-ken)

Koya-san is a mountain famous as the center of the Shingon-mikkyo (True Word) sect of Buddhism. On its flat top are more than 120 temples carrying on a tradition from 816 A.D. It is a place of pilgrimage for the faithful, especially for those with family members buried in the extensive cemetery, which is actually one of the most interesting things to see. Koya-san has also become a mountain resort providing an escape from the heat and humidity of the lower areas.

Information

Koya-san is best visited for its symbolic value, being a community of temples. But as an object of architectural study, compared with the beautiful buildings of Kyoto, it is not worth a special trip. The Tokyo TIC distributes a single-page information sheet that gives some more details on Koya-san, although its map is typically not to scale.

Things to See

Buses run from the upper cable-car station into the center of the small community, or you can take a taxi or walk the three km or so into town. The road is lined with tall cedars and leads to the main temple on the west side of the community.

Gobyo

If a bus is available, it is better to go directly to Gobyo. This is the mausoleum of Kobodaishi, the founder of the temples and a great teacher of Shingon, who also devised the *hiragana* syllabary for writing Japanese in a form simpler than *kanji*. From Gobyo there is a very pleasant and peaceful walk through the great cemetery, where tombs and memorials are set amidst a forest of very tall cedar trees. The path leads to Ichinohashi (First Bridge), from

To Hashimoto & Osaka
Gokuraku-bashi stn
Cable car
N
Koya-san
Gobyo mausoleum
Kongobu-ji temple
Daimon gate
Pagoda
Tourist info. office
To Hashimoto
Rte 371

where you can walk through the town and visit any of the large number of temples on the way. There is only one main street, so it is impossible to get lost. At the intersection with the main road is an information office that can supply a map, some literature, and give assistance in finding a room.

Kongobu-ji Temple

Just a short distance beyond the town is Kongobu-ji (Temple of the Diamond Mountain, rebuilt in 1861), the chief temple of the sect and the best one to visit if time is limited.

Other Sights

Nearby (downhill and across the road) is the pagoda Daito, located in a large courtyard, and built in a style uncommon in Japan (rebuilt 1937). The interior features brilliantly colored beams and houses five sacred images of Buddha in different incarnations. Other buildings are the Golden Hall (for ceremonies) and Miedo. (The pamphlet from the information center identifies the buildings.)

Farther along the road below the latter cluster of buildings is Daimon (Great Gate), a large wooden structure from 1705; it is similar to such gates at other old temples. The youth hostel (at Henjosan-ji) is near here.

Places To Stay

There are 53 temples on the mountain that provide accommodation. Most, if not all, have been developed into attractive places to stay, with lovely little gardens. Each of these temples is virtually owned by its abbot, and then inherited by his son (natural or adopted). By charging about double the tariff of most temples elsewhere in Japan (about ¥5000 a night), the abbots have turned them into a very lucrative business, and many are reputedly quite weak in the

theology of their sect. Since wealth is required to advance in the religious hierarchy of the sect, this operation of the temples as money-making ventures is encouraged. (Remember that these comments apply to the Shingon-mikkyo sect. Although there are some other groups that appear to exist more for money-making than for religious purposes, most Buddhist sects are still close to the original tenets of their faith.)

Getting There

The direct route is by Nankai private railway from Namba station (Osaka) to the terminus at Gokuraku-bashi station. From cities such as Kyoto and Nara, you can go via JR to Hashimoto station and change there for the final 21 km by the Nankai line. At the terminus a cable-car runs to the top of Koya-san.

Continuing from Koya-san

From Koya-san you can go west to Wakayama and continue around the Kii-hanto peninsula. From Gojo, Route 168 runs south to Hongu, Shingu, and other attractions of the peninsula (described in the Mie-ken section) covering the more interesting parts of the area.

Three buses daily make the scenic run between Gojo and Shingu, and another two go from Gojo to Hongu.

Yoshino

The view of the cherry blossoms on the side of Yoshino-yama (northeast of Koya-san) is famous throughout Japan. There are about 100,000 cherry trees, and in season the blossoms form a massive blanket of pink stretching a long distance up the slope. Because of the differences in temperature from the top of the mountain to the bottom, the trees mature at different times, so the *sakura* season on Yoshino can last for a couple of weeks.

From Yoshino station of the Kintetsu railway, a nearby cable car rises to the main road that passes through the settled areas of the mountainside. You can then walk or take a taxi to the main temple area.

The mountain has been regarded as sacred for centuries, and is a center of *yamabushi* religious activities. The main temple, Kimpusen-ji, is of this sect; the old wooden gate (*Karamon*) encountered during the climb up the road from the cable car belongs to the temple. Kimpusen-ji is a National Treasure, and its age shows in the weathered timbers and inside pillars. It is reputed to be the second largest wooden building in Japan.

Typical of almost any tourist destination in Japan, the main street is lined with souvenir shops and eating and drinking places. Several of the latter have balconies overlooking the trees on the hillside. The little shop with the giant toad sells Chinese-type traditional medicines.

Partway along this level stretch, just past the small temple with an unusual low pagoda, stands a stone *torii* gate. Pass through through it, on the road downhill, and you come to the most historic place on Yoshino. Sho-in dates from 1336, and was a resort villa used by a number of emperors through the years. It is very famous in Japanese history, although it would be of more interest to students of traditional architecture than to the casual visitor. The small garden is only of passing interest, but near the parking lot there is a lookout offering the best single view over the sea of cherry trees covering the facing mountainside. When the blossoms are at their peak, the sight is magnificent, and explains the popularity of Yoshino for successive emperors.

Near the *torii* gate, the road forks; take the road uphill to Kizo-ji temple, which is now a combination youth hostel and commercial *ryokan* providing accommodation for travellers and pilgrims.

Nearby is Chikurin-in, a villa built by the famous tea master Sen-no-rikyu, who was forced to commit *seppuku* (ritual suicide) for preventing shogun Hideyoshi from taking his daughter as a concubine. The present main building is a highly regarded (and priced) *ryokan* open to the public when not being used by visiting members of the royal family. The beautiful garden behind the *ryokan* should not be missed.

Numerous roads wind their way up and across the Yoshino mountainside, and can be followed into the mass of cherry trees. There are several large maps posted in prominent places in the village.

To the east and south of Yoshino is a heavily-wooded wilderness area that would appeal to hikers. Accessible from the Nara plain side of the mountains is a point on the flank of Mt. Odaigahara (1695 meters) that is the starting point for hikes to Owase (on the east coast of Kii-hanto peninsula) and Doro Gorge to the south. These are both described in the section on Southern Kii-hanto peninsula, along with the rest of the coastal region. (The Odaigahara area is the wettest region of Japan and the mountain top is often fog-bound.)

Getting There

Yoshino station is the terminus of the Kintetsu line from Abeno-bashi station (Osaka); travellers from Kyoto transfer at Kashihara-jingu-mae. You can also go most of the way by JR, changing to the Kintetsu line at Yoshino-guchi.

During many months of the year there are three buses a day to Odaigahara from Nara-Kintetsu station. The bus passes through Yamato-kami-ichi (two stops before Yoshinoyama station). There are also two buses a day between Nara and Kumano (on the southeast coast) which pass Wasabi-dani, the point where the toll road to Odaigahara branches off Route 169; it should be possible to get off there and transfer to the other bus (if schedules match) or hitch the rest of the way.

MIE-KEN ■■■■■■■■■■■■

Mie-ken, east of Nara-ken, is divided by a coastal ridge of mountains. On the Nara side of this ridge is the area around Iga-ueno. Most of the other attractions of Mie-ken are on the coastal side of the mountains. From there you can conveniently travel in a clockwise route around the Kii-hanto peninsula and up the west coast to Wakayama and Osaka as described in the following pages. (The part of Mie-ken adjacent to Nagoya was described immediately after the section on Nagoya.)

Iga-ueno

This small city east of Nara has some unusual history and an attraction almost unique in Japan. (The name simply means "Ueno of the Iga region", to distinguish it from other places called Ueno, which is a common name in Japan.)

Information

A pamphlet on Ueno in quite good English is given out at Ueno castle, and may also be available at the TICs in Kyoto and Tokyo. It also contains information on some other places of lesser interest.

Things to See

Ueno Castle

Ueno has a small but picturesque castle. Although the present building dates from only 1953, it is a reminder of when the rulers of Iga had to defend their fertile lands against neighboring, powerful Kyoto and Yamato. As part of their defences (beginning around the 1200s) they developed the *ninjutsu* art

of stealthy combat to defeat foreign armies in the mountains. *Ninja*, the practitioners, were trained in invisibility, poisons, sabotage, espionage, assassination, and other genteel arts. (*Ninja* are featured in the James Clavell novel *Shogun*, and have become well known in the west through films [that are often quite inaccurate], plus a TV series featuring four testudinata.)

In the grounds of the castle is Ninja-Yashiki (Ninja House), an ordinary-looking building that actually has a number of hidden passages, hiding places, and weapons caches. These are demonstrated frequently during the day for visitors by a lithe, black-dressed young woman.

Elsewhere in the grounds is Ninjutsu Shiryokan, a museum of weapons, clothing, climbing devices, and other ingenious items used by ninja in their work—such as an iron claw that would tear a victim as if by the claw of a bear, armor, and several kinds of throwing weapons. This is one of very few places in Japan with such a large display of items of this black "art". (Another is nearby at Akame 48 Falls, described below.) Ninjutsu is explained well in Stephen Hayes' book *The Ninja and Their Fighting Art* (Tuttle).

Festival

October 23–25: Tenjin Matsuri festival is a 400-year-old Demon Procession. It features more than 100 "demons" in masks and costumes, as well as nine ornate festival wagons, similar to but smaller than those of Kyoto's Gion Matsuri. Masks and other items from the procession are displayed at the museum beside the Ninja-yashiki.

Getting There

The castle is reached by walking up the hill from Ueno-shi station of the Kintetsu line; this can be reached by transferring from the JR Kansai Honsen line at Iga-ueno station, or by branching off the Kintetsu-Osaka line at Iga-kambe. The Kansai line runs between Osaka and Nagoya via Nara, the latter between Osaka and Matsusaka. Both are easily reached from Kyoto and Nara.

Akame 48 Falls

Due south of Iga-ueno is a very pleasant gorge known for its 48 waterfalls (*yonju-hachi taki*). Many are rather small, especially higher up near the source, but the large ones are quite impressive. The riverside walk is a rare way to enjoy nature with no sound but the shrilling cicadas, some birds, and the rushing water. There is a good chance you will see some of the large and very colorful butterflies for which Japan is noted. Higher up the gorge there is an inviting pool.

Just inside the entrance to the park is a very non-descript concrete cage containing some equally non-descript animals; they are giant salamanders, found only in this area.

Before the entrance to the park (on the left going in) is a small building that houses a good (if modest) museum of historic articles used in daily life. Possibly of greater interest is a sizeable collection of *ninja* weapons and devices. If you can't locate the building, ask for "Ninja hakubutsu-kan".

The entrance to the falls ("Akame Taki") is reached easily by bus (12 per day) from Akame-guchi station of the Kintetsu-Osaka line, three stations west of Iga-kambe station (the junction for Ueno city).

Kii Region

The broad peninsula that projects southward between Nagoya and Osaka can be broken into three major areas for sightseeing convenience as well as for "ranking" them in interest. They are: Nara & Area (described above), Shima-hanto & Ise, and Nanki & Southern Kii Peninsula.

"Shima-hanto & Ise" covers the small Shima-hanto peninsula area on the east side of the main peninsula. It is famous for pearl farming, and is the home of Mikimoto pearls. The most important Shinto shrines in Japan are located at Ise. There are also other attractions.

"Nanki & Southern Kii-hanto Peninsula" describes all the rest of the peninsula south of Osaka, Nara-ken, and the Shima-hanto area. It is best known for its natural attractions of mountains, forests, gorges, waterfalls, and rivers, although it is also home to some highly revered shrines. This description is followed by that of Osaka and area.

Shima-hanto & Ise

Shima-hanto (peninsula) and the vicinity of the city of Ise is one of the longest-settled parts of Japan. Passing through the area, one can easily understand its attraction to early settlers. The land is flat and ideal for rice farming, and the climate is the mildest in central-north Japan due to the warm Black Current that passes nearby. It was settled first by the Yamato tribe, which ultimately became the dominant power in Japan. (Quite possibly there were other people in the region originally.) Many legends come from this part of the country regarding the origin of Japan and its people. It is not surprising, therefore, that the most important Shinto shrine of the 80,000 or so around Japan is located here, at the city of Ise.

The other main place of interest around the peninsula is at Toba. It is a shrine of another sort, to the man who put beautiful pearls within the reach of most wallets.

The area is easily reached by train from Nagoya, Nara, Osaka, and Kyoto (as described at the end of this chapter).

Information

The TIC offices have notes for travellers to

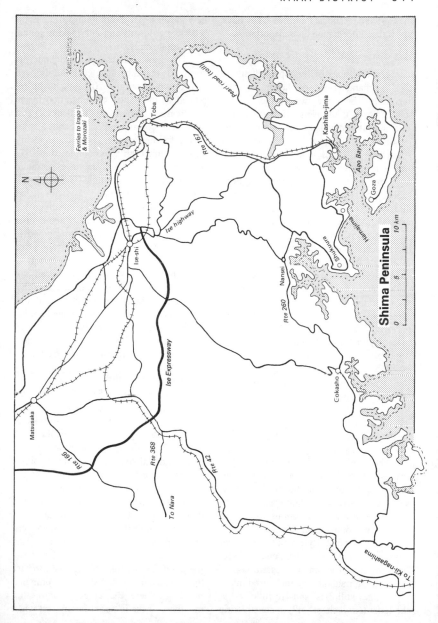

Shima Peninsula

the Ise-Shima National Park area. They have up-to-date information on transportation.

Ise

The grand shrines of Ise represent much that is characteristic of Japan and the Japanese. There are two shrines, Geku (Outer Shrine), and Naiku (Inner Shrine). The latter is somewhat more important, as it honors and is considered the abode of Amaterasu, the sun goddess. Prior to the war, when the emperor was still considered to be divine, it was claimed (and taught in schools) that the Japanese royal family was directly descended from this goddess. By extension, since all Japanese were descended from that family, they therefore had a special place in the world. The claims of divinity have been given up, and Shinto has been disestablished as the state religion (although the shrine is still regarded as the shrine of the royal family and thus of the Japanese), but the old beliefs regarding superiority have been preserved and promoted by a number of right-wing nationalist organizations and people of like mind.

When a memorable event occurs within the royal family, it is still reported here by an emissary, and the prime minister normally makes an annual New Year visit. There are many other ties between the shrine and the royal family and, therefore, the people in general.

The style of the buildings is identical to that used at least as long ago as the 8th century (possibly even further back), and is said to be the style that was used for palaces. Those who are curious about such things can compare the Yuitsu-shimmei-zukuri architectural style with that used for Hongu-taisha at Hongu (Kii Peninsula section) to see if it is similar. Descriptions of the building methods and tools used in ancient times still exist and are followed to the letter (*kanji* character?) in constructing

new shrines. All the buildings are assembled using dowels and interlocking joints; there are no nails.

The most interesting fact about the shrines is that they have customarily been torn down after only 20 years, to be replaced as the center of veneration by an identical set of buildings (220 in all) that have been constructed on adjacent lots reserved for the purpose. The last such reconstruction, the 60th, was completed in 1973 after nine years of work and the expenditure of more than ¥4500 million (U.S. $ 43 million at a 1996 exchange rate). Work has begun on construction of the buildings that will replace the present ones. The old ones will then be torn down and the wood in them distributed to shrines around the country. (One wonders how long this practice can continue into the future because of the high building costs plus the fact that building methods are changing and few young carpenters want to bother learning the traditional, specialized skills.)

Geku is located in Ise-shi (city) and Naiku is six km away, outside the city.

Geku (Outer Shrine)

Geku shrine is located within 15 minutes walk of the two stations (JR and Kintetsu lines). It honors Toyouke-no-omikami, Goddess of agriculture. Like those of Naiku, the buildings of Geku are built in the traditional style dating from the times before Chinese influence swept over the country. The shrine dates from 478 A.D. Also, like Naiku, the grounds are covered with magnificent, tall, ancient cedars.

The main entrance is easily seen from the road. You follow the path under two *torii* (gates) and past the large Magatama-ike pond. To the right of the first *torii* are the Anzaisho and Sanshido, a combined building where the emperor and other members of the imperial family rest when

Geku shrine

North Entrance

Main Entrance

1
2 3
6   5
4
Magatama-ike pond

Tsuchi-no-miya shrine
Kaze-no-miya shrine
Taka-no-miya shrine

the Shinto pantheon. The importance of the sun in Japanese history/mythology can be appreciated a little more by recalling that the name of Japan in Japanese is *Nippon* (or *Nihon*), which means "origin of the sun".

The shrine grounds are entered by crossing Isuzu-kawa river by Uji bridge, a picturesque structure. From here the faithful follow one of several paths to the riverside, where they wash their hands and rinse their mouths as purification. The many tall cedars on the grounds give a peaceful mood, and the size of the grounds (over 66 hectares) swallows up the large number of people who visit.

The usual route takes visitors through the first and second *torii*, past the Kagura-den (hall of sacred dances) and on to the main shrine Shoden. As with Geku, four rows of fences block a large part of the view of the buildings—after all, a lady (especially a goddess) needs her privacy. Photos toward the shrine building are prohibited, and it is customary for men to remove hats and overcoats.

Again the style of architecture is ancient and severely simple, with thatched roofs. Beside the shrine is the open space where the previous shrine stood until 1973, when the present buildings were finished and consecrated, and the goddess (along with her belongings) moved into her new quarters amidst very solemn ceremony. The accompanying map will be valid at least until 1993 (and any difference if new buildings are constructed would be negligible).

On the same compound with the Shoden (main hall) are two treasure houses, Tohoden and Saihoden (East and West Treasuries), in which are housed about 2500 treasures of the shrine—fine clothing, lacquerware, swords, etc. These are made anew each time along with the buildings, and represent the finest of craftsmanship in the

visiting. Just past the second *torii* is the Kagura-den, where performances of sacred dances are presented (fairly frequently).

A bridge to the left leads to the shrines Kaze-no-miya, Tsuchi-no-miya and Takano-miya. Continuing straight on leads to the main shrine. The architecture of the buildings is severely plain—unpainted, fine, hinoki (cypress) wood, with a thatched roof—but four fences surround the buildings and block much of the view from ordinary eyes; only members of the imperial family and their envoys are permitted beyond the Tonotamagaki gate.

The sightseeing is far from spectacular. You should enjoy/appreciate the mood and atmosphere of the wooded grounds and take it for what it is, one of the two most sacred shrines in the country. Don't spend too long here, as there is still Naiku, the inner shrine, to visit, and it is the more important of the two.

Naiku (Inner Shrine)

Naiku is easily reached from Geku by the regular bus that runs between the two shrines. The bus stop is "Naiku-mae".

Naiku is the sacred home of Amaterasu, the sun goddess, the highest deity in

Legend for both maps
1 Shoden (main hall)
2 Saihoden (west treasure hall)
3 Tohoden (east treasure hall)
4 First *torii*
5 Second *torii*
6 Kagura-den (sacred dance hall)

Naiku shrine

Aramatsuri-no-miya shrine

Isuzu-gawa river

Kazahinomi-no-miya shrine

best Japanese tradition. In previous times these were destroyed when the new shrines were opened. But today, because of the great value of these objects as representations of the work of perhaps the last generations who were part of the "old ways", they are preserved and displayed at Chokokan, the museum of the history of the shrine.

Included among the treasures in the two treasure buildings (not on display) is the sacred mirror, one of the three sacred treasures of the imperial throne. The others are the sword and jewel. (The sword was lost in the battle of Dan-no-ura in Kanmon Strait (Shimonoseki). The jewel is kept in Tokyo.)

A news item stated that some antique rickshaws (*jinriki-sha*) were being operated at the shrines (entrances). If you wish to try one, keep your eyes open. Proceeds are for charity.

Ise to Toba

There are two main routes to Toba, Ise-shima Skyline, and Route 167/railway.

Ise-shima Skyline

From a point near Naiku, a toll road runs along and over a ridge of the Asama mountains to Toba-shi (city). The scenery is pretty, with distant views of the water and the indented coast (though it is not worth a special trip from elsewhere just to partake of the view). At the top of the ridge is Kongoshoji temple. Two buses an hour make the trip from Naiku to Toba station, the last in mid-afternoon.

Route 167/Railway

Travellers by Route 167 or JR from Ise to Toba might want to stop for a look at a sight dear to the hearts of the Japanese, Futami-ga-ura. This is a pair of rocks that jut out of the sea close to each other, not far from shore. In keeping with the traditional Japanese view of nature as representations of *kami* (spirits/gods), or other "semi-animate" objects, the rocks have been regarded as male and female (exactly in the same manner as assigning gender to most or all mountains in the country). More specifically, they are likened to Izanagi and Izanami, the founders of Japan (in mythology at least), who are honored yearly by National Foundation Day, a national holiday.

Being male and female, and the parents of the country, what could be more natural than for them to be married? So, a couple they are (their name, *meoto-iwa*, means "wedded rocks"), joined by thick ropes of twisted and braided straw of the type used to make the *shimenawa* rope strung between the uprights of many torii after the harvest season. The ropes are replaced every January 5 in a colorful ceremony.

Near the rocks is an aquarium, Sea Lion House, and Marine House where women divers give demonstrations. There is a Youth Hostel (Taiko-ji; 4404) that is also a temple, not far from the rocks (tel. (05964) 3-2283).

The rocks are about a km from Futami-no-ura station (JR). Buses from the station, as well as from Toba, Ise-shi, Uji-yamada, Naiku, and Geku go close to the stretch of beach (Futami-ga-ura), sea wall, and hotels that preceed the short walkway around the base of the cliffs to the lookout near the rocks.

Toba

Toba is famous as the place where the cultivation of pearls was perfected. The Toba area is still one of the most important pearl farming areas of Japan.

Mikimoto Pearl Island

Until Kokichi Mikimoto began his research in the late 1800s, the only pearls were accidents of nature. If a grain of sand or other foreign material happened to find its way into the shell and irritate the oyster, the irritant would be covered with layers of nacre, forming a pearl. Mikimoto reasoned that it should be possible to introduce such an irritant artificially, so he began experimenting in 1888. By 1893 he had succeeded in producing a pearl, though it was not spherical, and by 1905 had succeeded completely.

Since then his company has continued to grow, and his name is well known around the world. (He died in 1954.) Always dedicated to top quality, and a bit of a showman, Mikimoto once burned hundreds of kilos of pearls of inferior quality that he had rejected, but which (as he let be known) his competitors would have sold. (Such pearls are now used to decorate items of lesser value, like ashtrays.)

Tatoku-shima island, where he performed his experiments, is now the site of a very interesting museum where all stages of producing cultured pearls are shown, both as a static display of photos and materials (with flawless English text), and exhibitions by young women of how they insert the irritant, remove a pearl from an oyster, match pearls by color and size, then drill and string them. Also on display are some fabulously valuable displays utilising pearls, such as a small scale model of the Liberty Bell in solid silver (16.9 kg), with 336 diamonds and 12,250 pearls.

The complete process of making pearls begins with a pearl oyster, of large enough

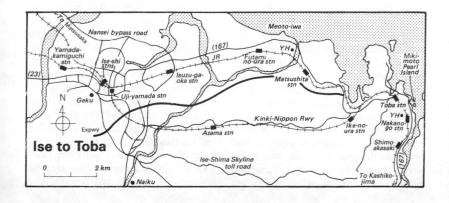

Ise to Toba

0   2 km

size and usually about two years of age. Its shell is pried open, an incision is made in its body, and two spheres about six mm in diameter (the irritant) are introduced into the wound. For collectors of trivia, the irritant is made from the pig toe shell, a variety found along the Mississippi River (the substance that Mikimoto found to be the best after trying thousands of materials). Along with the two spheres, a small piece of tissue about a mm square, from the body of another oyster, is introduced. This piece is cut from the band of tissue at the juncture between the body of the oyster and its shell, the tissue that excretes the nacre that deposits as Mother of Pearl. The oyster "adopts" this and uses it to coat the irritant with layer after layer of nacre. By this method, one oyster can be used to produce two pearls.

The oysters are suspended in special racks hung below rafts in the sea; these rafts can be seen in Ago Bay and other sheltered bodies of water in the region, where the temperature and other conditions are ideal. The nearby Black Current guarantees a plentiful supply of plankton, the food on which oysters thrive.

The racks are pulled up four to six times a year and the shells are cleaned of marine growths, then they are lowered again. After about three years they are lifted out a last time and the pearls are taken out, sorted to remove imperfections and odd shapes, classified by color, then drilled and strung. The range of colors is quite amazing to anyone who is not familiar with pearls, going from pink and gold through silver to a distinct blue tint.

Only about 50% of oysters produce pearls after all that effort, and only about 5% of these are suitable as gems. In past years, the lifespan of oysters was six to seven years, with the irritant being implanted at age two, but pollution is raising its ugly head these days, and the pearls must now be harvested after only two to three years in the water instead of four to five years as before. The quality of the pearls is also said to be slipping.

There is, if it needs to be said, absolutely no difference in composition between cultured and naturally-occurring pearls; the former just increases the harvest and guarantees consistent quality.

Where do the oysters come from? They grow on trees. When females are spawning, they release thousands of larvae into the water, to come to rest where they may. Trees are lowered into the water and, with luck, larvae will cling to the branches. After two to three months the trees are raised and the small oysters transferred to a better place where they can grow to sufficient maturity to allow the irritant implantation.

Every 40 minutes there is a display of women divers. Similar divers and the floating round baskets into which they drop their catch may be seen in action near Toba and in nearby sheltered bays and coves, like Ago Bay, and in waters in many other parts of Japan. There are still about 3500 nationwide, though this is only half the number of a few years ago. (It is a hard way to make a living, and the younger generation mostly is not interested.) They are noted for the peculiar whistling sound they make when when they breathe.

There is much nonsense written about these white-clothed divers. They do not dive for pearls, and publications and tour pamphlets that repeatedly refer to them as "women pearl divers" are misleading their readers (Business is business. . . .). Before Mikimoto's successful experimentation their ancestors *did* dive for the gems of the sea, but they could not make a living at it today. The whole idea of cultivating pearls is to sidestep the hit-or-miss (mostly miss) business of looking for natural pearls. Also, natural pearls are often misshapen and/or discolored, while cultivating them gives a good yield of nearly-perfect spherical ones.

What the women *do* dive for is seafood: shellfish (such as abalone), octopus, and edible seaweed. Any pearl oysters that they find are a bonus, and can be used to grow pearls by implantation of a nucleus.

Other Attractions of Toba

The aquarium at Toba is considered one of the best in Japan. Other related attractions are Dolphin Island (Iruka-jima) and the marine museum (Burajiru-maru).

Getting There

There are regular boat excursions out of Toba to nearby islands, including Kamishima, scene of Mishima's story *Sound of Waves*.

There is a ferry service across the bay to Irako at the tip of Atsuma-hanto peninsula (at least 13 times daily), as well as to Gamagori on the "mainland" between the peninsulas (at least six a day); these places are all on the east side of the bay, below Nagoya, and offer a convenient way to bypass that city if you're planning to travel to Tokyo via the south coast (though this is the least desirable or interesting way to get to Tokyo; inland routes via the Kiso or Tenryu river valleys (Chubu region), or a roundabout route via the Noto peninsula, would be much more interesting.)

Ago Bay

This bay, incredibly indented, and sheltered from the ocean tumult, offers the beauties of nature and the finest scenery of the Shima-hanto peninsula. A common sight is the numerous rafts from which pearl oysters are suspended in the water. They should not be confused with the even rows of poles protruding from the water near the shore; these have nets strung horizontally

among them on which edible seaweed grows. Ago Bay is ideal for pearl oysters because the water temperature is always between 17° and 22° C and there is plenty of food.

Kashikojima

This is the main town on Ago Bay. From it, sightseeing boats leave regularly on excursions that circle the bay. It would be a good way for a closer look at the rafts, and there is a good chance of seeing *ama* (women divers) at work. Near Kashikojima station is Shima Marineland, which houses an aquarium.

Goza

This town affords a good view, from Kompira-san hill, of both the Pacific Ocean and Ago Bay. It can be reached from Kashikojima by boat or by bus.

Places to Stay

There is a youth hostel at Isobe (not far from Kashikojima), Ise-shima YH (tel (05995) 5-0226). It sits on a hill, giving a good view over a smaller bay. However, it is a JYH hostel, and has some of the less-than-favorable characteristics of one, particularly since the housefather is a regional Youth Hostel Association executive. The biggest drawback of the place is that the rooms are almost hermetically sealed and are very stuffy, a shame because it is so close to all that fine sea air.

SOUTHERN KII PENINSULA (NANKI)

Most travellers who plan to continue from the Ago Bay area to detinations in the Nanki (Southern Kii region) like Shingu by road (hitching or own transportation) would find it preferable to backtrack to Ise and beyond to connect with Route 42 (or railway) rather than following Route 260 along the coast. Few roads in a civilized country require more time to travel a given distance than this one. It winds in, out, up, down, over, and around every combination of cape, ridge, hill, crest, valley, and promontory imaginable. The scenery is pleasant, for it passes through fishing villages and coves of pearl rafts or seaweed "frames", but it tends to quickly become variations on a theme rather than new melodies. From the youth hostel at Isobe I followed the road by motorcycle for what seemed like hours and only reached Shukuura, a relatively short distance down the coast, at which point I turned back to Ise and went around it.

The Kii Peninsula (Kii-hanto) is still relatively unpopulated due to its mountainous terrain. Two areas have been combined into a national park, the forest lands named for Yoshino, and the sea coast area, named after Kumano. Yoshino itself is in Nara-ken and is covered in the section on that part of

the country (earlier in this chapter).

The Japanese way of treating this area for tourist publicity purposes is a little frustrating. Mie-ken extends almost to Shingu, so literature issued by Mie-ken covers much of the southeast coast, but not Shingu, while Wakayama-ken literature describes Shingu and the rest of the southeast coast and all the southwest coast (but not the Mie area). This isn't of much use to travellers who are trying to see the whole region and who might have been able to obtain only one lot of literature. The following pages cover the Kii Peninsula in what seems like a logical manner, beginning in the east from above Owase, and going west around to Wakayama, taking in inland areas conveniently reached from the coast.

Places to Stay

As in all parts of Japan that are popular

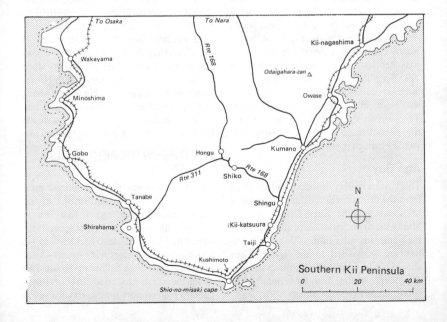

with tourists, there are accommodation facilities everywhere, including hotels, *ryokan*, *minshuku*, and youth hostels. Some hostel locations have been mentioned.

Getting Around Nanki Region

JR tracks loop around the outside of the entire Nanki region from Nagoya to Osaka, as well as branching off to Toba. The Kintetsu-Nippon line runs from Nagoya to Kashikojima in the Shima-hanto peninsula. There are many local bus services. The northern part of the peninsula is intensively served by a number of railway lines, as detailed early in the chapter.

SOUTHERN MIE-KEN ▬▬▬

Osugi-dani

Inland from a point 10 km or so above Owase (just a short distance below Funa station), a road leads inland to Osugi-dani, considered one of the grandest valleys in Japan. A publicity photo shows a very pretty series of cascades and pools and a rustic suspension bridge.

The valley leads close to Mt. Odaigahara, a mountain much more easily reached from Yoshino (and described in more detail in the section on Nara-ken). There are trails in the area between Odaigahara and Owase (32 km), and to Doro-kyo gorge (described below). Serious hikers can obtain more detailed information on the spot.

There is no scheduled transport in to Osugi-dani, and keep in mind that Odaigahara has the greatest rainfall of any area in Japan.

Owase

The town is an important fishing center, but of limited touristic interest. Along the shore of Owase Bay are rock formations of columnar basalt, similar (though smaller) to those of Land's End in Britain.

Kumano

The attractions of Kumano ("Bear Field") are the sea and cliffs. Two popular sights are Oniga-jo ("Ogre's Castle"), a large chamber in the cliffs. Near it the rock has been weathered to an unusual texture, slightly resembling the exterior of the brain. It is about a km east of the station, along the coast.

In the opposite direction, also along the coast, is a rock formation known as Shishi-iwa ("Lion Rock") because of its resemblance to a lion.

Kumano is the starting point for a trip by raft through the rapids of the scenic Doro-kyo gorge. Sightseeing information for the gorge, including this trip from Kumano, is given in the description of the area around Hongu, next.

Owase

Owase
—Kumano

N

Rte 311

Rte 42

Odomari stn

Kumano

Kumano-shi stn

Onigajo

Shishi-iwa

5 km

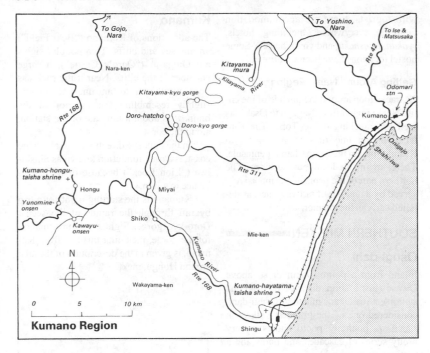

Kumano Region

WAKAYAMA-KEN ▰▰▰▰▰

Shingu

The name Shingu ("New Shrine") reveals Shingu's main attraction, Kumano-haya-tama-taisha (shrine), one of the three main shrines of the Kii-hanto peninsula. the others are at Hongu and Nachi. Unlike the weathered buildings of Hongu, those of Shingu are of more recent "tradition" and are brighter and more colorful. Its festival is on October 15.

Inland from Shingu

A short distance inland, up the valley of the Kumano River, are Hongu and Doro-kyo gorge. Between Shingu and Hongu the road passes through the Kumano-gawa valley.

The pretty, relatively-unspoiled scenery makes the trip enjoyable. Hills rise on both sides of the valley, and the water of the river is a beautiful emerald or jade green. In seasons of heavy rainfall, like the September–October typhoon season, several waterfalls thunder close to the road or can be seen clearly nearby.

Buses run from Shingu station to Hongu (70 minutes) and on to Gojo (4-3/4 hours).

Hongu

Hongu, which means "Main Shrine", is the most important of the three great shrines of Kii. Nearby are a couple of typical mountain hot spring resorts with *rotemburo* (open-air hot spring baths).

The areas near the Kii Peninsula were

settled early in Japanese history, and the mountains of the peninsula appealed to the religious feelings of the people. The early folk religion, the predecessor of Shinto ("Way of the Gods"), was animistic in nature, closely related to similar beliefs still found in Korea and in many other regions of Asia. The mountains, valleys, forests, rocks—in fact all of nature—appeared to be a special habitat of the gods, and were areas of special veneration 15 to 20 centuries ago. With the advent of Buddhism in Japan, the beliefs and form of worship changed somewhat as the people accepted the idea (promoted by Buddhist teachers in the manner used also by Christianity and other religions to make their new message acceptable) that their old religion was an earlier manifestation of the new one, and that the gods were manifestations of the Buddha. This culminated in the development of Shugendo. *Yamabushi* (pilgrims) of this belief may be seen here (as well as at areas like Haguro-san (near Tsuruoka) and elsewhere in Tohoku), dressed in white with unusual (and hard to describe) "ornaments", perhaps ringing bells as they proceed. Such *yamabushi* indulge in ascetic practices, like bathing under icy mountain waterfalls and other forms of corporal mortification. More information is included in the section on Tohoku.

The main shrine is at Hongu and is set in wooded land near the town of the same name. The present buildings are quite large and have a natural weathered color. Their architectural style is an uncommon form used in the early 10th century for palaces. Its festival is April 15.

Access is via a long path attractively lined with tall cedars. This is not too far from the wettest place in Japan, so lush greenery can be expected. In other areas of the Kii Peninsula there are still virgin forests with some trees 600 to 1000 years old. The name "Kii" is a contraction of *Ki-no-kuni*, or "country of trees".

Yunomine

In past days, *yamabushi* pilgrims included bathing in the hot springs of Yunomine as part of their devotions. These days it is more like a typical onsen, with visitors who indulge in the hot water for the same reasons as elsewhere, for health and pleasure. Along with hotels (large and small), and their private baths, there is also a *rotemburo*, a natural hot spring pool in the middle of the stream, surrounded by a simple wooden fence and an equally simple (and quite traditional) bathhouse.

Kawayu

This is another hot spring resort town. It also has a *rotemburo* open to all comers. There is a youth hostel (5612) here.

Doro-kyo Gorge

This gorge on the Kitayama-gawa river is considered the finest in Japan. Cliffs rise 50 meters vertically from the green water, nature-sculpted rocks decorate the way, and in June azaleas and rhododendrons bloom on the cliff faces. The gorge stretches several km along the river, with alternating rapids and wide, calm areas. The three major sections are Oku ("inner") doro, Kami ("upper") doro, and Doro-hatcho. Shimo-doro ("lower Doro") is the entrance and not so noteworthy. Doro-hatcho means "eight cho", signifying eight cho of tranquil water, a "cho" being an old measurement of 109 meters.

There are three ways to see the gorge. First, from the road through the valley, long glass-roofed boats leave from docks behind a building resembling a restaurant (which it is), and go as far upstream as Kami-doro. The day I went to the area (in mid-September), the river was swollen from heavy rains and boat trips were suspended. There are several trips a day, from 0800 to early afternoon. The trip up takes 50 minutes, there is a 20 minute rest, and the return takes 45 minutes. (Be sure to check with the TIC in Kyoto or Tokyo to ensure that these boats are in operation before making a trip there.)

The boat terminal can be reached by bus from Shingu station in 30 minutes, or from Kawayu-onsen in 20. The four buses a day from the latter are timed to meet a departure. Further information is available at the youth hostel.

Second, if you have your own transportation, you can see part of the gorge by taking the road to Doro-hatcho. Maps indicate future road construction to link this point with Kitayama-mura. An offshoot to join Route 311 to Kumano is also likely, but the completion date is uncertain.

The third way has been in operation for several years, so is likely to continue. It is a ride through all the rapids on a long, narrow 20-man raft. Rides are exciting, requiring "wettable" clothing because of frequent spray. Rides begin at Kitayama-mura, a village accessible from Kumano station by a once-a-day bus to Shima-oi, plus a minibus ride from there to the starting point. The ride lasts three hours, ending at Miyai, not far from the boat terminal, and costs about ¥5000. The contact telephone number is (073549) 2331, in Japanese. The TIC in Kyoto should know if this is still running.

Along the Coast

Between Shingu and Nachi-katsuura, the next major center along the coast, is the Nachi-katsuura terminal for regular long-distance ferry services to Tokyo and Kochi (on the island of Shikoku).

Schedule information is given in the general "Transportation" section early in the book.

The terminal ("ferry noriba") is close to Usui station, above Nachi. There are 12 trains a day between the two places, but note that the ferry leaves for Tokyo hours after the last train.

Nachi-katsuura

This is the collective name for the district between Nachi and Kii-katsuura; both are station names. The several attractions of the area give it the most concentrated sightseeing of the southern part of the peninsula.

Places to Stay

There are youth hostels at Nachi, Katsuura, and Taiji.

Nachi-taki

The highpoint of the Nachi area is the 130 meter high Nachi-taki waterfall—one of the deepest plunges in Japan. The falls are reached by taking a short bus ride from Nachi station. From the stop, the falls are reached after a brief and and enjoyable walk down steps, between rows of tall and very old cedars.

Nachi-taisha Shrine

Beside the falls and located there from ancient times because of its obvious strong connection with the Shinto spirit world, is Nachi-taisha (shrine), one of the three great shrines of the Kii area. It was founded in the 4th century. Its festivals are January 1–7 and July 14.

Seiganto-ji

Immediately beside Nachi-taisha is the temple Seiganto-ji.

Myoho-ji Temple

At the top of the twisty toll road is the temple Myoho-ji.

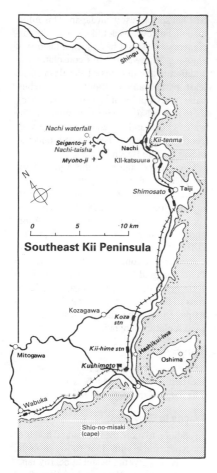

Southeast Kii Peninsula

bling a camel in silhouette, while others come in a variety of other pine-covered shapes. A good lookout point is from the narrow peninsula on which Katsuura-onsen is located.

Taiji

Taiji has been the center of the whaling industry in the Kumano district. On a small peninsula a little more than a km from Taiji station, five minutes by bus, is Kujirahama-koen (Whale Beach Park). Its main attraction is Geirui Hakubutsukan (Whale Museum), which has displays of articles associated with this now-criticized industry. As well, there are some full-size "reproductions" of whales to show their immense size. Unfortunately, Japan is one of the few countries still hunting these behemoths of the deep, though these days "only" for "research" purposes.

Kushimoto

This city is located at the base of the peninsula, and is the entrance to the Shio-no-misaki cape. A short distance northeast of the city, and a little closer to Kii-hime station, is the unusual rock formation Hashi-kui-iwa, a row of about 30 large rocks, spaced quite regularly in a line and stretching into the sea. They do resemble what their name means, "bridge pillars". Other writers have likened them to a procession of hooded medieval monks.

Kozagawa-kyo

Inland a short distance from Kushimoto is a pretty gorge, Kozagawa-kyo. The Kozagawa river has eroded the rocks of its bed and flanks into interesting shapes and textures. Much of the rock was apparently formed with trapped bubbles; the water has removed the solid surface, leaving a strange perforated appearance.

Kii-katsuura

From a place near Kii-katsuura station you can take a boat ride around a group of pine-covered islands called Kii-no-matsushima. The name implies a comparison with the "real" Matsushima near Sendai, one of the scenic "big three" that are supposed to send the Japanese into fits of ecstasy. The ones at Kii are also scenic, one islet being perforated, another (visible from shore) resembling

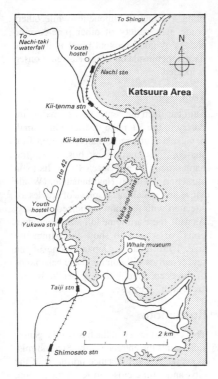

Katsuura Area

best hot spring resorts in Japan. This information, however, is not likely to excite foreigners who do not have such a history of enjoying "the waters". As consolation, in addition to the delights of the flesh (or at least partial amelioration of the aches, pains, and troubles of corporeal existence), there are also scenic pleasures at the water's edge and the enjoyment of a very good white sand beach; "Shirahama" means "White Beach".

A short distance to the north of the beach is the islet of Engetsu-to ("Round Moon Island"), known for the hole in its middle. South of the beach are the layers of rock "plates" of the Senjojiki formation, and just around the promontory are the cliffs of Sandanpeki. The seascapes are considered among the best on the Kii Peninsula, and there is a good view from Heisogen hill, behind the town. A cable car runs to the 130-meter summit from Shirahama. During the summer festival, large sand sculptures are built on the beach.

Tanabe

There are several beaches near this port city, the best-known of which is Ogigahama. The name of the station is Kii-tanabe.

Places to Stay

In addition to more than a hundred hotels of all types, some with floor shows at night, there is also a youth hostel at nearby tanabe, very close to Kii-tanabe station (third stop from Shirahama station).

Minabe

In late January to mid-February, Minabe-gawa-mura is a popular destination for tourists who flock to see the huge groves of plum trees (about 300,000) on the surrounding hills and valleys. They are a couple of km inland from the station; buses are available from the station.

The road through the gorge turns off Route 42 at Koza, and the gorge begins shortly after, at Taka-ike ("High Pond"). It continues for 15 km to Mito-gawa, from where a local road returns to the coast while the "main" road continues some distance inland before rejoining Route 42.

Northwest from Kushimoto along the southwest coast there are pleasant views from both the road and train, although there are not as many identifiable attractions as there are on the south-east coast.

Shirahama

Along with Atami and Beppu, this is regarded by the Japanese as one of the three

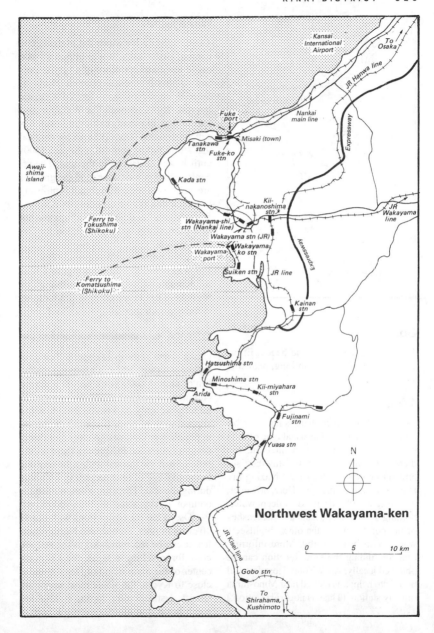

Northwest Wakayama-ken

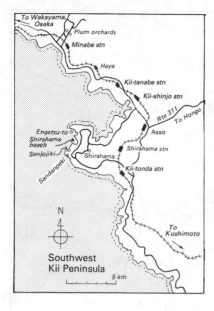

To Wakayama, Osaka
Plum orchards
Minabe stn
Haya
Kii-tanabe stn
Kii-shinjo stn
Rte 311
To Hongu
Engetsu-to
Shirahama beach
Senjojiki
Asso
Shirahama
Shirahama stn
Kii-tonda stn
Sandanpeki
N
To Kushimoto
Southwest Kii Peninsula
5 km

Gobo

There is a good white sand beach, Enju-ga-hama, about half a km long, near this small city.

Arida

On Arida-kawa river, there is nightly *ukai* (cormorant fishing). The usual type of ukai is described in the section on Gifu, but there is a difference here. Usually the fishermen ride in boats that have a blazing fire in an iron grate at the bow. Here, however, the fisherman wade in knee-deep water, holding a torch in one hand and the leashes of the cormorants in the other. Sightseers watch from boats nearby. More information for finding the exact location can be obtained locally. Arida Youth Hostel would be able to help; it is located near Minoshima railway station. (There is no Arida station.)

Wakayama

This is the city for which the prefecture is named. Historically, it was important as a castle town and residence of a very important *daimyo*. It is now a commercial and industrial center of very limited touristic interest. Its "trademark" is Wakayama-jo (castle) but, like many castles in Japan, it is a reconstruction (from 1958) of the original that stood on the spot from the late 1500s until it was destroyed in the war. The reconstruction is well done, and the grounds are an oasis of tranquility, but it is probably best regarded as an escape for city residents from their rather drab surroundings and not as a particularly special attraction for foreign visitors.

From ports near Wakayama (Fuke-ko and Wakayama-ko) there are regular ferries to Komatsushima and Tokushima on Shikoku. Details are given in the write-up in the Shikoku section.

OSAKA

Osaka is one of the most important cities in Japanese history, and was a thriving trading center almost 2000 years ago. It is now a commercial and industrial city, second in importance only to Tokyo, though it has slipped to third place (behind Yokohama) in population. Despite its history as a power center (as narrated in *Shogun*), there is very little of historic interest within the city due to the passage of time and heavy bombing during the war. There are a few attractions north of the city, across the Shin-yodo River.

Osaka has air connections with nearly 40 cities in Asia, Europe, and North America. It can be recommended as the starting point for travelling in Japan, for it is in the center of the main island of Honshu and is close to Kyoto, the single most important tourist destination in Japan. It also has much better and more convenient internal air connections than Narita (Tokyo). Osaka is a hub of train services, so it is easy to travel in any direction; there are also inter-city bus services and long-distance ferries to several cities.

Transportation within the Kinki district is covered at the beginning of the Kinki chapter. Major intercity services are described in the major Transportation section early in the book.

Information

At Osaka station there are two information offices, one at the front of the station, and one at the rear. The front one is more likely to have pamphlets. If out of stock, they should be able to refer you to the Osaka city information office. One of the offices should also be able to help with finding accommodation. There is a large-scale map of Osaka on the back of the JNTO map of Japan, available at the TICs in Tokyo and Kyoto as well as overseas JNTO offices.

A lavish publication simply called *Osaka*, of 48 glossy color pages, has been distributed at the Tokyo TIC, and should also be available at the Kyoto TIC and one of the offices in Osaka station. It is published by the Osaka government, and does an excellent job of making a silk purse out of what is generally regarded as a pig's ear of a city.

Home Visit

You can arrange a visit to the home of a Japanese family for a couple of hours in the evening. (For more details see the introductory section of this book.) A day or more is usually required to arrange a visit although, if you are in Osaka for only a short time, you might be able to arrange it on a same-day basis if you start early in the day. Contact Osaka Tourist Association (tel 261-3948) or Osaka Tourist Information Office (345-2189).

Things to See

Osaka is primarily a business city. Its day of political greatness and power is long past, and what relics were left from ancient times were obliterated during the war. Osaka was reconstructed with little plan other than for commerce, and with a notable lack of park space, even by Japanese standards (which are already lamentably low by western standards). The following section gives information on the few attractions that are definitely worth seeing because they are unique or at least uncommon elsewhere in Japan. The booklets *Your Guide To Osaka* and *Osaka* give information on everything there is to see in the city.

Osaka Castle

The original castle was destroyed long ago. In 1931 a reproduction was built, in concrete, so it preserves a similar exterior (though not interior, which even has elevators!) and gives an impression of its historic appearance. This was once the mightiest fortress in Japan (though it *was* captured in battle) and the huge foundation stones and gates (some original) testify to its former strength. The municipal museum is in the castle grounds.

From Osaka station, it is most easily reached by bus 2 (but check with the information center to verify this route number). Because it is a reconstruction, the castle is of limited historical interest; the finest castle in Japan is only an hour away, at Himeji, so a visit there can obviously be recommended much more strongly.

Sumiyoshi-taisha Shrine

This was the only historic structure to survive the war. It is believed to date from 202 A.D., though the present four main buildings (all national treasures) are from 1810. Their architectural style is unique; the

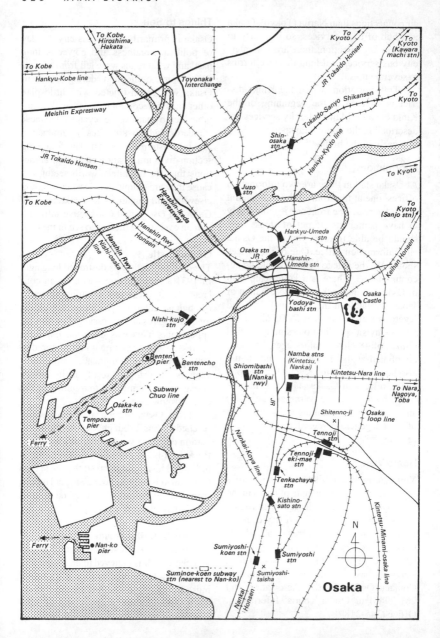

Osaka

roofs, for example, are not tiled, but covered with multiple layers of thin strips of wood. The grounds have many picturesque lanterns that have been donated by seamen, and an arched stone bridge.

The shrine can be reached easily from Sumiyoshi-koen station of the Nankai Honsen private line (main line) out of Nankai-Namba station. This line can be transferred to from the Nankai shuttle line out of Tennoji at Tengachaya, or from the Nankai-koya-sen line (out of Shiomibashi station, near Sakuragawa station of the Sennichi-mae subway line) at Kishinosato.

Shitenno-ji

Often mentioned as an attraction of Osaka, this temple was totally destroyed during the war and the main buildings later reconstructed in concrete, a material which cannot begin to reproduce the qualities inherent in Japanese wooden temple design.

Keitaku-en Garden

Located beside the Municipal Art Museum (Shiritsu Bijutsukan) in Tennoji-koen park, this very pretty garden is considered as an excellent example of the Japanese circular garden. It is open without reservation on Tuesdays, Thursdays, and Sundays, and with reservation on Wednesday, Fridays, and Saturdays. It is easily reached from Tennoji JR or subway stations.

The Mint

There is a museum of coins from around the world, but the main attraction is during the cherry-blossom season when the grounds are open to the public to allow viewing the many beautiful trees planted there.

Festivals

January 9–11: Imamiya Ebisu-jinja (Naniwa-ku).
April 22: Shitenno-ji temple.
June 14: Sumiyoshi-taisha.
June 24–5: Tenmangu shrine (Tenjin Matsuri).
July 30–August 1: Sumiyoshi-taisha.
August 11–12: Ikutama-jinja shrine (Osaka Takigi Noh performances at night).

Other Sights

There are few sights in Osaka itself that can't be found elsewhere; if you have time to kill in the area, look through *Your Guide to Osaka* for more ideas. For combined shopping and sightseeing, the underground shopping centers are worth a look, as they are usually very attractive. They are generally located at the terminuses of the various private railway lines. The arcade at Hankyu-Umeda station is a good starting point; it has one section that resembles the arched roof of a cathedral, with stained-glass windows.

Although Osaka is unlovely by day, with lots of large buildings, parts of it are quite pretty at night, particularly the Dotombori area where the lights of large multi-colored advertising signs are reflected in the water of a canal. Fountain sprays in the canal serve the double duty of adding a note of beauty while helping to purify the water. Many shops and restaurants line the nearby streets.

NORTH OF OSAKA

Expo 70 & Its Legacy

Osaka came to international attention by hosting the World Fair, Expo 70. The use of the structures as pavilions ended in September 1970, but some of them have been preserved and converted to other display purposes, and the famed garden has survived.

JAPANESE GARDEN   A garden incorporating the elements for which Japanese gardens have become famous—the placing of rocks, water, "hills", trees and other shrubbery—was created for Expo 70, and is one of the most pleasant places to visit in Osaka.

NATIONAL MUSEUM OF ETHNOLOGY This is located on the old Expo grounds, and has been rated as very worthwhile by all who have visited—some who live in the area have returned several times. Exhibits include items of daily use, plus video tapes of festivals, music, and other folk arts from a large number of countries. (It has been criticized, however, for having exhibits labelled only in Japanese.) Most interesting and exotic to the Japanese is Spanish flamenco. Access to both the garden and museum is by bus from Ibaraki-shi station of the JR Tokaido line, or Ibaraki-shi station of the Hankyu-Kyoto line. These stations are between Osaka and Kyoto (closer to the former) and can very easily be visited from Kyoto as a day trip.

Koriyama Honjin

This is in the same area. During the Edo era (1603–1867), feudal lords were compelled to spend part of their time in Edo (Tokyo) as virtual hostages, so there was much movement of their parties to and from Edo. To provide accommodation fit for people of such exalted rank, inns of the finest construction and facilities were set up along the route. Koriyama Honjin was one; it looks much as it did then. It is open for inspection, and has many historical items on display. It is accessible from JR Ibaraki station.

Japanese Farmhouse Museum (Nihon Minka Shuraku Hakubutsukan)

This open-air museum is an interesting collection of 12 traditional thatched-roof farmhouses of the type once common in Japan but now quite rare. They were brought to Hattori Ryokuchi Park and re-assembled in a village-like arrangement. The buildings house exhibits of traditional furniture and items used in daily life. There is an English language pamphlet available. Hattori Ryokuchi is accessible from Sone station (before Toyonaka) on the Hankyu-Takarazuka-sen line from Hankyu-Umeda station, or from Ryokuchi-koen subway station (closed Mondays).

SOUTH OF OSAKA

Nintoku Tomb Mound (Sakai)

The greatest tomb mound in Japan, covering a larger area than the Great Pyramid (about 460,000 sq meters), is located in Sakai, a short distance south of Osaka. The keyhole-shaped mound is 478 meters long, 300 meters wide at the flat end, and up to 35 meters high. An immense amount of work went into its construction, involving the movement of 1.45 million cubic meters of earth. Three moats surround it.

After this description, it is only fair to say that it is not worth the effort (for most people) to go to see it; from ground level it looks like little more than a broad ditch surrounding a low hill. (There is a tall tower at its base that looks like an observatory, but it was closed when I visited. If tomb mounds interest you, ask at the Kyoto TIC or other information source if it is open for this purpose.)

The mound is more interesting for what it represents. For several hundred years, from the fifth century onwards, the Osaka area was the residence of the rulers of Japan who had the power and resources to build such tombs. One theory is that Osaka was at the eastern tip of a crescent of the same ethnic group that stretched to Kyushu and into part of Korea, and that the laborers who built the tomb were captives from wars on the Korean peninsula. This is only interesting speculation at this point, but would explain how so many people could be assigned to non-productive work. The practice of building these mounds seems to have died out in the seventh century, possibly indicating a shift of power to a "native" clan.

Access is from Mozu station of the JR Hanwa-sen line (from Tennoji station), or from Mikuni-oka station of Nankai-Koya-sen line (from Shiomibashi station of Nankai line, near Sakuragawa subway station).

Yoshimura-ke House

This is a large farmhouse built in the 17th century and preserved in excellent condition. It is accessible from Takawashi station of Kintetsu-Minami-osaka line, which leads to Yoshino.

Entertainment in Osaka and Environs

Food

While Osaka has few "touristy" attractions, it has a well-deserved reputation for good dining.

Bunraku

Osaka's contribution to the world's performing arts is Bunraku puppet theater. The puppets are more than a meter tall, have realistic faces, and are beautifully costumed. (I say "faces" rather than "masks" because the mouths, eyebrows and eyes can move, making life-like expressions.) Each doll is manipulated by one to three people standing behind it, moving the head, arms, and legs in such a realistic manner that it seems to take on a life of its own. The master puppeteer is sometimes visible and dressed in traditional costume, while his masked assistants are dressed in black. There is a narrator, and musical accompaniment by shamisen.

In early 1984, Bunraku acquired a permanent home in Osaka, the Kokuritsu Bunraku Gekijo (National Bunraku Theater), a five-storey, ¥65 billion building in Minami-ku (ward). Inquire locally about performances of this interesting art. (The TIC in Kyoto should be able to help.)

Kabuki

Performances of Kabuki are also given at various times through the year; the theater is Shin Kabukiza, near Namba station of the subway or Nankai line. Information is available from the same sources mentioned for Bunraku.

Takarazuka Women's Opera

This is an "institution" in the Kansai area, a music hall in which all performers are young women. Programs include revues, musicals, and adaptations of light operas. The 4000-seat theater, the largest in the Orient, is part of Takarazuka Family Land, a large recreation center with cinemas, gardens, etc in Takarazuka city. Access is by Hankyu-Takarazuka line from Hankyu Umeda station. It was originally built to attract users to the Hankyu railroad, which had been built through new housing developments, but which was losing money.

Clubs & Bars

Being a large business center, Osaka has all the nightclubs, cabarets, hostess bars, etc., found in any large Japanese city. The same warnings also bear repeating—that many (if not most) are aimed at expense account spenders and can be *very* expensive. If prices aren't posted, ask before ordering anything.

Shopping

Because of the relatively small number of foreign visitors to Osaka, there is a correspondingly small number of tax-free shops for cameras and other high-tech goodies that overseas visitors like. Based on a very small sample, I found that discounts were smaller than those available in Tokyo, and about the same as (or a little less than) those in Kyoto, but it might be possible to shop around and do better than this. One place to look for would be Doi Camera, one of a chain of shops across the country; their Tokyo branch in Shinjuku has very favorable prices. Kimura Camera is another widespread chain, but prices in their Tokyo stores vary from branch to branch, so there is no assurance that their Osaka prices will be favorable.

Places to Stay

Because it is such an important business center, Osaka has a large number of hotels of various prices, from luxury class to business hotels, *ryokan*, etc. Help in finding a room is available at Osaka station. Most travel agents can make bookings if you are arriving from another part of Japan. International hotels are not listed here because any overseas travel agent worth his salt has the same information and can make bookings in advance at little or no extra cost.

There are several youth hostels in and near Osaka. Nagai YH (tel (06) 699-5631) is located in the municipal sports ground. It has 102 beds, is quite pleasant and one of the less costly hostels in Japan. It is reached from Nagai station of either the JR Hanwa line (south from Tennoji station) or Midosuji subway line. No card is required, only a passport. Hattori Ryokuchi YH (tel (06) 862-0600) is located north of the city in the same park as the Farmhouse Museum. It has 108 beds and is reached via Ryokuchi-koen station of Midosuji subway line. Other hostels in the region can be located with the help of the information service at the station. Failing that, a Japanese person could ask for additional phone numbers by telephoning any of the hostels listed. The

hostels of Kyoto and Nara are also within range of Osaka, but if Osaka hostels are full the others probably will be too.

Getting There

Air

Kansai International Airport serves the entire region around Osaka, including Kyoto and Kobe. For international flights it replaces the former Osaka International airport, now known widely as Itami airport, but the latter is still used for many internal flights. The new facility, often referred to in print as "KIA" (designation code "KIX"), was prompted by the need of an airport that could operate at night, and was built at the cost of multi billions of dollars on a man-made island five kilometers off the coast. It opened in September 1994.

Clearing Immigration and Customs is straight-forward; the immigration officials at Itami airport had a reputation for being quite reasonable, so we may hope that that continues. As at the Narita terminals, there are two exits to the arrivals concourse, so anyone meeting a flight has to determine the correct exit.

There is a choice of train, bus, taxi, and boat to get to Osaka and nearby destinations.

TRAIN Trains of the JR and Nankai lines run from the station, located at the NE end of the terminal building.

JR operates two services, the "Haruka" express, and the rapid service. Haruka trains run every 30 minutes and stop at only two stations in greater Osaka, Tennoji (on SE side of city, the only transfer to the Osaka loop line) and Shin-osaka (Shinkansen station for Osaka), then goes non-stop to Kyoto. The cost and times are ¥2230/29 min to Tennoji, ¥2930/45 min to Shin-osaka, and ¥3430/75 min to Kyoto. (Though not the cheapest, this is the most direct way to Kyoto station.) Rapid service trains make several stops en route into the city. Within Osaka, some go around the loop to Kyobashi, stopping at several stations along the way, while others go to JR Namba, inside the loop and toward the south of the city. The 29-minute trip to Namba costs ¥1250.

Nankai line offers the "Rapi:t" (sic; I don't have the kind of mind that can make these things up!) to Namba, also for ¥1250 and taking the same 29 minutes as JR, making the choice of line a toss-up.

BUS Buses leave from the terminus at the NE end of the terminal building for Osaka, Kyoto, and Kobe, as well as Nara, Wakayama, and the transfer to Itami (Osaka domestic) airport. For passengers bound for the greater Osaka area, buses go to JR Osaka (north) and Kintetsu-Uehon-machi (south central) stations (¥1300 and about 60 minutes each) and to Keihan-Moriguchi station (¥1600/80 min) several kilometers northest of central Osaka (toward Kyoto; the Keihan line could be taken from here to Kyoto as well). For Kobe, the bus to JR Sannomiya station (the main JR station in Kobe) takes about 70 minutes and costs ¥1800. And for Kyoto, the bus takes about 135 minutes and costs ¥2200, ending at Keihan-Uji station more than 10 kilometers southeast of Kyoto station. It also stops at JR Uji and Kintetsu-Okubo stations. A train of the Keihan, JR, or Kintetsu line may be taken from these stations to Kyoto station. All are commuter lines with frequent service. As mentioned above, one could also go by bus to Moriguchi and continue by Keihan train to Kyoto. There is also bus service to JR Nara station taking 95 minutes and costing ¥1800.

BOAT Kobe lies across Osaka harbor from the airport island and can be reached by jetfoil to Port Island (¥180 bus to KIA ferry

terminal then ¥2650/34 minute jetfoil trip) and then bus to Shin-kobe (¥400) or JR Sannomiya (¥320) stations. A ferry service also connects airport island with Tempozan harbor of Osaka (¥1650), but it would then be necessary to use local subway or bus service to continue.

ITAMI AIRPORT Buses that depart from the front of the terminal building are the most economical way to get in from the airport. The most useful destinations for most travellers will be Shin-osaka station (for Shinkansen trains), Osaka station (for most other JR services; posted as "Osaka-Umeda"), and Namba, on the south side of the city (in the Osaka City Air Terminal Building). There are also buses direct to Kyoto and Kobe. There are buses every 10 to 20 minutes to most destinations; the trip takes 30 minutes into Osaka and one hour to Kyoto.

Buses to the airport leave from several points in Osaka; one is in front of the Daimaru building, about three minutes walk to the right when leaving the front of Osaka station. Others leave from various city hotels (Shin-hankyu Hotel, Dai-ichi Hotel, etc.

Intercity Trains
Kyoto, Nara, and Kobe can be reached in less than an hour by train from Osaka, while Nagoya and a large number of other places in the Kinki district can be reached in a somewhat longer time. For details of services in the Kinki district, refer to the transportation section at the beginning of this chapter.

For longer distances, the Shinkansen offers very fast service to Tokyo (about three hours), and Hakata (Fukuoka, in northern Kyushu) is 3-1/2 hours in the opposite direction. Shinkansen services are detailed in the general Transportation section (covering all of Japan) early in the book.

Shinkansen trains use Shin-osaka (New Osaka) station (one stop from Osaka station), while Osaka station (the main JR station) is used by Tokaido and Sanyo JR lines, including the very useful Shin-kaisoku service to/from Kyoto, Hikone, Kobe, and Himeji. Shin-osaka station is on the Midosuji subway line, while Osaka station and the Umeda stations of the Hankyu and Hanshin lines are all served by the Midosuji, Yotsuhashi, and Tanimachi lines. The Keihan line intersects the Tanimachi, Sakaisuji, and Midosuji lines at the three stations following Kyobashi station (JR Sanyo line), and Kyobashi is also the transfer point from the Katamachi line (to/from Nara) before it terminates at Katamachi.

Tennoji, on the Kanjo, Tanimachi, and Midosuji lines, is the starting point for the JR line to Wakayama, the Kintetsu line to Koyasan, and the Nankai Koya-sen (to Koyasan), and Nankai Honsen to Wakayama.

Namba stations of the Kintetsu-Nara line (to Nara), JR line (to Nara; formerly Minatomachi station), and Nansai-Koya line (to Koyasan) are close to stations of the Yotsuhashi, Midosuji, and Sennichi-mae subway lines. (It is also possible to transfer to the Kintetsu-Nara line where these lines intersect the Sakaisuji and Tanimachi lines.)

Buses

See the beginning of this chapter for inter-city services.

Ferries

International: From Osaka there is regular service to Shanghai (China). Further details are given in the general "Transportation" section early in the book.
Domestic: From Osaka there are boats to Shikoku (Matsuyama, Kochi, Sakate,

Tokushima, and Takamatsu), Kyushu (Shin-moji, Beppu, Miyazaki, Shibushi), and Okinawa (Naha). From nearby Kobe there are also boats to Shikoku and Kyushu.

The long-distance domestic ferries generally sail overnight, enabling travellers to save the cost of accommodation. (See the general Transportation section early in the book for details.)

GETTING TO THE DOCKS Ferries from Osaka to points on Shikoku and Kyushu leave from three different docks—Benten-futo pier, Tempozan pier, and Osaka Nanko pier.

Benten-futo pier: Take the JR Kanjo-sen (loop line) or the subway Chuo line to Bentensho station. From there it is a five minute bus trip by regular city bus from the station. In addition you can take city bus 53 from Osaka station or bus 60 from Namba station to "Benten-futo" stop.

Tempozan pier: Tempozan pier is most easily reached by Chuo-sen subway line. The terminus, Osaka-ko station, is a three minute walk from the pier. In addition to the subway, buses 53 and 88 from Osaka station, 60 from Namba station, and 107 from Tenmabashi go to Tempozan terminal.

Osaka Nanko pier: Osaka Nanko can be reached easily by taking Yotsuhashi-sen subway line to its terminus, Suminoe-Koen, then taking a bus from there (15 minutes) to Osaka Nanko (the end of the line). There are also buses from Sumiyoshi-koen station of the Nankai-densha private railway line, but it is advisable to check the frequency of these buses in advance.

It will do no harm to confirm that these docks are still the correct ones, for the ferry schedules and departure points seem to change yearly.

Subways and City Trains

Osaka has seven subway lines: Midosuji,

Tanimachi, Yotsuhashi, Chuo, Sennichimae, Sakaisuji, and Tsurumi-ryokuchi. The subway lines criss-cross the central part of the city, while the JR Kanjo-sen loop line circles around the central district in both directions. The subway lines intersect each other at many places, making transfer simple. They also cross the Kanjo line at several points, but there is not always a station near the intersection where you can transfer between JR and subway lines.

Separate tickets are required for JR and subway lines, and tickets must be kept and surrendered when leaving the system. A subway map in English is available at the information center at Osaka station.

City Buses

A map of all city bus services in Osaka is available (Japanese only) at the small information office near the bus departure area in front of Osaka station (to the left when leaving the station). Ask for a "basu (bus) no chizu".

Hitching

Between Osaka and Kyoto, forget it. It takes too long to try to get a ride and back into the city at the other end. Take the train. For hitching to more distant points, it is necessary to reach the Meishin Kosokudoro expressway (between Kobe and Nagoya) or the Chugoku Kosokudoro expressway from Osaka to the western end of Honshu. There is no simple way to get started, as the interchanges are all to the north of Osaka, and it is necessary to take a train or local road to the entrance, or to start at an entrance in Osaka itself and try to get a car that will switch to the exact road you want to take. (The latter requires a sign indicating where you want to go, as hitching is not allowed on the expressways themselves.) One entrance is close to Osaka station and leads onto the Osaka–Ikeda route, which leads to

Toyonaka interchange (Meishin), and Ikeda interchange (Chugoku); the latter is near the interchange for Osaka airport. Somewhat to the northeast is another entrance to a local expressway (Kinki Expressway) that becomes the Chugoku Expressway and intersects the Meishin at Suita. The starting point is the Kadoma interchange, which is about a km from Kadoma station of the Keihan-Kyoto line. (Ibaraki, on the Meishin Expressway, is about two km from the Ibaraki JR station, and there may be a bus passing close to it.) Alternatively, you can use the slower national highways which switch from Route 1 (from Tokyo) to Route 2 (to Shimonoseki at the far west) in front of Osaka station. However, this is in the middle of Osaka, so hitching could be rather poor. If you are near the station, ask at the information office for a map and suggestions for getting a better starting point.

HYOGO-KEN ▬▬▬▬

Kobe

Kobe is an international port of entry to Japan, mostly for passengers of cruise liners, and also an industrial and commercial city. In a reversal of the old saying, it is considered a nice place to live but you wouldn't want to visit there. Mt. Rokko provides a view over the city, and there is an area of foreign-style houses from the last century that belonged to European merchants. These are of great interest to Japanese sightseers, but these would be of quite limited interest to the average foreigner. There is relatively little else for a short-term visitor to see. (Those arriving to reside there will have the more subtle points of interest described by old hands soon after arrival.) In January 1995, a large earthquake here killed over 6,000 people.

Most of the following information refers to getting to the nearby, and more interesting, cities of Kyoto, Nara, and Himeji.

Visiting liners dock at Pier 4. From there a wide road (known among foreigners as The Bund) goes straight to Sannomiya station, effectively the main station of Kobe. Bus 92 runs between the station and the port, and taxis are also available.

Home Visit

A visit to the home of a Japanese family (afternoon or evening) is an enjoyable experience and can be arranged by contacting the organizers (Sannomiya Kotsu Center Building, 2F, near Sannomiya station; tel 078-391-4753), or arrange through your hotel or shipping company.

Food

Kobe is famous for a type of beef that takes the name of the city. It has a reputation for delicious taste (and for very high cost, even more so than the already high prices charged for beef of any kind in Japan), but it is very fatty and might not appeal if you are accustomed to lean beef.

Places to Stay

Kobe has many hotels, business hotels, etc. There are four youth hostels in the Kobe area. Kobe Tarumi YH (tel 078-707-21330) and Chorin-ji YH (tel 078-911-4727) are to the west of Kobe, toward Himeji, while Kobe Mudo-ji YH (tel 078-581-0250) is within the city, to the north, while Ashiya YH (tel 0797-38-0109) is to the east, toward Osaka. (The two "-ji" hostels are temples, and likely to be more pleasant and interesting.)

Getting There

Air

Like Kyoto, Kobe is served by Osaka's airports, Kansai International for international flights and many domestic flights and Itami airport for the majority of domestic flights. Information on transportation from Kansai International is given in the section on Osaka, and there are buses from Itami to various points in Kobe.

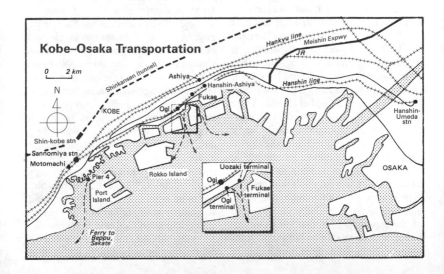

Trains

Kyoto, Osaka, and Himeji can all be reached quickly and conveniently from Kobe. Even passengers on cruise liners could reach Kyoto for some sightseeing and be back at the ship the same day. (An alternative is to leave the ship at Kobe and rejoin it at Yokohama, if the ship goes there next, or vice versa.) All major train services in the region are detailed in the Kinki district transportation section early in this chapter.

Shinkansen super-express trains use Shin-kobe station, which nestles at the foot of the mountain that over-shadows the city. This station can be reached from the main JR station, Sannomiya, in about 10 minutes by bus 4 or by taxi. (The extra speed of the Shinkansen train may be counter-balanced by the less convenient station (and cost) for going to Osaka or Kyoto.)

Regular JR services, including the speedy *Shin-kaisoku* expresses (non-surcharge expresses through the Himeji–Kobe–Osaka–Kyoto–Maibara corridor), use Sannomiya; Kobe station is relatively unimportant.

The main station of the Hankyu line (to Osaka and Kyoto) is Hankyu Sannomiya. Similarly for the Hanshin line (to Osaka only), the main station is Hanshin Sannomiya, terminating at Hanshin Motomachi. All the Sannomiya stations are close to each other.

Ferries

There are ferries from Kobe to Shikoku (Konoura, Tosa-shimizu, Matsuyama, Imabari, Takamatsu, Tokushima, Niihima, and Kawanoe), Kyushu (Shin-moji, Oita, Hyuga, and Beppu) and Okinawa (Naha). Details of the sailings to/from the destinations on Kyushu and Okinawa plus Matsuyama, Konnoura, and Tosa-shimizu are given in the general Transportation section early in the book. Services to the relatively close points on Shikoku are detailed in the write-ups on the places on Shikoku.

Naka-tottei pier is in Kobe harbor, in central Kobe, at the end of the broad avenue known as "The Bund". The pier is easily identified by the red Port Tower. Boats to Okinawa leave from near the end of the pier; passenger ferries to Kyushu leave from the end nearer land; and car ferries to Kyushu leave from the middle.

The other ports, Ogi, Uozaki, and Fukae, are collectively known as Higashi Kobe-ko (East Kobe port). The map shows their relative locations.

Ogi and Uozaki are reached most conveniently from Ogi station of the Hanshin line, and Fukae from Fukae station of the same line. At Ogi station, the docks are on the track-4 side of the station, on the far side of the expressway (Hwy 43); there is a guide map at the station.

Express trains do not stop at these stations, so it is necessary to take a local train from Kobe/Osaka, or an express from either city to Hanshin-Ashiya and change there to a local train. Trains from Osaka leave Hanshin-Umeda station. From Kobe they leave Hanshin-Sannomiya and Hanshin-Motomachi stations.

The JR Tokaido Honsen line passes farther to the north of the Hanshin line; Setsumotoyama station would be the one for Uosaki and Ogi docks, while Fukae dock seems about equidistant from Setsumotoyama and Ashiya stations. A taxi would be recommended from either JR station, while the distance is not too great to go on foot from the Hanshin stations.

Akashi

Apart from the stone walls and two turrets remaining of the old castle, the main interest of Akashi is that it is one port for ferries to Iwaya on nearby Awaji-shima island; the trip takes 25 minutes.

Himeji

The city of Himeji is noteworthy for the finest castle in Japan. Begun on a modest scale in the 16th century, it was expanded by later daimyo until it reached its present form in the early 1800s, and was restored to nearly original condition in the 1960s. It is located on a hill not far from Himeji station, and its white form can be seen soon after leaving the station's front exit.

Himeji also offers the unusual cemetery of Nago-yama (15 minutes from the station by bus), and Enkyo Temple at the top of Shosha-san (eight km from the station). Access from Shosha station is by bus, then a cable-car.

Things to See

Himeji- (shirasagi-) jo Castle

Himeji-jo is often called White Egret Castle in Japanese because of its graceful appearancce. It is made up of 78 individual buildings, the main one standing five storeys high. It is a defensive castle despite its aesthetic appearance, approached by narrow paths that could be showered with arrows from slits in the walls. In contrast, the upper part (which was unassailable) was designed for the best in gracious living, as defined by the tastes of the day; this can be seen in the delicate wood carving and bronze decorations around the rooms.

A couple of hours can easily be spent exploring the interior and exterior, observing the defensive details, including the racks for spears, and wondering at the size of the massive wooden pillars that support the upper storeys.

The castle is easily reached on foot in 15 minutes from the station (less by taxi). The lighting for photos is most dramatic as the sun gets low in the sky. An interesting vantage point for those determined enough and with a telephoto lens, is the top of the

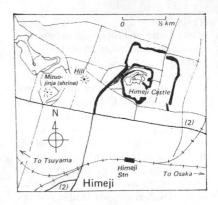

Himeji

hill where Mizuo-jinja shrine stands.

Festivals

April 3: Rice Planting festival at Hiromine-jinja.

April 17–18: Spring festival at Hiromine-jinja.

October 14–15: Kenka Matsuri is held at Matsubara Hichiman-jinja (near Shirahama-no-miya station)

Places to Stay

There are many hotels, *ryokan*, and *minshuku* because Himeji is a major destination for Japanese sightseers as well. There is a youth hostel, Tegarayama YH (tel 0792-93-2716). Another YH in the region is Joun-ji YH (tel 07932-4-0030), a temple to the west of Himeji.

Getting There

Information on trains connecting Himeji with Kyoto, Osaka, and Kobe is given early in this chapter. Westward you can use regular JR Sanyo line services (to Hiroshima, etc.) as well as the super-express Shinkansen trains. It is necessary to consult a timetable because not all Shinkansen trains stop at Himeji.

This section describes the region known as *Chugoku* ("Middle Country"), the western end of the main island, Honshu. The description begins from Himeji and follows a route clockwise along the south shore (Sanyo-kaigan), around the end of the island, and back along the northern shore (Sanin-kaigan) almost to Kyoto.

The name *Chugoku* implies that this was in the center of Japanese civilization in the past. Archaeological remains can be found near Okayama and other places, and the nation's most venerated ancient shrine site is at Izumo (near Matsue, Sanin coast).

Himeji properly belongs in this region, but it was described with the Kinki section because it can easily be reached from Kyoto as a day trip, and thus is most conveniently dealt with as part of the Kinki region.

The Sanin coast is by far the more enjoyable for scenery and uncrowded, largely non-developed conditions. The route is excellent for cyclists as it is mostly flat and road traffic is reasonable (as is the continuation described in the Hokuriku section, up through Fukui, Kanazawa, and around the Noto Peninsula).

The Sanyo coast is very heavily developed through to Hiroshima, and road traffic moves very slowly. However it has a larger number of specific places to visit.

TRANSPORTATION

There are major highways and rail lines along the full length of both the Sanyo and Sanin coasts, from the Kyoto–Osaka area to Shimonoseki at the west end. Chugoku is also criss-crossed with roads and train lines from one coast to the other. While no one route is particularly outstanding, any such route is almost sure to lead through scenic mountain-and-valley terrain, with many rice fields and typical farmhouses. If you are on your own transportation, a mild warning: I found (when crossing from Matsue to Fukuyama) that the route markers sometimes vanished, and at one memorable intersection there was no guidance whatever, which caused me to waste two hours finding the continuation of the road. This sort of thing happened more than once.

The Chugoku expressway (Chugoku Kosokudoro) runs through the middle from Osaka to Shimonoseki, where it connects with the Kyushu Expressway via the Kanmon-ohashi bridge. The expressway is the route for hitchhikers in a hurry; the scenery, though pleasant, is not outstanding.

There are numerous ferry connections from points in the Chugoku region to Shikoku and Kyushu. These are identified in the write-up on each place, although details of frequency, etc., are given only for the connecting locale in Shikoku and Kyushu.

Further details on road conditions and a summary of things to see along the way may be found in the section on Shimonoseki later.

NOTE: In some of the following write-ups there will be references to viewing the Inland Sea. Keep in mind that visibility is frequently very limited during the warmer months. It is best not to make plans specifically and exclusively for such sightseeing.

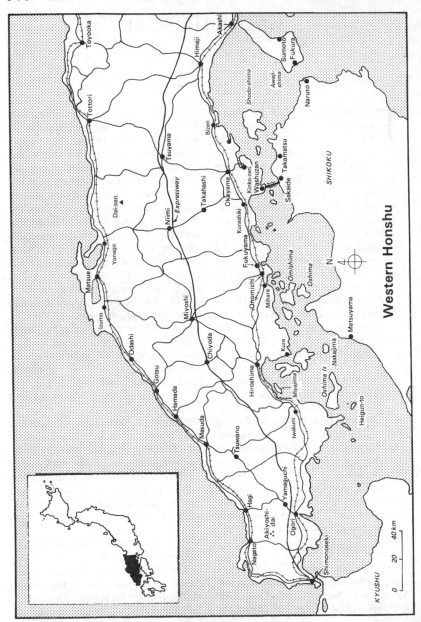

Western Honshu

OKAYAMA-KEN

Bizen

The city of Bizen is famous in Japan for the pottery known as *Bizen-yaki*; numerous potteries and kilns can be found in and around the city. The pottery is of a very old (1200 years) and simple style, obtaining its characteristic finish and patterns from the firing rather than the glazing.

An interesting sidelight of the pottery craft is a reported reduction in the number of birds in the coastal area. So many pine trees have been cut down over the centuries for fuel that the roosts and sources of insects have been reduced.

Shizutani School

This historical school may not be recognizable as such to westerners. It dates from 1666 and resembles classical schools of China and Korea. It was the first school in Japan for commoners. The white-walled buildings are roofed with Bizen-ware tiles and surrounded with a rock-covered earthen wall broken by small picturesque gates. It is located at the foot of a tree-covered hill that is colorful in autumn. The appearance of the school is very uncommon in a Japanese setting.

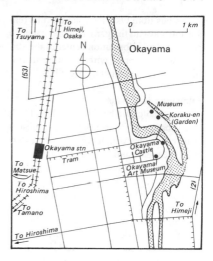

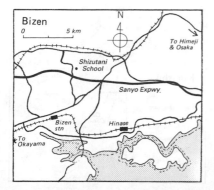

Okayama

Okayama is the better known city of the pair Okayama-Kurashiki, but they can best be regarded as two parts of a whole. The city centers are only 16 km apart, so travel between them is convenient.

Things to See

Koraku-en Garden

The main attraction of Okayama, this is one of the "Big Three" gardens of Japan, as rated by the Japanese. The "strolling" landscape garden was laid out more than 300 years ago. In places, it has the features westerners associate with a Japanese garden— careful placement of rocks, water, miniature hills, etc., plus plots of blooms and a teahouse. However, I was rather disappointed by it, for much of its expanse is open lawn similar to that found in any western park. This is a novelty to the Japanese, where space is at such a premium, but not to westerners. To be sure, it is pretty, but do not expect too much of it. Near the garden is a museum (*hakubutsukan*).

A bus from Okayama station runs reasonably close to the garden; a taxi can also be used. The information center at the station (well equipped with literature in English) can help you get the right bus.

Okayama-jo Castle

The original castle here was built in 1573, but subsequently destroyed. The present concrete reconstruction preserves the external appearance and adds a traditional note to Koraku-en, which it overlooks. It is black, in contrast with the white of the castle at Himeji (Japan's finest); its nickname, *Ujo* (crow) is a joke on the name of Himeji's pride, which translates as "white egret". The castle is only a short distance from Koraku-en, and is accessible by a bridge across the river. Nearby is Okayama Bijutsukan (Art Museum).

Festivals

On the night of the first Saturday in February, Saidai-ji temple is the scene of an interesting festival, when loin-clothed young men vie to grab and keep two sacred wands (*shingi*) that are thrown into their midst; the wands are supposed to bring lifelong happiness.

Near Okayama

Tsuyama

Inland, due north of Okayama, lies Tsuyama. In cherry-blossom season, the site of the old castle (destroyed in 1873 during the civil war known as the Meiji Restoration) is very beautiful, for the grounds (now Kakuzan-koen) are planted with 8000 cherry trees. Of interest at any time to historians is the site of a Yayoi-era (pre-Yamato Japanese civilization) pit dwelling that has been excavated. Little is known of the people of that era, but their pottery and the remnants of their dwellings of 2000 years

ago have been found in many parts of Japan. About 2.5 km northeast of Numa station, one Yayoi-type dwelling has been reconstructed and is open to the public. (Refer to the section on Shizuoka for more information on pit dwellings.)

Kurashiki

This is possibly the most charming town in Japan (parts of it, at least). It was extremely prosperous in feudal days, when rice from the very productive inland region was shipped through here. Merchants built large and elaborate storehouses of dark stone and contrasting white mortar, which still stand in one section of the town. A canal (also stone-walled and once used to transport rice to and from the storehouses) passes by the buildings, and willows droop gracefully over the water. Although the architecture is Japanese, the mood of the area is almost that of old Europe. You can enjoy just walking around, absorbing the appearance and atmosphere,

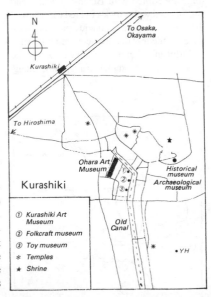

and possibly taking a short rickshaw ride along the narrow streets. I first saw the area late in the afternoon when the sun was low, and was captivated; but I could never quite recapture the lighting and that mood again. May every visitor have such an opportunity. The area is not large, so a stroll of half an hour or so down the back streets will probably be enough before returning to the warehouse-museums along the canal.

Information

The city has an information office near the Ohara Museum. If you are beginning your travels in Tokyo, you should pick up a copy of the photocopied information sheet on Kurashiki at the TIC.

Things to See

The Warehouses

Several of the *kura* (warehouses, hence the name Kurashiki) have been converted into museums, and are worth visiting. They are described in the order that they are encountered along the canal bank.

TOY MUSEUM (KYODO GANGUKAN) This houses a collection of toys from all over Japan, including many types no longer used. They are interesting for the simplicity of their designs (using local materials).

FOLKCRAFT MUSEUM (KURASHIKI MINGEIKAN) Several adjoining kura have been combined so you can walk back and forth within them, up and down floors, while admiring a large collection of folkcraft, articles of daily utility made of indigenous materials. Most are of Japanese origin, but enough pieces have been brought from other countries and cultures to stress the similarities and individualities. (Closed Mondays.)

KURASHIKI ART MUSEUM (KURASHIKI BIJU-TSUKAN) This museum houses mostly Eu-ropean art, including some ancient Mediterranean works.

KURASHIKI ARCHAEOLOGICAL MUSEUM (KURASHIKI KOKOKAN) Many relics excavated in the region are on display here to show the cultures that have flourished around Kurashiki and Okayama since ancient times, particularly the Kibi culture that survived into the fifth century; it is known for a number of tomb mounds in the vicinity of the city. (Closed Mondays.)

Ohara Art Museum (Ohara Bijutsukan)

No, not founded by an errant Irishman, but by a wealthy Japanese textile manufacturer, Magosaburo Ohara, who collected western art. To house his collection, he constructed a large Greek-style building complete with columns. The collection is interesting but not exciting, at least for those who have had access to the great Western museums. In the grounds behind this building are other museums housing contemporary Japanese art, pottery, Chinese art, and other assorted collections. Some regard these as more interesting than the main museum.

Kurashiki Historical Museum (Kurashiki Rekishikan)

This museum is apart from the others and can be reached in 10 to 15 minutes on foot.

Ivy Square

Built as a textile factory soon after the Meiji Restoration in 1868, this ivy-covered red brick complex has been converted into a cluster of tourist attractions. It is of greatest interest to the Japanese (to whom such a brick structure is exotic), but there is a small museum of the Kurashiki textile industry which may interest foreign visitors, plus restaurants, coffee houses, an open square, and a hotel.

Places to Stay

In addition to the hotel in Ivy Square, there are many other hotels and ryokan of various price ranges, as well as the pleasant, hilltop Kurashiki YH (tel (0864) 22-7355). Assistance in finding accommodation is available at the information office in the railway station.

Getting There

Kurashiki is accessible by Shinkansen via Shin-kurashiki station, but the connections make it simpler to transfer from Okayama station (also on the Shinkansen), which allows a short visit to Okayama as well.

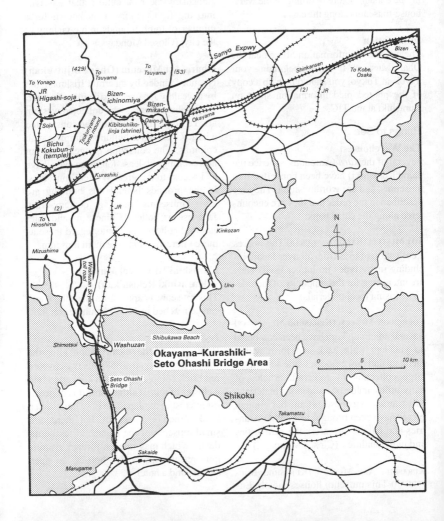

Okayama–Kurashiki– Seto Ohashi Bridge Area

Near Kurashiki

Just north of Kurashiki is the Kibi plain, which was settled long before recorded history; many historic and prehistoric remains may be found in the area. Kibitsuhiko-jinja shrine (a national treasure) at the foot of a forested hill (near Bizen-mikado station) is one of the attractions; its main building is built in an unusual Kibitsu-style, and dates from 1425.

Tsukuriyama Tomb Mound

In the same area is the Tsukuriyama tomb mound, the largest such burial site in the Kibi area, and the fourth largest in Japan. Similar mounds are found in Kyushu, near Osaka (including the largest), and near Tokyo. The practice of building such mounds was also prevalent in Korea, so the question remains whether these people were Korean in origin, or if they were only influenced by the culture across the water. (Such tombs were built only in the third through seventh centuries.) It is a keyhole-shaped mound of earth 350 meters long, 238 meters wide at the greatest point, and 25 meters high. It is of limited interest to most people, however, because it simply looks like any other hill, even though man-made; its historical significance is what makes it interesting.

Another place to visit in the same area is Bicchu-kokubun-ji temple. It has a picturesque five-storey pagoda. To reach these attractions, make enquiries locally.

Coastal Attractions

A broad peninsula below Okayama and Kurashiki offers some sightseeing and beaches, as well as boat services to Shikoku.

Kinko-zan

On the eastern side of the peninsula is Kinko-zan hill (403 meters), which offers an excellent view of the Inland Sea (Seto Naikai), atmospherics permitting. En route it passes by Kojima Bay, which is interesting (though not spectacularly so) for being the second largest man-made lake in the world (after one in Holland). It allowed the reclamation of a large area of farm land. One bus a day goes from Okayama station to Kinko-zan (one hour), waits 40 minutes, then returns.

Shibukawa-hama Beach

One of the best beaches (white sand, etc.) is about eight km from Uno station, accessible by bus from Uno in 25 minutes.

Washuzan

Another excellent view over the Inland Sea is available (also atmospherics permitting) at Washuzan, almost due south of Kurashiki on the western side of the peninsula. (Washuzan is very close to the very large Seto Ohashi series of bridges to Shikoku, so it will be prominent in the view.) There are several buses through the day from Kurashiki station (70 min; ¥790); buses are more frequent from nearby Kojima station, which is on the JR line from Okayama (22 minutes; ¥240). From Kojima there are many buses through the day to Uno (also on the coast), and from there a bus service

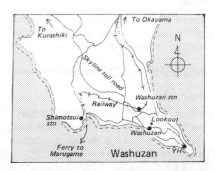

is indicated on the map in *jikokuhyo*, though I could not find the schedule (probably also regular; check locally). These would enable making a circling route close to the coast from Kurashiki to Okayama.

There is a youth hostel near Washuzan (tel (0864) 79-9280).

Access to Shikoku

Ferries
Shimotsui
A regular ferry service runs between nearby Shimotsui and Marugame on Shikoku (¥650). Details are given in the Marugame section.

Uno
From Uno (terminal station of a JR line from Okayama, and probably linked to Okayama by bus as well) there is frequent ferry service through the day across to Takamatsu on Shikoku (¥380).

Train
With the opening of the Seto Ohashi series of bridges, JR trains can be used to cross to Shikoku. Many trains cross daily from Okayama station (and others along the line on the Honshu side) to Sakaide, on Shikoku. Further details are given in the Shikoku section.

Road
There is also a road link between Honshu (at Kojima) and Shikoku (near Utazu) via the Seto Ohashi bridge system.

HIROSHIMA-KEN▬▬▬▬

Fukuyama
This industrial city is of little touristic interest, although it has a 1966 reproduction of its historic castle. It is best known for the nearby town of Tomo-no-ura.

There is a regular boat service between Fukuyama (Higashi-fukuyama port) and Tadotsu and Takamatsu on Shikoku. (Details given in the write-ups of those places.)

Tomo-no-ura
The port for Fukuyama has long been regarded as one of the most picturesque places in the Inland Sea area (and Japan). Undoubtedly Tomo-no-ura fitted the description when it was made up entirely of single-storey tile-roofed houses . . . but before the intrusion of two- and three-storey concrete structures amidst them, construction of the large and prominent hotel across the harbor, building of the breakwater out to the small islands in the middle of the harbor (Sensui, Benten, and Kogo), and other modern intrusions in conflict with the original appearance.

For those with their own transportation, a road leads up the high hill behind the town to a lookout over the Inland Sea. When I was there in August, the view extended little beyond the harbor below, perhaps a km at most; such hazy conditions prevail through much of the warm season.

Abuto-Kannon Temple
This temple to the Goddess of Mercy, four km from Tomo-no-ura, is built on a cape less than 30 meters above the water and is noted for its superb view over the water. It is accessible from Tomo-no-ura by bus or boat, or from Fukuyama by bus to Abuto-guchi, from where it is a 20-minute walk.

Onomichi
One of the best views of the Inland Sea may be had (when visibility permits) from the heights of Senko-ji temple. (In August I couldn't see beyond the shoreline, a km or so away.) It is accessible from the station in 20 minutes by direct bus, or by bus (five minutes) to Nagaeguchi, then by cable car

to the top. The park at the top is noted for cherry blossoms in season, and picturesque rocks that you scramble over and around.

The city was not touched by the war, so many older houses and buildings have survived, but with each year more will disappear. The city is noted for a number of temples, such as Jodo-ji, Saigo-ji, Saikoku-ji, and Tennei-ji. (There are many others.) A map of the city, showing the temples, is available at the station, and can be used as a guide while strolling around.

There is a regular boat service between Onomichi and Matsuyama and Imabari on Shikoku, the latter offering a service to Omishima island as well. (Details are given in the write-ups of those places.)

Mukai-shima

Located near Onomichi, and accessible by a bridge, Mukai-shima island has a lookout (*tembodai*) that features an excellent view of the Inland Sea and Onomichi (atmospherics permitting).

Mihara & Ikuchi Island

The industrial city of Mihara is the gateway to the island of Ikuchi, 12 km to the south. Setoda, on Ikuchi, is noted for its interesting temple, Kosan-ji. Dating from 1946, the temple has several buildings modelled on those of famous temples elsewhere in Japan (e.g., the Hall of Dreams in Nara) as well as a collection of cultural and religious objects. It is regarded as rather kitschy, so don't make a special trip just to see it. Access is by ferry (50 minutes) or fast boat (20 minutes) from Mihara to Setoda; the temple is about 10 minutes on foot east of the dock.

There is a regular boat service between Mihara and Matsuyama and Imabari on Shikoku. (Details are given in the sections on those places.) The terminal is close to the station.

Kure

Along the coast east of Hiroshima is the shipbuilding center of Kure. During the war, the giant battleship *Yamato* was built here. The largest of its day, carrying 18-inch guns, it was sunk by U.S. aircraft without the chance to make any contribution to the Japanese war effort. In post-war days Kure has produced many of the world's super-tankers that would dwarf the Yamato. If you want to visit the shipyards, inquire in advance; the city has no other attractions, being a typical industrial port city.

There are regular boat services between Kure and Matsuyama on Shikoku (details in the section on Matsuyama), and between Niigata and Imabari on Shikoku (details in the section on Imabari).

Nikyu Gorge

About 15 km northeast of Kure lies this scenic gorge, most noted for many waterfalls and potholes. It can be reached by bus from Kure in 40 minutes.

Takehara

There is a regular boat service between Takehara and Imabari and Namikata on Shikoku, the former offering service en route to Omishima island. (Details are given in the write-ups of those places.)

Taishaku-kyo Gorge

This scenic gorge stretches about 20 km upstream from Taishaku-mura village along the Taishaku River. About 2.4 km from the village is Oni-wa-iwaya (Demon Cave), known for its stalactites. Further along there are two natural rock bridges. The gorge is in one part of Hiba-Taishaku Quasi National Park. Other attractions of the region include mountain, marsh, and forest views. Taishaku-mura can be reached by bus in about one hour from Bingo-sho-bara station.

Miyoshi Area

The inland areas of Chugoku have not gained a great name for tourist attractions, but the scenery along the expressway from Miyoshi to Osaka is enjoyable.

Ukai (cormorant fishing) is carried out through June, July, and August near the junction of three rivers, not far from Nishi-miyoshi station.

Sandan-kyo Gorge

A pleasant excursion from Hiroshima is northwest to Sandan-kyo. Its 16 km length, covered on foot, takes in a number of waterfalls and scenery ranging from pretty to spectacular. Access is by train to Sandan-kyo station (JR) or by bus, both from Hiroshima.

Hiroshima

The city of Hiroshima is known to the in-habitants of every civilized country in the world because of an instant in 1945 when it was destroyed by an atom bomb. For this reason, large numbers of tourists visit the city during a stay in Japan, but be aware that there is relatively little else in Hiroshima city itself, as it is first and foremost an industrial city (which is why it was chosen as a target).

Hiroshima is built on the flat estuary of the Ota river and has little natural beauty, although this is more than offset by the beauties of nearby Itsukushima Island (aka Miyajima). However, the relics and exhibits related to the A-bomb do make Hiroshima a recommended destination—if for no other reason than to make everyone aware of the true horrors of nuclear warfare.

The bomb exploded almost directly over the Industrial Promotion Hall, formerly an architecturally noteworthy structure. It is the only ruined building still allowed to stand, its dome the symbol of the destruction. It is easily reached from Hiroshima station by tram 2 or 6, or bus 3 (but it is advisable to check on these routes).

Information

There is an information center in front of the station that supplies a good map and brochure in English. They should also be able to help with tram information, etc., but don't expect great proficiency in English. Travellers starting from Tokyo can pick up information at the TIC there, including a printed pamphlet (MG-19).

Things to See

Peace Memorial Museum

The area around the remains of the Industrial Promotion Hall building has been made into Peace Park, Heiwa-koen, with a peaceful canal (row-boats for rent), greenery, etc. From the dome, it is an easy and

To Matsue
N
Mitaki temple
•YH
Mitaki stn
Hiroshima
0   1 km
Yokogawa stn
Castle
Hiroshima stn
Bus Term. (Sogo dept store)
Peace Memorial Park
Atomic Bomb Dome
To Hiroshima Port Tram 5
Miyajima
Peace Memorial Museum
Okayama
Osaka

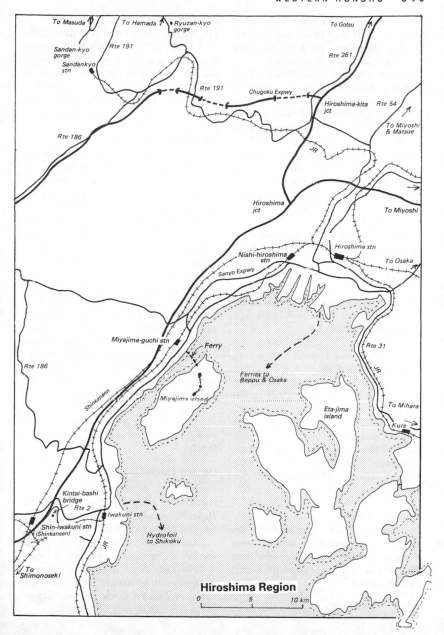

Hiroshima Region

0   5   10 km

pleasant walk through the park to the Peace Memorial Museum, a broad, low building standing on pillars; along the way one passes the saddle-shaped cenotaph.

Every visitor to Japan should try to visit the museum (or its equivalent in Nagasaki, though this one is possibly better). Its purpose is to show the effects of the bomb on Hiroshima, and to serve as a warning to national leaders about the horrors of such weapons. It should be kept in mind that the terrific destruction was done by a bomb equivalent to about 20,000 tonnes of TNT; the average nuclear weapon in the world today is equivalent to 2000 Hiroshima bombs.

The museum has film showings (in English) at 1000, 1125, 1250, 1415, and 1540, as well as a film of Hiroshima in wartime (in Japanese only) every hour from 0930 to 1530. There are signposts in the lobby. (Changes in the program and schedule are possible, so check beforehand rather than relying on these times.)

Most visitors leave the museum in a sombre or depressed mood; it is a very sobering emotional experience, but not to be missed. An excellent book showing the effects of the bombing is worth looking for; the title is simply *Hiroshima-Nagasaki*. Two Hiroshima bookstores which have sold the book are Kinokuniya (Sogo Department Store, sixth floor), and Maruzen Department Store (third floor). The publishers are Hiroshima Heiwa Kaikan, 1-4-9 Shiba, Minato-ku, Tokyo.

Shukkei-en Garden

This landscape garden was originally designed in 1620, though its form has been changed. It offers a pleasant respite from the busy city, and is only about 700 meters from the station.

Hiroshima Castle

The original castle stood here from 1589 until destroyed by the bomb. It was rebuilt in concrete and preserves the external appearance of the former building. It is now a local museum and gives some idea of the appearance of old Hiroshima. The late afternoon offers the best light for photographs.

Places to Stay

There are many hotels and other commercial accommodation in Hiroshima, as well as a youth hostel (tel 082-221-5343). The information center may have directions on how to get to the youth hostel; if not, walk toward the post office (to the right at the front of the station), cross the street and turn right. A short distance along should be a sign "50 meters to Hiroshima Youth Hostel bus stop". More than one bus uses the same stop, so ask the driver before boarding, and get off at Ushita-shin-machi or Ushita-itchome; signs from there should be clear guides up the hill to the hostel. It is one of the best-marked hostels in Japan, and is one of the more pleasant (apart from the 0630 reveille); it is also an excellent source of travel information. (Another YH is Higashi Hiroshima YH (tel (0824) 29-0305).

Another accommodation center is the World Friendship Association; the information center at the station should be able to help.

Getting There

Trains

Hiroshima is one of the major stops on the JR Shinkansen superexpress train that runs between Tokyo and Hakata (Kyushu). Tokyo is about five hours away (depending on the number of stops made), while Kyoto is two to three hours away. There are also slower, less expensive JR services. Shinkansen services are detailed in the general "Transportation" section early in the book.

Ferries

There is a daily overnight ferry service between Hiroshima and Beppu (each way), making this a convenient and relatively inexpensive way of getting to Kyushu, saving the cost of one night's accommodation. Details of this service are given in the general "Transportation" section. There are also regular boats (including speedy hydrofoils) between Hiroshima and Matsuyama and Imabari, both on Shikoku. (Details are given in the write-ups of these places.) The dock area can be reached from Hiroshima station by tram or bus. The information center can give assistance. There are also boats from nearby Iwakuni to Shikoku.

Hitching

Hitching along the south coast is very slow and unpleasant, although unavoidable if you wish to go directly toward Okayama and beyond (unless you go to the bother of getting to the expressway at one end and back out to the coast at the other). Route 2 passes through the city and can be intercepted by a tram No. 8 going south.

To use the Chugoku Expressway to/from Kyushu (west) or Osaka/Kyoto (east), the most convenient interchange is Hiroshima-kita, about 25 km out of the city. From Hiroshima it can be reached by taking Route 54 to Kami-ga-hara, then going left about seven km. The interchange is close to the west (far) end of the tunnel. The interchange can also be reached from Aki-imuro, which is a little more than an hour out of Hiroshima station (some trains begin only at Yokogawa station, through which all pass), but there are only about five trains a day. The interchange is about three km east of Aki-imuro station.

Getting Around

The simplest way to get around Hiroshima is by tram; one goes to the A-bomb dome, and you can return by the same route or walk along Peace Boulevard (Heiwa Dori) and across the river, returning to the station by another line.

The reason for the weird and wonderful variety in the color scheme of the trams is that Hiroshima (which wisely kept its tram tracks) bought up trams from other cities as they phased out tram services. The cars retain their original colors.

There are buses to Hiroshima station from various parts of the city. The bus station is in the Sogo Department Store; it serves both city buses and those to other cities. Any red or orange bus goes to the station; red-and-white striped ones pass by the castle.

Miyajima

Many of the buildings of the shrine on Miyajima were severely damaged by a typhoon at the end of September, 1991; TV and newspaper photos showed some buildings collapsed, the Noh theater partly submerged in the sea, others with roofs stripped off, and general mayhem prevailing. It was not known at the time of completing this revision how long repairs would take. The write-up from the previous edition has been retained for guidance, because the buildings will be rebuilt as closely as possible to the originals.

Things to See

The major attraction of the Hiroshima area is Miyajima (Shrine Island), more correctly known as Itsukushima. Its best known feature is one of the most famous symbols of all Japan, the huge off-shore *torii* gate that is seen in every travelog and book on Japan. The island is ranked traditionally as one of the three most beautiful sights in Japan (along with Matsushima, near Sendai, and Amanohashidate, on the north coast). There is much to see while walking

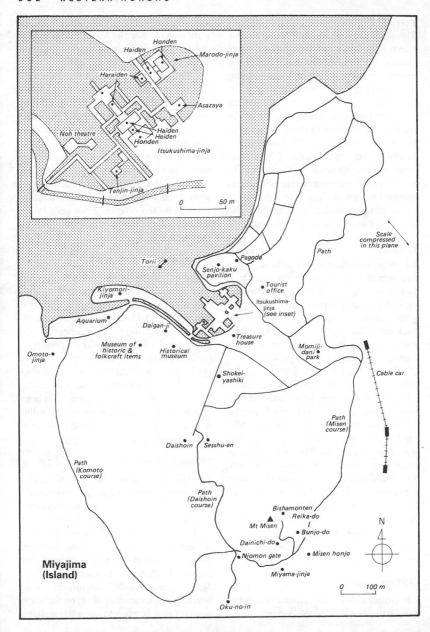

Honden
Haiden
Honden
Marodo-jinja
Haraiden
Asazaya
Noh theatre
Haiden
Heiden
Honden
Itsukushima-jinja
Tenjin-jinja

0   50 m

Torii
Pagoda
Senjo-kaku pavilion
Path
Scale compressed in this plane
Tourist office
Kiyomori-jinja
Itsukushima-jinja (see inset)
Aquarium
Daigan-ji
Treasure house
Omoto-jinja
Museum of historic & folkcraft items
Historical museum
Momiji-dani park
Shokei-yashiki
Cable car
Daishoin
Sesshu-en
Path (Misen course)
Path (Komoto course)
Path (Daishoin course)
Bishamonten
Reika-do
Mt Misen
Bunjo-do
Dainichi-do
Misen honjo
Niomon gate
Miyama-jinja
Oku-no-in

N

Miyajima (Island)

0   100 m

around the island—the famous shrine, the *torii*, the heavy woods to stroll through, the sound of the *semi* in summer, the tame deer—and a visit is sure to be enjoyed. A half-day will take in a good number of the features of the island, but an overnight stay would allow greater relaxation and time to absorb the mood.

The ferry from Miyajima-guchi on the mainland arrives at Miyajima-ko in 10 minutes. In front of the building at the entrance to the dock is a large three-dimensional information board for orientation. Most visitors set off immediately to the right, to the main attraction of the island, Itsukushima jinja shrine.

Itsukushima-jinja

The shrine is unusual because the buildings are built on piles over the shallows at the water's edge, and are joined by narrow galleries. One explanation of the unusual construction is that the island has been regarded as sacred from ancient times, and Taira no Kiyomori had the shrine built in this way in the 12th century so that it could be approached by boat without setting foot on land. (Earlier shrines had stood on the same spot since 593.)

The principal buildings of Itsukushima Shrine are the *honden* (main hall), *heiden* (offering hall), *haiden* (hall of worship), and *haraiden* (purification hall). In the *Asazaya* (morning prayer room), dance costumes and masks, etc., are displayed. The public is allowed only as far as the outer sanctuary of the honden; all these buildings, plus the corridors, are ranked as National Treasures.

The great *torii* gate in the water (accessible on foot at low tide for those who don't mind mud) dates from 1875, and is the largest wooden *torii* in Japan, 16.2 meters high and 23.3 meters wide. The large stone *torii* on the shore dates from 1905.

The first shrine structure seen when approaching from the ferry dock is Marodo-jinja, the largest shrine after Itsukushima-jinja itself.

Noh Theater

Most of the shrine buildings are of comparatively recent construction, but the Noh theater dates from 1568, and was rebuilt in Edo times. It is the oldest Noh theater in Japan, and one of the only stages in the world where the audience is unlikely to crowd around and block the view, especially at high tide.

Dances

The shrine is noted for performances of Bugaku and Kagura dances on the *takabutai* stage at the end of the shrine nearest the channel; every brochure on Japan is likely to feature a photo of a masked dancer with the *torii* in the background. However, performances do not seem to be regularly scheduled, but are performed according to the payment of a suitable fee, so seeing one may be hit-or-miss, depending on the arrival of a tour group.

Treasure Hall

On the shore near the shrine is the Treasure Hall (Homotsukan), which contains more than 3500 historical and cultural items, including a number of national treasures. The building resembles a simple temple, but was built specifically to house these items, as a replacement for an older wooden building. A folklore museum (*mingeikan*) is located in an old, traditional-style house nearby.

Other Sights

Apart from a visit to the shrine, there are several walking paths. A popular route passes a five-storey pagoda (*gojunoto*), which dates from 1407, and Senjokaku, an old pavilion (1587) of little particular interest.

Further inland, other sights (besides the pleasant forest and semi-tame deer) await, including Momiji-dani maple-grove park, a number of lesser shrines scattered through the woods, and the cable-car to the top of Mt. Misen. Near the upper station is a number of temple and shrine buildings, along with an observation platform (*tembodai*) that gives a good view.

Festivals

Colorful festivals are held on June 17 and July 18 of the lunar calendar. The former, Kangen Matsuri, is the biggest festival of the year. On April 15 and November 15, monks walk on fire; and on April 16 to 18, a special Noh performance is given.

Places to Stay

Accommodation ranges from the Miyajima-guchi YH (tel (0829) 56-1444) to ryokan of high quality (and price).

Getting There

Miyajima is easily reached from Hiroshima by rail, via Miyajima-guchi station, by both JR and by private line. The private line is shown on maps as starting at Higashi-hiroshima station. However, some trams from Hiroshima station go directly to Miyajima-guchi without transfer. Inquire locally about the correct tram.

YAMAGUCHI-KEN ▬▬▬

Iwakuni

The small city of Iwakuni is most famous for a very graceful and unusual wooden bridge of five arches, Kintai-kyo (Bridge of the Silver Brocade Sash). It is unusual because, not only does the understructure form an arch, but the actual walkway also rises and falls five times in its 193 meter length.

Things to See
Kintai-bashi Bridge

The present bridge dates from 1953, and is an exact replica of the historic one that stood from 1673 to 1950, when it was swept away by a flood. No nails were used in its construction. It is the only one of its kind in Japan, probably because the steepness of the walkway makes it so utterly impractical.

Cormorant Fishing

From June to August, *ukai* is performed nightly at the bridge, except on nights of full moon or after heavy rains, when the water is muddy.

Nishimura Museum

Near the bridge is the excellent Nishimura Hakubutsukan. Its collection comprises mostly samurai armor and weapons, along with other objects used in daily life (especially by warriors), and is one of the best such collections in Japan. It is worth a special visit by anyone at all interested in how samurai warriors dressed, fought, and lived (or died). The museum also has many pieces of superb lacquerware. The collection was put together over a period of 45 years from all over Japan, and was opened in 1963.

Shiroyama

On the top of Shiroyama, one of the hills overlooking the museum and bridge, is a novelty—a southern-European-style castle! A Japanese-style one stood here for the brief period 1608–15 before being torn down. The present building was constructed in 1960. Easiest access is by the cable-car that rises from Kikko-en park (close to both the bridge and museum). All are easily reached from Iwakuni or Shin-iwakuni (Shinkansen) stations by bus.

Places to Eat

Because of the U.S. military base near Iwakuni, there are several restaurants, fast food joints, etc., that serve U.S. or pseudo-U.S. food, which may be of interest to those suffering advanced junk-food withdrawal symptoms.

Hofu

Located here is one of Japan's better-known shrines, Hofu Tenmangu (Matsugasaki) shrine. The buildings are large, colorful, and impressive.

Tokuyama

There is a regular boat service between Tokuyama (Shinnanyo port) and Taketazu, on the Kunisaki Peninsula of Kyushu. Details are given in the Taketazu write-up.

Yanai

There is a regular boat service between Yanai and Matsuyama on Shikoku. More details are given in the section on Matsuyama.

Ogori

There are no notable tourist attractions at Ogori other than its summer steam-train excursions to and from Tsuwano. These are detailed in the general "Transportation" section early in the book.

Yamaguchi

Formerly a castle town, Yamaguchi reached its zenith in the 1500s and declined when the *daimyo* found himself on the losing side in the civil war. Relics from those days include Ruriko-ji (from the 14th century) and its five-storey pagoda, and a landscape garden by the famous designer Sesshu at Joei-ji temple. A modern cathedral was built to commemorate the time spent in Yamaguchi by St. Francis Xavier in 1551, but all of it except the facade was destroyed in a fire in 1991.

Chomon-kyo Gorge

About 20 km from Yamaguchi is the pretty gorge Chomon-kyo. It begins close to the station of the same name and extends for 12 km to Uzugahara. The Abu-kawa river has sculpted the rock into fanciful shapes, pools, falls, and Jacob's wells.

Akiyoshi

Clumps of limestone rocks dot the rolling Akiyoshi-dai tableland, looking like thousands of sheep or tombstones. Although the rocks appear small from a distance, many are as tall as a man.

Things to See

Akiyoshi Cave

Beneath the plateau is Akiyoshi-do, the largest cave in the Far East. It extends sev-

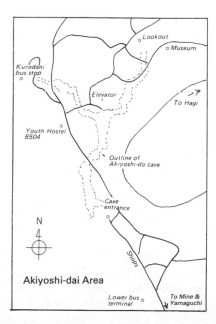

Akiyoshi-dai Area

eral km into the ground, of which about one km is accessible to visitors. Electric lights and walkways make the expedition simple, and you pass typical features of limestone caves, like stalagmites and stalactites (as geologists remember it, the mites go up and the tites go down), as well as other fantastic forms that the limestone takes as it precipitates out of solution.

Well into the cave there is an elevator that rises near Kuro-dani (Black Valley), which is located among the rocks of the plateau. A path leads up to a lookout (*tembodai*) and a museum of specimens associated with the cave and plateau. Buses run between the Kuro-dani area and the terminal near the entrance to the cave, so you can return to one entrance from the other by bus or retrace your steps through the cave.

Places to Stay

There is a large variety of accommodation in the area, particularly around Kuro-dani (including a youth hostel: tel (08376) 2-0341). There are places to stay near the lower entrance as well.

Getting There

Buses run throughout the day to and from Shimonoseki, Yamaguchi, Mine, and Ogori (south coast), and Higashi-hagi (north coast).

Shimonoseki

Shimonoseki (known to locals as "Shimo") is located at the far west end of Honshu, and is important as a crossing point to Kyushu as well as an international port of entry for the daily ferry service to and from Pusan, Korea. The name of the city has the well-earned meaning "Lower Gate".

Things to See

If this is your first time in Japan, you can get a good idea of the prosperity of the country by a quick walk around either

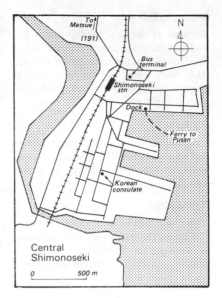

Central Shimonoseki

0   500 m

Daiei or Daimaru department stores on the square facing the station.

One of the major attractions of Shimonoseki is Akamon-jinja, a large and colorful shrine. It is made of concrete, not the traditional wood, and is thus not really representative of Japan's best. It is named for its red gate of uncommon Chinese shape. (There are many shrines in Japan that are more exciting.) The shrine can be reached by the same bus that goes to the youth hostel.

The other attraction is a view over the Kanmon Strait from Hinoyama (Fire Mountain). Those staying at the youth hostel are only a couple of minutes walk away. It is also easy to reach from the city by bus, either the hourly one from stand 3 to "Kokumin-shukusha-mae", which goes right up to and past the top station, or any bus going past "Ropeway-mae", where you get off and either take the cable car or walk up the hill.

Along the way out of Shimo you may see a sign pointing to the site of the battle of Dan-no-ura in 1185. Don't get out to look for anything, for most of the action took place in the water, and whatever beach might have existed has disappeared under the tall pillars of the graceful Kanmon-ohashi suspension bridge.

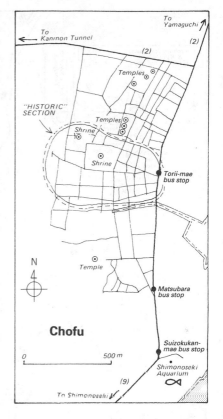

Shimonoseki Aquarium

Another attraction of Shimo is its aquarium, claimed to be the largest in the Orient. It has a collection of some truly weird and wonderful creatures of the deep; dolphin and seal shows are also part of the entertainment. The aquarium (*suizokukan*) is easily reached from Shimo station or by bus; the name of the bus stop is Suizokukan-mae.

Chofu

This is a separate town that is included as part of Shimo. Its claim to fame lies in a couple of streets with earth-walled samurai-style houses, and a few shrines and temples. It is an enjoyable walk for those with time to pass.

Korean Visas

These are available at the Korean consulate. See following explanation for details.

Places to Stay

Along with several hotels, etc., Shimo has the very pleasant Hinoyama YH (tel (0832) 22-3753), beautifully located overlooking the Kanmon Strait and the suspension bridge. It has one of the best vantage points in the city, with a view second only to that from the top of Hinoyama, 100 meters away. Access is as described above for Hinoyama. Only a passport is required to stay at the YH. If it is full, there may be vacancies at others nearby at Toyota (tel (08376) 6-8271) or Akiyoshi-dai (tel (08376) 2-0341), or in northern Kyushu

(covered in the Kyushu section).

Getting There—From Korea

The dock for the ferry from Korea is a 10-minute walk from Shimo station.

For those arriving from Korea, the only problem is likely to be the immigration officials, who have a reputation for being the most unpleasant and officious in Japan: passports are rigorously scrutinized, and an entry stamp given as if it were a precious gift. Travellers re-entering Japan can expect to be questioned as to the purpose of entry.

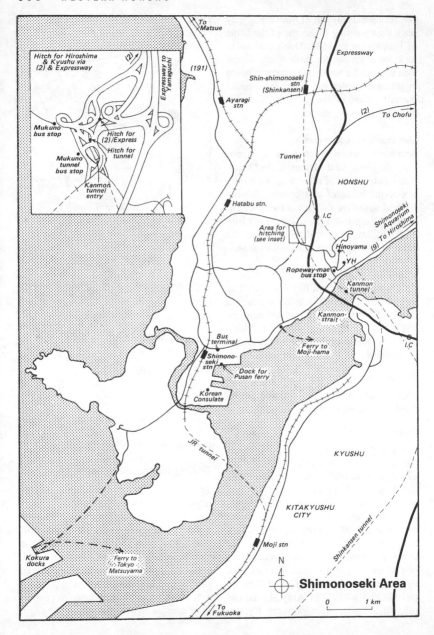

Shimonoseki Area

0   1 km

Because the ferry is the cheapest way to and from a foreign country, many people make the trip to renew visas. If you have any reason to anticipate difficulties (many prior entries to Japan, etc.), it might be simpler just to fly in through Narita, Osaka, Nagoya, etc., where the officials are more reasonable. (Officials at Fukuoka, in nearby Kyushu, are close runners-up to those at Shimo, so there is no likely advantage in going that way if you expect problems at Shimo).

There is a money changer in the ferry terminus; the rate is the same as that given at local banks. Be sure to exchange all Korean money *before* leaving Korea, as it is worthless outside the country (except at Korean banks in Tokyo and Osaka, and then only if you have exchange certificates from Korea). There is an exchange office at the Pusan terminal.

Getting to Korea

Boat Connection

There is a daily sailing in each direction by the Kampu ferry *Pukwan* between Shimonoseki and Pusan in Korea. It leaves from Shimo at 1700, arriving at Pusan next morning at 0830, and from Pusan at 1800, reaching Shimo at 0930. The lowest fare is ¥6800 (less 20% with a student card) for an open tatami area; smaller open rooms and cabins with bunks are available at higher cost. Shimonoseki International Port Terminal is 10-minute walk from Shimo station.

It is advisable to buy your ticket as early in the day as possible. By doing so, you get a reservation number that will save queuing near boarding time; try to get on board ship early to guarantee a place to lie at night. Once under way, it is also advisable to get to sleep early, as fellow passengers have been known to be up at 3 am standing in line (noisily) even though they do not begin to disembark until 7; there is

no need to rush, because there is a separate immigration line for aliens. (One reason for getting in line early, unless things have changed, is to observe if the "Passing of the Bribe" Ceremony is still held, when a herd of women collectively give to the immigration and customs official their stack of extension-paged passports, interleaved with U.S. banknotes, for processing, so that they can get the household appliances that they have bought in Japan landed in Korea without hassles.

The Tokyo TIC has a hand-out sheet with up-to-date fares and sailings. Kampu office telephone numbers: Tokyo (03) 3567-0971; Shimo (0832) 666-8211.

Visas

Visas are obtained with the least hassle at the visa annex of the Korean embassy in Tokyo, but are also available at the consulate at Shimo, Fukuoka, Osaka, and other cities.

In Shimonoseki, the Korean consulate, *Kankoku ryojikan*, is near the ferry dock. Here, visas *can* be obtained within the day if applied for early in the morning, but more than one traveller has reported rather brusque treatment.

Transportation out of Shimonoseki

Trains

Regular JR services to points in Honshu and Kyushu leave from Shimonoseki station. The Shinkansen super-expresses (the fastest service to Hiroshima, Kyoto, Tokyo, etc.) leave from Shin-shimonoseki station, two stops away by local train, and also accessible by bus from Shimo station; local trains are scheduled to reach Shin-shimo station in time for each train. There is a schedule of all services posted in Shimo station in adequate English, and staff at the information center should be able to give basic information. (As advised elsewhere, always speak slowly and clearly, avoid slang, and watch the person's face for signs of non-comprehension.) To cross to Kyushu, the simplest way is by train through the tunnel to Moji, Kokura, etc.

Ferries

A convenient way to get from Shimonoseki to points farther east on Honshu and to Shikoku is by overnight ferry from places in nearby northern Kyushu. Overnight ferries run from Kokura (part of Kitakyushu city), one to Tokyo (stopping en route at Tokushima, on Shikoku), and another to Matsuyama (on Shikoku); from nearby Shin-moji-ko, ferries run to Kobe and Osaka.

Further information on these ferries is given in the sections on Kokura and Shin-moji-ko, and details are to be found in the general "Transportation" section earlier in the book. However, the ports of departure and destination cities change with annoying regularity (for a guide book writer), so some of the routes described may have stopped, and others may have started. Learn how to use *jikokuhyo* and inquire locally about available ferries.

From Shimonoseki (Karato district) a ferry crosses to Moji-ko (on the upper right-hand tip of Kyushu) every 15–30 minutes between 0600 and 2130 (¥260). (Note that Moji-ko is in Kitakyushu city, and that Shin-moji-ko is some distance away.)

Road

By road eastward from Shimonoseki toward Osaka/Kyoto and Tokyo there are three main routes, north along the Sanin-kaigan coast (Route 191 out of Shimo), south along the Sanyo-kaigan coast (Route 2 out of Shimo), and the Chugoku expressway (*kosokudoro*).

The San-in route has only a few specific places to visit, like Hagi and Matsue,

but it is one of the most pleasant areas in Japan to travel through for seascapes, peaceful landscapes of farms, mountains (generally low), and even sand dunes. The road is quite flat along the coast, so it can be particularly recommended for cyclists; traffic is not too heavy either. At the end of the Sanin region it is easy to get to Kyoto and other attractions of central Honshu, or you can even take a ferry to Hokkaido.

The Sanyo route is quite pleasant and scenic as far as Hiroshima, with many hilly roads, large farmhouses, and some interesting side trips. East of Hiroshima is heavily populated and industrialized and road traffic moves at snail's pace most of the way to Kyoto. The route cannot be recommended to those on two wheels because the air along the road is filthy with diesel exhaust, as are all buildings close to the road. (I made the Hiroshima–Kyoto trip by motorcycle in less-crowded 1971; it took 17 hours almost non-stop, at the end of which I could have been mistaken for African.) However, the attractions of Okayama, Kurashiki, and Himeji are on this road, and there are some views of the Inland Sea.

A "compromise" route can be followed by travellers who do not have the option of going by one coast in one direction and returning via the other; that is to cut across country one or more times using any of several road or rail links traversing the island. The width of the island in the Chugoku region is approximately 70–110 km, as the crow flies (but not as he would be driving or in a train). The countryside is attractive along most of the inland roads.

The quickest road route eastward would be via the Chugoku Kosokudoro (expressway) to Osaka; there it connects directly with the Meishin Expressway past Kyoto to Nagoya, where you can continue (without stopping) via the Tomei Expressway to Tokyo (and onward nonstop (if desired) to the north of Tohoku). The scenery along the expressway is pleasant, but not outstanding. For hitchhikers in a hurry it is the only way.

Buses

With the completion of expressways through much of the length of the country, long-distance bus routes have been established, and are increasing yearly. At the time of writing there is a bus from Shimo to Osaka via the expressway, with a number of feeder routes running to the north and south coasts. For up to date routes, consult a *jikokuhyo*, which has one map exclusively of bus routes.

A bus can be useful at Shimo for getting out of the city to start hitching, as well, and there is a direct bus service (seven per day) from Shimo station to the Akiyoshi area, described earlier.

Hitching

As described at the beginning of the book, hitching is easy in Japan and one of the best ways to travel, both for economy and for experiencing the kindness of the Japanese people. The following section details the starting points for hitching out of Shimo.

EASTBOUND—SOUTH SHORE The road along the south shore is labelled Route 9, but it runs only a few km before becoming Route 2, and doesn't resume a separate identity until Ogori, 60 km away. Route 2 to Osaka (where it ends) is more direct than Route 191, and takes in Hiroshima, Kurashiki/ Okayama, and Himeji, but travellers should be aware that this road, along with Route 1 from Osaka to Tokyo, is one of the busiest in Japan and is almost one continuous urban area from Ogori to Tokyo. The road does pass along much of the Inland Sea, but the few glimpses of it from the road are not memorable. All roads in Japan, other than expressways, have an absurd maximum speed of 60 km/h, and actual averages are much lower than this because of an endless succession of red lights and urban areas. To make time, though without views, it is fastest to hitch at night with a truck (and they use the expressway to go any appreciable distance).

EXPRESSWAY/ROUTE 2 The Chugoku Kosokudoro (expressway) runs from Shimo east to Osaka. The expressway from Shimo also runs west to Kyushu across the graceful Kammon-ohashi suspension bridge. Eastbound, Route 2 curves to meet the coast and generally runs parallel to it as far as Osaka, passing virtually the only non-built-up area of the entire road, with good views of countryside, farms, etc. The expressway, on the other hand, saves time in terms of distance covered.

To hitch on the expressway or Route 2 toward Kyushu (via either bridge or tunnel), the best starting point is in a maze of interchanges, a map of which resembles the result of an explosion in a spaghetti factory. To reach it from Shimo station, take a bus from stand 2, but be sure that it is not an express: the destination is Mukuno Tunnel, where you get off and continue walking in the same direction. This should lead to a junction identified with direction signs to Kawatana (left) and Hiroshima/expressway/tunnel (right): follow the road to the right, and another set of signs will come into view. Traffic heading left to the expressway will subsequently split into streams going west to Kyushu and east toward Yamaguchi, while that to the right will branch off either toward the tunnel to Kyushu or to Hiroshima. Position yourself for the stream you want; there is one place that catches all traffic, but it is very busy so you must have a very large sign with the name of your destination in *kanji*, and there must be a clear place for a car to stop safely. It might be advisable to make a choice between trying for the expressway or Route 2 tunnel, as the approach road to each offers better stopping places than the point where they divide. If you want only the tunnel, it would be better to stand near the entrance (quite close to Mukuno bus stop).

For those hitching to the Shimo area, a bus from Mukuno bus stop goes into the station, but quite infrequently during the day. If you are coming through the tunnel you should try to get out of the vehicle as soon as possible after clearing the tunnel exit. If crossing the bridge, get off at or before the Shimonoseki/Dannoura exit and scramble back to the road, which leads back to the youth hostel.

Sanin Coast

The northern Sanin-kaigan coast is relatively undeveloped, mostly lush green farms (in summer) and prosperous-looking farm houses, plus coastal scenery. It is a much more pleasant area to travel through than the heavily industrialised southern coast (Sanyo-kaigan). Compared with the southern coast however, it has few specific attractions.

The area between Shimonoseki and Hagi was quite off the beaten track until comparatively recently. In the early '70s there were still many houses made of mud and wattle. Along the main road they have now all been replaced by wood or concrete buildings with aluminium doors and windows—vastly more practical and comfortable, but representing yet another vanished Japanese tradition.

There are several picturesque fishing villages along the way and many views of the sea.

Nagato

Off the end of Omi-shima island, near Nagato city, is a picturesque promontory of rocks, including twin pillars that jut more than 40 meters straight out of the sea. Access is by bus, and a cruise around the island is available.

The caves of Akiyoshi (described earlier) are accessible from Nagato. You can go by train to Mine and to Akiyoshi by bus, then carry on from there to Hagi (north

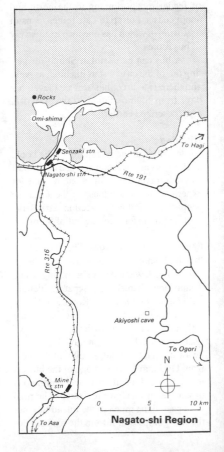

Nagato-shi Region

coast) or Mine to Yamaguchi, etc., on the south coast.

Hagi

The city of Hagi is a very popular holiday destination for the Japanese, partly for what there is to see, but also for its historical associations, particularly those leading to the Meiji Restoration. The latter are invisible to foreigners of course, so the importance of Hagi is less for non-Japanese. However, there are areas with a traditional appearance, and it can be worth a look around.

Many of the features that give Hagi its particular charm date back to the period when it was the castle town of the Mori clan. The castle stood from 1604 to 1871, when it was torn down—unfortunately, because the remaining walls and moats are quite picturesque.

Things to See

Visitors will be most interested in the castle fortifications, the grounds (which now make up Shizuki-koen park, and house its historical museum as well as a shrine), and a lovely beach. Hagi is built on the delta of several rivers. The nearby attractions, good for an hour or two of exploration on foot or by bicycle (available at the youth hostel across the road from the castle), include the narrow streets, samurai barracks of the feudal days, and a number of old houses. Several are best known as the former residences of well-known figures in the history of Japan just prior to the Meiji Restoration (and instrumental in it), but they can be appreciated just for their appearance as well.

Hagi is well known for pottery. Three potteries are located near the castle: Shiroyama, Shogetsu, and Hagi-jo.

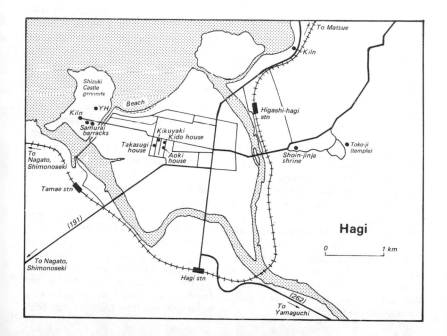

The castle area is closest to Tamae station, one stop beyond Hagi station. Buses are also available, the closest stop being Shizuku-bashi.

Shoin Shrine

Another area of touristic interest centers around Shoin-jinja. In the grounds is a building that served as the village school where local hero Yoshida Shoin taught; he was loyal to the emperor, and was executed by the Tokugawa government.

Near Shoin-jinja is Toko-ji, the family temple of the Mori family and famous for 494 stone lanterns erected by their subordinates over several generations. The Shoin-jinja area is easily reached by bus from Higashi-hagi station (Nakano-kuru stop).

Myojin-ike Lake

Lake Built as a retreat by the Mori, this lake outside the city is connected to the ocean and follows its tides.

Potteries

There are four potteries in the vicinity of Shoin-jinja: Miwa, Shodo, Renzokan, and Hosen.

Other Sights

Of lesser interest is a pretty little shrine to the right of the road when going into Hagi from Hagi station. I was interested in a stone turtle statue bearing a commemorative stone on its back, a common sight in Korea, but almost unknown in Japan. It may have some relationship to the Korean potters who were brought here in the early 1600s by the Tokugawa following an invasion of Korea, or it may indicate earlier ties with that country. The latter is logical in view of the short distance across the water to Korea, and it is known that this area was settled in very early times by people from Korea.

Places to Stay

There are numerous hotels, *ryokan, minshuku* and other accommodation in Hagi, as well as a youth hostel (tel (08382) 2-0733) near the castle. Across the street from it is a kokumin-shukusha.

Continuing Along the Coast

East from Hagi to Tottori the coast is pleasant, with a succession of towns and cities, some fishing villages, and many farms. It is one of the better areas for observing unpolluted rural Japan. Foreigners are quite rare, so the people are even nicer than usual.

SHIMANE-KEN ▬▬▬

Masuda

In the somewhat industrial city of Masuda the attractions are Manpuku-ji and Iko-ji, both of which have noted landscape gardens.

From Masuda, Route 9 and the train cross diagonally to Yamaguchi via Tsuwano, while Route 191 and rail continue along the coast to Hagi and Shimonoseki at the western tip of Kyushu.

Tsuwano

The old castle town of Tsuwano has long been known for carp, and recently for steam as well. The former come in a variety of beautiful colors, number in the tens of thousands, and measure up to a meter in length. They may be found in ponds in front of most business establishments, and even in the channels passing beside the road in the Tonomachi district of the town.

Inari-jinja is the best known shrine in Tsuwano, and is noted for its huge, bright-orange *torii* gate. Near the shrine is a museum (Kyodokan) of historical items.

The other reason for fame is that Tsuwano is the northeast terminus of a steam train run from Ogori (Yamaguchi-ken), one of only two such runs surviving in Japan. Further details are given in the section on rail transport in the introductory section of the book.

Mt. Sambe

The next major attraction is inland from Oda. The mountain can be climbed easily in an hour from Sambe-onsen (hot-spring resort), which is accessible by bus (12 per day) from Oda. Nearby is a large lava field and a small lake, Ukinu-no-ike.

Easily reached from the area is the Dangyo-kei ravine that stretches four km along the Yagami-kawa river. The ravine is six km from Imbara, on the railway line passing close to Sambe-onsen; a bus runs toward the ravine from Imbara.

Izumo

Not far from Matsue is Izumo, site of Izumo-taisha, the oldest Shinto shrine in Japan and ranking only behind the grand shrines of Ise in importance. It is most easily reached from Matsue by the Ichihata private railway line; the 40 km trip takes less than an hour, and 21 trains a day run from Matsue-onsen to Izumo-taisha-mae station. Turn right when leaving the station and walk up the hill. If travelling by the private line, note the tall trees grown as windbreaks on the windswept flat peninsula.

Typical of shrines in Japan, although the site is ancient, the buildings are comparatively recent, dating from 1874 (the main shrine from 1744). They are built in the oldest style of architecture known in Japan, and are quite imposing. The grounds are covered with tall old trees, and the shrine is backdropped by Yakumo hill. There is a museum in the grounds.

This area was one of the earliest settled by the post-Yayoi people. They most likely came from nearby Korea, although their ancestry is not known with any certainty.

(There is strong evidence that the present Japanese are, to a large extent, descendants of settlers from Korea. But, because most Japanese hold Koreans in very regard, such findings have been given little regard.)

By the old (lunar) calendar, the month of October was the time when all the Shinto gods met at Izumo, so the month was known in the Izumo area as *Kami-arizuki* (month with gods) and as *Kannazuki* (month without gods) everywhere else in Japan.

Inasano-hama

This is a beach close to Izumo-taisha shrine, about two km from the stations; swimming is good. About 6.5 km northwest of the beach is Cape Hino-misaki, site of ancient Hino-misaki shrine and a lighthouse, and with very pretty coastal scenery. Buses run to both the beach and the cape (35 minutes to the latter from the station).

Tachikue-kyo Gorge

Near Izumo-shi is the pretty one-km-long Tachikue-kyo, formed of cliffs, picturesquely eroded rock, and basalt columns. It is easily reached from Izumo-shi station by train to Tachikue-kyo station in 30 minutes.

Hirata

Between Matsue-onsen and Izumo is Hirata, where Gakuen-ji temple is noted for the brilliant autumn colors of trees in its grounds.

Matsue

Picturesquely located between a lake (Shinji) and a lagoon (Naka-umi), the city of Matsue is the proud owner of one of the few original castles surviving in Japan, a small but attractive structure dating from 1611.

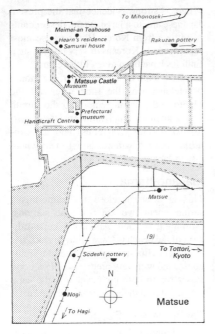

To Mihonoseki

Meimei-an Teahouse

Hearn's residence
Samurai house

Rakuzan pottery

Matsue Castle
Museum

Prefectural
museum

Handicraft Centre

Matsue

(9)

To Tottori,
Kyoto

Sodeshi pottery

N

Nogi

To Hagi

Matsue

Things to See

Matsue-jo Castle and Surroundings

Near the castle is *buke-yashiki*, an old samurai residence that has been well preserved; it is open to the public. Nearby is the former residence of Lafcadio Hearn, an English writer who lived in Matsue during the 1890's and wrote a number of books about the Japan of that day, most of which are still readily available as reprints. Close to his old house is Yakumo-kinenkan, a museum of his manuscripts and other memorabilia.

Fudoki-no-oka Hill

The Matsue area was one of the regions settled before the Yamato conquest of the Japanese islands. There is an archaeological site of an ancient village to the south of Matsue at Fudoki-no-oka, with a museum displaying artefacts of this old civilization. On the grounds are reproductions of ancient dwellings. Inquire locally for information on how to get to the museum. (Closed Monday.)

Kaga

A stretch of picturesque coast may be found at Kaga, north of Matsue. The most interesting part is the cave Kaga-no-kukedo, which is entered by boat; the opening is small but the interior is large. Access is by bus from Matsue, taking a little over an hour.

Festivals

Annual festivals at Izumo-taisha are on May 14–16 and October 11–17 (lunar calendar); October 22 through November 3 are very popular for weddings at Izumo, so it should be possible to see gorgeous bridal kimonos against the backdrop of the shrine.

At Matsue, festivals are held in the first half of April (Castle Festival), and the last third of July (Matsue-odori dance and fireworks display); there is also the summer festival of Tenmangu jinja shrine.

On August 16 (Toro-nagashi), many paper lanterns on tiny boats are released on Shinji-ko lake. In the middle of the month is the *obon* festival, and Takeuchi-jinja shrine festival is at the end. There are also various festivals on November 3, 5, and 6.

Oki Islands

These islands, almost due north of Matsue, are known for their high steep cliffs and generally wild scenery. Access is by boat from near Matsue (Sakai-minato and Nanarui) to Saigocho on the main island. There are two youth hostels on Dogo-shima, and one each on the three lesser islands.

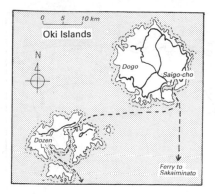

Oki Islands

0   5   10 km

N

Dogo

Saigo-cho

Dozen

Ferry to
Sakaiminato

TOTTORI-KEN ■■■■■■■

Mt. Daisen

For a considerable distance along the way, the form of Daisen is visible. It is interesting because, although it presents a conical face from the west, it is seen as a succession of smaller peaks from the north or south. It may be climbed quite easily and offers a good view over the coast (including the Oki Islands) and nearby peaks. In clear weather it is possible to see Shikoku to the south. The climb begins at Daisen-ji temple, which is easily reached by bus from Daisen-guchi station. The 5.5 km climb takes about 3-1/2 hours going up and 1-1/2 hours coming down. The temple was founded in 718 and was once huge and powerful, but all its original buildings have been destroyed by fire.

Tottori

The best-known place along the Sanin-kaigan is the extensive area of sand dunes at Tottori, two km wide and 16 km long. They have a stark beauty all their own, their broad flanks rippled by the wind. Even though there are usually hundreds of sightseers on the dunes at any one time, they are swallowed in its expanse, and the

energetic can walk beyond the area usually tromped by the hordes. In the heat of the summer it is advisable to have a canteen of water or some soft drinks, for the air is very dehydrating. The dunes are slightly to the east of town; the entrance is easily reached by bus from Tottori.

In the city of Tottori itself, Tottori Mingei Hakubutsukan (Folk Art Museum) may be of interest, along with the garden of Kannon-in temple.

An alternative route for those headed toward the south coast is via Tsuyama, which is described in the Okayama-ken section.

The Sanin coast is considered to extend as far east as Amino. The road and rail line follow the coast closely, giving good views over the sea to contrast with spreads of farms and inland mountains. Although there is no particular attraction, the areas near Kasumi and Yoroi are highly regarded. Typical sea scenery is a succession of pretty views of small white beaches with rocks jutting sharply out of the water, many topped with one or more twisted "patented Japanese-type" pine trees. As mentioned earlier, the Sanin coast is quite level for much of its length, with relatively gentle grades where they do appear. Because of the sparse (by Japanese standards) traffic, the area can be particularly recommended to cyclists.

HYOGO-KEN (NORTH) ■■■■■

Toyooka

In the vicinity of this small city (pronounced "Toyo-oka") in northern Hyogo-ken are the well known and very interesting basalt grotto-like rock formations of Gembudo. Liquid lava cooled and crystallized. Some of it formed pillars six to nine meters in height, of five, six, seven, and eight sides, some parallel, others growing at odd angles. Other lava formed structures that

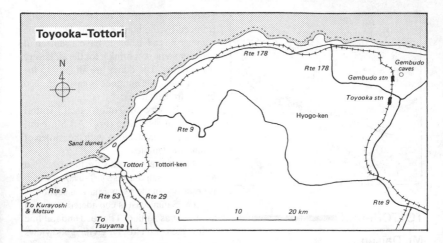

look like neatly stacked bricks. There are five grottos, of various heights. Access is by train to Gembudo station, 5.3 km out of Toyooka, and then by ferry across the river.

KYOTO-FU (NORTH)

Amanohashidate

About 30 km west of Maizuru, and almost due north of Kobe (in northern Kyoto-fu) lies one of the Japanese "Big Three" scenic places, traditionally regarded as the three finest views in Japan. (The other two are Matsushima, near Sendai, and Miyajima, near Hiroshima.)

The cause of this excitement is a sand bar that stretches 3.6 km across peaceful Miyazu Bay. It varies from 35 to 110 meters in width, and has many picturesque, twisted pine trees.

The best view is obtained from Kasamatsu-koen park to the northwest, accessible by cable-car, or from Ochi-toge (pass) on a local road to Tango-omiya. (The traditional way to look at the scene is by bending over and looking at it through your legs!) The former can be reached from

Amanohashidate station by bus to Ichinomiya (15 minutes), or by ferry from Amanohashidate or Miyazu (15 and 25 minutes respectively). You can also walk across the sandbar. Amanohashidate station is served by a private railway that runs between Toyooka and Nishi-maizuru.

It should be noted that the scenery is in fact, not terribly spectacular, and the modern generation of Japanese do not fall into raptures at the sight, though the town is full of young sightseers in summer. It's worth a look for those passing through, but not worth a special trip for itself alone.

Okutango Peninsula

A route taken by few travellers leads around the Okutango (or Yosa) Peninsula, which begins at Amanohashidate. There are several good sea views and picturesque fishing villages. The most scenic of the villages is Ine, about 20 km from Miyazu, which is built right to the water's edge around a semicircular bay, with the back part of the houses on stilts over the water. It is quite hilly, so not the best for bikes.

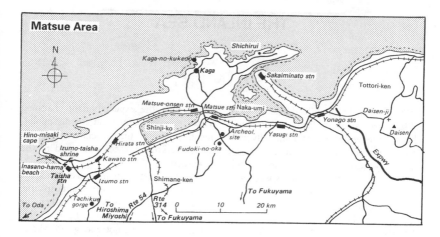

From here, the main routes are south-ward to Kyoto and vicinity, either through the mountains or around the western shore of Biwa-ko lake, or eastward around Wakasa Bay toward Fukui, with the option of going south along the eastern shore of Biwa ko to Hikone, etc. These areas are covered in the earlier section on the Kinki region, while the Wakasa Bay area is de-scribed at the end of the section on the Hokuriku region.

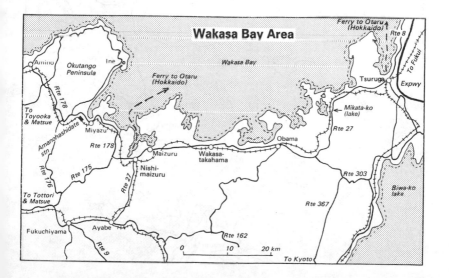

THE INLAND SEA

S eto Naikai, the Inland Sea, is one of those areas in Japan about which travel writers have traditionally written in superlatives and uncritically. There *are* many very lovely views around this body of water, but the reality is that much of it has changed greatly since it first came to the notice of western eyes. Many fishing villages have been replaced by modern industries—substituting "progress" and pollution for once idyllic scenes. The waters are filled with large numbers of ships, and the peace and serenity of 30 and more years ago have largely disappeared. Anyone arriving with the expectation of charming views at every turn is in for disappointment, although time spent seeking out some or all of the places mentioned may be rewarded.

The biggest problem with enjoying the scenery of the Inland Sea is atmospheric; during the months of warm weather, the visibility over the water may be only a few kilometers or less, not enough to take in distant views and often not even those just a short distance offshore.

The book *The Inland Sea*, by Japan expert Donald Richie, although in many ways

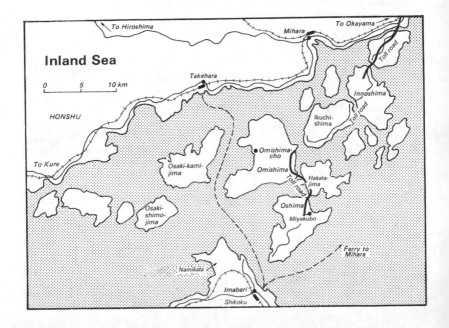

a narrative of personal development and change, gives a good description of the area as it was through the eyes of a Japanese-speaking foreigner. The book is beautifully illustrated, though it probably outdoes present reality.

Along the north shore of the sea, good views may be available (from east to west) near Okayama/Kurashiki, Onomichi, Tomo-no-Ura (near Fukuyama), and Itsukushima (Miyajima, near Hiroshima), as well as at Shimonoseki, at the western end of the sea. (Each vantage point is described under the appropriate city.) The most beautiful maritime views are in the area bounded on the east by Shodo Island and on the west by Tomo-no-ura (Honshu) and Tadotsu (Shikoku).

In addition to the numerous "shuttle" ferries between Honshu and Shikoku that pass through various parts of the Inland Sea, the overnight ferry from Beppu to Kobe and Osaka (leaving Beppu at 2100) passes through some of the most scenic parts of the sea in the early morning. Because the sky is light as early as 0430 in the summer, early risers can have a couple of hours of sightseeing before the boat docks at Takamatsu at 0730 (and more after it leaves). It reaches Kobe at 1150 and Osaka at 1310. The boat that leaves Osaka at 2100 and Kobe at 2230 reaches Imabari at 0540, so this trip would provide some views of the western part of the Inland Sea by daylight, although you would have passed through the "best" part before sunrise.

There are numerous ferries and hydrofoils across the Inland Sea between Honshu and Shikoku. Terminals are shown on the map and the frequency and travel time information is given in the write-up for the places on Shikoku (not Honshu).

The best way to enjoy the mood of the Inland Sea (if you have time to spare) is to pick an island or two and spend some time there. Some have youth hostels, and an island of any size is sure to have a minshuku; an isolated area is the best place to enjoy the homely pleasures of minshuku accommodation.

The islands described fall into three groups: Awaji-shima; Shodo-shima and nearby islands; and Innoshima and nearby islands.

AWAJI-SHIMA

This is the largest island in the Inland Sea, and one of the most densely populated islands in Japan. It is relatively flat and agricultural, holding no fantastic visual delights. It serves as a bridge between the Kobe area (via Akashi) and Shikoku.

Things to See

Puppet Theater

Awaji appears to be the home of the oldest puppet theater in Japan, more ancient though less famous than the Bunraku of Osaka. Short (about 30 minutes) performances of puppet plays are given daily at Ningyo-za, the small puppet theater by the ferry dock at Fukura at 1100 between March 1 and November 30. At other times you must be content with a look at the large number of puppets on display around the walls.

It was feared that the puppetry tradition would die out completely, as the 15 performers at Fukura are the only ones left on Awaji and their average age is close to 70. However a renaissance seems to be under way, so there may be a return to the golden days of the start of the Meiji era, when there were 48 theaters on Awaji.

Naruto Whirlpools

The whirlpools are almost next door to Fukura. They are at their mightiest at high and low tide, when the water swirls into or out of the Inland Sea through the narrow

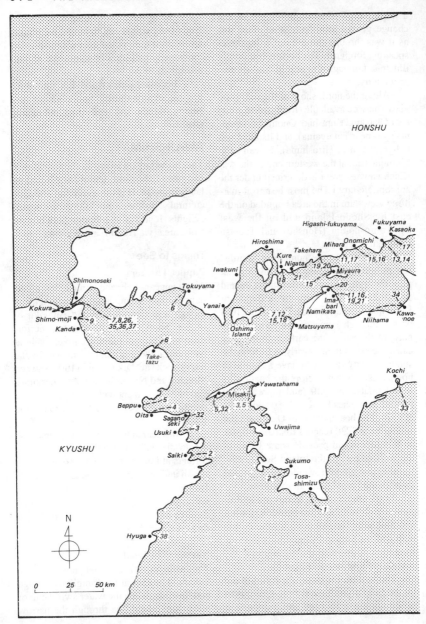

Ports with Ferry Services

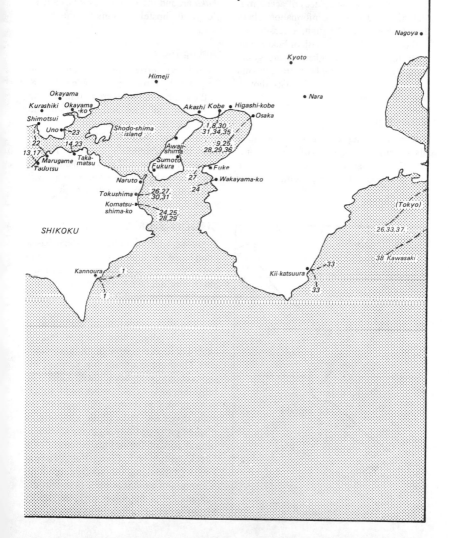

(1.3 km) Naruto Strait between Awaji and Shikoku. The rapids run in one direction at high tide and in the opposite at full ebb. It is necessary to catch them at either extreme to see the whirlpools at their greatest (over 20 meters across); tide tables are posted at touristed locales, and places of accommodation should also have information. There is a lookout over the strait, accessible by toll road, a little to the north of Fukura and near the pier of the giant bridge going across the strait. Cruise boats from Fukura travel very close to the whirlpools, though without danger.

Other Sights

Other sightseeing on Awaji-shima includes the beaches and sea views of Goshiki-hama and Kei-no-Matsubara. The former (meaning "five-colored beach") has multicolored pebbles. Each stretches several km, and both are accessible by bus from Sumoto in less than an hour.

Places to Stay

There are several hotels, *ryokan*, and *minshuku* around the island, as well as a temple youth hostel at Sumoto, the major town.

Getting There

From Kobe, ferries cross to Sumoto, and from Akashi, ferries are available to Iwaya. At the south end, ferries cross from Nandan to Naruto and from Anaga to Kame-ura (both destinations on Shikoku).

The graceful Naruto Ohashi suspension bridge stretches between Fukura (Awaji-shima) and Shikoku, making this link possible by road as well. A bridge will eventually link Awaji with Honshu, near Kobe.

SHODO-SHIMA

Everyone who visits Shodo Island has a good word for it. It is sufficiently off the beaten track not to be overrun with tourists, but it has adequate accommodation and travel facilities as well as lots of beautiful scenery.

The main attraction of the island is Kanka-kei gorge, near the east end. A cable-car descends through the most scenic part. There are also many fine views of unspoilt countryside, tidy terraced paddies up hillsides, mountains, farmers and fishermen, as well as quarries that supplied the giant stones for Osaka Castle. Other sights include groves of olives (in the south and central part of the island), a replica of a Greek temple (at Tayo-no-oka Heiwakoen) overlooking the sea and beautiful scenery, and a monkey park. (The friendly simians are in the lower park, unfriendly higher up; even a short-time visitor can get

Awaji-shima

N

Akashi
Iwaya
Tsuna-cho
Goshiki-cho
Goshiki-hama
Seidan
Toll road
Sumoto
Anaga
Naruto stn
Nandan
Onaruto bridge
Naruto

0   10   20 km

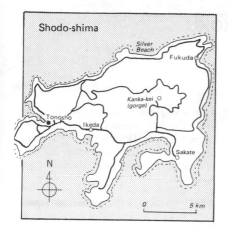

Shodo-shima

Silver Beach
Fukuda
Kanka-kei (gorge)
Tonosho
Ikeda
Sakate
N
0   5 km

Kobe, and Osaka. Check the schedules in *jikokuhyo*, or get help at an information center or travel agency.

OTHER ISLANDS

From Shodo-shima you can island-hop via Toyo-shima to Uno, near Okayama. Other pleasant, really off-the-beaten-track islands (some are listed below) are located between Imabari (Shikoku) and Mihara (Honshu) and are accessible (along with nearby islands) from both places. Anyone really interested in this type of exploring might try to obtain an old copy of Nancy Phelan's book *A Pillow of Grass*.

Ikuchi-shima

The island offers views of orange groves, shrines, temples, and most important, an atmosphere of rural Japan. Besides the youth hostel overlooking a quiet village, there are also *ryokan* and *minshuku*.

Innoshima

This island is also worth a visit but has no youth hostel. Ikuchi-shima is "next-door" however.

Omishima

Fifteen km off Imabari city, Omishima is noted for Oyamazumi-jinja shrine, dedicated to the guardian gods of sailors. In historic times, it was visited by many warriors off to battle, and a large amount of the finest armor was donated in supplication for good fortune in battle. As a result, 80% of all the armor in Japan that has survived and been given the rating "national treasure" or "important cultural property" belongs to this shrine. Most of it is on display, unlike at other museums which show only a small sample of their collections. The shrine is near Miyaura, the town where the ferries dock.

a feel for the social organisation within their community.)

Places to Stay

There are two youth hostels on the island, but budget accommodation is generally otherwise scarce. The information center at both Tonosho and Sakate may be of assistance in finding a room.

Getting Around

Getting around Shodo is no problem, as buses run regularly—both special and sightseeing coaches, and scheduled public transport. The usual starting point is Tonosho, but tour buses also leave from Sakata and possibly from other ports served by ferries. Generally it seems there is a tour bus waiting for each ferry arrival. More than one person has liked the relaxed pace of Shodo life and stayed for several days. You can get a good idea of its attractions by taking a bus tour on arrival, then explore by public bus afterward.

Ferries connect the towns of Tonosho, Ikeda, Sakata, and Fukudo (on Shodo) with Takamatsu, Ono, Okayama, Hinase, Himeji,

SHIKOKU

Shikoku is the fourth main island of the Japanese group. It is generally rural and gets left by most travellers as a place to see if time permits, not an unrealistic evaluation. With available time, however, it can be worth a visit for a couple of unique attractions.

On Shikoku you are almost sure to see large numbers of people dressed in white, making pilgrimages to the 88 temples related to the priest Kobo Daishi. It should not be difficult to locate the temples, for they are marked by road signs (in Japanese only). As places of touristic interest to foreigners, however, none is really outstanding. Apart from scenery, the most noteworthy place on Shikoku is Ritsurin-koen garden in Takamatsu, one of the finest in Japan.

GETTING THERE

There is a great variety of ship services to and from Honshu and Kyushu. Connections are described in the text. Note, however, that these services change very much from year to year, so information given here can be only a guide, and is as likely as not to indicate services that no longer exist. The book of timetables, *jikokuhyo*, shows all current services.

There are also air services from the principal cities in each of the four prefectures that give Shikoku its name, which translates as "Four Districts".

In 1985 the graceful 1629-meter-long Naruto Ohashi suspension bridge was put into service between Awaji-shima and Naruto, across the Naruto Strait. It is the longest suspension bridge in the Orient. In 1988, the Seto Ohashi bridge system also opened, joining Honshu (near Okayama) and Shikoku (near Takamatsu). Another will eventually link Awaji Island with the Kobe area.

TOKUSHIMA-KEN

Naruto

The great whirlpools of the Naruto Strait have already been described in the section on Awaji-shima (Inland Sea). From the Shikoku side, an excellent view is available from Naruto Park on Oge-jima Island (eight km northeast of Naruto city); buses run from Naruto station. The park is also accessible from Awaji-shima by ferry from Anaga (a little above Fukura).

Tokushima

This city is known for a crazy dance, puppets, and a fine garden. One of the most famous festivals in Japan is the Awa-odori (August 15–18) when large numbers of celebrants dressed in traditional costume dance in the city streets through much of the night.

Things to See
Puppet Theater
Along with Awaji-shima and Osaka, Tokushima has a tradition of puppet theater. Performances are usually given by farmers, so they are more likely to be seen after harvest time and before planting; make inquiries locally.

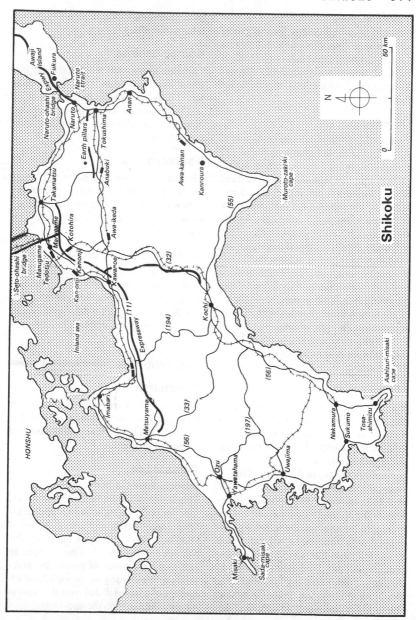

Tokushima Park

This park contains a garden that was part of the mansion associated with Tokushima Castle (now ruined) and dates from 1586. It is a landscape garden typical of the Momoyama period. The park is 400 meters east of the station.

Other Sights

East from Tokushima you can go to Anabuki station and then take a bus (15 minutes) northeast to an interesting natural phenomenon. Pillars of earth have been formed by erosion, and stand 12 to 18 meters high. They are similar to the Hoodoos in Alberta (Canada) and other formations in the Tyrol.

South from Tokushima lies Anan, beside Tachibana Bay. It offers a good view of many islands, and is compared by local boosters to the famous Matsushima (near Sendai), although the slightest resemblance in any way to a more famous sight in Japan receives similar comparisons.

From a point one km south of Mugi, Yasakahama beach stretches for about 10 km.

Getting There

The ferry between Tokyo and Kokura (Kyushu) every two days stops at Tokushima en route each way. For details refer to the general "Transportation" section early in the book.

Locally, boats run from Tokushima to various docks in Wakayama-ko (¥3390) and Fuke-ko (near Wakayama; ¥1410), Osaka, and Kobe. These boats are too numerous to list here, and the schedules (and ports) change from year to year, but typical times are 2 hours from Osaka by passenger boat (¥4530) and 3-1/2 hours (¥1970) by car ferry. From Kobe, the hydrofoil takes two hours (¥4530), the ferry 190 minutes (¥1970). For up-to-date information and ports of departure, consult *jikokuhyo* or an information office.

Komatsushima

There are many boats through the day between Komatsushima-ko and Wakayama-ko (¥1700), and a couple to Osaka.

From Komatsushima you can continue down to Cape Muroto at the far southeast tip of the island.

Kannoura

The daily boat between Kobe and Tosa-shimizu (southwest Shikoku) stops en route both ways at Kannoura (¥3090), but the arrival time from Kobe is awkward. (To Kobe is OK.)

Northwest from Naruto

From Naruto to Takamatsu, the main road runs parallel to the coast and offers several pretty views. (Lookouts are provided beside the road.) The rafts visible in the water are used to grow edible seaweed, not pearls.

KAGAWA-KEN ■■■■■

Takamatsu

Probably the most enjoyable city on Shikoku, Takamatsu features one of the finest gardens in Japan, as well as a number of other attractions.

Things to See

Ritsurin-koen Garden

This is one of the finest gardens in Japan, superior (in my eyes) to at least two of the "Big Three" gardens—those at Mito and Okayama—and at least the equal of Kenroku-en in Kanazawa. It is built around an interconnected series of ponds, and comprises a large variety of views, taking advantage of a large hill and natural forests in its plan. It dates from the mid-1600s.

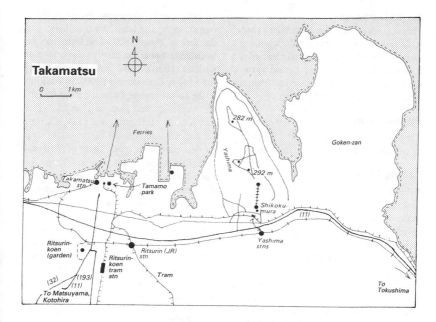

A folkcraft museum in the park features an excellent collection of hand-crafted utensils, etc. It has two sections, one for Shikoku crafts, the other for those from other regions of Japan.

The garden is easily reached by tram; the stop is Ritsurin-koen.

Takamatsu-jo Castle

Most of the castle has been destroyed, but the remaining walls, three turrets, and one original gate are quite picturesque. It is close to Takamatsu station and pier, and is thus easy to reach. The site is now called Tamamo-koen park.

Yashima

Technically this is an island because a narrow channel surrounds it, but it appears to be a high hill (292 meters) on the east of the city. Historically it is famous for a battle,

one of a seemingly endless number throughout western Japan between the Taira and Minamoto clans in the late 1100s which the Taira usually lost.

The top of the hill is accessible directly by bus from the station or by tram and cable-car to the south peak. At the top, Yashima-ji temple has a display of relics from the battles, while the north peak offers a good view over the Inland Sea.

Shikoku-mura

This is a collection of typical, traditional buildings from various locations around the island, and includes a vine suspension bridge of the type once common in isolated valleys. It is interesting if you have not visited such a village elsewhere, but could be a bit of a letdown if you have already been to Takayama.

Megishima Island

This tiny island (eight km in circumference) is famous in Japan through the children's story of Momotaro, a boy who cleaned out a pack of demons. It offers a good view of the Inland Sea; it is only four km from the city, and easily reached by ferry.

Places to Stay

There are two youth hostels at Takamatsu, as well as *ryokan*, *minshuku*, and hotels.

Getting There

Ferries

One of the Osaka–Beppu overnight ferries stops at Takamatsu en route each way (evening from Osaka, morning from Beppu). Several boats run to Shodo-shima island from Matsuyama; details are given in the write-up on Shodo.

Takamatsu is linked with Kobe and Osaka by ferries (from ¥2370); three/day; 4 and 5-1/2 hours, resp.), and hydrofoils (¥5990; four/day from Osaka (two from Kobe; 2 and 2-l/2 hours, resp.).

Between Takamatsu and Uno (near Okayama), three lines operate ferries with departures at 30 and 40 minute intervals through the day (60–75 min; ¥380). (These boat services have remained viable despite the opening of the giant Seto Ohashi bridge system linking Honshu and Shikoku by road and rail.)

The Shikoku end of the bridge system begins at Sakaide, which is only about 20 km from Takamatsu.

Train

There is regular JR train service between Takamatsu and Okayama, on Honshu, via the Seto Ohashi chain of bridges across the Inland Sea. A Japan Rail Pass is valid for these. The "ordinary" service is the more than 30 daily *kaisoku* (non-surcharge express) trains in each direction between Okayama and Takamatsu. Between these two cities the trip takes about an hour, and the fare is about ¥800. The train can be boarded/left near the start of the bridge at Kojima (Honshu) and Sakaide (Shikoku) for a lower fare (around ¥400). In addition to the *kaisoku* trains, there are about 9 daily 'L' expresses that stop only at Okayama and Kojima on Honshu and only at Utazu (one at Sakaide instead) before continuing to destinations in other parts of Shikoku (not Takamatsu). There is a surcharge for these trains if one is paying cash fare (non Rail Pass). (Utazu and Sakaide are about 20km west of Takamatsu.)

Road

The Seto Ohashi bridges also carry road traffic, so it is possible to hitch across the strait by starting on the access highway.

For up-to-date details, consult a copy of *jikokuhyo* or a travel agent.

Sakaide

This port city is the starting point on the Shikoku end of the Seto Ohashi bridge system from Honshu. This combination of 11 bridges and linking roadway is a marvel of construction totalling 13.1 km, and cost ¥1.1 trillion. The longest span is 1100 meters, which is 180 meters shorter than the Golden Gate bridge, and 300 less than the world's longest, Britain's Humber Bridge, but it is the longest double-decker bridge span in the world.

Marugame

The town still has some gates and structures of Marugame Castle (built in 1597) remaining. The castle is about one km south of the station.

Between Marugame and Shimotsui (near Kurashiki) there are 14 ferry crossings daily in each direction (65 min/¥650; 45 min/¥870). Between Marugame and

Fukuyama there are four daily crossings each way (¥3100, 70 minutes).

Tadotsu

Tadotsu is interesting in *sakura* time when 10,000 cherry trees in Toryo-koen park (1.5 km west of the station) are in bloom. The same park gives a good view over the sea, and there is a good beach nearby.

Between Tadotsu and Fukuyama there are 11 boat crossings a day in each direction (¥1340; 100 min).

Kotohira & Kompira-san

One of the best-known shrines in Japan is Kotohira-gu, on Kompira-san. It was, for a long time, the shrine for mariners who brought their boats nearby to be blessed. The shrine is on a high hill and is accessible only by a very long climb.

From the top there is a good view of the nearby countryside, and there are several attractive shrine buildings, lanterns, etc., to see on the way up. These include paintings by Maruyama on the doors of the Shoin (built 1659). However, this shrine is little different from a number of other old shrines in Japan, and the one km climb (it seems like 10) is not rewarded in proportion to the effort.

A single male wandering the back streets at night might get the impression that not all visitors to Kotohira come for religious experience. A woman in a dimly-lit window beckoned conspiringly to me and offered "Korean women". (Korean women are widely and mistakenly believed by many Japanese men to be "easy".)

Places to Stay

Of interest to anyone wanting to sample gracious *ryokan* living would be a small cluster of high-class (and price) inns at the foot of the hill where the path (and rows of souvenir stands) begins. Several have very ornate carved wooden panels, intimate gardens, and other "typical" Japanalia, that are in fact not often seen. Of minor interest, just a little to the south, is an old-style bridge with a decorative roof.

Getting There

Kotohira is easily reached from Takamatsu by Takamatsu-Kotohira Dentetsu railway (the same line that can be taken from Takamatsu station to Ritsurin), or by bus, both taking about an hour.

Kan-onji

An unusual sight here, visible from Kotohiki-koen park (1.5 km north of Kan-onji station) is Zenigata, the huge outline of an ancient square-holed coin, with four kanji characters. It is made of a series of trenches in the ground and is 345 meters wide. It dates from the Kan-ei era (1624–44), and is explained by one source as having been made by the people as a reminder to their feudal lord that they would be careful not to waste money. (In view of the heavy taxes of those days, it was more likely a reminder to the lord not to waste *their* money.) A good view of the Inland Sea is available from Kotohiki Hachiman shrine (atmospherics permitting).

EHIME-KEN (EAST) ■■■■■■

Kawanoe

From here you can go east via Route 192 to Awa-ikeda, to travel south by the (recommended) route described below. There is also a ferry service to Kobe; see the section on Niihama below. You can also travel west from here, but the north coast is more industrialised and of little interest. The following description follows a route south from Takamatsu.

Niihama

There is a regular ferry service between Niihama/Kawanoe and Kobe and Osaka. Two boats from Osaka, one day and one night, go first to Kobe, then to Kawanoe, then to Niihama (7-1/4, 8-3/4 hours respectively, from Kobe, 85 min more from Osaka; ¥3600 to both). In the return direction the day boat leaves Niihama, then goes to Kawanoe, while the night boat takes the opposite course before going to Kobe.

TOKUSHIMA-KEN (WEST) ▬

Awa-ikeda to Kochi

South of Kompira-san lies some lovely inland scenery of the mountain and valley type. The starting point is Awa-ikeda, not far below Kompira. You can either follow the main road (Route 32 and JR), or branch inland for a while. Road and rail continue through the valley of the Yoshino river, passing the biggest gorge in Shikoku, which is particularly noteworthy for a 7.5 km stretch that includes two picturesque rock formations (Koboke and Oboke). There is a JR station near each, both of which are accessible by train or bus from Awa-ikeda station. From a point two km north of Oboke, a boat is available for a descent of the river (30 to 40 minutes), ending about 3.5 km from Koboke station. A toll road links Oboke to Iya-keiGorge.

Iya-kei Gorge

This is a lovely valley rather off the beaten track. The gorge extends from a point near Iyaguchi for about 45 km to Sugeoi. After only a few km a toll road branches west to rejoin Route 32. A short distance past the junction is the 45 meter-long Iya-no-kazura-bashi, the last surviving original vine suspension bridge of the type once common in the region. (They had the ad-

vantage of being easily cut to block the ingress of invaders.) The inhabitants of the valley are believed to be descendants of the Taira clan who survived the defeat at Yashima and retreated here, much as other Taira descendants are found in the Shirakawago area of Gifu-ken. (The bridge is of the same type as the one at Shikoku-mura in Takamatsu; those in a rush can be content with the latter.) There is a fee for crossing the bridge, and the keeper becomes angry if you even set foot on it without paying.

There are several buses daily running through the very pretty valley to Sugeoi. Beyond that the bus continues in a near-circle north to Sadamitsu station, an area where a foreigner is sure to be a rarity. From there it would be simple to return to Awa-ikeda. Alternatively, you can backtrack to the toll road and out to Oboke to

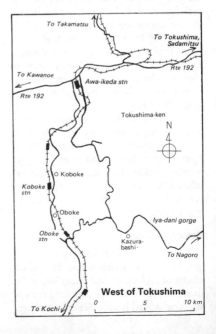

To Takamatsu

To Tokushima, Sadamitsu

Rte 192

To Kawanoe

Awa-ikeda stn

Rte 192

Tokushima-ken

N

O Koboke

Koboke stn

Oboke

Iya-dani gorge

Oboke stn

O Kazura-bashi·

To Nagoro

West of Tokushima

0   5   10 km

To Kochi

take the boat ride or just continue south toward Kochi.

KOCHI-KEN ▬▬▬▬▬

Jofuki-ji

On the way to Kochi, Toyonaga station is the landmark for Jofuki-ji. Not a famous "sight", it is a temple/youth hostel (tel (0887) 74-0301). The young priest speaks good English, is very friendly, well-travelled, and happy to introduce guests to Zen, including meditation. Travellers have been known to stay here for weeks, and it's easy to understand why—the surroundings are peaceful and beautiful. The temple is located high on the side of the valley among tall trees; it is 1.7 km from the station. Ask for directions on arrival.

Buraku-ji

Located one km north of Otaguchi station, this temple is noted for the architecture of its main hall, Yakushido, which was built in 1151. It is a national treasure and a good example of Fujiwara architecture (897–1192 A.D.).

Ryugado Cave

Discovered in 1931, this cave contained clay dishes of a prehistoric people. It features stalagmites and stalactites and other sights of a typical limestone cave. It is accessible in 20 minutes by bus from Tosayamada station.

Oshino

The Kochi area is noted historically for the raising of roosters with incredible tail plumage, sometimes more than six meters in length. The village of Oshino is the center where such birds are raised (said to be a fading interest). Oshino is a district in the city of Nankoku, accessible from Gomen station. Local inquiries in the city (or possi-

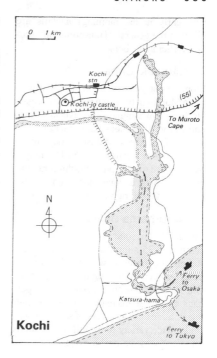

Kochi

bly in Kochi) would be required to track down these birds.

Kochi

The main attraction of Kochi is its five-storey castle. The present buildings date from 1748. It gives an open view of the city and surrounding hills (which I found to be pleasant enough, but of quite limited interest).

Getting There

There is a daily overnight ferry in each direction between Kochi and Osaka (¥4530), and an overnight boat every second day between Kochi and Tokyo (¥13,910). The latter stops at Kii-katsuura (each direction) on the Kii-hanto peninsula south of Osaka and Nagoya (¥5560 from Kochi, but arriving very early in the morning). Details are given in the general "Transportation" section earlier in the book.

Muroto-zaki Cape

From Kochi you can make a side-trip to Cape Muroto in the southeast (also accessible from Tokushima). The five km tip is known for its lighthouse and generally wild atmosphere. About 10 buses a day run to the cape from Kochi or nearby Harimaya-bashi. Close to the tip is Higashi-dera temple; it is both a youth hostel and worth seeing in its own right.

Katsura-hama Beach

Located 13 km southeast of Kochi, and accessible in 35 minutes by bus from Kochi station, this beach is well worth avoiding unless you enjoy wading through rubbish. One traveller described a visit as, " . . . perhaps the most disappointing trip I ever made in Japan." Collectors of seashells will find a wide variety of beautiful specimens on sale at very reasonable prices.

Ino

This is a town noted for producing hand-made paper. It may be possible to arrange to watch the process. Inquire locally for directions. The town is the last stop of the Kochi tram system.

Ashizuri-misaki Cape

The beauties of this cape and the surrounding area are reached from Tosa-shimizu. Three roads, each with their own bus service, run to the tip. The coastal road is adventurously narrow, while the central (toll) road—the Ashizuri Skyline—passes over the central ridge, skirting 433-meter Shiraou-san. (The name Ashizuri translates as "leg grazing", quite possibly a reference to the narrowness of the paths of olden times.) Attractions of the tip are the wildness, the

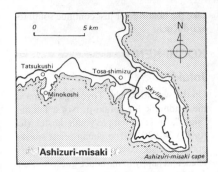

lighthouse, and Kongofuku-ji temple, close enough to the sea for you to hear the crash of the surf. Today's temple dates back 300 years, but there has been one on the site for more than 1100 years. The vegetation verges on tropical, with palms and banyan trees, and there are coral reefs to contrast with granite cliffs.

Tosa-shimizu

There is a daily boat between Tosa-Shimizu and Kobe, stopping en route (both ways) at Kannoura on the southeast coast of Shikoku. Details are given in the general "Transportation" section early in the book.

Minokoshi Area

Continuing west from Tosa-shimizu takes you to the coastal area of Minokoshi, which contains some of the most beautiful views of all. Glass-bottomed boats can be hired to see the colorful fish of the coral reefs. Beside the road are eroded limestone cliffs of wondrous shapes, which lead up to another strange rock formation at Tatsukushi. Tatsukushi means "dragon skewers", a name taken from the number of slim cylinders of stone.

The Hall of Shells

At Tatsukushi town there is an interesting museum that displays nothing but seashells— about 50,000 of them, including many rare and beautiful types. The building is modern and the displays are well planned. Many typhoons pass through this area and stir up the sea bottom, bringing large numbers of shells onto the shore.

North from Minokoshi

The coast north from the Minokoshi area is also very scenic, although of the rias type (submerged fingers of land). There are views of the sea and the coast to the west, orange groves and other greenery to the east—sometimes in both directions when the road goes a little inland.

Sukumo

Ferries run between Sukumo and Saiki (Kyushu) usually six times a day (three hours; ¥1640; up to six/day).

EHIME-KEN ■■■■■■

Uwajima

Uwajima has several attractions. Places of interest include Uwajima Castle (dating from 1665) and Atago-koen park on a hill high enough to give a good view of the city and sea. The impression of this city and the entire coast is of unusually lush foliage. There is a fine landscape garden, Tensha-en

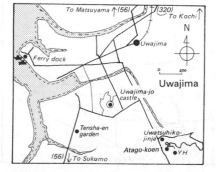

("Heavenly Forgiveness Garden"), two km south of the city.

World War II buffs might be interested in looking for the remains of the Shidenkai fighter aircraft that was raised from the bottom of Kure Bay in 1979, where it had lain since being shot down in July 1945. It was to be put on display in a local park, without restoration, and is believed to be the only example of its type in Japan.

There is one ferry daily each way to Beppu (3-1/4 hours; ¥5590).

Bull Fights

Uwajima is famous for its *togyu* bull fights. These are not the kind that pit matador against animal with the result of hundreds of kg of beef, but are contests between two animals that lock horns and try to push the other backwards. Generally there is a fight every month but, with the exception of Wareisai summer festival (July 23–24), dates vary from year to year. Information offices such as the TIC in Tokyo or Kyoto, as well as travel agencies, should be able to provide details. Ehime-ken also maintains an office in Tokyo and other large cities, so a friend can phone in Japanese for up-to-date information. The fights are held at Togyu jo at the foot of Tenman-yama, a 30 minute walk from Uwajima station.

Ozu

There is *ukai* (cormorant fishing) on the river at Ozu from June 1 to September 20.

Yawatahama

The hillsides behind this port city are noted for the scenic appearance of their terraces, as well as the many orange groves. Kinzan Shusseki Temple, at the top of Kinzan, gives an excellent view of the Inland Sea and as far away as Kyushu. Yawatahama is a convenient port for ferries to Usuki and Beppu, both in Kyushu. There are five boats in each direction for Beppu (three hours, ¥1740), and up to nine a day each way for Usuki (three hours, ¥1300).

Sada-misaki Cape

This cape, more than 50 km long, projects toward Kyushu. Reports indicate, however, that there is nothing of exceptional interest to be found there.

Misaki

There are four ferries a day (each direction) between Misaki and Saganoseki on Kyushu (70 minutes; ¥400).

Matsuyama

Things to See

Matsuyama-jo Castle

The main attraction in Matsuyama is its castle. Matsuyama-jo is a three-storey building dating from 1602, one of the best-preserved castles in Japan. It also functions as a museum. It is atop Shiroyama hill, which is accessible by climbing, or by cable-car (gondola) from the east side (remote from the station).

Dogo-onsen

Matsuyama is famous among the Japanese for its nearby hot-spring resort, Dogo-onsen, which is known for the traditional architecture of its municipal bathhouse (Shinrokaku) and the variety of waters available there. However, Japanese sources continually overstress hotsprings in tourist literature, so this one will be of limited interest to most foreign visitors.

Ishite Temple

Near the hot spring, this is the only temple

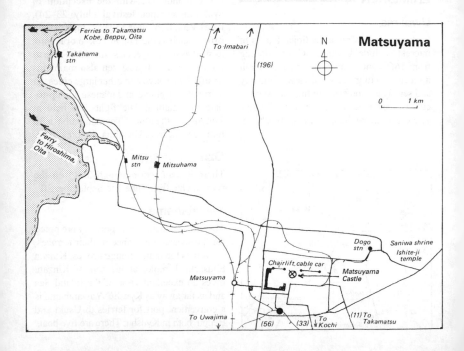

of note in the area. It dates back to 1318 and illustrates the Kamakura style of architecture.

Getting There & Getting Around

Kyushu

Overnight ferries between Beppu (Kyushu) and Osaka/Kobe, stop at Matsuyama, as do boats between Oita (Kyushu) and Kobe. Schedule and fare information on these is given in the general "Transportation" section early in the book. Between Kokura (northern Kyushu) and Matsuyama (Kanko-ko port) there is one daily ferry (in each direction), overnight from Matsuyama, daytime from Kokura (seven hours; ¥3500).

Honshu

Matsuyama is connected via four nearby ports to a number of ports on Honshu by ferries. Get local asssistance in getting to the correct port, and for checking on currently-available service; these are changed and cancelled with great abandon.

There are daily boats between Matsuyama and Kobe (Nakatottei port). Sailing time is about 8 hours (¥4900).

There is a fast hydrofoil service between Matsuyama and Hiroshima (66 min (75 if via Kure); ¥5700; 16/day), in addition to conventional ferries between Matsuyama (Kanko-ko port) and Hiroshima (2-3/4 hours; ¥2130; 11/day); the same boats also go to/from nearby Mitsuhama port (three hours, ¥2130).

Another hydrofoil service runs between Matsuyama (Kanko-ko port) and Onomichi, stopping at two islands en route (six/day; ¥5700).

Between Mitsuhama and Iwakuni (west of Hiroshima) there are also hydrofoils (seven/day; 85 min; ¥4250); these stop en route at Inoda on Oshima island.

Between Mitsuhama and Yanai (west of Iwakuni) there are 21 ferries/day (2 hr 25 min; ¥2310).

Namikata

Between Namikata (two stations west from Imabari) and Takehara there are up to 23 boats a day each way (70 minutes; ¥980); some of these stop en route at Miyaura on Omishima island.

Imabari

Imabari is near Kurushima strait, which is famous for its whirlpools that form at high and low tide like those at Naruto. The city is industrial and of no touristic interest, but it has useful ferry connections.

Getting There

Imabari has several ferry connections with Honshu.

The daily boats between Matsuyama and Kobe (Aoki port) stop en route at Imabari in both directions. Sailing time is about eight hours (¥5000). Some sailings are overnight, and others are entirely in daytime, allowing a good view of much of the scenic part of the Inland Sea area.

Between Imabari and Hiroshima there are five boats each way daily (about 2 hours, ¥4300).

Between Imabari and Mihara there are fast and slow ferry services. The "slow" ones (18/day; ¥2410) take 1-3/4 hours and leave on the hour (both directions) through most of the day. The "fast" boats take one hour (18/day; ¥3400), but have a more restricted period of operation.

There are two ferry services between Imabari and Onomichi with differing patterns of stops at islands en route, nine/day by one, and four/day by the other; all take about 1-1/2 hours (¥3400).

Between Imabari and Nigata (not Niigata!) there are five boats daily each way (1-1/2 hours; ¥3300).

KYUSHU

Kyushu, the southernmost of the four main islands of Japan, is regarded as the "cradle of Japanese civilization", and has many places of interest. It was from here that the Yamato tribe (probably of continental origin) spread to the Kobe–Osaka–Ise area and then the rest of the country. However, because of the antiquity of these events (dating from about 600 B.C.), only archaeological remains are left, mostly in the Usuki and Miyazaki areas. Kyushu has also been substantially influenced by Chinese and Korean civilizations because it is the part of Japan closest to Korea, which acted as a conduit for Chinese culture (in addition to its own).

The main attractions of Kyushu are Mt. Aso, the Yamanami Highway, Kagoshima/ Sakura-jima, Kirishima, various islands off the coasts, some interesting hot springs, temples, shrines, Nagasaki, the anti-Mongol wall, and many gardens. The people of Kyushu also have a reputation for being more friendly than in most other parts of Japan (although there can be no complaints about the people elsewhere!).

Even if you have studied Japanese and speak it well, you can still expect great difficulties in speaking to people in Kyushu, especially around Kagoshima, as the local dialects are quite different from standard Japanese. The old dialect of Kagoshima, *Satsuma-ben*, now spoken only by older generations, is totally incomprehensible even to other Japanese. The story given (and apparently believed by most Japanese) is that a local feudal lord commanded that the people change their way of speaking so that spies from Honshu could be detected. (But as any school teacher can certify, correcting even one grammatical error like "I seen" can be a hopeless task, so this explanation can be taken "cum grano salis".) The almost certain explanation is that the accent is a carry-over from languages spoken by early inhabitants from other areas (such as neighboring Korea), in the same way that accents in England reflect intonations brought by the various tribes and groups from the continent. The dialect of Okinawa, for example, only a relatively short distance to the south, is virtually a separate language.

The description for travel begins at Kitakyushu in the north, and follows a counter-clockwise route back. Some side-trips and shortcuts are also suggested that will assist travellers with limited time, or those who begin their Kyushu travels at a different part of the island.

GETTING THERE

Kyushu can be reached by land, air and sea.

Rail

Shinkansen super express train links Fukuoka (northern Kyushu) via rail tunnel to Shimonoseki, at the southern end of Honshu, to all the major cities of Honshu, such as Hiroshima, Kyoto, and Tokyo, in a few hours; Tokyo is about seven hours away. Fukuoka and Kokura are the only stops on Kyushu. There are also ordinary train services to Honshu (at lower cost) via Shimonoseki.

Kyushu

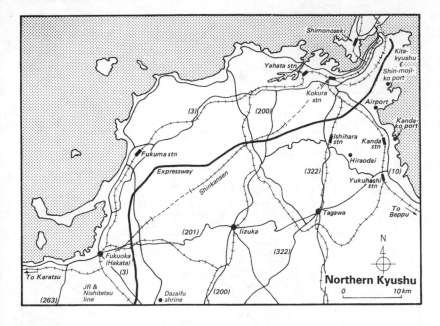

Northern Kyushu

Road

The road links are a tunnel and bridge from Shimonoseki.

Air

There are airports at or near the major cities Hakata (Fukuoka), Nagazaki, Kumamoto, Kagoshima, Miyazaki, and Oita/Beppu, in addition to several small islands off the north and northwest coasts. Access information is given in the write-up for each city. All the major cities are linked to other cities around Japan by air; many flights pass through Fukuoka, the regional air transport center (hub). The cities of Fukuoka, Nagasaki, Kumamoto, and Kagoshima are international air ports of entry. The overseas cities connected to them are listed in the write-up on those cities. Check with a travel agent if you are travelling from Asia to Japan and wish to land in Kyushu, because services seem to change often.

Boat

There are numerous boat and ferry connections to Kyushu from both Honshu and Shikoku. (The word "ferry" is generally used here; many of the ships plying Japanese waters are ferries that carry both passengers and vehicles, but some are purely passenger boats. If you have a motor vehicle, check *jikokuhyo* precisely before showing up at the dock with the expectation of getting onto the boat. Voice of experience.) Ferries leave from the Kyushu ports of Kokura and Moji (Kitakyushu city), Beppu, Oita, Hyuga, Miyazaki, and Shibushi to various ports on Honshu, such as Hiroshima, Osaka, Kobe, Tokyo, and Kawasaki. Also, there are boats to Okinawa and some of the other southern islands of

Japan from Kagoshima and Fukuoka. In addition, there are several ferries across the relatively narrow Hoyo Straits to/from Shikoku and Honshu. These "local" ferries connect the following cities: Beppu–Yawatahama and Misaki (Shikoku); Saganoseki–Misaki; Usuki–Yawatahama; Saiki–Sukumo (Shikoku); Taketazu–Shin-nanyo (near Tokuyama, western Honshu). There are generally several sailings every day for each of these. Details are given in the write-ups for the places in Shikoku and Honshu.

There are also international boat connections to Korea from Fukuoka and Nagasaki.

GETTING AROUND

Rail

There is an extensive network of JR lines in the north of Kyushu, a line around the periphery of the island, a couple of lines across the island roughly in the middle, and some shorter lines partway inland and in the south.

Bus

There is quite an extensive network also of buses, particularly in the north, center, and far south, but also between major cities, such as Fukuoka–Oita and Fukuoka–Nagasaki. For all these services, refer to *jikokuhyo*.

FUKUOKA-KEN ▬▬▬▬▬

Kitakyushu

After crossing from Shimonoseki (on western Honshu) to Kyushu, you will first encounter Kitakyushu (North Kyushu city), a composite of five formerly separate cities (Moji, Kokura, Tobata, Yahata, and Wakamatsu) that stretches a considerable distance along the northeastern coast of the

island. Few people visit this city for its tourist attractions, unless they are enamored of steel mills, smoke stacks, and other appurtenances of a modern industrial city. Fortunately, it is the only major city of this kind in Kyushu; most of the island is still green and natural attractions abound. (It has been pushing for development in producing semiconductor products and has achieved about 40 per cent of present Japanese production, so Kyushu has been nicknamed "Silicon island".)

If you do have a reason for staying in the area, there are some places worth visiting. About 500 meters west of Kokura station there is a reconstruction of (parts of) the once-great Kokura-jo castle. The original was destroyed in 1866 during the fighting that attended the Meiji Restoration. Not far out of town is Hiraodai.

Things to See
Hiraodai

An unusual geological feature that makes for a pleasant excursion and hike in the open countryside (a rarity close to cities in most of Japan) is Hiraodai. This is a rolling plateau covered by weathered and rounded outcroppings of limestone, many taller than a person. For the benefit of non-geologists (like myself) this is known as a karst tableland. (A similar sight can be seen at Akiyoshidai in Yamaguchi-ken (Honshu).) At the east end of Hiraodai lies the limestone grotto of Sembutsu.

Hiraodai can be reached most easily by JR (or Route 322) from Kokura to Ishihara, from where a local road leading to Yukuhashi passes Hiraodai. There might be direct bus transport from Kokura; make inquiries at the station.

Festival

July 10–12: The Daiko (drum) Matsuri, when over 100 floats carrying drums and

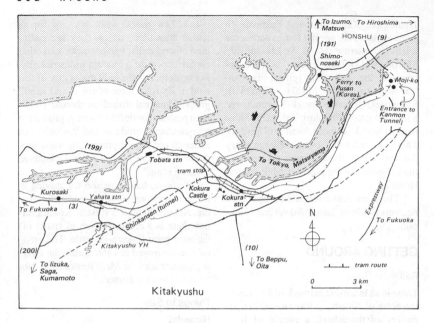

Kitakyushu

drummers parade through the city. Japanese drumming is both complex and unexpectedly primitive, so such a festival is interesting.

Places to Stay

In addition to the usual hotels and ryokan, there is also a nice youth hostel, Kitakyushu YH (tel (093) 681-8142), accessible from Yahata station. It offers a good view.

Getting There

There are convenient connections to Tokyo and the Kobe/Osaka area by ferries leaving from two ports in the Kitakyushu area.

From Kokura (one of the cities making up Kitakyushu) there is a daily boat to Tokyo, via Tokushima (Shikoku), arriving at Tokyo the morning of the second day.

There are two daily boats between Moji (Shin-moji-ko port) and Osaka, leaving late in the afternoon and in late evening and arriving at Osaka the next morning. This is a way to cover a long distance while saving a night's accommodation costs. Schedule information is given in the general "Transportation" section early in the book.

Kitakyushu-ko (harbor) dock is not far from Kokura station; there should be a bus. Likewise from JR Moji station to Shin-moji-ko, but check on the spot. Fare and schedule information on these boats is given in the general "Transportation" section early in the book.

The simplest way of getting to and from Shimonoseki, on the other side of the Kanmon Strait, is by JR train (which goes through a tunnel). Shimonoseki is the station on the other side; any of the several stations on the Kyushu side can be used as the starting point, such as Moji, Kokura, etc. (Moji is the first after exiting the tunnel.)

Hitching from central Kitakyushu to the other side is not exactly simple, as the city is the seventh largest in Japan and is very spread out. To Honshu, I would recommend taking the train across and following the instructions in the Shimonoseki write-up for hitching from there. Likewise, it is simpler to take a train or a bus some distance out of Kitakyushu before trying to hitch elsewhere in Kyushu. For the adventurous who would nevertheless like to try to hitch out of Kitakyushu, the entrance to the Kanmon tunnel for cars (where it should be possible to get a lift in either direction, to either Shimonoseki or into Kyushu) is not far from Moji station (the final stop of the tram line that passes through the city) or JR Moji-ko station. As for the expressway across Kanmon-ohashi bridge and on to Hiroshima, Osaka and

Tokyo or through Kyushu to Kumamoto, etc., the nearest interchange is some distance from the center of the city and quite difficult to reach; local help would be required to find out how to get to it.

Fukuoka/Hakata

The largest city of Kyushu, Fukuoka has a limited number of attractions worth looking at. It is also an international port of entry by air and ship (from Korea).

Information

If setting out from Hakata station, first stop at the Travel Center and pick up a copy of their map of the Fukuoka area. Everything is marked in both Japanese and English, so it can be useful for finding your way almost anywhere.

There is a Korean consulate in Fukuoka,

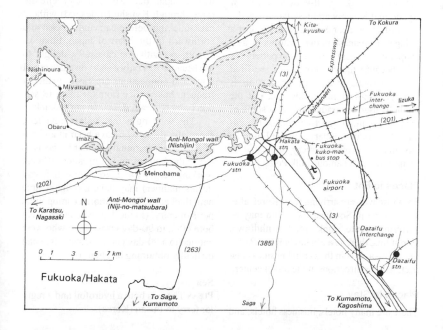

making it a convenient place to obtain a visa.

If you need film, Doi camera shop, near the station, has good prices.

Things to See

Sumiyoshi-jinja Shrine

This shrine, less than one km from Hakata station, has buildings dating from 400 years ago. Its annual festival is held on October 12–14.

Shofuku-ji Temple

Also located not far from Hakata station, this temple was the first center of Zen teachings in Japan, from 1195.

Potteries

There are several pottery making centers in northern Kyushu. Some, if not all, are the legacy of Korean potters who came to Japan about 200 years ago. Within Fukuoka are the well-known towns of Agano and Koishiwara; less famous is the town of Onta, near Koishiwara, the last a village of Japanese potters who work as a cooperative. There is usually no pottery for sale, because the climbing kilns are fired only occasionally and the production is generally spoken for in advance, but the methods used are traditional, as is some of the equipment. Of the 14 houses in the village, 10 produce pottery. On the Fukuoka city map is another pottery, indicated as "Takatori Kiln (Famous Folk Pottery)".

Places to Eat

For those who are arriving from Korea after a long time in Southeast Asia and may be suffering acute junk food withdrawal symptoms, there is a Shakey's Pizza Parlor in Fukuoka. It is in the central business district; ask for directions at the travel center.

Places to Stay

There are many hotels, business hotels, and ryokan in Fukuoka, as well as in nearby hot-spring resorts. Assistance is available at the information center at Hakata station. Daizaifu YH is a temple and temples are usually the nicest kind of hostel in Japan, but it has only 24 beds (tel (092) 922-8740). (It is close to Dazaifu-jinja shrine, one of the major places to see in Fukuoka). Other hostels in the area include Yakiyama-kogen YH (90 beds; tel (0948) 22-6385), which is about half-way to Kitakyushu, or Kitakyushu YH (96 beds, tel (093) 681-8142).

Getting There—International

Air

Fukuoka is connected by air with Hong Kong, Honolulu, Manila, Taipei, Seoul, and Pusan—the latter being the cheapest flight from Korea. It is a convenient gateway to Japan because it allows a circling route through Kyushu (if desired) without back-tracking before carrying on east and northward to the heart of Japan. Fukuoka airport is—with one caveat—a delight to use because it is only a short distance out of town and connections are easily made by frequent bus service from the main JR station (which is called Hakata, not Fukuoka).

The warning is that budget travellers, especially those who have been in and out of Japan on a seemingly regular basis (as if, to the thinking of an Immigration official, working illegally and prolonging their stay in this manner) may have a rougher time here than at the larger, more cosmopolitan ports of entry. (In the days when there were both 60- and 90-day visas, those who were entitled to a 90-day period of stay often had difficulty obtaining one here.)

Sea

Pusan There is both a hydrofoil and a regular ferry to Pusan (Korea).

The ferry leaves Fukuoka three days a week (Tue/Thur/Sat), at 1700 (¥8500), reaching Pusan the next morning at 0840; departure time from Pusan (Mon/Wed/Fri) is the same, arrival at 0900.

The hydrofoil leaves Fukuoka daily at 0930, arriving in Pusan at 1225 (¥12,400). From Pusan it leaves at 1400, arriving at 1655.

CHEJU A hydrofoil leaves Fukuoka every Friday at 1200 for Ryeosudo, in the coastal-island national park in southern Korea (5-1/4 hours; ¥18,000). From Korea, the boat leaves on Sunday at 0925.

Getting There—Domestic

In addition to several flights a day to various points within Japan, there is a good train service. Hakata is the western terminus of the Shinkansen, and the trip to or from Tokyo takes less than seven hours by the fastest trains.

Things to See—South of Fukuoka

Dazaifu Temmangu Shrine

Less than an hour south of Fukuoka by train is the famous shrine Dazaifu Temmangu, one of the highest ranking shrines in Japan. The grounds and picturesque bright-orange buildings (dating from 1590) are attractive (though not outstanding; skip the place if in a hurry), and include an arched stone bridge. From the 7th to the 14th century, Dazaifu was the residence of the Kyushu governor. The shrine's annual festival takes place on September 23–25, and features a procession.

The shrine is easily reached by the Nishitetsu line, leaving from Nishitetsu Fukuoka station, first to Nishitetsu Futsukaichi (12 minutes by *kyuko* express), where it is necessary to change trains and go two stops to Dazaifu station. From there the shrine is about 500 meters away. If you

are beginning at Hakata station, it is simpler to go by JR to Futsukaichi station, where there should be a bus to the shrine (otherwise go to Nishitetsu-Futsukaichi station and take the train). Dazaifu YH is near the shrine.

Close to Dazaifu-jinja are Komyo-ji and Kanzeon-ji temples, as well as the Fukuoka-ken Rekishi Hakubutsukan (historical museum). Komyo-ji has a very pretty Zen-style garden. Kanzeon-ji has a number of valued Buddhist images on display.

Pottery Towns

If you are interested in pottery, it is worth visiting the kilns and potters in the towns of Koishiwara, Hoju, and Ichinose, all in the vicinity of Kurume.

Hot Springs

Two hot-spring resort towns, Harazuru (in southern Fukuoka-ken) and Hita (just across the boundary in Oita-ken) feature *ukai* (cormorant fishing) on the nearby river; the dates are May to September in Harazuru, and until the end of October in Hita.

Things to See—West of Fukuoka

The major route westward from Fukuoka takes you along the coast toward Nagasaki.

Anti-Mongol Wall

To combine a swim on a white-sand beach with a bit of history, visit the remnants of the 20 km wall built around Hakata Bay to prevent the landing of the Mongol hordes in 1281. Kublai Khan had made one try to invade in 1274, but was beaten off. A defensive wall was built over the following years, but it was feared that the next wave of invaders would nevertheless overpower the defenders. However, a typhoon sank the Mongol fleet, thus saving the Japanese the need to use the wall. This was the last at-

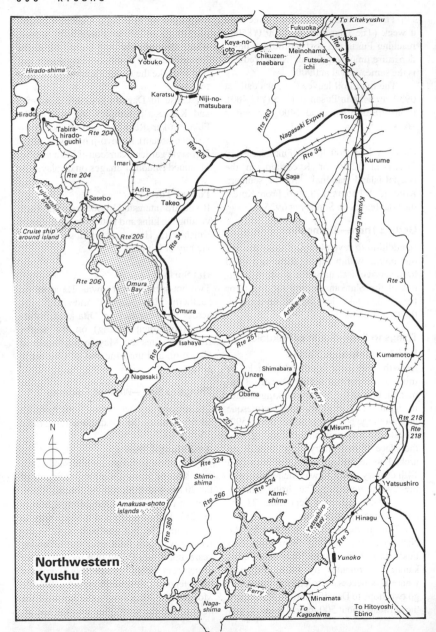

Northwestern Kyushu

tempted invasion until 1945 (which explains the great shock felt at the end of the last war). Because this wind saved Japan, it was named *Kamikaze* (wind of the gods), a word revived in the last war but with less effective results.

Only traces of the walls (originally three meters high) remain. Near Imazu, one stretch of 100 meters or so has been excavated from the sand. Once you see this remnant (still nearly two meters high), you realise that the traces of rocks just below the sand through the groves of picturesque, twisted pine trees near the shore, are the top of the wall. From here it is only a short walk to the beach. To take the bus from Hakata station, ask for the *Nishi-no-ura yuki* bus, which probably leaves from gate 3 on the second floor. The location is shown on the handout map in Japanese as well as English. The wall is marked as "Genko Fort", but ask for "boheki", which is its local name. The bus trip takes about two hours.

Genkai Park

The anti-Mongol wall at Imazu, and others (shown on the handout map, but said to be in much poorer condition), are part of Genkai Quasi National Park that extends about 90 km along the north coast of Kyushu into Saga-ken. Other features are more white sand beaches and more groves of gnarled pine trees, the best-known of which is at Niji-no-matsubara.

Keya-no-oto

The main attraction of the park is "the Great Cave of Keya", a rocky promontory at the western end of Itoshima Peninsula. It juts 60 meters out of the sea, and is formed of groups of parallel columns of basalt projecting at different angles (probably created as lava cooled in a large mass and formed giant crystals). The sea has eroded a cave 9

meters high and 18 meters wide that extends more than 50 meters into the rock. (Like most attractions in Japan it will have many tourists and tour buses.)

Keya-no-oto can be reached by bus from either Chikuzen-maebaru station (40 minutes) or directly from Hakata station (95 minutes).

SAGA-KEN ▬▬▬▬▬

There are three famous pottery towns in Saga-ken: Karatsu, Imari, and Arita. The pottery there is noted for its very colorful glazes and is considered more artistic than that from the kilns of Seto (near Nagoya in central Honshu). You can get to the Imari potteries in 15 minutes by bus from Imari station, passing through pretty countryside with thatched-roof houses.

Karatsu

Festival

November 3–5: Giant floats of papier-mache figures are drawn through the streets of Karatsu.

NAGASAKI-KEN ▬▬▬▬▬

Islands Off the Northwest Coast

There are three large islands off the northwest coast of Kyushu: Iki, Tsushima, and Hirado. While none has any particular sightseeing attractions, nearly all are relatively isolated and visited by only a few foreigners. The people are therefore "unspoilt" and friendly, though even less able to communicate with outsiders than other Japanese, as they have still less incentive than other Japanese to learn foreign languages, and their dialects are usually incomprehensible even to other Japanese. (Japanese remark that the language sounds like Korean, though it is said to be basically Japanese.) Iki and Tsushima are both accessible from Saga-ken and Fukuoka-ken. For up-to-date information on transport to these two islands, as well as scheduled services to a number of smaller islands not mentioned here, consult *jikokuhyo*.

Iki-shima

This island was recommended particularly by a cyclist friend who liked its flat terrain and beautiful beaches; the island is small and the sea always close. There are several campsites, plus ryokan. There are four boats a day between Iki and Yobuko on the tip of the peninsula near Karatsu, which take just over an hour, as well as others from Hakata (2-1/2 hours). There are also three flights a day from Fukuoka.

Tsushima

Very close to Korea, this island is much larger and more rugged than Iki, and you will need a bus or car for transport. One traveller reported several quizzings by police during his visit, because foreigners are very rare and there is a lot of drug smuggling from Korea. Just prior to his arrival a smuggler had come out on the wrong side of police bullets, so the authorities were edgy.

In addition to *ryokan*, there are two youth hostels on the island (one a temple) and a *kokumin-shukusha*.

There is a boat service to Kokura as well as to Iki. There are also four daily flights to and from Fukuoka.

Hirado-shima

At the north of Nagasaki-ken is Hirado Island, accessible by bridge from Tabira-hirado-guchi (JR station). The island is hilly with many high cliffs.

Kujukushima

Between Hirado Island and Sasebo (on the coast of Nagasaki-ken) is Kujukushima ("99 islands"), in fact a group of about 170

islets. A cruise boat makes two trips daily from Sasebo (Kashi-mae pier).

Goto-retto Archipelago

This is the name of five islands west of Kujukushima. Like other islands in the area, they are mostly agricultural and fishing communities. The coast is rugged. Access is by boat from Nagasaki, Sasebo, and other centers, as well as by air from Fukuoka. (Again, consult *jikokuhyo* for more detailed information.)

Nagasaki

So much has been written about Nagasaki that it is difficult for another travel writer to try to follow suit. However, although I enjoyed my visit to Nagasaki, I would not claim that it is the one and only place in Japan (or in Kyushu for that matter) to visit, as implied by some writers who have gone before. It certainly has several attractions, but reality should temper enthusiasm. It definitely lacks the "haunting beauty" and "fatal charm" gushed by one writer (unless I missed something).

Nagasaki has an interesting history and has long flourished as a port. During the period when Japan was closed to the outside world (the early 1600s to 1867), Nagasaki was virtually the only gateway open for trade. Formerly a point of contact with the Asian continent, it became the entry point for western knowledge (mainly via the Dutch) and religion (Roman Catholicism).

Nagasaki gained some fame through Puccini's "Madame Butterfly", but it might never have become so well known if it had not been the second city to be A-bombed, having been picked as a target because of the huge Mitsubishi shipyards across the harbor from the city (which the bomb missed, exploding instead over the other side of the harbor.

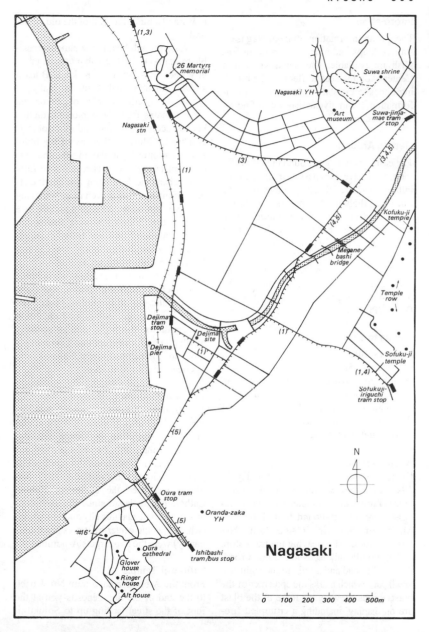

(1,3)

26 Martyrs
memorial

Suwa shrine

Nagasaki YH

Suwa-jinja-
mae tram
stop

Art
museum

Nagasaki
stn

(3)

(1)

(3,4,5)

Kofuku-ji
temple

(4,5)

Megane-
bashi
bridge

Temple
row

Dejima
tram
stop

Dejima
site

(1)

Sofuku-ji
temple

Dejima
pier

(1)

(1,4)

Sofukuji-
iriguchi
tram stop

(5)

N

Oura tram
stop

Oranda-zaka
YH

(5)

'#16'

Nagasaki

Oura
cathedral

Ishibashi
tram/bus stop

Glover
house

Ringer
house

Alt house

0   100   200   300   400   500m

Information

There is an information office at Nagasaki station. Maps and tourist literature in English are available. The Nagasaki Tourist Center is on the second floor of the building opposite the station. In addition to information, it can give assistance in finding accommodation.

Getting Around

The easiest way to get around the city is by tram, as the five lines pass near all points of interest and are clearly numbered. (The lines and their turning points are shown on the map.) City buses cover much more extensive routes, but they are difficult to use because they are identified only in Japanese.

The following route covers all the major places of interest. It is based on the tram routes, beginning and ending at the Dejima Pier/Nagasaki Station area.

Things to See

Martyrs' Site

On February 5, 1597, twenty Japanese and six foreign Christians were crucified in an effort by Hideyoshi Toyotomi to stamp out Christianity. A church-like building of somewhat unusual features (dating from 1962) stands on the site.

A-Bomb Relics

Everything related to that fateful day in 1945 is clustered within easy walking distance. From Nagasaki station, easiest access is by a north-bound tram 1 or 3 to Matsuyama-cho, eighth stop from Nagasaki station. After leaving the tram stop, a short uphill walk leads to the main road. Across the road and a little to the right is a small park which marks the epicenter of the blast. Relics showing the force of the blast are on display, including a crumpled fire-

tower and a bit of the wall of the old cathedral.

Atop the hill behind the park (accessible by stairs) is the A-bomb museum, properly known as Nagasaki Kokusai Bunka-kaikan (International Cultural Hall). It houses an excellent display of photos and other remains from the explosion; melted bottles, scorched stones, and other objects graphically illustrate the fury of the blast. Every visitor to Japan should see either this museum or the one at Hiroshima to fully comprehend the devastating and horrific effects of the bomb. It is even more terrifying when you realise the damage was done by a weapon that rates as a mere firecracker when measured against today's super-bombs. (Of the two museums, I would rate Hiroshima's a little higher.)

North of the park and museum is Peace Park (Heiwa-koen), with ponds, fountains, and a statue said to symbolize peace. The statue is a little grotesque, the head being too small for the body, and is scarcely worth going to see except that it is on every brochure and pamphlet from Nagasaki and has become a bit of an icon.

Urakami Catholic Cathedral

The original church on this site was finished in 1914 after 32 years of work. It was the largest church in the Orient until destroyed by the bomb. Part of one of its pillars stands in the epicenter park. The present building was finished in 1959. Nagasaki has been the center of Roman Catholicism in Japan since the 16th century; it is ironic that this city and Hiroshima (which was the center of Protestant Christianity) were the two targets A-bombed.

Sofuku-ji Temple

From the A-bomb area, a tram No. 1 back to the end of the line deposits you at the foot of the street leading up to Sofuku-ji.

This temple dates back to 1629 and is noted for its Chinese architecture, particularly the second gate and main hall (Hondo), which were built in late Ming-dynasty style. From the temple, the athletic can walk along the row of temples shown on the map (the best known of which is Kofuku-ji) via Megane-bashi bridge to Suwa-jinja shrine. An alternative route is tram 4 to Suwa-jinja-mae.

Megane-bashi Bridge

"Spectacles Bridge" has two steep arches, and when the river level is high enough, the reflection forms two ovals that look like eyeglasses. The original bridge was built in 1634 with the help of Chinese Buddhist priests, but was swept away in a flood caused by a typhoon in 1983. The bridge was rebuilt in three months in its original form.

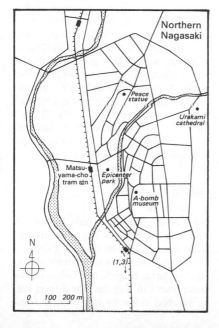

Suwa-jinja

Although there is no particular "sight" here, the buildings are attractive and typical of large shrines throughout Japan. There is a good view over the city from the hill on which Suwa-jinja stands. The grounds are heavily wooded and offer a haven from city buildings. Okunchi is the shrine's annual festival (October 7–9), and its dragon dance dates from the days of trade with China.

Glover House

From the shrine area, tram 5 (southbound) leads to Glover House. Get off at the first stop after the tram turns left to run beside a canal. A nearby bridge leads to the house.

One of the best-known landmarks of Nagasaki, Glover House is a large English-style mansion that was the home of a remarkable Englishman named (what else?) Glover. He supervised the construction of railways and the opening of mines, and introduced a tremendous amount of modern technology to Japan after it was opened to the world in the latter part of the 19th century.

The house has a lovely garden, and the view from the porch out over the harbor is probably the finest in the city. The interior of the house is well preserved. Attesting to the numbers of visitors is an outdoor escalator that lifts people up the hill on which the house is perched.

In the grounds, observe (for humor's sake) the statue of Madame Butterfly. Whether there ever was such a person is not really known (some say "no", but a friend says there is a chance that one of her forebears could have been a model for Lt. Pinkerton, though the woman in that instance did not do herself in), but in any case there is certainly no connection with this house. However, local tourist authorities are pushing the story for all it's worth, and a poll would probably show a high rate of belief.

Nearby are three other houses of the same era, two of which are also known for their former residents, Alt and Ringer. The third house ("No. 16") has considerable quantities of Victorian bric-a-brac. In the bottom of the building is a museum of portable shrines, costumes, and a dragon—all of which are carried in the annual Okunchi festival. A videotape shows scenes from the celebrations.

Oura Tenshu-do Catholic Cathedral
This is the oldest Gothic-style structure in Japan, dating from 1865. It was built in memory of the 26 Christian martyrs. A museum (*shiryokan*) in front of the cathedral has exhibits showing the history of the persecution of the Christians under the Tokugawa.

From this area, tram 5 returns to the Dejima Pier area.

Koshibyo-tojinkan
This building is in very traditional Chinese style, with red pillars and walls, and a yellow roof with dragons cavorting on the peaks. The original temple, built by the many Chinese merchants once in the city, was destroyed by the A-bomb. The present structure is now a museum of traditional Chinese art.

Dejima
The pier where visiting cruise ships dock is named after Dejima Island, a small body of land to which Dutch traders were restricted during the "closed" years when Japan's only connection with the rest of the world was through Nagasaki. The island no longer exists, as the harbor was filled in to make the pier, and the dock area is now farther out than the island used to be. A garden and reproduction of an old warehouse now stand on the site of the former island.

Nagasaki Aquarium
There is an aquarium about 12 km from the city; access is by bus or taxi from Nagasaki station.

Views of the City
The best view of the city is from the top of Mt. Inasa (332 meters). A cable-car runs to the top from a point about one km from Nagasaki station. The view at night is especially attractive, somewhat resembling Hong Kong, although the lights are not so numerous nor so bright.

Places to Stay
As can be expected at a very popular destination for domestic travel, there is plenty of accommodation available, with many hotels and ryokan clustered around the station. As in any city of reasonable size in Japan, assistance in finding a place to stay can be obtained from the station or the tourist center. There are three youth hostels: two are in town, the third is quite far away.

Nagasaki YH (tel 0958-23-5032) is a 12 minute walk from Nagasaki station. Go up to the end of the little street opposite the station, then turn right and cross seven intersections of various sizes. It is a little to the left from there. Oranda-zaka YH (tel 0958-22-2730) is farther away, and can be reached by taking a 1 tram as far as Ishibashi-sh'ta tram stop. Staff at the information office could help.

Getting There
International
AIR Internationally, Nagasaki has an air link with Shanghai, a city with historic trade ties, and Pusan (Korea). Domestically, there are air links to major cities, such as Osaka, Nagoya, and Tokyo, and to some points in Kyushu. The airport can be reached either by bus directly from

Nagasaki station (90 minutes), or by taking a JR train to Omura station and continuing by bus (10 minutes). The train to Omura passes briefly along the shore of Omura Bay en route from Nagasaki; the main highway goes inland most of the way and is less scenic.

SEA Nagasaki is connected by hydrofoil to Cheju-do island (Korea) Monday–Thursday plus Saturday (and return the same day). The trip takes 4-1/2 hours (¥17,000).

Domestic
RAIL Nagasaki is served by JR lines that link it to Fukuoka (north), Kagoshima (south), and Beppu (cross-island).

BUS Intercity buses leave from the terminal across from Nagasaki station, and link the city to a number of points on Kyushu, as well as long-distance (generally overnight) buses to such distant cities as Hiroshima, Osaka, Kyoto, and Nagoya. A special excursion bus to Beppu is described below.

HITCHING If travelling by aid of the thumb, you will find it simplest to take a train or bus to Isahaya and start hitching from there.

Nagasaki to Sasebo

Omura

One sightseeing attraction in the Omura area (location of the airport for Nagasaki) is Oranda-mura, the Dutch Village. This is a reproduction of an idealized Dutch town with the appearance of typical traditional street scenes and buildings. (The relationship to Holland is the historic trading connection through Nagasaki.) A major feature is a full-scale exact replica, built in Holland in the mid-80s, of the Dutch warship "Prins Willem", the original of which was launched in 1650. It is typical of the ships

that sailed between the Netherlands and Asia at that time—sea trade which brought great riches and gave disproportionate power to that small European country. The replica serves as a museum, and is moored in Omura Bay.

The Dutch Village is very expensive, so it will not be for the budget traveller. It is mainly of interest to the Japanese.

In March 1992, Huis Ten Bosch, another reproduction of a Dutch village, also in the Omura area but on a much larger scale than Oranda-mura, was opened. This town's features include theaters, hotels, museums, shopping malls, etc.—not necessarily "Dutch". Huis Ten Bosch is now a major attraction of Nagasaki, reputedly interesting not only to Japanese. Entrance fee is ¥3900. Joint pass with Oranda-mura available.

Sasebo

Sasebo is the site of a U.S. Navy base, but is not known for any specific places of interest to visitors. However, the trip northward from Nagasaki offers pleasant views by road and JR, both of which pass along the shore of Omura Bay for most of the distance. The scenery includes the rafts of pearl farms, for this is the second largest pearl-producing area in Japan after Ise.

Nagasaki to Beppu

A popular trip is by bus from Nagasaki through to Beppu, on the other side of Kyushu (or the reverse). The bus passes by way of Kumamoto, goes to the top of Mt. Aso (described below), through the immense crater valley of the same volcanic mountain, and goes on to Beppu by way of the scenic Yamanami Highway (also described below). The bus trip is aimed at taking in the best places of touristic interest (it is an excursion bus, not just point-to-point transportation). At least one bus makes the entire Nagasaki–Beppu trip in one long day. In addition, several buses go as far as the Aso area, others from Aso on to Beppu (and vice versa).

Nagasaki to Kumamoto

Another popular route from Nagasaki is via Obama and Unzen to Shimabara, from where frequent ferries ply to and from Misumi on the Uto Peninsula. From Misumi it is only a short distance north to Kumamoto. The route south leads to Kagoshima.

Unzen

The following description was valid until 1991, and parts may apply again in the future, so it is being retained. After 200 years of dormancy, part of Mt. Unzen (Unzen Fugen-dake) erupted repeatedly in 1991, taking more than 30 lives and introducing foreign residents of Japan to the technical term "pyroclastic flow", which describes the violent release of superhot gas, steam, and ash that swept down the mountainside and destroyed towns, crops, and the topography of Mt. Unzen. (Mt. St. Helens erupted in the same way.) At the time of writing, all people have been evacuated from on and near the mountain, and life in nearby Shimabara is also far from normal.

Historic Unzen

In the days of the British Empire, Unzen was a favorite resort for colonial officials and old China hands, breeds now vanished. There are still some noteworthy features, though most travellers stop only for a look around before continuing. Unzen has golf courses and other recreational facilities, but its raison d'etre is the hotspring waters. These boil up—violently in places—in a steaming and desolate, but colorful, area near town. The waters are conducted to the various hotels for the baths. The claims of curative properties would get hotels in plenty of hot water of another kind if made in countries with strong consumer-protection laws. During the days of Christian persecution, these boiling waters were put to another use—disposing of those who refused to renounce their faith.

Rather a curiosity in Unzen is the Roman Catholic church, a ¥130 million brick-clad building, for there were only eight known catholics in the area when it was built in 1982. This anomaly makes a little more sense with the knowledge that the area's relics, remains, and evidence of the exotic Christian history and tradition constitute one of the mainstays of what had been a declining tourist industry.

A toll road loops up between Nodake and Myoken mountains. The view from the road itself is not spectacular, but from the top cable-car station there is a beautiful view of the ocean and off-shore islands. Wildflowers are pretty in spring and summer, while leaves are the attraction in autumn. The youth hostel at Unzen is unusually large.

Shimabara

Another place of interest on the Shimabara Peninsula is Shimabara itself, with its reconstructed castle. The original was destroyed in 1637 in an episode during the government's effort to eradicate Christianity. About 30,000 of the faithful captured the castle, but it was later retaken by the authorities and the defenders were slaughtered. The castle was ruined at that time, but a large reproduction, built in 1964, recreates the beautiful appearance of the white original and serves as a museum. Among the exhibits are *fumi-e* ("trampling images"), images of Christian significance upon which people had to tread in order to prove that they were not Christians. The castle is about 400 meters west of the station. Ferries to Misumi are frequent.

KUMAMOTO-KEN ▬▬▬▬

Misumi

From Misumi it is 27 km to the main north-south road (Route 3) at Uto, from where it is only 15 km to Kumamoto. An alternative is a visit to the Amakusa Islands.

Kumamoto

Kumamoto is the third largest city on Kyushu and was one of the major military centers of Japan until the last century. The two major attractions of Kumamoto are Suizenji-koen garden and Kumamoto-jo castle, plus a shrine or two.

Information

A small handout map showing the tram lines and major sightseeing spots is available at the station. It has sufficient English to be useful.

Things to See

Suizenji-koen Park

This is a very attractive landscape garden, larger than most in Japan. I would rate it ahead of two of the "Big Three" gardens, behind only Kenroku-en in Kanazawa. The hills and water have been arranged to resemble famous natural features, such as Mt. Fuji and Lake Biwa, and there is a teahouse identical in every feature to one of the most famous of such buildings in Kyoto. The garden dates from 1632, so it is much older than the more celebrated ones mentioned above. It was part of a villa of the Hosokawa clan, who once commanded the region.

The park is easily reached by tram from

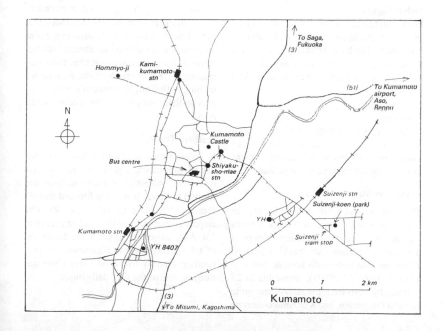

Kumamoto

Kumamoto station; the stop is Sui-zenji.

Kumamoto-jo Castle

Kumamoto was once one of the principal castle towns of Japan, ranking only behind Osaka and Nagoya. The original castle was finished in 1607 and stood until 1867, when most of it was burned in a siege during the civil war period that was part of the Meiji Restoration. In 1960 the structure was reproduced in concrete, and now houses a good museum. I usually play down such reproductions for their lack of authenticity, but this one is so large, reproduces details well, and is set in such attractive surroundings of tall trees and stone walls, that it is worth at least a look if you are passing through.

The castle is easily reached on foot or by tram from the station; the stop is "Shi-yakusho-mae" (town hall).

Other Sights

Other interesting sights that can be singled out are Hommyo-ji temple and Tatsuta-koen park. The latter houses a folk-art museum (*mingei hakubutsukan*), as well as an attractive garden and teahouse from 350 years ago.

Festivals

September 15: At Fujisaki Hachiman-gu shrine, there is an annual procession of "warriors" on horseback wearing ancient armor to escort three portable shrines.

Places to Stay

There are several hotels, minshuku, etc., in Kumamoto. Assistance in finding a room can be obtained at information centers at the airport, station, or travel agencies. There are also two youth hostels: Suizenji YH (tel (096) 371-9193), accessible in 25 minutes by tram from the station and quite close to the garden, and Kumamoto-shiritsu

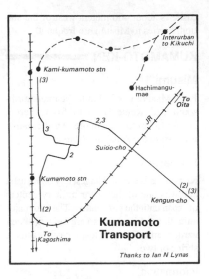

Kumamoto Transport

Thanks to Ian N Lynas

YH (tel (096) 352-2441), a municipal hostel that I gave up trying to find on motorcycle; with the map in the YH Handbook this should not be a problem. Hostels in the Aso area can be considered as alternatives because of the short travelling time from Kumamoto (100 minutes by train, 80 minutes by bus, both from Kumamoto station). Details on them are given in the section on Mt. Aso.

Getting There

In recent times, Kumamoto has joined the list of international ports of entry for air travellers. Although the connections are limited to Seoul, it is a step forward and offers an alternative to, say, Fukuoka. The airport is located near the road/rail route to Mt. Aso, so on arrival you have the option of taking the bus into Kumamoto or proceeding directly to the Aso area (Aso station) on one of the four daily buses.

The Aso Region

Aso-san

The present Aso-san mountain sits in the midst of the largest volcanic crater on earth, and is still fuming after 80 million years of activity. Several routes go to the top if you have your own vehicle, but for travellers using public transportation from within the area, the simplest way is by bus from either Aso or Miyaji JR station (five/day; ¥170/390) to the east side (Kako-higashi), or from Aso JR station (seven/day; ¥570) or Akamizu station (two/day; ¥620) to the west entrance (Kako-nishi). There are also two buses from Kumamoto station to Kako-nishi (¥1580). As described earlier, one or two daily special sightseeing cross-island buses from both Nagasaki and Beppu go to Kako-nishi along their route. (Complete schedules are printed in *jikokuhyo*.)

Unless the path is blocked for safety reasons, it is possible to walk between Kako-nishi and Kako-higashi. (At one time there were buses at the top between "nishi" and "higashi", but they have not operated for a number of years.)

The following describes the trip to the west (nishi) side of the crater (Kako-nishi) from Aso town. En route, the road twists and turns up the flank of the mountain (passing Aso YH, 1.5 km from Aso station). At the lush, sloping meadows along the way you may see Japanese tourists jumping out of their cars to photograph an exotic species of animal life—a cow. Clearly visible in the green are the shape of fingers of lava from prehistoric flows. The road also passes a smallish cone, Komezuka, an "afterthought" of a later mini eruption.

Eventually the road reaches the flattened top of Aso-san. From the first lookout near the crest of the uphill road, you can finally see (on a clear day, at least) the enormity of the crater, or bowl, in which Aso-san sits. The cliffs several km away are, in fact, the walls of the original hole. Its dimensions are given variously as 23 or 32 km north–south, 16 km east–west, and 80 or 128 km in circumference. Any way you measure it, it's huge, and the mind boggles at the amount of energy that has been released over the eons from this place. Although the volcano has been active for about 30 million years, the present form probably dates back a little more than 120 millennia.

The road circles around a lake before reaching the base station of the Kako-nishi cable-car (four minutes to the top). A toll road also goes the short distance to the top, and you can also walk. The view from the top is one of great desolation, mostly black ash thrown out over the centuries. A path leads to the very rim of the main crater (no guard rail—caution!) in the side of Naka-dake, on the far side of which can be seen layers of ash and lava—mostly black, but with colorful streaks of dark red. In its own sombre way it is very picturesque.

Far below, down in the deep black cavity, steam billows forth continuously, sometimes diminishing only to burst forth in greater volume. Is it safe? Generally yes, as a constant watch is kept and visitors are barred from the rim area when it is active. However, in September 1979, while access was barred, a particularly violent explosion hurled head-sized rocks nearly a km away into an area thought safe, killing three sightseers. Prior to this, the last eruption had been in November 1977. These eruptions explain the presence of the numerous concrete domes near the rim, built as emergency shelters after an unexpected eruption in 1958 killed 12 people.

Another good overall view of the crater can be had from Taka-dake ("High Peak"),

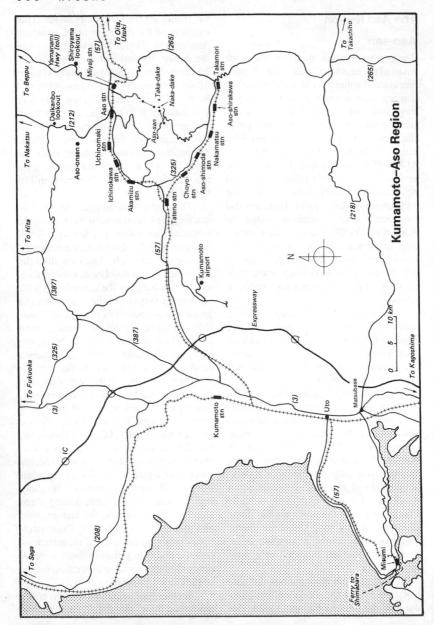

Kumamoto–Aso Region

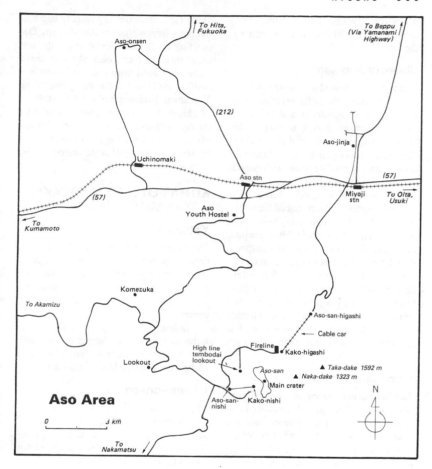

Aso Area

0   3 km

an easy hike to the east from the upper station at Kako-higashi.

Miyaji

A short distance from Miyaji station lies Aso-jinja shrine. This is one of those attractions that can be described as "nice if you haven't seen one before". There are some attractive carvings on the buildings.

Places to Stay

In addition to hotels, ryokan, and minshuku, there are three youth hostels around the base of the mountain. I stayed at Aso YH (tel 0967-34-0804) and found it pleasant; it can be reached by the bus to Kakonishi, and is a claimed 16 minute walk (*up*) from Aso station. The others are Aso YMCA Camp YH (tel 0967-35-0124), and

Murataya Ryokan (tel 09676-2-0066), though one traveller gave a low rating to the latter.

Views of Aso-san

There are also two places on the northern rim of the valley that offer excellent views of the present mountain and the valley floor, with its patchwork of small fields. One is Daikanbo, a little distance above Aso-onsen (also known as Uchinomaki-onsen) and accessible from Uchinomaki station. The other is Shiroyama tembodai, at the rim of the old crater where the Yamanami Highway climbs out of the valley. But the view from almost any point along the road here is memorable. These are most accessible if you have your own transportation; I stopped my motorcycle a number of times for enjoyable looks. Unfortunately, little regard had been paid to maintaining visibility; when I was last there, the view from most lookouts was being progressively blocked by the growth of trees. Unless they are cut at some time soon, there will be no view left.

Yamanami Highway

Aso lies partway along the highway that links Beppu with Nagasaki. Between Aso and Beppu it traverses some of the nicest countryside in Kyushu, and some of the most unusual in Japan. It is a rolling highland plateau that passes a number of mountain peaks, like Kuju-san, at 1788 meters the highest in Kyushu. The overall effect is memorable in all seasons: in spring it is made colorful by wildflowers, in summer it is a lush green, and the autumn has its own beauty, for even though all is reduced to shades of brown, the tall pampas grass moves gracefully with the wind.

There are several buses each day that make the run between Aso and Beppu along the Yamanami Highway (8/day Kumamoto–Beppu plus one Aso–Beppu). Depending on the number of stops, the trip takes three to four hours. An alternative route northward from Aso (for those in a rush) is via Hita, but the attractions of the Yamanami Highway make it preferable.

From Aso, another route is southeast through Takachiho Gorge, a very pleasant place to visit. Like Beppu however, it lies in Miyazaki-ken and is described in that section.

KUMAMOTO TO MIYAZAKI TO KAGOSHIMA

Yatsushiro

This is an industrial city of little interest except for pottery addicts; it is the place of origin for Koda-yaki (or Yatsushiro-yaki) pottery, carrying on a tradition started by Korean potters who came here in the 16th century.

In late August–early September strange lights can be seen in the sea late at night. Known as *shiranui*, it is caused by phosphorescence from a kind of marine life.

Hinagu-onsen

The view from the shore near this hotspring resort (accessible from Hinagu JR station) is regarded as particularly appealing, taking in the Amakusa islands and the bay in front of them.

Minamata

This is another industrial city of no touristic merit, but it was brought to world attention in the early 1970s because of the illness caused by mercury poisoning, now known as Minamata disease.

Yunoko

The swimming is regarded as partially good here.

Hitoyoshi

Travellers descending from the Kumamoto area bound for Kagoshima could do far worse than to turn inland at Yatsushiro and travel through the pretty, wooded valley to Hitoyoshi by rail or road (Route 219). The Kuma River, flowing through the valley, is intensely green. At Hitoyoshi, both rail and road turn southward: the road (Route 221) to Ebino and Kobayashi, rail to Yoshimatsu and Kagoshima. A branch from Yoshimatsu goes to Ebino and Kobayashi.

From Hitoyoshi, you can shoot the rapids in a 2-1/2 hour trip on the Kuma river for 18 km to Osakahama (on the JR). The starting point is 1.5 km southeast of Hitoyoshi station, opposite the grounds of the former castle, Hitoyoshi-jo. The rapids are rated among the three swiftest in Japan, but there is no risk involved.

I was struck by the strange appearance of one town along routes 219–221 (possibly Hitoyoshi itself—memory fails), which looked as if every building along the main street had been built from the same pre-fab components (of non-Japanese style) with only the colors varying. It's nothing special, just a curiosity to look out for.

Kobayashi

This is one entry point for a trip through the very scenic Kirishima National Park. Several buses a day leave for Ebino-kogen, the changing point for the most scenic parts. (This same trip can be made in reverse from Kagoshima.) There are also buses to Kobayashi from Miyazaki many times a day. The trip takes 1-1/2 to two hours.

Kirishima Area

The Kirishima area is very scenic and well known for the two peaks Karakuni-dake (1700 meters), and Takachiho-no-mine (1574 meters) which are 16 km apart; between them stand 21 lesser peaks. Easily

visible from the Kirishima Skyline toll road (along which the bus passes) are colorful caldera lakes, craters, and much other evidence of volcanic activity. It is unusual scenery and definitely worth seeing.

Ebino-kogen

From Kobayashi, the local road passes under the freeway, twists along to the entrance of the toll road, then twists a great deal more up to Ebino-kogen (Ebino highland plateau). This is the terminus of the bus and the transfer point for another bus bound for Kagoshima.

At Ebino-kogen there are three small lakes, or rather "ponds". They are volcano calderas, and quite round; all are of different colors, including one of the most intense green I have ever encountered. (Use a polarising filter to photograph them, otherwise reflection from the water will wash out the color.) There are several paths to follow for different views. Karakuni-dake is visible from here as well.

From Ebino-kogen south along the toll road to Shinyu-onsen, various views of Karakuni-dake unfold to the east. A short distance later is Onami-ike, a caldera lake even more circular than the others mentioned above. (Shinsho lookout gives a good view.) Here and there along the road steam pours out of the ground, sometimes beside the road (or even through the cracks in the pavement)—evidence of the potential geological forces underfoot.

A fork east at the junction of the toll roads (Shinyu-onsen) leads to Takachiho-kawara. From here, there is a good view of Takachiho-no-mine, an ugly, scenic, still-active volcano. Its rim is red-brown, heat-discolored rock; the conical top vanished in prehistoric eruptions. The gaping crater, backdropped by yet more craters and peaks, gives an other-worldly look to the area. Takachiho-kawara is the starting point

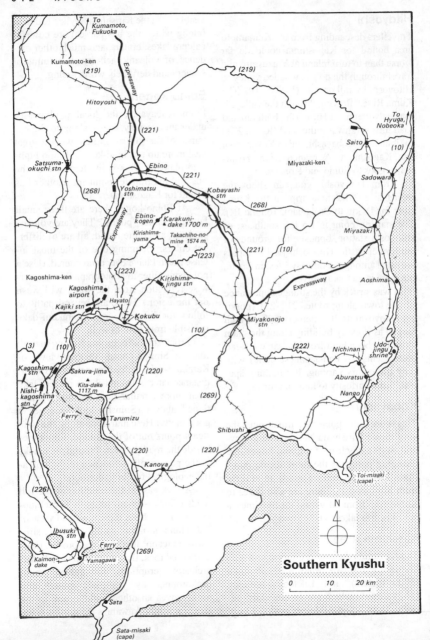

Southern Kyushu

0   10   20 km

for hiking to the picturesque cratered cone.

KAGOSHIMA-KEN ▬▬▬

Kirishima

Kirishima-jingu shrine (in Kirishima town, which is 15 minutes from the JR Kirishima-jingu station) is colorful, with wood carvings, and is set amidst tall cedars. There is a youth hostel in the town, as well as ryokan and hotels.

There are several bus services through the Ebino–Kirishima area. The main routes are: Miyazaki–Kobayashi (two bus routes; the cheaper goes from Miyazaki station); Kobayashi–Ebino-kogen/Hayashida-onsen; Ebino-kogen/Hayashida-onsen–Kirishima-jingu–Nishi-kagoshima. A map in *jikokuhyo* shows a bus route past Takachiho-kawara, but the schedules show no stop; it would seem that service is available. Routes and schedules change from year to year, so

check what is available locally.

Kagoshima

The largest city in southern Kyushu, Kagoshima is an international airport, as well as a seaport for regular boats to and from Okinawa and other southern islands. It is also a stop-over point for some cruise ships.

There are some things to see in Kagoshima itself, and enough attractions nearby that two or three days can easily be spent looking around.

Kagoshima is one of the few cities in the world where an umbrella is useful, rain or shine. The reason is Kagoshima's most spectacular sight—the massive smoking cone of Sakura-jima, across the harbor. Sakura-jima has an awesome history of eruptions, and its south peak is still active, regularly spewing fine black ash into the air. With an unfavorable wind it blows over Kagoshima and covers the streets with a thin layer, or drifts into shallow piles, and is the bane of housewives with washing. A good view of Sakura-jima may be had from the top of Shiroyama, the hill behind the city. Bus 25 runs close to the top, and you can also walk up from Shiroyama tram stop. The park was formerly the site of a castle.

The main attractions of the city are located a little to the north, and are associated (like most history of Kagoshima up to the time of the Meiji Restoration in 1868) with the Shimazu family, who controlled the area for only five years short of seven centuries.

Information

There is an excellent information center at Nishi-kagoshima station (which is the main JR station). The person on duty when I was there spoke excellent English and was very helpful. The office keeps generous hours (0600 to 2200), has literature in English,

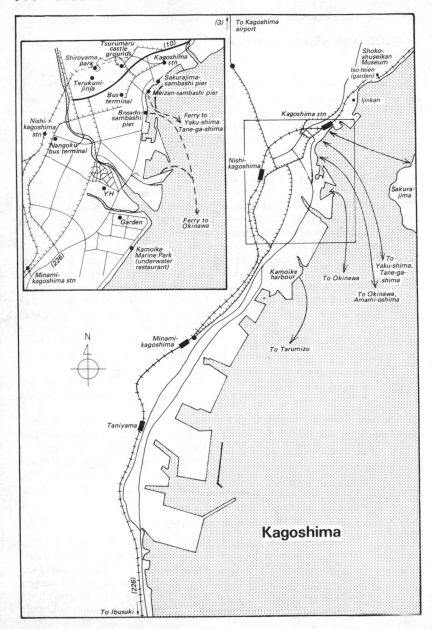

Kagoshima

and can give any information required for further travel connections, access to boat docks for Okinawa, etc.

Home Visit

At the information center at Nishi-kagoshima station you can arrange a visit to a private home. Families who speak English or other foreign languages have been selected for this programme. Arrangements can also be made by phone (tel 099-24-1111).

Things to See

Iso-teien

This is a large landscape garden over 300 years old, one of the nicest in Japan, employing ponds and plants in artistic arrangement. It stretches along the coast, overlooking the magnificence of Sakura-jima and overlooked by nearby Isoyama (which has a cable-car). In the midst of the garden stands a 13-room villa (traditional Japanese style), and there is a good beach nearby. Iso-teien can be reached by city bus 1 in 20 minutes.

Shoko-shuseikan Museum

This building was formerly a factory, built in the second quarter of the 19th century by Shimazu Nariakira, an exceptionally enlightened *daimyo* of the area. He introduced his people to a number of western skills, like photography, telegraphy, cotton-spinning, glass, armaments making, etc. The museum displays items from 700 years of the Shimazu family, and is located beside Iso-teien garden.

Ijinkan

A short distance back toward the city from the museum is Ijinkan ("foreigners residence"), built for overseas advisors in the last century. It is a large wooden house of distinctively foreign architecture—probably early Victorian—and is an anomaly in Japan, especially when contrasted with the lovely and traditional villa in Iso-teien garden.

Other Sights

Another (lesser) attraction of Kagoshima is the foundation stones and walls of the former Tsurumaru Castle. The north-bound tram line passes it, and the closest stop is also the most convenient for walking up to Shiroyama ("Castle Mountain"). The castle was built in 1602 but was destroyed in the 1870s when the local Satsuma rulers under Saigo opposed the Meiji restoration. There isn't space here to describe Saigo's activities, but his battle was futile and he committed *seppuku* (ritual suicide) in a cave near the castle. His name will be found in many places in Kagoshima, and Terukuni-jinja shrine at the foot of Shiroyama honors him. (There is also a statue to him in Ueno (Tokyo).)

Other attractions include the Tropical Plants Botanical Garden, and nearby Kamoike Marine Park with its underwater restaurant.

There are three potteries in the Kagoshima area: Satsuma Toki, Urushima Togei, and Chotaro-yaki. You can arrange to visit them through the tourist office at the station.

Places to Stay

There are many hotels in Kagoshima and nearby resort towns like Ibusuki and the hot-spring town of Furusato. Help in finding a room can be obtained at Nishi-kagoshima station. The nearest youth hostel is Sakurajima YH (tel 0992-93-2150) on Sakura-jima across the harbor. Another two are at Ibusuki: Ibusuki YH (tel 0993-22-2758), and Tamaya YH (tel 0993-22-3553). There was once a hostel in Kagoshima, but none was shown in the 1995 Handbook. It

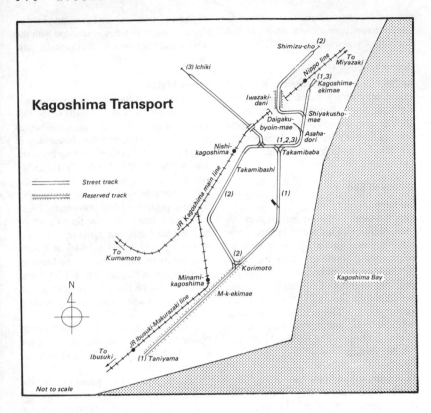

Kagoshima Transport

Shimizu-cho (2)

Nippo line   To Miyazaki

(1,3) Kagoshima-ekimae

(3) Ichiki

Iwazaki-dani

Daigaku-byoin-mae

Shiyakusho-mae

Asaha-dori

Nishi-kagoshima

(1,2,3)

Takamibaba

Takamibashi

JR Kagoshima main line

Street track

Reserved track

(2)   (1)

To Kumamoto

(2)

Korimoto

Kagoshima Bay

N

Minami-kagoshima

M-k-ekimae

JR Ibusuki-Makurazaki line

To Ibusuki   (1) Taniyama

Not to scale

will do no harm to inquire at the information office in the station.

Getting There & Getting Around

Air

In addition to flights to other parts of Japan, Kagoshima is linked internationally with Hong Kong and Seoul by regular flights, which makes it a convenient port of entry for travellers from those areas who wish to start their Japan travels in the south. The airport is north of the city, which is connected to Nishi-kagoshima station by bus. Departures are every 20 minutes, and the trip takes about an hour. If you want to make your way immediately to the Kirishima area, try to get to Kajiki station, from where seven trains a day run directly to Kirishima-jingu station. Inquire at the airport about schedules.

Airport buses make more than one stop in Kagoshima; Nishi-kagoshima station (West Kagoshima) is close to the post office and the central business district.

Sea

There is a regular (but not daily) boat service to Naha, on Okinawa, plus a daily boat to several of the Nansei islands south of Kyushu. For details refer to the general

"Transportation" section early in the book. There is no service to central Japan from Kagoshima, but there is a daily boat to Osaka from Shibushi, which is not far away. Shibushi can be reached by taking the ferry to the Sakurajima side and a bus from there, or train to Nishi-miyakonojo and a bus from there.

Down the Coast and Inland

Chiran

This little town, a bit over an hour diagonally inland from Kagoshima by bus, preserves one corner much as it was two centuries ago. Several samurai houses are open to the public and are worth visiting to see the lovely gardens and large residences of this formerly privileged class. Buses to Chiran leave Kagoshima from Yamagataya bus terminal (Yamagataya department store), and make trips in each direction 11 times a day.

Ibusuki

About an hour south of Kagoshima by train or bus (from Nishi-kagoshima station), Ibusuki is a pleasant hot-spring resort town. Unlike most such towns, this one can be readily enjoyed by Westerners as well as Japanese, because it isn't necessary to stay at a ryokan and to be familiar with Japanese customs, etc.

Information

At Ibusuki station, your first stop should be the tourist information office to pick up a map of the area; it has enough English to be useful. The girls at the office probably won't speak English, but they will be friendly and helpful.

For the day's nibbles you could try to find the Lotteria coffee shop near the station; a shop in the building sells a variety of tempura, good for a picnic lunch.

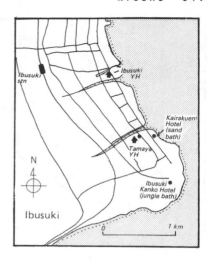

Things to See

Sand Bath (Sunamushi)

One of the most enjoyably unusual sensations of Japan is to be buried up to the neck in hot sand. This is possible where a hot spring surfaces near a beach, permeating the sand and heating it to a high but still bearable temperature. Go to the Kairaku-en Hotel and ask for a *sunamushi*; you'll be directed to a small area on the beach behind the hotel next to the sea-wall, where the attendant will dig a hole and shovel you in. The experience is wonderfully relaxing, probably better left for the end of a day's explorations lest all your energy be sapped at the start!

Jungle Bath (Janguru-buro)

A km or so down the road is the huge Ibusuki Kanko Hotel, a very popular destination for Japanese honeymooners and recommended to anyone travelling on a non-budget basis. Its facilities are quite luxurious and on a grand scale.

The Jungle Bath is a building the size

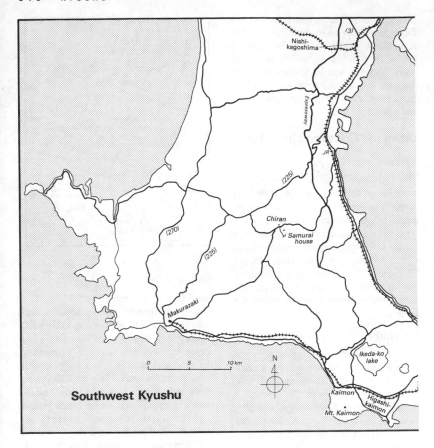

Southwest Kyushu

of an aircraft hangar, to the left of the main hotel building. It contains over 15 pools of hot-spring water of different temperatures, size, shape, and mineral content. Luxuriant growths of tropical plants decorate the room. Depending on the season it may be crowded or you may have the place almost to yourself. The sensation of relaxing in the various pools is marvellous, but it is best to go with a friend because the experience can become boring without someone to talk to. Formerly it didn't matter whether the friend were male or female, for mixed bathing used to be the practice here until recent years, but the shy younger generation (and active peepers among the male contingent) has brought about a division of the facilities. (Unfortunately for females, the pools open to them are fewer in number.) Nevertheless, the place is definitely worth the ¥500 or so. The baths are open from 0700 to 0100.

There is also a sand bath adjacent to the pools, but it is indoors and the water is

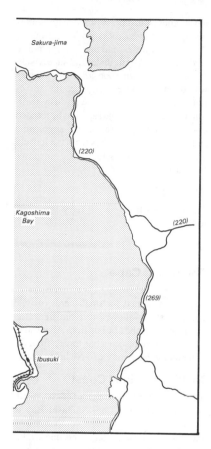

from Kaimon-dake bus stop. Another nearby feature is the round caldera lake, Ikeda-ko, and projecting below the body of the peninsula is a spit, Nagasaki-bana (Long Cape Harbor), which offers an excellent view of Kaimon-dake and the sea.

Bus Tours

Several bus tours begin at Ibusuki station and make sightseeing in the area very easy. All but one begin in the morning; some return to Ibusuki, and some terminate in Kagoshima. The basic tours take in Kaimon-dake and Ikeda-ko; others take in destinations such as Ibusuki Skyline Highway, Chiran, and Sakura-jima, while yet others cross the bay and travel to Sata-misaki Cape, ending at Kagoshima. Information on these tours, and others beginning at Kagoshima, is available from the information centers at Nishi-Kagoshima and Ibusuki stations.

Around the East Side of Kagoshima Bay

Sakura-jima

Across the harbor, the cone of Sakurajima dominates the skyline of Kagoshima. Because of it, Kagoshima is sometimes compared with Naples, and this is one time that the comparison is not far-fetched (as it often is elsewhere). Sakura-jima was an island until 1914, when an immense eruption poured out an estimated 3 billion tons of lava and ash, and bridged the gap to the mainland on the side facing away from Kagoshima. The peninsula is virtually one lava and ash field, and it is interesting to spend some time looking around the huge and jagged masses of ugly but fascinating black rock. You can take a sightseeing bus from the Sakura-jima ferry dock; the trip takes 1-3/4 hours. The lava field begins about 10 minutes walk away from the dock.

piped, so the sunamushi at the beach would be more "authentic".

Kaimon-dake

Another attraction of the Ibusuki area is the graceful conical shape of Kaimon-dake. Buses run from Yamagawa (near the Kanko Hotel) past the mountain to Maku-razaki; from there buses run to Kagoshima via Chiran, allowing a circular route around the bottom of the peninsula. Kaimon-dake can be climbed in about two hours, starting

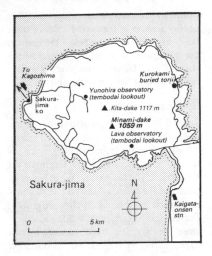

Only Minami-dake (south peak) is still active; it occasionally ejects rock, so climbing is prohibited. Large clouds of smoke and fine ash are also common, and are the cause of the problem in Kagoshima.

One of the interesting sights on the island is the torii (gate) of a shrine at Kurokami. It was once four meters tall, but the eruption buried so much of it that only the top meter still shows above the ground.

There is a lava observation point (*tembodai*) on the south side of the island, giving a good view of the great expanse of lava hurled out during the 20 or so known eruptions during recorded history. On the peninsula are farms that produce the largest radishes in the world—some 50 cm in diameter and 45 kg in weight!

Ferries to Sakurajima leave the Kagoshima side regularly; the dock (Sakurajima-sambashi) is close to Kagoshima station.

Sata-misaki Cape

Sata-misaki, at the bottom of the peninsula on the eastern side of Kagoshima Bay, is the southern-most point of the main islands of Japan. Rugged rocks projecting out of the sea, blue water, and the first lighthouse in the country (built under the supervision of an Englishman soon after the country was opened to foreigners), are the attractions. The area is a park with lush semi-tropical vegetation. The cape can be reached easily by tour bus from Nishi-kagoshima station or by ferry and bus from the Ibusuki area. (The ferry crosses from Yamagawa to Sata.)

Shibushi

There is a daily overnight ferry from here to Osaka.

MIYAZAKI-KEN ▬▬▬▬▬

Toi-misaki Cape

This is another scenic cape, northeast of Cape Sata, famed for small herds of wild horses that are allowed to roam free. It is most easily reached by bus from Aburatsu or Miyazaki; a sightseeing bus travels from the latter along the picturesque Nichinan coast.

Nichinan-kaigan Coast

This is a very pretty stretch of coast extending about 100 km from Shibushi Bay to Miyazaki city. It has been compared with the Amalfi coast of Italy, and one cyclist friend said he was tempted to turn around and return the way he had come because he found it so enjoyable. Because the climate is so mild, semi-tropical plants, such as palms, flourish.

Along the way is Udo-jingu shrine, perched on cliffs at the edge of the sea, partly in a cave.

Ao-shima

Ao-shima is a small island, now connected to the mainland by a causeway. It is covered with betel-nut palms, and the surrounding beach has many tiny sea shells mixed with the sand. It is famous for the Ogres' Washboard, formed over the ages when sedimentary rock became up-ended and eroded to form a series of parallel ridges of rock a meter or so apart. It is quite interesting at low tide.

There is good swimming at Ao-shima. Other places to visit are the Cactus Park (with a reputed million plants) and the Subtropical Plant Garden. Because it is a popular tourist destination, there are many hotels, etc. There is also a youth hostel close by.

Miyazaki

The city of Miyazaki sits in the middle of the area that was the center of early Japanese civilization (as we know it). Because this period predates written history, much of its story is mythical and no structures survive. However some interesting remains have been excavated and are worth visiting. The name Miyazaki means "shrine promontory"

There is a daily ferry each way between Miyazaki and Osaka. (Details of schedules and fares are given in the general Transportation section early in the book.)

Things to See

Heiwadai Park

The city of Miyazaki is quite ordinary, but you can spend your time profitably by visiting Heiwadai-koen park. Heiwa means "peace", so it is somewhat ironic that the 36-meter tower was built in 1940. The tower is of little interest unless you look for the marker on the path leading to the main staircase, stand there, and clap your hands. The result will be a strange groaning echo. The main feature of the park, along with the many flowers, is Haniwa-niwa.

Haniwa-koen

Haniwa are charming and sometimes hu-

morous clay figures that have been excavated from the many burial mounds found in the vicinity. Reproductions of many of these have been located around the park, surrounded by flowers, under shrubs, beside trees. Most of the figures are about a meter tall, so the details of their expressions are clearly discernible. There are knights with horses, court ladies, even a vacant-faced village idiot—I found it an excellent introduction to archaeology. Miniature reproductions of many of the figures are on

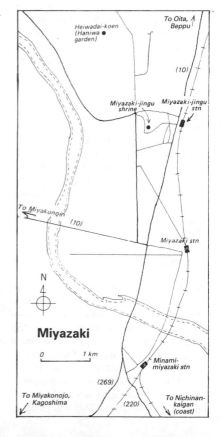

sale at the administrative building near the garden. They can also be bought in Tokyo and other places, but finding them elsewhere can be a problem without time to look around, and the selection may not be as great.

Miyazaki-jingu Shrine

The first emperor of Japan is said to have been Jimmu, a man known more from myths than actual fact. He is believed to have been the ruler of this area of Kyushu about 600 BC; his descendants—the Yamato tribe—went on to conquer all of Japan, thus determining its culture. He is enshrined in Miyazaki-jingu, and in the grounds there is a museum of items excavated from nearby tombs.

Both Heiwadai and Miyazaki-jingu are accessible from Miyazaki station by bus; the first station north of Miyazaki (called Miyazaki-jingu) is also close to the shrine.

Saitobaru

The early settlers of this area brought with them the practice of building tomb mounds (*kofun*), which was carried on into at least the 7th century—culminating in the largest at Sakai, near Osaka. Similar mound building customs existed in Korea, especially in the Kyongju area, not too far from the coast facing Japan.

It would seem likely that the origin of the early settlers was Korea, but debates among scholars still continue. Other evidence suggesting continental ties are *haniwa* funerary clay figures of horses and horsemen found in the tombs; horses were not known in Japan until the 3rd century A.D. The figures were buried with important people, in place of live humans, in the same way as had become the practice in China.

This is intended as an introduction to Saitobaru, where about 300 tomb mounds dot the flat countryside. They will probably be of limited interest to most visitors, because they are little more than grassy mounds of earth. Some are only a meter or so in height, others are large enough to be mistaken for hills; they will be of greater interest to archaeologists. Items excavated from the tombs *are* interesting, and are displayed at the museums in Saito and at Miyazaki-jingu; the figures at Haniwa-koen are reproductions of funerary items from this area.

The tomb area is close to Saito on Route 219, which leads to Hitoyoshi; the closest railway station is Tsuki, reached by branching off the main line at Sadowara.

Hyuga

The city of Hyuga is nothing special touristically, but it is connected by daily ferries with Kobe and Kawasaki (near Tokyo). (Details of schedules and fares are given in the general Transportation section early in the book.)

Takachiho-kyo Gorge

Inland from Nobeoka by road (Route 218) or JR, or south-east from the Aso area by Routes 325 or 265/218, is the lovely Takachiho-kyo gorge. The cliffs are formed of columnar basalt, lava that has cooled into parallel pillars of rock up to 80 meters high. The green water of the Gokase river passes through the narrow valley, and waterfalls splash down here and there.

Also of interest is Takachiho-jinja shrine. This sacred site is said to be the "Cradle of Japan", so the shrine is quite important. Of special interest is the sacred dance, Iwato Kagura, which is performed every day.

Places to Stay

In addition to other accommodation in the area, there are three youth hostels. One traveller had nothing but the highest praise for the food at Yamatoya YH (tel (0982) 72-2243); however I tried three times to obtain accommodation there without success. The others are Takachiho YH (tel (0982) 72-3021), and Iwato Furusato YH (tel (0982) 74-8254).

OITA-KEN

Saiki

There is a regular boat service between Saiki and Sukumo and Yawatahama, both on Shikoku. Details are given in the write-ups on the latter two.

Usuki Area

The attraction of the Usuki area is a number of statues of Buddha dating from the 10th through 12th centuries. The most artistic and numerous of these are located near Usuki; several are largely intact, while elsewhere only the heads have survived (but these heads are well formed and some of the original coloring remains). The Usuki

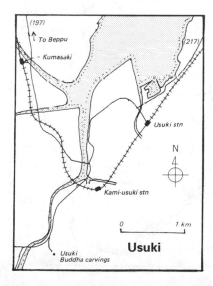

Usuki

images, *seki-butsu*, are displayed in a small ravine a couple of km from Kami-usuki station (JR). A good descriptive pamphlet in English is given out when you enter.

Other rock sculptures are scattered through the valleys of the Oita and Ono rivers at Motomachi, Takase, Sugao, Ogata, and Fukoji, as well as on the Kunisaki Peninsula to the north; Motomachi has some of the best preserved images, those at Magari are badly weathered, and those at Takase are so-so.

Saganoseki

There is a ferry service between Saganoseki and Misaki on Shikoku. Details are given in the Misaki write-up.

Taketa

Ogata and Fukoji are quite close to Taketa (Bungo-taketa station) where Oka-jo castle once stood. The castle was destroyed in the late 19th century and only its foundation stones and walls still stand, rising high up a hillside. It inspired the very famous composition *Kojo-no-tsuki* ("Moon over Castle Ruins"), a hauntingly beautiful piece of music, especially when played on the intended *koto* and *shakuhachi*. Its composer, Rentaro Taki, was influenced by western music, so western ears will find it very pleasing. (A record including this composition would make a good souvenir of Japan.) Also in this area is Harajiki-taki waterfall.

Oita

There is a daily overnight ferry service (some days, two) each way between Oita and Kobe, with a stop at Matsuyama (Shikoku). For details refer to the general "Transportation" section.

The fastest way from Oita airport to Oita is hovercraft (up to 14/day). There are also buses.

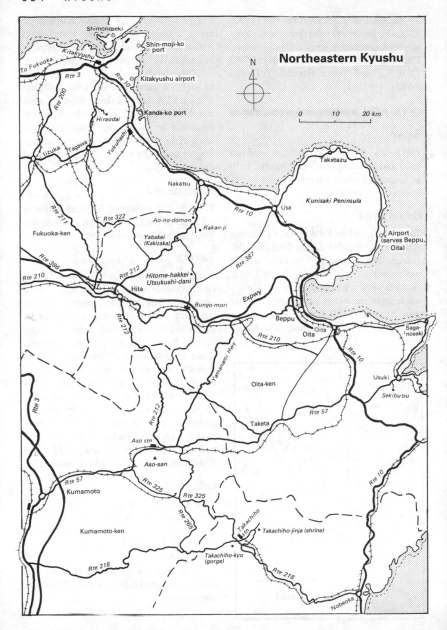

Northeastern Kyushu

Beppu

Beppu is one of the best-known hot-spring resorts in Japan, ideal for sybaritic delights and interesting sightseeing. There are eight "towns" with hot-springs within the bounds of Beppu; the total water outflow exceeds 100 million liters per day.

There are other *onsen* quite a distance outside Beppu, such as Mugen-no-sato and Tsuru-no-yu. Getting to them would require your own transportation or a knowledgeable taxi driver. Talk with the people at the Information Center.

Information

The Foreign Tourist Information Service (tel. 0977-23-1119) near the JR Beppu station gives out maps and other literature, some in English. As usual with Japanese maps, some may have only a superficial resemblance to true scale and actual locations.

Things to See

The Hells (Jigoku)

For those not particularly interested in hot-spring bathing, there is another attraction—the *jigoku* or "hells". In several places around the city, subterranean water of boiling temperature comes to the surface, sometimes violently, sometimes quietly but colorfully—would you believe a pond of naturally red water? Other malevolent emanations include geysers and dark, malodorous, bubbling pools of mud.

The hells are located in two areas of Beppu. Several are clustered close together at Kannawa, about six km from Beppu station, and the other two are a couple of km farther away. The first cluster can be reached from Beppu station by bus 16, 17, 24, 25, or 27, getting off at Kannawa. A ticket for entry to most of the nine hells is available for the price of five. (In actuality, only about five of them are really worth visiting.) The following list describes the hells from west to east, and then the separate ones.

HON-BOZU JIGOKU Not included on the multiple ticket, and some distance up a long hill (accessible from Hon-bozu bus stop, the second after Kannawa), this hell features a number of grey mud pools that plurp and plop in a humorous manner. Recommended more to those who will not have any other opportunity to see such boiling mud.

UMI JIGOKU *Umi* means sea, and the water here is a very picturesque green. It is hot enough to boil eggs, as demonstrated by a basket of them suspended in the water. Around the grounds are torii gates. There is a second pond, also green, but cooler.

YAMA JIGOKU This is of minimal proportions, and wild animals on display are the gimmick that is supposed to pull in the customers. Their living conditions demonstrate an unfortunate general Japanese lack of concern for the comfort of animals despite their world-reknowned "oneness with nature". (One thinks, "oneness with cliche", after a while.) Not recommended.

GARDEN The garden on the corner between the hells is pleasant, but not particularly noteworthy. Admittance is separate.

ONIYAMA JIGOKU The hell content here is negligible; the drawcard is a number of crocodiles.

PHALLIC SHRINE Amidst the hells is this unusual "museum", which houses a sizeable collection of carved phalluses and other erotica (appropriate for a hot spring town, where these sum up a major industry). For those with an earthy sense of humor and

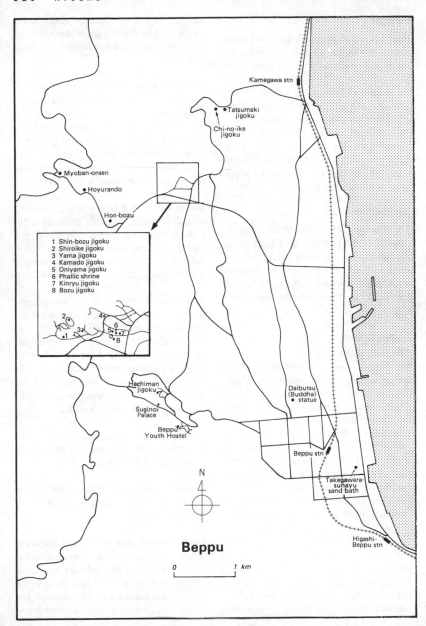

1 Shin-bozu jigoku
2 Shiroike jigoku
3 Yama jigoku
4 Kamado jigoku
5 Oniyama jigoku
6 Phallic shrine
7 Kinryu jigoku
8 Bozu jigoku

Kamegawa stn

Tatsumaki
jigoku

Chi-no-ike
jigoku

Myoban-onsen

Hoyurando

Hon-bozu

Hachiman
jigoku

Suginoi
Palace

Beppu
Youth Hostel

Daibutsu
(Buddha)
statue

Beppu stn

Takegawara-
sunayu
sand bath

N

Higashi-
Beppu stn

Beppu

0   1 km

¥1500 to spare, recommendable; for those easily shocked, to be avoided. It can be recognized by the Indian sculptures in metal.

KINRYU JIGOKU The name means "golden dragon". There is nothing to see except clouds of steam and gaudy, faded, tacky Buddhist images. A waste of time.

SHIROIKE JIGOKU The curiosities here are a cloudy-white pond and several small aquaria of fish not native to Japan, including large, ungainly pirarucu from the Amazon. The pond is similar to that at Hoyurando (described later) but of minor interest. The name, imaginatively, means "white pond".

KAMADO JIGOKU One of the main attractions here is the noise, as steam jets non-stop out of the ground with a great roar. Also interesting is red-brown bubbling mud. If one dares to believe signs, the precipitated minerals on sale are good for the following (verbatim) collection of ailments: "chronic mascular rheumatism, mascular rigidity, neuralgia, arthritis, gout, swelling of gland and syphilis, anaemia, weakness after illness, chronic gastroenteric catarrhs and fatigue, evidation after getting a wind, haemorrhoids, scabies, honeycomb ringworm, scaly tetter, moist tetter, leucodermia and other chronic skin diseases and ulcers".

CHI-NO-IKE JIGOKU The name means "blood hell" and comes from the surprising red of the water (due to ferrous oxide). It is worth seeing for its unusual color. To reach this and the following jigoku, it is necessary to take a bus or taxi to Chinoike stop. The two hells are a short walk back up the hill.

TATSUMAKI JIGOKU This is the only geyser of the Beppu hells. The name means "waterspout hell" and it erupts frequently enough to be worth waiting for.

TSURUMI JIGOKU Not on the "regular" route, this jigoku is close to the Suginoi Hotel. It also has a number of Buddha statues, said to be "in good taste".

Hyotan-onsen

Also in the Kannawa area is this public bath. It is very large, and has a number of baths of different kinds.

Takasaki-yama

One of the other sightseeing "targets", this mountain is known for its semi-wild monkeys (tame enough to have no fear of humans, but wild enough not to trust). The mountain is most easily reached by bus from Beppu station; ask at the information center for directions.

Daibutsu

This large concrete figure of Buddha is a rather unusual sight in Beppu, mostly of curiosity value. Unlike the usual benevolent visage, this Buddha scowls and looks generally unpleasant. Mixed into the concrete are the ashes of thousands of cremated Buddhists.

Hoyurando Hot-Spring Baths

The best outdoor hot-spring pools around Beppu are located at Hoyurando, a hotel-style resort; the name translates as either "Recreation land" or "Recuperation land". Behind the hotel building are two outdoor pools of bluish-white water, strongly sulfurous to the nose; bathing in them is mixed, but there are segregated pools inside the buildings for those who prefer them.

To use the baths, you enter the hotel lobby, pay the fee, then leave by the rear and follow the long covered walkway downhill to the baths. After disrobing and washing you then enter the chosen bath or pool. The outdoor pools are most enjoyable in warm, sunny weather, although the warm water guarantees comfort in any season while submerged. There are also two kinds of mud baths. (A friend amused himself by building an eight cm nose; the Japanese didn't know what to make of him.)

Behind the hotel and to the left is the source of the hot water, marked by the bright colors of chemicals precipitated from the subterranean water as it cools.

Hoyurando is a couple of km beyond the *jigoku* of the Kannawa area, on the road that forks off to the right. There is a bus service (en route to Ajimu); the stop is Hoyurando. On the way the bus passes through another of the eight active hot-spring areas, Myoban. Numbers of little tent-like grass huts have been built over the sources of underground steam and heat to form natural steam baths.

Suginoi Hotel

The huge Suginoi Hotel can be recommended for its annex, Suginoi Palace. Along with arcade games, it has a large stage with a nightly production of a play, mini-circus, or other act. In the same complex are two gigantic bath rooms, both the size of an aircraft hangar, one each for men and women (no mixed section). In each are several pools of different size and temperature, from two-people size to gigantic, from frigid to *very* hot. Decorations on the men's side include a waterfall, a slide, *torii* gate, and a Chinese-style temple with heated marble floor. The ladies' side has a large and benevolent Buddha and equally lush greenery.

Oishi-so Bath

This smaller-scale bath is open to the public. It has tastefully decorated pools, with rock walls and floors. It is located a short distance down from the cluster of *jigoku*

on the main road. (It also offers accommodation.) A sand bath is included in the amenities.

Hot-Sand Baths

Another activity to enjoy in Beppu is a sand bath, where you can be buried to the neck in naturally hot, steaming sand. Public sand baths (*suna*) are found both on the beach and indoors at Takegawara. The latter is a large, oldish, wooden building where you pay at the entrance, put your clothes in a locker, rinse at the small concrete tub, pick up your towel (or one of the many lying around), and follow one of the ladies to the hole she has dug for you in the sand. Lie down, put the towel where it will do the most good, and relax while she piles hot sand over your body. A feeling of infinite relaxation will overtake you as the warmth permeates. When your time is up, rinse off the sand, soap, rinse again, and it's all over. (Take your own soap and towel.) Definitely worthwhile and it costs only a few hundred yen.

It's quite common to have your picture taken in the sand bath; pre-set your camera, and use sign language to explain to the "burier" what you want. It is best to keep your camera in a plastic bag until it is time to take the picture, otherwise the lens will steam up. (It may do so anyway.)

There is also an open-air sand bath on the beach near Kamegawa station; ask for "sunayu".

Places to Stay

In addition to countless hotels, ryokan, and minshuku, there is also the Beppu YH (tel (0977) 23-4116). The information center should have instructions on how to get there. It is very close to the Suginoi Hotel.

Getting There

In addition to train services and flights from

nearby Oita airport (which is actually north of Beppu, on the Kunisaki Peninsula), there are also ferries to several destinations. (Two hovercraft/day connect Beppu with the airport, in addition to the usual bus.)

There are three daily overnight boats between Beppu and Kobe/Osaka. These stop at various ports in Shikoku en route, and the last boat of the evening passes through much of the most scenic part of the Inland Sea in daylight. (These do not carry vehicles, not even motorcycles, as I learned to my annoyance.) There is also daily service with Hiroshima from Beppu. In addition, there is another service between nearby Oita and Kobe (stopping at Matsuyama (Shikoku) en route). For details, refer to the general "Transportation" section. The docks are 10 minutes from the station by bus.

Yufuin-onsen

This is another hot-spring resort town, not too far from Beppu. Accommodation is in the ¥10,000 a night range, so not for budget travellers, but if you are not worried about money you would enjoy staying at one of the thatched-roof farmhouses that serve as inns. The town reputedly has the only free public bath in Japan. The setting is very scenic, with a mountain in the background. It can be reached by bus directly from Beppu or indirectly via Oita by train.

Yamanami Highway

Beppu is the eastern terminus of this highway that crosses Kyushu via Mt. Aso and Kumamoto, ending in Nagasaki. It passes through some of the prettiest countryside in Kyushu and can be recommended. (There is further description in the Nagasaki section.) Eight buses/day go from Beppu to Kumamoto, two of which continue to Nagasaki.

Usa

To the north of Beppu lies the shrine city of Usa. The bright-orange shrine buildings are decorated with carvings; the style of the buildings is of the Heian era (794–1192) but the shrine was founded earlier (725). The hill on which the shrine is built is an old burial mound.

Usa was once the political, economic, and cultural center of Kyushu. At one time there were 65 temples in the area, but through the years they have disappeared—only the carved Buddha heads and tombstones scattered around nearby Kunisaki-hanto peninsula testify to its former importance and strong Buddhist influence.

A story, probably dubious, reported that interest in Usa picked up in the immediate post-war occupation period because of companies who wanted to be able to mark their manufactures "MADE IN USA."

Kunisaki Peninsula

There are eight ferries a day in each direction between Taketazu (Kunisaki Peninsula) and Tokuyama (western Honshu). Sailings are scheduled through the day, around the clock (¥1330, 2 hours).

Yaba-kei Gorge

Attractive scenery may be found along the Yamakuni-gawa river in Yaba-kei gorge. It is "pleasant" rather than "spectacular", as the cliffs on either side of the river (along which the road passes) are often too far apart and do not soar skyward as do those of some other gorges in Japan.

The gorge is easily seen by bus from Nakatsu. The starting point of the main gorge is near Ao-no-domon, about 16 km out of Nakatsu, and continues for about 10 km to Kakizaka. Apart from the main gorge (Hon-yaba-kei), there are several gorges that branch off from it, the most attractive of which is Shin-yaba-kei ("deep Yabakei"), beginning at Kakizaka. The main attractions begin about eight km into the valley, and include Hitome-hakkei ("one look—eight views") and Utsukushi-dani ("beautiful valley"). However, despite the fame and reputation of the valley, I was somewhat underwhelmed, and would suggest it mostly for those with a little extra time.

From Nakatsu station, buses run at least as far as Kakizaka (23 a day); of these, three a day turn and go through Shin-yaba-kei (with another four a day that originate at Kakizaka) as far as Bungo-mori (on Route 210 and JR). There are six buses a day returning from Bungo-mori to Kakizaka and a much greater number from there back to Nakatsu (or on to Hita), so a one-day excursion out of Nakatsu is possible.

From here it is not far to Kokura (Kitakyushu city), described at the beginning of the Kyushu section, from where it is easy to carry on to Honshu by rail and ferries (from Kokura and Shin-moji).

There are two chains of islands to the south of the main islands of Japan: the Nansei-shoto group, extending south and east from southern Kyushu, and the Ogasawara-shoto group (the Bonin islands), more-or-less due south of Tokyo, a continuation of the Izu islands.

NANSEI ISLANDS

South of Kyushu and stretching to Taiwan are the Nansei (southwest) Islands. Some are mere atolls, while others support sizeable populations. As far south as Yoron-jima is Kagoshima-ken; this group takes in Tane-ga-shima and Yaku-shima, close to Kagoshima, plus the Amami-shoto group farther south, which includes Amami-oshima, Toku-no-shima, Okinoerabu-jima, and Yoron-jima.

Okinawa and all the islands south of it make up Okinawa-ken. These comprise the Ryukyu group (made up of Okinawa and the islands around it), the Saki group (around Miyako), and the Yaeyama group (Ishigaki, Iriomote, and Yonaguni). All offer a semi-tropical flavor not found in the main islands of Japan.

The culture of the Nansei Islands is basically Japanese, but there is also a Chinese element. The islands closest to Kagoshima were most strongly influenced by the Satsuma culture of the Kagoshima area, while the islands closest to Taiwan had the greatest Chinese influence. The unfortunate islanders had the misfortune of being squeezed between two powers, and had to pay tribute to both, causing much misery in olden times. Until quite recently there was a distinct Okinawan language, related to Japanese but quite incomprehensible to main-island Japanese, even to those of the Satsuma area. (The dialect in common use now is still incomprehensible.) Many place names use unique local pronunciation of *kanji*; these are used in this book as much as possible, and may differ from other sources that use standard Japanese (but incorrect) pronunciation.

Snake Warning

Nearly all islands except Miyako are inhabited by a venomous snake—the *habu*. Every year about 300 people are bitten, four or five of whom die. (Prompt medical treatment from special clinics keeps the toll this low.) The snakes are nocturnal, so be especially careful at night. Carry a bright light (which they dislike) and make lots of noise, particularly walking heavily; although snakes are deaf, they can feel the vibrations. They are always found in pineapple plantations.

Getting There—Nansei Islands

There are boat services from Tokyo, Osaka/Kobe, Hakata, Fukuoka (northern Kyushu), and Kagoshima (southern Kyushu) to Naha on Okinawa. Many of these ships stop at some of the Amami-shoto group of islands en route, a group beginning just north of Okinawa). In addition, there are separate services from Kagoshima to just this group, as well as to the two closer islands of Tane-ga-shima and Yaku-shima. All these services are detailed in the general "Transportation" section early in the book.

There are also air services to Tane-

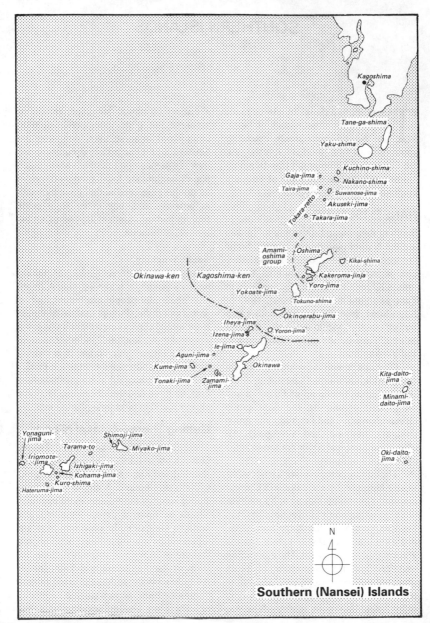

Kagoshima

Tane-ga-shima

Yaku-shima

Kuchino-shima

Gaja-jima

Nakano-shima

Taira-jima

Suwanose-jima

Akuseki-jima

Takara-jima

Amami-
oshima
group

Oshima

Kikai-shima

Kakeroma-jinja

Okinawa-ken

Kagoshima-ken

Yoro-jima

Yokoate-jima

Tokuno-shima

Okinoerabu-jima

Iheya-jima

Izena-jima

Yoron-jima

Ie-jima

Aguni-jima

Kume-jima

Okinawa

Kita-daito-
jima

Tonaki-jima

Zamami-
jima

Minami-
daito-jima

Yonaguni-
jima

Shimoji-jima

Tarama-to

Miyako-jima

Oki-daito-
jima

Iriomote-
jima

Ishigaki-jima

Kohama-jima

Kuro-shima

Hateruma-jima

N

Southern (Nansei) Islands

ga-shima, Yaku-shima, Amami-oshima, Kikai-shima, Toku-no-shima, Kume-jima, Kita-daito-jima, Minami-daito-jima, Miyako-jima, Shimoji-jima, Tarama-to, Ishigaki-jima, Yonaguni-jima, and Hateruma- jima. Information on flights to these places can be obtained from any travel agent in Japan.

TANE-GA-SHIMA

Both this island and Yaku-shima are close to southern Kyushu, and are easily reached by boat (two or more sailings a day to each island), or by air from Kagoshima.

There is no special attraction on Tanega-shima other than its relative remoteness; the island is flat and agricultural. There are campsites, and a bus service runs several times a day between the north and south. The main city and boat landing point is Nishino-omote.

YAKU-SHIMA

Whereas Tane-ga-shima is quite flat, Yaku-shima has the highest mountain in Kyushu, Miyanoura-dake (1935 meters), plus a number of lesser peaks. The island is well-known for huge centuries-old cedar trees (*yaku-sugi*). Boats from Kagoshima dock at Miyanoura, and there are several buses daily covering three-quarters of the distance around the island.

Amami Islands (Amami-shoto)

The Amami group comprises the main islands of Amami-oshima, Kikai-shima, Tokuno-shima, Okinoerabu-jima, and Yoron-jima. While there are no particular attractions that can be singled out (these islands are also basically agricultural, producing semi-tropical crops such as bananas, pineapples, and sugar), there are many good beaches for relaxation and diving.

The scenery of Amami-oshima and the other islands is beautiful. There is a bus service through Amami, or you can rent a bicycle or motorcycle. Camping is good. In contrast with the emerald of the coral sea around Okinawa, the water here is deep blue.

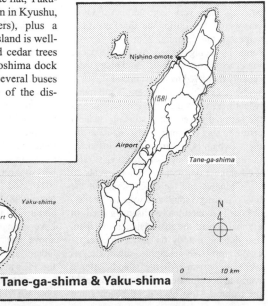

Tane-ga-shima & Yaku-shima

OKINAWA-KEN ▬▬▬▬▬

Ryukyu Islands

Okinawa

The largest of the southwest islands is Okinawa. From the 14th to the 19th century, this was a nominally independent kingdom with its own language and culture. Both were related to Japanese but there was a strong Chinese influence. The rulers of both Japan and China claimed suzerainty of the islands, and the people were kept poor by having to provide tribute to both governments. In the last century the Japanese connection became dominant, but the people have generally been regarded as somewhat second-class citizens. After World War II, the American military occupation continued, making travel there difficult until 1972, when it reverted to Japanese control.

During the war, the Japanese military treated the Okinawans much like subject peoples, and a very large number of civilians were killed during the allied invasion, some by the fighting, some by suicide, some by being forced by the Japanese forces to "commit suicide", and many were actually murdered by the mainland Japanese soldiers. For this reason there is still much resentment toward both the mainland and the national government, so many schools refuse to sing the song used as national anthem (which is not, in actuality, officially the anthem), and have been refusing to raise the Japanese flag at many school events.

Okinawa and the other islands of the Ryukyu group (south and west to Taiwan) are still economically disadvantaged in comparison to the main islands of Japan, and depend mainly on agriculture (especially crops like pineapple, sugar, etc.) as well as tourism. All the islands offer a warm to hot climate, very similar to that of the tropics. Most have good beaches and

clear water, so they have become popular destinations for the main-island Japanese, especially in winter. Diving is rated as very good off Okinawa, as well as off the other islands in the area. The conditions, such as water clarity, may change with the seasons, so it is advisable to inquire at the tourist information office or other source for current information.

Getting There

International

There are flights between Naha and Taipei, Hong Kong, Guam, Honolulu, San Francisco, and Los Angeles.

Arimura Sangyo shipping company operates boats to Taiwan, alternating between Keelung and Kaohsiung in northern Taiwan. The following describes the services of spring 1996. Boats sail at approximately one-week intervals, but there is variation of a day or two from such regularity. The ship leaves Naha at 2000 and reaches Keelung at 0700 or Kaohsiung at 0900 the third day. En route it stops at Miyako and Ishigaki islands on the second day. It leaves Keelung and Kaohsiung at 1600; the boat from Keelung sails direct to Naha, arriving at 1400 of the second day, while the boat from Kaohsiung stops at Ishigaki the next day, and reaches Naha at 0900 of the third day. The lowest fare (shared, open tatami mat area) is ¥15,600 (Keelung), ¥18,000 (Kaohsiung). Reservations are recommended. The phone numbers of Arimura Sangyo offices are: Tokyo (03) 3562-2091; Osaka (06) 531-9271; Naha (098) 868-2191. (Note: The departure and arrival times and stops made en route have changed from year to year, so the above information is for guidance only. Obtain current schedules from the agents or the TICs in Tokyo, Narita, and Kyoto.

Travellers en route to Taiwan must obtain a visa in advance (unless exempt)

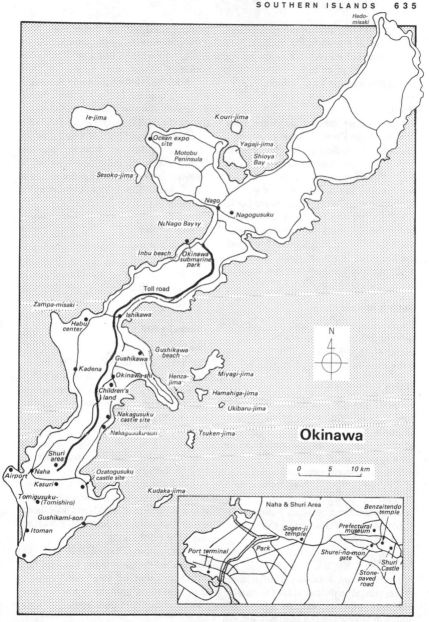

Hedo-misaki

Ie-jima

Kouri-jima

Ocean expo site

Motobu Peninsula

Yagaji-jima

Shioya Bay

Sesoko-jima

Nago

Nagogusuku

Nₐ Nago Bayₛy

Inbu beach

Okinawa submarine park

Toll road

Zampa-misaki

Ishikawa

Habu center

Gushikawa beach

Gushikawa

Kadena

Okinawa-shi

Henza-jima

Miyagi-jima

Hamahiga-jima

Children's land

Ukibaru-jima

Nakagusuku castle site

Nakagusuku-son

Tsuken-jima

N

Okinawa

Shuri area

Naha

Airport

Kasuri

Ozatogusuku castle site

0   5   10 km

Tomigusuku- (Tomishiro)

Kudaka-jima

Gushikami-son

Itoman

Naha & Shuri Area

Benzaitendo temple

Sogen-ji temple

Prefectural museum

Port terminal

Park

Shurei-no-mon gate

Shuri Castle

Stone-paved road

from the representative of the government of Taiwan, the Association of East Asia Relations in Tokyo. The address and access information are given earlier in the book in the chapter on Facts for the Visitor.

Domestic

There are boat services to Naha from Tokyo, Osaka/Kobe, Hakata (Fukuoka), and Kagoshima. Because several of these stop at islands between Kagoshima and Naha, island hopping is feasible. The various services are detailed in the general "Transportation" section early in the book.

There are also flights from Sendai, Tokyo, Osaka, Nagoya, Fukuoka, Nagasaki, Kumamoto, Kagoshima, Miyazaki, and the more important small Nansei islands nearby. (Nearly all the main small islands are accessible by air.)

Getting Around

There are several bus tours (in Japanese only) to different destinations on Okinawa lasting 4-1/2 to 9-1/2 hours. There are also many local buses for the adventurous.

Naha

Today the administrative center of Okinawa-ken, Naha was the capital of the Ryukyu kingdom for about 400 years. Remnants of three major castles and several lesser ones still stand from those days, along with some historic gates and other relics of Ryukyu design. Although the design of some of these structures appears Chinese, the architecture is an authentically Ryukyuan style that evolved through the centuries.

Information

A good first stop is the tourist information office, located on the city side of the harbor and river near the end of Meiji-bashi bridge. It is near the bus terminal and can be recognised by its red roof tiles. Staff there can provide ample information for getting around, and can also make hotel bookings.

Additional information on Okinawa is available from the TIC in Tokyo, including the booklet *Okinawa Japan*, and the photocopied sheets *How to Get to Keelung* (No. 20), and *Okinawa* (No. 54) which give updated information on ships to Naha and Taiwan, hotels, etc. Information can also be obtained from the Okinawa-ken office in the Kokusai Kanko-kaikan building in Marunouchi (Tokyo).

Places to Stay

In addition to several hotels of good quality, there are also many ryokan. Bookings may be made at the information center. The youth hostels are listed in the Naha section.

Things to See

The Boulevards

The main area of Naha is the 1.6 km Kok'sai-dori (International Boulevard). It has several large department stores, as well many shops catering for tourists, with well-known Okinawa products like *bingata* textiles, and shell and coral products. Near the end of Kok'sai-dori is Sogen-ji temple, known for the stone gates on two sides. Heavily damaged during the war, they were restored afterward. A uniquely Okinawan program of classical and folk dances and music is performed weekly at Oki-e theater (near Mitsukoshi department store) and would be worth seeing.

Heiwa-dori (Peace Boulevard) runs off Kok'sai-dori, and is the site for a typical Okinawa-style market. Women sit by their baskets of produce in a scene more like Southeast Asia than Japan.

Shuri

Shuri is the location of the former castle of the kings of Okinawa during the zenith of the Ryukyu civilization. The centerpiece, and symbol of this era, is Shurei-no-mon gate. The original, dating from the founding of the castle, was destroyed during the war and faithfully rebuilt afterward. Much of the original castle wall still stands, but a university now occupies the site of the castle itself.

Nearby is attractive Ryutan-ike pond and surrounding park, and not far away is Benzaitendo temple. The original was built in 1502, but it too was destroyed during the war; it was rebuilt in 1968. On the north side of the pond is the very good prefectural museum, Kenritsu Hakubutsukan, which is housed in the large and traditional residence of the Osho family.

A charming walk goes along the stone-paved street of Kin-jo (golden castle) town. It leads down from the castle site to the harbor and is lined with many fine traditional houses.

Other attractions of the area are Sono hiyan-utaki stone gate, Kankaimon gate, of typical Ryukyu style (first built in the early 1500s and rebuilt after the war), and Enkaku-ji somon temple (pre-1500s and also rebuilt after the war).

The Shuri area can be reached by bus 25 or 26 from the bus center.

Arts and Crafts

A little farther away you can find a workshop where *bingata* textiles are produced. The dyes and patterns are very bright, quite different from the more subdued and restrained colors used on the main islands.

Another craft to look for is pottery. Tsuboya ware (named for the area where it is made) is quite simple and intended mainly for use as storage vessels for water, etc. The forms and finishes owe more to Chinese and southern areas than to Japanese influences. The workshops are open to the public.

Tomigusuku

A castle once stood at Tomigusuku, south of Naha, but today only depressions in the ground indicate its site. More interesting, at least to those concerned with events of World War II, is the nearby former headquarters of the Imperial Navy, easily reached on foot. The entire building is underground and was so well concealed that it was not discovered by the victorious American forces until three weeks after the landing. To their horror, they found that 4000 men and officers had committed suicide in the underground tunnels rather than surrender. The tunnels and rooms are now open for inspection, with no hint of that grisly occurrence in 1945. Buses to Tomigusuku leave from Naha bus center.

Places to Stay

As well as hotels and ryokan, there are three youth hostels in Naha. The Harumi YH (tel 098-867-3218) has the best reputation. There is also the Okinawa International YH (tel 098-857-0073). The Maeda-Misaki YH (tel 098-964-2497), 70 minutes north by bus and not far from the habu center, is also spoken of well.

Around the South Coast

As you travel south of Naha along town and country roads, a common sight is Okinawan houses with tiled roofs. All the tiles are firmly cemented to guard against wind storms, and surmounted by a fierce *shiisaa*, the guardian lion that keeps evil spirits from the house. (Very similar tiling can be seen in India and Bali.) In former times, the tiles were shaped and fired on site, and the shiisaa was sculpted from the same clay, but these days most are made in factories and lack individuality.

The south coast was the scene of the heaviest fighting of the landings of World War II—at Mabuni hill alone, 200,000 people died. If you are interested in the various memorial sites, visit the tourist information office for more details. (Note: Residents still find live ordnance on the battlefields. If you discover anything, do not touch it. Notify the police, or contact the USAF Kadena base.)

Gyokusendo

This is a limestone cave with a claimed 460,000 stalactites and other limestone configurations, many of which have interesting and lovely colors. About 800 meters of the cave is open for inspection.

Kasuri

If you are interested in weaving, visit the village of *kasuri* (comprising Kiyan, Motobo, and Teruya) where the handwoven, vegetable-dyed *kasuri* fabrics (mostly silk) are made.

Along the East Coast

Continuing around the south coast and up the east, you are constantly in view of the deep-emerald sea. Along this coast and others you are likely to see uniquely Okinawan tombs—large structures with a surrounding semicircular wall, set into hillsides overlooking the coast. There is nothing like them anywhere else in Japan.

Nakagusuku Castle Site

This is possibly the finest of such sites on Okinawa; the length and height of the remaining walls and three citadels give a good idea of the scale of the former buildings. From the ramparts you can see the Pacific Ocean in one direction and the East China Sea in the other. It is located close to Nakagusuku-son ("Central Castle Village").

Nakumuru House (Nakumuru-ke)

In the same area as Nakagusuku Castle, this is probably the finest residence on Okinawa. It was built in the mid-1700s by a wealthy farmer, and the five structures embody the best of traditional Okinawan building and decorative techniques.

Okinawa-shi

Much of this city is aimed at providing recreation for the U.S. airmen of nearby Kadena Air Force Base. With its many clubs and bars, it bears little resemblance to anything typically Okinawan or Japanese. The mood is American, or at least the Japanese impression of American.

Of great interest to the Japanese is Plaza House shopping center, complete with large car park (an unaffordable luxury in most of Japan because of land costs). The Tuttle Bookshop stocks a large number of books on Okinawa.

Things to See

OKINAWA CHILDREN'S LAND (KODOMO-NO-KUNI) To the southeast of the city, this aquarium raises more than 60 kinds of reptiles, and has exhibitions of more than 200 kinds of tropical freshwater fish.

MUNICIPAL COLOSSEUM At Gushikawa, near Children's Land, is this venue of Sunday bullfights. These are not like the Spanish variety, but are "bull sumo"—trying to force the opponent out of the ring by locking horns and pushing. Similar fights are found on several other islands of Japan, including Shikoku, and as far south as Indonesia.

SOUTHEAST BOTANICAL GARDEN This has a large variety and huge number of tropical plants, 600 kinds of flowers, and 200 types of tropical fruit trees, and is intended to emphasize the island's nearly-tropical climate.

There is a small lake, and rental boats are available.

Hedo-misaki Cape

The view from this northern tip of Okinawa is very pretty. On a clear day you can see Yoron-jima island on the horizon. The view is definitely worth the trip, which involves passing a number of attractive villages along the way.

Along the West Coast

Much of the west coast has been set aside as Okinawa Coast Quasi National Park, which takes in the area from Hedo-misaki to the northern side of Motobu-hanto peninsula, and resumes from the south side almost an equal distance to Zampa-misaki. The main attraction is the view of the coast and the beautiful colors of the water.

Motobu-hanto Peninsula

At the northeast neck of the peninsula, there is a beautiful view overlooking Ya-gachi and Okubu islands (large and small respectively).

Ocean Expo

In 1975 a mini World Expo was held near the northwest tip of the peninsula, based on the theme of using oceans. Although the exhibition lasted only six months, sufficient attractions have been carried over or added to offer an enjoyable day's outing.

The Okinawa Village Pavilion demonstrates the old culture of Okinawa, and has examples of houses in both traditional and modern styles. The Oceanic Culture Pavilion shows the rich variety of cultures found among the races and ethnic groups of the South Pacific. On the same site is the largest aquarium in the world, featuring three display areas that show tropical, ocean, and deep sea fish, as well as a number of performing dolphins (at Okichan Theater). Floating City is a science-fiction writer's delight, a large steel multi-columned structure in the water that supposedly represents the way we will live in the future (with appropriate phrases such as "new era", "producing harmony between science and nature", and other such slogans which the Japanese are so adept at inventing). It's interesting, but not to be taken seriously. (All attractions are closed on Mondays.)

At the northern end of the site is the graceful arc of beautiful Expo beach.

Accommodation in the vicinity of the Expo site is generally not inexpensive. Okinawa Resort Station is a resort village for young people, and uses retired JNR/JR sleeping cars for accommodation. They had to be brought to Okinawa, along with an idled steam engine, for there are no railways on the island.

Nago

Located at the southern neck of the peninsula, Nago was little damaged during the war, so you can still see several houses in the traditional Okinawan style. There are also tall gajumaru trees, 300 years old, on the southeast approaches to the city. In late January and early February, the cherry blossoms are beautiful on the site of former Nago-gusuku castle, reached via a long stone staircase. At the top, you can enjoy an excellent view of the surrounding sea and land.

OKINAWA MARINE PARK A long walkway extends beyond the shallows of a reef here, to a column with underwater glasswindows, so visitors may look out from beneath sea level. Depending on conditions the number of fish in view may be rather limited; visitors generally tend to visit Ocean Expo instead.

In addition to the "reverse aquarium", where fish can come to look at people, there is a museum showing many of the seashells found around the island. Glass-bottomed boats may be rented as well.

A short distance to the south are three fine beaches, beginning with Inbu Beach.

HABU CENTER Here you can see the venomous *habu* snake in perfect safety. A feature is a fight between a *habu* and a mongoose; the agile animal wins about 99% of the time, particularly because the nocturnal snake is at a disadvantage. The fights are staged relatively frequently, probably a reflection of the plentiful supply. Recent research has shown that mature snakes can survive two to three years without any food whatsoever.

Other Ryukyu Islands

Ie-jima

Off the Motobu-hanto peninsula, Ie island is easily traversed in a short time. There are many lovely views of the deep-blue sea. The Travel Village (on the side nearest Okinawa) is especially aimed at young travellers.

Minna-jima

This island is claimed to offer the most beautiful sunsets in Okinawa.

Kudaka-jima

The "Island of the Gods", just off Okinawa, is quite sacred to Okinawans. There are many burials here, and funerary practices in the past were rather unusual. Many bodies were exposed to the elements in special places, and only after decomposition were the bones cleaned and buried. (This practice may still be found in mountain villages on the island of Bali in Indonesia.)

Especially on Kudaka, but true everywhere on Okinawa, foreigners are ill-advised to enter cemeteries. It will upset many

of the local people, who believe that the presence of an outsider (especially a foreigner) will disturb the spirits of the dead, with bad results for the living. It is worth reading up in advance of a visit to Kudaka to avoid misunderstanding. (The Tuttle bookstore in Naha has books on the subject.)

Other Islands

Other islands that may be visited from Okinawa are Iheya, Izena, Kerama (a group of about 20), and Kume. Information on how to get there can be obtained at the information center in Naha or from travel agents.

Miyako-jima

There are many beautiful views on Miyako, as well as fine beaches. Miyako-jima was not damaged during the war, so its appearance is more traditional than Okinawa. Most houses are surrounded by walls of coral as protection against the frequent typhoons. Unfortunately it can be a little difficult actually seeing the houses, because a screen of wood, rock, etc., blocks the view through the gateway. Its purpose is to keep out evil spirits, believed able to hop only in straight lines (a belief shared with the Chinese). Such superstitions are still strong, and a talisman will often be seen on a wall in line with a road ending at a T-junction. Miyako-jima is at least as interesting for culture as for its basically agricultural landscapes. It is one of the few islands free of the deadly *habu* snake.

Things to See

ONOYAMA-MURA Miyako Tropical Botanical Garden near here occupies 226 hectares of land, and boasts 40,000 trees and more than 1200 kinds of flowering plants from Central and South America, Africa, and the Philippines.

The "poll stone" near Onoyama is a

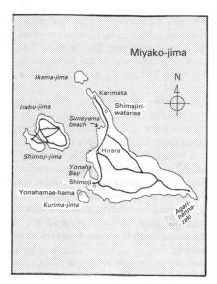

Jofu Fabric A common sight following the rainy season is great lengths of yarn draped over any available support to dry in the sun after dyeing. It is then woven into Jofu fabric, a well-known product of the island and historically an item used in payment of taxes.

Places to Stay
There are several minshuku, near the harbor. A good one is Ueno-so.

Getting There
In addition to regular air services, there are scheduled boats between Okinawa (Naha) and Taiwan. They stop at both Ishigaki and Miyako en route. From Taiwan, they skip Miyako.

Getting Around
The best way to get around is by bicycle or motorcycle rented from one of the shops near the harbor of the main city, Hirara.

Yaeyama Islands
The Yaeyama group of islands extends from Ishigaki to Yonaguni in a southwesterly arc.

Ishigaki-jima
The most important of the group, Ishigaki, is famed for its many beautiful beaches. The main city and port is Ishigaki.

Things to See
Miyara Dunchi This is the house of a noble of the old Ryukyu kingdom, dating from 1819. It follows the plan of houses for people of equal rank that were built around the castle at Shuri on Okinawa; here it is unique, the island's most valued cultural asset. (It may be described in some literature as a samurai house, but there were no true samurai in this region.) It houses a

relic of harsh times in the past, when the islanders were little more than slaves, being taxed by both Chinese and Satsuma (Kyushu) authorities. A person was compelled to pay taxes when his or her height equalled that of this stone. Its name is *Jintozeiseki* or *Bubakariisu*, depending on the dialect.

Yonahamae Beach Four km of white sand stretch along the blue waters and offer excellent swimming.

Sunayama Beach The name means "Sand Mountain". The attraction is good swimming, and nearby Miyako-jinja shrine is worth a visit.

Agari-henna-zaki Cape The view over the sea here is beautiful. Cliffs drop to the sea, rocks jut above its surface, and with the exception of a solitary lighthouse, there are no nearby buildings to interfere with the wild atmosphere.

small museum of the period, and is also noted for its garden and stone wall.

YAEYAMA SHIRITSU MUSEUM Exhibits relating to the culture of the Yaeyama islands are on display at this very interesting museum. Labels, unfortunately, are only in Japanese, but most displays can be understood.

TORIN-JI This temple has some beautiful old Buddhist sculptures.

CHINESE CEMETERY The very Chinese-looking monument here commemorates 128 Chinese who were killed in a fight on a British ship in the last century. It is considered a general monument to peace.

KABIRA-WAN BAY Most visitors consider this the most beautiful place on the island. Pearls are cultivated here, and are of an unusual (and thus very costly) black hue. They take the name of the island group, Yaeyama. The bay can be reached by bus.

THE BEACHES Most visitors will want to enjoy the fine beaches of Ishigaki; skin-diving and scuba gear are available for rent. Since there are many types of incredible and beautiful tropical fish in the waters around this (and all the other) islands, diving can be recommended. Water-skiing and fishing are other potential activities.

At the time of revising this book there were still good coral reefs around much of the island, with the usual complement of colorful fish, clear water, etc.; they have been one of the main attractions of Ishigaki. An extension to the airport runway had

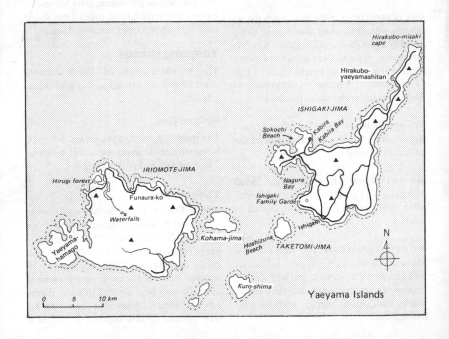

Yaeyama Islands

once been planned. Some work, in fact, had been done, but appears to be in suspension pending further study. This project would have required extension into the sea, with consequent landfill that would have destroyed much or all of the reefs near Shiraho, one of the best reef areas of all the islands. Fortunately, common sense seems to have overcome the greed of contractors (and the strong likelihood of kickbacks to politicians) promoting the plan, which would have destroyed one of the main reasons why tourists would want to go there.

Places to Stay
Accommodation is plentiful, mostly in the form of minshuku, but there are two camping grounds as well. There are two youth hostels, Yashima Ryokan (tel 09808-2-3157) and Trek Ishigaki-Jima YH (tel 09808-6-8257), both in Ishigaki city.

Getting Around
Bicycles, motorcycles, and cars can be rented from several shops near the center of town (even by bicycle it is possible to see the island in a day), and there is also a bus service.

Getting to Other Islands
Nearby Taketomi can be reached in about 20 minutes (around ¥300, eight trips a day), and Iriomote is accessible by regular boat or hovercraft.

The boats between Naha and Taiwan all stop at Ishigaki en route to Taiwan, and about half of them stop on the return trip as well. There is air service to and from Naha on Okinawa as well as to Yonaguni, Tarama, and Hateruma islands.

Taketomi-jima
Just a short distance west of Ishigaki, tiny Taketomi (11 km in circumference) can be explored easily in a day on bicycle (avail-

able near the boat dock). The island is very popular with day-trippers from Ishigaki, as its magnificent beaches virtually surround the island.

Because it was an untouristed backwater until only a decade or so ago, the pace of life and traditions on Taketomi are much as they always were. The people are friendly and houses are still of the traditional style, surrounded by walls of coral. It is common to see people preparing the thread for weaving *minsaori* fabric, a craft going back to the 17th century; the yarn may be stretched by the side of the street. An exhibition of weaving may be seen at the Folk Art Museum in the village; small items are on sale.

Some water-buffalo may be seen on the island, either working in the fields or pulling carts for tourists.

STAR SAND (HOSHI-ZUNA) Taketomi's beaches are noted for "star sand"; what looks like ordinary white sand is actually the five-pointed skeletal remains of tiny sea creatures. Most of it has been collected by visitors (or souvenir sellers), but it may be possible to find some in pockets in the coral, particularly on the south side of the island. The sand is stirred up from the depths by storms and washed ashore, so the supply is renewed periodically. (Not generally known is that this sand is found on all the Yaeyama islands.) If you find a "deposit", remember the motto: "Take a little and it will bring lots of happiness; take a lot and it will bring little happiness". Leave some for the next person.

Places to Stay
There are minshuku and a youth hostel, Takana Ryokan (tel 09808-5-2151) in Taketomi.

Iriomote-jima

More than 80% of this island (plus nearby Kohama, Taketomi, Kuroshima, and Aragusuku islands) forms Iriomote National Park, habitat of the primitive Iriomote wildcat. Thought to have remained unchanged in five to 10 million years, this "living fossil" is the size of a domestic cat. It is nocturnal, so it is seldom seen, even by residents. Authorities believe that there are only 30 to 40 still living. Star sand is also found on the island, but you are not allowed to collect it because Iriomote is a national park. The island also has habu snakes, so take care.

Things to See

URA-UCHI-KAWA The best single excursion on the island is up the Ura-uchi River. Beginning at the mouth of the river, the boat usually carries about 12 people. There is no trouble making up a party, because many day-trippers cross from Ishigaki. After half an hour or so, you disembark and walk for about 40 minutes through canopied near-jungle to two pretty waterfalls, Mariyudo and Kampira. The first has three drops totaling 33 meters, ending in a deep pool; the latter is a long incline with numerous Jacob's wells ("pot holes" formed by small rocks swirling around in depressions and grinding the holes larger).

SKIN DIVING As on many of the other islands, skin-diving in the colorful coral beds among equally colorful fish is to be recommended. A barrier reef surrounds the island.

Places to Stay

There are several minshuku as well as two youth hostels at Funaura. Of the latter, Irumote-so YH has been rated as the better (tel 09808-5-6255), with pleasant staff and a nice view over the countryside. The other is Iriomote-jima YH (tel 09808-5-6526.

Getting There & Getting Around

The boat, and possibly a hydrofoil, from Ishigaki (60 to 90 minutes) docks at Ohara, from where a bus leaves soon afterward for the other side of the island and the trip up the Ura-uchi River. You can rent bicycles and motorcycles at a shop two minutes from Irumote-so Youth Hostel.

Kohama-jima

Once bypassed by tourists, Kohama now has full-scale facilities (Japanese-style) and is attracting more visitors to its fine beaches of white sand and the coral reefs offshore.

Yonaguni-jima

This is the westernmost part of Japan, and on a clear day you can see Taiwan from Irizaki (West Cape). The main attraction is scenery, beaches, warm water, and the largest moths in the world. A beautiful view waits at the top of the 231-meter hill overlooking the village of Sonae.

Kubura-wari One curiosity is this natural hole in the ground near Kubura. Legend has it that anyone able to jump over it won't have to pay taxes and will have a long life, and women will give birth easily. It is wide enough that few are known to test the legend. It is surrounded by interesting rock formations and is located behind Kubura school.

Places to Stay

There are only minshuku, no youth hostels.

Getting Around

Bicycles and motorcycles may be rented for convenient transportation.

Hateruma-jima

This small island is the southernmost part of Japan and a pleasant place to visit. One good place to stay is a room adjacent to the Ishino-ume Restaurant.

OGASAWARA ISLANDS

South of the Izu Islands is another group, the Ogasawara-shoto Islands. These are part of the Tokyo-to administrative district and extend to latitudes as far south as Okinawa.

The islands are ideal for really getting away from it all; access is only by ship from Tokyo (generally twice a week), and they are beyond TV and regular radio range. The climate is semi-tropical (slightly cooler than Okinawa), small palm trees grow, and there are frequent rain showers. While the Izu islands offer a good weekend excursion for swimming and meeting other people, the Ogasawara Islands are better for quiet exploration and adventure.

The main islands are named after family members, such as Chichi-jima (father), Haha-jima (mother), and Ani-jima (elder brother). The first two are the main islands; Ani is a small island just above Chichi-jima. Muko-jima is a cluster of small islands to the north. To the south are the Kazan (Volcano) islands, which include Io-jima (better known in English as Iwo-jima), famed as a battle site in World War II and memorialized in the photo of Marines raising the U.S. flag atop 185-meter Suribachi-yama. Tourists are not allowed onto Io-jima because large areas still have live ordnance from the fighting, and the remains of many Japanese soldiers lie entombed in the caves where they died. Only Chichi and Haha are regularly populated.

Chichi-jima

This largest island has peaks up to 600 meters, and also has beaches and good swimming. It is small enough to walk across in two hours, or around in a day; roads are good, and there is a bus service. Bougainvil-lea and hibiscus give a tropical air.

There are three beaches, one of which is sandy, while another has some coral. Skin diving can be recommended at many places around the island, especially between Chichi-jima and Ani-jima, because of the many fantastically colored tropical fish; they are not afraid of people, and come close. There are also turtles and rays. Scuba and less complex diving equipment is available for hire. You can also rent a boat and circle the island, stopping to dive where desired. It is reminiscent of Australia's Great Barrier Reef. Throwing bread on the water from shore results in "instant fish". The water is a darker blue than that of the Okinawa area and is not as clear.

On the west side, the rusting hull of a small ship is a relic of the war. There are also caves around the shore that were used for defence purposes; some are now used by fishermen for storage, and others are blocked by gates.

There are minshuku on the island, but they tend to be crowded and generally do not serve meals, so you have to eat at restaurants or buy food at a local store. The few shops close by 1830; the hottest nightspot, a coffee shop, is closed by 2200.

Because the island was under U.S. control for a long time both in the 1800s (many people have American ancestors) and after WWII, many people can communicate in English, and there are several U.S.-style buildings, a curiosity to the Japanese.

Getting There

Access is from Tokyo to Futami-ko in Chichi-jima (¥22,400 one way). There are one or two sailings a week in each direction (depending on season); the trip takes a little over a day. Further information is available at the Tourist Information Center, Tokyo.

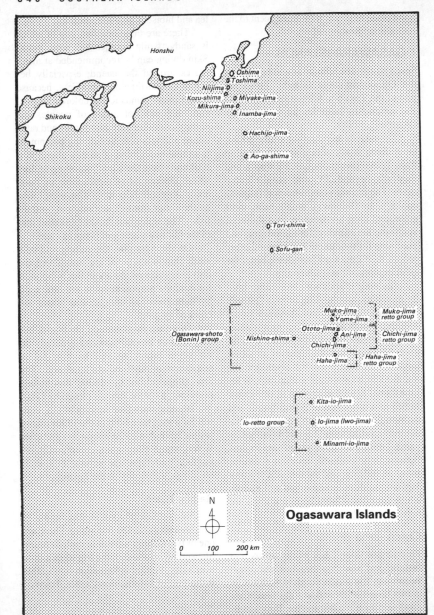

Ogasawara Islands

INDEX

The Author

Ian L. McQueen is a Canadian who has been living in Tokyo for a number of years. He grew up in the port city of Saint John, New Brunswick, and later graduated in Chemical Engineering from the University of New Brunswick (Fredericton) and worked a few years in that field. Travels over the years in South America, Europe, and the Caribbean were followed by an extended stay in Japan in 1970–1, during which he travelled widely, from the north of Hokkaido to Okinawa. This was followed by a year and a half travelling through Korea, Taiwan, Hong Kong, and most countries of Southeast Asia. He then spent nearly five years in Australia during which he did graduate studies in Chemical Engineering at Melbourne University leading to an MEngSc degree. He returned to Japan in 1978 to research the guide book originally released as *Japan—A Travel Survival Kit*. He remained in Japan for fifteen more years, working as a technical editor and preparing revisions for subsequent editions of the book. He now lives in Saint John.

Acknowledgments

Many individuals and organisations have given information or other forms of assistance in researching and producing this book.

The Japan National Tourist Organisation, through both its head office and its Tourist Information Centers in Tokyo and Kyoto, have provided invaluable assistance of many kinds. The staff at the TICs deserve special thanks for their friendly helpfulness.

Grateful acknowledgment is made to the Australia-Japan Foundation and the Japan National Tourist Organization for supporting the initial research.

The following individuals deserve specific mention for their assistance: D. Britton, D. Green, T. Kaihata, N-J Kang, H. Kawatsura, M. Kira, Ian N. Lynas, K. Matsumoto, R. Morley, A. Miyaji, J. Morris, N. Nagayoshi, K. Osada, S. Onda, J. Pearce, D. Petersen, K. Sasaki, H. Suzuki, D. Weber, W. Wetherall, J. Yamamoto, and Dr. G. Zobel.

Gilles Pineau was an invaluable source for most of the detailed information on Okinawa and other islands of southern Japan.

My apologies for not being able to single out everyone who has supplied useful information.

最新版・上手な日本の旅
JAPAN: A BUDGET TRAVEL GUIDE

年5月16日　第1刷発行

著　者　　イアン・マックィーン
発行者　　野間佐和子
発行所　　講談社インターナショナル株式会社
　　　　　〒112　東京都文京区音羽 1-17-14
　　　　　電話：03-3944-6493

印刷所　　株式会社　平河工業社
製本所　　株式会社　堅省堂

落丁本・乱丁本は、小社営業部宛にお送りください。送料小
社負担にてお取替えします。本書の無断複写（コピー）、転載
は著作権法の例外を除き、禁じられています。

定価はカバーに表示してあります。
© 講談社インターナショナル　1997
Printed in Japan
ISBN4-7700-2047-3